Finance

Corporate Finance
MBA 8135

Georgia State University
Robinson College of Business – Department of Finance

McGraw-Hill/Irwin

A Division of The McGraw·Hill Companies

McGraw–Hill Primis

ISBN–10: 0–39–080084–8
ISBN–13: 978–0–39–080084–8

Text:

Corporate Finance, Eighth Edition
Ross–Westerfield–Jaffe

Fundamentals of Corporate Finance, Eighth
Edition, Standard
Ross–Westerfield–Jordan

This book was printed on recycled paper.

Finance

http://www.primisonline.com

111   FINAGEN   ISBN-10: 0-39-080084-8   ISBN-13: 978-0-39-080084-8

Finance

Contents

CHAPTER 1

Introduction to Corporate Finance

In July 1999, Carleton "Carly" Fiorina assumed the position of CEO of Hewlett-Packard (HP). Investors were pleased with her view of HP's future: She promised 15 percent annual growth in sales and earnings, quite a goal for a company with five consecutive years of declining revenue. Ms. Fiorina also changed the way HP was run. Rather than continuing to operate as separate product groups, which essentially meant the company operated as dozens of minicompanies, Ms. Fiorina reorganized the company into just two divisions.

In 2002, HP announced that it would merge with Compaq Computers. However, in one of the more acrimonious recent corporate battles, a group led by Walter Hewlett, son of one of HP's cofounders, fought the merger. Ms. Fiorina ultimately prevailed, and the merger took place. With Compaq in the fold, the company began

a two-pronged strategy. It would compete with Dell in the lower-cost, more commodity-like personal computer segment and with IBM in the more specialized, high-end computing market.

Unfortunately for HP's shareholders, Ms. Fiorina's strategy did not work out as planned; in February 2005, under pressure from HP's board of directors, Ms. Fiorina resigned her position as CEO. Evidently investors also felt a change in direction was a good idea; HP's stock price jumped almost 7 percent the day the resignation was announced.

Understanding Ms. Fiorina's rise from corporate executive to chief executive officer, and finally to ex-employee, takes us into issues involving the corporate form of organization, corporate goals, and corporate control, all of which we discuss in this chapter.

1.1 What Is Corporate Finance?

Suppose you decide to start a firm to make tennis balls. To do this you hire managers to buy raw materials, and you assemble a workforce that will produce and sell finished tennis balls. In the language of finance, you make an investment in assets such as inventory, machinery, land, and labor. The amount of cash you invest in assets must be matched by an equal amount of cash raised by financing. When you begin to sell tennis balls, your firm will generate cash. This is the basis of value creation. The purpose of the firm is to create value for you, the owner. The value is reflected in the framework of the simple balance sheet model of the firm.

The Balance Sheet Model of the Firm

Suppose we take a financial snapshot of the firm and its activities at a single point in time. Figure 1.1 shows a graphic conceptualization of the balance sheet, and it will help introduce you to corporate finance.

Figure 1.1

The Balance Sheet Model of the Firm

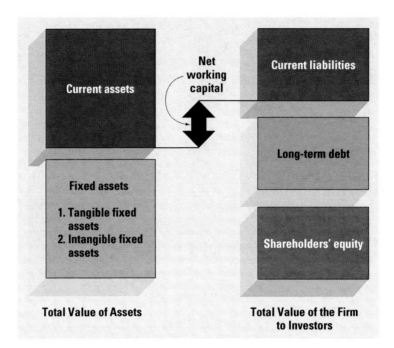

The assets of the firm are on the left side of the balance sheet. These assets can be thought of as current and fixed. *Fixed assets* are those that will last a long time, such as buildings. Some fixed assets are tangible, such as machinery and equipment. Other fixed assets are intangible, such as patents and trademarks. The other category of assets, *current assets*, comprises those that have short lives, such as inventory. The tennis balls that your firm has made, but has not yet sold, are part of its inventory. Unless you have overproduced, they will leave the firm shortly.

Before a company can invest in an asset, it must obtain financing, which means that it must raise the money to pay for the investment. The forms of financing are represented on the right side of the balance sheet. A firm will issue (sell) pieces of paper called *debt* (loan agreements) or *equity shares* (stock certificates). Just as assets are classified as long-lived or short-lived, so too are liabilities. A short-term debt is called a *current liability*. Short-term debt represents loans and other obligations that must be repaid within one year. Long-term debt is debt that does not have to be repaid within one year. Shareholders' equity represents the difference between the value of the assets and the debt of the firm. In this sense, it is a residual claim on the firm's assets.

From the balance sheet model of the firm, it is easy to see why finance can be thought of as the study of the following three questions:

1. In what long-lived assets should the firm invest? This question concerns the left side of the balance sheet. Of course the types and proportions of assets the firm needs tend to be set by the nature of the business. We use the term **capital budgeting** to describe the process of making and managing expenditures on long-lived assets.

2. How can the firm raise cash for required capital expenditures? This question concerns the right side of the balance sheet. The answer to this question involves the firm's **capital structure**, which represents the proportions of the firm's financing from current and long-term debt and equity.

3. How should short-term operating cash flows be managed? This question concerns the upper portion of the balance sheet. There is often a mismatch between the timing of

Figure 1.2

Two Pie Models of the Firm

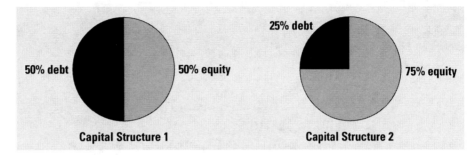

cash inflows and cash outflows during operating activities. Furthermore, the amount and timing of operating cash flows are not known with certainty. Financial managers must attempt to manage the gaps in cash flow. From a balance sheet perspective, short-term management of cash flow is associated with a firm's **net working capital**. Net working capital is defined as current assets minus current liabilities. From a financial perspective, short-term cash flow problems come from the mismatching of cash inflows and outflows. This is the subject of short-term finance.

Capital Structure

Financing arrangements determine how the value of the firm is sliced up. The people or institutions that buy debt from (i.e., lend money to) the firm are called *creditors*.[1] The holders of equity shares are called *shareholders*.

Sometimes it is useful to think of the firm as a pie. Initially the size of the pie will depend on how well the firm has made its investment decisions. After a firm has made its investment decisions, it determines the value of its assets (e.g., its buildings, land, and inventories).

The firm can then determine its capital structure. The firm might initially have raised the cash to invest in its assets by issuing more debt than equity; now it can consider changing that mix by issuing more equity and using the proceeds to buy back (pay off) some of its debt. Financing decisions like this can be made independently of the original investment decisions. The decisions to issue debt and equity affect how the pie is sliced.

The pie we are thinking of is depicted in Figure 1.2. The size of the pie is the value of the firm in the financial markets. We can write the value of the firm, V, as

$$V = B + S$$

where B is the market value of the debt and S is the market value of the equity. The pie diagrams consider two ways of slicing the pie: 50 percent debt and 50 percent equity, and 25 percent debt and 75 percent equity. The way the pie is sliced could affect its value. If so, the goal of the financial manager will be to choose the ratio of debt to equity that makes the value of the pie—that is, the value of the firm, V—as large as it can be.

The Financial Manager

In large firms, the finance activity is usually associated with a top officer of the firm, such as the vice president and chief financial officer, and some lesser officers. Figure 1.3 depicts a general organizational structure emphasizing the finance activity within the firm. Reporting to the chief financial officer are the treasurer and the controller. The treasurer is

For current issues facings CFOs, see www.cfo.com.

---

[1]We tend to use the words *creditors*, *debtholders*, and *bondholders* interchangeably. In later chapters we examine the differences among the kinds of creditors. In algebraic notation, we will usually refer to the firm's debt with the letter B (for bondholders).

Figure 1.3

Hypothetical
Organization Chart

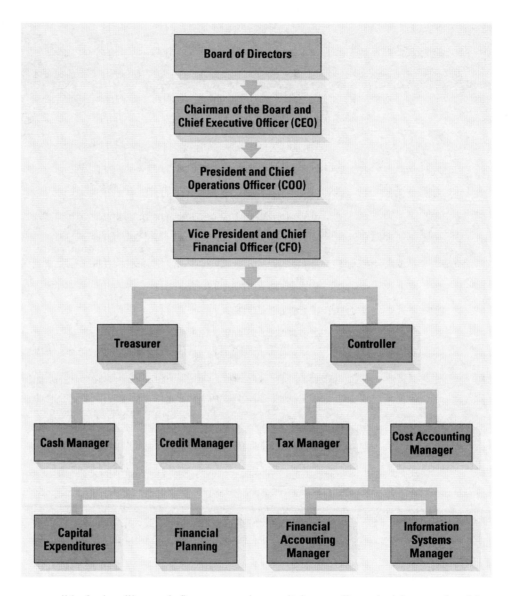

responsible for handling cash flows, managing capital expenditure decisions, and making financial plans. The controller handles the accounting function, which includes taxes, cost and financial accounting, and information systems.

The most important job of a financial manager is to create value from the firm's capital budgeting, financing, and net working capital activities. How do financial managers create value? The answer is that the firm should:

1. Try to buy assets that generate more cash than they cost.

2. Sell bonds and stocks and other financial instruments that raise more cash than they cost.

Thus, the firm must create more cash flow than it uses. The cash flows paid to bondholders and stockholders of the firm should be greater than the cash flows put into the firm by the bondholders and stockholders. To see how this is done, we can trace the cash flows from the firm to the financial markets and back again.

In Their Own Words

SKILLS NEEDED FOR THE CHIEF FINANCIAL OFFICERS OF eFINANCE.COM

Chief strategist: CFOs will need to use real-time financial information to make crucial decisions fast.

Chief deal maker: CFOs must be adept at venture capital, mergers and acquisitions, and strategic partnerships.

Chief risk officer: Limiting risk will be even more important as markets become more global and hedging instruments become more complex.

Chief communicator: Gaining the confidence of Wall Street and the media will be essential.

SOURCE: *BusinessWeek*, August 28, 2000, p. 120.

The interplay of the firm's activities with the financial markets is illustrated in Figure 1.4. The arrows in Figure 1.4 trace cash flow from the firm to the financial markets and back again. Suppose we begin with the firm's financing activities. To raise money, the firm sells debt and equity shares to investors in the financial markets. This results in cash flows from the financial markets to the firm (*A*). This cash is invested in the investment activities (assets) of the firm (*B*) by the firm's management. The cash generated by the firm (*C*) is paid to shareholders and bondholders (*F*). The shareholders receive cash in the form of dividends; the bondholders who lent funds to the firm receive interest and, when the initial loan is repaid, principal. Not all of the firm's cash is paid out. Some is retained (*E*), and some is paid to the government as taxes (*D*).

Over time, if the cash paid to shareholders and bondholders (*F*) is greater than the cash raised in the financial markets (*A*), value will be created.

Identification of Cash Flows Unfortunately, it is not easy to observe cash flows directly. Much of the information we obtain is in the form of accounting statements, and much of the work of financial analysis is to extract cash flow information from accounting statements. The following example illustrates how this is done.

Figure 1.4

Cash Flows between the Firm and the Financial Markets

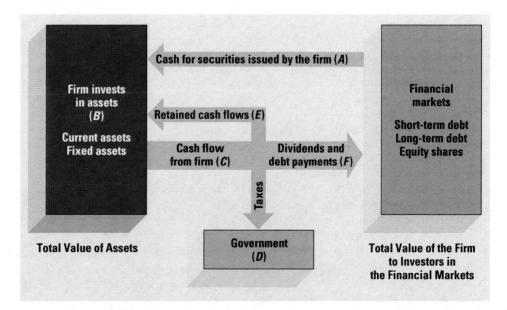

EXAMPLE 1.1

Accounting Profit versus Cash Flows   The Midland Company refines and trades gold. At the end of the year, it sold 2,500 ounces of gold for $1 million. The company had acquired the gold for $900,000 at the beginning of the year. The company paid cash for the gold when it was purchased. Unfortunately it has yet to collect from the customer to whom the gold was sold. The following is a standard accounting of Midland's financial circumstances at year-end:

The Midland Company
Accounting View
Income Statement
Year Ended December 31

Sales	$1,000,000
− Costs	−900,000
Profit	$ 100,000

By generally accepted accounting principles (GAAP), the sale is recorded even though the customer has yet to pay. It is assumed that the customer will pay soon. From the accounting perspective, Midland seems to be profitable. However, the perspective of corporate finance is different. It focuses on cash flows:

The Midland Company
Financial View
Income Statement
Year Ended December 31

Cash inflow	$ 0
Cash outflow	−900,000
	−$ 900,000

The perspective of corporate finance is interested in whether cash flows are being created by the gold trading operations of Midland. Value creation depends on cash flows. For Midland, value creation depends on whether and when it actually receives $1 million.

Timing of Cash Flows   The value of an investment made by a firm depends on the timing of cash flows. One of the most important principles of finance is that individuals prefer to receive cash flows earlier rather than later. One dollar received today is worth more than one dollar received next year.

EXAMPLE 1.2

Cash Flow Timing   The Midland Company is attempting to choose between two proposals for new products. Both proposals will provide additional cash flows over a four-year period and will initially cost $10,000. The cash flows from the proposals are as follows:

Year	New Product A	New Product B
1	$ 0	$ 4,000
2	0	4,000
3	0	4,000
4	20,000	4,000
Total	$20,000	$16,000

(continued)

At first it appears that new product A would be best. However, the cash flows from proposal B come earlier than those of A. Without more information, we cannot decide which set of cash flows would create the most value for the bondholders and shareholders. It depends on whether the value of getting cash from B up front outweighs the extra total cash from A. Bond and stock prices reflect this preference for earlier cash, and we will see how to use them to decide between A and B.

Risk of Cash Flows   The firm must consider risk. The amount and timing of cash flows are not usually known with certainty. Most investors have an aversion to risk.

Risk   The Midland Company is considering expanding operations overseas. It is evaluating Europe and Japan as possible sites. Europe is considered to be relatively safe, whereas operating in Japan is seen as very risky. In both cases the company would close down operations after one year.

After doing a complete financial analysis, Midland has come up with the following cash flows of the alternative plans for expansion under three scenarios—pessimistic, most likely, and optimistic:

	Pessimistic	Most Likely	Optimistic
Europe	$75,000	$100,000	$125,000
Japan	0	150,000	200,000

If we ignore the pessimistic scenario, perhaps Japan is the best alternative. When we take the pessimistic scenario into account, the choice is unclear. Japan appears to be riskier, but it also offers a higher expected level of cash flow. What is risk and how can it be defined? We must try to answer this important question. Corporate finance cannot avoid coping with risky alternatives, and much of our book is devoted to developing methods for evaluating risky opportunities.

EXAMPLE 1.3

1.2   The Corporate Firm

The firm is a way of organizing the economic activity of many individuals. A basic problem of the firm is how to raise cash. The corporate form of business—that is, organizing the firm as a corporation—is the standard method for solving problems encountered in raising large amounts of cash. However, businesses can take other forms. In this section we consider the three basic legal forms of organizing firms, and we see how firms go about the task of raising large amounts of money under each form.

The Sole Proprietorship

A **sole proprietorship** is a business owned by one person. Suppose you decide to start a business to produce mousetraps. Going into business is simple: You announce to all who will listen, "Today, I am going to build a better mousetrap."

Most large cities require that you obtain a business license. Afterward, you can begin to hire as many people as you need and borrow whatever money you need. At year-end all the profits and the losses will be yours.

Here are some factors that are important in considering a sole proprietorship:

1. The sole proprietorship is the cheapest business to form. No formal charter is required, and few government regulations must be satisfied for most industries.

For more about small business organization, see the "Business and Human Resources" section at **www.nolo.com**.

2. A sole proprietorship pays no corporate income taxes. All profits of the business are taxed as individual income.

3. The sole proprietorship has unlimited liability for business debts and obligations. No distinction is made between personal and business assets.

4. The life of the sole proprietorship is limited by the life of the sole proprietor.

5. Because the only money invested in the firm is the proprietor's, the equity money that can be raised by the sole proprietor is limited to the proprietor's personal wealth.

The Partnership

Any two or more people can get together and form a **partnership**. Partnerships fall into two categories: (1) general partnerships and (2) limited partnerships.

In a *general partnership* all partners agree to provide some fraction of the work and cash and to share the profits and losses. Each partner is liable for all of the debts of the partnership. A partnership agreement specifies the nature of the arrangement. The partnership agreement may be an oral agreement or a formal document setting forth the understanding.

Limited partnerships permit the liability of some of the partners to be limited to the amount of cash each has contributed to the partnership. Limited partnerships usually require that (1) at least one partner be a general partner and (2) the limited partners do not participate in managing the business. Here are some things that are important when considering a partnership:

1. Partnerships are usually inexpensive and easy to form. Written documents are required in complicated arrangements, including general and limited partnerships. Business licenses and filing fees may be necessary.

2. General partners have unlimited liability for all debts. The liability of limited partners is usually limited to the contribution each has made to the partnership. If one general partner is unable to meet his or her commitment, the shortfall must be made up by the other general partners.

3. The general partnership is terminated when a general partner dies or withdraws (but this is not so for a limited partner). It is difficult for a partnership to transfer ownership without dissolving. Usually all general partners must agree. However, limited partners may sell their interest in a business.

4. It is difficult for a partnership to raise large amounts of cash. Equity contributions are usually limited to a partner's ability and desire to contribute to the partnership. Many companies, such as Apple Computer, start life as a proprietorship or partnership, but at some point they choose to convert to corporate form.

5. Income from a partnership is taxed as personal income to the partners.

6. Management control resides with the general partners. Usually a majority vote is required on important matters, such as the amount of profit to be retained in the business.

It is difficult for large business organizations to exist as sole proprietorships or partnerships. The main advantage to a sole proprietorship or partnership is the cost of getting started. Afterward, the disadvantages, which may become severe, are (1) unlimited liability, (2) limited life of the enterprise, and (3) difficulty of transferring ownership. These three disadvantages lead to (4) difficulty in raising cash.

The Corporation

Of the forms of business enterprises, the **corporation** is by far the most important. It is a distinct legal entity. As such, a corporation can have a name and enjoy many of the legal powers of natural persons. For example, corporations can acquire and exchange property. Corporations can enter contracts and may sue and be sued. For jurisdictional purposes the corporation is a citizen of its state of incorporation (it cannot vote, however).

Starting a corporation is more complicated than starting a proprietorship or partnership. The incorporators must prepare articles of incorporation and a set of bylaws. The articles of incorporation must include the following:

1. Name of the corporation.
2. Intended life of the corporation (it may be forever).
3. Business purpose.
4. Number of shares of stock that the corporation is authorized to issue, with a statement of limitations and rights of different classes of shares.
5. Nature of the rights granted to shareholders.
6. Number of members of the initial board of directors.

The bylaws are the rules to be used by the corporation to regulate its own existence, and they concern its shareholders, directors, and officers. Bylaws range from the briefest possible statement of rules for the corporation's management to hundreds of pages of text.

In its simplest form, the corporation comprises three sets of distinct interests: the shareholders (the owners), the directors, and the corporation officers (the top management). Traditionally, the shareholders control the corporation's direction, policies, and activities. The shareholders elect a board of directors, who in turn select top management. Members of top management serve as corporate officers and manage the operations of the corporation in the best interest of the shareholders. In closely held corporations with few shareholders, there may be a large overlap among the shareholders, the directors, and the top management. However, in larger corporations, the shareholders, directors, and the top management are likely to be distinct groups.

The potential separation of ownership from management gives the corporation several advantages over proprietorships and partnerships:

1. Because ownership in a corporation is represented by shares of stock, ownership can be readily transferred to new owners. Because the corporation exists independently of those who own its shares, there is no limit to the transferability of shares as there is in partnerships.
2. The corporation has unlimited life. Because the corporation is separate from its owners, the death or withdrawal of an owner does not affect the corporation's legal existence. The corporation can continue on after the original owners have withdrawn.
3. The shareholders' liability is limited to the amount invested in the ownership shares. For example, if a shareholder purchased $1,000 in shares of a corporation, the potential loss would be $1,000. In a partnership, a general partner with a $1,000 contribution could lose the $1,000 plus any other indebtedness of the partnership.

Limited liability, ease of ownership transfer, and perpetual succession are the major advantages of the corporation form of business organization. These give the corporation an enhanced ability to raise cash.

Table 1.1   A Comparison of Partnerships and Corporations

	Corporation	Partnership
Liquidity and marketability	Shares can be exchanged without termination of the corporation. Common stock can be listed on a stock exchange.	Units are subject to substantial restrictions on transferability. There is usually no established trading market for partnership units.
Voting rights	Usually each share of common stock entitles the holder to one vote per share on matters requiring a vote and on the election of the directors. Directors determine top management.	Some voting rights by limited partners. However, general partners have exclusive control and management of operations.
Taxation	Corporations have double taxation: Corporate income is taxable, and dividends to shareholders are also taxable.	Partnerships are not taxable. Partners pay personal taxes on partnership profits.
Reinvestment and dividend payout	Corporations have broad latitude on dividend payout decisions.	Partnerships are generally prohibited from reinvesting partnership profits. All profits are distributed to partners.
Liability	Shareholders are not personally liable for obligations of the corporation.	Limited partners are not liable for obligations of partnerships. General partners may have unlimited liability.
Continuity of existence	Corporations may have a perpetual life.	Partnerships have limited life.

There is, however, one great disadvantage to incorporation. The federal government taxes corporate income (the states do as well). This tax is in addition to the personal income tax that shareholders pay on dividend income they receive. This is double taxation for shareholders when compared to taxation on proprietorships and partnerships. Table 1.1 summarizes our discussion of partnerships and corporations.

Today all 50 states have enacted laws allowing for the creation of a relatively new form of business organization, the limited liability company (LLC). The goal of this entity is to operate and be taxed like a partnership but retain limited liability for owners, so an LLC is essentially a hybrid of partnership and corporation. Although states have differing definitions for LLCs, the more important scorekeeper is the Internal Revenue Service (IRS). The IRS will consider an LLC a corporation, thereby subjecting it to double taxation, unless it meets certain specific criteria. In essence, an LLC cannot be too corporation-like, or it will be treated as one by the IRS. LLCs have become common. For example, Goldman, Sachs and Co., one of Wall Street's last remaining partnerships, decided to convert from a private partnership to an LLC (it later "went public," becoming a publicly held corporation). Large accounting firms and law firms by the score have converted to LLCs.

To find out more about LLCs, visit **www.corporate.com**.

A Corporation by Another Name . . .

The corporate form of organization has many variations around the world. The exact laws and regulations differ from country to country, of course, but the essential features of public ownership and limited liability remain. These firms are often called *joint stock companies*, *public limited companies*, or *limited liability companies*, depending on the specific nature of the firm and the country of origin.

Table 1.2 gives the names of a few well-known international corporations, their countries of origin, and a translation of the abbreviation that follows each company name.

Table 1.2

International Corporations

		Type of Company	
Company	**Country of Origin**	**In Original Language**	**Interpretation**
Bayerische Moterenwerke (BMW) AG	Germany	Aktiengesellschaft	Corporation
Dornier GmBH	Germany	Gesellschaft mit Baschraenkter Haftung	Limited liability company
Rolls-Royce PLC	United Kingdom	Public limited company	Public ltd. company
Shell UK Ltd.	United Kingdom	Limited	Corporation
Unilever NV	Netherlands	Naamloze Vennootschap	Joint stock company
Fiat SpA	Italy	Societa per Azioni	Joint stock company
Volvo AB	Sweden	Aktiebolag	Joint stock company
Peugeot SA	France	Société Anonyme	Joint stock company

1.3 The Goal of Financial Management

Assuming that we restrict our discussion to for-profit businesses, the goal of financial management is to make money or add value for the owners. This goal is a little vague, of course, so we examine some different ways of formulating it to come up with a more precise definition. Such a definition is important because it leads to an objective basis for making and evaluating financial decisions.

Possible Goals

If we were to consider possible financial goals, we might come up with some ideas like the following:

- Survive.
- Avoid financial distress and bankruptcy.
- Beat the competition.
- Maximize sales or market share.
- Minimize costs.
- Maximize profits.
- Maintain steady earnings growth.

These are only a few of the goals we could list. Furthermore, each of these possibilities presents problems as a goal for the financial manager.

For example, it's easy to increase market share or unit sales: All we have to do is lower our prices or relax our credit terms. Similarly, we can always cut costs simply by doing away with things such as research and development. We can avoid bankruptcy by never borrowing any money or never taking any risks, and so on. It's not clear that any of these actions are in the stockholders' best interests.

Profit maximization would probably be the most commonly cited goal, but even this is not a precise objective. Do we mean profits this year? If so, then we should note that actions such as deferring maintenance, letting inventories run down, and taking other short-run cost-cutting measures will tend to increase profits now, but these activities aren't necessarily desirable.

12

Ross–Westerfield–Jaffe:
Corporate Finance, Eighth
Edition

I. Overview

1. Introduction to Corporate
Finance

© The McGraw–Hill
Companies, 2008

The goal of maximizing profits may refer to some sort of "long-run" or "average" profits, but it's still unclear exactly what this means. First, do we mean something like accounting net income or earnings per share? As we will see in more detail in the next chapter, these accounting numbers may have little to do with what is good or bad for the firm. Second, what do we mean by the long run? As a famous economist once remarked, in the long run, we're all dead! More to the point, this goal doesn't tell us what the appropriate trade-off is between current and future profits.

The goals we've listed here are all different, but they tend to fall into two classes. The first of these relates to profitability. The goals involving sales, market share, and cost control all relate, at least potentially, to different ways of earning or increasing profits. The goals in the second group, involving bankruptcy avoidance, stability, and safety, relate in some way to controlling risk. Unfortunately, these two types of goals are somewhat contradictory. The pursuit of profit normally involves some element of risk, so it isn't really possible to maximize both safety and profit. What we need, therefore, is a goal that encompasses both factors.

The Goal of Financial Management

The financial manager in a corporation makes decisions for the stockholders of the firm. So, instead of listing possible goals for the financial manager, we really need to answer a more fundamental question: From the stockholders' point of view, what is a good financial management decision?

If we assume that stockholders buy stock because they seek to gain financially, then the answer is obvious: Good decisions increase the value of the stock, and poor decisions decrease the value of the stock.

From our observations, it follows that the financial manager acts in the shareholders' best interests by making decisions that increase the value of the stock. The appropriate goal for the financial manager can thus be stated quite easily:

The goal of financial management is to maximize the current value per share of the existing stock.

The goal of maximizing the value of the stock avoids the problems associated with the different goals we listed earlier. There is no ambiguity in the criterion, and there is no short-run versus long-run issue. We explicitly mean that our goal is to maximize the *current* stock value.

If this goal seems a little strong or one-dimensional to you, keep in mind that the stockholders in a firm are residual owners. By this we mean that they are entitled only to what is left after employees, suppliers, and creditors (and everyone else with legitimate claims) are paid their due. If any of these groups go unpaid, the stockholders get nothing. So if the stockholders are winning in the sense that the leftover, residual portion is growing, it must be true that everyone else is winning also.

Because the goal of financial management is to maximize the value of the stock, we need to learn how to identify investments and financing arrangements that favorably impact the value of the stock. This is precisely what we will be studying. In fact, we could have defined *corporate finance* as the study of the relationship between business decisions and the value of the stock in the business.

A More General Goal

If our goal is as stated in the preceding section (to maximize the value of the stock), an obvious question comes up: What is the appropriate goal when the firm has no traded stock? Corporations are certainly not the only type of business; and the stock in many corporations rarely changes hands, so it's difficult to say what the value per share is at any particular time.

Business ethics are considered at **www. business-ethics.com**.

As long as we are considering for-profit businesses, only a slight modification is needed. The total value of the stock in a corporation is simply equal to the value of the owners' equity. Therefore, a more general way of stating our goal is as follows: Maximize the market value of the existing owners' equity.

With this in mind, we don't care whether the business is a proprietorship, a partnership, or a corporation. For each of these, good financial decisions increase the market value of the owners' equity, and poor financial decisions decrease it. In fact, although we choose to focus on corporations in the chapters ahead, the principles we develop apply to all forms of business. Many of them even apply to the not-for-profit sector.

Finally, our goal does not imply that the financial manager should take illegal or unethical actions in the hope of increasing the value of the equity in the firm. What we mean is that the financial manager best serves the owners of the business by identifying goods and services that add value to the firm because they are desired and valued in the free marketplace.

1.4 The Agency Problem and Control of the Corporation

We've seen that the financial manager acts in the best interests of the stockholders by taking actions that increase the value of the stock. However, in large corporations ownership can be spread over a huge number of stockholders. This dispersion of ownership arguably means that management effectively controls the firm. In this case, will management necessarily act in the best interests of the stockholders? Put another way, might not management pursue its own goals at the stockholders' expense? In the following pages we briefly consider some of the arguments relating to this question.

Agency Relationships

The relationship between stockholders and management is called an *agency relationship*. Such a relationship exists whenever someone (the principal) hires another (the agent) to represent his or her interests. For example, you might hire someone (an agent) to sell a car that you own while you are away at school. In all such relationships there is a possibility of a conflict of interest between the principal and the agent. Such a conflict is called an **agency problem**.

Suppose you hire someone to sell your car and you agree to pay that person a flat fee when he or she sells the car. The agent's incentive in this case is to make the sale, not necessarily to get you the best price. If you offer a commission of, say, 10 percent of the sales price instead of a flat fee, then this problem might not exist. This example illustrates that the way in which an agent is compensated is one factor that affects agency problems.

Management Goals

To see how management and stockholder interests might differ, imagine that a firm is considering a new investment. The new investment is expected to favorably impact the share value, but it is also a relatively risky venture. The owners of the firm will wish to take the investment (because the stock value will rise), but management may not because there is the possibility that things will turn out badly and management jobs will be lost. If management does not take the investment, then the stockholders may lose a valuable opportunity. This is one example of an *agency cost*.

More generally, the term *agency costs* refers to the costs of the conflict of interest between stockholders and management. These costs can be indirect or direct. An indirect agency cost is a lost opportunity, such as the one we have just described.

Direct agency costs come in two forms. The first type is a corporate expenditure that benefits management but costs the stockholders. Perhaps the purchase of a luxurious and unneeded corporate jet would fall under this heading. The second type of direct agency cost is an expense that arises from the need to monitor management actions. Paying outside auditors to assess the accuracy of financial statement information could be one example.

It is sometimes argued that, left to themselves, managers would tend to maximize the amount of resources over which they have control or, more generally, corporate power or wealth. This goal could lead to an overemphasis on corporate size or growth. For example, cases in which management is accused of overpaying to buy up another company just to increase the size of the business or to demonstrate corporate power are not uncommon. Obviously, if overpayment does take place, such a purchase does not benefit the stockholders of the purchasing company.

Our discussion indicates that management may tend to overemphasize organizational survival to protect job security. Also, management may dislike outside interference, so independence and corporate self-sufficiency may be important goals.

Do Managers Act in the Stockholders' Interests?

Whether managers will, in fact, act in the best interests of stockholders depends on two factors. First, how closely are management goals aligned with stockholder goals? This question relates, at least in part, to the way managers are compensated. Second, can managers be replaced if they do not pursue stockholder goals? This issue relates to control of the firm. As we will discuss, there are a number of reasons to think that, even in the largest firms, management has a significant incentive to act in the interests of stockholders.

Managerial Compensation   Management will frequently have a significant economic incentive to increase share value for two reasons. First, managerial compensation, particularly at the top, is usually tied to financial performance in general and often to share value in particular. For example, managers are frequently given the option to buy stock at a bargain price. The more the stock is worth, the more valuable is this option. In fact, options are often used to motivate employees of all types, not just top management.

The second incentive managers have relates to job prospects. Better performers within the firm will tend to get promoted. More generally, managers who are successful in pursuing stockholder goals will be in greater demand in the labor market and thus command higher salaries.

In fact, managers who are successful in pursuing stockholder goals can reap enormous rewards. For example, the best-paid executive in 2005 was Terry Semel, the CEO of Yahoo; according to *Forbes* magazine, he made about $231 million. By way of comparison, Semel made quite a bit more than George Lucas ($180 million), but only slightly more than Oprah Winfrey ($225 million), and way more than Judge Judy ($28 million). Over the period 2001–2005, Oracle CEO Larry Ellison was the highest-paid executive, earning about $868 million.

Control of the Firm   Control of the firm ultimately rests with stockholders. They elect the board of directors, who, in turn, hire and fire management. The fact that stockholders control the corporation was made abundantly clear by Carly Fiorina's experience at HP, which we described to open the chapter. Even though she had reorganized the corporation,

Ross–Westerfield–Jaffe:
Corporate Finance, Eighth
Edition

I. Overview

1. Introduction to Corporate
Finance

© The McGraw–Hill
Companies, 2008

15

there came a time when shareholders, through their elected directors, decided that HP would be better off without her, so out she went.

An important mechanism by which unhappy stockholders can replace existing management is called a *proxy fight*. A proxy is the authority to vote someone else's stock. A proxy fight develops when a group solicits proxies in order to replace the existing board and thereby replace existing management. For example, the proposed merger between HP and Compaq, which we mentioned in our chapter opener, triggered one of the most widely followed, bitterly contested, and expensive proxy fights in history, with an estimated price tag of well over $100 million.

Another way that management can be replaced is by takeover. Firms that are poorly managed are more attractive as acquisitions than well-managed firms because a greater profit potential exists. Thus, avoiding a takeover by another firm gives management another incentive to act in the stockholders' interests. For example, in 2004, Comcast, the cable television giant, announced a surprise bid to buy Disney when Disney's management was under close scrutiny for its performance. Not too surprisingly, Disney's management strongly opposed being acquired, and Comcast ultimately decided to withdraw, in part because of improvements in Disney's financial performance.

Conclusion   The available theory and evidence are consistent with the view that stockholders control the firm and that stockholder wealth maximization is the relevant goal of the corporation. Even so, there will undoubtedly be times when management goals are pursued at the expense of the stockholders, at least temporarily.

Stakeholders

Our discussion thus far implies that management and stockholders are the only parties with an interest in the firm's decisions. This is an oversimplification, of course. Employees, customers, suppliers, and even the government all have a financial interest in the firm.

Taken together, these various groups are called **stakeholders** in the firm. In general, a stakeholder is someone other than a stockholder or creditor who potentially has a claim on the cash flows of the firm. Such groups will also attempt to exert control over the firm, perhaps to the detriment of the owners.

1.5   Financial Markets

As indicated in Section 1.1, firms offer two basic types of securities to investors. *Debt securities* are contractual obligations to repay corporate borrowing. *Equity securities* are shares of common stock and preferred stock that represent noncontractual claims to the residual cash flow of the firm. Issues of debt and stock that are publicly sold by the firm are then traded in the financial markets.

The financial markets are composed of the **money markets** and the **capital markets**. Money markets are the markets for debt securities that will pay off in the short term (usually less than one year). Capital markets are the markets for long-term debt (with a maturity of over one year) and for equity shares.

The term *money market* applies to a group of loosely connected markets. They are dealer markets. Dealers are firms that make continuous quotations of prices for which they stand ready to buy and sell money market instruments for their own inventory and at their own risk. Thus, the dealer is a principal in most transactions. This is different from a stockbroker acting as an agent for a customer in buying or selling common stock on most stock exchanges; an agent does not actually acquire the securities.

At the core of the money markets are the money market banks (these are large banks mostly in New York), government securities dealers (some of which are the large banks), and many money brokers. Money brokers specialize in finding short-term money for borrowers and placing money for lenders. The financial markets can be classified further as the *primary market* and the *secondary markets*.

The Primary Market: New Issues

The primary market is used when governments and corporations initially sell securities. Corporations engage in two types of primary market sales of debt and equity: public offerings and private placements.

Most publicly offered corporate debt and equity come to the market underwritten by a syndicate of investment banking firms. The *underwriting* syndicate buys the new securities from the firm for the syndicate's own account and resells them at a higher price. Publicly issued debt and equity must be registered with the United States Securities and Exchange Commission (SEC). *Registration* requires the corporation to disclose any and all material information in a registration statement.

The legal, accounting, and other costs of preparing the registration statement are not negligible. In part to avoid these costs, privately placed debt and equity are sold on the basis of private negotiations to large financial institutions, such as insurance companies and mutual funds, and other investors. Private placements are not registered with the SEC.

Secondary Markets

A secondary market transaction involves one owner or creditor selling to another. Therefore, the secondary markets provide the means for transferring ownership of corporate securities. Although a corporation is directly involved only in a primary market transaction (when it sells securities to raise cash), the secondary markets are still critical to large corporations. The reason is that investors are much more willing to purchase securities in a primary market transaction when they know that those securities can later be resold if desired.

Dealer versus Auction Markets   There are two kinds of secondary markets: *dealer* markets and *auction* markets. Generally speaking, dealers buy and sell for themselves, at their own risk. A car dealer, for example, buys and sells automobiles. In contrast, brokers and agents match buyers and sellers, but they do not actually own the commodity that is bought or sold. A real estate agent, for example, does not normally buy and sell houses.

Dealer markets in stocks and long-term debt are called *over-the-counter* (OTC) markets. Most trading in debt securities takes place over the counter. The expression *over the counter* refers to days of old when securities were literally bought and sold at counters in offices around the country. Today a significant fraction of the market for stocks and almost all of the market for long-term debt have no central location; the many dealers are connected electronically.

Auction markets differ from dealer markets in two ways. First, an auction market or exchange has a physical location (like Wall Street). Second, in a dealer market, most of the buying and selling is done by the dealer. The primary purpose of an auction market, on the other hand, is to match those who wish to sell with those who wish to buy. Dealers play a limited role.

Trading in Corporate Securities   The equity shares of most large firms in the United States trade in organized auction markets. The largest such market is the New York Stock Exchange (NYSE), which accounts for more than 85 percent of all the shares traded in auction markets. Other auction exchanges include the American Stock Exchange (AMEX) and regional exchanges such as the Pacific Stock Exchange.

In addition to the stock exchanges, there is a large OTC market for stocks. In 1971, the National Association of Securities Dealers (NASD) made available to dealers and brokers an electronic quotation system called NASDAQ (which originally stood for NASD Automated Quotation system and is pronounced "naz-dak"). There are roughly two times as many companies on NASDAQ as there are on the NYSE, but they tend to be much smaller and trade less actively. There are exceptions, of course. Both Microsoft and Intel trade OTC, for example. Nonetheless, the total value of NASDAQ stocks is much less than the total value of NYSE stocks.

There are many large and important financial markets outside the United States, of course, and U.S. corporations are increasingly looking to these markets to raise cash. The Tokyo Stock Exchange and the London Stock Exchange (TSE and LSE, respectively) are two well-known examples. The fact that OTC markets have no physical location means that national borders do not present a great barrier, and there is now a huge international OTC debt market. Because of globalization, financial markets have reached the point where trading in many investments never stops; it just travels around the world.

Exchange Trading of Listed Stocks

Auction markets are different from dealer markets in two ways. First, trading in a given auction exchange takes place at a single site on the floor of the exchange. Second, transaction prices of shares traded on auction exchanges are communicated almost immediately to the public by computer and other devices.

The NYSE is one of the preeminent securities exchanges in the world. All transactions in stocks listed on the NYSE occur at a particular place on the floor of the exchange called a *post*. At the heart of the market is the specialist. Specialists are members of the NYSE who *make a market* in designated stocks. Specialists have an obligation to offer to buy and sell shares of their assigned NYSE stocks. It is believed that this makes the market liquid because the specialist assumes the role of a buyer for investors if they wish to sell and a seller if they wish to buy.

Listing

Stocks that trade on an organized exchange are said to be *listed* on that exchange. To be listed, firms must meet certain minimum criteria concerning, for example, asset size and number of shareholders. These criteria differ from one exchange to another.

NYSE has the most stringent requirements of the exchanges in the United States. For example, to be listed on the NYSE, a company is expected to have a market value for its publicly held shares of at least $100 million. There are additional minimums on earnings, assets, and number of shares outstanding. The listing requirements for non–U.S. companies are somewhat more stringent. Table 1.3 gives the market value of NYSE-listed stocks and bonds.

Listed companies face significant disclosure requirements. In response to corporate scandals at companies such as Enron, WorldCom, Tyco, and Adelphia, Congress enacted the Sarbanes-Oxley Act in 2002. The act, better known as "Sarbox" or "SOX," is intended to protect investors from corporate abuses. For example, one section of Sarbox prohibits personal loans from a company to its officers, such as the ones that were received by WorldCom CEO Bernie Ebbers.

One of the key sections of Sarbox took effect on November 15, 2004. Section 404 requires, among other things, that each company's annual report must have an assessment

To learn more about the exchanges, visit **www.nyse.com** and **www.nasdaq.com**.

To find out more about Sarbanes-Oxley, go to **www.sarbanes-oxley.com**.

Table 1.3

Market Value of NYSE-Listed Securities

End-of-Year	Number of Listed Companies	Market Value ($ in trillions)
NYSE-listed stocks*		
2005	2,779	$21.2
2004	2,768	19.8
2003	2,750	17.3
2002	2,783	13.4
2001	2,798	16.0
2000	2,862	17.1

End-of-Year	Number of Issues	Market Value ($ in trillions)
NYSE-listed bonds†		
2005	971	$1.0
2004	1,059	1.1
2003	1,273	1.4
2002	1,323	1.4
2001	1,447	1.7
2000	1,627	2.1

*Includes preferred stock and common stock.

†Includes bonds issued by U.S. companies, foreign companies, the U.S. government, international banks, foreign governments, and municipalities. The bond value shown is the face value.

SOURCE: Data from the NYSE Web site, www.nyse.com.

of the company's internal control structure and financial reporting. The auditor must then evaluate and attest to management's assessment of these issues.

Sarbox contains other key requirements. For example, the officers of the corporation must review and sign the annual reports. They must explicitly declare that the annual report does not contain any false statements or material omissions; that the financial statements fairly represent the financial results; and that they are responsible for all internal controls. Finally, the annual report must list any deficiencies in internal controls. In essence, Sarbox makes company management responsible for the accuracy of the company's financial statements.

Of course, as with any law, there are compliance costs, and Sarbox has increased the cost of corporate audits, sometimes dramatically. Estimates of the increase in company audit costs to comply with Sarbox range from $500,000 to over $5 million, which has led to some unintended consequences. For example, in 2004, 134 firms delisted their shares from exchanges, or "went dark." This was up from 30 delistings in 1999. Most of the companies that delisted stated that their reason was to avoid the cost of compliance with Sarbox. Some conservative estimates put the national Sarbox compliance tab at $35 billion in the first year alone, which is roughly 20 times the amount originally estimated by the SEC. For a large multibillion-dollar-revenue company, the cost might be .05 percent of revenues; but it could be 4 percent or so for smaller companies, an enormous cost.

A company that goes dark does not have to file quarterly or annual reports. Annual audits by independent auditors are not required, and executives do not have to certify the accuracy of the financial statements, so the savings can be huge. Of course there are costs. Stock prices typically fall when a company announces it is going dark. Further, such companies will typically have limited access to capital markets and usually will pay higher interest on bank loans.

Summary and Conclusions

This chapter introduced you to some of the basic ideas in corporate finance:

1. Corporate finance has three main areas of concern:
   a. *Capital budgeting:* What long-term investments should the firm take?
   b. *Capital structure:* Where will the firm get the long-term financing to pay for its investments? Also, what mixture of debt and equity should it use to fund operations?
   c. *Working capital management:* How should the firm manage its everyday financial activities?

2. The goal of financial management in a for-profit business is to make decisions that increase the value of the stock, or, more generally, increase the market value of the equity.

3. The corporate form of organization is superior to other forms when it comes to raising money and transferring ownership interests, but it has the significant disadvantage of double taxation.

4. There is the possibility of conflicts between stockholders and management in a large corporation. We called these conflicts *agency problems* and discussed how they might be controlled and reduced.

5. The advantages of the corporate form are enhanced by the existence of financial markets. Financial markets function as both primary and secondary markets for corporate securities and can be organized as either dealer or auction markets.

Of the topics we've discussed thus far, the most important is the goal of financial management: maximizing the value of the stock. Throughout the text we will be analyzing many different financial decisions, but we will always ask the same question: How does the decision under consideration affect the value of the stock?

Concept Questions

1. **Agency Problems** Who owns a corporation? Describe the process whereby the owners control the firm's management. What is the main reason that an agency relationship exists in the corporate form of organization? In this context, what kinds of problems can arise?

2. **Not-for-Profit Firm Goals** Suppose you were the financial manager of a not-for-profit business (a not-for-profit hospital, perhaps). What kinds of goals do you think would be appropriate?

3. **Goal of the Firm** Evaluate the following statement: Managers should not focus on the current stock value because doing so will lead to an overemphasis on short-term profits at the expense of long-term profits.

4. **Ethics and Firm Goals** Can the goal of maximizing the value of the stock conflict with other goals, such as avoiding unethical or illegal behavior? In particular, do you think subjects like customer and employee safety, the environment, and the general good of society fit in this framework, or are they essentially ignored? Think of some specific scenarios to illustrate your answer.

5. **International Firm Goal** Would the goal of maximizing the value of the stock differ for financial management in a foreign country? Why or why not?

6. **Agency Problems** Suppose you own stock in a company. The current price per share is $25. Another company has just announced that it wants to buy your company and will pay $35 per share to acquire all the outstanding stock. Your company's management immediately begins fighting off this hostile bid. Is management acting in the shareholders' best interests? Why or why not?

7. **Agency Problems and Corporate Ownership** Corporate ownership varies around the world. Historically, individuals have owned the majority of shares in public corporations in the United States. In Germany and Japan, however, banks, other large financial institutions, and other companies own most of the stock in public corporations. Do you think agency problems are likely to be more or less severe in Germany and Japan than in the United States?

8. **Agency Problems and Corporate Ownership** In recent years, large financial institutions such as mutual funds and pension funds have become the dominant owners of stock in the

United States, and these institutions are becoming more active in corporate affairs. What are the implications of this trend for agency problems and corporate control?

9. **Executive Compensation**   Critics have charged that compensation to top management in the United States is simply too high and should be cut back. For example, focusing on large corporations, Larry Ellison of Oracle has been one of the best-compensated CEOs in the United States, earning about $41 million in 2004 alone and $836 million over the 2000–2004 period. Are such amounts excessive? In answering, it might be helpful to recognize that superstar athletes such as Tiger Woods, top entertainers such as Mel Gibson and Oprah Winfrey, and many others at the top of their respective fields earn at least as much, if not a great deal more.

10. **Goal of Financial Management**   Why is the goal of financial management to maximize the current share price of the company's stock? In other words, why isn't the goal to maximize the future share price?

S&P Problems

STANDARD &POOR'S

www.mhhe.com/edumarketinsight

1. **Industry Comparison**   On the Market Insight home page, follow the "Industry" link at the top of the page. You will be on the industry page. You can use the drop-down menu to select different industries. Answer the following questions for these industries: airlines, automobile manufacturers, biotechnology, computer hardware, homebuilding, marine, restaurants, soft drinks, and wireless telecommunications.
   a. How many companies are in each industry?
   b. What are the total sales for each industry?
   c. Do the industries with the largest total sales have the most companies in the industry? What does this tell you about competition in the various industries?

CHAPTER 1
INTRODUCTION TO CORPORATE FINANCE

Answers to Concept Questions

1. In the corporate form of ownership, the shareholders are the owners of the firm. The shareholders elect the directors of the corporation, who in turn appoint the firm's management. This separation of ownership from control in the corporate form of organization is what causes agency problems to exist. Management may act in its own or someone else's best interests, rather than those of the shareholders. If such events occur, they may contradict the goal of maximizing the share price of the equity of the firm.

2. Such organizations frequently pursue social or political missions, so many different goals are conceivable. One goal that is often cited is revenue minimization; i.e., provide whatever goods and services are offered at the lowest possible cost to society. A better approach might be to observe that even a not-for-profit business has equity. Thus, one answer is that the appropriate goal is to maximize the value of the equity.

3. Presumably, the current stock value reflects the risk, timing, and magnitude of all future cash flows, both short-term *and* long-term. If this is correct, then the statement is false.

4. An argument can be made either way. At the one extreme, we could argue that in a market economy, all of these things are priced. There is thus an optimal level of, for example, ethical and/or illegal behavior, and the framework of stock valuation explicitly includes these. At the other extreme, we could argue that these are non-economic phenomena and are best handled through the political process. A classic (and highly relevant) thought question that illustrates this debate goes something like this: "A firm has estimated that the cost of improving the safety of one of its products is $30 million. However, the firm believes that improving the safety of the product will only save $20 million in product liability claims. What should the firm do?"

5. The goal will be the same, but the best course of action toward that goal may be different because of differing social, political, and economic institutions.

6. The goal of management should be to maximize the share price for the current shareholders. If management believes that it can improve the profitability of the firm so that the share price will exceed $35, then they should fight the offer from the outside company. If management believes that this bidder or other unidentified bidders will actually pay more than $35 per share to acquire the company, then they should still fight the offer. However, if the current management cannot increase the value of the firm beyond the bid price, and no other higher bids come in, then management is not acting in the interests of the shareholders by fighting the offer. Since current managers often lose their jobs when the corporation is acquired, poorly monitored managers have an incentive to fight corporate takeovers in situations such as this.

B-2   SOLUTIONS

7.   We would expect agency problems to be less severe in other countries, primarily due to the relatively small percentage of individual ownership. Fewer individual owners should reduce the number of diverse opinions concerning corporate goals. The high percentage of institutional ownership might lead to a higher degree of agreement between owners and managers on decisions concerning risky projects. In addition, institutions may be better able to implement effective monitoring mechanisms on managers than can individual owners, based on the institutions' deeper resources and experiences with their own management.

8.   The increase in institutional ownership of stock in the United States and the growing activism of these large shareholder groups may lead to a reduction in agency problems for U.S. corporations and a more efficient market for corporate control. However, this may not always be the case. If the managers of the mutual fund or pension plan are not concerned with the interests of the investors, the agency problem could potentially remain the same, or even increase since there is the possibility of agency problems between the fund and its investors.

9.   How much is too much? Who is worth more, Jack Welch or Tiger Woods? The simplest answer is that there is a market for executives just as there is for all types of labor. Executive compensation is the price that clears the market. The same is true for athletes and performers. Having said that, one aspect of executive compensation deserves comment. A primary reason executive compensation has grown so dramatically is that companies have increasingly moved to stock-based compensation. Such movement is obviously consistent with the attempt to better align stockholder and management interests. In recent years, stock prices have soared, so management has cleaned up. It is sometimes argued that much of this reward is simply due to rising stock prices in general, not managerial performance. Perhaps in the future, executive compensation will be designed to reward only differential performance, i.e., stock price increases in excess of general market increases.

10.   Maximizing the current share price is the same as maximizing the future share price at any future period. The value of a share of stock depends on all of the future cash flows of company. Another way to look at this is that, barring large cash payments to shareholders, the expected price of the stock must be higher in the future than it is today. Who would buy a stock for $100 today when the share price in one year is expected to be $80?

Ross–Westerfield–Jordan:
Fundamentals of Corporate
Finance, Eighth Edition,
Standard

III. Valuation of Future
Cash Flows

5. Introduction to
Valuation: The Time Value
of Money

© The McGraw–Hill
Companies, 2008

23

INTRODUCTION TO VALUATION: THE TIME VALUE OF MONEY

5

PART 3

Valuation of Future Cash Flows

On April 21, 2006, Toyota Motor Credit Corporation (TMCC), a subsidiary of Toyota Motors, offered some securities for sale to the public. Under the terms of the deal, TMCC promised to repay the owner of one of these securities $10,000 on April 23, 2036, but investors would receive nothing until then. Investors paid TMCC $1,163 for each of these securities; so they gave up $1,163 on April 21, 2006, for the promise of a $10,000 payment 30 years later. Such a security, for which you pay some amount today in exchange for a promised lump sum to be received at a future date, is about the simplest possible type.

Is giving up $1,163 in exchange for $10,000 in 30 years a good deal? On the plus side, you get back about $9 for every $1 you put up. That probably sounds good; but on the down side, you have to wait 30 years to get it. What you need to know is how to analyze this trade-off; this chapter gives you the tools you need.

Visit us at www.mhhe.com/rwj

DIGITAL STUDY TOOLS
- Self-Study Software
- Multiple-Choice Quizzes
- Flashcards for Testing and Key Terms

One of the basic problems faced by the financial manager is how to determine the value today of cash flows expected in the future. For example, the jackpot in a PowerBall™ lottery drawing was $110 million. Does this mean the winning ticket was worth $110 million? The answer is no because the jackpot was actually going to pay out over a 20-year period at a rate of $5.5 million per year. How much was the ticket worth then? The answer depends on the time value of money, the subject of this chapter.

In the most general sense, the phrase *time value of money* refers to the fact that a dollar in hand today is worth more than a dollar promised at some time in the future. On a practical level, one reason for this is that you could earn interest while you waited; so a dollar today would grow to more than a dollar later. The trade-off between money now and money later thus depends on, among other things, the rate you can earn by investing. Our goal in this chapter is to explicitly evaluate this trade-off between dollars today and dollars at some future time.

A thorough understanding of the material in this chapter is critical to understanding material in subsequent chapters, so you should study it with particular care. We will present a number of examples in this chapter. In many problems, your answer may differ from ours slightly. This can happen because of rounding and is not a cause for concern.

122   **PART 3** Valuation of Future Cash Flows

5.1 Future Value and Compounding

future value (FV)
The amount an investment is worth after one or more periods.

The first thing we will study is future value. **Future value (FV)** refers to the amount of money an investment will grow to over some period of time at some given interest rate. Put another way, future value is the cash value of an investment at some time in the future. We start out by considering the simplest case: a single-period investment.

INVESTING FOR A SINGLE PERIOD

Suppose you invest $100 in a savings account that pays 10 percent interest per year. How much will you have in one year? You will have $110. This $110 is equal to your original *principal* of $100 plus $10 in interest that you earn. We say that $110 is the future value of $100 invested for one year at 10 percent, and we simply mean that $100 today is worth $110 in one year, given that 10 percent is the interest rate.

In general, if you invest for one period at an interest rate of r, your investment will grow to $(1 + r)$ per dollar invested. In our example, r is 10 percent, so your investment grows to $1 + .10 = 1.1$ dollars per dollar invested. You invested $100 in this case, so you ended up with $100 \times 1.10 = \$110$.

INVESTING FOR MORE THAN ONE PERIOD

Going back to our $100 investment, what will you have after two years, assuming the interest rate doesn't change? If you leave the entire $110 in the bank, you will earn $110 \times .10 = \$11$ in interest during the second year, so you will have a total of $110 + 11 = \$121$. This $121 is the future value of $100 in two years at 10 percent. Another way of looking at it is that one year from now you are effectively investing $110 at 10 percent for a year. This is a single-period problem, so you'll end up with $1.10 for every dollar invested, or $110 \times 1.1 = \$121$ total.

This $121 has four parts. The first part is the $100 original principal. The second part is the $10 in interest you earned in the first year, and the third part is another $10 you earn in the second year, for a total of $120. The last $1 you end up with (the fourth part) is interest you earn in the second year on the interest paid in the first year: $10 \times .10 = \$1$.

compounding
The process of accumulating interest on an investment over time to earn more interest.

This process of leaving your money and any accumulated interest in an investment for more than one period, thereby *reinvesting* the interest, is called **compounding**. Compounding the interest means earning **interest on interest**, so we call the result **compound interest**. With **simple interest**, the interest is not reinvested, so interest is earned each period only on the original principal.

interest on interest
Interest earned on the reinvestment of previous interest payments.

| **EXAMPLE 5.1** | **Interest on Interest** |

Suppose you locate a two-year investment that pays 14 percent per year. If you invest $325, how much will you have at the end of the two years? How much of this is simple interest? How much is compound interest?

At the end of the first year, you will have $325 \times (1 + .14) = \$370.50$. If you reinvest this entire amount and thereby compound the interest, you will have $370.50 \times 1.14 = \$422.37$ at the end of the second year. The total interest you earn is thus $422.37 - 325 = \$97.37$. Your $325 original principal earns $325 \times .14 = \$45.50$ in interest each year, for a two-year total of $91 in simple interest. The remaining $97.37 - 91 = \$6.37$ results from compounding. You can check this by noting that the interest earned in the first year is $45.50. The interest on interest earned in the second year thus amounts to $45.50 \times .14 = \$6.37$, as we calculated.

We now take a closer look at how we calculated the $121 future value. We multiplied $110 by 1.1 to get $121. The $110, however, was $100 also multiplied by 1.1. In other words:

$$\begin{aligned} \$121 &= \$110 \times 1.1 \\ &= (\$100 \times 1.1) \times 1.1 \\ &= \$100 \times (1.1 \times 1.1) \\ &= \$100 \times 1.1^2 \\ &= \$100 \times 1.21 \end{aligned}$$

At the risk of belaboring the obvious, let's ask, How much would our $100 grow to after three years? Once again, in two years, we'll be investing $121 for one period at 10 percent. We'll end up with $1.10 for every dollar we invest, or $121 × 1.1 = $133.10 total. This $133.10 is thus:

$$\begin{aligned} \$133.10 &= \$121 \times 1.1 \\ &= (\$110 \times 1.1) \times 1.1 \\ &= (\$100 \times 1.1) \times 1.1 \times 1.1 \\ &= \$100 \times (1.1 \times 1.1 \times 1.1) \\ &= \$100 \times 1.1^3 \\ &= \$100 \times 1.331 \end{aligned}$$

You're probably noticing a pattern to these calculations, so we can now go ahead and state the general result. As our examples suggest, the future value of $1 invested for t periods at a rate of r per period is this:

Future value $= \$1 \times (1 + r)^t$ [5.1]

The expression $(1 + r)^t$ is sometimes called the *future value interest factor* (or just *future value factor*) for $1 invested at r percent for t periods and can be abbreviated as FVIF(r, t).

In our example, what would your $100 be worth after five years? We can first compute the relevant future value factor as follows:

$(1 + r)^t = (1 + .10)^5 = 1.1^5 = 1.6105$

Your $100 will thus grow to:

$100 × 1.6105 = $161.05

The growth of your $100 each year is illustrated in Table 5.1. As shown, the interest earned in each year is equal to the beginning amount multiplied by the interest rate of 10 percent.

compound interest
Interest earned on both the initial principal and the interest reinvested from prior periods.

simple interest
Interest earned only on the original principal amount invested.

For a discussion of time value concepts (and lots more) see www.financeprofessor.com.

Year	Beginning Amount	Simple Interest	Compound Interest	Total Interest Earned	Ending Amount
1	$100.00	$10	$ 0.00	$10.00	$110.00
2	110.00	10	1.00	11.00	121.00
3	121.00	10	2.10	12.10	133.10
4	133.10	10	3.31	13.31	146.41
5	146.41	10	4.64	14.64	161.05
		Total $50 simple interest	Total $11.05 compound interest	Total $61.05 interest	

TABLE 5.1

Future Value of $100 at 10 percent

FIGURE 5.1

Future Value, Simple Interest, and Compound Interest

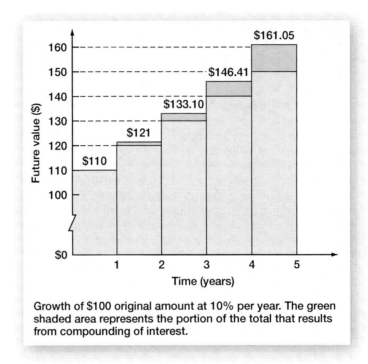

Growth of $100 original amount at 10% per year. The green shaded area represents the portion of the total that results from compounding of interest.

A brief introduction to key financial concepts is available at www.teachmefinance.com.

In Table 5.1, notice the total interest you earn is $61.05. Over the five-year span of this investment, the simple interest is $100 × .10 = $10 per year, so you accumulate $50 this way. The other $11.05 is from compounding.

Figure 5.1 illustrates the growth of the compound interest in Table 5.1. Notice how the simple interest is constant each year, but the amount of compound interest you earn gets bigger every year. The amount of the compound interest keeps increasing because more and more interest builds up and there is thus more to compound.

Future values depend critically on the assumed interest rate, particularly for long-lived investments. Figure 5.2 illustrates this relationship by plotting the growth of $1 for different rates and lengths of time. Notice the future value of $1 after 10 years is about $6.20 at a 20 percent rate, but it is only about $2.60 at 10 percent. In this case, doubling the interest rate more than doubles the future value.

To solve future value problems, we need to come up with the relevant future value factors. There are several different ways of doing this. In our example, we could have multiplied 1.1 by itself five times. This would work just fine, but it would get to be very tedious for, say, a 30-year investment.

Fortunately, there are several easier ways to get future value factors. Most calculators have a key labeled "y^x." You can usually just enter 1.1, press this key, enter 5, and press the "=" key to get the answer. This is an easy way to calculate future value factors because it's quick and accurate.

Alternatively, you can use a table that contains future value factors for some common interest rates and time periods. Table 5.2 contains some of these factors. Table A.1 in the appendix at the end of the book contains a much larger set. To use the table, find the column that corresponds to 10 percent. Then look down the rows until you come to five periods. You should find the factor that we calculated, 1.6105.

Tables such as 5.2 are not as common as they once were because they predate inexpensive calculators and are available only for a relatively small number of rates. Interest rates

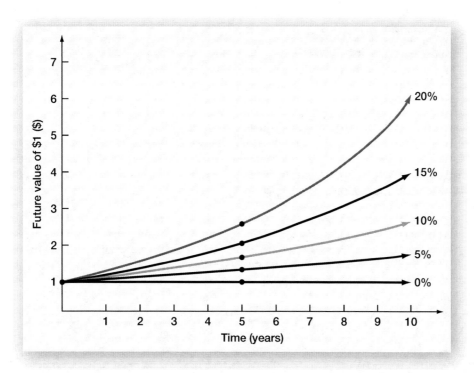

FIGURE 5.2

Future Value of $1 for Different Periods and Rates

TABLE 5.2

Future Value Interest Factors

	Interest Rate			
Number of Periods	**5%**	**10%**	**15%**	**20%**
1	1.0500	1.1000	1.1500	1.2000
2	1.1025	1.2100	1.3225	1.4400
3	1.1576	1.3310	1.5209	1.7280
4	1.2155	1.4641	1.7490	2.0736
5	1.2763	1.6105	2.0114	2.4883

are often quoted to three or four decimal places, so the tables needed to deal with these accurately would be quite large. As a result, the real world has moved away from using them. We will emphasize the use of a calculator in this chapter.

These tables still serve a useful purpose. To make sure you are doing the calculations correctly, pick a factor from the table and then calculate it yourself to see that you get the same answer. There are plenty of numbers to choose from.

Compound Interest	**EXAMPLE 5.2**

You've located an investment that pays 12 percent. That rate sounds good to you, so you invest $400. How much will you have in three years? How much will you have in seven years? At the end of seven years, how much interest will you have earned? How much of that interest results from compounding?

Based on our discussion, we can calculate the future value factor for 12 percent and three years as follows:

$$(1 + r)^t = 1.12^3 = 1.4049$$

(continued)

126   **PART 3** Valuation of Future Cash Flows

Your $400 thus grows to:

$$\$400 \times 1.4049 = \$561.97$$

After seven years, you will have:

$$\$400 \times 1.12^7 = \$400 \times 2.2107 = \$884.27$$

Thus, you will more than double your money over seven years.

Because you invested $400, the interest in the $884.27 future value is $884.27 − 400 = $484.27. At 12 percent, your $400 investment earns $400 × .12 = $48 in simple interest every year. Over seven years, the simple interest thus totals 7 × $48 = $336. The other $484.27 − 336 = $148.27 is from compounding.

The effect of compounding is not great over short time periods, but it really starts to add up as the horizon grows. To take an extreme case, suppose one of your more frugal ancestors had invested $5 for you at a 6 percent interest rate 200 years ago. How much would you have today? The future value factor is a substantial $1.06^{200} = 115,125.90$ (you won't find this one in a table), so you would have $5 × 115,125.90 = $575,629.52 today. Notice that the simple interest is just $5 × .06 = $.30 per year. After 200 years, this amounts to $60. The rest is from reinvesting. Such is the power of compound interest!

EXAMPLE 5.3 **How Much for That Island?**

To further illustrate the effect of compounding for long horizons, consider the case of Peter Minuit and the American Indians. In 1626, Minuit bought all of Manhattan Island for about $24 in goods and trinkets. This sounds cheap, but the Indians may have gotten the better end of the deal. To see why, suppose the Indians had sold the goods and invested the $24 at 10 percent. How much would it be worth today?

About 380 years have passed since the transaction. At 10 percent, $24 will grow by quite a bit over that time. How much? The future value factor is roughly:

$$(1 + r)^t = 1.1^{380} \approx 5{,}400{,}000{,}000{,}000{,}000$$

That is, 5.4 followed by 14 zeroes. The future value is thus on the order of $24 × 5.4 = $130 *quadrillion* (give or take a few hundreds of trillions).

Well, $130 quadrillion is a lot of money. How much? If you had it, you could buy the United States. All of it. Cash. With money left over to buy Canada, Mexico, and the rest of the world, for that matter.

This example is something of an exaggeration, of course. In 1626, it would not have been easy to locate an investment that would pay 10 percent every year without fail for the next 380 years.

CALCULATOR HINTS

Using a Financial Calculator

Although there are the various ways of calculating future values we have described so far, many of you will decide that a financial calculator is the way to go. If you are planning on using one, you should read this extended hint; otherwise, skip it.

A financial calculator is simply an ordinary calculator with a few extra features. In particular, it knows some of the most commonly used financial formulas, so it can directly compute things like future values.

(continued)

Financial calculators have the advantage that they handle a lot of the computation, but that is really all. In other words, you still have to understand the problem; the calculator just does some of the arithmetic. In fact, there is an old joke (somewhat modified) that goes like this: Anyone can make a mistake on a time value of money problem, but to really screw one up takes a financial calculator! We therefore have two goals for this section. First, we'll discuss how to compute future values. After that, we'll show you how to avoid the most common mistakes people make when they start using financial calculators.

How to Calculate Future Values with a Financial Calculator

Examining a typical financial calculator, you will find five keys of particular interest. They usually look like this:

| N | I/Y | PMT | PV | FV |

For now, we need to focus on four of these. The keys labeled **PV** and **FV** are just what you would guess: present value and future value. The key labeled **N** refers to the number of periods, which is what we have been calling t. Finally, **I/Y** stands for the interest rate, which we have called r.[1]

If we have the financial calculator set up right (see our next section), then calculating a future value is very simple. Take a look back at our question involving the future value of $100 at 10 percent for five years. We have seen that the answer is $161.05. The exact keystrokes will differ depending on what type of calculator you use, but here is basically all you do:

1. Enter −100. Press the **PV** key. (The negative sign is explained in the next section.)
2. Enter 10. Press the **I/Y** key. (Notice that we entered 10, not .10; see the next section.)
3. Enter 5. Press the **N** key.

Now we have entered all of the relevant information. To solve for the future value, we need to ask the calculator what the FV is. Depending on your calculator, either you press the button labeled "CPT" (for compute) and then press **FV**, or you just press **FV**. Either way, you should get 161.05. If you don't (and you probably won't if this is the first time you have used a financial calculator!), we will offer some help in our next section.

Before we explain the kinds of problems you are likely to run into, we want to establish a standard format for showing you how to use a financial calculator. Using the example we just looked at, in the future, we will illustrate such problems like this:

Enter	5	10		−100	
	N	I/Y	PMT	PV	

Here is an important tip: Appendix D (which can be found on our Web site) contains more detailed instructions for the most common types of financial calculators. See if yours is included; if it is, follow the instructions there if you need help. Of course, if all else fails, you can read the manual that came with the calculator.

How to Get the Wrong Answer Using a Financial Calculator

There are a couple of common (and frustrating) problems that cause a lot of trouble with financial calculators. In this section, we provide some important *dos* and *don'ts*. If you just can't seem to get a problem to work out, you should refer back to this section.

There are two categories we examine: three things you need to do only once and three things you need to do every time you work a problem. The things you need to do just once deal with the following calculator settings:

1. *Make sure your calculator is set to display a large number of decimal places.* Most financial calculators display only two decimal places; this causes problems because we frequently work with numbers—like interest rates—that are very small.

(*continued*)

---

[1] The reason financial calculators use N and I/Y is that the most common use for these calculators is determining loan payments. In this context, N is the number of payments and I/Y is the interest rate on the loan. But as we will see, there are many other uses of financial calculators that don't involve loan payments and interest rates.

2. *Make sure your calculator is set to assume only one payment per period or per year.* Most financial calculators assume monthly payments (12 per year) unless you say otherwise.

3. *Make sure your calculator is in "end" mode.* This is usually the default, but you can accidently change to "begin" mode.

If you don't know how to set these three things, see Appendix D on our Web site or your calculator's operating manual. There are also three things you need to do *every time you work a problem:*

1. *Before you start, completely clear out the calculator.* This is very important. Failure to do this is the number one reason for wrong answers; you simply must get in the habit of clearing the calculator every time you start a problem. How you do this depends on the calculator (see Appendix D on our Web site), but you must do more than just clear the display. For example, on a Texas Instruments BA II Plus you must press `2nd` then `CLR TVM` for *clear time value of money.* There is a similar command on your calculator. Learn it!

   Note that turning the calculator off and back on won't do it. Most financial calculators remember everything you enter, even after you turn them off. In other words, they remember all your mistakes unless you explicitly clear them out. Also, if you are in the middle of a problem and make a mistake, *clear it out and start over.* Better to be safe than sorry.

2. *Put a negative sign on cash outflows.* Most financial calculators require you to put a negative sign on cash outflows and a positive sign on cash inflows. As a practical matter, this usually just means that you should enter the present value amount with a negative sign (because normally the present value represents the amount you give up today in exchange for cash inflows later). By the same token, when you solve for a present value, you shouldn't be surprised to see a negative sign.

3. *Enter the rate correctly.* Financial calculators assume that rates are quoted in percent, so if the rate is .08 (or 8 percent), you should enter 8, not .08.

If you follow these guidelines (especially the one about clearing out the calculator), you should have no problem using a financial calculator to work almost all of the problems in this and the next few chapters. We'll provide some additional examples and guidance where appropriate.

A NOTE ABOUT COMPOUND GROWTH

If you are considering depositing money in an interest-bearing account, then the interest rate on that account is just the rate at which your money grows, assuming you don't remove any of it. If that rate is 10 percent, then each year you simply have 10 percent more money than you had the year before. In this case, the interest rate is just an example of a compound growth rate.

The way we calculated future values is actually quite general and lets you answer some other types of questions related to growth. For example, your company currently has 10,000 employees. You've estimated that the number of employees grows by 3 percent per year. How many employees will there be in five years? Here, we start with 10,000 people instead of dollars, and we don't think of the growth rate as an interest rate, but the calculation is exactly the same:

$$10,000 \times 1.03^5 = 10,000 \times 1.1593 = 11,593 \text{ employees}$$

There will be about 1,593 net new hires over the coming five years.

To give another example, according to Value Line (a leading supplier of business information for investors), Wal-Mart's 2005 sales were about $313 billion. Suppose sales are projected to increase at a rate of 15 percent per year. What will Wal-Mart's sales be in the year 2010 if this is correct? Verify for yourself that the answer is about $630 billion—just over twice as large.

Ross–Westerfield–Jordan:
Fundamentals of Corporate
Finance, Eighth Edition,
Standard

III. Valuation of Future
Cash Flows

5. Introduction to
Valuation: The Time Value
of Money

© The McGraw–Hill
Companies, 2008

31

Dividend Growth	EXAMPLE 5.4

The TICO Corporation currently pays a cash dividend of $5 per share. You believe the dividend will be increased by 4 percent each year indefinitely. How big will the dividend be in eight years?

Here we have a cash dividend growing because it is being increased by management; but once again the calculation is the same:

Future value = $5 × 1.04^8 = $5 × 1.3686 = $6.84

The dividend will grow by $1.84 over that period. Dividend growth is a subject we will return to in a later chapter.

Concept Questions

5.1a What do we mean by the future value of an investment?

5.1b What does it mean to compound interest? How does compound interest differ from simple interest?

5.1c In general, what is the future value of $1 invested at r per period for t periods?

Present Value and Discounting

5.2

When we discuss future value, we are thinking of questions like: What will my $2,000 investment grow to if it earns a 6.5 percent return every year for the next six years? The answer to this question is what we call the future value of $2,000 invested at 6.5 percent for six years (verify that the answer is about $2,918).

Another type of question that comes up even more often in financial management is obviously related to future value. Suppose you need to have $10,000 in 10 years, and you can earn 6.5 percent on your money. How much do you have to invest today to reach your goal? You can verify that the answer is $5,327.26. How do we know this? Read on.

THE SINGLE-PERIOD CASE

We've seen that the future value of $1 invested for one year at 10 percent is $1.10. We now ask a slightly different question: How much do we have to invest today at 10 percent to get $1 in one year? In other words, we know the future value here is $1, but what is the **present value (PV)**? The answer isn't too hard to figure out. Whatever we invest today will be 1.1 times bigger at the end of the year. Because we need $1 at the end of the year:

Present value × 1.1 = $1

Or solving for the present value:

Present value = $1/1.1 = $.909

In this case, the present value is the answer to the following question: What amount, invested today, will grow to $1 in one year if the interest rate is 10 percent? Present value is thus just the reverse of future value. Instead of compounding the money forward into the future, we **discount** it back to the present.

present value (PV)
The current value of future cash flows discounted at the appropriate discount rate.

discount
Calculate the present value of some future amount.

EXAMPLE 5.5   Single-Period PV

Suppose you need $400 to buy textbooks next year. You can earn 7 percent on your money. How much do you have to put up today?

We need to know the PV of $400 in one year at 7 percent. Proceeding as in the previous example:

Present value $\times$ 1.07 = $400

We can now solve for the present value:

Present value = $400 $\times$ (1/1.07) = $373.83

Thus, $373.83 is the present value. Again, this just means that investing this amount for one year at 7 percent will give you a future value of $400.

From our examples, the present value of $1 to be received in one period is generally given as follows:

$$PV = \$1 \times [1/(1 + r)] = \$1/(1 + r)$$

We next examine how to get the present value of an amount to be paid in two or more periods into the future.

PRESENT VALUES FOR MULTIPLE PERIODS

Suppose you need to have $1,000 in two years. If you can earn 7 percent, how much do you have to invest to make sure you have the $1,000 when you need it? In other words, what is the present value of $1,000 in two years if the relevant rate is 7 percent?

Based on your knowledge of future values, you know the amount invested must grow to $1,000 over the two years. In other words, it must be the case that:

$$\$1,000 = PV \times 1.07 \times 1.07$$
$$= PV \times 1.07^2$$
$$= PV \times 1.1449$$

Given this, we can solve for the present value:

Present value = $1,000/1.1449 = $873.44

Therefore, $873.44 is the amount you must invest to achieve your goal.

EXAMPLE 5.6   Saving Up

You would like to buy a new automobile. You have $50,000 or so, but the car costs $68,500. If you can earn 9 percent, how much do you have to invest today to buy the car in two years? Do you have enough? Assume the price will stay the same.

What we need to know is the present value of $68,500 to be paid in two years, assuming a 9 percent rate. Based on our discussion, this is:

PV = $68,500/1.09^2 = $68,500/1.1881 = $57,655.08

You're still about $7,655 short, even if you're willing to wait two years.

Number of Periods	Interest Rate			
	5%	**10%**	**15%**	**20%**
1	.9524	.9091	.8696	.8333
2	.9070	.8264	.7561	.6944
3	.8638	.7513	.6575	.5787
4	.8227	.6830	.5718	.4823
5	.7835	.6209	.4972	.4019

TABLE 5.3

Present Value Interest Factors

As you have probably recognized by now, calculating present values is quite similar to calculating future values, and the general result looks much the same. The present value of $1 to be received t periods into the future at a discount rate of r is:

$$PV = \$1 \times [1/(1 + r)^t] = \$1/(1 + r)^t \qquad\qquad [5.2]$$

The quantity in brackets, $1/(1 + r)^t$, goes by several different names. Because it's used to discount a future cash flow, it is often called a *discount factor*. With this name, it is not surprising that the rate used in the calculation is often called the **discount rate**. We will tend to call it this in talking about present values. The quantity in brackets is also called the *present value interest factor* (or just *present value factor*) for $1 at r percent for t periods and is sometimes abbreviated as PVIF(r, t). Finally, calculating the present value of a future cash flow to determine its worth today is commonly called **discounted cash flow (DCF) valuation**.

discount rate
The rate used to calculate the present value of future cash flows.

discounted cash flow (DCF) valuation
Calculating the present value of a future cash flow to determine its value today.

To illustrate, suppose you need $1,000 in three years. You can earn 15 percent on your money. How much do you have to invest today? To find out, we have to determine the present value of $1,000 in three years at 15 percent. We do this by discounting $1,000 back three periods at 15 percent. With these numbers, the discount factor is:

$$1/(1 + .15)^3 = 1/1.5209 = .6575$$

The amount you must invest is thus:

$$\$1,000 \times .6575 = \$657.50$$

We say that $657.50 is the present or discounted value of $1,000 to be received in three years at 15 percent.

There are tables for present value factors just as there are tables for future value factors, and you use them in the same way (if you use them at all). Table 5.3 contains a small set. A much larger set can be found in Table A.2 in the book's appendix.

In Table 5.3, the discount factor we just calculated (.6575) can be found by looking down the column labeled "15%" until you come to the third row.

CALCULATOR HINTS

You solve present value problems on a financial calculator just as you do future value problems. For the example we just examined (the present value of $1,000 to be received in three years at 15 percent), you would do the following:

Enter   3   15   1,000

            N   I/Y   PMT   FV

Notice that the answer has a negative sign; as we discussed earlier, that's because it represents an outflow today in exchange for the $1,000 inflow later.

EXAMPLE 5.7   **Deceptive Advertising?**

Businesses sometimes advertise that you should "Come try our product. If you do, we'll give you $100 just for coming by!" If you read the fine print, what you find out is that they will give you a savings certificate that will pay you $100 in 25 years or so. If the going interest rate on such certificates is 10 percent per year, how much are they really giving you today?

What you're actually getting is the present value of $100 to be paid in 25 years. If the discount rate is 10 percent per year, then the discount factor is:

$$1/1.1^{25} = 1/10.8347 = .0923$$

This tells you that a dollar in 25 years is worth a little more than nine cents today, assuming a 10 percent discount rate. Given this, the promotion is actually paying you about .0923 × $100 = $9.23. Maybe this is enough to draw customers, but it's not $100.

As the length of time until payment grows, present values decline. As Example 5.7 illustrates, present values tend to become small as the time horizon grows. If you look out far enough, they will always approach zero. Also, for a given length of time, the higher the discount rate is, the lower is the present value. Put another way, present values and discount rates are inversely related. Increasing the discount rate decreases the PV and vice versa.

The relationship between time, discount rates, and present values is illustrated in Figure 5.3. Notice that by the time we get to 10 years, the present values are all substantially smaller than the future amounts.

FIGURE 5.3

Present Value of $1 for Different Periods and Rates

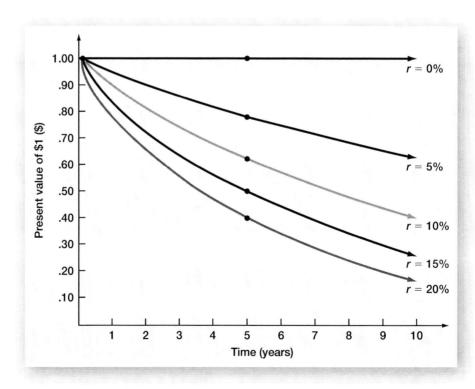

Concept Questions

5.2a What do we mean by the present value of an investment?

5.2b The process of discounting a future amount back to the present is the opposite of doing what?

5.2c What do we mean by discounted cash flow, or DCF, valuation?

5.2d In general, what is the present value of $1 to be received in t periods, assuming a discount rate of r per period?

More about Present and Future Values   5.3

If you look back at the expressions we came up with for present and future values, you will see a simple relationship between the two. We explore this relationship and some related issues in this section.

PRESENT VERSUS FUTURE VALUE

What we called the present value factor is just the reciprocal of (that is, 1 divided by) the future value factor:

Future value factor $= (1 + r)^t$

Present value factor $= 1/(1 + r)^t$

In fact, the easy way to calculate a present value factor on many calculators is to first calculate the future value factor and then press the "$1/x$" key to flip it over.

If we let FV_t stand for the future value after t periods, then the relationship between future value and present value can be written simply as one of the following:

$$PV \times (1 + r)^t = FV_t$$
$$PV = FV_t/(1 + r)^t = FV_t \times [1/(1 + r)^t]$$

[5.3]

This last result we will call the *basic present value equation*. We will use it throughout the text. A number of variations come up, but this simple equation underlies many of the most important ideas in corporate finance.

Evaluating Investments   EXAMPLE 5.8

To give you an idea of how we will be using present and future values, consider the following simple investment. Your company proposes to buy an asset for $335. This investment is very safe. You would sell off the asset in three years for $400. You know you could invest the $335 elsewhere at 10 percent with very little risk. What do you think of the proposed investment?

This is not a good investment. Why not? Because you can invest the $335 elsewhere at 10 percent. If you do, after three years it will grow to:

$$\$335 \times (1 + r)^t = \$335 \times 1.1^3$$
$$= \$335 \times 1.331$$
$$= \$445.89$$

134   **PART 3** Valuation of Future Cash Flows

Because the proposed investment pays out only $400, it is not as good as other alternatives we have. Another way of seeing the same thing is to notice that the present value of $400 in three years at 10 percent is:

$$\$400 \times [1/(1 + r)^t] = \$400/1.1^3 = \$400/1.331 = \$300.53$$

This tells us that we have to invest only about $300 to get $400 in three years, not $335. We will return to this type of analysis later on.

For a down-loadable, Windows-based financial calculator, go to www.calculator.org.

DETERMINING THE DISCOUNT RATE

We frequently need to determine what discount rate is implicit in an investment. We can do this by looking at the basic present value equation:

$$PV = FV_t /(1 + r)^t$$

There are only four parts to this equation: the present value (PV), the future value (FV_t), the discount rate (r), and the life of the investment (t). Given any three of these, we can always find the fourth.

EXAMPLE 5.9   **Finding *r* for a Single-Period Investment**

You are considering a one-year investment. If you put up $1,250, you will get back $1,350. What rate is this investment paying?

First, in this single-period case, the answer is fairly obvious. You are getting a total of $100 in addition to your $1,250. The implicit rate on this investment is thus $100/1,250 = 8 percent.

More formally, from the basic present value equation, the present value (the amount you must put up today) is $1,250. The future value (what the present value grows to) is $1,350. The time involved is one period, so we have:

$$\$1,250 = \$1,350 /(1 + r)^1$$
$$1 + r = \$1,350 /1,250 = 1.08$$
$$r = 8\%$$

In this simple case, of course, there was no need to go through this calculation. But as we describe next, it gets a little harder with more than one period.

To illustrate what happens with multiple periods, let's say we are offered an investment that costs us $100 and will double our money in eight years. To compare this to other investments, we would like to know what discount rate is implicit in these numbers. This discount rate is called the *rate of return,* or sometimes just the *return,* on the investment. In this case, we have a present value of $100, a future value of $200 (double our money), and an eight-year life. To calculate the return, we can write the basic present value equation as:

$$PV = FV_t /(1 + r)^t$$
$$\$100 = \$200/(1 + r)^8$$

It could also be written as:

$$(1 + r)^8 = \$200/100 = 2$$

We now need to solve for r. There are three ways we could do it:

1. Use a financial calculator.
2. Solve the equation for $1 + r$ by taking the eighth root of both sides. Because this is the same thing as raising both sides to the power of $1/8$ or .125, this is actually easy to do with the "y^x" key on a calculator. Just enter 2, then press "y^x," enter .125, and press the "=" key. The eighth root should be about 1.09, which implies that r is 9 percent.
3. Use a future value table. The future value factor after eight years is equal to 2. If you look across the row corresponding to eight periods in Table A.1, you will see that a future value factor of 2 corresponds to the 9 percent column, again implying that the return here is 9 percent.

Actually, in this particular example, there is a useful "back of the envelope" means of solving for r—the Rule of 72. For reasonable rates of return, the time it takes to double your money is given approximately by $72/r\%$. In our example, this means that $72/r\% = 8$ years, implying that r is 9 percent, as we calculated. This rule is fairly accurate for discount rates in the 5 percent to 20 percent range.

Baseball Collectibles as Investments

EXAMPLE 5.10

In June 2005, the contract between the Boston Red Sox and New York Yankees that sold Babe Ruth to the Yankees (and thereby cursed Red Sox fans to decades of frustration) was auctioned for an astonishing $996,000. "Experts" on such collectibles often argue that collectibles such as this will double in value over a 10-year period.

So would the contract have been a good investment? By the Rule of 72, you already know the experts were predicting that the contract would double in value in 10 years; so the return predicted would be about $72/10 = 7.2$ percent per year, which is only so-so.

At one time at least, a rule of thumb in the rarefied world of fine art collecting was "your money back in 5 years, double your money in 10 years." Given this, let's see how an investment stacked up. In 1998, the Alberto Giacometti bronze statue *Homme Qui Marche III* sold for $2,972,500. Five years later, the statue was sold again, walking out the door at a price of $4,039,500. How did the seller do?

The rule of thumb has us doubling our money in 10 years; so, from the Rule of 72, we have that 7.2 percent per year was the norm. The statue was resold in almost exactly five years. The present value is $2,972,500, and the future value is $4,039,500. We need to solve for the unknown rate, r, as follows:

Why does the Rule of 72 work? See www.datachimp.com.

$$\$2,972,500 = \$4,039,500/(1 + r)^5$$
$$(1 + r)^5 = 1.3590$$

Solving for r, we find the seller earned about 6.33 percent per year—less than the 7.2 percent rule of thumb. At least the seller made his money back.

What about other collectibles? To a philatelist (a stamp collector to you and us), one of the most prized stamps is the 1918 24-cent inverted Jenny C3a. The stamp is a collectible because it has a picture of an upside-down biplane. A block of four of these stamps sold at auction for $2,970,000 in 2005. At what rate did its value grow? Verify for yourself that the answer is about 18.74 percent, assuming an 87-year period.

Perhaps the most desired coin for numismatics (coin collectors) is the 1933 $20 gold double eagle. Outside of the U.S. Mint and the Smithsonian, only one of these coins is in circulation. In 2002, the coin sold at auction for $7,590,020. See if you agree that this collectible gained about 20.5 percent per year.

A slightly more extreme example involves money bequeathed by Benjamin Franklin, who died on April 17, 1790. In his will, he gave 1,000 pounds sterling to Massachusetts and the city of Boston. He gave a like amount to Pennsylvania and the city of Philadelphia. The money had been paid to Franklin when he held political office, but he believed that politicians should not be paid for their service (it appears that this view is not widely shared by modern politicians).

Franklin originally specified that the money should be paid out 100 years after his death and used to train young people. Later, however, after some legal wrangling, it was agreed that the money would be paid out in 1990, 200 years after Franklin's death. By that time, the Pennsylvania bequest had grown to about $2 million; the Massachusetts bequest had grown to $4.5 million. The money was used to fund the Franklin Institutes in Boston and Philadelphia. Assuming that 1,000 pounds sterling was equivalent to $1,000, what rate of return did the two states earn? (The dollar did not become the official U.S. currency until 1792.)

For Pennsylvania, the future value is $2 million and the present value is $1,000. There are 200 years involved, so we need to solve for r in the following:

$$\$1,000 = \$2 \text{ million}/(1 + r)^{200}$$
$$(1 + r)^{200} = 2,000$$

Solving for r, we see that the Pennsylvania money grew at about 3.87 percent per year. The Massachusetts money did better; verify that the rate of return in this case was 4.3 percent. Small differences in returns can add up!

CALCULATOR HINTS

We can illustrate how to calculate unknown rates using a financial calculator with these numbers. For Pennsylvania, you would do the following:

Enter	200		−1,000	2,000,000
	N	**PMT**	**PV**	**FV**

As in our previous examples, notice the minus sign on the present value, representing Franklin's outlay made many years ago. What do you change to work the problem for Massachusetts?

EXAMPLE 5.11 | **Saving for College**

You estimate that you will need about $80,000 to send your child to college in eight years. You have about $35,000 now. If you can earn 20 percent per year, will you make it? At what rate will you just reach your goal?

(continued)

If you can earn 20 percent, the future value of your $35,000 in eight years will be:

$$FV = \$35,000 \times 1.20^8 = \$35,000 \times 4.2998 = \$150,493.59$$

So, you will make it easily. The minimum rate is the unknown r in the following:

$$FV = \$35,000 \times (1 + r)^8 = \$80,000$$

$$(1 + r)^8 = \$80,000/35,000 = 2.2857$$

Therefore, the future value factor is 2.2857. Looking at the row in Table A.1 that corresponds to eight periods, we see that our future value factor is roughly halfway between the ones shown for 10 percent (2.1436) and 12 percent (2.4760), so you will just reach your goal if you earn approximately 11 percent. To get the exact answer, we could use a financial calculator or we could solve for r:

$$(1 + r)^8 = \$80,000/35,000 = 2.2857$$

$$1 + r = 2.2857^{(1/8)} = 2.2857^{.125} = 1.1089$$

$$r = 10.89\%$$

Only 18,262.5 Days to Retirement   **EXAMPLE 5.12**

You would like to retire in 50 years as a millionaire. If you have $10,000 today, what rate of return do you need to earn to achieve your goal?

The future value is $1,000,000. The present value is $10,000, and there are 50 years until payment. We need to calculate the unknown discount rate in the following:

$$\$10,000 = \$1,000,000/(1 + r)^{50}$$

$$(1 + r)^{50} = 100$$

The future value factor is thus 100. You can verify that the implicit rate is about 9.65 percent.

Not taking the time value of money into account when computing growth rates or rates of return often leads to some misleading numbers in the real world. For example, the most loved (and hated) team in baseball, the New York Yankees, had the highest payroll during the 1988 season, about $19 million. In 2006, the Yankees again had the highest payroll, a staggering $195 million: an increase of 926 percent! If history is any guide, we can get a rough idea of the future growth in baseball payrolls. See if you don't agree that this represents an annual increase of 13.8 percent, a substantial growth rate, but much less than the gaudy 926 percent.

How much do you need at retirement? Check out the "Money/Retirement" link at www.about.com.

How about classic maps? A few years ago, the first map of America, printed in Rome in 1507, was valued at about $135,000, 69 percent more than the $80,000 it was worth 10 years earlier. Your return on investment if you were the proud owner of the map over those 10 years? Verify that it's about 5.4 percent per year—far worse than the 69 percent reported increase in price.

Whether with maps or baseball payrolls, it's easy to be misled when returns are quoted without considering the time value of money. However, it's not just the uninitiated who are guilty of this slight form of deception. The title of a feature article in a leading business magazine predicted the Dow Jones Industrial Average would soar to a 70 percent gain over the coming five years. Do you think it meant a 70 percent return per year on your money? Think again!

FINDING THE NUMBER OF PERIODS

Suppose we are interested in purchasing an asset that costs $50,000. We currently have $25,000. If we can earn 12 percent on this $25,000, how long until we have the $50,000? Finding the answer involves solving for the last variable in the basic present value equation, the number of periods. You already know how to get an approximate answer to this particular problem. Notice that we need to double our money. From the Rule of 72, this will take about $72/12 = 6$ years at 12 percent.

To come up with the exact answer, we can again manipulate the basic present value equation. The present value is $25,000, and the future value is $50,000. With a 12 percent discount rate, the basic equation takes one of the following forms:

$$\$25,000 = \$50,000/1.12^t$$
$$\$50,000/25,000 = 1.12^t = 2$$

We thus have a future value factor of 2 for a 12 percent rate. We now need to solve for t. If you look down the column in Table A.1 that corresponds to 12 percent, you will see that a future value factor of 1.9738 occurs at six periods. It will thus take about six years, as we calculated. To get the exact answer, we have to explicitly solve for t (or use a financial calculator). If you do this, you will see that the answer is 6.1163 years, so our approximation was quite close in this case.

CALCULATOR HINTS

If you use a financial calculator, here are the relevant entries:

Enter		12		$-25,000$	50,000
		I/Y	PMT	PV	FV

EXAMPLE 5.13   Waiting for Godot

You've been saving up to buy the Godot Company. The total cost will be $10 million. You currently have about $2.3 million. If you can earn 5 percent on your money, how long will you have to wait? At 16 percent, how long must you wait?

At 5 percent, you'll have to wait a long time. From the basic present value equation:

$$\$2.3 \text{ million} = \$10 \text{ million}/1.05^t$$
$$1.05^t = 4.35$$
$$t = 30 \text{ years}$$

At 16 percent, things are a little better. Verify for yourself that it will take about 10 years.

SPREADSHEET STRATEGIES

Using a Spreadsheet for Time Value of Money Calculations

More and more, businesspeople from many different areas (not just finance and accounting) rely on spreadsheets to do all the different types of calculations that come up in the real world. As a result, in this section, we will show you how to use a spreadsheet to handle the various time value of money problems we presented in this chapter. We will use Microsoft Excel™, but the commands are similar for other types of software. We assume you are already familiar with basic spreadsheet operations.

As we have seen, you can solve for any one of the following four potential unknowns: future value, present value, the discount rate, or the number of periods. With a spreadsheet, there is a separate formula for each. In Excel, these are shown in a nearby box.

In these formulas, pv and fv are present and future value, nper is the number of periods, and rate is the discount, or interest, rate.

Two things are a little tricky here. First, unlike a financial calculator, the spreadsheet requires that the rate be entered as a decimal. Second, as with most financial calculators, you have to put a negative sign on either the present value or the future value to solve

To Find	Enter This Formula
Future value	= FV (rate,nper,pmt,pv)
Present value	= PV (rate,nper,pmt,fv)
Discount rate	= RATE (nper,pmt,pv,fv)
Number of periods	= NPER (rate,pmt,pv,fv)

for the rate or the number of periods. For the same reason, if you solve for a present value, the answer will have a negative sign unless you input a negative future value. The same is true when you compute a future value.

To illustrate how you might use these formulas, we will go back to an example in the chapter. If you invest $25,000 at 12 percent per year, how long until you have $50,000? You might set up a spreadsheet like this:

	A	B	C	D	E	F	G	H
1								
2		Using a spreadsheet for time value of money calculations						
3								
4	If we invest $25,000 at 12 percent, how long until we have $50,000? We need to solve							
5	for the unknown number of periods, so we use the formula NPER(rate, pmt, pv, fv).							
6								
7	Present value (pv):	$25,000						
8	Future value (fv):	$50,000						
9	Rate (rate):	0.12						
10								
11	Periods:	6.1162554						
12								
13	The formula entered in cell B11 is =NPER(B9,0,-B7,B8); notice that pmt is zero and that pv							
14	has a negative sign on it. Also notice that rate is entered as a decimal, not a percentage.							

U.S. EE Savings Bonds are a familiar investment for many. You purchase them for half of their $100 face value. In other words, you pay $50 today and get $100 at some point in the future when the bond "matures." You receive no interest in between, and the interest rate is adjusted every six months, so the length of time until your $50 grows to $100 depends on future interest rates. However, at worst, the bonds are guaranteed to be worth $100 at the end of 17 years, so this is the longest you would ever have to wait. If you do have to wait the full 17 years, what rate do you earn?

Because this investment is doubling in value in 17 years, the Rule of 72 tells you the answer right away: $72/17 = 4.24\%$. Remember, this is the minimum guaranteed return, so

Learn more about using Excel for time value and other calculations at www.studyfinance.com.

WORK THE WEB

How important is the time value of money? A recent search on one Web search engine returned over 259 million hits! Although you must understand the calculations behind the time value of money, the advent of financial calculators and spreadsheets has eliminated the need for tedious calculations. In fact, many Web sites offer time value of money calculators. The following is one example from www.investopedia.com. You have $12,000 today and will invest it at 10.5 percent for 22 years. How much will it be worth at that time? With the Investopedia calculator, you simply enter the values and hit Calculate. The results look like this:

Interest Rate Per Time Period: 10.5 %

Number of Time Periods: 25

Present Value: 12000

Calculate

Future Value: **$145,625.76**

Who said time value of money calculations are hard?

TABLE 5.4

Summary of Time Value Calculations

I. Symbols:
PV = Present value, what future cash flows are worth today
FV_t = Future value, what cash flows are worth in the future
r = Interest rate, rate of return, or discount rate per period—typically, but not always, one year
t = Number of periods—typically, but not always, the number of years
C = Cash amount
II. Future Value of C Invested at r Percent for t Periods:
$FV_t = C \times (1 + r)^t$
The term $(1 + r)^t$ is called the *future value factor*.
III. Present Value of C to Be Received in t Periods at r Percent per Period:
$PV = C/(1 + r)^t$
The term $1/(1 + r)^t$ is called the *present value factor*.
IV. The Basic Present Value Equation Giving the Relationship between Present and Future Value:
$PV = FV_t/(1 + r)^t$

you might do better. This example finishes our introduction to basic time value concepts. Table 5.4 summarizes present and future value calculations for future reference. As our nearby *Work the Web* box shows, online calculators are widely available to handle these calculations; but it is still important to know what is really going on.

Concept Questions

5.3a What is the basic present value equation?

5.3b What is the Rule of 72?

Summary and Conclusions 5.4

This chapter has introduced you to the basic principles of present value and discounted cash flow valuation. In it, we explained a number of things about the time value of money, including these:

1. For a given rate of return, we can determine the value at some point in the future of an investment made today by calculating the future value of that investment.
2. We can determine the current worth of a future cash flow or series of cash flows for a given rate of return by calculating the present value of the cash flow(s) involved.
3. The relationship between present value (PV) and future value (FV) for a given rate r and time t is given by the basic present value equation:

$$PV = FV_t/(1 + r)^t$$

As we have shown, it is possible to find any one of the four components (PV, FV_t, r, or t) given the other three.

The principles developed in this chapter will figure prominently in the chapters to come. The reason for this is that most investments, whether they involve real assets or financial assets, can be analyzed using the discounted cash flow (DCF) approach. As a result, the DCF approach is broadly applicable and widely used in practice. Before going on, therefore, you might want to do some of the problems that follow.

CHAPTER REVIEW AND SELF-TEST PROBLEMS

5.1 **Calculating Future Values** Assume you deposit $10,000 today in an account that pays 6 percent interest. How much will you have in five years?

5.2 **Calculating Present Values** Suppose you have just celebrated your 19th birthday. A rich uncle has set up a trust fund for you that will pay you $150,000 when you turn 30. If the relevant discount rate is 9 percent, how much is this fund worth today?

5.3 **Calculating Rates of Return** You've been offered an investment that will double your money in 10 years. What rate of return are you being offered? Check your answer using the Rule of 72.

5.4 **Calculating the Number of Periods** You've been offered an investment that will pay you 9 percent per year. If you invest $15,000, how long until you have $30,000? How long until you have $45,000?

ANSWERS TO CHAPTER REVIEW AND SELF-TEST PROBLEMS

5.1 We need to calculate the future value of $10,000 at 6 percent for five years. The future value factor is:

$$1.06^5 = 1.3382$$

The future value is thus $10,000 × 1.3382 = $13,382.26.

5.2 We need the present value of $150,000 to be paid in 11 years at 9 percent. The discount factor is:

$$1/1.09^{11} = 1/2.5804 = .3875$$

The present value is thus about $58,130.

PART 3 Valuation of Future Cash Flows

5.3 Suppose you invest $1,000. You will have $2,000 in 10 years with this investment. So, $1,000 is the amount you have today, or the present value, and $2,000 is the amount you will have in 10 years, or the future value. From the basic present value equation, we have:

$$\$2,000 = \$1,000 \times (1 + r)^{10}$$
$$2 = (1 + r)^{10}$$

From here, we need to solve for r, the unknown rate. As shown in the chapter, there are several different ways to do this. We will take the 10th root of 2 (by raising 2 to the power of $1/10$):

$$2^{(1/10)} = 1 + r$$
$$1.0718 = 1 + r$$
$$r = 7.18\%$$

Using the Rule of 72, we have $72/t = r\%$, or $72/10 = 7.2\%$, so, our answer looks good (remember that the Rule of 72 is only an approximation).

5.4 The basic equation is this:

$$\$30,000 = \$15,000 \times (1 + .09)^{t}$$
$$2 = (1 + .09)^{t}$$

If we solve for t, we find that $t = 8.04$ years. Using the Rule of 72, we get $72/9 = 8$ years, so once again our answer looks good. To get $45,000, verify for yourself that you will have to wait 12.75 years.

CONCEPTS REVIEW AND CRITICAL THINKING QUESTIONS

1. **Present Value** The basic present value equation has four parts. What are they?
2. **Compounding** What is compounding? What is discounting?
3. **Compounding and Period** As you increase the length of time involved, what happens to future values? What happens to present values?
4. **Compounding and Interest Rates** What happens to a future value if you increase the rate r? What happens to a present value?
5. **Ethical Considerations** Take a look back at Example 5.7. Is it deceptive advertising? Is it unethical to advertise a future value like this without a disclaimer?

   To answer the next five questions, refer to the TMCC security we discussed to open the chapter.
6. **Time Value of Money** Why would TMCC be willing to accept such a small amount today ($1,163) in exchange for a promise to repay about 9 times that amount ($10,000) in the future?
7. **Call Provisions** TMCC has the right to buy back the securities on the anniversary date at a price established when the securities were issued (this feature is a term of this particular deal). What impact does this feature have on the desirability of this security as an investment?
8. **Time Value of Money** Would you be willing to pay $1,163 today in exchange for $10,000 in 30 years? What would be the key considerations in answering yes or no? Would your answer depend on who is making the promise to repay?
9. **Investment Comparison** Suppose that when TMCC offered the security for $1,163, the U.S. Treasury had offered an essentially identical security. Do you think it would have had a higher or lower price? Why?

10. **Length of Investment** The TMCC security is bought and sold on the New York Stock Exchange. If you looked at the price today, do you think the price would exceed the $1,163 original price? Why? If you looked in the year 2015, do you think the price would be higher or lower than today's price? Why?

QUESTIONS AND PROBLEMS

1. **Simple Interest versus Compound Interest** First City Bank pays 6 percent simple interest on its savings account balances, whereas Second City Bank pays 6 percent interest compounded annually. If you made a $5,000 deposit in each bank, how much more money would you earn from your Second City Bank account at the end of 10 years?

BASIC
(Questions 1–15)

2. **Calculating Future Values** For each of the following, compute the future value:

Present Value	Years	Interest Rate	Future Value
$ 2,250	16	10%	
8,752	13	8	
76,355	4	17	
183,796	12	7	

3. **Calculating Present Values** For each of the following, compute the present value:

Present Value	Years	Interest Rate	Future Value
	6	4%	$ 15,451
	7	11	51,557
	23	20	886,073
	18	13	550,164

4. **Calculating Interest Rates** Solve for the unknown interest rate in each of the following:

Present Value	Years	Interest Rate	Future Value
$ 240	2		$ 307
360	10		896
39,000	15		174,384
38,261	30		483,500

5. **Calculating the Number of Periods** Solve for the unknown number of years in each of the following:

Present Value	Years	Interest Rate	Future Value
$ 560		8%	$ 1,284
810		9	4,341
18,400		21	364,518
21,500		13	173,439

6. **Calculating Interest Rates** Assume the total cost of a college education will be $280,000 when your child enters college in 18 years. You presently have $50,000 to invest. What annual rate of interest must you earn on your investment to cover the cost of your child's college education?

7. **Calculating the Number of Periods** At 9 percent interest, how long does it take to double your money? To quadruple it?

8. **Calculating Interest Rates** In 2005, the average vehicle selling price in the United States was $27,958. Seven years earlier, the average price was $21,608. What was the annual increase in vehicle selling price?

9. **Calculating the Number of Periods** You're trying to save to buy a new $170,000 Ferrari. You have $40,000 today that can be invested at your bank. The bank pays 6.2 percent annual interest on its accounts. How long will it be before you have enough to buy the car?

10. **Calculating Present Values** Imprudential, Inc., has an unfunded pension liability of $700 million that must be paid in 20 years. To assess the value of the firm's stock, financial analysts want to discount this liability back to the present. If the relevant discount rate is 8.5 percent, what is the present value of this liability?

11. **Calculating Present Values** You have just received notification that you have won the $1 million first prize in the Centennial Lottery. However, the prize will be awarded on your 100th birthday (assuming you're around to collect), 80 years from now. What is the present value of your windfall if the appropriate discount rate is 9 percent?

12. **Calculating Future Values** Your coin collection contains fifty 1952 silver dollars. If your grandparents purchased them for their face value when they were new, how much will your collection be worth when you retire in 2054, assuming they appreciate at a 4.5 percent annual rate?

13. **Calculating Interest Rates and Future Values** In 1895, the first U.S. Open Golf Championship was held. The winner's prize money was $150. In 2006, the winner's check was $1,170,000. What was the percentage increase in the winner's check over this period? If the winner's prize increases at the same rate, what will it be in 2040?

14. **Calculating Present Values** The first comic book featuring Superman was sold in 1938. In 2005, the estimated price for this comic book in good condition was about $485,000. This represented a return of 25.90 percent per year. For this to be true, what must the comic book have sold for when new?

15. **Calculating Rates of Return** Although appealing to more refined tastes, art as a collectible has not always performed so profitably. During 2003, Sotheby's sold the Edgar Degas bronze sculpture *Petite Danseuse de Quartorze Ans* at auction for a price of $10,311,500. Unfortunately for the previous owner, he had purchased it in 1999 at a price of $12,377,500. What was his annual rate of return on this sculpture?

INTERMEDIATE
(Questions 16–20)

16. **Calculating Rates of Return** Referring to the TMCC security we discussed at the very beginning of the chapter:
   a. Based on the $1,163 price, what rate was TMCC paying to borrow money?
   b. Suppose that, on April 21, 2015, this security's price is $2,500. If an investor had purchased it for $1,163 at the offering and sold it on this day, what annual rate of return would she have earned?
   c. If an investor had purchased the security at market on April 21, 2015, and held it until it matured, what annual rate of return would she have earned?

17. **Calculating Present Values** Suppose you are still committed to owning a $170,000 Ferrari (see Problem 9). If you believe your mutual fund can achieve an 11 percent annual rate of return and you want to buy the car in 10 years on the day you turn 30, how much must you invest today?

18. **Calculating Future Values** You have just made your first $2,000 contribution to your individual retirement account. Assuming you earn a 12 percent rate of return and make no additional contributions, what will your account be worth when you retire in 45 years? What if you wait 10 years before contributing? (Does this suggest an investment strategy?)

19. **Calculating Future Values** You are scheduled to receive $25,000 in two years. When you receive it, you will invest it for six more years at 7.9 percent per year. How much will you have in eight years?

20. **Calculating the Number of Periods** You expect to receive $10,000 at graduation in two years. You plan on investing it at 11 percent until you have $100,000. How long will you wait from now?

WEB EXERCISES

5.1 **Calculating Future Values** Go to www.dinkytown.net and find the basic financial calculator. If you currently have $10,000 and invest this money at 9 percent, how much will you have in 30 years? Assume you will not make any additional contributions. How much will you have if you can earn 11 percent?

5.2 **Calculating the Number of Periods** Go to www.dinkytown.net and find the "Cool Million" calculator. You want to be a millionaire. You can earn 11.5 percent per year. Using your current age, at what age will you become a millionaire if you have $25,000 to invest, assuming you make no other deposits (ignore inflation)?

5.3 **Future Values and Taxes** Taxes can greatly affect the future value of your investment. The Financial Calculators Web site at www.fincalc.com has a financial calculator that adjusts your return for taxes. Suppose you have $50,000 to invest today. If you can earn a 12 percent return and no additional annual savings, how much will you have in 20 years? (Enter 0 percent as the tax rate.) Now assume that your marginal tax rate is 27.5 percent. How much will you have at this tax rate?

Visit us at www.mhhe.com/rwj

PART 3 Valuation of Future Cash Flows

6

DISCOUNTED CASH FLOW VALUATION

THE SIGNING OF BIG-NAME ATHLETES is often accompanied by great fanfare, but the numbers are often misleading. For example, in 2006, catcher Ramon Hernandez joined the Baltimore Orioles, signing a contract with a reported value of $27.5 million. Not bad, especially for someone who makes a living using the "tools of ignorance" (jock jargon for catcher's equipment). Another example is the contract signed by wide receiver Chad Johnson of the Cincinnati Bengals, which had a stated value of about $35.5 million.

A closer look at the numbers shows that both Ramon and Chad did pretty well, but nothing like the quoted figures. Using Chad's contract as an example, while the value was reported to be $35.5 million, this amount was actually payable over several years. It consisted of $8.25 million in the first year plus $27.25 million in future salary and bonuses paid in the years 2007 through 2011. Ramon's payments were similarly spread over time. Because both contracts called for payments that are made at future dates, we must consider the time value of money, which means neither player received the quoted amounts. How much did they really get? This chapter gives you the "tools of knowledge" to answer this question.

Visit us at www.mhhe.com/rwj

DIGITAL STUDY TOOLS
- Self-Study Software
- Multiple-Choice Quizzes
- Flashcards for Testing and Key Terms

In our previous chapter, we covered the basics of discounted cash flow valuation. However, so far, we have dealt with only single cash flows. In reality, most investments have multiple cash flows. For example, if Sears is thinking of opening a new department store, there will be a large cash outlay in the beginning and then cash inflows for many years. In this chapter, we begin to explore how to value such investments.

When you finish this chapter, you should have some very practical skills. For example, you will know how to calculate your own car payments or student loan payments. You will also be able to determine how long it will take to pay off a credit card if you make the minimum payment each month (a practice we do not recommend). We will show you how to compare interest rates to determine which are the highest and which are the lowest, and we will also show you how interest rates can be quoted in different—and at times deceptive—ways.

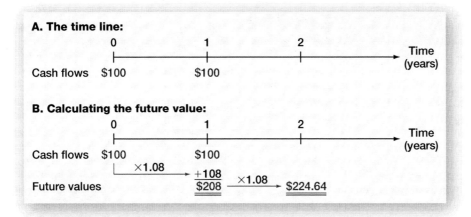

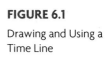

FIGURE 6.1

Drawing and Using a Time Line

Future and Present Values of Multiple Cash Flows

6.1

Thus far, we have restricted our attention to either the future value of a lump sum present amount or the present value of some single future cash flow. In this section, we begin to study ways to value multiple cash flows. We start with future value.

FUTURE VALUE WITH MULTIPLE CASH FLOWS

Suppose you deposit $100 today in an account paying 8 percent. In one year, you will deposit another $100. How much will you have in two years? This particular problem is relatively easy. At the end of the first year, you will have $108 plus the second $100 you deposit, for a total of $208. You leave this $208 on deposit at 8 percent for another year. At the end of this second year, it is worth:

$$\$208 \times 1.08 = \$224.64$$

Figure 6.1 is a *time line* that illustrates the process of calculating the future value of these two $100 deposits. Figures such as this are useful for solving complicated problems. Almost anytime you are having trouble with a present or future value problem, drawing a time line will help you see what is happening.

In the first part of Figure 6.1, we show the cash flows on the time line. The most important thing is that we write them down where they actually occur. Here, the first cash flow occurs today, which we label as time 0. We therefore put $100 at time 0 on the time line. The second $100 cash flow occurs one year from today, so we write it down at the point labeled as time 1. In the second part of Figure 6.1, we calculate the future values one period at a time to come up with the final $224.64.

Saving Up Revisited   **EXAMPLE 6.1**

You think you will be able to deposit $4,000 at the end of each of the next three years in a bank account paying 8 percent interest. You currently have $7,000 in the account. How much will you have in three years? In four years?

At the end of the first year, you will have:

$$\$7,000 \times 1.08 + 4,000 = \$11,560$$

148 **PART 3** Valuation of Future Cash Flows

At the end of the second year, you will have:

$11,560 × 1.08 + 4,000 = $16,484.80

Repeating this for the third year gives:

$16,484.80 × 1.08 + 4,000 = $21,803.58

Therefore, you will have $21,803.58 in three years. If you leave this on deposit for one more year (and don't add to it), at the end of the fourth year, you'll have:

$21,803.58 × 1.08 = $23,547.87

When we calculated the future value of the two $100 deposits, we simply calculated the balance as of the beginning of each year and then rolled that amount forward to the next year. We could have done it another, quicker way. The first $100 is on deposit for two years at 8 percent, so its future value is:

$100 × 1.08² = $100 × 1.1664 = $116.64

The second $100 is on deposit for one year at 8 percent, and its future value is thus:

$100 × 1.08 = $108

The total future value, as we previously calculated, is equal to the sum of these two future values:

$116.64 + 108 = $224.64

Based on this example, there are two ways to calculate future values for multiple cash flows: (1) Compound the accumulated balance forward one year at a time or (2) calculate the future value of each cash flow first and then add them up. Both give the same answer, so you can do it either way.

To illustrate the two different ways of calculating future values, consider the future value of $2,000 invested at the end of each of the next five years. The current balance is zero, and the rate is 10 percent. We first draw a time line, as shown in Figure 6.2.

On the time line, notice that nothing happens until the end of the first year, when we make the first $2,000 investment. This first $2,000 earns interest for the next four (not five) years. Also notice that the last $2,000 is invested at the end of the fifth year, so it earns no interest at all.

Figure 6.3 illustrates the calculations involved if we compound the investment one period at a time. As illustrated, the future value is $12,210.20.

FIGURE 6.2

Time Line for $2,000 per Year for Five Years

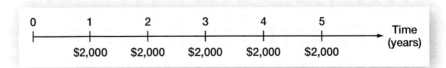

FIGURE 6.3 Future Value Calculated by Compounding Forward One Period at a Time

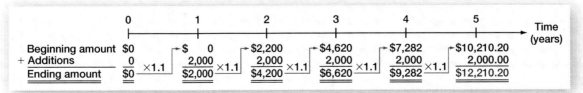

FIGURE 6.4   Future Value Calculated by Compounding Each Cash Flow Separately

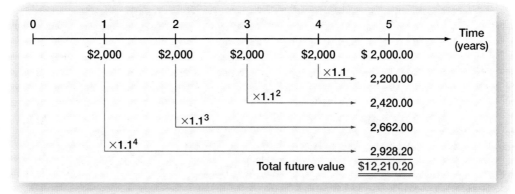

Figure 6.4 goes through the same calculations, but the second technique is used. Naturally, the answer is the same.

Saving Up Once Again   EXAMPLE 6.2

If you deposit $100 in one year, $200 in two years, and $300 in three years, how much will you have in three years? How much of this is interest? How much will you have in five years if you don't add additional amounts? Assume a 7 percent interest rate throughout.

We will calculate the future value of each amount in three years. Notice that the $100 earns interest for two years, and the $200 earns interest for one year. The final $300 earns no interest. The future values are thus:

$$\$100 \times 1.07^2 \quad = \$114.49$$
$$\$200 \times 1.07 \quad\ \ = \ \ 214.00$$
$$+\$300 \qquad\qquad = \ \ \underline{300.00}$$
$$\text{Total future value} = \underline{\$628.49}$$

The total future value is thus $628.49. The total interest is:

$$\$628.49 - (100 + 200 + 300) = \$28.49$$

How much will you have in five years? We know that you will have $628.49 in three years. If you leave that in for two more years, it will grow to:

$$\$628.49 \times 1.07^2 = \$628.49 \times 1.1449 = \$719.56$$

Notice that we could have calculated the future value of each amount separately. Once again, be careful about the lengths of time. As we previously calculated, the first $100 earns interest for only four years, the second deposit earns three years' interest, and the last earns two years' interest:

$$\$100 \times 1.07^4 = \$100 \times 1.3108 = \$131.08$$
$$\$200 \times 1.07^3 = \$200 \times 1.2250 = \ \ 245.01$$
$$+\$300 \times 1.07^2 = \$300 \times 1.1449 = \ \ \underline{343.47}$$
$$\qquad\qquad\text{Total future value} = \underline{\$719.56}$$

PRESENT VALUE WITH MULTIPLE CASH FLOWS

We often need to determine the present value of a series of future cash flows. As with future values, there are two ways we can do it. We can either discount back one period at a time, or we can just calculate the present values individually and add them up.

Suppose you need $1,000 in one year and $2,000 more in two years. If you can earn 9 percent on your money, how much do you have to put up today to exactly cover these amounts in the future? In other words, what is the present value of the two cash flows at 9 percent?

The present value of $2,000 in two years at 9 percent is:

$$\$2,000/1.09^2 = \$1,683.36$$

The present value of $1,000 in one year is:

$$\$1,000/1.09 = \$917.43$$

Therefore, the total present value is:

$$\$1,683.36 + 917.43 = \$2,600.79$$

To see why $2,600.79 is the right answer, we can check to see that after the $2,000 is paid out in two years, there is no money left. If we invest $2,600.79 for one year at 9 percent, we will have:

$$\$2,600.79 \times 1.09 = \$2,834.86$$

We take out $1,000, leaving $1,834.86. This amount earns 9 percent for another year, leaving us with:

$$\$1,834.86 \times 1.09 = \$2,000$$

This is just as we planned. As this example illustrates, the present value of a series of future cash flows is simply the amount you would need today to exactly duplicate those future cash flows (for a given discount rate).

An alternative way of calculating present values for multiple future cash flows is to discount back to the present, one period at a time. To illustrate, suppose we had an investment that was going to pay $1,000 at the end of every year for the next five years. To find the present value, we could discount each $1,000 back to the present separately and then add them up. Figure 6.5 illustrates this approach for a 6 percent discount rate; as shown, the answer is $4,212.37 (ignoring a small rounding error).

FIGURE 6.5

Present Value Calculated by Discounting Each Cash Flow Separately

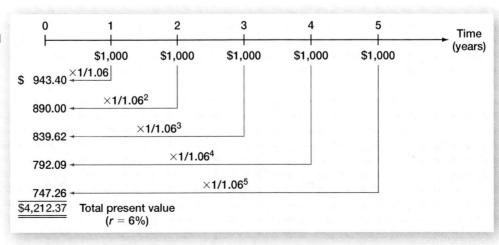

FIGURE 6.6 Present Value Calculated by Discounting Back One Period at a Time

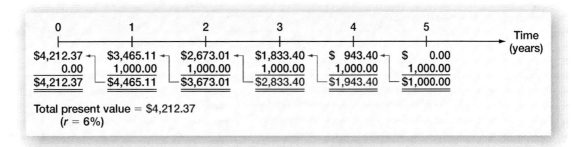

Alternatively, we could discount the last cash flow back one period and add it to the next-to-the-last cash flow:

$$(\$1,000/1.06) + 1,000 = \$943.40 + 1,000 = \$1,943.40$$

We could then discount this amount back one period and add it to the year 3 cash flow:

$$(\$1,943.40/1.06) + 1,000 = \$1,833.40 + 1,000 = \$2,833.40$$

This process could be repeated as necessary. Figure 6.6 illustrates this approach and the remaining calculations.

How Much Is It Worth?   EXAMPLE 6.3

You are offered an investment that will pay you $200 in one year, $400 the next year, $600 the next year, and $800 at the end of the fourth year. You can earn 12 percent on very similar investments. What is the most you should pay for this one?

We need to calculate the present value of these cash flows at 12 percent. Taking them one at a time gives:

$$\$200 \times 1/1.12^1 = \$200/1.1200 = \$\ 178.57$$
$$\$400 \times 1/1.12^2 = \$400/1.2544 = \ 318.88$$
$$\$600 \times 1/1.12^3 = \$600/1.4049 = \ 427.07$$
$$+\$800 \times 1/1.12^4 = \$800/1.5735 = \ \underline{508.41}$$
$$\text{Total present value} = \underline{\$1,432.93}$$

If you can earn 12 percent on your money, then you can duplicate this investment's cash flows for $1,432.93, so this is the most you should be willing to pay.

How Much Is It Worth? Part 2   EXAMPLE 6.4

You are offered an investment that will make three $5,000 payments. The first payment will occur four years from today. The second will occur in five years, and the third will follow in six years. If you can earn 11 percent, what is the most this investment is worth today? What is the future value of the cash flows?

We will answer the questions in reverse order to illustrate a point. The future value of the cash flows in six years is:

$$(\$5,000 \times 1.11^2) + (5,000 \times 1.11) + 5,000 = \$6,160.50 + 5,550 + 5,000$$
$$= \$16,710.50$$

(continued)

54

Ross–Westerfield–Jordan:
Fundamentals of Corporate
Finance, Eighth Edition,
Standard

III. Valuation of Future
Cash Flows

6. Discounted Cash Flow
Valuation

© The McGraw–Hill
Companies, 2008

PART 3 Valuation of Future Cash Flows

The present value must be:

$16,710.50/1.11^6 = $8,934.12$

Let's check this. Taking them one at a time, the PVs of the cash flows are:

$$\$5,000 \times 1/1.11^6 = \$5,000/1.8704 = \$2,673.20$$
$$\$5,000 \times 1/1.11^5 = \$5,000/1.6851 = 2,967.26$$
$$+\$5,000 \times 1/1.11^4 = \$5,000/1.5181 = \underline{3,293.65}$$
$$\text{Total present value} = \$8,934.12$$

This is as we previously calculated. The point we want to make is that we can calculate present and future values in any order and convert between them using whatever way seems most convenient. The answers will always be the same as long as we stick with the same discount rate and are careful to keep track of the right number of periods.

CALCULATOR HINTS

How to Calculate Present Values with Multiple Future Cash Flows Using a Financial Calculator

To calculate the present value of multiple cash flows with a financial calculator, we will simply discount the individual cash flows one at a time using the same technique we used in our previous chapter, so this is not really new. However, we can show you a shortcut. We will use the numbers in Example 6.3 to illustrate.

To begin, of course we first remember to clear out the calculator! Next, from Example 6.3, the first cash flow is $200 to be received in one year and the discount rate is 12 percent, so we do the following:

Enter	1	12			200
	N	**I/Y**	**PMT**		**FV**

Now, you can write down this answer to save it, but that's inefficient. All calculators have a memory where you can store numbers. Why not just save it there? Doing so cuts way down on mistakes because you don't have to write down and/or rekey numbers, and it's much faster.

Next we value the second cash flow. We need to change N to 2 and FV to 400. As long as we haven't changed anything else, we don't have to reenter I/Y or clear out the calculator, so we have:

Enter	2				400
	N	**I/Y**	**PMT**		**FV**

You save this number by adding it to the one you saved in our first calculation, and so on for the remaining two calculations.

As we will see in a later chapter, some financial calculators will let you enter all of the future cash flows at once, but we'll discuss that subject when we get to it.

SPREADSHEET STRATEGIES

How to Calculate Present Values with Multiple Future Cash Flows Using a Spreadsheet

Just as we did in our previous chapter, we can set up a basic spreadsheet to calculate the present values of the individual cash flows as follows. Notice that we have simply calculated the present values one at a time and added them up:

	A	B	C	D	E
1					
2		**Using a spreadsheet to value multiple future cash flows**			
3					
4	What is the present value of $200 in one year, $400 the next year, $600 the next year, and				
5	$800 the last year if the discount rate is 12 percent?				
6					
7	Rate:	0.12			
8					
9		Year	Cash flows	Present values	Formula used
10		1	$200	$178.57	=PV($B$7,A10,0,−B10)
11		2	$400	$318.88	=PV($B$7,A11,0,−B11)
12		3	$600	$427.07	=PV($B$7,A12,0,−B12)
13		4	$800	$508.41	=PV($B$7,A13,0,−B13)
14					
15			Total PV:	$1,432.93	=SUM(C10:C13)
16					
17	Notice the negative signs inserted in the PV formulas. These just make the present values have				
18	positive signs. Also, the discount rate in cell B7 is entered as $B$7 (an "absolute" reference)				
19	because it is used over and over. We could have just entered ".12" instead, but our approach is more				
20	flexible.				
21					
22					

A NOTE ABOUT CASH FLOW TIMING

In working present and future value problems, cash flow timing is critically important. In almost all such calculations, it is implicitly assumed that the cash flows occur at the *end* of each period. In fact, all the formulas we have discussed, all the numbers in a standard present value or future value table, and (very important) all the preset (or default) settings on a financial calculator assume that cash flows occur at the end of each period. Unless you are explicitly told otherwise, you should always assume that this is what is meant.

As a quick illustration of this point, suppose you are told that a three-year investment has a first-year cash flow of $100, a second-year cash flow of $200, and a third-year cash flow of $300. You are asked to draw a time line. Without further information, you should always assume that the time line looks like this:

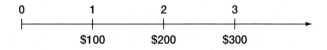

On our time line, notice how the first cash flow occurs at the end of the first period, the second at the end of the second period, and the third at the end of the third period.

154   **PART 3** Valuation of Future Cash Flows

We will close this section by answering the question we posed at the beginning of the chapter concerning Chad Johnson's NFL contract. Recall that the contract called for $8.25 million in the first year. The remaining $27.25 million was to be paid as $7.75 million in 2007, $3.25 million in 2008, $4.75 million in 2009, $5.25 million in 2010, and $6.25 million in 2011. If 12 percent is the appropriate interest rate, what kind of deal did the Bengals' wide receiver catch?

To answer, we can calculate the present value by discounting each year's salary back to the present as follows (notice we assume that all the payments are made at year-end):

Year 1 (2006): $8,250,000 \times 1/1.12^1 = $7,366,071.43$

Year 2 (2007): $7,750,000 \times 1/1.12^2 = $6,178,252.55$

Year 3 (2008): $3,250,000 \times 1/1.12^3 = $2,313,285.81$

.

.

Year 6 (2011): $6,250,000 \times 1/1.12^6 = $3,166,444.51$

If you fill in the missing rows and then add (do it for practice), you will see that Johnson's contract had a present value of about $25 million, or about 70 percent of the stated $35.5 million value.

Concept Questions

6.1a Describe how to calculate the future value of a series of cash flows.

6.1b Describe how to calculate the present value of a series of cash flows.

6.1c Unless we are explicitly told otherwise, what do we always assume about the timing of cash flows in present and future value problems?

6.2 Valuing Level Cash Flows: Annuities and Perpetuities

We will frequently encounter situations in which we have multiple cash flows that are all the same amount. For example, a common type of loan repayment plan calls for the borrower to repay the loan by making a series of equal payments over some length of time. Almost all consumer loans (such as car loans) and home mortgages feature equal payments, usually made each month.

More generally, a series of constant or level cash flows that occur at the end of each period for some fixed number of periods is called an ordinary **annuity**; more correctly, the cash flows are said to be in *ordinary annuity form*. Annuities appear frequently in financial arrangements, and there are some useful shortcuts for determining their values. We consider these next.

annuity
A level stream of cash flows for a fixed period of time.

PRESENT VALUE FOR ANNUITY CASH FLOWS

Suppose we were examining an asset that promised to pay $500 at the end of each of the next three years. The cash flows from this asset are in the form of a three-year, $500 annuity. If we wanted to earn 10 percent on our money, how much would we offer for this annuity?

From the previous section, we know that we can discount each of these $500 payments back to the present at 10 percent to determine the total present value:

$$
\begin{aligned}
\text{Present value} &= (\$500/1.1^1) + (500/1.1^2) + (500/1.1^3) \\
&= (\$500/1.1) + (500/1.21) + (500/1.331) \\
&= \$454.55 + 413.22 + 375.66 \\
&= \$1,243.43
\end{aligned}
$$

This approach works just fine. However, we will often encounter situations in which the number of cash flows is quite large. For example, a typical home mortgage calls for monthly payments over 30 years, for a total of 360 payments. If we were trying to determine the present value of those payments, it would be useful to have a shortcut.

Because the cash flows of an annuity are all the same, we can come up with a handy variation on the basic present value equation. The present value of an annuity of C dollars per period for t periods when the rate of return or interest rate is r is given by:

$$
\begin{aligned}
\text{Annuity present value} &= C \times \left(\frac{1 - \text{Present value factor}}{r} \right) \\
&= C \times \left\{ \frac{1 - [1/(1 + r)^t]}{r} \right\}
\end{aligned}
\qquad \text{[6.1]}
$$

The term in parentheses on the first line is sometimes called the *present value interest factor* for annuities and abbreviated PVIFA(r, t).

The expression for the annuity present value may look a little complicated, but it isn't difficult to use. Notice that the term in square brackets on the second line, $1/(1 + r)^t$, is the same present value factor we've been calculating. In our example from the beginning of this section, the interest rate is 10 percent and there are three years involved. The usual present value factor is thus:

$$
\text{Present value factor} = 1/1.1^3 = 1/1.331 = .751315
$$

To calculate the annuity present value factor, we just plug this in:

$$
\begin{aligned}
\text{Annuity present value factor} &= (1 - \text{Present value factor})/r \\
&= (1 - .751315)/.10 \\
&= .248685/.10 = 2.48685
\end{aligned}
$$

Just as we calculated before, the present value of our $500 annuity is then:

$$
\text{Annuity present value} = \$500 \times 2.48685 = \$1,243.43
$$

How Much Can You Afford?   EXAMPLE 6.5

After carefully going over your budget, you have determined you can afford to pay $632 per month toward a new sports car. You call up your local bank and find out that the going rate is 1 percent per month for 48 months. How much can you borrow?

To determine how much you can borrow, we need to calculate the present value of $632 per month for 48 months at 1 percent per month. The loan payments are in ordinary annuity form, so the annuity present value factor is:

$$
\begin{aligned}
\text{Annuity PV factor} &= (1 - \text{Present value factor})/r \\
&= [1 - (1/1.01^{48})]/.01 \\
&= (1 - .6203)/.01 = 37.9740
\end{aligned}
$$

(continued)

156   **PART 3** Valuation of Future Cash Flows

With this factor, we can calculate the present value of the 48 payments of $632 each as:

Present value = $632 × 37.9740 = $24,000

Therefore, $24,000 is what you can afford to borrow and repay.

Annuity Tables   Just as there are tables for ordinary present value factors, there are tables for annuity factors as well. Table 6.1 contains a few such factors; Table A.3 in the appendix to the book contains a larger set. To find the annuity present value factor we calculated just before Example 6.5, look for the row corresponding to three periods and then find the column for 10 percent. The number you see at that intersection should be 2.4869 (rounded to four decimal places), as we calculated. Once again, try calculating a few of these factors yourself and compare your answers to the ones in the table to make sure you know how to do it. If you are using a financial calculator, just enter $1 as the payment and calculate the present value; the result should be the annuity present value factor.

TABLE 6.1

Annuity Present Value Interest Factors

Number of Periods	Interest Rate			
	5%	10%	15%	20%
1	.9524	.9091	.8696	.8333
2	1.8594	1.7355	1.6257	1.5278
3	2.7232	2.4869	2.2832	2.1065
4	3.5460	3.1699	2.8550	2.5887
5	4.3295	3.7908	3.3522	2.9906

CALCULATOR HINTS

Annuity Present Values

To find annuity present values with a financial calculator, we need to use the **PMT** key (you were probably wondering what it was for). Compared to finding the present value of a single amount, there are two important differences. First, we enter the annuity cash flow using the **PMT** key. Second, we don't enter anything for the future value, **FV**. So, for example, the problem we have been examining is a three-year, $500 annuity. If the discount rate is 10 percent, we need to do the following (after clearing out the calculator!):

Enter	3	10	500		
	N	I/Y	PMT		FV

As usual, we get a negative sign on the PV.

SPREADSHEET STRATEGIES

Annuity Present Values

Using a spreadsheet to find annuity present values goes like this:

	A	B	C	D	E	F	G
1							
2	**Using a spreadsheet to find annuity present values**						
3							
4	What is the present value of $500 per year for 3 years if the discount rate is 10 percent?						
5	We need to solve for the unknown present value, so we use the formula PV(rate, nper, pmt, fv).						
6							
7	Payment amount per period:	$500					
8	Number of payments:	3					
9	Discount rate:	0.1					
10							
11	Annuity present value:	**$1,243.43**					
12							
13	The formula entered in cell B11 is =PV(B9,B8,-B7,0); notice that fv is zero and that						
14	pmt has a negative sign on it. Also notice that rate is entered as a decimal, not a percentage.						
15							
16							
17							

Finding the Payment Suppose you wish to start up a new business that specializes in the latest of health food trends, frozen yak milk. To produce and market your product, the Yakkee Doodle Dandy, you need to borrow $100,000. Because it strikes you as unlikely that this particular fad will be long-lived, you propose to pay off the loan quickly by making five equal annual payments. If the interest rate is 18 percent, what will the payment be?

In this case, we know the present value is $100,000. The interest rate is 18 percent, and there are five years. The payments are all equal, so we need to find the relevant annuity factor and solve for the unknown cash flow:

$$\text{Annuity present value} = \$100,000 = C \times [(1 - \text{Present value factor})/r]$$
$$= C \times \{[1 - (1/1.18^5)]/.18\}$$
$$= C \times [(1 - .4371)/.18]$$
$$= C \times 3.1272$$
$$C = \$100,000/3.1272 = \$31,978$$

Therefore, you'll make five payments of just under $32,000 each.

CALCULATOR HINTS

Annuity Payments

Finding annuity payments is easy with a financial calculator. In our yak example, the PV is $100,000, the interest rate is 18 percent, and there are five years. We find the payment as follows:

Enter	5	18		100,000	
	N	I/Y		PV	FV

Here, we get a negative sign on the payment because the payment is an outflow for us.

SPREADSHEET STRATEGIES

Annuity Payments

Using a spreadsheet to work the same problem goes like this:

	A	B	C	D	E	F	G
1							
2	**Using a spreadsheet to find annuity payments**						
3							
4	What is the annuity payment if the present value is $100,000, the interest rate is 18 percent, and						
5	there are 5 periods? We need to solve for the unknown payment in an annuity, so we use the						
6	formula PMT(rate, nper, pv, fv).						
7							
8	Annuity present value:	$100,000					
9	Number of payments:	5					
10	Discount rate:	0.18					
11							
12	Annuity payment:	**$31,977.78**					
13							
14	The formula entered in cell B12 is =PMT(B10, B9, -B8,0); notice that fv is zero and that the payment						
15	has a negative sign because it is an outflow to us.						
16							

EXAMPLE 6.6	**Finding the Number of Payments**

You ran a little short on your spring break vacation, so you put $1,000 on your credit card. You can afford only the minimum payment of $20 per month. The interest rate on the credit card is 1.5 percent per month. How long will you need to pay off the $1,000?

What we have here is an annuity of $20 per month at 1.5 percent per month for some unknown length of time. The present value is $1,000 (the amount you owe today). We need to do a little algebra (or use a financial calculator):

$$\$1,000 = \$20 \times [(1 - \text{Present value factor})/.015]$$
$$(\$1,000/20) \times .015 = 1 - \text{Present value factor}$$
$$\text{Present value factor} = .25 = 1/(1 + r)^t$$
$$1.015^t = 1/.25 = 4$$

At this point, the problem boils down to asking. How long does it take for your money to quadruple at 1.5 percent per month? Based on our previous chapter, the answer is about 93 months:

$$1.015^{93} = 3.99 \approx 4$$

It will take you about 93/12 = 7.75 years to pay off the $1,000 at this rate. If you use a financial calculator for problems like this, you should be aware that some automatically round up to the next whole period.

CALCULATOR HINTS

Finding the Number of Payments

To solve this one on a financial calculator, do the following:

Enter		1.5	−20	1,000	
		I/Y	PMT	PV	FV

Notice that we put a negative sign on the payment you must make, and we have solved for the number of months. You still have to divide by 12 to get our answer. Also, some financial calculators won't report a fractional value for N; they automatically (without telling you) round up to the next whole period (not to the nearest value). With a spreadsheet, use the function =NPER(rate,pmt,pv,fv); be sure to put in a zero for fv and to enter −20 as the payment.

Finding the Rate   The last question we might want to ask concerns the interest rate implicit in an annuity. For example, an insurance company offers to pay you $1,000 per year for 10 years if you will pay $6,710 up front. What rate is implicit in this 10-year annuity?

In this case, we know the present value ($6,710), we know the cash flows ($1,000 per year), and we know the life of the investment (10 years). What we don't know is the discount rate:

$$\$6,710 = \$1,000 \times [(1 - \text{Present value factor})/r]$$
$$\$6,710/1,000 = 6.71 = \{1 - [1/(1 + r)^{10}]\}/r$$

So, the annuity factor for 10 periods is equal to 6.71, and we need to solve this equation for the unknown value of r. Unfortunately, this is mathematically impossible to do directly. The only way to do it is to use a table or trial and error to find a value for r.

If you look across the row corresponding to 10 periods in Table A.3, you will see a factor of 6.7101 for 8 percent, so we see right away that the insurance company is offering just about 8 percent. Alternatively, we could just start trying different values until we got very close to the answer. Using this trial-and-error approach can be a little tedious, but fortunately machines are good at that sort of thing.[1]

To illustrate how to find the answer by trial and error, suppose a relative of yours wants to borrow $3,000. She offers to repay you $1,000 every year for four years. What interest rate are you being offered?

The cash flows here have the form of a four-year, $1,000 annuity. The present value is $3,000. We need to find the discount rate, r. Our goal in doing so is primarily to give you a feel for the relationship between annuity values and discount rates.

We need to start somewhere, and 10 percent is probably as good a place as any to begin. At 10 percent, the annuity factor is:

Annuity present value factor $= [1 - (1/1.10^4)]/.10 = 3.1699$

---

[1]Financial calculators rely on trial and error to find the answer. That's why they sometimes appear to be "thinking" before coming up with the answer. Actually, it is possible to directly solve for r if there are fewer than five periods, but it's usually not worth the trouble.

The present value of the cash flows at 10 percent is thus:

Present value = $1,000 × 3.1699 = $3,169.90

You can see that we're already in the right ballpark.

Is 10 percent too high or too low? Recall that present values and discount rates move in opposite directions: Increasing the discount rate lowers the PV and vice versa. Our present value here is too high, so the discount rate is too low. If we try 12 percent, we're almost there:

Present value = $1,000 × \{[1 − (1/1.12^4)]/.12\} = $3,037.35

We are still a little low on the discount rate (because the PV is a little high), so we'll try 13 percent:

Present value = $1,000 × \{[1 − (1/1.13^4)]/.13\} = $2,974.47

This is less than $3,000, so we now know that the answer is between 12 percent and 13 percent, and it looks to be about 12.5 percent. For practice, work at it for a while longer and see if you find that the answer is about 12.59 percent.

To illustrate a situation in which finding the unknown rate can be useful, let us consider that the Tri-State Megabucks lottery in Maine, Vermont, and New Hampshire offers you a choice of how to take your winnings (most lotteries do this). In a recent drawing, participants were offered the option of receiving a lump sum payment of $250,000 or an annuity of $500,000 to be received in equal installments over a 25-year period. (At the time, the lump sum payment was always half the annuity option.) Which option was better?

To answer, suppose you were to compare $250,000 today to an annuity of $500,000/25 = $20,000 per year for 25 years. At what rate do these have the same value? This is the same problem we've been looking at; we need to find the unknown rate, *r*, for a present value of $250,000, a $20,000 payment, and a 25-year period. If you grind through the calculations (or get a little machine assistance), you should find that the unknown rate is about 6.24 percent. You should take the annuity option if that rate is attractive relative to other investments available to you. Notice that we have ignored taxes in this example, and taxes can significantly affect our conclusion. Be sure to consult your tax adviser anytime you win the lottery.

CALCULATOR HINTS

Finding the Rate

Alternatively, you could use a financial calculator to do the following:

Enter   4   1,000   −3,000

N   PMT   PV   FV

Notice that we put a negative sign on the present value (why?). With a spreadsheet, use the function =RATE(nper,pmt,pv,fv); be sure to put in a zero for fv and to enter 1,000 as the payment and −3,000 as the pv.

FUTURE VALUE FOR ANNUITIES

On occasion, it's also handy to know a shortcut for calculating the future value of an annuity. As you might guess, there are future value factors for annuities as well as present value factors. In general, here is the future value factor for an annuity:

$$\text{Annuity FV factor} = (\text{Future value factor} - 1)/r$$
$$= [(1 + r)^t - 1]/r \qquad \textbf{[6.2]}$$

To see how we use annuity future value factors, suppose you plan to contribute $2,000 every year to a retirement account paying 8 percent. If you retire in 30 years, how much will you have?

The number of years here, t, is 30, and the interest rate, r, is 8 percent; so we can calculate the annuity future value factor as:

$$\text{Annuity FV factor} = (\text{Future value factor} - 1)/r$$
$$= (1.08^{30} - 1)/.08$$
$$= (10.0627 - 1)/.08$$
$$= 113.2832$$

The future value of this 30-year, $2,000 annuity is thus:

$$\text{Annuity future value} = \$2,000 \times 113.28$$
$$= \$226,566$$

Sometimes we need to find the unknown rate, r, in the context of an annuity future value. For example, if you had invested $100 per month in stocks over the 25-year period ended December 1978, your investment would have grown to $76,374. This period had the *worst* stretch of stock returns of any 25-year period between 1925 and 2005. How bad was it?

CALCULATOR HINTS

Future Values of Annuities

Of course, you could solve this problem using a financial calculator by doing the following:

Enter	30	8	−2,000		
		I/Y	PMT	PV	FV

Notice that we put a negative sign on the payment (why?). With a spreadsheet, use the function =FV(rate,nper, pmt,pv); be sure to put in a zero for pv and to enter −2,000 as the payment.

Here we have the cash flows ($100 per month), the *future* value ($76,374), and the time period (25 years, or 300 months). We need to find the implicit rate, r:

$$\$76,374 = \$100 \times [(\text{Future value factor} - 1)/r]$$
$$763.74 = [(1 + r)^{300} - 1]/r$$

Because this is the worst period, let's try 1 percent:

$$\text{Annuity future value factor} = (1.01^{300} - 1)/.01 = 1,878.85$$

We see that 1 percent is too high. From here, it's trial and error. See if you agree that r is about .55 percent per month. As you will see later in the chapter, this works out to be about 6.8 percent per year.

A NOTE ABOUT ANNUITIES DUE

annuity due
An annuity for which the cash flows occur at the beginning of the period.

So far we have only discussed ordinary annuities. These are the most important, but there is a fairly common variation. Remember that with an ordinary annuity, the cash flows occur at the end of each period. When you take out a loan with monthly payments, for example, the first loan payment normally occurs one month after you get the loan. However, when you lease an apartment, the first lease payment is usually due immediately. The second payment is due at the beginning of the second month, and so on. A lease is an example of an **annuity due**. An annuity due is an annuity for which the cash flows occur at the beginning of each period. Almost any type of arrangement in which we have to prepay the same amount each period is an annuity due.

There are several different ways to calculate the value of an annuity due. With a financial calculator, you simply switch it into "due" or "beginning" mode. Remember to switch it back when you are done! Another way to calculate the present value of an annuity due can be illustrated with a time line. Suppose an annuity due has five payments of $400 each, and the relevant discount rate is 10 percent. The time line looks like this:

0	1	2	3	4	5
$400	$400	$400	$400	$400	

Notice how the cash flows here are the same as those for a *four*-year ordinary annuity, except that there is an extra $400 at Time 0. For practice, check to see that the value of a four-year ordinary annuity at 10 percent is $1,267.95. If we add on the extra $400, we get $1,667.95, which is the present value of this annuity due.

Time value applications abound on the Web. See, for example, www.collegeboard.com, www.1stmortgagedirectory. com, and personal.fidelity. com.

There is an even easier way to calculate the present or future value of an annuity due. If we assume cash flows occur at the end of each period when they really occur at the beginning, then we discount each one by one period too many. We could fix this by simply multiplying our answer by $(1 + r)$, where r is the discount rate. In fact, the relationship between the value of an annuity due and an ordinary annuity is just this:

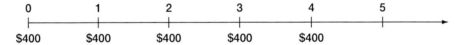

Annuity due value = Ordinary annuity value $\times (1 + r)$ **[6.3]**

This works for both present and future values, so calculating the value of an annuity due involves two steps: (1) Calculate the present or future value as though it were an ordinary annuity, and (2) multiply your answer by $(1 + r)$.

PERPETUITIES

perpetuity
An annuity in which the cash flows continue forever.

consol
A type of perpetuity.

We've seen that a series of level cash flows can be valued by treating those cash flows as an annuity. An important special case of an annuity arises when the level stream of cash flows continues forever. Such an asset is called a **perpetuity** because the cash flows are perpetual. Perpetuities are also called **consols**, particularly in Canada and the United Kingdom. See Example 6.7 for an important example of a perpetuity.

Because a perpetuity has an infinite number of cash flows, we obviously can't compute its value by discounting each one. Fortunately, valuing a perpetuity turns out to be the easiest possible case. The present value of a perpetuity is simply:

PV for a perpetuity = C/r **[6.4]**

I. Symbols:

PV = Present value, what future cash flows are worth today

FV_t = Future value, what cash flows are worth in the future

r = Interest rate, rate of return, or discount rate per period—typically, but not always, one year

t = Number of periods—typically, but not always, the number of years

C = Cash amount

II. Future Value of C per Period for t Periods at r Percent per Period:

$$FV_t = C \times \{[(1 + r)^t - 1]/r\}$$

A series of identical cash flows is called an *annuity*, and the term $[(1 + r)^t - 1]/r$ is called the *annuity future value factor.*

III. Present Value of C per Period for t Periods at r Percent per Period:

$$PV = C \times \{1 - [1/(1 + r)^t]\}/r$$

The term $\{1 - [1/(1 + r)^t]\}/r$ is called the *annuity present value factor.*

IV. Present Value of a Perpetuity of C per Period:

$$PV = C/r$$

A *perpetuity* has the same cash flow every year forever.

TABLE 6.2

Summary of Annuity and Perpetuity Calculations

For example, an investment offers a perpetual cash flow of $500 every year. The return you require on such an investment is 8 percent. What is the value of this investment? The value of this perpetuity is:

$$\text{Perpetuity PV} = C/r = \$500/.08 = \$6,250$$

For future reference, Table 6.2 contains a summary of the annuity and perpetuity basic calculations we described. By now, you probably think that you'll just use online calculators to handle annuity problems. Before you do, see our nearby *Work the Web* box!

Preferred Stock   **EXAMPLE 6.7**

Preferred stock (or preference stock) is an important example of a perpetuity. When a corporation sells preferred stock, the buyer is promised a fixed cash dividend every period (usually every quarter) forever. This dividend must be paid before any dividend can be paid to regular stockholders—hence the term *preferred.*

Suppose the Fellini Co. wants to sell preferred stock at $100 per share. A similar issue of preferred stock already outstanding has a price of $40 per share and offers a dividend of $1 every quarter. What dividend will Fellini have to offer if the preferred stock is going to sell?

The issue that is already out has a present value of $40 and a cash flow of $1 every quarter forever. Because this is a perpetuity:

$$\text{Present value} = \$40 = \$1 \times (1/r)$$
$$r = 2.5\%$$

To be competitive, the new Fellini issue will also have to offer 2.5 percent *per quarter;* so if the present value is to be $100, the dividend must be such that:

$$\text{Present value} = \$100 = C \times (1/.025)$$
$$C = \$2.50 \text{ (per quarter)}$$

GROWING ANNUITIES AND PERPETUITIES

Annuities commonly have payments that grow over time. Suppose, for example, that we are looking at a lottery payout over a 20-year period. The first payment, made one year from now, will be $200,000. Every year thereafter, the payment will grow by 5 percent, so the payment in the second year will be $200,000 × 1.05 = $210,000. The payment in the third year will be $210,000 × 1.05 = $220,500, and so on. What's the present value if the appropriate discount rate is 11 percent?

If we use the symbol g to represent the growth rate, we can calculate the value of a growing annuity using a modified version of our regular annuity formula:

$$\text{Growing annuity present value} = C \times \left[\frac{1 - \left(\frac{1+g}{1+r} \right)^t}{r - g} \right] \qquad [6.5]$$

Plugging in the numbers from our lottery example (and letting $g = .05$), we get:

$$PV = \$200,000 \times \left[\frac{1 - \left(\frac{1 + .05}{1 + .11} \right)^{20}}{.11 - .05} \right] = \$200,000 \times 11.18169 = \$2,236,337.06$$

WORK THE WEB

As we discussed in the previous chapter, many Web sites have financial calculators. One of these sites is MoneyChimp, which is located at www.moneychimp.com. Suppose you are lucky enough to have $2,000,000. You think you will be able to earn a 9 percent return. How much can you withdraw each year for the next 30 years? Here is what MoneyChimp says:

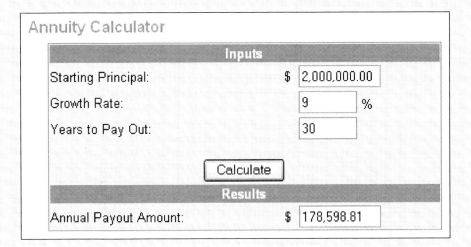

According to the MoneyChimp calculator, the answer is $178,598.81. How important is it to understand what you are doing? Calculate this one for yourself, and you should get $194,672.70. Which one is right? You are, of course! What's going on is that MoneyChimp assumes (but does not tell you) that the annuity is in the form of an annuity due, not an ordinary annuity. Recall that with an annuity due, the payments occur at the beginning of the period rather than the end of the period. The moral of the story is clear: *caveat calculator.*

There is also a formula for the present value of a growing perpetuity:

$$\text{Growing perpetuity present value} = C \times \left[\frac{1}{r - g}\right] = \frac{C}{r - g} \qquad \text{[6.6]}$$

In our lottery example, now suppose the payments continue forever. In this case, the present value is:

$$PV = \$200,000 \times \frac{1}{.11 - .05} = \$200,000 \times 16.6667 = \$3,333,333.33$$

The notion of a growing perpetuity may seem a little odd because the payments get bigger every period forever; but, as we will see in a later chapter, growing perpetuities play a key role in our analysis of stock prices.

Before we go on, there is one important note about our formulas for growing annuities and perpetuities. In both cases, the cash flow in the formula, C, is the cash flow that is going to occur exactly one period from today.

Concept Questions

6.2a In general, what is the present value of an annuity of C dollars per period at a discount rate of r per period? The future value?

6.2b In general, what is the present value of a perpetuity?

Comparing Rates: The Effect of Compounding

6.3

The next issue we need to discuss has to do with the way interest rates are quoted. This subject causes a fair amount of confusion because rates are quoted in many different ways. Sometimes the way a rate is quoted is the result of tradition, and sometimes it's the result of legislation. Unfortunately, at times, rates are quoted in deliberately deceptive ways to mislead borrowers and investors. We will discuss these topics in this section.

EFFECTIVE ANNUAL RATES AND COMPOUNDING

If a rate is quoted as 10 percent compounded semiannually, this means the investment actually pays 5 percent every six months. A natural question then arises: Is 5 percent every six months the same thing as 10 percent per year? It's easy to see that it is not. If you invest $1 at 10 percent per year, you will have $1.10 at the end of the year. If you invest at 5 percent every six months, then you'll have the future value of $1 at 5 percent for two periods:

$$\$1 \times 1.05^2 = \$1.1025$$

This is $.0025 more. The reason is simple: Your account was credited with $1 × .05 = 5 cents in interest after six months. In the following six months, you earned 5 percent on that nickel, for an extra 5 × .05 = .25 cents.

As our example illustrates, 10 percent compounded semiannually is actually equivalent to 10.25 percent per year. Put another way, we would be indifferent between

stated interest rate
The interest rate expressed in terms of the interest payment made each period. Also known as the *quoted interest rate*.

effective annual rate (EAR)
The interest rate expressed as if it were compounded once per year.

10 percent compounded semiannually and 10.25 percent compounded annually. Anytime we have compounding during the year, we need to be concerned about what the rate really is.

In our example, the 10 percent is called a **stated**, or **quoted, interest rate**. Other names are used as well. The 10.25 percent, which is actually the rate you will earn, is called the **effective annual rate (EAR)**. To compare different investments or interest rates, we will always need to convert to effective rates. Some general procedures for doing this are discussed next.

CALCULATING AND COMPARING EFFECTIVE ANNUAL RATES

To see why it is important to work only with effective rates, suppose you've shopped around and come up with the following three rates:

Bank A: 15 percent compounded daily
Bank B: 15.5 percent compounded quarterly
Bank C: 16 percent compounded annually

Which of these is the best if you are thinking of opening a savings account? Which of these is best if they represent loan rates?

To begin, Bank C is offering 16 percent per year. Because there is no compounding during the year, this is the effective rate. Bank B is actually paying $.155/4 = .03875$ or 3.875 percent per quarter. At this rate, an investment of $1 for four quarters would grow to:

$$\$1 \times 1.03875^4 = \$1.1642$$

The EAR, therefore, is 16.42 percent. For a saver, this is much better than the 16 percent rate Bank C is offering; for a borrower, it's worse.

Bank A is compounding every day. This may seem a little extreme, but it is common to calculate interest daily. In this case, the daily interest rate is actually:

$$.15/365 = .000411$$

This is .0411 percent per day. At this rate, an investment of $1 for 365 periods would grow to:

$$\$1 \times 1.000411^{365} = \$1.1618$$

The EAR is 16.18 percent. This is not as good as Bank B's 16.42 percent for a saver, and not as good as Bank C's 16 percent for a borrower.

This example illustrates two things. First, the highest quoted rate is not necessarily the best. Second, compounding during the year can lead to a significant difference between the quoted rate and the effective rate. Remember that the effective rate is what you get or what you pay.

If you look at our examples, you see that we computed the EARs in three steps. We first divided the quoted rate by the number of times that the interest is compounded. We then added 1 to the result and raised it to the power of the number of times the interest is compounded. Finally, we subtracted the 1. If we let m be the number of times the interest is compounded during the year, these steps can be summarized simply as:

$$\text{EAR} = [1 + (\text{Quoted rate}/m)]^m - 1 \qquad \textbf{[6.7]}$$

For example, suppose you are offered 12 percent compounded monthly. In this case, the interest is compounded 12 times a year; so m is 12. You can calculate the effective rate as:

$$
\begin{aligned}
\text{EAR} &= [1 + (\text{Quoted rate}/m)]^m - 1 \\
&= [1 + (.12/12)]^{12} - 1 \\
&= 1.01^{12} - 1 \\
&= 1.126825 - 1 \\
&= 12.6825\%
\end{aligned}
$$

| **What's the EAR?** | **EXAMPLE 6.8** |

A bank is offering 12 percent compounded quarterly. If you put $100 in an account, how much will you have at the end of one year? What's the EAR? How much will you have at the end of two years?

The bank is effectively offering 12%/4 = 3% every quarter. If you invest $100 for four periods at 3 percent per period, the future value is:

$$
\begin{aligned}
\text{Future value} &= \$100 \times 1.03^4 \\
&= \$100 \times 1.1255 \\
&= \$112.55
\end{aligned}
$$

The EAR is 12.55 percent: $100 × (1 + .1255) = $112.55.

We can determine what you would have at the end of two years in two different ways. One way is to recognize that two years is the same as eight quarters. At 3 percent per quarter, after eight quarters, you would have:

$$\$100 \times 1.03^8 = \$100 \times 1.2668 = \$126.68$$

Alternatively, we could determine the value after two years by using an EAR of 12.55 percent; so after two years you would have:

$$\$100 \times 1.1255^2 = \$100 \times 1.2688 = \$126.68$$

Thus, the two calculations produce the same answer. This illustrates an important point. Anytime we do a present or future value calculation, the rate we use must be an actual or effective rate. In this case, the actual rate is 3 percent per quarter. The effective annual rate is 12.55 percent. It doesn't matter which one we use once we know the EAR.

| **Quoting a Rate** | **EXAMPLE 6.9** |

Now that you know how to convert a quoted rate to an EAR, consider going the other way. As a lender, you know you want to actually earn 18 percent on a particular loan. You want to quote a rate that features monthly compounding. What rate do you quote?

In this case, we know the EAR is 18 percent, and we know this is the result of monthly compounding. Let q stand for the quoted rate. We thus have:

$$
\begin{aligned}
\text{EAR} &= [1 + (\text{Quoted rate}/m)]^m - 1 \\
.18 &= [1 + (q/12)]^{12} - 1 \\
1.18 &= [1 + (q/12)]^{12}
\end{aligned}
$$

(continued)

We need to solve this equation for the quoted rate. This calculation is the same as the ones we did to find an unknown interest rate in Chapter 5:

$$1.18^{(1/12)} = 1 + (q/12)$$
$$1.18^{.08333} = 1 + (q/12)$$
$$1.0139 = 1 + (q/12)$$
$$q = .0139 \times 12$$
$$= 16.68\%$$

Therefore, the rate you would quote is 16.68 percent, compounded monthly.

EARs AND APRs

annual percentage rate (APR)
The interest rate charged per period multiplied by the number of periods per year.

Sometimes it's not altogether clear whether a rate is an effective annual rate. A case in point concerns what is called the **annual percentage rate (APR)** on a loan. Truth-in-lending laws in the United States require that lenders disclose an APR on virtually all consumer loans. This rate must be displayed on a loan document in a prominent and unambiguous way.

Given that an APR must be calculated and displayed, an obvious question arises: Is an APR an effective annual rate? Put another way, if a bank quotes a car loan at 12 percent APR, is the consumer actually paying 12 percent interest? Surprisingly, the answer is no. There is some confusion over this point, which we discuss next.

The confusion over APRs arises because lenders are required by law to compute the APR in a particular way. By law, the APR is simply equal to the interest rate per period multiplied by the number of periods in a year. For example, if a bank is charging 1.2 percent per month on car loans, then the APR that must be reported is $1.2\% \times 12 = 14.4\%$. So, an APR is in fact a quoted, or stated, rate in the sense we've been discussing. For example, an APR of 12 percent on a loan calling for monthly payments is really 1 percent per month. The EAR on such a loan is thus:

$$EAR = [1 + (APR/12)]^{12} - 1$$
$$= 1.01^{12} - 1 = 12.6825\%$$

| **EXAMPLE 6.10** | **What Rate Are You Paying?** |

Depending on the issuer, a typical credit card agreement quotes an interest rate of 18 percent APR. Monthly payments are required. What is the actual interest rate you pay on such a credit card?

Based on our discussion, an APR of 18 percent with monthly payments is really $.18/12 = .015$ or 1.5 percent per month. The EAR is thus:

$$EAR = [1 + (.18/12)]^{12} - 1$$
$$= 1.015^{12} - 1$$
$$= 1.1956 - 1$$
$$= 19.56\%$$

This is the rate you actually pay.

It is somewhat ironic that truth-in-lending laws sometimes require lenders to be *un*truthful about the actual rate on a loan. There are also truth-in-saving laws that require banks and other borrowers to quote an "annual percentage yield," or APY, on things like savings accounts.

To make things a little confusing, an APY is an EAR. As a result, by law, the rates quoted to borrowers (APRs) and those quoted to savers (APYs) are not computed the same way.

There can be a huge difference between the APR and EAR when interest rate are large. For example, consider "payday loans." Payday loans are short-term loans made to consumers, often for less than two weeks, and are offered by companies such as AmeriCash Advance and National Payday. The loans work like this: You write a check today that is postdated (the date on the check is in the future) and give it to the company. They give you some cash. When the check date arrives, you either go to the store and pay the cash amount of the check, or the company cashes it (or else automatically renews the loan).

For example, AmeriCash Advance allows you to write a check for $125 dated 15 days in the future, for which they give you $100 today. So what are the APR and EAR of this arrangement? First, we need to find the interest rate, which we can find by the FV equation as follows:

$$FV = PV \times (1 + r)^1$$
$$\$125 = \$100 \times (1 + r)^1$$
$$1.25 = (1 + r)$$
$$r = .25 \text{ or } 25\%$$

That doesn't seem too bad until you remember this is the interest rate for *15 days!* The APR of the loan is:

$$APR = .25 \times 365/15$$
$$APR = 6.08333 \text{ or } 608.33\%$$

And the EAR for this loan is:

$$EAR = (1 + \text{Quoted rate}/m)^m - 1$$
$$EAR = (1 + .25)^{365/15} - 1$$
$$EAR = 227.1096 \text{ or } 22{,}710.96\%$$

Now that's an interest rate! Just to see what a difference a day (or three) makes, let's look at National Payday's terms. This company will allow you to write a postdated check for the same amount, but will give you 18 days to repay. Check for yourself that the APR of this arrangement is 506.94 percent and the EAR is 9,128.26 percent. Still not a loan we would like to take out!

TAKING IT TO THE LIMIT:
A NOTE ABOUT CONTINUOUS COMPOUNDING

If you made a deposit in a savings account, how often could your money be compounded during the year? If you think about it, there isn't really any upper limit. We've seen that daily compounding, for example, isn't a problem. There is no reason to stop here, however. We could compound every hour or minute or second. How high would the EAR get in this case? Table 6.3 illustrates the EARs that result as 10 percent is compounded at shorter and shorter intervals. Notice that the EARs do keep getting larger, but the differences get very small.

As the numbers in Table 6.3 seem to suggest, there is an upper limit to the EAR. If we let q stand for the quoted rate, then, as the number of times the interest is compounded gets extremely large, the EAR approaches:

$$EAR = e^q - 1 \qquad \qquad \text{[6.8]}$$

TABLE 6.3

Compounding Frequency and Effective Annual Rates

Compounding Period	Number of Times Compounded	Effective Annual Rate
Year	1	10.00000%
Quarter	4	10.38129
Month	12	10.47131
Week	52	10.50648
Day	365	10.51558
Hour	8,760	10.51703
Minute	525,600	10.51709

where e is the number 2.71828 (look for a key labeled "e^x" on your calculator). For example, with our 10 percent rate, the highest possible EAR is:

$$EAR = e^q - 1$$
$$= 2.71828^{.10} - 1$$
$$= 1.1051709 - 1$$
$$= 10.51709\%$$

In this case, we say that the money is continuously, or instantaneously, compounded. Interest is being credited the instant it is earned, so the amount of interest grows continuously.

EXAMPLE 6.11   **What's the Law?**

At one time, commercial banks and savings and loan associations (S&Ls) were restricted in the interest rates they could offer on savings accounts. Under what was known as Regulation Q, S&Ls were allowed to pay at most 5.5 percent, and banks were not allowed to pay more than 5.25 percent (the idea was to give the S&Ls a competitive advantage; it didn't work). The law did not say how often these rates could be compounded, however. Under Regulation Q, then, what were the maximum allowed interest rates?

The maximum allowed rates occurred with continuous, or instantaneous, compounding. For the commercial banks, 5.25 percent compounded continuously would be:

$$EAR = e^{.0525} - 1$$
$$= 2.71828^{.0525} - 1$$
$$= 1.0539026 - 1$$
$$= 5.39026\%$$

This is what banks could actually pay. Check for yourself to see that S&Ls could effectively pay 5.65406 percent.

Concept Questions

6.3a If an interest rate is given as 12 percent compounded daily, what do we call this rate?

6.3b What is an APR? What is an EAR? Are they the same thing?

6.3c In general, what is the relationship between a stated interest rate and an effective interest rate? Which is more relevant for financial decisions?

6.3d What does continuous compounding mean?

Loan Types and Loan Amortization · 6.4

Whenever a lender extends a loan, some provision will be made for repayment of the principal (the original loan amount). A loan might be repaid in equal installments, for example, or it might be repaid in a single lump sum. Because the way that the principal and interest are paid is up to the parties involved, there are actually an unlimited number of possibilities.

In this section, we describe a few forms of repayment that come up quite often, and more complicated forms can usually be built up from these. The three basic types of loans are pure discount loans, interest-only loans, and amortized loans. Working with these loans is a very straightforward application of the present value principles that we have already developed.

PURE DISCOUNT LOANS

The *pure discount loan* is the simplest form of loan. With such a loan, the borrower receives money today and repays a single lump sum at some time in the future. A one-year, 10 percent pure discount loan, for example, would require the borrower to repay $1.10 in one year for every dollar borrowed today.

Because a pure discount loan is so simple, we already know how to value one. Suppose a borrower was able to repay $25,000 in five years. If we, acting as the lender, wanted a 12 percent interest rate on the loan, how much would we be willing to lend? Put another way, what value would we assign today to that $25,000 to be repaid in five years? Based on our work in Chapter 5, we know the answer is just the present value of $25,000 at 12 percent for five years:

$$\text{Present value} = \$25,000/1.12^5$$
$$= \$25,000/1.7623$$
$$= \$14,186$$

Pure discount loans are common when the loan term is short—say a year or less. In recent years, they have become increasingly common for much longer periods.

| **Treasury Bills** | **EXAMPLE 6.12** |

When the U.S. government borrows money on a short-term basis (a year or less), it does so by selling what are called *Treasury bills,* or *T-bills* for short. A T-bill is a promise by the government to repay a fixed amount at some time in the future—for example, 3 months or 12 months.

Treasury bills are pure discount loans. If a T-bill promises to repay $10,000 in 12 months, and the market interest rate is 7 percent, how much will the bill sell for in the market?

Because the going rate is 7 percent, the T-bill will sell for the present value of $10,000 to be repaid in one year at 7 percent:

Present value = $10,000/1.07 = $9,345.79

INTEREST-ONLY LOANS

A second type of loan repayment plan calls for the borrower to pay interest each period and to repay the entire principal (the original loan amount) at some point in the future. Loans with such a repayment plan are called *interest-only loans.* Notice that if there is just one period, a pure discount loan and an interest-only loan are the same thing.

For example, with a three-year, 10 percent, interest-only loan of $1,000, the borrower would pay $1,000 × .10 = $100 in interest at the end of the first and second years. At the end of the third year, the borrower would return the $1,000 along with another $100 in interest for that year. Similarly, a 50-year interest-only loan would call for the borrower to pay interest every year for the next 50 years and then repay the principal. In the extreme, the borrower pays the interest every period forever and never repays any principal. As we discussed earlier in the chapter, the result is a perpetuity.

Most corporate bonds have the general form of an interest-only loan. Because we will be considering bonds in some detail in the next chapter, we will defer further discussion of them for now.

AMORTIZED LOANS

With a pure discount or interest-only loan, the principal is repaid all at once. An alternative is an *amortized loan,* with which the lender may require the borrower to repay parts of the loan amount over time. The process of providing for a loan to be paid off by making regular principal reductions is called *amortizing* the loan.

A simple way of amortizing a loan is to have the borrower pay the interest each period plus some fixed amount. This approach is common with medium-term business loans. For example, suppose a business takes out a $5,000, five-year loan at 9 percent. The loan agreement calls for the borrower to pay the interest on the loan balance each year and to reduce the loan balance each year by $1,000. Because the loan amount declines by $1,000 each year, it is fully paid in five years.

In the case we are considering, notice that the total payment will decline each year. The reason is that the loan balance goes down, resulting in a lower interest charge each year, whereas the $1,000 principal reduction is constant. For example, the interest in the first year will be $5,000 × .09 = $450. The total payment will be $1,000 + 450 = $1,450. In the second year, the loan balance is $4,000, so the interest is $4,000 × .09 = $360, and the total payment is $1,360. We can calculate the total payment in each of the remaining years by preparing a simple *amortization schedule* as follows:

Year	Beginning Balance	Total Payment	Interest Paid	Principal Paid	Ending Balance
1	$5,000	$1,450	$ 450	$1,000	$4,000
2	4,000	1,360	360	1,000	3,000
3	3,000	1,270	270	1,000	2,000
4	2,000	1,180	180	1,000	1,000
5	1,000	1,090	90	1,000	0
Totals		$6,350	$1,350	$5,000	

Notice that in each year, the interest paid is given by the beginning balance multiplied by the interest rate. Also notice that the beginning balance is given by the ending balance from the previous year.

Probably the most common way of amortizing a loan is to have the borrower make a single, fixed payment every period. Almost all consumer loans (such as car loans) and mortgages work this way. For example, suppose our five-year, 9 percent, $5,000 loan was amortized this way. How would the amortization schedule look?

We first need to determine the payment. From our discussion earlier in the chapter, we know that this loan's cash flows are in the form of an ordinary annuity. In this case, we can solve for the payment as follows:

$$\$5,000 = C \times \{[1 - (1/1.09^5)]/.09\}$$
$$= C \times [(1 - .6499)/.09]$$

This gives us:

$$C = \$5,000/3.8897$$
$$= \$1,285.46$$

The borrower will therefore make five equal payments of $1,285.46. Will this pay off the loan? We will check by filling in an amortization schedule.

In our previous example, we knew the principal reduction each year. We then calculated the interest owed to get the total payment. In this example, we know the total payment. We will thus calculate the interest and then subtract it from the total payment to calculate the principal portion in each payment.

In the first year, the interest is $450, as we calculated before. Because the total payment is $1,285.46, the principal paid in the first year must be:

Principal paid = $1,285.46 − 450 = $835.46

The ending loan balance is thus:

Ending balance = $5,000 − 835.46 = $4,164.54

The interest in the second year is $4,164.54 × .09 = $374.81, and the loan balance declines by $1,285.46 − 374.81 = $910.65. We can summarize all of the relevant calculations in the following schedule:

Year	Beginning Balance	Total Payment	Interest Paid	Principal Paid	Ending Balance
1	$5,000.00	$1,285.46	$ 450.00	$ 835.46	$4,164.54
2	4,164.54	1,285.46	374.81	910.65	3,253.88
3	3,253.88	1,285.46	292.85	992.61	2,261.27
4	2,261.27	1,285.46	203.51	1,081.95	1,179.32
5	1,179.32	1,285.46	106.14	1,179.32	0.00
Totals		$6,427.30	$1,427.31	$5,000.00	

Because the loan balance declines to zero, the five equal payments do pay off the loan. Notice that the interest paid declines each period. This isn't surprising because the loan balance is going down. Given that the total payment is fixed, the principal paid must be rising each period.

If you compare the two loan amortizations in this section, you will see that the total interest is greater for the equal total payment case: $1,427.31 versus $1,350. The reason for this is that the loan is repaid more slowly early on, so the interest is somewhat higher. This doesn't mean that one loan is better than the other; it simply means that one is effectively paid off faster than the other. For example, the principal reduction in the first year is $835.46 in the equal total payment case as compared to $1,000 in the first case. Many Web sites offer loan amortization schedules. See our nearby *Work the Web* box for an example.

We will close this chapter with an example that may be of particular relevance. Federal Stafford loans are an important source of financing for many college students, helping to

WORK THE WEB

Preparing an amortization table is one of the more tedious time value of money applications. Using a spread-sheet makes it relatively easy, but there are also Web sites available that will prepare an amortization very quickly and simply. One such site is www.bankrate.com. This site has a mortgage calculator for home loans, but the same calculations apply to most other types of loans such as car loans and student loans. Suppose you graduate with a student loan of $20,000 and will repay the loan over the next 10 years at 6.25 percent. What are your monthly payments? Using the calculator we get:

Monthly mortgage payment and amortization calculator

Calculate your monthly mortgage payment. Click on the "?" next to the input box for an item to get help on that item. Find rates in your area

Mortgage amount $ | 20000.00 | [?] (Do not use commas.)

Mortgage term | 10 | [?] years

Interest rate | 6.25 | [?] % per year

Mortgage start date | Dec ⌄ | 1 ⌄ , | 2005 ⌄

Monthly mortgage payment $ | 224.56 | [?]

[Calculate]

[Show/Recalculate Amortization Table] [?]

Try this example yourself and click the "Show/Recalculate Amortization Table" button. You will find that your first payment will consist of $120.39 in principal and $104.17 in interest. Over the life of the loan you will pay a total of $6,947.22 in interest.

EXAMPLE 6.13 | Partial Amortization, or "Bite the Bullet"

A common arrangement in real estate lending might call for a 5-year loan with, say, a 15-year amortization. What this means is that the borrower makes a payment every month of a fixed amount based on a 15-year amortization. However, after 60 months, the borrower makes a single, much larger payment called a "balloon" or "bullet" to pay off the loan. Because the monthly payments don't fully pay off the loan, the loan is said to be partially amortized.

Suppose we have a $100,000 commercial mortgage with a 12 percent APR and a 20-year (240-month) amortization. Further suppose the mortgage has a five-year balloon. What will the monthly payment be? How big will the balloon payment be?

(continued)

The monthly payment can be calculated based on an ordinary annuity with a present value of $100,000. There are 240 payments, and the interest rate is 1 percent per month. The payment is:

$$\$100,000 = C \times [1 - (1/1.01^{240})/.01]$$
$$= C \times 90.8194$$
$$C = \$1,101.09$$

Now, there is an easy way and a hard way to determine the balloon payment. The hard way is to actually amortize the loan for 60 months to see what the balance is at that time. The easy way is to recognize that after 60 months, we have a $240 - 60 = 180$-month loan. The payment is still $1,101.09 per month, and the interest rate is still 1 percent per month. The loan balance is thus the present value of the remaining payments:

$$\text{Loan balance} = \$1,101.09 \times [1 - (1/1.01^{180})/.01]$$
$$= \$1,101.09 \times 83.3217$$
$$= \$91,744.69$$

The balloon payment is a substantial $91,744. Why is it so large? To get an idea, consider the first payment on the mortgage. The interest in the first month is $100,000 \times .01 = \$1,000$. Your payment is $1,101.09, so the loan balance declines by only $101.09. Because the loan balance declines so slowly, the cumulative "pay down" over five years is not great.

cover the cost of tuition, books, new cars, condominiums, and many other things. Sometimes students do not seem to fully realize that Stafford loans have a serious drawback: They must be repaid in monthly installments, usually beginning six months after the student leaves school.

Some Stafford loans are subsidized, meaning that the interest does not begin to accrue until repayment begins (this is a good thing). If you are a dependent undergraduate student under this particular option, the total debt you can run up is, at most, $23,000. The maximum interest rate is 8.25 percent, or $8.25/12 = 0.6875$ percent per month. Under the "standard repayment plan," the loans are amortized over 10 years (subject to a minimum payment of $50).

Suppose you max out borrowing under this program and also get stuck paying the maximum interest rate. Beginning six months after you graduate (or otherwise depart the ivory tower), what will your monthly payment be? How much will you owe after making payments for four years?

Given our earlier discussions, see if you don't agree that your monthly payment assuming a $23,000 total loan is $282.10 per month. Also, as explained in Example 6.13, after making payments for four years, you still owe the present value of the remaining payments. There are 120 payments in all. After you make 48 of them (the first four years), you have 72 to go. By now, it should be easy for you to verify that the present value of $282.10 per month for 72 months at 0.6875 percent per month is just under $16,000, so you still have a long way to go.

Of course, it is possible to rack up much larger debts. According to the Association of American Medical Colleges, medical students who borrowed to attend medical school and graduated in 2005 had an average student loan balance of $120,280. Ouch! How long will it take the average student to pay off her medical school loans?

SPREADSHEET STRATEGIES

Loan Amortization Using a Spreadsheet

Loan amortization is a common spreadsheet application. To illustrate, we will set up the problem that we examined earlier: a five-year, $5,000, 9 percent loan with constant payments. Our spreadsheet looks like this:

	A	B	C	D	E	F	G	H
1								
2			Using a spreadsheet to amortize a loan					
3								
4			Loan amount:	$5,000				
5			Interest rate:	0.09				
6			Loan term:	5				
7			Loan payment:	**$1,285.46**				
8				Note: Payment is calculated using PMT(rate,nper,-pv,fv).				
9		Amortization table:						
10								
11		Year	Beginning	Total	Interest	Principal	Ending	
12			Balance	Payment	Paid	Paid	Balance	
13		1	$5,000.00	$1,285.46	$450.00	$835.46	$4,164.54	
14		2	4,164.54	1,285.46	374.81	910.65	3,253.88	
15		3	3,253.88	1,285.46	292.85	992.61	2,261.27	
16		4	2,261.27	1,285.46	203.51	1,081.95	1,179.32	
17		5	1,179.32	1,285.46	106.14	1,179.32	0.00	
18		Totals		6,427.31	1,427.31	5,000.00		
19								
20		Formulas in the amortization table:						
21								
22		Year	Beginning	Total	Interest	Principal	Ending	
23			Balance	Payment	Paid	Paid	Balance	
24		1	=+D4	=$D$7	=+$D$5*C13	=+D13-E13	=+C13-F13	
25		2	=+G13	=$D$7	=+$D$5*C14	=+D14-E14	=+C14-F14	
26		3	=+G14	=$D$7	=+$D$5*C15	=+D15-E15	=+C15-F15	
27		4	=+G15	=$D$7	=+$D$5*C16	=+D16-E16	=+C16-F16	
28		5	=+G16	=$D$7	=+$D$5*C17	=+D17-E17	=+C17-F17	
29								
30		Note: Totals in the amortization table are calculated using the SUM formula.						
31								

Let's say she makes a monthly payment of $1,000, and the loan has an interest rate of 7 percent per year, or .5833 percent per month. See if you agree that it will take 208 months, or just over 17 years, to pay off the loan. Maybe MD really stands for "mucho debt"!

Concept Questions

6.4a What is a pure discount loan? An interest-only loan?

6.4b What does it mean to amortize a loan?

6.4c What is a balloon payment? How do you determine its value?

Summary and Conclusions   6.5

This chapter rounded out your understanding of fundamental concepts related to the time value of money and discounted cash flow valuation. Several important topics were covered:

1. There are two ways of calculating present and future values when there are multiple cash flows. Both approaches are straightforward extensions of our earlier analysis of single cash flows.

2. A series of constant cash flows that arrive or are paid at the end of each period is called an ordinary annuity, and we described some useful shortcuts for determining the present and future values of annuities.

3. Interest rates can be quoted in a variety of ways. For financial decisions, it is important that any rates being compared be first converted to effective rates. The relationship between a quoted rate, such as an annual percentage rate (APR), and an effective annual rate (EAR) is given by:

$$EAR = [1 + (Quoted\ rate/m)]^m - 1$$

where m is the number of times during the year the money is compounded or, equivalently, the number of payments during the year.

4. Many loans are annuities. The process of providing for a loan to be paid off gradually is called amortizing the loan, and we discussed how amortization schedules are prepared and interpreted.

The principles developed in this chapter will figure prominently in the chapters to come. The reason for this is that most investments, whether they involve real assets or financial assets, can be analyzed using the discounted cash flow (DCF) approach. As a result, the DCF approach is broadly applicable and widely used in practice. For example, the next two chapters show how to value bonds and stocks using an extension of the techniques presented in this chapter. Before going on, therefore, you might want to do some of the problems that follow.

Visit us at www.mhhe.com/rwj

CHAPTER REVIEW AND SELF-TEST PROBLEMS

6.1   Present Values with Multiple Cash Flows A first-round draft choice quarterback has been signed to a three-year, $25 million contract. The details provide for an immediate cash bonus of $2 million. The player is to receive $5 million in salary at the end of the first year, $8 million the next, and $10 million at the end of the last year. Assuming a 15 percent discount rate, is this package worth $25 million? If not, how much is it worth?

6.2   Future Value with Multiple Cash Flows You plan to make a series of deposits in an individual retirement account. You will deposit $1,000 today, $2,000 in two years, and $2,000 in five years. If you withdraw $1,500 in three years and $1,000 in seven years, assuming no withdrawal penalties, how much will you have after eight years if the interest rate is 7 percent? What is the present value of these cash flows?

6.3   Annuity Present Value You are looking into an investment that will pay you $12,000 per year for the next 10 years. If you require a 15 percent return, what is the most you would pay for this investment?

6.4 **APR versus EAR** The going rate on student loans is quoted as 8 percent APR. The terms of the loans call for monthly payments. What is the effective annual rate (EAR) on such a student loan?

6.5 **It's the Principal That Matters** Suppose you borrow $10,000. You are going to repay the loan by making equal annual payments for five years. The interest rate on the loan is 14 percent per year. Prepare an amortization schedule for the loan. How much interest will you pay over the life of the loan?

6.6 **Just a Little Bit Each Month** You've recently finished your MBA at the Darnit School. Naturally, you must purchase a new BMW immediately. The car costs about $21,000. The bank quotes an interest rate of 15 percent APR for a 72-month loan with a 10 percent down payment. You plan on trading the car in for a new one in two years. What will your monthly payment be? What is the effective interest rate on the loan? What will the loan balance be when you trade the car in?

ANSWERS TO CHAPTER REVIEW AND SELF-TEST PROBLEMS

6.1 Obviously, the package is not worth $25 million because the payments are spread out over three years. The bonus is paid today, so it's worth $2 million. The present values for the three subsequent salary payments are:

$$(\$5/1.15) + (8/1.15^2) + (10/1.15^3) = (\$5/1.15) + (8/1.32) + (10/1.52)$$
$$= \$16.9721 \text{ million}$$

The package is worth a total of $18.9721 million.

6.2 We will calculate the future values for each of the cash flows separately and then add them up. Notice that we treat the withdrawals as negative cash flows:

$$\$1,000 \times 1.07^8 = \quad \$1,000 \times 1.7812 = \$\ 1,718.19$$
$$\$2,000 \times 1.07^6 = \quad \$2,000 \times 1.5007 = \quad 3,001.46$$
$$-\$1,500 \times 1.07^5 = -\$1,500 \times 1.4026 = \ -2,103.83$$
$$\$2,000 \times 1.07^3 = \quad \$2,000 \times 1.2250 = \quad 2,450.09$$
$$-\$1,000 \times 1.07^1 = -\$1,000 \times 1.0700 = \ \underline{-1,070.00}$$
$$\text{Total future value} \qquad\qquad\qquad = \underline{\$\ 3,995.91}$$

This value includes a small rounding error.

To calculate the present value, we could discount each cash flow back to the present or we could discount back a single year at a time. However, because we already know that the future value in eight years is $3,995.91, the easy way to get the PV is just to discount this amount back eight years:

$$\text{Present value} = \$3,995.91/1.07^8$$
$$= \$3,995.91/1.7182$$
$$= \$2,325.64$$

We again ignore a small rounding error. For practice, you can verify that this is what you get if you discount each cash flow back separately.

6.3 The most you would be willing to pay is the present value of $12,000 per year for 10 years at a 15 percent discount rate. The cash flows here are in ordinary annuity form, so the relevant present value factor is:

Annuity present value factor $= (1 -$ Present value factor$)/r$

$$= [1 - (1/1.15^{10})]/.15$$
$$= (1 - .2472)/.15$$
$$= 5.0188$$

The present value of the 10 cash flows is thus:

Present value $= \$12,000 \times 5.0188$
$$= \$60,225$$

This is the most you would pay.

6.4 A rate of 8 percent APR with monthly payments is actually $8\%/12 = .67\%$ per month. The EAR is thus:

$$\text{EAR} = [1 + (.08/12)]^{12} - 1 = 8.30\%$$

6.5 We first need to calculate the annual payment. With a present value of $10,000, an interest rate of 14 percent, and a term of five years, the payment can be determined from:

$$\$10,000 = \text{Payment} \times \{[1 - (1/1.14^5)]/.14\}$$
$$= \text{Payment} \times 3.4331$$

Therefore, the payment is $10,000/3.4331 = $2,912.84 (actually, it's $2,912.8355; this will create some small rounding errors in the following schedule). We can now prepare the amortization schedule as follows:

Year	Beginning Balance	Total Payment	Interest Paid	Principal Paid	Ending Balance
1	$10,000.00	$ 2,912.84	$1,400.00	$ 1,512.84	$8,487.16
2	8,487.16	2,912.84	1,188.20	1,724.63	6,762.53
3	6,762.53	2,912.84	946.75	1,966.08	4,796.45
4	4,796.45	2,912.84	671.50	2,241.33	2,555.12
5	2,555.12	2,912.84	357.72	2,555.12	0.00
Totals		$14,564.17	$4,564.17	$10,000.00	

6.6 The cash flows on the car loan are in annuity form, so we need to find only the payment. The interest rate is $15\%/12 = 1.25\%$ per month, and there are 72 months. The first thing we need is the annuity factor for 72 periods at 1.25 percent per period:

Annuity present value factor $= (1 -$ Present value factor$)/r$

$$= [1 - (1/1.0125^{72})]/.0125$$
$$= [1 - (1/2.4459)]/.0125$$
$$= (1 - .4088)/.0125$$
$$= 47.2925$$

The present value is the amount we finance. With a 10 percent down payment, we will be borrowing 90 percent of $21,000, or $18,900. To find the payment, we need to solve for C:

$$\$18,900 = C \times \text{Annuity present value factor}$$
$$= C \times 47.2925$$

Rearranging things a bit, we have:

$$C = \$18,900 \times (1/47.2925)$$
$$= \$18,900 \times .02115$$
$$= \$399.64$$

Your payment is just under $400 per month.

The actual interest rate on this loan is 1.25 percent per month. Based on our work in the chapter, we can calculate the effective annual rate as:

$$EAR = (1.0125)^{12} - 1 = 16.08\%$$

The effective rate is about one point higher than the quoted rate.

To determine the loan balance in two years, we could amortize the loan to see what the balance is at that time. This would be fairly tedious to do by hand. Using the information already determined in this problem, we can instead simply calculate the present value of the remaining payments. After two years, we have made 24 payments, so there are $72 - 24 = 48$ payments left. What is the present value of 48 monthly payments of $399.64 at 1.25 percent per month? The relevant annuity factor is:

$$\text{Annuity present value factor} = (1 - \text{Present value factor})/r$$
$$= [1 - (1/1.0125^{48})]/.0125$$
$$= [1 - (1/1.8154)]/.0125$$
$$= (1 - .5509)/.0125$$
$$= 35.9315$$

The present value is thus:

$$\text{Present value} = \$399.64 \times 35.9315 = \$14,359.66$$

You will owe about $14,360 on the loan in two years.

CONCEPTS REVIEW AND CRITICAL THINKING QUESTIONS

1. **Annuity Factors** There are four pieces to an annuity present value. What are they?
2. **Annuity Period** As you increase the length of time involved, what happens to the present value of an annuity? What happens to the future value?
3. **Interest Rates** What happens to the future value of an annuity if you increase the rate r? What happens to the present value?
4. **Present Value** What do you think about the Tri-State Megabucks lottery discussed in the chapter advertising a $500,000 prize when the lump sum option is $250,000? Is it deceptive advertising?
5. **Present Value** If you were an athlete negotiating a contract, would you want a big signing bonus payable immediately and smaller payments in the future, or vice versa? How about looking at it from the team's perspective?
6. **Present Value** Suppose two athletes sign 10-year contracts for $80 million. In one case, we're told that the $80 million will be paid in 10 equal installments. In the other case, we're told that the $80 million will be paid in 10 installments, but the installments will increase by 5 percent per year. Who got the better deal?
7. **APR and EAR** Should lending laws be changed to require lenders to report EARs instead of APRs? Why or why not?

8. **Time Value** On subsidized Stafford loans, a common source of financial aid for college students, interest does not begin to accrue until repayment begins. Who receives a bigger subsidy, a freshman or a senior? Explain. In words, how would you go about valuing the subsidy on a subsidized Stafford loan?

9. **Time Value** Eligibility for a subsidized Stafford loan is based on current financial need. However, both subsidized and unsubsidized Stafford loans are repaid out of future income. Given this, do you see a possible objection to having two types?

10. **Time Value** A viatical settlement is a lump sum of money given to a terminally ill individual in exchange for his life insurance policy. When the insured person dies, the purchaser receives the payout from the life insurance policy. What factors determine the value of the viatical settlement? Do you think such settlements are ethical? Why or why not?

QUESTIONS AND PROBLEMS

1. **Present Value and Multiple Cash Flows** Seaborn Co. has identified an investment project with the following cash flows. If the discount rate is 10 percent, what is the present value of these cash flows? What is the present value at 18 percent? At 24 percent?

BASIC
(Questions 1–28)

Year	Cash Flow
1	$1,100
2	720
3	940
4	1,160

2. **Present Value and Multiple Cash Flows** Investment X offers to pay you $7,000 per year for eight years, whereas Investment Y offers to pay you $9,000 per year for five years. Which of these cash flow streams has the higher present value if the discount rate is 5 percent? If the discount rate is 22 percent?

3. **Future Value and Multiple Cash Flows** Paradise, Inc., has identified an investment project with the following cash flows. If the discount rate is 8 percent, what is the future value of these cash flows in year 4? What is the future value at a discount rate of 11 percent? At 24 percent?

Year	Cash Flow
1	$ 700
2	950
3	1,200
4	1,300

4. **Calculating Annuity Present Value** An investment offers $4,600 per year for 15 years, with the first payment occurring one year from now. If the required return is 8 percent, what is the value of the investment? What would the value be if the payments occurred for 40 years? For 75 years? Forever?

5. **Calculating Annuity Cash Flows** If you put up $28,000 today in exchange for a 8.25 percent, 15-year annuity, what will the annual cash flow be?

6. **Calculating Annuity Values** Your company will generate $65,000 in annual revenue each year for the next eight years from a new information database. If the appropriate interest rate is 8.5 percent, what is the present value of the savings?

7. **Calculating Annuity Values** If you deposit $3,000 at the end of each of the next 20 years into an account paying 10.5 percent interest, how much money will you have in the account in 20 years? How much will you have if you make deposits for 40 years?

8. **Calculating Annuity Values** You want to have $80,000 in your savings account 10 years from now, and you're prepared to make equal annual deposits into the account at the end of each year. If the account pays 6.5 percent interest, what amount must you deposit each year?

9. **Calculating Annuity Values** Dinero Bank offers you a $30,000, seven-year term loan at 8 percent annual interest. What will your annual loan payment be?

10. **Calculating Perpetuity Values** The Maybe Pay Life Insurance Co. is trying to sell you an investment policy that will pay you and your heirs $20,000 per year forever. If the required return on this investment is 8 percent, how much will you pay for the policy?

11. **Calculating Perpetuity Values** In the previous problem, suppose a sales associate told you the policy costs $280,000. At what interest rate would this be a fair deal?

12. **Calculating EAR** Find the EAR in each of the following cases:

Stated Rate (APR)	Number of Times Compounded	Effective Rate (EAR)
7%	Quarterly	
18	Monthly	
10	Daily	
14	Infinite	

13. **Calculating APR** Find the APR, or stated rate, in each of the following cases:

Stated Rate (APR)	Number of Times Compounded	Effective Rate (EAR)
	Semiannually	12.2%
	Monthly	9.4
	Weekly	8.6
	Infinite	23.8

14. **Calculating EAR** First National Bank charges 13.1 percent compounded monthly on its business loans. First United Bank charges 13.4 percent compounded semiannually. As a potential borrower, which bank would you go to for a new loan?

15. **Calculating APR** Tarpley Credit Corp. wants to earn an effective annual return on its consumer loans of 14 percent per year. The bank uses daily compounding on its loans. What interest rate is the bank required by law to report to potential borrowers? Explain why this rate is misleading to an uninformed borrower.

16. **Calculating Future Values** What is the future value of $1,400 in 20 years assuming an interest rate of 9.6 percent compounded semiannually?

17. **Calculating Future Values** Corpstein Credit Bank is offering 8.4 percent compounded daily on its savings accounts. If you deposit $6,000 today, how much will you have in the account in 5 years? In 10 years? In 20 years?

18. **Calculating Present Values** An investment will pay you $45,000 in six years. If the appropriate discount rate is 11 percent compounded daily, what is the present value?

19. **EAR versus APR** Big Dom's Pawn Shop charges an interest rate of 25 percent per month on loans to its customers. Like all lenders, Big Dom must report an APR to consumers. What rate should the shop report? What is the effective annual rate?

20. **Calculating Loan Payments** You want to buy a new sports coupe for $61,800, and the finance office at the dealership has quoted you a 7.4 percent APR loan for 60 months to buy the car. What will your monthly payments be? What is the effective annual rate on this loan?

21. **Calculating Number of Periods** One of your customers is delinquent on his accounts payable balance. You've mutually agreed to a repayment schedule of $300 per month. You will charge .9 percent per month interest on the overdue balance. If the current balance is $17,000, how long will it take for the account to be paid off?

22. **Calculating EAR** Friendly's Quick Loans, Inc., offers you "three for four or I knock on your door." This means you get $3 today and repay $4 when you get your paycheck in one week (or else). What's the effective annual return Friendly's earns on this lending business? If you were brave enough to ask, what APR would Friendly's say you were paying?

23. **Valuing Perpetuities** Live Forever Life Insurance Co. is selling a perpetuity contract that pays $1,200 monthly. The contract currently sells for $63,000. What is the monthly return on this investment vehicle? What is the APR? The effective annual return?

24. **Calculating Annuity Future Values** You are planning to make monthly deposits of $250 into a retirement account that pays 10 percent interest compounded monthly. If your first deposit will be made one month from now, how large will your retirement account be in 30 years?

25. **Calculating Annuity Future Values** In the previous problem, suppose you make $3,000 annual deposits into the same retirement account. How large will your account balance be in 30 years?

26. **Calculating Annuity Present Values** Beginning three months from now, you want to be able to withdraw $1,500 each quarter from your bank account to cover college expenses over the next four years. If the account pays .75 percent interest per quarter, how much do you need to have in your bank account today to meet your expense needs over the next four years?

27. **Discounted Cash Flow Analysis** If the appropriate discount rate for the following cash flows is 11 percent compounded quarterly, what is the present value of the cash flows?

Year	Cash Flow
1	$ 900
2	850
3	0
4	1,140

28. **Discounted Cash Flow Analysis** If the appropriate discount rate for the following cash flows is 8.45 percent per year, what is the present value of the cash flows?

Year	Cash Flow
1	$2,800
2	0
3	5,600
4	1,940

184   **PART 3**   Valuation of Future Cash Flows

INTERMEDIATE
(Questions 29–56)

29.   Simple Interest versus Compound Interest First Simple Bank pays 6 percent simple interest on its investment accounts. If First Complex Bank pays interest on its accounts compounded annually, what rate should the bank set if it wants to match First Simple Bank over an investment horizon of 10 years?

30.   Calculating EAR You are looking at an investment that has an effective annual rate of 18 percent. What is the effective semiannual return? The effective quarterly return? The effective monthly return?

31.   Calculating Interest Expense You receive a credit card application from Shady Banks Savings and Loan offering an introductory rate of 2.5 percent per year, compounded monthly for the first six months, increasing thereafter to 17 percent compounded monthly. Assuming you transfer the $5,000 balance from your existing credit card and make no subsequent payments, how much interest will you owe at the end of the first year?

32.   Calculating Annuities You are planning to save for retirement over the next 30 years. To do this, you will invest $600 a month in a stock account and $300 a month in a bond account. The return of the stock account is expected to be 12 percent, and the bond account will pay 7 percent. When you retire, you will combine your money into an account with a 9 percent return. How much can you withdraw each month from your account assuming a 25-year withdrawal period?

33.   Calculating Future Values You have an investment that will pay you 1.08 percent per month. How much will you have per dollar invested in one year? In two years?

34.   Calculating Annuity Payments You want to be a millionaire when you retire in 40 years. How much do you have to save each month if you can earn an 11 percent annual return? How much do you have to save if you wait 10 years before you begin your deposits? 20 years?

35.   Calculating Rates of Return Suppose an investment offers to quadruple your money in 12 months (don't believe it). What rate of return per quarter are you being offered?

36.   Comparing Cash Flow Streams You've just joined the investment banking firm of Dewey, Cheatum, and Howe. They've offered you two different salary arrangements. You can have $90,000 per year for the next two years, or you can have $65,000 per year for the next two years, along with a $45,000 signing bonus today. The bonus is paid immediately, and the salary is paid at the end of each year. If the interest rate is 10 percent compounded monthly, which do you prefer?

37.   Growing Annuity You have just won the lottery and will receive $1,000,000 in one year. You will receive payments for 25 years, which will increase 5 percent per year. If the appropriate discount rate is 9 percent, what is the present value of your winnings?

38.   Growing Annuity Your job pays you only once a year for all the work you did over the previous 12 months. Today, December 31, you just received your salary of $50,000 and you plan to spend all of it. However, you want to start saving for retirement beginning next year. You have decided that one year from today you will begin depositing 2 percent of your annual salary in an account that will earn 10 percent per year. Your salary will increase at 4 percent per year throughout your career. How much money will you have on the date of your retirement 40 years from today?

39.   Present Value and Interest Rates What is the relationship between the value of an annuity and the level of interest rates? Suppose you just bought a 10-year annuity of $7,000 per year at the current interest rate of 10 percent per year. What happens to the value of your investment if interest rates suddenly drop to 5 percent? What if interest rates suddenly rise to 15 percent?

40. Calculating the Number of Payments You're prepared to make monthly payments of $225, beginning at the end of this month, into an account that pays 9 percent interest compounded monthly. How many payments will you have made when your account balance reaches $20,000?

41. Calculating Annuity Present Values You want to borrow $55,000 from your local bank to buy a new sailboat. You can afford to make monthly payments of $1,120, but no more. Assuming monthly compounding, what is the highest rate you can afford on a 60-month APR loan?

42. Calculating Loan Payments You need a 30-year, fixed-rate mortgage to buy a new home for $220,000. Your mortgage bank will lend you the money at a 6.8 percent APR for this 360-month loan. However, you can afford monthly payments of only $1,100, so you offer to pay off any remaining loan balance at the end of the loan in the form of a single balloon payment. How large will this balloon payment have to be for you to keep your monthly payments at $1,100?

43. Present and Future Values The present value of the following cash flow stream is $6,785 when discounted at 10 percent annually. What is the value of the missing cash flow?

Year	Cash Flow
1	$1,500
2	?
3	1,800
4	2,400

44. Calculating Present Values You just won the TVM Lottery. You will receive $1 million today plus another 10 annual payments that increase by $400,000 per year. Thus, in one year, you receive $1.4 million. In two years you get $1.8 million, and so on. If the appropriate interest rate is 9 percent, what is the present value of your winnings?

45. EAR versus APR You have just purchased a new warehouse. To finance the purchase, you've arranged for a 30-year mortgage loan for 80 percent of the $2,400,000 purchase price. The monthly payment on this loan will be $13,000. What is the APR on this loan? The EAR?

46. Present Value and Break-Even Interest Consider a firm with a contract to sell an asset for $145,000 three years from now. The asset costs $94,000 to produce today. Given a relevant discount rate on this asset of 13 percent per year, will the firm make a profit on this asset? At what rate does the firm just break even?

47. Present Value and Multiple Cash Flows What is the present value of $2,000 per year, at a discount rate of 10 percent, if the first payment is received 9 years from now and the last payment is received 25 years from now?

48. Variable Interest Rates A 15-year annuity pays $1,500 per month, and payments are made at the end of each month. If the interest rate is 13 percent compounded monthly for the first seven years, and 10 percent compounded monthly thereafter, what is the present value of the annuity?

49. Comparing Cash Flow Streams You have your choice of two investment accounts. Investment A is a 15-year annuity that features end-of-month $1,000 payments and has an interest rate of 9.5 percent compounded monthly. Investment B is a 9 percent continuously compounded lump sum investment, also good for 15 years. How much money would you need to invest in B today for it to be worth as much as investment A 15 years from now?

50. **Calculating Present Value of a Perpetuity**   Given an interest rate of 5.7 percent per year, what is the value at date $t = 7$ of a perpetual stream of $5,000 payments that begins at date $t = 15$?

51. **Calculating EAR**   A local finance company quotes a 15 percent interest rate on one-year loans. So, if you borrow $20,000, the interest for the year will be $3,000. Because you must repay a total of $23,000 in one year, the finance company requires you to pay $23,000/12, or $1,916.67, per month over the next 12 months. Is this a 15 percent loan? What rate would legally have to be quoted? What is the effective annual rate?

52. **Calculating Present Values**   A 5-year annuity of ten $6,000 semiannual payments will begin 9 years from now, with the first payment coming 9.5 years from now. If the discount rate is 10 percent compounded monthly, what is the value of this annuity five years from now? What is the value three years from now? What is the current value of the annuity?

53. **Calculating Annuities Due**   As discussed in the text, an ordinary annuity assumes equal payments at the end of each period over the life of the annuity. An *annuity due* is the same thing except the payments occur at the beginning of each period instead. Thus, a three-year annual annuity due would have periodic payment cash flows occurring at years 0, 1, and 2, whereas a three-year annual ordinary annuity would have periodic payment cash flows occurring at years 1, 2, and 3.
    a. At a 9.5 percent annual discount rate, find the present value of an eight-year ordinary annuity contract of $950 payments.
    b. Find the present value of the same contract if it is an annuity due.

54. **Calculating Annuities Due**   You want to buy a new sports car from Muscle Motors for $61,000. The contract is in the form of a 60-month annuity due at an 8.15 percent APR. What will your monthly payment be?

55. **Amortization with Equal Payments**   Prepare an amortization schedule for a five-year loan of $36,000. The interest rate is 9 percent per year, and the loan calls for equal annual payments. How much interest is paid in the third year? How much total interest is paid over the life of the loan?

56. **Amortization with Equal Principal Payments**   Rework Problem 55 assuming that the loan agreement calls for a principal reduction of $7,200 every year instead of equal annual payments.

CHALLENGE
(Questions 57–78)

57. **Calculating Annuity Values**   Bilbo Baggins wants to save money to meet three objectives. First, he would like to be able to retire 30 years from now with retirement income of $20,000 per month for 20 years, with the first payment received 30 years and 1 month from now. Second, he would like to purchase a cabin in Rivendell in 10 years at an estimated cost of $325,000. Third, after he passes on at the end of the 20 years of withdrawals, he would like to leave an inheritance of $750,000 to his nephew Frodo. He can afford to save $2,000 per month for the next 10 years. If he can earn an 11 percent EAR before he retires and an 8 percent EAR after he retires, how much will he have to save each month in years 11 through 30?

58. **Calculating Annuity Values**   After deciding to buy a new car, you can either lease the car or purchase it on a three-year loan. The car you wish to buy costs $28,000.

The dealer has a special leasing arrangement where you pay $1 today and $380 per month for the next three years. If you purchase the car, you will pay it off in monthly payments over the next three years at an 8 percent APR. You believe you will be able to sell the car for $15,000 in three years. Should you buy or lease the car? What break-even resale price in three years would make you indifferent between buying and leasing?

59. Calculating Annuity Values An All-Pro defensive lineman is in contract negotiations. The team has offered the following salary structure:

Time	Salary
0	$8,000,000
1	$4,000,000
2	$4,800,000
3	$5,700,000
4	$6,400,000
5	$7,000,000
6	$7,500,000

All salaries are to be paid in lump sums. The player has asked you as his agent to renegotiate the terms. He wants a $9 million signing bonus payable today and a contract value increase of $750,000. He also wants an equal salary paid every three months, with the first paycheck three months from now. If the interest rate is 5.5 percent compounded daily, what is the amount of his quarterly check? Assume 365 days in a year.

60. Discount Interest Loans This question illustrates what is known as *discount interest*. Imagine you are discussing a loan with a somewhat unscrupulous lender. You want to borrow $20,000 for one year. The interest rate is 14 percent. You and the lender agree that the interest on the loan will be .14 × $20,000 = $2,800. So the lender deducts this interest amount from the loan up front and gives you $17,200. In this case, we say that the discount is $2,800. What's wrong here?

61. Calculating Annuity Values You are serving on a jury. A plaintiff is suing the city for injuries sustained after a freak street sweeper accident. In the trial, doctors testified that it will be five years before the plaintiff is able to return to work. The jury has already decided in favor of the plaintiff. You are the foreperson of the jury and propose that the jury give the plaintiff an award to cover the following: (a) The present value of two years' back pay. The plaintiff's annual salary for the last two years would have been $44,000 and $46,000, respectively. (b) The present value of five years' future salary. You assume the salary will be $49,000 per year. (c) $100,000 for pain and suffering. (d) $20,000 for court costs. Assume that the salary payments are equal amounts paid at the end of each month. If the interest rate you choose is a 9 percent EAR, what is the size of the settlement? If you were the plaintiff, would you like to see a higher or lower interest rate?

62. Calculating EAR with Points You are looking at a one-year loan of $10,000. The interest rate is quoted as 9 percent plus three points. A *point* on a loan is simply 1 percent (one percentage point) of the loan amount. Quotes similar to this one are common with home mortgages. The interest rate quotation in this example requires the borrower to pay three points to the lender up front and repay the loan later with 9 percent interest. What rate would you actually be paying here?

63. **Calculating EAR with Points** The interest rate on a one-year loan is quoted as 12 percent plus two points (see the previous problem). What is the EAR? Is your answer affected by the loan amount?

64. **EAR versus APR** Two banks in the area offer 30-year, $220,000 mortgages at 7.2 percent and charge a $1,500 loan application fee. However, the application fee charged by Insecurity Bank and Trust is refundable if the loan application is denied, whereas that charged by I.M. Greedy and Sons Mortgage Bank is not. The current disclosure law requires that any fees that will be refunded if the applicant is rejected be included in calculating the APR, but this is not required with nonrefundable fees (presumably because refundable fees are part of the loan rather than a fee). What are the EARs on these two loans? What are the APRs?

65. **Calculating EAR with Add-On Interest** This problem illustrates a deceptive way of quoting interest rates called *add-on interest*. Imagine that you see an advertisement for Crazy Judy's Stereo City that reads something like this: "$1,000 Instant Credit! 13% Simple Interest! Three Years to Pay! Low, Low Monthly Payments!" You're not exactly sure what all this means and somebody has spilled ink over the APR on the loan contract, so you ask the manager for clarification.

Judy explains that if you borrow $1,000 for three years at 13 percent interest, in three years you will owe:

$$\$1{,}000 \times 1.13^3 = \$1{,}000 \times 1.42290 = \$1{,}442.90$$

Now, Judy recognizes that coming up with $1,442.90 all at once might be a strain, so she lets you make "low, low monthly payments" of $1,442.90/36 = $40.08 per month, even though this is extra bookkeeping work for her.

Is this a 13 percent loan? Why or why not? What is the APR on this loan? What is the EAR? Why do you think this is called add-on interest?

66. **Calculating Annuity Payments** This is a classic retirement problem. A time line will help in solving it. Your friend is celebrating her 35th birthday today and wants to start saving for her anticipated retirement at age 65. She wants to be able to withdraw $90,000 from her savings account on each birthday for 20 years following her retirement; the first withdrawal will be on her 66th birthday. Your friend intends to invest her money in the local credit union, which offers 8 percent interest per year. She wants to make equal annual payments on each birthday into the account established at the credit union for her retirement fund.

    a. If she starts making these deposits on her 36th birthday and continues to make deposits until she is 65 (the last deposit will be on her 65th birthday), what amount must she deposit annually to be able to make the desired withdrawals at retirement?

    b. Suppose your friend has just inherited a large sum of money. Rather than making equal annual payments, she has decided to make one lump sum payment on her 35th birthday to cover her retirement needs. What amount does she have to deposit?

    c. Suppose your friend's employer will contribute $1,500 to the account every year as part of the company's profit-sharing plan. In addition, your friend expects a $25,000 distribution from a family trust fund on her 55th birthday, which she will also put into the retirement account. What amount must she deposit annually now to be able to make the desired withdrawals at retirement?

67. **Calculating the Number of Periods** Your Christmas ski vacation was great, but it unfortunately ran a bit over budget. All is not lost: You just received an offer in the mail to transfer your $10,000 balance from your current credit card, which charges an annual rate of 18.2 percent, to a new credit card charging a rate of 8.2 percent.

How much faster could you pay the loan off by making your planned monthly payments of $200 with the new card? What if there was a 2 percent fee charged on any balances transferred?

68.   **Future Value and Multiple Cash Flows** An insurance company is offering a new policy to its customers. Typically, the policy is bought by a parent or grandparent for a child at the child's birth. The details of the policy are as follows: The purchaser (say, the parent) makes the following six payments to the insurance company:

First birthday:	$ 800
Second birthday:	$ 800
Third birthday:	$ 900
Fourth birthday:	$ 900
Fifth birthday:	$1,000
Sixth birthday:	$1,000

After the child's sixth birthday, no more payments are made. When the child reaches age 65, he or she receives $350,000. If the relevant interest rate is 11 percent for the first six years and 7 percent for all subsequent years, is the policy worth buying?

69.   **Calculating a Balloon Payment** You have just arranged for a $450,000 mortgage to finance the purchase of a large tract of land. The mortgage has an 8.5 percent APR, and it calls for monthly payments over the next 30 years. However, the loan has an eight-year balloon payment, meaning that the loan must be paid off then. How big will the balloon payment be?

70.   **Calculating Interest Rates** A financial planning service offers a college savings program. The plan calls for you to make six annual payments of $5,000 each, with the first payment occurring today, your child's 12th birthday. Beginning on your child's 18th birthday, the plan will provide $15,000 per year for four years. What return is this investment offering?

71.   **Break-Even Investment Returns** Your financial planner offers you two different investment plans. Plan X is a $15,000 annual perpetuity. Plan Y is a 10-year, $20,000 annual annuity. Both plans will make their first payment one year from today. At what discount rate would you be indifferent between these two plans?

72.   **Perpetual Cash Flows** What is the value of an investment that pays $7,500 every *other* year forever, if the first payment occurs one year from today and the discount rate is 11 percent compounded daily? What is the value today if the first payment occurs four years from today?

73.   **Ordinary Annuities and Annuities Due** As discussed in the text, an annuity due is identical to an ordinary annuity except that the periodic payments occur at the beginning of each period and not at the end of the period. Show that the relationship between the value of an ordinary annuity and the value of an otherwise equivalent annuity due is:

Annuity due value = Ordinary annuity value $\times$ (1 + r)

Show this for both present and future values.

74.   **Calculating Growing Annuities** You have 30 years left until retirement and want to retire with $1 million. Your salary is paid annually, and you will receive $55,000 at the end of the current year. Your salary will increase at 3 percent per year, and you can earn a 10 percent return on the money you invest. If you save a constant percentage of your salary, what percentage of your salary must you save each year?

75. **Calculating EAR** A check-cashing store is in the business of making personal loans to walk-up customers. The store makes only one-week loans at 8 percent interest per week.

   a. What APR must the store report to its customers? What EAR are customers actually paying?

   b. Now suppose the store makes one-week loans at 8 percent discount interest per week (see Problem 60). What's the APR now? The EAR?

   c. The check-cashing store also makes one-month add-on interest loans at 8 percent discount interest per week. Thus if you borrow $100 for one month (four weeks), the interest will be ($100 × 1.08⁴) − 100 = $31.08. Because this is discount interest, your net loan proceeds today will be $68.92. You must then repay the store $100 at the end of the month. To help you out, though, the store lets you pay off this $100 in installments of $25 per week. What is the APR of this loan? What is the EAR?

76. **Present Value of a Growing Perpetuity** What is the equation for the present value of a growing perpetuity with a payment of C one period from today if the payments grow by C each period?

77. **Rule of 72** Earlier, we discussed the Rule of 72, a useful approximation for many interest rates and periods for the time it takes a lump sum to double in value. For a 10 percent interest rate, show that the "Rule of 73" is slightly better. For what rate is the Rule of 72 exact? (*Hint:* Use the Solver function in Excel.)

78. **Rule of 69.3** A corollary to the Rule of 72 is the Rule of 69.3. The Rule of 69.3 is exactly correct except for rounding when interest rates are compounded continuously. Prove the Rule of 69.3 for continuously compounded interest.

WEB EXERCISES

6.1 **Annuity Future Value** The St. Louis Federal Reserve Board has files listing historical interest rates on its Web site: www.stls.frb.org. Find the link for "FRED II," then "Interest Rates." You will find listings for Moody's Seasoned Aaa Corporate Bond Yield and Moody's Seasoned Baa Corporate Bond Yield. (These rates are discussed in the next chapter.) If you invest $2,000 per year for the next 40 years at the most recent Aaa yield, how much will you have? What if you invest the same amount at the Baa yield?

6.2 **Loan Payments** Finding the time necessary until you pay off a loan is simple if you make equal payments each month. However, when paying off credit cards many individuals make only the minimum monthly payment, which is generally $10 or 2 percent to 3 percent of the balance, whichever is greater. You can find a credit card calculator at www.fincalc.com. You currently owe $10,000 on a credit card with a 17 percent interest rate and a minimum payment of $10 or 2 percent of your balance, whichever is greater. How soon will you pay off this debt if you make the minimum payment each month? How much total interest will you pay?

6.3 **Annuity Payments** Go to www.moneychimp.com. Use the calculator to solve this problem. If you have $1,500,000 when you retire and want to withdraw an equal amount for the next 30 years, how much can you withdraw each year if you earn 7 percent? What if you earn 9 percent?

6.4 **Annuity Payments** The St. Louis Federal Reserve Board has files listing historical interest rates on its Web site: www.stls.frb.org. Find the link for "FRED II," then "Interest Rates." You will find a listing for the Bank Prime Loan Rate. The file lists the monthly prime rates since January 1949 (1949.01). What is the most recent prime rate? What is the highest prime rate over this period? If you bought a house for $150,000 at the current prime rate on a 30-year mortgage with monthly payments, how much are your payments? If you had purchased the house at the same price when the prime rate was its highest, what would your monthly payments have been?

6.5 **Loan Amortization** You can find a calculator that will prepare a loan amortization table at www.hsh.com. You want to buy a home for $200,000 on a 30-year mortgage with monthly payments at the rate quoted on the site. What percentage of your first month's payment is principal? What percentage of your last month's payment is principal? What is the total interest paid on the loan?

The MBA Decision

Ben Bates graduated from college six years ago with a finance undergraduate degree. Although he is satisfied with his current job, his goal is to become an investment banker. He feels that an MBA degree would allow him to achieve this goal. After examining schools, he has narrowed his choice to either Wilton University or Mount Perry College. Although internships are encouraged by both schools, to get class credit for the internship, no salary can be paid. Other than internships, neither school will allow its students to work while enrolled in its MBA program.

Ben currently works at the money management firm of Dewey and Louis. His annual salary at the firm is $50,000 per year, and his salary is expected to increase at 3 percent per year until retirement. He is currently 28 years old and expects to work for 35 more years. His current job includes a fully paid health insurance plan, and his current average tax rate is 26 percent. Ben has a savings account with enough money to cover the entire cost of his MBA program.

The Ritter College of Business at Wilton University is one of the top MBA programs in the country. The MBA degree requires two years of full-time enrollment at the university. The annual tuition is $60,000, payable at the beginning of each school year. Books and other supplies are estimated to cost $2,500 per year. Ben expects that after graduation from Wilton, he will receive a job offer for about $95,000 per year, with a $15,000 signing bonus. The salary at this job will increase at 4 percent per year. Because of the higher salary, his average income tax rate will increase to 31 percent.

The Bradley School of Business at Mount Perry College began its MBA program 16 years ago. The Bradley School is smaller and less well known than the Ritter College. Bradley offers an accelerated one-year program, with a tuition cost of $75,000 to be paid upon matriculation. Books and other supplies for the program are expected to cost $3,500. Ben thinks that he will receive an offer of $78,000 per year upon graduation, with a $10,000 signing bonus. The salary at this job will increase at 3.5 percent per year. His average tax rate at this level of income will be 29 percent.

Both schools offer a health insurance plan that will cost $3,000 per year, payable at the beginning of the year. Ben also estimates that room and board expenses will cost $20,000 per year at both schools. The appropriate discount rate is 6.5 percent.

1. How does Ben's age affect his decision to get an MBA?
2. What other, perhaps nonquantifiable, factors affect Ben's decision to get an MBA?
3. Assuming all salaries are paid at the end of each year, what is the best option for Ben from a strictly financial standpoint?
4. Ben believes that the appropriate analysis is to calculate the future value of each option. How would you evaluate this statement?
5. What initial salary would Ben need to receive to make him indifferent between attending Wilton University and staying in his current position?
6. Suppose, instead of being able to pay cash for his MBA, Ben must borrow the money. The current borrowing rate is 5.4 percent. How would this affect his decision?

Visit us at www.mhhe.com/rwj

CHAPTER 5

How to Value Bonds and Stocks

When the stock market closed on January 20, 2006, the common stock of McGraw-Hill, publisher of high-quality college textbooks, was going for $49.34 per share. On that same day, Eastman Chemical closed at $49.96, while pharmaceutical benefits manager Caremark Rx closed at $50.02. Because the stock prices of these three companies were so similar, you might expect that they would be offering similar dividends to their stockholders, but you would be wrong. In fact, Eastman Chemical's dividend was $1.76 per share,

McGraw-Hill's was $0.66 per share, and Caremark Rx paid no dividends at all!

As we will see in this chapter, the dividends currently being paid are one of the primary factors we look at when attempting to value common stocks. However, it is obvious from looking at Caremark that current dividends are not the end of the story, so this chapter explores dividends, stock values, and the connection between the two.

5.1 Definition and Example of a Bond

A *bond* is a certificate showing that a borrower owes a specified sum. To repay the money, the borrower has agreed to make interest and principal payments on designated dates. For example, imagine that Kreuger Enterprises just issued 100,000 bonds for $1,000 each, where the bonds have a coupon rate of 5 percent and a maturity of two years. Interest on the bonds is to be paid yearly. This means that:

1. $100 million (=100,000 × $1,000) has been borrowed by the firm.
2. The firm must pay interest of $5 million (=5% × $100 million) at the end of one year.
3. The firm must pay both $5 million of interest and $100 million of principal at the end of two years.

We now consider how to value a few different types of bonds.

5.2 How to Value Bonds

Pure Discount Bonds

The **pure discount bond** is perhaps the simplest kind of bond. It promises a single payment, say $1, at a fixed future date. If the payment is one year from now, it is called a *one-year discount bond*; if it is two years from now, it is called a *two-year discount bond*, and so on.

Figure 5.1

Different Types of Bonds: *C*, Coupon Paid Every 6 Months; *F*, Face Value at Year 4 (maturity for pure discount and coupon bonds)

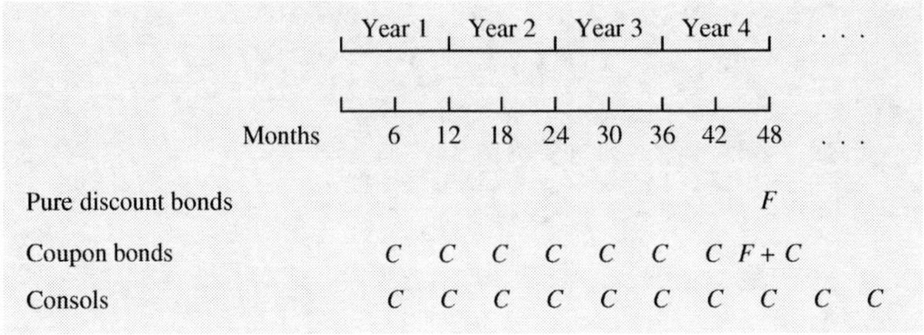

The date when the issuer of the bond makes the last payment is called the **maturity date** of the bond, or just its *maturity* for short. The bond is said to mature or *expire* on the date of its final payment. The payment at maturity ($1 in this example) is termed the bond's **face** or **par value**.

Pure discount bonds are often called *zero coupon bonds* or *zeros* to emphasize the fact that the holder receives no cash payments until maturity. We will use the terms *zero* and *discount* interchangeably to refer to bonds that pay no coupons.

The first row of Figure 5.1 shows the pattern of cash flows from a four-year pure discount bond. Note that the face value, *F*, is paid when the bond expires in the 48th month. There are no payments of either interest or principal prior to this date.

In the previous chapter, we indicated that one discounts a future cash flow to determine its present value. The present value of a pure discount bond can easily be determined by the techniques of the previous chapter. For short, we sometimes speak of the *value* of a bond instead of its present value.

Consider a pure discount bond that pays a face value of *F* in *T* years, where the interest rate is *R* in each of the *T* years. (We also refer to this rate as the *market interest rate.*) Because the face value is the only cash flow that the bond pays, the present value of this face amount is calculated as follows:

Value of a Pure Discount Bond:

$$PV = \frac{F}{(1 + R)^T}$$

The present value formula can produce some surprising results. Suppose that the interest rate is 10 percent. Consider a bond with a face value of $1 million that matures in 20 years. Applying the formula to this bond, its PV is given by:

$$PV = \frac{\$1 \text{ million}}{(1.1)^{20}}$$
$$= \$148,644$$

or only about 15 percent of the face value.

Level Coupon Bonds

Typical bonds issued by either governments or corporations offer cash payments not just at maturity, but also at regular times in between. For example, payments on U.S. government issues and American corporate bonds are made every six months until the bonds mature.

These payments are called the **coupons** of the bond. The middle row of Figure 5.1 illustrates the case of a four-year, *level coupon bond*: The coupon, C, is paid every six months and is the same throughout the life of the bond.

Note that the face value of the bond, F, is paid at maturity (end of year 4). F is sometimes called the *principal* or the *denomination*. Bonds issued in the United States typically have face values of $1,000, though this can vary with the type of bond.

As we mentioned before, the value of a bond is simply the present value of its cash flows. Therefore, the value of a level coupon bond is merely the present value of its stream of coupon payments plus the present value of its repayment of principal. Because a level coupon bond is just an annuity of C each period, together with a payment at maturity of $1,000, the value of a level coupon bond is calculated as follows:

Value of a Level Coupon Bond:

$$PV = \frac{C}{1+R} + \frac{C}{(1+R)^2} + \cdots + \frac{C}{(1+R)^T} + \frac{\$1,000}{(1+R)^T}$$

where C is the coupon and the face value, F, is $1,000. The value of the bond can be rewritten like this:

Value of a Level Coupon Bond:

$$PV = C \times A_R^T + \frac{\$1,000}{(1+R)^T}$$

As mentioned in the previous chapter, A_R^T is the present value of an annuity of $1 per period for T periods at an interest rate per period of R.

EXAMPLE 5.1

Bond Prices   Suppose it is November 2006 and we are considering a government bond. We see in *The Wall Street Journal* some *13s* of November 2010. This is jargon that means the annual coupon rate is 13 percent.[1] The face value is $1,000, implying that the yearly coupon is $130 (=13% × $1,000). Interest is paid each May and November, implying that the coupon every six months is $65 (=$130/2). The face value will be paid out in November 2010, four years from now. By this we mean that the purchaser obtains claims to the following cash flows:

5/07	11/07	5/08	11/08	5/09	11/09	5/10	11/10
$65	$65	$65	$65	$65	$65	$65	$65 + $1,000

If the stated annual interest rate in the market is 10 percent per year, what is the present value of the bond?

Our work on compounding in the previous chapter showed that the interest rate over any six-month interval is half of the stated annual interest rate. In the current example, this semiannual rate is 5 percent (=10%/2). Because the coupon payment in each six-month period is $65, and there are

(continued)

---

[1]The coupon rate is specific to the bond. The coupon rate indicates what cash flow should appear in the numerator of the NPV equation. The coupon rate does *not* appear in the denominator of the NPV equation.

eight of these six-month periods from November 2006 to November 2010, the present value of the bond is:

$$PV = \frac{\$65}{(1.05)} + \frac{\$65}{(1.05)^2} + \cdots + \frac{\$65}{(1.05)^8} + \frac{\$1,000}{(1.05)^8}$$

$$= \$65 \times A_{0.05}^8 + \$1,000/(1.05)^8$$

$$= (\$65 \times 6.463) + (\$1,000 \times 0.677)$$

$$= \$420.095 + \$677$$

$$= \$1,097.095$$

Traders will generally quote the bond as 109.7095,[2] indicating that it is selling at 109.7095 percent of the face value of $1,000.

At this point, it is worthwhile to relate the preceding example of bond pricing to the discussion of compounding in the previous chapter. At that time, we distinguished between the stated annual interest rate and the effective annual interest rate. In particular, we pointed out that the effective annual interest rate is:

$$(1 + R/m)^m - 1$$

where R is the stated annual interest rate and m is the number of compounding intervals. Because $R = 10\%$ and $m = 2$ (the bond makes semiannual payments), the effective annual interest rate is

$$[1 + (0.10/2)]^2 - 1 = (1.05)^2 - 1 = 10.25\%$$

In other words, because the bond is paying interest twice a year, the bondholder earns a 10.25 percent return when compounding is considered.[3]

One final note concerning level coupon bonds: Although the preceding example concerns government bonds, corporate bonds are identical in form. For example, Du Pont Corporation has a 4.75 percent bond maturing in 2012. This means that Du Pont will make semiannual payments of $23.75 (=4.75%/2 × $1,000) between now and 2012 for each face value of $1,000.

Consols

Not all bonds have a final maturity date. As we mentioned in the previous chapter, consols are bonds that never stop paying a coupon, have no final maturity date, and therefore never mature. Thus, a consol is a perpetuity. In the 18th century, the Bank of England issued such bonds, called "English consols." These were bonds that the Bank of England guaranteed would pay the holder a cash flow forever! Through wars and depressions, the Bank of England continued to honor this commitment, and you can still buy such bonds in London today. The U.S. government also once sold consols to raise money to build the Panama Canal. Even though these U.S. bonds were supposed to last forever and to pay their coupons

---

[2]U.S. government bond prices are actually quoted in 32nds of a dollar, so a quote this precise would not be given for such bonds.

[3]For an excellent discussion of how to value semiannual payments, see J. T. Lindley, B. P. Helms, and M. Haddad, "A Measurement of the Errors in Intra-Period Compounding and Bond Valuation," *The Financial Review* 22 (February 1987). We benefited from several conversations with the authors of this article.

forever, don't go looking for any. There is a special clause in the bond contract that gives the government the right to buy them back from the holders, and that is what the government has done. Such clauses are known as *call provisions*, and we study them later.

An important example of a consol, though, is called *preferred stock*. Preferred stock is stock that is issued by corporations and that provides the holder a fixed dividend in perpetuity. If there were never any question that the firm would actually pay the dividend on the preferred stock, such stock would in fact be a consol.

These instruments can be valued by the perpetuity formula of the previous chapter. For example, if the marketwide interest rate is 10 percent, a consol with a yearly interest payment of $50 is valued at:

$$\frac{\$50}{0.10} = \$500$$

5.3   Bond Concepts

We complete our discussion of bonds by considering two concepts concerning them. First we examine the relationship between interest rates and bond prices. Then we define the concept of yield to maturity.

Interest Rates and Bond Prices

The discussion of level coupon bonds allows us to relate bond prices to interest rates. Consider the following example:

EXAMPLE 5.2

Bond Valuation   The interest rate is 10 percent. A two-year bond with a 10 percent coupon pays interest of $100 (= $1,000 × 10%). For simplicity we assume that the interest is paid annually. In this case, we see that the bond is priced at its face value of $1,000:

$$\$1,000 = \frac{\$100}{1.10} + \frac{\$1,000 + \$100}{(1.10)^2}$$

If the interest rate unexpectedly rises to 12 percent, the bond sells at:

$$\$966.20 = \frac{\$100}{1.12} + \frac{\$1,000 + \$100}{(1.12)^2}$$

Because $966.20 is less than $1,000, the bond is said to sell at a **discount**. This is a sensible result. Now that the interest rate is 12 percent, a newly issued bond with a 12 percent coupon rate will sell at $1,000. This newly issued bond will have coupon payments of $120 (= 0.12 × $1,000). Because our bond has interest payments of only $100, investors will pay less than $1,000 for it.

If interest rates fell to 8 percent, the bond would sell at:

$$\$1,035.67 = \frac{\$100}{1.08} + \frac{\$1,000 + \$100}{(1.08)^2}$$

Because $1,035.67 is more than $1,000, the bond is said to sell at a **premium**.

Thus, we find that bond prices fall with a rise in interest rates and rise with a fall in interest rates. Furthermore, the general principle is that a level coupon bond sells in the following ways:

1. At the face value of $1,000 if the coupon rate is equal to the marketwide interest rate.
2. At a discount if the coupon rate is below the marketwide interest rate.
3. At a premium if the coupon rate is above the marketwide interest rate.

Yield to Maturity

Let's now consider the previous example *in reverse*. If our bond is selling at $1,035.67, what return is a bondholder receiving? This can be answered by considering the following equation:

$$\$1,035.67 = \frac{\$100}{1+y} + \frac{\$1,000 + \$100}{(1+y)^2}$$

The unknown, y, is the discount rate that equates the price of the bond with the discounted value of the coupons and face value. Our earlier work implies that $y = 8\%$. Thus, traders state that the bond is yielding an 8 percent return. Bond traders also state that the bond has a **yield to maturity** of 8 percent. The yield to maturity is frequently called the bond's *yield* for short. So, we would say the bond with its 10 percent coupon is priced to yield 8 percent at $1,035.67.

Bond Market Reporting

In 2002, data availability in the corporate bond market began to improve dramatically. Under new regulations, corporate bond dealers are now required to report trade information through what is known as the Transactions Report and Compliance Engine (TRACE). As this is written, transaction prices are now reported for more than 4,000 bonds. More bonds will be added over time.

The Present Value Formulas for Bonds

Pure Discount Bonds

$$PV = \frac{F}{(1+R)^T}$$

Level Coupon Bonds

$$PV = C\left[\frac{1}{R} - \frac{1}{R \times (1+R)^T}\right] + \frac{F}{(1+R)^T} = C \times A_R^T + \frac{F}{(1+R)^T}$$

where F is typically $1,000 for a level coupon bond.

Consols

$$PV = \frac{C}{R}$$

Figure 5.2

Sample *Wall Street Journal* Bond Quotation

SOURCE: Reprinted by permission of *The Wall Street Journal*, via Copyright Clearance Center. © 2006 Dow Jones and Company, Inc., January 19, 2006. All Rights Reserved Worldwide.

Corporate Bonds

Thursday, January 19, 2006

Forty most active fixed-coupon corporate bonds

COMPANY (TICKER)	COUPON	MATURITY	LAST PRICE	LAST YIELD	*EST SPREAD	UST†	EST $ VOL (000's)
Goldman Sachs Group Inc (GS)	4.500	Jun 15, 2010	97.984	5.016	71	5	116,790
JPMorgan Chase (JPM)	5.150	Oct 01, 2015	98.935	5.291	92	10	114,535
Wal-Mart Stores Inc (WMT)	5.250	Sep 01, 2035	97.286	5.435	89	30	106,785
Virginia Electric and Power Co (D)	6.000	Jan 15, 2036	101.113	5.920	138	30	102,050
Ameriprise Financial Inc (AMP)	5.650	Nov 15, 2015	101.670	5.427	105	10	78,419
Ameriprise Financial Inc (AMP)	5.350	Nov 15, 2010	101.107	5.086	78	5	77,720
AT&T Inc (SBC)	5.100	Sep 15, 2014	97.828	5.417	104	10	72,859
Telecom Italia Capital (TITIM)	6.375	Nov 15, 2033	100.195	6.359	181	30	71,279
Tyco International Group SA (TYC)	6.375	Oct 15, 2011	104.961	5.355	105	5	69,148
Marsh & McLennan Companies Inc (MMC)	5.150	Sep 15, 2010	99.773	5.204	90	5	68,850
COX Communications Inc (COXENT)	7.125	Oct 01, 2012	106.810	5.876	149	5	65,891
Mohawk Industries Inc (MHK)	6.125	Jan 15, 2016	101.159	5.969	159	10	65,400
Time Warner Inc (TWX)	7.700	May 01, 2032	113.181	6.632	209	30	63,575
iStar Financial Inc (SFI)	5.375	Apr 15, 2010	99.981	5.378	107	5	60,530
Kroger Co (KR)	5.500	Feb 01, 2013	98.542	5.755	138	10	58,626
Ohio Power Co (AEP)	5.500	Feb 15, 2013	101.661	5.215	84	10	55,150
Kroger Co (KR)	7.500	Apr 01, 2031	112.406	6.492	195	30	54,720
Toyota Motor Credit Corp (TOYOTA)	5.125	Jan 11, 2011	99.930	5.141	83	5	54,000
General Electric Capital Corp (GE)	5.875	Feb 15, 2012	104.601	4.985	61	5	53,751
Time Warner Inc (TWX)	6.875	May 01, 2012	106.527	5.623	124	5	53,436
Vale Overseas Ltd (VALE)	6.250	Jan 11, 2016	100.600	6.168	179	10	52,735
Morgan Stanley (MWD)	5.050	Jan 21, 2011	100.030	5.036	73	5	51,415
HSBC Finance Corp (HSBC)	4.625	Jan 15, 2008	99.514	4.885	53	2	51,115
Albertson's Inc (ABS)	8.000	May 01, 2031	99.093	8.083	353	30	50,549
United Technologies Corp (UTX)	7.125	Nov 15, 2010	109.487	4.885	58	5	50,420
Convergys Corp (CVG)	4.875	Dec 15, 2009	96.769	5.813	150	3	50,400
General Electric Capital Corp (GE)	6.125	Feb 22, 2011	105.465	4.895	59	5	49,912
Bear Stearns Companies Inc (BSC)	6.500	May 01, 2006	100.506	4.531	n.a.	n.a.	49,769
Wal-Mart Stores Inc (WMT)	4.550	May 01, 2013	97.800	4.912	54	10	49,352
Fortune Brands Inc (FO)	5.375	Jan 15, 2016	99.287	5.468	109	10	48,700
Lear Corp (LEA)	5.750	Aug 01, 2014	79.125	9.359	499	10	48,466
HSBC Finance Corp (HSBC)	5.500	Jan 19, 2016	100.418	5.445	107	10	48,195
Wells Fargo (WFC)	4.875	Jan 12, 2011	99.919	4.893	57	5	46,830
BellSouth Corp (BLS)	5.200	Sep 15, 2014	99.587	5.259	89	10	45,588
Johnson Controls Inc (JCI)	5.250	Jan 15, 2011	100.351	5.169	86	5	45,325
Comcast Corp (CMCSA)	4.950	Jun 15, 2016	93.867	5.741	137	10	44,279
GlaxoSmithKline Capital Inc (GSK)	4.375	Apr 15, 2014	96.153	4.949	58	10	43,249
WellPoint Inc (WLP)	5.850	Jan 15, 2036	101.016	5.778	123	30	42,600
Countrywide Home Loans Inc (CFC)	5.500	Feb 01, 2007	100.539	4.950	n.a.	n.a.	41,744
GlaxoSmithKline Capital Inc (GSK)	2.375	Apr 16, 2007	97.254	4.700	34	2	41,704
Time Warner Companies Inc (TWX)	9.150	Feb 01, 2023	122.903	6.850	230	30	41,109

Volume represents total volume for each issue; price/yield data are for trades of $1 million and greater. * Estimated spreads, in basis points (100 basis points is one percentage point), over the 2, 3, 5, 10 or 30-year hot run Treasury note/bond. 2-year: 4.375 12/07; 3-year: 4.375 11/08; 5-year: 4.250 01/11; 10-year: 4.500 11/15; 30-year: 5.375 02/31. †Comparable U.S. Treasury issue.

Source: MarketAxess Corporate BondTicker

To learn more about TRACE, visit **www.nasd.com**.

TRACE bond quotes are available at www.nasdbondinfo.com. We went to the site and entered "Deere" for the well-known manufacturer of green tractors. We found a total of eight bond issues outstanding. Here you can see the information we found for three of these:

Issue: DE.GG DEERE & CO. 7.125 03/03/2031				Time and Sales	Descriptive Data	
In Portfolio	Rating Moody's/S&P/Fitch	Date	Last Sale Price	Yield	Most Recent Date	Price	Yield
☐	A3 / A- / A	01/20/2006	122.333	5.476993	01/20/2006	122.33	5.476993

Issue: DE.GA DEERE & COMPANY 8.95 06/15/2019				Time and Sales	Descriptive Data	
In Portfolio	Rating Moody's/S&P/Fitch	Date	Last Sale Price	Yield	Most Recent Date	Price	Yield
☐	A3 / A- / A	01/20/2006	113.50	4.599	01/20/2006	113.50	4.599

Issue: DE.GB DEERE & COMPANY 8.50 01/09/2022				Time and Sales	Descriptive Data	
In Portfolio	Rating Moody's/S&P/Fitch	Date	Last Sale Price	Yield	Most Recent Date	Price	Yield
☐	A3 / A- / A	01/05/2006	132.115	5.463	01/05/2006	132.12	5.463

Most of the information is self-explanatory. The price and yield columns show the price and yield to maturity of the most recent sales. Notice the last sale dates for the issue maturing in 2022. This bond had not had a reported trade for the last two weeks. A great feature of this Web site is the "Descriptive Data" link, which gives you more information about the bond issue such as call dates and coupon dates.

102

Ross–Westerfield–Jaffe:
Corporate Finance, Eighth
Edition

II. Valuation and Capital
Budgeting

5. How to Value Bonds and
Stocks

© The McGraw–Hill
Companies, 2008

The Federal Reserve
Bank of St. Louis main-
tains dozens of online
files containing
macroeconomic data
as well as rates on U.S.
Treasury issues. Go to
**www.stls.frb.org/fred/
files**.

As shown in Figure 5.2, *The Wall Street Journal* provides a daily snapshot of the data from TRACE by reporting the 40 most active issues. The information reported is again largely self-explanatory. The EST Spread is the estimated yield spread over a particular U.S. Treasury issue (a yield spread is just the difference in yields). The spread is reported in basis points, where 1 basis point is equal to .01 percent. The selected Treasury issue's maturity is given under UST, which is a standard abbreviation in the bond markets for U.S. Treasury. A "hot run" Treasury is the most recently issued of a particular maturity, better known as an on-the-run issue. Finally, the reported volume is the face value of bonds traded.

5.4 The Present Value of Common Stocks

Dividends versus Capital Gains

Our goal in this section is to value common stocks. We learned in the previous chapter that an asset's value is determined by the present value of its future cash flows. A stock provides two kinds of cash flows. First, stocks often pay dividends on a regular basis. Second, the stockholder receives the sale price when selling the stock. Thus, to value common stocks, we need to answer an interesting question. Which of the following is the value of a stock equal to?

1. The discounted present value of the sum of next period's dividend plus next period's stock price.

2. The discounted present value of all future dividends.

This is the kind of question that students would love to see on a multiple-choice exam: Both (1) and (2) are right.

To see that (1) and (2) are the same, let's start with an individual who will buy the stock and hold it for one year. In other words, she has a one-year *holding period*. In addition, she is willing to pay P_0 for the stock today. That is, she calculates:

$$P_0 = \frac{\text{Div}_1}{1 + R} + \frac{P_1}{1 + R} \tag{5.1}$$

Div_1 is the dividend paid at year's end, and P_1 is the price at year's end. P_0 is the PV of the common stock investment. The term in the denominator, R, is the appropriate discount rate for the stock.

That seems easy enough; but where does P_1 come from? P_1 is not pulled out of thin air. Rather, there must be a buyer at the end of year 1 who is willing to purchase the stock for P_1. This buyer determines price as follows:

$$P_1 = \frac{\text{Div}_2}{1 + R} + \frac{P_2}{1 + R} \tag{5.2}$$

Substituting the value of P_1 from Equation 5.2 into Equation 5.1 yields:

$$P_0 = \frac{1}{1+R}\left[\text{Div}_1 + \left(\frac{\text{Div}_2 + P_2}{1+R}\right)\right]$$

$$= \frac{\text{Div}_1}{1+R} + \frac{\text{Div}_2}{(1+R)^2} + \frac{P_2}{(1+R)^2} \tag{5.3}$$

We can ask a similar question for Equation 5.3: Where does P_2 come from? An investor at the end of year 2 is willing to pay P_2 because of the dividend and stock price at year 3. This process can be repeated *ad nauseam*.[4] At the end, we are left with this:

$$P_0 = \frac{Div_1}{1+R} + \frac{Div_2}{(1+R)^2} + \frac{Div_3}{(1+R)^3} + \cdots = \sum_{t=1}^{\infty} \frac{Div_t}{(1+R)^t} \qquad (5.4)$$

Thus, the value of a firm's common stock to the investor is equal to the present value of all of the expected future dividends.

This is a very useful result. A common objection to applying present value analysis to stocks is that investors are too shortsighted to care about the long-run stream of dividends. These critics argue that an investor will generally not look past his or her time horizon. Thus, prices in a market dominated by short-term investors will reflect only near-term dividends. However, our discussion shows that a long-run dividend discount model holds even when investors have short-term time horizons. Although an investor may want to cash out early, she must find another investor who is willing to buy. The price this second investor pays is dependent on dividends *after* his date of purchase.

Valuation of Different Types of Stocks

The preceding discussion shows that the value of the firm is the present value of its future dividends. How do we apply this idea in practice? Equation 5.4 represents a very general model and is applicable regardless of whether the level of expected dividends is growing, fluctuating, or constant. The general model can be simplified if the firm's dividends are expected to follow some basic patterns: (1) zero growth, (2) constant growth, and (3) differential growth. These cases are illustrated in Figure 5.3.

Case 1 (Zero Growth)   The value of a stock with a constant dividend is given by

$$P_0 = \frac{Div_1}{1+R} + \frac{Div_2}{(1+R)^2} + \cdots = \frac{Div_1}{R}$$

Here it is assumed that $Div_1 = Div_2 = \cdots = Div$. This is just an application of the perpetuity formula from a previous chapter.

Case 2 (Constant Growth)   Dividends grow at rate g, as follows:

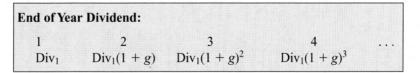

End of Year Dividend:				
1	2	3	4	$\cdots$
Div_1	$Div_1(1+g)$	$Div_1(1+g)^2$	$Div_1(1+g)^3$	

Note that Div_1 is the dividend at the end of the *first* period.

----

[4] This procedure reminds us of the physicist lecturing about the origins of the universe. He was approached by an elderly gentleman in the audience who disagreed with the lecture. The attendee said that the universe rests on the back of a huge turtle. When the physicist asked what the turtle rested on, the gentleman said another turtle. Anticipating the physicist's objections, the attendee said, "Don't tire yourself out, young fellow. It's turtles all the way down."

Figure 5.3

Zero Growth,
Constant Growth, and
Differential Growth
Patterns

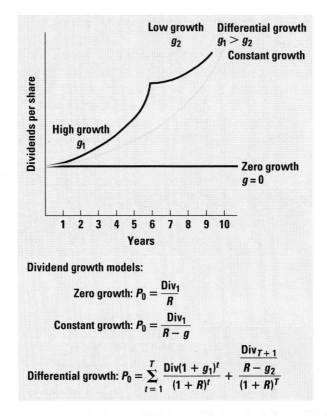

Dividend growth models:

Zero growth: $P_0 = \dfrac{\text{Div}_1}{R}$

Constant growth: $P_0 = \dfrac{\text{Div}_1}{R - g}$

Differential growth: $P_0 = \displaystyle\sum_{t=1}^{T} \dfrac{\text{Div}(1 + g_1)^t}{(1 + R)^t} + \dfrac{\dfrac{\text{Div}_{T+1}}{R - g_2}}{(1 + R)^T}$

Projected Dividends   Hampshire Products will pay a dividend of $4 per share a year from now. Financial analysts believe that dividends will rise at 6 percent per year for the foreseeable future. What is the dividend per share at the end of each of the first five years? With 6 percent growth we have this:

End of Year Dividend:				
1	2	3	4	5
$4.00	$4 × (1.06)	$4 × (1.06)^2	$4 × (1.06)^3	$4 × (1.06)^4
	= $4.24	= $4.4944	= $4.7641	= $5.0499

The value of a common stock with dividends growing at a constant rate is

$$P_0 = \frac{\text{Div}_1}{1 + R} + \frac{\text{Div}_1 (1 + g)}{(1 + R)^2} + \frac{\text{Div}_1 (1 + g)^2}{(1 + R)^3} + \frac{\text{Div}_1 (1 + g)^3}{(1 + R)^4} + \cdots = \frac{\text{Div}_1}{R - g}$$

where g is the growth rate. Div_1 is the dividend on the stock at the end of the first period. This is the formula for the present value of a growing perpetuity, which we derived in a previous chapter.

Stock Valuation   Suppose an investor is considering the purchase of a share of the Utah Mining Company. The stock will pay a $3 dividend a year from today. This dividend is expected to grow at 10 percent per year ($g = 10\%$) for the foreseeable future. The investor thinks that the required return (R) on this stock is 15 percent, given her assessment of Utah Mining's risk. (We also refer to R as the discount rate for the stock.) What is the value of a share of Utah Mining Company's stock?

Using the constant growth formula of case 2, we assess the value to be $60:

$$\$60 = \frac{\$3}{.15 - .10}$$

(continued)

P_0 is quite dependent on the value of g. If g had been estimated to be 12.5 percent, the value of the share would have been:

$$\$120 = \frac{\$3}{.15 - .125}$$

The stock price doubles (from \$60 to \$120) when g increases only 25 percent (from 10 percent to 12.5 percent). Because of P_0's dependence on g, one must maintain a healthy sense of skepticism when using this constant growth of dividends model.

Furthermore, note that P_0 is equal to infinity when the growth rate, g, equals the discount rate, R. Because stock prices do not grow infinitely, an estimate of g greater than R implies an error in estimation. More will be said about this point later.

Case 3 (Differential Growth)   In this case, an algebraic formula would be too unwieldy. Instead we present examples.

EXAMPLE 5.5

Differential Growth   Consider the stock of Elixir Drug Company, which has a new massage ointment and is enjoying rapid growth. The dividend for a share of stock a year from today will be \$1.15. During the following four years the dividend will grow at 15 percent per year ($g_1 = 15\%$). After that, growth (g_2) will equal 10 percent per year. Can you calculate the present value of the stock if the required return (R) is 15 percent?

Figure 5.4 displays the growth in the dividends. We need to apply a two-step process to discount these dividends. We first calculate the net present value of the dividends growing at 15 percent per annum. That is, we first calculate the present value of the dividends at the end of each of the first five years. Second, we calculate the present value of the dividends that begin at the end of year 6.

Figure 5.4

Growth in Dividends for Elixir Drug Company

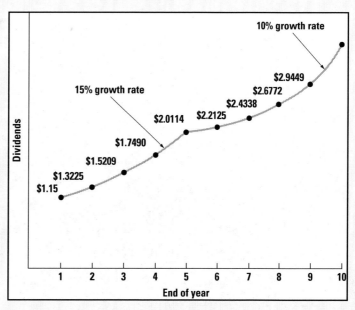

(*continued*)

Calculate Present Value of First Five Dividends   The present value of dividend payments in years 1 through 5 is as follows:

Future Year	Growth Rate (g_1)	Expected Dividend	Present Value
1	.15	$1.15	$1
2	.15	1.3225	1
3	.15	1.5209	1
4	.15	1.7490	1
5	.15	2.0114	1
Years 1–5	The present value of dividends = $5		

The growing annuity formula of the previous chapter could normally be used in this step. However, note that dividends grow at 15 percent, which is also the discount rate. Because $g = R$, the growing annuity formula cannot be used in this example.

Calculate Present Value of Dividends Beginning at End of Year 6   This is the procedure for deferred perpetuities and deferred annuities that we mentioned in the previous chapter. The dividends beginning at the end of year 6 are as follows:

End of Year Dividend:			
6	7	8	9
$\text{Div}_5 \times (1 + g_2)$	$\text{Div}_5 \times (1 + g_2)^2$	$\text{Div}_5 \times (1 + g_2)^3$	$\text{Div}_5 \times (1 + g_2)^4$
2.0114×1.10	$2.0114 \times (1.10)^2$	$2.0114 \times (1.10)^3$	$2.0114 \times (1.10)^4$
= $2.2125	= $2.4338	= $2.6772	= $2.9449

As stated in the previous chapter, the growing perpetuity formula calculates present value as of one year prior to the first payment. Because the payment begins at the end of year 6, the present value formula calculates present value as of the end of year 5.

The price at the end of year 5 is given by

$$P_5 = \frac{\text{Div}_6}{R - g_2} = \frac{\$2.2125}{.15 - .10}$$
$$= \$44.25$$

The present value of P_5 today is

$$\frac{P_5}{(1 + R)^5} = \frac{\$44.25}{(1.15)^5} = \$22$$

The present value of *all* dividends today is $27 (=$22 + 5).

5.5   Estimates of Parameters in the Dividend Growth Model

The value of the firm is a function of its growth rate, g, and its discount rate, R. How do we estimate these variables?

Where Does g Come From?

The previous discussion of stocks assumed that dividends grow at the rate *g*. We now want to estimate this rate of growth. This section extends the discussion of growth contained in Chapter 3. Consider a business whose earnings next year are expected to be the same as earnings this year unless a *net investment* is made. This situation is likely to occur because net investment is equal to gross, or total, investment less depreciation. A net investment of zero occurs when *total investment* equals depreciation. If total investment is equal to depreciation, the firm's physical plant is maintained, consistent with no growth in earnings.

Net investment will be positive only if some earnings are not paid out as dividends— that is, only if some earnings are retained.[5] This leads to the following equation:

$$
\underset{\text{year}}{\underset{\text{next}}{\text{Earnings}}} = \underset{\text{year}}{\underset{\text{this}}{\text{Earnings}}} + \underbrace{\underset{\text{this year}}{\underset{\text{earnings}}{\text{Retained}}} \times \underset{\text{earnings}}{\underset{\text{retained}}{\text{Return on}}}}_{\text{Increase in earnings}} \qquad (5.5)
$$

The increase in earnings is a function of both the *retained earnings* and the *return on the retained earnings.*

We now divide both sides of Equation 5.5 by earnings this year, yielding

$$
\frac{\text{Earnings next year}}{\text{Earnings this year}} = \frac{\text{Earnings this year}}{\text{Earnings this year}} + \left(\frac{\text{Retained earnings this year}}{\text{Earnings this year}} \right) \times \text{Return on retained earnings} \qquad (5.6)
$$

The left side of Equation 5.6 is simply 1 plus the growth rate in earnings, which we write as $1 + g$. The ratio of retained earnings to earnings is called the **retention ratio**. Thus we can write

$$1 + g = 1 + \text{Retention ratio} \times \text{Return on retained earnings} \qquad (5.7)$$

It is difficult for a financial analyst to determine the return to be expected on currently retained earnings: The details on forthcoming projects are not generally public information. However, it is frequently assumed that the projects selected in the current year have an anticipated return equal to returns from projects in other years. Here we can estimate the anticipated return on current retained earnings by the historical **return on equity** or ROE. After all, ROE is simply the return on the firm's entire equity, which is the return on the cumulation of all the firm's past projects.

From Equation 5.7, we have a simple way to estimate growth:

Formula for Firm's Growth Rate:

$$g = \text{Retention ratio} \times \text{Return on retained earnings} \qquad (5.8)$$

Previously, *g* referred to growth in dividends. However, the growth in earnings is equal to the growth rate in dividends in this context, because as we will presently see, the ratio of dividends to earnings is held constant. In fact, as you have probably figured out, *g* is the sustainable growth rate we introduced in Chapter 3.

---

[5]We ignore the possibility of the issuance of stocks or bonds to raise capital. These possibilities are considered in later chapters.

EXAMPLE 5.6

Earnings Growth   Pagemaster Enterprises just reported earnings of $2 million. It plans to retain 40 percent of its earnings. The historical return on equity (ROE) has been 16 percent, a figure that is expected to continue into the future. How much will earnings grow over the coming year?

We first perform the calculation without reference to Equation 5.8. Then, we use Equation 5.8 as a check.

Calculation without Reference to Equation 5.8   The firm will retain $800,000 ($= 40\% \times$ $2 million). Assuming that historical ROE is an appropriate estimate for future returns, the anticipated increase in earnings is:

$$\$800,000 \times .16 = \$128,000$$

The percentage growth in earnings is:

$$\frac{\text{Change in earnings}}{\text{Total earnings}} = \frac{\$128,000}{\$2 \text{ million}} = .064$$

This implies that earnings in one year will be $2,128,000 ($= \$2,000,000 \times 1.064$).

Check Using Equation 5.8   We use $g =$ Retention ratio $\times$ ROE. We have:

$$g = .4 \times .16 = .064$$

Where Does R Come From?

Thus far, we have taken the required return, or discount rate R, as given. We will have quite a bit to say about this subject in later chapters. For now, we want to examine the implications of the dividend growth model for this required return. Earlier we calculated P_0 as follows:

$$P_0 = \text{Div}_1/(R - g)$$

If we rearrange this to solve for R, we get:

$$R - g = \text{Div}_1/P_0$$
$$R = \text{Div}_1/P_0 + g \tag{5.9}$$

This tells us that the total return, R, has two components. The first of these, Div_1/P_0, is called the **dividend yield**. Because this is calculated as the expected cash dividend divided by the current price, it is conceptually similar to the current yield on a bond, which is the annual coupon divided by the bond's price.

The second part of the total return is the growth rate, g. As we will verify shortly, the dividend growth rate is also the rate at which the stock price grows. Thus, this growth rate can be interpreted as the **capital gains yield**—that is, the rate at which the value of the investment grows.

To illustrate the components of the required return, suppose we observe a stock selling for $20 per share. The next dividend will be $1 per share. You think that the dividend will grow by 10 percent per year more or less indefinitely. What return does this stock offer you if this is correct?

The dividend growth model calculates total return as:

$$R = \text{Dividend yield} + \text{Capital gains yield}$$
$$R = \text{Div}_1/P_0 \qquad + \qquad g$$

Ross−Westerfield−Jaffe:
Corporate Finance, Eighth
Edition

II. Valuation and Capital
Budgeting

5. How to Value Bonds and
Stocks

© The McGraw−Hill
Companies, 2008

109

In this case, total return works out to be:

$$R = \$1/20 + 10\%$$
$$= 5\% + 10\%$$
$$= 15\%$$

This stock, therefore, has an expected return of 15 percent.

We can verify this answer by calculating the price in one year, P_1, using 15 percent as the required return. Based on the dividend growth model, this price is:

$$P_1 = \text{Div}_1 \times (1 + g)/(R - g)$$
$$= \$1 \times 1.10/(.15 - .10)$$
$$= \$1.10/.05$$
$$= \$22$$

Notice that this $22 is $20 × 1.1, so the stock price has grown by 10 percent as it should. If you pay $20 for the stock today, you will get a $1 dividend at the end of the year, and you will have a $22 − 20 = $2 gain. Your dividend yield is thus $1/20 = 5 percent. Your capital gains yield is $2/20 = 10 percent, so your total return would be 5 percent + 10 percent = 15 percent.

To get a feel for actual numbers in this context, consider that, according to the 2006 Value Line *Investment Survey*, Procter & Gamble's dividends were expected to grow by 9.5 percent over the next 5 or so years, compared to a historical growth rate of 10.5 percent over the preceding 5 years and 11.5 percent over the preceding 10 years. In 2006, the projected dividend for the coming year was given as $1.12. The stock price at that time was about $58 per share. What is the return investors require on P&G? Here the dividend yield is 1.9 percent and the capital gains yield is 9.5 percent, giving a total required return of 11.4 percent on P&G stock.

EXAMPLE 5.7

Calculating the Required Return   Pagemaster Enterprises, the company examined in the previous example, has 1,000,000 shares of stock outstanding. The stock is selling at $10. What is the required return on the stock?

Because the retention ratio is 40 percent, the **payout ratio** is 60 percent (=1 − retention ratio). The payout ratio is the ratio of dividends/earnings. Because earnings a year from now will be $2,128,000 (=$2,000,000 × 1.064), dividends will be $1,276,800 (=.60 × $2,128,000). Dividends per share will be $1.28 (=$1,276,800/1,000,000). Given our previous result that $g = .064$, we calculate R from (5.9) as follows:

$$.192 = \frac{\$1.28}{10.00} + .064$$

A Healthy Sense of Skepticism

It is important to emphasize that our approach merely *estimates* g; our approach does not *determine* g precisely. We mentioned earlier that our estimate of g is based on a number of assumptions. For example, we assume that the return on reinvestment of future retained earnings is equal to the firm's past ROE. We assume that the future retention ratio is equal to the past retention ratio. Our estimate for g will be off if these assumptions prove to be wrong.

Unfortunately, the determination of R is highly dependent on g. For example, if g is estimated to be 0 in our example, R equals 12.8 percent (=$1.28/$10.00). If g is estimated to be 12 percent, R equals 24.8 percent (=$1.28/$10.00 + 12%). Thus, one should view estimates of R with a healthy sense of skepticism.

Because of the preceding, some financial economists generally argue that the estimation error for R or a single security is too large to be practical. Therefore, they suggest calculating the average R for an entire industry. This R would then be used to discount the dividends of a particular stock in the same industry.

One should be particularly skeptical of two polar cases when estimating R for individual securities. First, consider a firm currently paying no dividend. The stock price will be above zero because investors believe that the firm may initiate a dividend at some point or the firm may be acquired at some point. However, when a firm goes from no dividends to a positive number of dividends, the implied growth rate is *infinite*. Thus, Equation 5.9 must be used with extreme caution here, if at all—a point we emphasize later in this chapter.

Second, we mentioned earlier that the value of the firm is infinite when g is equal to R. Because prices for stocks do not grow infinitely, an analyst whose estimate of g for a particular firm is equal to or above R must have made a mistake. Most likely the analyst's high estimate for g is correct for the next few years. However, firms simply cannot maintain an abnormally high growth rate *forever*. The analyst's error was to use a short-run estimate of g in a model requiring a perpetual growth rate.

5.6 Growth Opportunities

We previously spoke of the growth rate of dividends. We now want to address the related concept of growth opportunities. Imagine a company with a level stream of earnings per share in perpetuity. The company pays all of these earnings out to stockholders as dividends. Hence we have:

$$EPS = Div$$

where EPS is *earnings per share* and Div is dividends per share. A company of this type is frequently called a *cash cow*.

The perpetuity formula of the previous chapter gives the value of a share of stock:

Value of a Share of Stock When a Firm Acts as a Cash Cow:

$$\frac{EPS}{R} = \frac{Div}{R}$$

where R is the discount rate on the firm's stock.

This policy of paying out all earnings as dividends may not be the optimal one. Many firms have *growth* opportunities: opportunities to invest in profitable projects. Because these projects can represent a significant fraction of the firm's value, it would be foolish to forgo them in order to pay out all earnings as dividends.

Although firms frequently think in terms of a *set* of growth opportunities, let's focus on only one opportunity—that is, the opportunity to invest in a single project. Suppose the firm retains the entire dividend at date 1 to invest in a particular capital budgeting project. The net present value *per share* of the project as of date 0 is *NPVGO*, which stands for the *net present value (per share) of the growth opportunity.*

What is the price of a share of stock at date 0 if the firm decides to take on the project at date 1? Because the per share value of the project is added to the original stock price, the stock price must now be this:

Stock Price after Firm Commits to New Project:

$$\frac{EPS}{R} + NPVGO \qquad\qquad (5.10)$$

Thus Equation 5.10 indicates that the price of a share of stock can be viewed as the sum of two different items. The first term (EPS/R) is the value of the firm if it rested on its laurels—that is, if it simply distributed all earnings to the stockholders. The second term is the *additional* value if the firm retains earnings to fund new projects.

EXAMPLE 5.8

Growth Opportunities   Sarro Shipping, Inc., expects to earn $1 million per year in perpetuity if it undertakes no new investment opportunities. There are 100,000 shares of stock outstanding, so earnings per share equal $10 (= $1,000,000/100,000). The firm will have an opportunity at date 1 to spend $1,000,000 on a new marketing campaign. The new campaign will increase earnings in every subsequent period by $210,000 (or $2.10 per share). This is a 21 percent return per year on the project. The firm's discount rate is 10 percent. What is the value per share before and after deciding to accept the marketing campaign?

The value of a share of Sarro Shipping before the campaign is

Value of a Share of Sarro When Firm Acts as a Cash Cow:

$$\frac{EPS}{R} = \frac{\$10}{.1} = \$100$$

The value of the marketing campaign as of date 1 is

Value of Marketing Campaign at Date 1:

$$-\$1,000,000 + \frac{\$210,000}{.1} = \$1,100,000 \qquad (5.11)$$

Because the investment is made at date 1 and the first cash inflow occurs at date 2, Equation 5.11 represents the value of the marketing campaign as of date 1. We determine the value at date 0 by discounting back one period as follows:

Value of Marketing Campaign at Date 0:

$$\frac{\$1,100,000}{1.1} = \$1,000,000$$

Thus NPVGO per share is $10 (= $1,000,000/100,000).

The price per share is

$$EPS/R + NPVGO = \$100 + 10 = \$110$$

The calculation in our example can also be made on a straight net present value basis. Because all the earnings at date 1 are spent on the marketing effort, no dividends are paid to stockholders at that date. Dividends in all subsequent periods are $1,210,000 (= $1,000,000 + $210,000). In this case $1,000,000 is the annual dividend when Sarro is a cash cow. The additional contribution to the dividend from the marketing effort is $210,000. Dividends per share are $12.10 (= $1,210,000/100,000). Because these dividends start at date 2, the price per share at date 1 is $121 (= $12.10/.1). The price per share at date 0 is $110 (= $121/1.1).

Note that value is created in this example because the project earned a 21 percent rate of return when the discount rate was only 10 percent. No value would have been created had the project earned a 10 percent rate of return. The NPVGO would have been zero, and value would have been negative had the project earned a percentage return below 10 percent. The NPVGO would be negative in that case.

Two conditions must be met in order to increase value:

1. Earnings must be retained so that projects can be funded.[6]
2. The projects must have positive net present value.

Surprisingly, a number of companies seem to invest in projects known to have *negative* net present values. For example, in the late 1970s, oil companies and tobacco companies were flush with cash. Due to declining markets in both industries, high dividends and low investment would have been the rational action. Unfortunately, a number of companies in both industries reinvested heavily in what were widely perceived to be negative NPVGO projects.

Given that NPV analysis (such as that presented in the previous chapter) is common knowledge in business, why would managers choose projects with negative NPVs? One conjecture is that some managers enjoy controlling a large company. Because paying dividends in lieu of reinvesting earnings reduces the size of the firm, some managers find it emotionally difficult to pay high dividends.

Growth in Earnings and Dividends versus Growth Opportunities

As mentioned earlier, a firm's value increases when it invests in growth opportunities with positive NPVGOs. A firm's value falls when it selects opportunities with negative NPVGOs. However, dividends grow whether projects with positive NPVs or negative NPVs are selected. This surprising result can be explained by the following example.

EXAMPLE 5.9

NPV versus Dividends   Lane Supermarkets, a new firm, will earn $100,000 a year in perpetuity if it pays out all its earnings as dividends. However, the firm plans to invest 20 percent of its earnings in projects that earn 10 percent per year. The discount rate is 18 percent. An earlier formula tells us that the growth rate of dividends is:

$$g = \text{Retention ratio} \times \text{Return on retained earnings} = .2 \times .10 = 2\%$$

For example, in this first year of the new policy, dividends are $80,000 [= (1 − .2) × $100,000]. Dividends next year are $81,600 (= $80,000 × 1.02). Dividends the following year are $83,232 [= $80,000 × (1.02)^2] and so on. Because dividends represent a fixed percentage of earnings, earnings must grow at 2 percent a year as well.

However, note that the policy reduces value because the rate of return on the projects of 10 percent is less than the discount rate of 18 percent. That is, the firm would have had a higher value at date 0 if it had a policy of paying all its earnings out as dividends. Thus, a policy of investing in projects with negative NPVs rather than paying out earnings as dividends will lead to growth in dividends and earnings, but will reduce value.

Dividends or Earnings: Which to Discount?

As mentioned earlier, this chapter applied the growing perpetuity formula to the valuation of stocks. In our application, we discounted dividends, not earnings. This is sensible because investors select a stock for what they can get out of it. They get only two things out of a stock: dividends and the ultimate sale price, which is determined by what future investors expect to receive in dividends.

---

[6]Later in the text, we speak of issuing stock or debt to fund projects.

The calculated stock price would be too high were earnings to be discounted instead of dividends. As we saw in our estimation of a firm's growth rate, only a portion of earnings goes to the stockholders as dividends. The remainder is retained to generate future dividends. In our model, retained earnings are equal to the firm's investment. To discount earnings instead of dividends would be to ignore the investment a firm must make today to generate future returns.

The No-Dividend Firm

Students frequently ask the following questions: If the dividend discount model is correct, why aren't no-dividend stocks selling at zero? This is a good question and gets at the goals of the firm. A firm with many growth opportunities faces a dilemma. The firm can pay out dividends now, or it can forgo dividends now so that it can make investments that will generate even greater dividends in the future.[7] This is often a painful choice because a strategy of dividend deferment may be optimal yet unpopular among certain stockholders.

Many firms choose to pay no dividends—and these firms sell at positive prices. For example, most Internet firms, such as Amazon.com, Google, and eBay, pay no dividends. Rational shareholders believe that either they will receive dividends at some point or they will receive something just as good. That is, the firm will be acquired in a merger, with the stockholders receiving either cash or shares of stock at that time.

Of course, the actual application of the dividend discount model is difficult for firms of this type. Clearly the model for constant growth of dividends does not apply. Though the differential growth model can work in theory, the difficulties of estimating the date of first dividend, the growth rate of dividends after that date, and the ultimate merger price make application of the model quite difficult in reality.

Empirical evidence suggests that firms with high growth rates are likely to pay lower dividends, a result consistent with the analysis here. For example, consider McDonald's Corporation. The company started in the 1950s and grew rapidly for many years. It paid its first dividend in 1975, though it was a billion-dollar company (in both sales and market value of stockholders' equity) prior to that date. Why did it wait so long to pay a dividend? It waited because it had so many positive growth opportunities (additional locations for new hamburger outlets) to take advantage of.

5.7　The Dividend Growth Model and the NPVGO Model

This chapter has revealed that the price of a share of stock is the sum of its price as a cash cow plus the per-share value of its growth opportunities. The Sarro Shipping example illustrated this formula using only one growth opportunity. We also used the growing perpetuity formula to price a stock with a steady growth in dividends. When the formula is applied to stocks, it is typically called the *dividend growth model*. A steady growth in dividends results from a continual investment in growth opportunities, not just investment in a single opportunity. Therefore, it is worthwhile to compare the dividend growth model with the *NPVGO model* when growth occurs through continual investing.

We can use an example to illustrate the main points. Suppose Cumberland Book Publishers has EPS of $10 at the end of the first year, a dividend payout ratio of 40 percent, a

---

[7]A third alternative is to issue stock so the firm has enough cash both to pay dividends and to invest. This possibility is explored in a later chapter.

discount rate of 16 percent, and a return on its retained earnings of 20 percent. Because the firm retains some of its earnings each year, it is selecting growth opportunities each year. This is different from Sarro Shipping, which had a growth opportunity in only one year. We wish to calculate the price per share using both the dividend growth model and the NPVGO model.

The Dividend Growth Model

The dividends at date 1 are $.40 \times \$10 = \$4$ per share. The retention ratio is .60 $(1 - .40)$, implying a growth rate in dividends of .12 $(= .60 \times .20)$.

From the dividend growth model, the price of a share of stock today is

$$\frac{\text{Div}_1}{R - g} = \frac{\$4}{.16 - .12} = \$100$$

The NPVGO Model

Using the NPVGO model, it is more difficult to value a firm with growth opportunities each year (like Cumberland) than a firm with growth opportunities in only one year (like Sarro). To value according to the NPVGO model, we need to calculate on a per-share basis (1) the net present value of a single growth opportunity, (2) the net present value of all growth opportunities, and (3) the stock price if the firm acts as a cash cow—that is, the value of the firm without these growth opportunities. The value of the firm is the sum of (2) + (3).

1. *Value per share of a single growth opportunity*: Out of the earnings per share of $10 at date 1, the firm retains $6 $(= .6 \times \$10)$ at that date. The firm earns $1.20 $(= \$6 \times .20)$ per year in perpetuity on that $6 investment. The NPV from the investment is calculated as follows:

   Per-Share NPV Generated from Investment of Date 1:

   $$-\$6 + \frac{\$1.20}{.16} = \$1.50 \tag{5.12}$$

   That is, the firm invests $6 to reap $1.20 per year on the investment. The earnings are discounted at 16 percent, implying a value per share from the project of $1.50. Because the investment occurs at date 1 and the first cash flow occurs at date 2, $1.50 is the value of the investment at *date 1*. In other words, the NPV from the date 1 investment has *not* yet been brought back to date 0.

2. *Value per share of all opportunities*: As pointed out earlier, the growth rate of earnings and dividends is 12 percent. Because retained earnings are a fixed percentage of total earnings, retained earnings must also grow at 12 percent a year. That is, retained earnings at date 2 are $6.72 $(= \$6 \times 1.12)$, retained earnings at date 3 are $7.5264 $[= \$6 \times (1.12)^2]$, and so on.

   Let's analyze the retained earnings at date 2 in more detail. Because projects will always earn 20 percent per year, the firm earns $1.344 $(= \$6.72 \times .20)$ in each future year on the $6.72 investment at date 2.

   Here is the NPV from the investment:

   NPV per Share Generated from Investment at Date 2:

   $$-\$6.72 + \frac{\$1.344}{.16} = \$1.68 \tag{5.13}$$

$1.68 is the NPV as of date 2 of the investment made at date 2. The NPV from the date 2 investment has *not* yet been brought back to date 0.

Now consider the retained earnings at date 3 in more detail. The firm earns $1.5053 ($= \$7.5264 \times .20$) per year on the investment of $7.5264 at date 3.

The NPV from the investment is thus:

NPV per Share Generated from Investment at Date 3:

$$-\$7.5264 + \frac{\$1.5053}{.16} = \$1.882 \tag{5.14}$$

From Equations 5.12, 5.13, and 5.14, the NPV per share of all of the growth opportunities, discounted back to date 0, is:

$$\frac{\$1.50}{1.16} + \frac{\$1.68}{(1.16)^2} + \frac{\$1.882}{(1.16)^3} + \cdots \tag{5.15}$$

Because it has an infinite number of terms, this expression looks quite difficult to compute. However, there is an easy simplification. Note that retained earnings are growing at 12 percent per year. Because all projects earn the same rate of return per year, the NPVs in Equations 5.12, 5.13, and 5.14 are also growing at 12 percent per year. Hence, we can write Equation 5.15 as:

$$\frac{\$1.50}{1.16} + \frac{\$1.50 \times 1.12}{(1.16)^2} + \frac{\$1.50 \times (1.12)^2}{(1.16)^3} + \cdots$$

This is a growth perpetuity whose value is:

$$\text{NPVGO} = \$\frac{1.50}{.16 - .12} = \$37.50$$

Because the first NPV of $1.50 occurs at date 1, the NPVGO is $37.50 as of date 0. In other words, the firm's policy of investing in new projects from retained earnings has an NPV of $37.50.

3. *Value per share if the firm is a cash cow*: We now assume that the firm pays out all of its earnings as dividends. The dividends would be $10 per year in this case. Because there would be no growth, the value per share would be evaluated by the perpetuity formula:

$$\frac{\text{Div}}{R} = \frac{\$10}{.16} = \$62.50$$

Summation

Equation 5.10 states that value per share is the value of a cash cow plus the value of the growth opportunities. This is

$$\$100 = \$62.50 + 37.50$$

Hence, value is the same whether calculated by a discounted dividend approach or a growth opportunities approach. The share prices from the two approaches must be equal because the approaches are different yet equivalent methods of applying concepts of present value.

5.8   Price–Earnings Ratio

We argued earlier that one should not discount earnings to determine price per share. Nevertheless, financial analysts frequently relate earnings and price per share, as made evident by their heavy reliance on the price–earnings (or PE) ratio.

Our previous discussion stated that:

$$\text{Price per share} = \frac{\text{EPS}}{R} + \text{NPVGO}$$

Dividing by EPS yields:

$$\frac{\text{Price per share}}{\text{EPS}} = \frac{1}{R} + \frac{\text{NPVGO}}{\text{EPS}}$$

The left side is the formula for the price–earnings ratio. The equation shows that the PE ratio is related to the net present value of growth opportunities. As an example, consider two firms, each having just reported earnings per share of $1. However, one firm has many valuable growth opportunities, whereas the other firm has no growth opportunities at all. The firm with growth opportunities should sell at a higher price because an investor is buying both current income of $1 and growth opportunities. Suppose that the firm with growth opportunities sells for $16 and the other firm sells for $8. The $1 earnings per share number appears in the denominator of the PE ratio for both firms. Thus, the PE ratio is 16 for the firm with growth opportunities but only 8 for the firm without the opportunities.

This explanation seems to hold fairly well in the real world. Electronic and other high-tech stocks generally sell at very high PE ratios (or *multiples*, as they are often called) because they are perceived to have high growth rates. In fact, some technology stocks sell at high prices even though the companies have never earned a profit. Conversely, railroads, utilities, and steel companies sell at lower multiples because of the prospects of lower growth. Table 5.1 contains PE ratios in 2006 for some well-known companies and the S&P 500 Index. Notice the variation across industries.

Of course, the market is merely pricing *perceptions* of the future, not the future itself. We will argue later in the text that the stock market generally has realistic perceptions of a firm's prospects. However, this is not always true. In the late 1960s, many electronics firms were selling at multiples of 200 times earnings. The high perceived growth rates did not materialize, causing great declines in stock prices during the early 1970s. In earlier decades, fortunes were made in stocks like IBM and Xerox because the high growth rates were not anticipated by investors. Most recently, we have experienced the dot-com collapse when many Internet stocks were trading at multiples of thousands of times annual earnings. In fact, most Internet stocks had no earnings.

There are two additional factors explaining the PE ratio. The first is the discount rate, *R*. The previous formula shows that the PE ratio is *negatively* related to the firm's discount

Table 5.1

Selected PE Ratios

Company	Industry	PE Ratio
Ford	Automobiles	7.69
Bear Stearns	Investment banking	11.60
Caterpillar	Heavy equipment	16.79
S&P 500 average	n/a	19.00
Cisco Systems	Computer networking	21.47
Amgen	Biotechnology	27.18
Starbucks	Expensive coffee	50.01

rate. We have already suggested that the discount rate is positively related to the stock's risk or variability. Thus the PE ratio is negatively related to the stock's risk. To see that this is a sensible result, consider two firms, *A* and *B*, behaving as cash cows. The stock market *expects* both firms to have annual earnings of $1 per share forever. However, the earnings of firm *A* are known with certainty, whereas the earnings of firm *B* are quite variable. A rational stockholder is likely to pay more for a share of firm *A* because of the absence of risk. If a share of firm *A* sells at a higher price and both firms have the same EPS, the PE ratio of firm *A* must be higher.

The second additional factor concerns the firm's choice of accounting methods. Under current accounting rules, companies are given a fair amount of leeway. For example, consider inventory accounting where either FIFO or LIFO may be used. In an inflationary environment, *FIFO (first in–first out)* accounting understates the true cost of inventory and hence inflates reported earnings. Inventory is valued according to more recent costs under *LIFO (last in–first out)*, implying that reported earnings are lower here than they would be under FIFO. Thus LIFO inventory accounting is a more *conservative* method than FIFO. Similar accounting leeway exists for construction costs (*completed contracts* versus *percentage-of-completion methods*) and depreciation (*accelerated depreciation* versus *straight-line depreciation*).

As an example, consider two identical firms, *C* and *D*. Firm *C* uses LIFO and reports earnings of $2 per share. Firm *D* uses the less conservative accounting assumptions of FIFO and reports earnings of $3 per share. The market knows that both firms are identical and prices both at $18 per share. This price–earnings ratio is 9 (= $18/$2) for firm *C* and 6 (= $18/$3) for firm *D*. Thus, the firm with the more conservative principles has the higher PE ratio.

This last example depends on the assumption that the market sees through differences in accounting treatments. A significant portion of the academic community believes that the market sees through virtually all accounting differences. These academics are adherents of the hypothesis of *efficient capital markets*, a theory that we explore in great detail later in the text. Though many financial people might be more moderate in their beliefs regarding this issue, the consensus view is certainly that many of the accounting differences are seen through. Thus, the proposition that firms with conservative accountants have high PE ratios is widely accepted.

5.9   Stock Market Reporting

If you look through the pages of *The Wall Street Journal* (or another financial newspaper), you will find information about a large number of stocks in several different markets. Figure 5.5 reproduces a small section of the stock page for the New York Stock Exchange from January 20, 2006. Information on most NASDAQ issues is reported in the same way. In Figure 5.5, locate the line for motorcycle maker Harley-Davidson (HarleyDav). With the column headings, the line reads:

| 52-WEEK | | STOCK (DIV) | YLD % | PE | VOL 100s | CLOSE | NET CHG |
HI	LO						
62.49	44.40	HarleyDav .64	1.2	16	70028	54.05	2.56

You can get real-time stock quotes on the Web. See **finance.yahoo. com** for details.

The first two numbers, 62.49 and 44.40, are the highest and lowest prices for the stock over the past 52 weeks. The .64 is the annual dividend in dollars. Because Harley, like most companies, pays dividends quarterly, this $.64 is actually the latest quarterly dividend multiplied by 4. So the cash dividend paid was $.64/4 = $.16, or 16 cents per share.

Jumping ahead just a bit, "CLOSE" is the closing price of the day (i.e., the last price at which a trade took place before the NYSE closed for the day). The "Net Chg" of 2.56 tells us that the closing price of \$54.05 is \$2.56 higher than it was the day before; so we say that Harley was up 2.56 for the day.

The column marked "Yld %" gives the dividend yield based on the current dividend and the closing price. For Harley, this is \$.64/54.05 = .0118, or about 1.2 percent, the number shown. The next column, labeled "PE," is the price–earnings ratio we discussed earlier. It is calculated as the closing price divided by annual earnings per share (based on

Figure 5.5
Sample Stock Quotation from *The Wall Street Journal*

SOURCE: Reprinted by permission of *The Wall Street Journal*, Friday, January 20, 2006. Reprinted by permission of Dow Jones & Company, Inc. via Copyright Clearance Center, Inc. © 2006 Dow Jones & Company, Inc. All Rights Reserved Worldwide.

FRIDAY, JANUARY 20, 2006 C5

NYSE COMPOSITE TRANSACTIONS

52-WEEK HI	52-WEEK LO	STOCK (DIV)	YLD %	PE	VOL 100s	CLOSE	NET CHG
		F					
33.10	25.15	♣FBL Fnl A .42	1.3	12	229	32.69	0.48
63.87	43.25	FMC	...	11	4249	53.19	−0.29
48.04	28.62	♣FMC Tech	...	25	8011	47.25	1.03
21	16.18	FNB Cp .94f	5.5	14	1006	17.19	0.20
48.11	36.89	FPL Gp s 1.42	3.3	19	19334	43.24	0.62
13.95	9.20	FTD Grp n	...	dd	755	10	−0.23
30.54	17.01	FTI Cnsltng	...	26	1264	27.73	0.39
42.30	27.06	FactsetRsch s .20	.5	27	1365	39.85	0.19
48.47	32.26	FairIsaac .08	.2	25	4654	46.37	0.16
3.84	2.11	FairchldCp	...	dd	235	2.44	−0.04
18.62	12.80	FrchldSemi	...	dd	49721	19.66	1.76
179.90	126.73	FairfaxFnl 1.40e	.9	dd	431	153.70	2.45
43.75	29.90	FairmntHtlRt .12	.3	33	5864	41.90	0.28
18.55	10.01	FairpntComm n1.59	13.2	dd	1995	12.03	...
31.15	15.42	Falconbridge .48g	...	...	696	29.74	0.41
35.25	19.40	FamilyDlr .38	1.6	19	7430	24.07	−0.11
66.50	41.34	FannieMae lf 1.04	1.9	7	27571	54.10	0.84
3.32	1.22	Fedders .09j	...	...	1040	1.33	−0.05
23.15	12.89	FedAgrMtg A .40	1.9	8	2	20.96	0.15
32.47	15.53	FedAgri C .40	1.4	11	215	29.04	0.24
65.98	46.19	FedRlty 2.22a	3.3	40	1059	66.80	1.82
17.95	13.80	FedSgnl .24	1.4	29	3843	16.63	0.50
78.05	54.20	FedDeptStr 1.00	1.4	12	17955	71.92	0.33
38.54	26.99	FedInv B .60	1.6	27	5613	38.48	0.12
105.82	76.81	FedExCp .32	.3	20	18187	102.72	2.10
18.80	11.78	Felcor .15e	.8	dd	2031	18.69	0.18
14.70	8.63	FldmnMallProp .91	7.4	...	120	12.25	0.59
22.49	20.13	Ferrellgas 2.00	9.3	14	826	21.54	...
23.22	16.27	Ferro lf .58	3.0	36	1034	19.55	0.38
10.28	5.76	Fiat ADS	...	...	304	10.11	−0.05
41.11	27.01	FidNtlFnl s 1.00	2.7	6	17489	37.50	0.10
26	19.50	FidNtlTitle n .25p	...	...	2130	25.60	0.45
45.19	32.70	FnlFed .60	1.4	20	1679	42.96	0.01
10.95	8.23	FstAcceptance	...	19	271	10.31	0.14
49.50	30	FstAmCp .72	1.6	10	3607	46.20	0.84
29.71	10.37	FstBcp slf .28	2.3	6	1830	12.39	0.16
14.70	12.63	FstCmwlthFnl .68f	5.1	15	1274	13.39	0.07
45	36.50	♣FstData .24	.6	21	28954	42.81	−0.24
44.80	34.78	FstHorizonNat 1.80	4.7	11	14298	38.62	−0.33
42.80	36.70	FstIndRlty 2.80f	7.2	23	4795	38.90	0.03
73.27	20.89	FstMarblehead .24e	.7	14	4764	32.64	−0.05
28.30	20.87	FstPotomac 1.20f	4.2	84	507	28.51	0.42
40.22	30.96	♣FstRepBnk s .50	1.2	20	2255	40.27	1.16
53.36	38.54	FstEngy 1.80f	3.5	20	7906	51.51	0.40
65.32	47.84	FstFedFnl	...	12	2309	57.40	−0.55
67.50	53.50	FisherSci	...	26	10349	65.68	0.28
22.42	12.62	Flagstar .60m	4.2	11	2071	14.41	0.09
13.69	7.33	♣FleetwdEnt	...	dd	7381	11.65	0.31
48.49	38.90	FL ECstInd .24	.5	19	1828	47.45	0.79
67.98	36	♣FL RockInd s .60	1.2	21	5062	50	−0.15
30.61	18.51	FlwrsFoods s .40	1.5	30	1459	26.92	−0.25
43.35	23.69	Flowserve lf	...	40	2966	43.77	0.61
82.50	50.11	FluorCp .64	.8	33	6302	81.75	−0.15
79.60	50.47	Fomento ADS .60e	.8	...	2188	76.51	0.61
29.95	18.74	FootLocker .36f	1.6	14	6989	22.45	−0.08
13.54	7.57	FordMotor .40	4.9	8	195015	8.22	0.01
45.15	24.77	FrdgCndn s 4.77e	...	...	8274	39.70	0.75
41	28.61	♣ForestCtyA s .24	.6	63	834	38.37	−0.18
40.90	29.05	♣ForestCtyB s .24	.6	63	10	38.16	−0.29
45.21	32.46	ForestLabs	...	22	19929	43.26	0.63
54.76	31.65	ForestOil	...	23	6110	50.24	1.14
90.57	73.02	FortBrnds 1.44	1.8	17	5826	78.59	0.16
44.30	20.65	FoundtnCoal .18e	.4	30	3641	44.37	1.46
23	15.46	♣4KidsEntn	...	25	681	17.78	0.37
82.20	46.85	FourSeasons .11g	...	...	1908	54.74	0.19
31.90	23	FraTelecm .68e	2.9	...	2255	23.15	−0.28
62.49	44.40	HarleyDav .64	1.2	16	70028	54.05	2.56
126.69	68.54	HarmanInt .05	...	28	4741	101.80	0.68
15.41	5.96	HrmnyGld ADS	...	...	19553	15.47	0.97
79.69	57.29	HarrahEntn 1.45	2.0	22	12208	71.83	−0.11
47.60	26.94	Harris s .32	.7	31	4478	47.54	0.04
71.68	49.87	Harsco 1.20	1.7	21	2653	71.41	2.25
31.47	25.04	HarteHanks .20	.8	20	1355	26.43	−0.07
89.49	65.35	HrtfrdFnl 1.20f	1.4	11	14241	87.32	0.43
80.30	61.58	HrtfrdFnl 7.0un 3.50	4.5	...	530	78.25	0.36
79.17	60.90	HrtfrdFnl un 3.00	3.9	...	19	77.66	0.76
10.48	6.09	♣Hartmarx	...	13	2425	7.85	0.29
33.69	23.85	HvstEngyTr nu 4.20g	12.8	...	1702	32.70	0.48
13.93	7.83	HarvstNatRes	...	7	2983	9.49	0.47
22.35	17.75	Hasbro .36	1.7	21	12330	21.76	0.30
18	11.53	HavrtyFurn .27f	2.0	19	938	13.75	0.05
17.69	11.92	HavrtyFurn A .25f	1.9	19	4	13.40	0.12
29.79	24.60	HawElInd 1.24	4.7	19	1626	26.50	0.24
4.40	2.45	Head	...	48	1	3.38	−0.01
45.75	29.08	Headwaters	...	13	9083	35.98	0.11
28.92	23.13	HlthCrProp 1.68	6.1	24	2870	27.59	0.59
39.20	31.15	HlthCr Reit 2.48	6.7	39	1493	37	0.44
27	20.75	HlthMgt A .24f	1.1	16	13862	22.27	−0.02
54.11	27.63	HealthNet	...	91	6973	51.21	−0.23
41.36	31.01	HlthcrRlty 2.64	7.7	31	2025	34.48	0.49
26.34	23.15	♣HearstArgyl .28	1.2	18	1171	23.95	0.14
27.73	20.77	HeartlndPymnt n	...	...	2032	21.75	0.03
6.22	2.95	HeclaMin	...	dd	11349	4.23	0.23
27.45	18.32	Heico .08f	.3	29	419	25.39	0.01
21.93	14.52	Heico A .08f	.4	23	106	20.26	−0.04
38.16	33.55	Heinz 1.20	3.5	17	14395	33.99	0.10
11.35	8.36	Hellenic	...	...	975	11.35	0.28
72.58	33.89	HelmPayne .33	.5	29	8435	71.66	1.61
34.10	14.52	Herbalife	...	...	1299	31.90	−0.40
15.55	10	Hercules	...	14	5657	11.10	0.05
37.89	29.16	HeritageProp 2.10	6.1	43	1995	34.63	0.40
67.37	52.49	Hershey .98	1.8	27	7545	55.16	0.06
31.43	23.94	Hewitt	...	22	9320	26.14	−0.49
31.90	18.89	HewlettPk .32	1.0	39	184228	32.24	0.57
20.15	13.81	Hexcel	...	dd	7124	19.34	...
12.24	9.78	HighlndHspty .56	5.1	78	2953	10.93	−0.01
31.86	24.27	HighwdProp lf 1.70	5.5	67	1698	30.72	0.61
40.45	31.75	♣HillbRogl .46	1.2	27	2085	39	−0.21
57	44.81	Hillenbrnd 1.13f	2.2	dd	1357	51	0.09
25.81	18.78	Hilton .16	.6	24	29325	25.03	0.65
75.40	57.36	Hitachi .96e	1.3	...	591	71.57	1.46
11.95	8.45	HollingrInt A s .20a	2.2	...	870	8.94	0.09
66.47	25.28	HollyCp .40	.6	16	2793	67.74	2.99
47	32.25	HllyEngyPtnr 2.40	5.8	...	167	41.50	−0.25
43.98	34.56	HomeDpt .60f	1.5	16	122154	41.28	−0.62
46.44	35.36	♣HmProp 2.56f	5.7	33	4920	44.70	0.45
10.34	6.70	Homebanc .95e	11.7	dd	1823	8.12	0.03
30.36	23.75	♣HondaMtr ADS .30e	1.1	...	12846	27.67	0.30
39.50	32.68	Honeywell .83	2.2	20	37918	37.19	0.17
20.80	15.86	HoraceMn .42	2.2	10	1960	19.47	0.27
13.10	10.24	HorizonLine n .11p	...	...	108	12.25	−0.12
35.44	29.16	♣HormelFood .56f	1.7	18	3270	33.59	−0.42
38.55	20.10	HrnbkOffshr	...	68	3137	38.59	1.78
42.82	26.83	♣DR Horton s .40f	1.0	8	31354	38.86	−1.14
45.50	28.35	Hospira	...	28	6291	45.40	0.15
45.04	38	HsptlyProp 2.92	6.9	26	2593	42.29	0.94
19.81	15.46	HostMar Reit .41e	2.1	60	14033	19.81	0.21
71.47	45.60	HoustonExplr	...	13	4939	55.95	2.23
73.40	42.50	♣HovnanEnt	...	7	7354	50.91	−0.32
46.75	34	HSBC Fin un 2.22a	5.2	...	10	42.85	−0.40
32.75	25.94	HuanengPwr 1.21r	4.3	...	909	28.10	0.32
27.05	16.80	HubIntl .24	.9	34	330	27	0.17
49.75	39.19	HubbellA 1.32	3.2	16	4661	41.35	−1.00
54.20	42.56	HubbellB 1.32	2.9	17	2966	45.24	−1.21
42.95	31.31	HudsnUtdBcp 1.48	3.5	17	1890	42.40	0.11
56.22	43.54	KindrMrgEgy 3.20f	6.3	23	4768	50.62	0.52
99.97	72.47	KindrMorgan 3.50f	3.5	23	16197	101.44	5.15
49.25	37.44	KindrMrgMg 3.20f	6.9	31	1040	46.67	0.65
42.11	24.74	Kindred	...	9	19081	26.80	−0.94
74.20	33	KineticCnpts	...	27	2945	41.20	0.08
18.85	7.50	KingPharm	...	19	19771	18.03	0.04
21.07	14.70	KingswayFin .20g	...	...	110	20.74	0.03
10.68	4.61	KinrossGld lf	...	1	19305	10.46	0.46
55.54	37.19	KirbyCp	...	22	931	53.02	1.26
16.52	13.40	KiteRltyTr .75	4.9	...	691	15.28	0.03
25.07	20.71	KKR Fnl n .72e	3.1	...	1295	23.25	−0.16
11.30	7.84	KMG America	...	...	276	8.78	−0.07
22.51	13.83	KnightTrnsp s .16f	.8	29	7943	20.89	−0.38
69.09	52.42	KnghtRidder 1.48	2.3	9	7479	63.54	−0.65
19	14.75	Knoll .25e	1.5	26	356	16.81	−0.07
58.90	43.63	KohlsCp	...	19	37830	44.48	−0.10
24.10	19	Konami ADS .49e	2.1	...	8	22.99	0.59
78.65	40.65	Kookmin ADS	...	...	6436	69.57	0.74
13.29	9.50	♣KoorInd	...	...	167	10.63	0.08
21.92	13.05	KoreaElecPwr .56e	2.6	...	6622	21.90	0.85
20.40	13.92	KornFerry	...	19	1458	19.55	0.14
34.35	27.44	KftFoods .92	3.2	20	24975	29.07	0.01
9.49	3.35	KrspyKrm lf	...	dd	15355	5.19	−0.06
20.88	15.15	Kroger	...	cc	51806	19	−0.07
49.20	27.50	KronosWrldwd 1.00	3.3	20	43	30.20	0.15
45.90	24.20	Kubota ADS .37e	.9	...	503	43.39	1.25
82.97	62.58	Kyocera .92e	1.2	...	406	79.78	0.27
		L					
8.29	1.90	LLE RoyalTr j	...	...	324	3.25	−0.01
10.75	5.01	LSI Logic	...	dd	55657	8.86	0.22
23.92	16.50	LTC Prop x 1.44f	6.4	15	735	22.60	0.14
84.84	64.66	L 3Comm .50	.7	19	8717	74.58	−0.32
11.19	7.75	LaQuinta	...	dd	7502	11.19	0.01
16.40	10.13	♣LaZ Boy .44	2.9	29	4966	15.16	0.06
26.50	15.25	LaborRdy	...	20	3497	21.64	−0.01
58.14	44.63	LabCpAm	...	22	9475	57.39	0.42
11.87	5.25	LaBranche	...	23	5746	10.89	0.21
34.31	26.90	LacledeGrp 1.38	4.5	16	448	30.85	0.18
26.35	19.81	Lafarge ADS .72e	3.1	...	732	23.57	1.07
70.47	50.85	♣LafargeNoAm .96	1.6	21	5252	58.81	1.24
27.56	20.41	LaidlawIntl .30e	1.1	12	6321	27.31	0.06
31.69	8.77	LamsonSes	...	29	3324	27.24	0.65
40.40	30.06	LanAirline ADS .69e	1.8	...	591	38.25	0.02
70.09	46.50	LandAmFnl .72	1.1	9	2945	66.64	−0.42
54	43.90	♣Landauer 1.80f	3.7	25	136	48.05	1.25
33	25.39	LandryRes .20	.7	13	2704	29.25	0.25
51.40	29.08	LasVegasSands	...	66	7548	47.78	−0.04
38.47	27.34	LaSalleHtl 1.20	3.1	64	1751	38.21	0.34
35.48	20.40	Lazard n .14e	.4	...	3362	34	0.70
15.35	9.20	LeapFrog A	...	dd	3217	11.77	−0.03
54.55	23.28	Lear 1.00	4.1	dd	25619	24.35	1.04
45.96	36.11	LeeEnt .72	2.0	23	1670	36.66	0.15
131.40	69.82	LeggMason .72	.5	34	12325	131.10	4.69
29.61	18.19	LegPlatt .64	2.7	17	7160	23.80	0.15
16.15	14.16	LehmnFstTrInco x 1.32n	8.9	...	345	14.87	−0.06
136.63	85.92	LehmnHldg .96f	.7	13	28223	137.49	4.12
68.86	50.30	Lennar A .64	1.0	8	13277	62.62	−0.65
64	46.90	Lennar B .64	1.1	7	1116	57.55	−0.75
31.16	18.65	♣LennoxIntl .44f	1.4	20	1861	30.70	0.42
17.94	9.85	LenoxGrp	...	11	252	12.83	0.03
49.65	32.40	LeucdaNat .25	.5	4	2203	48.94	0.46
33.85	18.86	Levitt A .08	.3	8	1773	23.90	0.43
25.26	20.26	LexgtnProp 1.46f	6.4	45	1660	22.70	0.29
86.62	39.33	LexmarkIntl	...	14	8880	46.75	0.05
26.60	18.01	LG PhilipsADS	...	...	10777	21.05	0.34
25.03	10.03	Libbey .40	3.8	46	869	10.60	0.43
48.05	34.32	LbtyCp 1.00a	2.1	27	255	47.22	0.01

the most recent four quarters). In the jargon of Wall Street, we might say that Harley "sells for 16 times earnings."

Finally, the column marked "Vol 100s" tells us how many shares traded during the day (in hundreds). For example, the 70028 for Harley tells us that about 7 million shares changed hands on this day alone. If the average price during the day was $54 or so, then the dollar volume of transactions was on the order of $54 × 7 million = $378 million worth for Harley alone. This was a fairly heavy day of trading in Harley shares, and it serves to illustrate how active the market can be for well-known companies.

If you look over Figure 5.5, you will notice quite a few footnote indicators (small letters) and special symbols. To learn more about these, pick up any *Wall Street Journal* and consult the stock pages.

Summary and Conclusions

In this chapter, we used general present value formulas from the previous chapter to price bonds and stock.

1. Pure discount bonds and perpetuities can be viewed as the polar cases of bonds. The value of a pure discount bond (also called a zero coupon bond, or simply a zero) is:

$$PV = \frac{F}{(1 + R)^T}$$

The value of a perpetuity (also called a *consol*) is:

$$PV = \frac{C}{R}$$

2. Level payment bonds can be viewed as an intermediate case. The coupon payments form an annuity, and the principal repayment is a lump sum. The value of this type of bond is simply the sum of the values of its two parts.

3. The yield to maturity on a bond is the single rate that discounts the payments on the bond to its purchase price.

4. A stock can be valued by discounting its dividends. We mentioned three types of situations:
   a. The case of zero growth of dividends.
   b. The case of constant growth of dividends.
   c. The case of differential growth.

5. An estimate of the growth rate of a stock is needed for the formulas for situations 4(b) or 4(c). A useful estimate of the growth rate is

$$g = \text{Retention ratio} \times \text{Return on retained earnings}$$

6. It is worthwhile to view a share of stock as the sum of its worth if the company behaves like a cash cow (the company does no investing) and the value per share of its growth opportunities. We write the value of a share as:

$$\frac{EPS}{R} + NPVGO$$

We showed that, in theory, share price must be the same whether the dividend growth model or the formula here is used.

7. From accounting, we know that earnings are divided into two parts: dividends and retained earnings. Most firms continually retain earnings to create future dividends. One should not

discount earnings to obtain price per share because part of earnings must be reinvested. Only dividends reach the stockholders, and only they should be discounted to obtain share price.

8. We suggested that a firm's price–earnings ratio is a function of three factors:
   a. The per-share amount of the firm's valuable growth opportunities.
   b. The risk of the stock.
   c. The type of accounting method used by the firm.

Concept Questions

1. **Coupon Rate** How does a bond issuer decide on the appropriate coupon rate to set on its bonds? Explain the difference between the coupon rate and the required return on a bond.

2. **Bond Market** What are the implications for bond investors of the lack of transparency in the bond market?

3. **Stock Valuation** Why does the value of a share of stock depend on dividends?

4. **Stock Valuation** A substantial percentage of the companies listed on the NYSE and the NASDAQ don't pay dividends, but investors are nonetheless willing to buy shares in them. How is this possible given your answer to the previous question?

5. **Dividend Policy** Referring to the previous two questions, under what circumstances might a company choose not to pay dividends?

6. **Dividend Growth Model** Under what two assumptions can we use the dividend growth model presented in the chapter to determine the value of a share of stock? Comment on the reasonableness of these assumptions.

7. **Common versus Preferred Stock** Suppose a company has a preferred stock issue and a common stock issue. Both have just paid a $2 dividend. Which do you think will have a higher price, a share of the preferred or a share of the common?

8. **Growth Rate** In the context of the dividend growth model, is it true that the growth rate in dividends and the growth rate in the price of the stock are identical?

9. **Price–Earnings Ratio** What are the three factors that determine a company's price–earnings ratio?

10. **Stock Valuation** Evaluate the following statement Managers should not focus on the current stock value because doing so will lead to an overemphasis on short-term profits at the expense of long-term profits.

Questions and Problems

BASIC
(Questions 1–9)

1. **Valuing Bonds** What is the price of a 10-year, pure discount bond paying $1,000 at maturity if the YTM is
   a. 5 percent?
   b. 10 percent?
   c. 15 percent?

2. **Valuing Bonds** Microhard has issued a bond with the following characteristics:
   Par: $1,000
   Time to maturity: 20 years
   Coupon rate: 8 percent
   Semiannual payments

   Calculate the price of this bond if the YTM is
   a. 8 percent.
   b. 10 percent.
   c. 6 percent.

3. **Bond Yields** Raines Umbrella Corp. issued 12-year bonds 2 years ago at a coupon rate of 8.6 percent. The bonds make semiannual payments. If these bonds currently sell for 97 percent of par value, what is the YTM?

4. **Stock Values** The Brennan Co. just paid a dividend of $1.40 per share on its stock. The dividends are expected to grow at a constant rate of 6 percent per year indefinitely. If investors require a 12 percent return on the Brennan Co. stock, what is the current price? What will the price be in three years? In 15 years?

5. **Stock Values** The next dividend payment by MUG, Inc., will be $3.10 per share. The dividends are anticipated to maintain a 5 percent growth rate forever. If MUG stock currently sells for $48.00 per share, what is the required return?

6. **Stock Values** Warren Corporation will pay a $3.60 per share dividend next year. The company pledges to increase its dividend by 4.5 percent per year indefinitely. If you require a 13 percent return on your investment, how much will you pay for the company's stock today?

7. **Stock Valuation** Suppose you know that a company's stock currently sells for $70 per share and the required return on the stock is 12 percent. You also know that the total return on the stock is evenly divided between a capital gains yield and a dividend yield. If it's the company's policy to always maintain a constant growth rate in its dividends, what is the current dividend per share?

8. **Stock Valuation** Gruber Corp. pays a constant $12 dividend on its stock. The company will maintain this dividend for the next eight years and will then cease paying dividends forever. If the required return on this stock is 10 percent, what is the current share price?

9. **Growth Rate** The newspaper reported last week that Bradley Enterprises earned $20 million this year. The report also stated that the firm's return on equity is 14 percent. Bradley retains 60 percent of its earnings. What is the firm's earnings growth rate? What will next year's earnings be?

INTERMEDIATE (Questions 10–31)

10. **Bond Price Movements** Miller Corporation has a premium bond making semiannual payments. The bond pays an 8 percent coupon, has a YTM of 6 percent, and has 13 years to maturity. The Modigliani Company has a discount bond making semiannual payments. This bond pays a 6 percent coupon, has a YTM of 8 percent, and also has 13 years to maturity. If interest rates remain unchanged, what do you expect the price of these bonds to be 1 year from now? In 3 years? In 8 years? In 12 years? In 13 years? What's going on here? Illustrate your answers by graphing bond prices versus time to maturity.

11. **Bond Yields** Stealers Wheel Software has 8.4 percent coupon bonds on the market with nine years to maturity. The bonds make semiannual payments and currently sell for 104 percent of par. What is the current yield on the bonds? The YTM? The effective annual yield?

12. **Bond Yields** Petty Co. wants to issue new 20-year bonds for some much-needed expansion projects. The company currently has 8 percent coupon bonds on the market that sell for $1,095, make semiannual payments, and mature in 20 years. What coupon rate should the company set on its new bonds if it wants them to sell at par?

13. **Stock Valuation** Ferson, Inc., just paid a dividend of $3.00 on its stock. The growth rate in dividends is expected to be a constant 5 percent per year indefinitely. Investors require a 16 percent return on the stock for the first three years, a 14 percent return for the next three years, and then an 11 percent return thereafter. What is the current share price for Ferson stock?

14. **Nonconstant Growth** Metallica Bearings, Inc., is a young start-up company. No dividends will be paid on the stock over the next nine years because the firm needs to plow back its earnings to fuel growth. The company will pay an $8 per share dividend in 10 years and will increase the dividend by 6 percent per year thereafter. If the required return on this stock is 13 percent, what is the current share price?

15. **Nonconstant Dividends** Corn, Inc., has an odd dividend policy. The company has just paid a dividend of $9 per share and has announced that it will increase the dividend by $3 per share for each of the next four years, and then never pay another dividend. If you require an 11 percent return on the company's stock, how much will you pay for a share today?

16. **Nonconstant Dividends** South Side Corporation is expected to pay the following dividends over the next four years: $8, $6, $3, and $2. Afterward the company pledges to maintain a constant 5 percent growth rate in dividends forever. If the required return on the stock is 13 percent, what is the current share price?

17. **Nonconstant Growth**   Rizzi Co. is growing quickly. Dividends are expected to grow at a 25 percent rate for the next three years, with the growth rate falling off to a constant 7 percent thereafter. If the required return is 13 percent and the company just paid a $2.80 dividend, what is the current share price?

18. **Nonconstant Growth**   Janicek Corp. is experiencing rapid growth. Dividends are expected to grow at 30 percent per year during the next three years, 18 percent over the following year, and then 8 percent per year indefinitely. The required return on this stock is 14 percent, and the stock currently sells for $70.00 per share. What is the projected dividend for the coming year?

19. **Finding the Dividend**   Hollin Corporation stock currently sells for $50 per share. The market requires a 14 percent return on the firm's stock. If the company maintains a constant 8 percent growth rate in dividends, what was the most recent dividend per share paid on the stock?

20 **Valuing Preferred Stock**   Mark Bank just issued some new preferred stock. The issue will pay a $9 annual dividend in perpetuity, beginning six years from now. If the market requires a 7 percent return on this investment, how much does a share of preferred stock cost today?

21. **Negative Growth**   Calamity Mining Company's iron ore reserves are being depleted, and its costs of recovering a declining quantity of ore are rising each year. As a result, the company's earnings are declining at a rate of 10 percent per year. If the dividend per share to be paid tomorrow is $5 and the required rate of return is 14 percent, what is the value of the firm's stock? Assume that the dividend payments are based on a fixed percentage of the firm's earnings.

22. **Nonconstant Growth and Quarterly Dividends**   Pasqually Mineral Water, Inc., will pay a quarterly dividend per share of $1 at the end of each of the next 12 quarters. Thereafter the dividend will grow at a quarterly rate of 0.5 percent forever. The appropriate rate of return on the stock is 10 percent, compounded quarterly. What is the current stock price?

23. **Nonconstant Growth**   To buy back its own shares, Pennzoil Co. has decided to suspend its dividends for the next two years. It will resume its annual cash dividend of $2.00 in year 3 and year 4. Thereafter its dividend payments will grow at an annual growth rate of 6 percent forever. The required rate of return on Pennzoil's stock is 16 percent. According to the discounted dividend model, what should Pennzoil's current share price be?

24. **Finding the Dividend**   Allen, Inc., is expected to pay equal dividends at the end of each of the next two years. Thereafter, the dividend will grow at a constant annual rate of 4 percent forever. The current stock price is $30. What is next year's dividend payment if the required rate of return is 12 percent?

25. **Finding the Required Return**   Juggernaut Satellite Corporation earned $10 million for the fiscal year ending yesterday. The firm also paid out 25 percent of its earnings as dividends yesterday. The firm will continue to pay out 25 percent of its earnings as annual, end-of-year dividends. The remaining 75 percent of earnings is retained by the company for use in projects. The company has 1.25 million shares of common stock outstanding. The current stock price is $40. The historical return on equity (ROE) of 11 percent is expected to continue in the future. What is the required rate of return on the stock?

26. **Dividend Growth**   Four years ago, Bling Diamond, Inc., paid a dividend of $.90 per share. Bling paid a dividend of $1.66 per share yesterday. Dividends will grow over the next five years at the same rate they grew over the last four years. Thereafter dividends will grow at 8 percent per year. The required return on the stock is 18 percent. What will Bling Diamond's cash dividend be in seven years?

27. **Price–Earnings Ratio**   Consider Pacific Energy Company and U.S. Bluechips, Inc., both of which reported earnings of $800,000. Without new projects, both firms will continue to generate earnings of $800,000 in perpetuity. Assume that all earnings are paid as dividends and that both firms require a 15 percent rate of return.
    a. What is the current PE ratio for each company?
    b. Pacific Energy Company has a new project that will generate additional earnings of $100,000 each year in perpetuity. Calculate the new PE ratio of the company.

Chapter 5 How to Value Bonds and Stocks 157

    c. U. S. Bluechips has a new project that will increase by $200,000 in perpetuity. Calculate the new PE ratio of the firm.

28. **Growth Opportunities** The Stambaugh Corporation currently has earnings per share of $7.00. The company has no growth and pays out all earnings as dividends. It has a new project that will require an investment of $1.75 per share in one year. The project will only last two years and will increase earnings in the two years following the investment by $1.90 and $2.10, respectively. Investors require a 12 percent return on Stambaugh stock.

    a. What is the value per share of the company's stock assuming the firm does not undertake the investment opportunity?

    b. If the company does undertake the investment, what is the value per share now?

    c. Again assume the company undertakes the investment. What will the price per share be four years from today?

29. **Growth Opportunities** Rite Bite Enterprises sells toothpicks. Gross revenues last year were $3 million, and total costs were $1.5 million. Rite Bite has 1 million shares of common stock outstanding. Gross revenues and costs are expected to grow at 5 percent per year. Rite Bite pays no income taxes. All earnings are paid out as dividends.

    a. If the appropriate discount rate is 15 percent and all cash flows are received at year's end, what is the price per share of Rite Bite stock?

    b. Rite Bite has decided to produce toothbrushes. The project requires an immediate outlay of $15 million. In one year, another outlay of $5 million will be needed. The year after that, earnings will increase by $6 million. That profit level will be maintained in perpetuity. What effect will undertaking this project have on the price per share of the stock?

30. **Growth Opportunities** California Real Estate, Inc., expects to earn $110 million per year in perpetuity if it does not undertake any new projects. The firm has an opportunity to invest $12 million today and $7 million in one year in real estate. The new investment will generate annual earnings of $10 million in perpetuity, beginning two years from today. The firm has 20 million shares of common stock outstanding, and the required rate of return on the stock is 15 percent. Land investments are not depreciable. Ignore taxes.

    a. What is the price of a share of stock if the firm does not undertake the new investment?

    b. What is the value of the investment?

    c. What is the per-share stock price if the firm undertakes the investment?

31. **Growth Opportunities** The annual earnings of Avalanche Skis, Inc., will be $5 per share in perpetuity if the firm makes no new investments. Under such a situation the firm would pay out all of its earnings as dividends. Assume the first dividend will be received exactly one year from now.

    Alternatively, assume that three years from now, and in every subsequent year in perpetuity, the company can invest 25 percent of its earnings in new projects. Each project will earn 40 percent at year-end in perpetuity. The firm's discount rate is 14 percent.

    a. What is the price per share of Avalanche Skis, Inc., stock today without the company making the new investment?

    b. If Avalanche announces that the new investment will be made, what will the per-share stock price be today?

CHALLENGE
(Questions 32–40)

32. **Components of Bond Returns** Bond P is a premium bond with a 10 percent coupon. Bond D is a 6 percent coupon bond currently selling at a discount. Both bonds make annual payments, have a YTM of 8 percent, and have five years to maturity. What is the current yield for Bond P? For Bond D? If interest rates remain unchanged, what is the expected capital gains yield over the next year for Bond P? For Bond D? Explain your answers and the interrelationship among the various types of yields.

33. **Holding Period Yield** The YTM on a bond is the interest rate you earn on your investment if interest rates don't change. If you actually sell the bond before it matures, your realized return is known as the holding period yield (HPY).

a. Suppose that today you buy an 8 percent annual coupon bond for $1,150. The bond has 10 years to maturity. What rate of return do you expect to earn on your investment?

b. Two years from now, the YTM on your bond has declined by 1 percent, and you decide to sell. What price will your bond sell for? What is the HPY on your investment? Compare this yield to the YTM when you first bought the bond. Why are they different?

34. Valuing Bonds The Mallory Corporation has two different bonds currently outstanding. Bond M has a face value of $20,000 and matures in 20 years. The bond makes no payments for the first six years, then pays $1,200 every six months over the subsequent eight years, and finally pays $1,500 every six months over the last six years. Bond N also has a face value of $20,000 and a maturity of 20 years; it makes no coupon payments over the life of the bond. If the required return on both these bonds is 10 percent compounded semiannually, what is the current price of Bond M? Of Bond N?

35. Capital Gains versus Income Consider four different stocks, all of which have a required return of 15 percent and a most recent dividend of $4.50 per share. Stocks W, X, and Y are expected to maintain constant rates in dividends for the foreseeable future of 10 percent, 0 percent, and −5 percent per year, respectively. Stock Z is a growth stock that will increase its dividend by 20 percent for the next two years and then maintain a constant 12 percent growth rate thereafter. What is the dividend yield for each of these four stocks? What is the expected capital gains yield? Discuss the relationship among the various returns that you find for each of these stocks.

36. Stock Valuation Most corporations pay quarterly rather than annual dividends on their common stock. Barring any unusual circumstances during the year, the board raises, lowers, or maintains the current dividend once a year and then pays this dividend out in equal quarterly installments to its shareholders.

a. Suppose a company currently pays a $3.00 annual dividend on its common stock in a single annual installment, and management plans on raising this dividend by 6 percent per year indefinitely. If the required return on this stock is 14 percent, what is the current share price?

b. Now suppose that the company in (a) actually pays its annual dividend in equal quarterly installments; thus this company has just paid a $.75 dividend per share, as it has for the previous three quarters. What is your value for the current share price now? (*Hint:* Find the equivalent annual end-of-year dividend for each year.) Comment on whether you think that this model of stock valuation is appropriate.

37. Growth Opportunities Lewin Skis, Inc., (today) expects to earn $6 per share for each of the future operating periods (beginning at time 1) if the firm makes no new investments and returns the earnings as dividends to the shareholders. However, Clint Williams, president and CEO, has discovered an opportunity to retain and invest 30 percent of the earnings beginning three years from today. This opportunity to invest will continue for each period indefinitely. He expects to earn 12 percent on this new equity investment, the return beginning one year after each investment is made. The firm's equity discount rate is 14 percent throughout.

a. What is the price per share of Lewin Skis, Inc., stock without making the new investment?

b. If the new investment is expected to be made, per the preceding information, what would the price of the stock be now?

c. Suppose the company could increase the investment in the project by whatever amount it chose. What would the retention ratio need to be to make this project attractive?

38. Nonconstant Growth Storico Co. just paid a dividend of $3.50 per share. The company will increase its dividend by 20 percent next year and will then reduce its dividend growth rate by 5 percentage points per year until it reaches the industry average of 5 percent dividend growth, after which the company will keep a constant growth rate forever. If the required return on Storico stock is 13 percent, what will a share of stock sell for today?

39. Nonconstant Growth This one's a little harder. Suppose the current share price for the firm in the previous problem is $98.65 and all the dividend information remains the same. What required return must investors be demanding on Storico stock? (*Hint:* Set up the valuation formula with all the relevant cash flows, and use trial and error to find the unknown rate of return.)

40.   Growth Opportunities   Shane, Inc., has earnings of $10 million and is projected to grow at a constant rate of 5 percent forever because of the benefits gained from the learning curve. Currently all earnings are paid out as dividends. The company plans to launch a new project two years from now that would be completely internally funded and require 20 percent of the earnings that year. The project would start generating revenues one year after the launch of the project, and the earnings from the new project in any year are estimated to be constant at $5 million. The company has 10 million shares of stock outstanding. Estimate the value of Shane stock. The discount rate is 10 percent.

S&P Problems

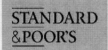

www.mhhe.com/edumarketinsight

1.   **Dividend Discount Model**   Enter the ticker symbol "WMT" for Wal-Mart. Using the most recent balance sheet and income statement under the "Excel Analytics" link, calculate the sustainable growth rate for Wal-Mart. Now download the "Mthly. Adj. Price" and find the closing stock price for the same month as the balance sheet and income statement you used. What is the implied required return on Wal-Mart according to the dividend growth model? Does this number make sense? Why or why not?

2.   **Growth Opportunities**   Assume that investors require an 11 percent return on Harley-Davidson (HDI) stock. Under the "Excel Analytics" link find the "Mthly. Adj. Price" and find the closing price for the month of the most recent fiscal year end for HDI. Using this stock price and the EPS for the most recent year, calculate the NPVGO for Harley-Davidson. What is the appropriate PE ratio for Harley-Davidson using these calculations?

Mini Case

Stock Valuation at Ragan Thermal Systems

Ragan Thermal Systems, Inc., was founded nine years ago by brother and sister Carrington and Genevieve Ragan. The company manufactures and installs commercial heating, ventilation, and cooling (HVAC) units. Ragan has experienced rapid growth because of a proprietary technology that increases the energy efficiency of its systems. The company is equally owned by Carrington and Genevieve. The original agreement between the siblings gave each 50,000 shares of stock. In the event either wished to sell the stock, the shares first had to be offered to the other at a discounted price.

Although neither sibling wants to sell any shares at this time, they have decided they should value their holdings in the company for financial planning purposes. To accomplish this, they have gathered the following information about their main competitors.

Ragan Thermal Systems, Inc., Competitors					
	EPS	DPS	Stock Price	ROE	R
Arctic Cooling, Inc.	$ .82	$ .16	$15.19	11%	10%
National Heating & Cooling	1.32	.52	12.49	14	13
Expert HVAC Corp.	−.47	.54	48.60	14	12
Industry average	$0.56	$0.41	$25.43	13%	11.67%

Expert HVAC Corp.'s negative earnings per share (EPS) were the result of an accounting write-off last year. Without the write-off, EPS for the company would have been $2.34.

Last year, Ragan had an EPS of $4.32 and paid a dividend to Carrington and Genevieve of $54,000 each. The company also had a return on equity of 25 percent. The siblings believe a required return for the company of 20 percent is appropriate.

1.   Assuming the company continues its current growth rate, what is the value per share of the company's stock?

2. To verify their calculations, Carrington and Genevieve have hired Josh Schlessman as a consultant. Josh was previously an equity analyst, and he has covered the HVAC industry. Josh has examined the company's financial statements as well as those of its competitors. Although Ragan currently has a technological advantage, Josh's research indicates that Ragan's competitors are investigating other methods to improve efficiency. Given this, Josh believes that Ragan's technological advantage will last for only the next five years. After that period, the company's growth will likely slow to the industry average. Additionally, Josh believes that the required return the company uses is too high. He believes the industry average required return is more appropriate. Under Josh's assumptions, what is the estimated stock price?

3. What is the industry average price–earnings ratio? What is Ragan's price–earnings ratio? Comment on any differences and explain why they may exist.

4. Assume the company's growth rate declines to the industry average after five years. What percentage of the stock's value is attributable to growth opportunities?

5. Assume the company's growth rate slows to the industry average in five years. What future return on equity does this imply?

6. After discussions with Josh, Carrington and Genevieve agree that they would like to try to increase the value of the company stock. Like many small business owners, they want to retain control of the company and do not want to sell stock to outside investors. They also feel that the company's debt is at a manageable level and do not want to borrow more money. What steps can they take to increase the price of the stock? Are there any conditions under which this strategy would not increase the stock price?

Appendix 5A   The Term Structure of Interest Rates, Spot Rates, and Yield to Maturity

To access the appendix for this chapter, please go to www.mhhe.com/rwj.

CHAPTER 5
HOW TO VALUE STOCKS AND BONDS

Answers to Concepts Review and Critical Thinking Questions

1. Bond issuers look at outstanding bonds of similar maturity and risk. The yields on such bonds are used to establish the coupon rate necessary for a particular issue to initially sell for par value. Bond issuers also simply ask potential purchasers what coupon rate would be necessary to attract them. The coupon rate is fixed and simply determines what the bond's coupon payments will be. The required return is what investors actually demand on the issue, and it will fluctuate through time. The coupon rate and required return are equal only if the bond sells exactly at par.

2. Lack of transparency means that a buyer or seller can't see recent transactions, so it is much harder to determine what the best price is at any point in time.

3. The value of any investment depends on the present value of its cash flows; i.e., what investors will actually receive. The cash flows from a share of stock are the dividends.

4. Investors believe the company will eventually start paying dividends (or be sold to another company).

5. In general, companies that need the cash will often forgo dividends since dividends are a cash expense. Young, growing companies with profitable investment opportunities are one example; another example is a company in financial distress. This question is examined in depth in a later chapter.

6. The general method for valuing a share of stock is to find the present value of all expected future dividends. The dividend growth model presented in the text is only valid (i) if dividends are expected to occur forever; that is, the stock provides dividends in perpetuity, and (ii) if a constant growth rate of dividends occurs forever. A violation of the first assumption might be a company that is expected to cease operations and dissolve itself some finite number of years from now. The stock of such a company would be valued by applying the general method of valuation explained in this chapter. A violation of the second assumption might be a start-up firm that isn't currently paying any dividends, but is expected to eventually start making dividend payments some number of years from now. This stock would also be valued by the general dividend valuation method explained in this chapter.

7. The common stock probably has a higher price because the dividend can grow, whereas it is fixed on the preferred. However, the preferred is less risky because of the dividend and liquidation preference, so it is possible the preferred could be worth more, depending on the circumstances.

8. Yes. If the dividend grows at a steady rate, so does the stock price. In other words, the dividend growth rate and the capital gains yield are the same.

9. The three factors are: 1) The company's future growth opportunities. 2) The company's level of risk, which determines the interest rate used to discount cash flows. 3) The accounting method used.

10. Presumably, the current stock value reflects the risk, timing and magnitude of all future cash flows, both short-term and long-term. If this is correct, then the statement is false.

Solutions to Questions and Problems

NOTE: All end-of-chapter problems were solved using a spreadsheet. Many problems require multiple steps. Due to space and readability constraints, when these intermediate steps are included in this solutions manual, rounding may appear to have occurred. However, the final answer for each problem is found without rounding during any step in the problem.

NOTE: Most problems do not explicitly list a par value for bonds. Even though a bond can have any par value, in general, corporate bonds in the United States will have a par value of $1,000. We will use this par value in all problems unless a different par value is explicitly stated.

Basic

1. The price of a pure discount (zero coupon) bond is the present value of the par. Even though the bond makes no coupon payments, the present value is found using semiannual compounding periods, consistent with coupon bonds. This is a bond pricing convention. So, the price of the bond for each YTM is:

a. $P = \$1,000/(1 + .025)^{20} = \$610.27$

b. $P = \$1,000/(1 + .05)^{20} = \$376.89$

c. $P = \$1,000/(1 + .075)^{20} = \$235.41$

2. The price of any bond is the PV of the interest payment, plus the PV of the par value. Notice this problem assumes an annual coupon. The price of the bond at each YTM will be:

a. $P = \$40(\{1 - [1/(1 + .04)]^{40}\} / .04) + \$1,000[1 / (1 + .04)^{40}]$
$P = \$1,000.00$
When the YTM and the coupon rate are equal, the bond will sell at par.

b. $P = \$40(\{1 - [1/(1 + .05)]^{40}\} / .05) + \$1,000[1 / (1 + .05)^{40}]$
$P = \$828.41$
When the YTM is greater than the coupon rate, the bond will sell at a discount.

c. $P = \$40(\{1 - [1/(1 + .03)]^{40}\} / .03) + \$1,000[1 / (1 + .03)^{40}]$
$P = \$1,231.15$
When the YTM is less than the coupon rate, the bond will sell at a premium.

B-102 SOLUTIONS

We would like to introduce shorthand notation here. Rather than write (or type, as the case may be) the entire equation for the PV of a lump sum, or the PVA equation, it is common to abbreviate the equations as:

$$PVIF_{R,t} = 1 / (1 + r)^t$$

which stands for $\underline{P}$resent $\underline{V}$alue $\underline{I}$nterest $\underline{F}$actor, and:

$$PVIFA_{R,t} = (\{1 - [1/(1 + r)]^t\} / r)$$

which stands for $\underline{P}$resent $\underline{V}$alue $\underline{I}$nterest $\underline{F}$actor of an $\underline{A}$nnuity

These abbreviations are short hand notation for the equations in which the interest rate and the number of periods are substituted into the equation and solved. We will use this shorthand notation in the remainder of the solutions key.

3. Here we are finding the YTM of a semiannual coupon bond. The bond price equation is:

$$P = \$970 = \$43(PVIFA_{R\%,20}) + \$1,000(PVIF_{R\%,20})$$

Since we cannot solve the equation directly for R, using a spreadsheet, a financial calculator, or trial and error, we find:

$$R = 4.531\%$$

Since the coupon payments are semiannual, this is the semiannual interest rate. The YTM is the APR of the bond, so:

$$YTM = 2 \times 4.531\% = 9.06\%$$

4. The constant dividend growth model is:

$$P_t = D_t \times (1 + g) / (R - g)$$

So, the price of the stock today is:

$$P_0 = D_0 (1 + g) / (R - g) = \$1.40 (1.06) / (.12 - .06) = \$24.73$$

The dividend at year 4 is the dividend today times the FVIF for the growth rate in dividends and four years, so:

$$P_3 = D_3 (1 + g) / (R - g) = D_0 (1 + g)^4 / (R - g) = \$1.40 (1.06)^4 / (.12 - .06) = \$29.46$$

We can do the same thing to find the dividend in Year 16, which gives us the price in Year 15, so:

$$P_{15} = D_{15} (1 + g) / (R - g) = D_0 (1 + g)^{16} / (R - g) = \$1.40 (1.06)^{16} / (.12 - .06) = \$59.27$$

There is another feature of the constant dividend growth model: The stock price grows at the dividend growth rate. So, if we know the stock price today, we can find the future value for any time in the future we want to calculate the stock price. In this problem, we want to know the stock price in three years, and we have already calculated the stock price today. The stock price in three years will be:

$$P_3 = P_0(1 + g)^3 = \$24.73(1 + .06)^3 = \$29.46$$

And the stock price in 15 years will be:

$$P_{15} = P_0(1 + g)^{15} = \$24.73(1 + .06)^{15} = \$59.27$$

5. We need to find the required return of the stock. Using the constant growth model, we can solve the equation for R. Doing so, we find:

$$R = (D_1 / P_0) + g = (\$3.10 / \$48.00) + .05 = 11.46\%$$

6. Using the constant growth model, we find the price of the stock today is:

$$P_0 = D_1 / (R - g) = \$3.60 / (.13 - .045) = \$42.35$$

7. We know the stock has a required return of 12 percent, and the dividend and capital gains yield are equal, so:

Dividend yield = $1/2(.12) = .06$ = Capital gains yield

Now we know both the dividend yield and capital gains yield. The dividend is simply the stock price times the dividend yield, so:

$$D_1 = .06(\$70) = \$4.20$$

This is the dividend next year. The question asks for the dividend this year. Using the relationship between the dividend this year and the dividend next year:

$$D_1 = D_0(1 + g)$$

We can solve for the dividend that was just paid:

$$\$4.20 = D_0 (1 + .06)$$

$$D_0 = \$4.20 / 1.06 = \$3.96$$

8. The price of any financial instrument is the PV of the future cash flows. The future dividends of this stock are an annuity for eight years, so the price of the stock is the PVA, which will be:

$$P_0 = \$12.00(PVIFA_{10\%,8}) = \$64.02$$

B-104 SOLUTIONS

9. The growth rate of earnings is the return on equity times the retention ratio, so:

$g = \text{ROE} \times b$
$g = .14(.60)$
$g = .084$ or 8.40%

To find next year's earnings, we simply multiply the current earnings times one plus the growth rate, so:

Next year's earnings = Current earnings$(1 + g)$
Next year's earnings = $\$20,000,000(1 + .084)$
Next year's earnings = $\$21,680,000$

Intermediate

10. Here we are finding the YTM of semiannual coupon bonds for various maturity lengths. The bond price equation is:

$$P = C(\text{PVIFA}_{R\%,t}) + \$1,000(\text{PVIF}_{R\%,t})$$

Miller Corporation bond:
$P_0 = \$40(\text{PVIFA}_{3\%,26}) + \$1,000(\text{PVIF}_{3\%,26}) = \$1,178.77$
$P_1 = \$40(\text{PVIFA}_{3\%,24}) + \$1,000(\text{PVIF}_{3\%,24}) = \$1,169.36$
$P_3 = \$40(\text{PVIFA}_{3\%,20}) + \$1,000(\text{PVIF}_{3\%,20}) = \$1,148.77$
$P_8 = \$40(\text{PVIFA}_{3\%,10}) + \$1,000(\text{PVIF}_{3\%,10}) = \$1,085.30$
$P_{12} = \$40(\text{PVIFA}_{3\%,2}) + \$1,000(\text{PVIF}_{3\%,2}) = \$1,019.13$
$P_{13} = \$1,000$

Modigliani Company bond:
Y: $P_0 = \$30(\text{PVIFA}_{4\%,26}) + \$1,000(\text{PVIF}_{4\%,26}) = \$840.17$
$P_1 = \$30(\text{PVIFA}_{4\%,24}) + \$1,000(\text{PVIF}_{4\%,24}) = \$847.53$
$P_3 = \$30(\text{PVIFA}_{4\%,20}) + \$1,000(\text{PVIF}_{4\%,20}) = \$864.10$
$P_8 = \$30(\text{PVIFA}_{4\%,10}) + \$1,000(\text{PVIF}_{4\%,10}) = \$918.89$
$P_{12} = \$30(\text{PVIFA}_{4\%,2}) + \$1,000(\text{PVIF}_{4\%,2}) = \$981.14$
$P_{13} = \$1,000$

All else held equal, the premium over par value for a premium bond declines as maturity approaches, and the discount from par value for a discount bond declines as maturity approaches. This is called "pull to par." In both cases, the largest percentage price changes occur at the shortest maturity lengths.

Also, notice that the price of each bond when no time is left to maturity is the par value, even though the purchaser would receive the par value plus the coupon payment immediately. This is because we calculate the clean price of the bond.

11. The bond price equation for this bond is:

$P_0 = \$1,040 = \$42(\text{PVIFA}_{R\%,18}) + \$1,000(\text{PVIF}_{R\%,18})$

Using a spreadsheet, financial calculator, or trial and error we find:

$R = 3.887\%$

This is the semiannual interest rate, so the YTM is:

$\text{YTM} = 2 \times 3.887\% = 7.77\%$

The current yield is:

Current yield = Annual coupon payment / Price = \$84 / \$1,040 = 8.08%

The effective annual yield is the same as the EAR, so using the EAR equation from the previous chapter:

Effective annual yield $= (1 + 0.03887)^2 - 1 = 7.92\%$

12. The company should set the coupon rate on its new bonds equal to the required return. The required return can be observed in the market by finding the YTM on outstanding bonds of the company. So, the YTM on the bonds currently sold in the market is:

$P = \$1,095 = \$40(\text{PVIFA}_{R\%,40}) + \$1,000(\text{PVIF}_{R\%,40})$

Using a spreadsheet, financial calculator, or trial and error we find:

$R = 3.55\%$

This is the semiannual interest rate, so the YTM is:

$\text{YTM} = 2 \times 3.55\% = 7.10\%$

13. This stock has a constant growth rate of dividends, but the required return changes twice. To find the value of the stock today, we will begin by finding the price of the stock at Year 6, when both the dividend growth rate and the required return are stable forever. The price of the stock in Year 6 will be the dividend in Year 7, divided by the required return minus the growth rate in dividends. So:

$P_6 = D_6(1 + g) / (R - g) = D_0(1 + g)^7 / (R - g) = \$3.00(1.05)^7 / (.11 - .05) = \$70.36$

Now we can find the price of the stock in Year 3. We need to find the price here since the required return changes at that time. The price of the stock in Year 3 is the PV of the dividends in Years 4, 5, and 6, plus the PV of the stock price in Year 6. The price of the stock in Year 3 is:

$P_3 = \$3.00(1.05)^4 / 1.14 + \$3.00(1.05)^5 / 1.14^2 + \$3.00(1.05)^6 / 1.14^3 + \$70.36 / 1.14^3$
$P_3 = \$56.35$

B-106 SOLUTIONS

Finally, we can find the price of the stock today. The price today will be the PV of the dividends in Years 1, 2, and 3, plus the PV of the stock in Year 3. The price of the stock today is:

$$P_0 = \$3.00(1.05) / 1.16 + \$3.00(1.05)^2 / (1.16)^2 + \$3.00(1.05)^3 / (1.16)^3 + \$56.35 / (1.16)^3$$
$$= \$43.50$$

14. Here we have a stock that pays no dividends for 10 years. Once the stock begins paying dividends, it will have a constant growth rate of dividends. We can use the constant growth model at that point. It is important to remember that general form of the constant dividend growth formula is:

$$P_t = [D_t \times (1 + g)] / (R - g)$$

This means that since we will use the dividend in Year 10, we will be finding the stock price in Year 9. The dividend growth model is similar to the PVA and the PV of a perpetuity: The equation gives you the PV one period before the first payment. So, the price of the stock in Year 9 will be:

$$P_9 = D_{10} / (R - g) = \$8.00 / (.13 - .06) = \$114.29$$

The price of the stock today is simply the PV of the stock price in the future. We simply discount the future stock price at the required return. The price of the stock today will be:

$$P_0 = \$114.29 / 1.13^9 = \$38.04$$

15. The price of a stock is the PV of the future dividends. This stock is paying four dividends, so the price of the stock is the PV of these dividends using the required return. The price of the stock is:

$$P_0 = \$12 / 1.11 + \$15 / 1.11^2 + \$18 / 1.11^3 + \$21 / 1.11^4 = \$49.98$$

16. With supernormal dividends, we find the price of the stock when the dividends level off at a constant growth rate, and then find the PV of the future stock price, plus the PV of all dividends during the supernormal growth period. The stock begins constant growth in Year 5, so we can find the price of the stock in Year 4, one year before the constant dividend growth begins, as:

$$P_4 = D_4 (1 + g) / (R - g) = \$2.00(1.05) / (.13 - .05) = \$26.25$$

The price of the stock today is the PV of the first four dividends, plus the PV of the Year 4 stock price. So, the price of the stock today will be:

$$P_0 = \$8.00 / 1.13 + \$6.00 / 1.13^2 + \$3.00 / 1.13^3 + \$2.00 / 1.13^4 + \$26.25 / 1.13^4 = \$31.18$$

17. With supernormal dividends, we find the price of the stock when the dividends level off at a constant growth rate, and then find the PV of the future stock price, plus the PV of all dividends during the supernormal growth period. The stock begins constant growth in Year 4, so we can find the price of the stock in Year 3, one year before the constant dividend growth begins as:

$$P_3 = D_3 (1 + g) / (R - g) = D_0 (1 + g_1)^3 (1 + g_2) / (R - g_2) = \$2.80(1.25)^3(1.07) / (.13 - .07) = \$97.53$$

The price of the stock today is the PV of the first three dividends, plus the PV of the Year 3 stock price. The price of the stock today will be:

$P_0 = 2.80(1.25) / 1.13 + \$2.80(1.25)^2 / 1.13^2 + \$2.80(1.25)^3 / 1.13^3 + \$97.53 / 1.13^3$
$P_0 = \$77.90$

18. Here we need to find the dividend next year for a stock experiencing supernormal growth. We know the stock price, the dividend growth rates, and the required return, but not the dividend. First, we need to realize that the dividend in Year 3 is the current dividend times the FVIF. The dividend in Year 3 will be:

$D_3 = D_0 (1.30)^3$

And the dividend in Year 4 will be the dividend in Year 3 times one plus the growth rate, or:

$D_4 = D_0 (1.30)^3 (1.18)$

The stock begins constant growth in Year 4, so we can find the price of the stock in Year 4 as the dividend in Year 5, divided by the required return minus the growth rate. The equation for the price of the stock in Year 4 is:

$P_4 = D_4 (1 + g) / (R - g)$

Now we can substitute the previous dividend in Year 4 into this equation as follows:

$P_4 = D_0 (1 + g_1)^3 (1 + g_2) (1 + g_3) / (R - g_3)$

$P_4 = D_0 (1.30)^3 (1.18) (1.08) / (.14 - .08) = 46.66D_0$

When we solve this equation, we find that the stock price in Year 4 is 46.66 times as large as the dividend today. Now we need to find the equation for the stock price today. The stock price today is the PV of the dividends in Years 1, 2, 3, and 4, plus the PV of the Year 4 price. So:

$P_0 = D_0(1.30)/1.14 + D_0(1.30)^2/1.14^2 + D_0(1.30)^3/1.14^3 + D_0(1.30)^3(1.18)/1.14^4 + 46.66D_0/1.14^4$

We can factor out D_0 in the equation, and combine the last two terms. Doing so, we get:

$P_0 = \$70.00 = D_0\{1.30/1.14 + 1.30^2/1.14^2 + 1.30^3/1.14^3 + [(1.30)^3(1.18) + 46.66] / 1.14^4\}$

Reducing the equation even further by solving all of the terms in the braces, we get:

$\$70 = \$33.04D_0$

$D_0 = \$70.00 / \$33.04 = \$2.12$

This is the dividend today, so the projected dividend for the next year will be:

$D_1 = \$2.12(1.30) = \$2.75$

B-108 SOLUTIONS

19. We are given the stock price, the dividend growth rate, and the required return, and are asked to find the dividend. Using the constant dividend growth model, we get:

$$P_0 = \$50 = D_0 \, (1 + g) / (R - g)$$

Solving this equation for the dividend gives us:

$$D_0 = \$50(.14 - .08) / (1.08) = \$2.78$$

20. The price of a share of preferred stock is the dividend payment divided by the required return. We know the dividend payment in Year 6, so we can find the price of the stock in Year 5, one year before the first dividend payment. Doing so, we get:

$$P_5 = \$9.00 / .07 = \$128.57$$

The price of the stock today is the PV of the stock price in the future, so the price today will be:

$$P_0 = \$128.57 / (1.07)^5 = \$91.67$$

21. If the company's earnings are declining at a constant rate, the dividends will decline at the same rate since the dividends are assumed to be a constant percentage of income. The dividend next year will be less than this year's dividend, so

$$P_0 = D_0 \, (1 + g) / (R - g) = \$5.00(1 - .10) / [(.14 - (-.10)] = \$18.75$$

22. Here we have a stock paying a constant dividend for a fixed period, and an increasing dividend thereafter. We need to find the present value of the two different cash flows using the appropriate quarterly interest rate. The constant dividend is an annuity, so the present value of these dividends is:

$$PVA = C(PVIFA_{R,t})$$
$$PVA = \$1(PVIFA_{2.5\%,12})$$
$$PVA = \$10.26$$

Now we can find the present value of the dividends beyond the constant dividend phase. Using the present value of a growing annuity equation, we find:

$$P_{12} = D_{13} / (R - g)$$
$$P_{12} = \$1(1 + .005) / (.025 - .005)$$
$$P_{12} = \$50.25$$

This is the price of the stock immediately after it has paid the last constant dividend. So, the present value of the future price is:

$$PV = \$50.25 / (1 + .025)^{12}$$
$$PV = \$37.36$$

The price today is the sum of the present value of the two cash flows, so:

$$P_0 = \$10.26 + 37.36$$
$$P_0 = \$47.62$$

23. We can find the price of the stock in Year 4 when it begins a constant increase in dividends using the growing perpetuity equation. So, the price of the stock in Year 4, immediately after the dividend payment, is:

$P_4 = D_4(1 + g) / (R - g)$
$P_4 = \$2(1 + .06) / (.16 - .06)$
$P_4 = \$21.20$

The stock price today is the sum of the present value of the two fixed dividends plus the present value of the future price, so:

$P_0 = \$2 / (1 + .16)^3 + \$2 / (1 + .16)^4 + \$21.20 / (1 + .16)^4$
$P_0 = \$14.09$

24. Here we need to find the dividend next year for a stock with nonconstant growth. We know the stock price, the dividend growth rates, and the required return, but not the dividend. First, we need to realize that the dividend in Year 3 is the constant dividend times the FVIF. The dividend in Year 3 will be:

$D_3 = D(1.04)$

The equation for the stock price will be the present value of the constant dividends, plus the present value of the future stock price, or:

$P_0 = D / 1.12 + D / 1.12^2 + D(1.04)/(.12 - .04)/1.12^2$
$\$30 = D / 1.12 + D / 1.12^2 + D(1.04)/(.12 - .04)/1.12^2$

We can factor out D_0 in the equation, and combine the last two terms. Doing so, we get:

$\$30 = D\{1/1.12 + 1/1.12^2 + [(1.04)/(.12 - .04)] / 1.12^2\}$

Reducing the equation even further by solving all of the terms in the braces, we get:

$\$30 = D(12.0536)$

$D = \$30 / 12.0536 = \$2.49$

25. The required return of a stock consists of two components, the capital gains yield and the dividend yield. In the constant dividend growth model (growing perpetuity equation), the capital gains yield is the same as the dividend growth rate, or algebraically:

$R = D_1/P_0 + g$

B-110 SOLUTIONS

We can find the dividend growth rate by the growth rate equation, or:

$g = ROE \times b$
$g = .11 \times .75$
$g = .0825$ or 8.25%

This is also the growth rate in dividends. To find the current dividend, we can use the information provided about the net income, shares outstanding, and payout ratio. The total dividends paid is the net income times the payout ratio. To find the dividend per share, we can divide the total dividends paid by the number of shares outstanding. So:

Dividend per share = (Net income × Payout ratio) / Shares outstanding
Dividend per share = ($10,000,000 × .25) / 1,250,000
Dividend per share = $2.00

Now we can use the initial equation for the required return. We must remember that the equation uses the dividend in one year, so:

$R = D_1/P_0 + g$
$R = \$2(1 + .0825)/\$40 + .0825$
$R = .1366$ or 13.66%

26. First, we need to find the annual dividend growth rate over the past four years. To do this, we can use the future value of a lump sum equation, and solve for the interest rate. Doing so, we find the dividend growth rate over the past four years was:

$FV = PV(1 + R)^t$
$\$1.66 = \$0.90(1 + R)^4$
$R = (\$1.66 / \$0.90)^{1/4} - 1$
$R = .1654$ or 16.54%

We know the dividend will grow at this rate for five years before slowing to a constant rate indefinitely. So, the dividend amount in seven years will be:

$D_7 = D_0(1 + g_1)^5(1 + g_2)^2$
$D_7 = \$1.66(1 + .1654)^5(1 + .08)^2$
$D_7 = \$4.16$

27. *a.* We can find the price of the all the outstanding company stock by using the dividends the same way we would value an individual share. Since earnings are equal to dividends, and there is no growth, the value of the company's stock today is the present value of a perpetuity, so:

P = D / R
P = $800,000 / .15
P = $5,333,333.33

The price-earnings ratio is the stock price divided by the current earnings, so the price-earnings ratio of each company with no growth is:

P/E = Price / Earnings
P/E = \$5,333,333.33 / \$800,000
P/E = 6.67 times

b. Since the earnings have increased, the price of the stock will increase. The new price of the all the outstanding company stock is:

P = D / R
P = (\$800,000 + 100,000) / .15
P = \$6,000,000.00

The price-earnings ratio is the stock price divided by the current earnings, so the price-earnings with the increased earnings is:

P/E = Price / Earnings
P/E = \$6,000,000 / \$800,000
P/E = 7.50 times

c. Since the earnings have increased, the price of the stock will increase. The new price of the all the outstanding company stock is:

P = D / R
P = (\$800,000 + 200,000) / .15
P = \$6,666,666.67

The price-earnings ratio is the stock price divided by the current earnings, so the price-earnings with the increased earnings is:

P/E = Price / Earnings
P/E = \$6,666,666.67 / \$800,000
P/E = 8.33 times

28. a. If the company does not make any new investments, the stock price will be the present value of the constant perpetual dividends. In this case, all earnings are paid dividends, so, applying the perpetuity equation, we get:

P = Dividend / R
P = \$7 / .12
P = \$58.33

b. The investment is a one-time investment that creates an increase in EPS for two years. To calculate the new stock price, we need the cash cow price plus the NPVGO. In this case, the NPVGO is simply the present value of the investment plus the present value of the increases in EPS. SO, the NPVGO will be:

$$NPVGO = C_1 / (1 + R) + C_2 / (1 + R)^2 + C_3 / (1 + R)^3$$
$$NPVGO = -\$1.75 / 1.12 + \$1.90 / 1.12^2 + \$2.10 / 1.12^3$$
$$NPVGO = \$1.45$$

Ross−Westerfield−Jaffe:
Corporate Finance, Eighth
Edition

II. Valuation and Capital
Budgeting

Answers for Chapter 5

© The McGraw−Hill
Companies, 2008

139

B-112 SOLUTIONS

So, the price of the stock if the company undertakes the investment opportunity will be:

P = $58.33 + 1.45
P = $59.78

    c.   After the project is over, and the earnings increase no longer exists, the price of the stock will revert back to $58.33, the value of the company as a cash cow.

29. *a.*   The price of the stock is the present value of the dividends. Since earnings are equal to dividends, we can find the present value of the earnings to calculate the stock price. Also, since we are excluding taxes, the earnings will be the revenues minus the costs. We simply need to find the present value of all future earnings to find the price of the stock. The present value of the revenues is:

$PV_{Revenue} = C_1 / (R - g)$
$PV_{Revenue} = \$3,000,000(1 + .05) / (.15 - .05)$
$PV_{Revenue} = \$31,500,000$

And the present value of the costs will be:

$PV_{Costs} = C_1 / (R - g)$
$PV_{Costs} = \$1,500,000(1 + .05) / (.15 - .05)$
$PV_{Costs} = \$15,750,000$

So, the present value of the company's earnings and dividends will be:

$PV_{Dividends} = \$31,500,000 - 15,750,000$
$PV_{Dividends} = \$15,750,000$

Note that since revenues and costs increase at the same rate, we could have found the present value of future dividends as the present value of current dividends. Doing so, we find:

$D_0 = Revenue_0 - Costs_0$
$D_0 = \$3,000,000 - 1,500,000$
$D_0 = \$1,500,000$

Now, applying the growing perpetuity equation, we find:

$PV_{Dividends} = C_1 / (R - g)$
$PV_{Dividends} = \$1,500,000(1 + .05) / (.15 - .05)$
$PV_{Dividends} = \$15,750,000$

This is the same answer we found previously. The price per share of stock is the total value of the company's stock divided by the shares outstanding, or:

P = Value of all stock / Shares outstanding
P = $15,750,000 / 1,000,000
P = $15.75

b. The value of a share of stock in a company is the present value of its current operations, plus the present value of growth opportunities. To find the present value of the growth opportunities, we need to discount the cash outlay in Year 1 back to the present, and find the value today of the increase in earnings. The increase in earnings is a perpetuity, which we must discount back to today. So, the value of the growth opportunity is:

$$NPVGO = C_0 + C_1 / (1 + R) + (C_2 / R) / (1 + R)$$
$$NPVGO = -\$15,000,000 - \$5,000,000 / (1 + .15) + (\$6,000,000 / .15) / (1 + .15)$$
$$NPVGO = \$15,434,782.61$$

To find the value of the growth opportunity on a per share basis, we must divide this amount by the number of shares outstanding, which gives us:

$$NPVGO_{Per\ share} = \$15,434,782.61 / \$1,000,000$$
$$NPVGO_{Per\ share} = \$15.43$$

The stock price will increase by $15.43 per share. The new stock price will be:

New stock price = $15.75 + 15.43
New stock price = $31.18

30. a. If the company continues its current operations, it will not grow, so we can value the company as a cash cow. The total value of the company as a cash cow is the present value of the future earnings, which are a perpetuity, so:

Cash cow value of company = C / R
Cash cow value of company = $110,000,000 / .15
Cash cow value of company = $733,333,333.33

The value per share is the total value of the company divided by the shares outstanding, so:

Share price = $733,333,333.33 / 20,000,000
Share price = $36.67

b. To find the value of the investment, we need to find the NPV of the growth opportunities. The initial cash flow occurs today, so it does not need to be discounted. The earnings growth is a perpetuity. Using the present value of a perpetuity equation will give us the value of the earnings growth one period from today, so we need to discount this back to today. The NPVGO of the investment opportunity is:

$$NPVGO = C_0 + C_1 + (C_2 / R) / (1 + R)$$
$$NPVGO = -\$12,000,000 - 7,000,000 + (\$10,000,000 / .15) / (1 + .15)$$
$$NPVGO = \$39,884,057.97$$

B-114 SOLUTIONS

c. The price of a share of stock is the cash cow value plus the NPVGO. We have already calculated the NPVGO for the entire project, so we need to find the NPVGO on a per share basis. The NPVGO on a per share basis is the NPVGO of the project divided by the shares outstanding, which is:

NPVGO per share = $39,884,057.97 / 20,000,000
NPVGO per share = $1.99

This means the per share stock price if the company undertakes the project is:

Share price = Cash cow price + NPVGO per share
Share price = $36.67 + 1.99
Share price = $38.66

31. *a.* If the company does not make any new investments, the stock price will be the present value of the constant perpetual dividends. In this case, all earnings are paid as dividends, so, applying the perpetuity equation, we get:

P = Dividend / R
P = $5 / .14
P = $35.71

b. The investment occurs every year in the growth opportunity, so the opportunity is a growing perpetuity. So, we first need to find the growth rate. The growth rate is:

g = Retention Ratio × Return on Retained Earnings
g = 0.25 × 0.40
g = 0.10 or 10%

Next, we need to calculate the NPV of the investment. During year 3, twenty-five percent of the earnings will be reinvested. Therefore, $1.25 is invested ($5 × .25). One year later, the shareholders receive a 40 percent return on the investment, or $0.50 ($1.25 × .40), in perpetuity. The perpetuity formula values that stream as of year 3. Since the investment opportunity will continue indefinitely and grows at 10 percent, apply the growing perpetuity formula to calculate the NPV of the investment as of year 2. Discount that value back two years to today.

NPVGO = [(Investment + Return / R) / (R − g)] / (1 + R)^2
NPVGO = [(−$1.25 + $0.50 / .14) / (0.14 − 0.1)] / (1.14)^2
NPVGO = $44.66

The value of the stock is the PV of the firm without making the investment plus the NPV of the investment, or:

P = PV(EPS) + NPVGO
P = $35.71 + $44.66
P = $80.37

Challenge

32. To find the capital gains yield and the current yield, we need to find the price of the bond. The current price of Bond P and the price of Bond P in one year is:

P: $P_0 = \$100(\text{PVIFA}_{8\%,5}) + \$1,000(\text{PVIF}_{8\%,5}) = \$1,079.85$

$P_1 = \$100(\text{PVIFA}_{8\%,4}) + \$1,000(\text{PVIF}_{8\%,4}) = \$1,066.24$

Current yield = $\$100 / \$1,079.85 = 9.26\%$

The capital gains yield is:

Capital gains yield = (New price – Original price) / Original price

Capital gains yield = $(\$1,066.24 - 1,079.85) / \$1,079.85 = -1.26\%$

The current price of Bond D and the price of Bond D in one year is:

D: $P_0 = \$60(\text{PVIFA}_{8\%,5}) + \$1,000(\text{PVIF}_{8\%,5}) = \$920.15$

$P_1 = \$60(\text{PVIFA}_{8\%,4}) + \$1,000(\text{PVIF}_{8\%,4}) = \$933.76$

Current yield = $\$60 / \$920.15 = 6.52\%$

Capital gains yield = $(\$933.76 - 920.15) / \$920.15 = +1.48\%$

All else held constant, premium bonds pay high current income while having price depreciation as maturity nears; discount bonds do not pay high current income but have price appreciation as maturity nears. For either bond, the total return is still 8%, but this return is distributed differently between current income and capital gains.

33. *a.* The rate of return you expect to earn if you purchase a bond and hold it until maturity is the YTM. The bond price equation for this bond is:

$P_0 = \$1,150 = \$80(\text{PVIFA}_{R\%,10}) + \$1,000(\text{PVIF}_{R\%,10})$

Using a spreadsheet, financial calculator, or trial and error we find:

$R = \text{YTM} = 5.97\%$

b. To find our HPY, we need to find the price of the bond in two years. The price of the bond in two years, at the new interest rate, will be:

$P_2 = \$80(\text{PVIFA}_{4.97\%,8}) + \$1,000(\text{PVIF}_{4.97\%,8}) = \$1,196.41$

B-116 SOLUTIONS

To calculate the HPY, we need to find the interest rate that equates the price we paid for the bond with the cash flows we received. The cash flows we received were $80 each year for two years, and the price of the bond when we sold it. The equation to find our HPY is:

$$P_0 = \$1,150 = \$80(PVIFA_{R\%,2}) + \$1,196.41(PVIF_{R\%,2})$$

Solving for R, we get:

$$R = HPY = 8.89\%$$

The realized HPY is greater than the expected YTM when the bond was bought because interest rates dropped by 1 percent; bond prices rise when yields fall.

34. The price of any bond (or financial instrument) is the PV of the future cash flows. Even though Bond M makes different coupons payments, to find the price of the bond, we just find the PV of the cash flows. The PV of the cash flows for Bond M is:

$$P_M = \$1,200(PVIFA_{5\%,16})(PVIF_{5\%,12}) + \$1,500(PVIFA_{5\%,12})(PVIF_{5\%,28}) + \$20,000(PVIF_{5\%,40})$$
$$P_M = \$13,474.20$$

Notice that for the coupon payments of $1,500, we found the PVA for the coupon payments, and then discounted the lump sum back to today.

Bond N is a zero coupon bond with a $20,000 par value; therefore, the price of the bond is the PV of the par, or:

$$P_N = \$20,000(PVIF_{5\%,40}) = \$2,840.91$$

35. We are asked to find the dividend yield and capital gains yield for each of the stocks. All of the stocks have a 15 percent required return, which is the sum of the dividend yield and the capital gains yield. To find the components of the total return, we need to find the stock price for each stock. Using this stock price and the dividend, we can calculate the dividend yield. The capital gains yield for the stock will be the total return (required return) minus the dividend yield.

W: $P_0 = D_0(1 + g) / (R - g) = \$4.50(1.10)/(.15 - .10) = \$99.00$

Dividend yield $= D_1/P_0 = 4.50(1.10)/99.00 = 5\%$

Capital gains yield $= .15 - .05 = 10\%$

X: $P_0 = D_0(1 + g) / (R - g) = \$4.50/(.15 - 0) = \$30.00$

Dividend yield $= D_1/P_0 = 4.50/30.00 = 15\%$

Capital gains yield $= .15 - .15 = 0\%$

Y: $P_0 = D_0(1 + g) / (R - g) = \$4.50(1 - .05)/(.15 + .05) = \$21.38$

Dividend yield $= D_1/P_0 = 4.50(0.95)/21.38 = 20\%$

Capital gains yield $= .15 - .20 = -5\%$

Z: $P_2 = D_2(1 + g) / (R - g) = D_0(1 + g_1)^2(1 + g_2)/(R - g) = \$4.50(1.20)^2(1.12)/(.15 - .12) = \$241.92$

$P_0 = \$4.50\ (1.20) / (1.15) + \$4.50\ (1.20)^2 / (1.15)^2 + \$241.92 / (1.15)^2 = \$192.52$

Dividend yield $= D_1/P_0 = \$4.50(1.20)/\$192.52 = 2.8\%$

Capital gains yield $= .15 - .028 = 12.2\%$

In all cases, the required return is 15%, but the return is distributed differently between current income and capital gains. High-growth stocks have an appreciable capital gains component but a relatively small current income yield; conversely, mature, negative-growth stocks provide a high current income but also price depreciation over time.

36. *a.* Using the constant growth model, the price of the stock paying annual dividends will be:

$P_0 = D_0(1 + g) / (R - g) = \$3.00(1.06)/(.14 - .06) = \$39.75$

b. If the company pays quarterly dividends instead of annual dividends, the quarterly dividend will be one-fourth of annual dividend, or:

Quarterly dividend: $\$3.00(1.06)/4 = \$0.795$

To find the equivalent annual dividend, we must assume that the quarterly dividends are reinvested at the required return. We can then use this interest rate to find the equivalent annual dividend. In other words, when we receive the quarterly dividend, we reinvest it at the required return on the stock. So, the effective quarterly rate is:

Effective quarterly rate: $1.14^{.25} - 1 = .0333$

The effective annual dividend will be the FVA of the quarterly dividend payments at the effective quarterly required return. In this case, the effective annual dividend will be:

Effective $D_1 = \$0.795(FVIFA_{3.33\%,4}) = \$3.34$

Now, we can use the constant growth model to find the current stock price as:

$P_0 = \$3.34/(.14 - .06) = \$41.78$

Note that we can not simply find the quarterly effective required return and growth rate to find the value of the stock. This would assume the dividends increased each quarter, not each year.

37. *a.* If the company does not make any new investments, the stock price will be the present value of the constant perpetual dividends. In this case, all earnings are paid dividends, so, applying the perpetuity equation, we get:

P = Dividend / R
P = \$6 / .14
P = \$42.86

B-118 SOLUTIONS

  b. The investment occurs every year in the growth opportunity, so the opportunity is a growing perpetuity. So, we first need to find the growth rate. The growth rate is:

  g = Retention Ratio × Return on Retained Earnings
  g = 0.30 × 0.12
  g = 0.036 or 3.60%

  Next, we need to calculate the NPV of the investment. During year 3, 30 percent of the earnings will be reinvested. Therefore, $1.80 is invested ($6 × .30). One year later, the shareholders receive a 12 percent return on the investment, or $0.216 ($1.80 × .12), in perpetuity. The perpetuity formula values that stream as of year 3. Since the investment opportunity will continue indefinitely and grows at 3.6 percent, apply the growing perpetuity formula to calculate the NPV of the investment as of year 2. Discount that value back two years to today.

  $$NPVGO = [(\text{Investment} + \text{Return} / R) / (R - g)] / (1 + R)^2$$
  $$NPVGO = [(-\$1.80 + \$0.216 / .14) / (0.14 - 0.036)] / (1.14)^2$$
  $$NPVGO = -\$1.90$$

  The value of the stock is the PV of the firm without making the investment plus the NPV of the investment, or:

  $$P = PV(EPS) + NPVGO$$
  $$P = \$42.86 - 1.90$$
  $$P = \$40.95$$

  c. Zero percent! There is no retention ratio which would make the project profitable for the company. If the company retains more earnings, the growth rate of the earnings on the investment will increase, but the project will still not be profitable. Since the return of the project is less than the required return on the company stock, the project is never worthwhile. In fact, the more the company retains and invests in the project, the less valuable the stock becomes.

38. Here we have a stock with supernormal growth but the dividend growth changes every year for the first four years. We can find the price of the stock in Year 3 since the dividend growth rate is constant after the third dividend. The price of the stock in Year 3 will be the dividend in Year 4, divided by the required return minus the constant dividend growth rate. So, the price in Year 3 will be:

$$P_3 = \$3.50(1.20)(1.15)(1.10)(1.05) / (.13 - .05) = \$69.73$$

The price of the stock today will be the PV of the first three dividends, plus the PV of the stock price in Year 3, so:

$$P_0 = \$3.50(1.20)/(1.13) + \$3.50(1.20)(1.15)/1.13^2 + \$3.50(1.20)(1.15)(1.10)/1.13^3 + \$69.73/1.13^3$$
$$P_0 = \$59.51$$

39. Here we want to find the required return that makes the PV of the dividends equal to the current stock price. The equation for the stock price is:

$$P = \$3.50(1.20)/(1 + R) + \$3.50(1.20)(1.15)/(1 + R)^2 + \$3.50(1.20)(1.15)(1.10)/(1 + R)^3$$
$$+ [\$3.50(1.20)(1.15)(1.10)(1.05)/(R - .05)]/(1 + R)^3 = \$98.65$$

We need to find the roots of this equation. Using spreadsheet, trial and error, or a calculator with a root solving function, we find that:

$R = 9.85\%$

40. In this problem, growth is occurring from two different sources: The learning curve and the new project. We need to separately compute the value from the two difference sources. First, we will compute the value from the learning curve, which will increase at 5 percent. All earnings are paid out as dividends, so we find the earnings per share are:

EPS = Earnings/total number of outstanding shares
EPS = ($10,000,000 × 1.05) / 10,000,000
EPS = $1.05

From the NPVGO mode:

$P = E/(k - g) + NPVGO$
$P = \$1.05/(0.10 - 0.05) + NPVGO$
$P = \$21 + NPVGO$

Now we can compute the NPVGO of the new project to be launched two years from now. The earnings per share two years from now will be:

$EPS_2 = \$1.00(1 + .05)^2$
$EPS_2 = \$1.1025$

Therefore, the initial investment in the new project will be:

Initial investment = .20($1.1025)
Initial investment = $0.22

The earnings per share of the new project is a perpetuity, with an annual cash flow of:

Increased EPS from project = $5,000,000 / 10,000,000 shares
Increased EPS from project = $0.50

So, the value of all future earnings in year 2, one year before the company realizes the earnings, is:

PV = $0.50 / .10
PV = $5.00

B-120 SOLUTIONS

Now, we can find the NPVGO per share of the investment opportunity in year 2, which will be:

$NPVGO_2 = -\$0.22 + 5.00$
$NPVGO_2 = \$4.78$

The value of the NPVGO today will be:

$NPVGO = \$4.78 / (1 + .10)^2$
$NPVGO = \$3.95$

Plugging in the NPVGO model we get;

$P = \$21 + 3.95$
$P = \$24.95$

Note that you could also value the company and the project with the values given, and then divide the final answer by the shares outstanding. The final answer would be the same.

CHAPTER 5, *APPENDIX*
THE TERM STRUCTURE OF INTEREST RATES, SPOT RATES, AND YIELD TO MATURITY

Solutions to Questions and Problems

NOTE: All end-of-chapter problems were solved using a spreadsheet. Many problems require multiple steps. Due to space and readability constraints, when these intermediate steps are included in this solutions manual, rounding may appear to have occurred. However, the final answer for each problem is found without rounding during any step in the problem.

1. *a.* The present value of any coupon bond is the present value of its coupon payments and face value. Match each cash flow with the appropriate spot rate. For the cash flow that occurs at the end of the first year, use the one-year spot rate. For the cash flow that occurs at the end of the second year, use the two-year spot rate. Doing so, we find the price of the bond is:

$$P = C_1 / (1 + r_1) + (C_2 + F) / (1 + r_2)^2$$
$$P = \$60 / (1.08) + (\$60 + 1,000) / (1.10)^2$$
$$P = \$931.59$$

   b. The yield to the maturity is the discount rate, y, which sets the cash flows equal to the price of the bond. So, the YTM is:

$$P = C_1 / (1 + y) + (C_2 + F) / (1 + y)^2$$
$$\$931.59 = \$60 / (1 + y) + (\$60 + 1,000) / (1 + y)^2$$
$$y = .0994 \text{ or } 9.94\%$$

2. The present value of any coupon bond is the present value of its coupon payments and face value. Match each cash flow with the appropriate spot rate.

$$P = C_1 / (1 + r_1) + (C_2 + F) / (1 + r_2)^2$$
$$P = \$50 / (1.11) + (\$50 + 1,000) / (1.08)^2$$
$$P = \$945.25$$

3. Apply the forward rate formula to calculate the one-year rate over the second year.

$$(1 + r_1)(1 + f_2) = (1 + r_2)^2$$
$$(1.07)(1 + f_2) = (1.085)^2$$
$$f_2 = .1002 \text{ or } 10.02\%$$

B-122 SOLUTIONS

4. *a.* We apply the forward rate formula to calculate the one-year forward rate over the second year. Doing so, we find:

$$(1 + r_1)(1 + f_2) = (1 + r_2)^2$$
$$(1.04)(1 + f_2) = (1.055)^2$$
$$f_2 = .0702 \text{ or } 7.02\%$$

b. We apply the forward rate formula to calculate the one-year forward rate over the third year. Doing so, we find:

$$(1 + r_2)^2(1 + f_3) = (1 + r_3)^3$$
$$(1.055)^2(1 + f_3) = (1.065)^3$$
$$f_3 = .0853 \text{ or } 8.53\%$$

5. The spot rate for year 1 is the same as forward rate for year 1, or 4.5 percent. To find the two year spot rate, we can use the forward rate equation:

$$(1 + r_1)(1 + f_2) = (1 + r_2)^2$$
$$r_2 = [(1 + r_1)(1 + f_2)]^{1/2} - 1$$
$$r_2 = [(1.045)(1.06)]^{1/2} - 1$$
$$r_2 = .0525 \text{ or } 5.25\%$$

6. Based upon the expectation hypotheses, strategy 1 and strategy 2 will be in equilibrium at:

$$(1 + f_1)(1 + f_2) = (1 + r_2)^2$$

That is, if the expected spot rate for 2 years is equal to the product of successive one year forward rates. If the spot rate in year 2 is higher than implied by f_2 then strategy 1 is best. If the spot rate in year 2 is lower than implied by f_2, strategy 1 is best.

CHAPTER 6

Net Present Value and Other Investment Rules

In 2005, the automobile market in North America faced chronic overcapacity. By some estimates, General Motors may have had as many as 15 factories more than it needed. But not all automobile manufacturers faced this problem. For example, Toyota Motors announced plans for its seventh North American assembly plant, and then began a search for a site to accommodate its eighth North American plant. Each plant represents an investment of $1 billion or more. For example, Toyota's truck factory in southern Indiana was built at a cost of $2.5 billion.

Toyota's new plants are an example of a capital budgeting decision. Decisions such as these, with a price tag of over $1 billion each, are obviously major undertakings, and the risks and rewards must be carefully weighed. In this chapter, we discuss the basic tools used in making such decisions.

In Chapter 1, we saw that increasing the value of the stock in a company is the goal of financial management. Thus, what we need to know is how to tell whether a particular investment will achieve that. This chapter considers a variety of techniques that are used in practice for this purpose. More important, it shows how many of these techniques can be misleading, and it explains why the net present value approach is the right one.

6.1 Why Use Net Present Value?

This chapter, as well as the next two, focuses on *capital budgeting*, the decision-making process for accepting or rejecting projects. This chapter develops the basic capital budgeting methods, leaving much of the practical application to subsequent chapters. But we don't have to develop these methods from scratch. In Chapter 4, we pointed out that a dollar received in the future is worth less than a dollar received today. The reason, of course, is that today's dollar can be reinvested, yielding a greater amount in the future. And we showed in Chapter 4 that the exact worth of a dollar to be received in the future is its present value. Furthermore, Section 4.1 suggested calculating the *net present value* of any project. That is, the section suggested calculating the difference between the sum of the present values of the project's future cash flows and the initial cost of the project.

Find out more about capital budgeting for small businesses at www. missouribusiness.net.

The net present value (NPV) method is the first one to be considered in this chapter. We begin by reviewing the approach with a simple example. Then, we ask why the method leads to good decisions.

EXAMPLE 6.1

Net Present Value   The Alpha Corporation is considering investing in a riskless project costing $100. The project receives $107 in one year and has no other cash flows. The discount rate is 6 percent.

The NPV of the project can easily be calculated as

$$\$.94 = -\$100 + \frac{\$107}{1.06} \tag{6.1}$$

From Chapter 4, we know that the project should be accepted because its NPV is positive. Had the NPV of the project been negative, as would have been the case with an interest rate greater than 7 percent, the project should be rejected.

The basic investment rule can be generalized thus:

> Accept a project if the NPV is greater than zero.
>
> Reject a project if NPV is less than zero.

We refer to this as the **NPV rule**.

Why does the NPV rule lead to good decisions? Consider the following two strategies available to the managers of Alpha Corporation:

1. Use $100 of corporate cash to invest in the project. The $107 will be paid as a dividend in one year.

2. Forgo the project and pay the $100 of corporate cash as a dividend today.

If strategy 2 is employed, the stockholder might deposit the dividend in a bank for one year. With an interest rate of 6 percent, strategy 2 would produce cash of $106 (= $100 × 1.06) at the end of the year. The stockholder would prefer strategy 1 because strategy 2 produces less than $107 at the end of the year.

Our basic point is this: Accepting positive NPV projects benefits the stockholders.

How do we interpret the exact NPV of $0.94? This is the increase in the value of the firm from the project. For example, imagine that the firm today has productive assets worth $V and has $100 of cash. If the firm forgoes the project, the value of the firm today would simply be:

$$\$V + \$100$$

If the firm accepts the project, the firm will receive $107 in one year but will have no cash today. Thus, the firm's value today would be:

$$\$V + \frac{\$107}{1.06}$$

The difference between these equations is just $0.94, the present value of Equation 6.1. Thus: The value of the firm rises by the NPV of the project.

Note that the value of the firm is merely the sum of the values of the different projects, divisions, or other entities within the firm. This property, called **value additivity**, is quite important. It implies that the contribution of any project to a firm's value is simply the NPV of the project. As we will see later, alternative methods discussed in this chapter do not generally have this nice property.

One detail remains. We assumed that the project was riskless, a rather implausible assumption. Future cash flows of real-world projects are invariably risky. In other words, cash flows can only be estimated, rather than known. Imagine that the managers of Alpha *expect* the cash flow of the project to be $107 next year. That is, the cash flow could be higher, say $117, or lower, say $97. With this slight change, the project is risky. Suppose the project is about as risky as the stock market as a whole, where the expected return this year is perhaps 10 percent. Then 10 percent becomes the discount rate, implying that the NPV of the project would be:

$$-\$2.73 = -\$100 + \frac{\$107}{1.10}$$

Because the NPV is negative, the project should be rejected. This makes sense: A stockholder of Alpha receiving a $100 dividend today could invest it in the stock market, expecting a 10 percent return. Why accept a project with the same risk as the market but with an expected return of only 7 percent?

Conceptually, the discount rate on a risky project is the return that one can expect to earn on a financial asset of comparable risk. This discount rate is often referred to as an *opportunity cost* because corporate investment in the project takes away the stockholder's opportunity to invest the dividend in a financial asset. If the actual calculation of the discount rate strikes you as extremely difficult in the real world, you are probably right. Although you can call a bank to find out the current interest rate, whom do you call to find the expected return on the market this year? And, if the risk of the project differs from that of the market, how do you make the adjustment? However, the calculation is by no means impossible. We forgo the calculation in this chapter, but we present it in later chapters of the text.

Having shown that NPV is a sensible approach, how can we tell whether alternative methods are as good as NPV? The key to NPV is its three attributes:

1. *NPV uses cash flows.* Cash flows from a project can be used for other corporate purposes (such as dividend payments, other capital budgeting projects, or payments of corporate interest). By contrast, earnings are an artificial construct. Although earnings are useful to accountants, they should not be used in capital budgeting because they do not represent cash.

2. *NPV uses all the cash flows of the project.* Other approaches ignore cash flows beyond a particular date; beware of these approaches.

3. *NPV discounts the cash flows properly.* Other approaches may ignore the time value of money when handling cash flows. Beware of these approaches as well.

6.2 The Payback Period Method

Defining the Rule

One of the most popular alternatives to NPV is **payback**. Here is how payback works: Consider a project with an initial investment of −$50,000. Cash flows are $30,000, $20,000, and $10,000 in the first three years, respectively. These flows are illustrated in Figure 6.1. A useful way of writing down investments like the preceding is with the notation

$$(-\$50,000, \$30,000, \$20,000, \$10,000)$$

Figure 6.1

Cash Flows of an Investment Project

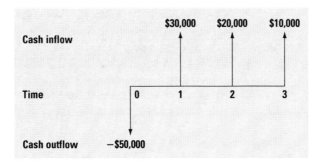

The minus sign in front of the $50,000 reminds us that this is a cash outflow for the investor, and the commas between the different numbers indicate that they are received—or if they are cash outflows, that they are paid out—at different times. In this example we are assuming that the cash flows occur one year apart, with the first one occurring the moment we decide to take on the investment.

The firm receives cash flows of $30,000 and $20,000 in the first two years, which add up to the $50,000 original investment. This means that the firm has recovered its investment within two years. In this case two years is the *payback period* of the investment.

The **payback period rule** for making investment decisions is simple. A particular cutoff date, say two years, is selected. All investment projects that have payback periods of two years or less are accepted, and all of those that pay off in more than two years—if at all—are rejected.

Problems with the Payback Method

There are at least three problems with payback. To illustrate the first two problems, we consider the three projects in Table 6.1. All three projects have the same three-year payback period, so they should all be equally attractive—right?

Actually, they are not equally attractive, as can be seen by a comparison of different *pairs* of projects.

Problem 1: Timing of Cash Flows within the Payback Period   Let us compare project *A* with project *B*. In years 1 through 3, the cash flows of project *A* rise from $20 to $50, while the cash flows of project *B* fall from $50 to $20. Because the large cash flow of $50 comes earlier with project *B*, its net present value must be higher. Nevertheless, we just saw that the payback periods of the two projects are identical. Thus, a problem with the payback method is that it does not consider the timing of the cash flows within the payback period. This example shows that the payback method is inferior to NPV because, as we pointed out earlier, the NPV method *discounts the cash flows properly.*

Problem 2: Payments after the Payback Period   Now consider projects *B* and *C*, which have identical cash flows within the payback period. However, project *C* is clearly preferred because it has a cash flow of $60,000 in the fourth year. Thus, another problem

Table 6.1

Expected Cash Flows for Projects *A* through *C* ($)

Year	A	B	C
0	−$100	−$100	−$100
1	20	50	50
2	30	30	30
3	50	20	20
4	60	60	60,000
Payback period (years)	3	3	3

with the payback method is that it ignores all cash flows occurring after the payback period. Because of the short-term orientation of the payback method, some valuable long-term projects are likely to be rejected. The NPV method does not have this flaw because, as we pointed out earlier, this method *uses all the cash flows of the project.*

Problem 3: Arbitrary Standard for Payback Period   We do not need to refer to Table 6.1 when considering a third problem with the payback method. Capital markets help us estimate the discount rate used in the NPV method. The riskless rate, perhaps proxied by the yield on a Treasury instrument, would be the appropriate rate for a riskless investment. Later chapters of this textbook show how to use historical returns in the capital markets to estimate the discount rate for a risky project. However, there is no comparable guide for choosing the payback cutoff date, so the choice is somewhat arbitrary.

Managerial Perspective

The payback method is often used by large, sophisticated companies when making relatively small decisions. The decision to build a small warehouse, for example, or to pay for a tune-up for a truck is the sort of decision that is often made by lower-level management. Typically, a manager might reason that a tune-up would cost, say, $200, and if it saved $120 each year in reduced fuel costs, it would pay for itself in less than two years. On such a basis the decision would be made.

Although the treasurer of the company might not have made the decision in the same way, the company endorses such decision making. Why would upper management condone or even encourage such retrograde activity in its employees? One answer would be that it is easy to make decisions using payback. Multiply the tune-up decision into 50 such decisions a month, and the appeal of this simple method becomes clearer.

The payback method also has some desirable features for managerial control. Just as important as the investment decision itself is the company's ability to evaluate the manager's decision-making ability. Under the NPV method, a long time may pass before one decides whether a decision was correct. With the payback method we know in two years whether the manager's assessment of the cash flows was correct.

It has also been suggested that firms with good investment opportunities but no available cash may justifiably use payback. For example, the payback method could be used by small, privately held firms with good growth prospects but limited access to the capital markets. Quick cash recovery enhances the reinvestment possibilities for such firms.

Finally, practitioners often argue that standard academic criticisms of payback overstate any real-world problems with the method. For example, textbooks typically make fun of payback by positing a project with low cash inflows in the early years but a huge cash inflow right after the payback cutoff date. This project is likely to be rejected under the payback method, though its acceptance would, in truth, benefit the firm. Project *C* in our Table 6.1 is an example of such a project. Practitioners point out that the pattern of cash flows in these textbook examples is much too stylized to mirror the real world. In fact, a number of executives have told us that for the overwhelming majority of real-world projects, both payback and NPV lead to the same decision. In addition, these executives indicate that if an investment like project *C* were encountered in the real world, decision makers would almost certainly make ad hoc adjustments to the payback rule so that the project would be accepted.

Notwithstanding all of the preceding rationale, it is not surprising to discover that as the decisions grow in importance, which is to say when firms look at bigger projects, NPV becomes the order of the day. When questions of controlling and evaluating the manager become less important than making the right investment decision, payback is used less frequently. For big-ticket decisions, such as whether or not to buy a machine, build a factory, or acquire a company, the payback method is seldom used.

Summary of Payback

The payback method differs from NPV and is therefore conceptually wrong. With its arbitrary cutoff date and its blindness to cash flows after that date, it can lead to some flagrantly foolish decisions if it is used too literally. Nevertheless, because of its simplicity, as well as its other mentioned advantages, companies often use it as a screen for making the myriad minor investment decisions they continually face.

Although this means that you should be wary of trying to change approaches such as the payback method when you encounter them in companies, you should probably be careful not to accept the sloppy financial thinking they represent. After this course, you would do your company a disservice if you used payback instead of NPV when you had a choice.

6.3 The Discounted Payback Period Method

Aware of the pitfalls of payback, some decision makers use a variant called the **discounted payback period method**. Under this approach, we first discount the cash flows. Then we ask how long it takes for the discounted cash flows to equal the initial investment.

For example, suppose that the discount rate is 10 percent and the cash flows on a project are given by:

$$(-\$100, \$50, \$50, \$20)$$

This investment has a payback period of two years because the investment is paid back in that time.

To compute the project's discounted payback period, we first discount each of the cash flows at the 10 percent rate. These discounted cash flows are:

$$[-\$100, \$50/1.1, \$50/(1.1)^2, \$20/(1.1)^3] = (-\$100, \$45.45, \$41.32, \$15.03)$$

The discounted payback period of the original investment is simply the payback period for these discounted cash flows. The payback period for the discounted cash flows is slightly less than three years because the discounted cash flows over the three years are $101.80 (=$45.45 + 41.32 + 15.03). As long as the cash flows and discount rate are positive, the discounted payback period will never be smaller than the payback period because discounting reduces the value of the cash flows.

At first glance discounted payback may seem like an attractive alternative, but on closer inspection we see that it has some of the same major flaws as payback. Like payback, discounted payback first requires us to make a somewhat magical choice of an arbitrary cutoff period, and then it ignores all cash flows after that date.

If we have already gone to the trouble of discounting the cash flows, any small appeal to simplicity or to managerial control that payback may have has been lost. We might just as well add up all the discounted cash flows and use NPV to make the decision. Although discounted payback looks a bit like NPV, it is just a poor compromise between the payback method and NPV.

6.4 The Average Accounting Return Method

Defining the Rule

Another attractive, but fatally flawed, approach to financial decision making is the **average accounting return**. The average accounting return is the average project earnings after taxes and depreciation, divided by the average book value of the investment during its life.

In spite of its flaws, the average accounting return method is worth examining because it is used frequently in the real world.

EXAMPLE 6.2

Average Accounting Return   Consider a company that is evaluating whether to buy a store in a new mall. The purchase price is $500,000. We will assume that the store has an estimated life of five years and will need to be completely scrapped or rebuilt at the end of that time. The projected yearly sales and expense figures are shown in Table 6.2.

Table 6.2   **Projected Yearly Revenue and Costs for Average Accounting Return**

	Year 1	Year 2	Year 3	Year 4	Year 5
Revenue	$433,333	$450,000	$266,667	$200,000	$133,333
Expenses	200,000	150,000	100,000	100,000	100,000
Before-tax cash flow	233,333	300,000	166,667	100,000	33,333
Depreciation	100,000	100,000	100,000	100,000	100,000
Earnings before taxes	133,333	200,000	66,667	0	− 66,667
Taxes ($t_c = .25$)*	33,333	50,000	16,667	0	− 16,667
Net income	$100,000	$150,000	$ 50,000	$ 0	−$ 50,000

$$\text{Average net income} = \frac{(\$100,000 + 150,000 + 50,000 + 0 - 50,000)}{5} = \$50,000$$

$$\text{Average investment} = \frac{\$500,000 + 0}{2} = \$250,000$$

$$\text{AAR} = \frac{\$50,000}{\$250,000} = 20\%$$

*Corporate tax rate $= t_c$. The tax rebate in year 5 of −$16,667 occurs if the rest of the firm is profitable. Here the loss in the project reduces the taxes of the entire firm.

It is worth examining Table 6.2 carefully. In fact, the first step in any project assessment is a careful look at projected cash flows. First-year sales for the store are estimated to be $433,333. Before-tax cash flow will be $233,333. Sales are expected to rise and expenses are expected to fall in the second year, resulting in a before-tax cash flow of $300,000. Competition from other stores and the loss in novelty will reduce before-tax cash flow to $166,667, $100,000, and $33,333, respectively, in the next three years.

To compute the average accounting return (AAR) on the project, we divide the average net income by the average amount invested. This can be done in three steps.

Step 1: Determining Average Net Income   Net income in any year is net cash flow minus depreciation and taxes. Depreciation is *not* a cash outflow.[1] Rather, it is a charge reflecting the fact that the investment in the store becomes less valuable every year.

We assume the project has a useful life of five years, at which time it will be worthless. Because the initial investment is $500,000 and because it will be worthless in five years, we assume that it loses value at the rate of $100,000 each year. This steady loss in value of $100,000 is called *straight-line depreciation*. We subtract both depreciation and taxes from before-tax cash flow to derive net income, as shown in Table 6.2. Net income is $100,000

---

[1]Depreciation will be treated in more detail in the next chapter.

in the first year, $150,000 in year 2, $50,000 in year 3, zero in year 4, and −$50,000 in the last year. The average net income over the life of the project is therefore:

Average Net Income:

$$[\$100,000 + 150,000 + 50,000 + 0 + (-50,000)]/5 = \$50,000$$

Step 2: Determining Average Investment   We stated earlier that, due to depreciation, the investment in the store becomes less valuable every year. Because depreciation is $100,000 per year, the value at the end of year zero is $500,000, the value at the end of year 1 is $400,000, and so on. What is the average value of the investment over the life of the investment?

The mechanical calculation is:

Average Investment:

$$(\$500,000 + 400,000 + 300,000 + 200,000 + 100,000 + 0)/6 \qquad \textbf{(6.2)}$$
$$= \$250,000$$

We divide by 6, not 5, because $500,000 is what the investment is worth at the beginning of the five years and $0 is what it is worth at the beginning of the sixth year. In other words, there are six terms in the parentheses of Equation 6.2.

Step 3: Determining AAR   The average return is simply:

$$AAR = \frac{\$50,000}{\$250,000} = 20\%$$

If the firm had a targeted accounting rate of return greater than 20 percent, the project would be rejected; if its targeted return were less than 20 percent, it would be accepted.

Analyzing the Average Accounting Return Method

By now you should be able to see what is wrong with the AAR method.

The most important flaw with AAR is that it does not work with the right raw materials. It uses net income and book value of the investment, both of which come from the accounting books. Accounting numbers are somewhat arbitrary. For example, certain cash outflows, such as the cost of a building, are depreciated under current accounting rules. Other flows, such as maintenance, are expensed. In real-world situations, the decision to depreciate or expense an item involves judgment. Thus, the basic inputs of the AAR method, income and average investment, are affected by the accountant's judgment. Conversely, the NPV method *uses cash flows*. Accounting judgments do not affect cash flow.

Second, AAR takes no account of timing. In the previous example, the AAR would have been the same if the $100,000 net income in the first year had occurred in the last year. However, delaying an inflow for five years would have lowered the NPV of the investment. As mentioned earlier in this chapter, the NPV approach *discounts properly*.

Third, just as payback requires an arbitrary choice of the cutoff date, the AAR method offers no guidance on what the right targeted rate of return should be. It could be the discount rate in the market. But then again, because the AAR method is not the same as the present value method, it is not obvious that this would be the right choice.

Given these problems, is the AAR method employed in practice? Like the payback method, the AAR (and variations of it) is frequently used as a "backup" to discounted cash flow methods. Perhaps this is so because it is easy to calculate and uses accounting numbers readily available from the firm's accounting system. In addition, both stockholders and the media pay a lot of attention to the overall profitability of a firm. Thus, some managers

Figure 6.2

Cash Flows for a Simple Project

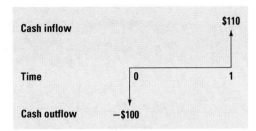

may feel pressured to select projects that are profitable in the near term, even if the projects come up short in terms of NPV. These managers may focus on the AAR of individual projects more than they should.

6.5 The Internal Rate of Return

Now we come to the most important alternative to the NPV method: the internal rate of return, universally known as the IRR. The IRR is about as close as you can get to the NPV without actually being the NPV. The basic rationale behind the IRR method is that it provides a single number summarizing the merits of a project. That number does not depend on the interest rate prevailing in the capital market. That is why it is called the internal rate of return; the number is internal or intrinsic to the project and does not depend on anything except the cash flows of the project.

For example, consider the simple project (−$100, $110) in Figure 6.2. For a given rate, the net present value of this project can be described as:

$$NPV = -\$100 + \frac{\$110}{1+R}$$

where R is the discount rate. What must the discount rate be to make the NPV of the project equal to zero?

We begin by using an arbitrary discount rate of .08, which yields:

$$\$1.85 = -\$100 + \frac{\$110}{1.08}$$

Because the NPV in this equation is positive, we now try a higher discount rate, such as .12. This yields:

$$-\$1.79 = -\$100 + \frac{\$110}{1.12}$$

Because the NPV in this equation is negative, we try lowering the discount rate to .10. This yields:

$$0 = -\$100 + \frac{\$110}{1.10}$$

This trial-and-error procedure tells us that the NPV of the project is zero when R equals 10 percent.[2] Thus, we say that 10 percent is the project's **internal rate of return** (IRR). In

---

[2] Of course, we could have directly solved for R in this example after setting NPV equal to zero. However, with a long series of cash flows, one cannot generally directly solve for R. Instead, one is forced to use trial and error (or let a machine use trial and error).

Figure 6.3

Cash Flows for a More Complex Project

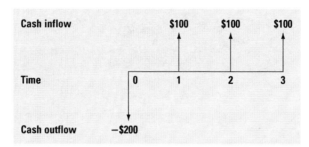

general, the IRR is the rate that causes the NPV of the project to be zero. The implication of this exercise is very simple. The firm should be equally willing to accept or reject the project if the discount rate is 10 percent. The firm should accept the project if the discount rate is below 10 percent. The firm should reject the project if the discount rate is above 10 percent.

The general investment rule is clear:

Accept the project if the IRR is greater than the discount rate. Reject the project if the IRR is less than the discount rate.

We refer to this as the **basic IRR rule**. Now we can try the more complicated example (−$200, $100, $100, $100) in Figure 6.3.

As we did previously, let's use trial and error to calculate the internal rate of return. We try 20 percent and 30 percent, yielding the following:

Discount Rate	NPV
20%	$10.65
30	−18.39

After much more trial and error, we find that the NPV of the project is zero when the discount rate is 23.37 percent. Thus, the IRR is 23.37 percent. With a 20 percent discount rate, the NPV is positive and we would accept it. However, if the discount rate were 30 percent, we would reject it.

Algebraically, IRR is the unknown in the following equation:[3]

$$0 = -\$200 + \frac{\$100}{1 + IRR} + \frac{\$100}{(1 + IRR)^2} + \frac{\$100}{(1 + IRR)^3}$$

Figure 6.4 illustrates what the IRR of a project means. The figure plots the NPV as a function of the discount rate. The curve crosses the horizontal axis at the IRR of 23.37 percent because this is where the NPV equals zero.

It should also be clear that the NPV is positive for discount rates below the IRR and negative for discount rates above the IRR. This means that if we accept projects like this one when the discount rate is less than the IRR, we will be accepting positive NPV projects. Thus, the IRR rule coincides exactly with the NPV rule.

If this were all there were to it, the IRR rule would always coincide with the NPV rule. This would be a wonderful discovery because it would mean that just by computing the

---

[3]One can derive the IRR directly for a problem with an initial outflow and up to four subsequent inflows. In the case of two subsequent inflows, for example, the quadratic formula is needed. In general, however, only trial and error will work for an outflow and five or more subsequent inflows.

Figure 6.4

Net Present Value (NPV) and Discount Rates for a More Complex Project

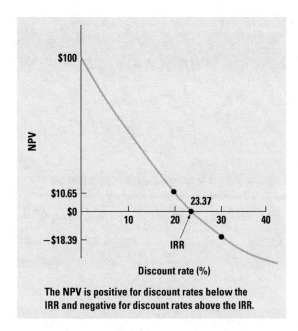

The NPV is positive for discount rates below the IRR and negative for discount rates above the IRR.

IRR for a project we would be able to tell where it ranks among all of the projects we are considering. For example, if the IRR rule really works, a project with an IRR of 20 percent will always be at least as good as one with an IRR of 15 percent.

But the world of finance is not so kind. Unfortunately, the IRR rule and the NPV rule are the same only for examples like the one just discussed. Several problems with the IRR approach occur in more complicated situations.

6.6 Problems with the IRR Approach

Definition of Independent and Mutually Exclusive Projects

An **independent project** is one whose acceptance or rejection is independent of the acceptance or rejection of other projects. For example, imagine that McDonald's is considering putting a hamburger outlet on a remote island. Acceptance or rejection of this unit is likely to be unrelated to the acceptance or rejection of any other restaurant in its system. The remoteness of the outlet in question ensures that it will not pull sales away from other outlets.

Now consider the other extreme, **mutually exclusive investments**. What does it mean for two projects, A and B, to be mutually exclusive? You can accept A or you can accept B or you can reject both of them, but you cannot accept both of them. For example, A might be a decision to build an apartment house on a corner lot that you own, and B might be a decision to build a movie theater on the same lot.

We now present two general problems with the IRR approach that affect both independent and mutually exclusive projects. Then we deal with two problems affecting mutually exclusive projects only.

Two General Problems Affecting Both Independent and Mutually Exclusive Projects

We begin our discussion with project A, which has the following cash flows:

$$(-\$100, \$130)$$

Table 6.3   The Internal Rate of Return and Net Present Value

	Project A			Project B			Project C		
Dates:	0	1	2	0	1	2	0	1	2
Cash flows	−$100	$130		$100	−$130		−$100	$230	−$132
IRR		30%			30%		10%	and	20%
NPV @10%		$18.2			−$18.2			0	
Accept if market rate		<30%			>30%		>10%	but	<20%
Financing or investing		Investing			Financing			Mixture	

Figure 6.5   Net Present Value and Discount Rates for Projects *A*, *B*, and *C*

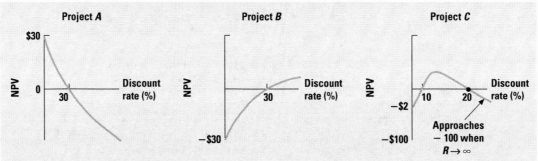

Project *A* has a cash outflow at date 0 followed by a cash inflow at date 1. Its NPV is negatively related to the discount rate.
Project *B* has a cash inflow at date 0 followed by a cash outflow at date 1. Its NPV is positively related to the discount rate.
Project *C* has two changes of sign in its cash flows. It has an outflow at date 0, an inflow at date 1, and an outflow at date 2.
Projects with more than one change of sign can have multiple rates of return.

The IRR for project *A* is 30 percent. Table 6.3 provides other relevant information about the project. The relationship between NPV and the discount rate is shown for this project in Figure 6.5. As you can see, the NPV declines as the discount rate rises.

Problem 1: Investing or Financing?   Now consider project *B*, with cash flows of:

$$(\$100, -\$130)$$

These cash flows are exactly the reverse of the flows for project *A*. In project *B*, the firm receives funds first and then pays out funds later. While unusual, projects of this type do exist. For example, consider a corporation conducting a seminar where the participants pay in advance. Because large expenses are frequently incurred at the seminar date, cash inflows precede cash outflows.

Consider our trial-and-error method to calculate IRR:

$$-\$4 = +\$100 - \frac{\$130}{1.25}$$
$$\$0 = +\$100 - \frac{\$130}{1.30}$$
$$\$3.70 = +\$100 - \frac{\$130}{1.35}$$

As with project *A*, the internal rate of return is 30 percent. However, notice that the net present value is *negative* when the discount rate is *below* 30 percent. Conversely, the net present value is positive when the discount rate is above 30 percent. The decision rule is exactly

Ross–Westerfield–Jaffe:
Corporate Finance, Eighth
Edition

II. Valuation and Capital
Budgeting

6. Net Present Value and
Other Investment Rules

© The McGraw–Hill
Companies, 2008

163

the opposite of our previous result. For this type of a project, the following rule applies:

Accept the project when the IRR is less than the discount rate. Reject the project when the IRR is greater than the discount rate.

This unusual decision rule follows from the graph of project B in Figure 6.5. The curve is upward sloping, implying that NPV is *positively* related to the discount rate.

The graph makes intuitive sense. Suppose the firm wants to obtain $100 immediately. It can either (1) accept project B or (2) borrow $100 from a bank. Thus, the project is actually a substitute for borrowing. In fact, because the IRR is 30 percent, taking on project B is tantamount to borrowing at 30 percent. If the firm can borrow from a bank at, say, only 25 percent, it should reject the project. However, if a firm can borrow from a bank only at, say, 35 percent, it should accept the project. Thus project B will be accepted if and only if the discount rate is *above* the IRR.[4]

This should be contrasted with project A. If the firm has $100 of cash to invest, it can either (1) accept project A or (2) lend $100 to the bank. The project is actually a substitute for lending. In fact, because the IRR is 30 percent, taking on project A is tantamount to lending at 30 percent. The firm should accept project A if the lending rate is below 30 percent. Conversely, the firm should reject project A if the lending rate is above 30 percent.

Because the firm initially pays out money with project A but initially receives money with project B, we refer to project A as an *investing type project* and project B as a *financing type project*. Investing type projects are the norm. Because the IRR rule is reversed for financing type projects, be careful when using it with this type of project.

Problem 2: Multiple Rates of Return   Suppose the cash flows from a project are:

$$(-\$100, \$230, -\$132)$$

Because this project has a negative cash flow, a positive cash flow, and another negative cash flow, we say that the project's cash flows exhibit two changes of sign, or "flip-flops." Although this pattern of cash flows might look a bit strange at first, many projects require outflows of cash after receiving some inflows. An example would be a strip-mining project. The first stage in such a project is the initial investment in excavating the mine. Profits from operating the mine are received in the second stage. The third stage involves a further investment to reclaim the land and satisfy the requirements of environmental protection legislation. Cash flows are negative at this stage.

Projects financed by lease arrangements may produce a similar pattern of cash flows. Leases often provide substantial tax subsidies, generating cash inflows after an initial investment. However, these subsidies decline over time, frequently leading to negative cash flows in later years. (The details of leasing will be discussed in a later chapter.)

It is easy to verify that this project has not one but two IRRs, 10 percent and 20 percent.[5] In a case like this, the IRR does not make any sense. What IRR are we to use—10 percent

---

[4]This paragraph implicitly assumes that the cash flows of the project are risk-free. In this way we can treat the borrowing rate as the discount rate for a firm needing $100. With risky cash flows, another discount rate would be chosen. However, the intuition behind the decision to accept when the IRR is less than the discount rate would still apply.

[5]The calculations are

$$-\$100 + \frac{\$230}{1.1} - \frac{\$132}{(1.1)^2}$$
$$-\$100 + 209.09 - 109.09 = 0$$

and

$$-\$100 + \frac{\$230}{1.2} - \frac{\$132}{(1.2)^2}$$
$$-\$100 + 191.67 - 91.67 = 0$$

Thus, we have multiple rates of return.

or 20 percent? Because there is no good reason to use one over the other, IRR simply cannot be used here.

Why does this project have multiple rates of return? Project C generates multiple internal rates of return because both an inflow and an outflow occur after the initial investment. In general, these flip-flops or changes in sign produce multiple IRRs. In theory, a cash flow stream with K changes in sign can have up to K sensible internal rates of return (IRRs above -100 percent). Therefore, because project C has two changes in sign, it can have as many as two IRRs. As we pointed out, projects whose cash flows change sign repeatedly can occur in the real world.

NPV Rule   Of course, we should not be too worried about multiple rates of return. After all, we can always fall back on the NPV rule. Figure 6.5 plots the NPV of project C ($-\$100$, $\$230$, $-\$132$) as a function of the discount rate. As the figure shows, the NPV is zero at both 10 percent and 20 percent and negative outside the range. Thus, the NPV rule tells us to accept the project if the appropriate discount rate is between 10 percent and 20 percent. The project should be rejected if the discount rate lies outside this range.

Modified IRR   As an alternative to NPV, we now introduce the **modified IRR (MIRR)** method, which handles the multiple IRR problem by combining cash flows until only one change in sign remains. To see how it works, consider project C again. With a discount rate of, say, 14 percent, the value of the last cash flow, $-\$132$, is:

$$-\$132/1.14 = -\$115.79$$

as of date 1. Because $\$230$ is already received at that time, the "adjusted" cash flow at date 1 is $\$114.21$ ($= \$230 - 115.79$). Thus, the MIRR approach produces the following two cash flows for the project:

$$(-\$100, \$114.21)$$

Note that by discounting and then combining cash flows, we are left with only one change in sign. The IRR rule can now be applied. The IRR of these two cash flows is 14.21 percent, implying that the project should be accepted given our assumed discount rate of 14 percent.

Of course, project C is relatively simple to begin with: It has only three cash flows and two changes in sign. However, the same procedure can easily be applied to more complex projects—that is, just keep discounting and combining the later cash flows until only one change of sign remains.

Although this adjustment does correct for multiple IRRs, it appears, at least to us, to violate the "spirit" of the IRR approach. As stated earlier, the basic rationale behind the IRR method is that it provides a single number summarizing the merits of a project. That number does not depend on the discount rate. In fact, that is why it is called the internal rate of return: The number is *internal*, or intrinsic, to the project and does not depend on anything except the cash flows of the project. By contrast, MIRR is clearly a function of the discount rate. However, a firm using this adjustment will avoid the multiple IRR problem, just as a firm using the NPV rule will avoid it.

The Guarantee against Multiple IRRs   If the first cash flow of a project is negative (because it is the initial investment) and if all of the remaining flows are positive, there can be only a single, unique IRR, no matter how many periods the project lasts. This is easy to understand by using the concept of the time value of money. For example, it is simple to verify that project A in Table 6.3 has an IRR of 30 percent because using a 30-percent discount rate gives

$$NPV = -\$100 + \$130/(1.3)$$
$$= \$0$$

How do we know that this is the only IRR? Suppose we were to try a discount rate greater than 30 percent. In computing the NPV, changing the discount rate does not change the value of the initial cash flow of −$100 because that cash flow is not discounted. But raising the discount rate can only lower the present value of the future cash flows. In other words, because the NPV is zero at 30 percent, any increase in the rate will push the NPV into the negative range. Similarly, if we try a discount rate of less than 30 percent, the overall NPV of the project will be positive. Though this example has only one positive flow, the above reasoning still implies a single, unique IRR if there are many inflows (but no outflows) after the initial investment.

If the initial cash flow is positive—and if all of the remaining flows are negative—there can only be a single, unique IRR. This result follows from similar reasoning. Both these cases have only one change of sign or flip-flop in the cash flows. Thus, we are safe from multiple IRRs whenever there is only one sign change in the cash flows.

General Rules   The following chart summarizes our rules:

Flows	Number of IRRs	IRR Criterion	NPV Criterion
First cash flow is negative and all remaining cash flows are positive.	1	Accept if IRR > R. Reject if IRR < R.	Accept if NPV > 0. Reject if NPV < 0.
First cash flow is positive and all remaining cash flows are negative.	1	Accept if IRR < R. Reject if IRR > R.	Accept if NPV > 0. Reject if NPV < 0.
Some cash flows after first are positive and some cash flows after first are negative.	May be more than 1.	No valid IRR.	Accept if NPV > 0. Reject if NPV < 0.

Note that the NPV criterion is the same for each of the three cases. In other words, NPV analysis is always appropriate. Conversely, the IRR can be used only in certain cases. When it comes to NPV, the preacher's words, "You just can't lose with the stuff I use," clearly apply.

Problems Specific to Mutually Exclusive Projects

As mentioned earlier, two or more projects are mutually exclusive if the firm can accept only one of them. We now present two problems dealing with the application of the IRR approach to mutually exclusive projects. These two problems are quite similar, though logically distinct.

The Scale Problem   A professor we know motivates class discussions of this topic with this statement: "Students, I am prepared to let one of you choose between two mutually exclusive 'business' propositions. Opportunity 1—You give me $1 now and I'll give you $1.50 back at the end of the class period. Opportunity 2—You give me $10 and I'll give you $11 back at the end of the class period. You can choose only one of the two opportunities. And you cannot choose either opportunity more than once. I'll pick the first volunteer."

Which would you choose? The correct answer is opportunity 2.[6] To see this, look at the following chart:

	Cash Flow at Beginning of Class	Cash Flow at End of Class (90 Minutes Later)	NPV[7]	IRR
Opportunity 1	−$ 1	+$ 1.50	$ .50	50%
Opportunity 2	− 10	+ 11.00	1.00	10

As we have stressed earlier in the text, one should choose the opportunity with the highest NPV. This is opportunity 2 in the example. Or, as one of the professor's students explained it, "I'm bigger than the professor, so I know I'll get my money back. And I have $10 in my pocket right now so I can choose either opportunity. At the end of the class, I'll be able to play two rounds of my favorite electronic game with opportunity 2 and still have my original investment, safe and sound.[8] The profit on opportunity 1 buys only one round."

This business proposition illustrates a defect with the internal rate of return criterion. The basic IRR rule indicates the selection of opportunity 1 because the IRR is 50 percent. The IRR is only 10 percent for opportunity 2.

Where does IRR go wrong? The problem with IRR is that it ignores issues of *scale*. Although opportunity 1 has a greater IRR, the investment is much smaller. In other words, the high percentage return on opportunity 1 is more than offset by the ability to earn at least a decent return[9] on a much bigger investment under opportunity 2.

Because IRR seems to be misguided here, can we adjust or correct it? We illustrate how in the next example.

EXAMPLE 6.3

NPV versus IRR   Stanley Jaffe and Sherry Lansing have just purchased the rights to *Corporate Finance: The Motion Picture*. They will produce this major motion picture on either a small budget or a big budget. Here are the estimated cash flows:

	Cash Flow at Date 0	Cash Flow at Date 1	NPV @25%	IRR
Small budget	−$10 million	$40 million	$22 million	300%
Large budget	− 25 million	65 million	27 million	160

Because of high risk, a 25 percent discount rate is considered appropriate. Sherry wants to adopt the large budget because the NPV is higher. Stanley wants to adopt the small budget because the IRR is higher. Who is right?

(continued)

---

[6]The professor uses real money here. Though many students have done poorly on the professor's exams over the years, no student ever chose opportunity 1. The professor claims that his students are "money players."

[7]We assume a zero rate of interest because his class lasted only 90 minutes. It just seemed like a lot longer.

[8]At press time for this text, electronic games cost $0.50 apiece.

[9]A 10 percent return is more than decent over a 90-minute interval!

For the reasons espoused in the classroom example, NPV is correct. Hence Sherry is right. However, Stanley is very stubborn where IRR is concerned. How can Sherry justify the large budget to Stanley using the IRR approach?

This is where *incremental IRR* comes in. Sherry calculates the incremental cash flows from choosing the large budget instead of the small budget as follows:

	Cash Flow at Date 0 (in $ millions)	Cash Flow at Date 1 (in $ millions)
Incremental cash flows from choosing large budget instead of small budget	−$25 − (−10) = −$15	$65 − 40 = $25

This chart shows that the incremental cash flows are −$15 million at date 0 and $25 million at date 1. Sherry calculates incremental IRR as follows:

Formula for Calculating the Incremental IRR:

$$0 = -\$15 \text{ million} + \frac{\$25 \text{ million}}{1 + IRR}$$

IRR equals 66.67 percent in this equation, implying that the **incremental IRR** is 66.67 percent. Incremental IRR is the IRR on the incremental investment from choosing the large project instead of the small project.

In addition, we can calculate the NPV of the incremental cash flows:

NPV of Incremental Cash Flows:

$$-\$15 \text{ million} + \frac{\$25 \text{ million}}{1.25} = \$5 \text{ million}$$

We know the small-budget picture would be acceptable as an independent project because its NPV is positive. We want to know whether it is beneficial to invest an additional $15 million to make the large-budget picture instead of the small-budget picture. In other words, is it beneficial to invest an additional $15 million to receive an additional $25 million next year? First, our calculations show the NPV on the incremental investment to be positive. Second, the incremental IRR of 66.67 percent is higher than the discount rate of 25 percent. For both reasons, the incremental investment can be justified, so the large-budget movie should be made. The second reason is what Stanley needed to hear to be convinced.

In review, we can handle this example (or any mutually exclusive example) in one of three ways:

1. *Compare the NPVs of the two choices.* The NPV of the large-budget picture is greater than the NPV of the small-budget picture. That is, $27 million is greater than $22 million.

2. *Calculate the incremental NPV from making the large-budget picture instead of the small-budget picture.* Because the incremental NPV equals $5 million, we choose the large-budget picture.

3. *Compare the incremental IRR to the discount rate.* Because the incremental IRR is 66.67 percent and the discount rate is 25 percent, we take the large-budget picture.

All three approaches always give the same decision. However, we must *not* compare the IRRs of the two pictures. If we did, we would make the wrong choice. That is, we would accept the small-budget picture.

Although students frequently think that problems of scale are relatively unimportant, the truth is just the opposite. A well-known chef on TV often says, "I don't know about your flour, but the flour I buy don't come seasoned." The same thing applies to capital budgeting. No real-world project comes in one clear-cut size. Rather, the firm has to *determine* the best size for the project. The movie budget of $25 million is not fixed in stone. Perhaps an extra $1 million to hire a bigger star or to film at a better location will increase the movie's gross. Similarly, an industrial firm must decide whether it wants a warehouse of, say, 500,000 square feet or 600,000 square feet. And, earlier in the chapter, we imagined McDonald's opening an outlet on a remote island. If it does this, it must decide how big the outlet should be. For almost any project, someone in the firm has to decide on its size, implying that problems of scale abound in the real world.

One final note here. Students often ask which project should be subtracted from the other in calculating incremental flows. Notice that we are subtracting the smaller project's cash flows from the bigger project's cash flows. This leaves an *outflow* at date 0. We then use the basic IRR rule on the incremental flows.[10]

The Timing Problem   Next we illustrate another, quite similar problem with the IRR approach to evaluating mutually exclusive projects.

EXAMPLE 6.4

Mutually Exclusive Investments   Suppose that the Kaufold Corporation has two alternative uses for a warehouse. It can store toxic waste containers (investment A) or electronic equipment (investment B). The cash flows are as follows:

	Cash Flow at Year				NPV			
Year:	0	1	2	3	@0%	@10%	@15%	IRR
Investment A	−$10,000	$10,000	$1,000	$ 1,000	$2,000	$669	$109	16.04%
Investment B	−10,000	1,000	1,000	12,000	4,000	751	−484	12.94

We find that the NPV of investment B is higher with low discount rates, and the NPV of investment A is higher with high discount rates. This is not surprising if you look closely at the cash flow patterns. The cash flows of A occur early, whereas the cash flows of B occur later. If we assume a high discount rate, we favor investment A because we are implicitly assuming that the early cash flow (for example, $10,000 in year 1) can be reinvested at that rate. Because most of investment B's cash flows occur in year 3, B's value is relatively high with low discount rates.

The patterns of cash flow for both projects appear in Figure 6.6. Project A has an NPV of $2,000 at a discount rate of zero. This is calculated by simply adding up the cash flows without discounting them. Project B has an NPV of $4,000 at the zero rate. However, the NPV of project B declines more rapidly as the discount rate increases than does the NPV

---

[10] Alternatively, we could have subtracted the larger project's cash flows from the smaller project's cash flows. This would have left an *inflow* at date 0, making it necessary to use the IRR rule for financing situations. This would work, but we find it more confusing.

Figure 6.6

Net Present Value and the Internal Rate of Return for Mutually Exclusive Projects

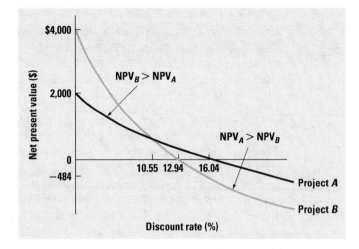

of project A. As we mentioned, this occurs because the cash flows of B occur later. Both projects have the same NPV at a discount rate of 10.55 percent. The IRR for a project is the rate at which the NPV equals zero. Because the NPV of B declines more rapidly, B actually has a lower IRR.

As with the movie example, we can select the better project with one of three different methods:

1. *Compare NPVs of the two projects.* Figure 6.6 aids our decision. If the discount rate is below 10.55 percent, we should choose project B because B has a higher NPV. If the rate is above 10.55 percent, we should choose project A because A has a higher NPV.

2. *Compare incremental IRR to discount rate.* Method 1 employed NPV. Another way of determining that B is a better project is to subtract the cash flows of A from the cash flows of B and then to calculate the IRR. This is the incremental IRR approach we spoke of earlier.

Here are the incremental cash flows:

						NPV of Incremental Cash Flows		
Year:	0	1	2	3	Incremental IRR	@0%	@10%	@15%
$B - A$	0	−$9,000	0	$11,000	10.55%	$2,000	$83	−$593

This chart shows that the incremental IRR is 10.55 percent. In other words, the NPV on the incremental investment is zero when the discount rate is 10.55 percent. Thus, if the relevant discount rate is below 10.55 percent, project B is preferred to project A. If the relevant discount rate is above 10.55 percent, project A is preferred to project B.[11]

---

[11]In this example, we first showed that the NPVs of the two projects are equal when the discount rate is 10.55 percent. We next showed that the incremental IRR is also 10.55 percent. This is not a coincidence; this equality must *always* hold. The incremental IRR is the rate that causes the incremental cash flows to have zero NPV. The incremental cash flows have zero NPV when the two projects have the same NPV.

3. *Calculate NPV on incremental cash flows.* Finally, we could calculate the NPV on the incremental cash flows. The chart that appears with the previous method displays these NPVs. We find that the incremental NPV is positive when the discount rate is either 0 percent or 10 percent. The incremental NPV is negative if the discount rate is 15 percent. If the NPV is positive on the incremental flows, we should choose *B*. If the NPV is negative, we should choose *A*.

In summary, the same decision is reached whether we (1) compare the NPVs of the two projects, (2) compare the incremental IRR to the relevant discount rate, or (3) examine the NPV of the incremental cash flows. However, as mentioned earlier, we should *not* compare the IRR of project *A* with the IRR of project *B*.

We suggested earlier that we should subtract the cash flows of the smaller project from the cash flows of the bigger project. What do we do here when the two projects have the same initial investment? Our suggestion in this case is to perform the subtraction so that the *first* nonzero cash flow is negative. In the Kaufold Corp. example we achieved this by subtracting *A* from *B*. In this way, we can still use the basic IRR rule for evaluating cash flows.

The preceding examples illustrate problems with the IRR approach in evaluating mutually exclusive projects. Both the professor–student example and the motion picture example illustrate the problem that arises when mutually exclusive projects have different initial investments. The Kaufold Corp. example illustrates the problem that arises when mutually exclusive projects have different cash flow timing. When working with mutually exclusive projects, it is not necessary to determine whether it is the scale problem or the timing problem that exists. Very likely both occur in any real-world situation. Instead, the practitioner should simply use either an incremental IRR or an NPV approach.

Redeeming Qualities of IRR

IRR probably survives because it fills a need that NPV does not. People seem to want a rule that summarizes the information about a project in a single rate of return. This single rate gives people a simple way of discussing projects. For example, one manager in a firm might say to another, "Remodeling the north wing has a 20 percent IRR."

To their credit, however, companies that employ the IRR approach seem to understand its deficiencies. For example, companies frequently restrict managerial projections of cash flows to be negative at the beginning and strictly positive later. Perhaps, then, the ability of the IRR approach to capture a complex investment project in a single number and the ease of communicating that number explain the survival of the IRR.

A Test

To test your knowledge, consider the following two statements:

1. You must know the discount rate to compute the NPV of a project, but you compute the IRR without referring to the discount rate.

2. Hence, the IRR rule is easier to apply than the NPV rule because you don't use the discount rate when applying IRR.

The first statement is true. The discount rate is needed to *compute* NPV. The IRR is *computed* by solving for the rate where the NPV is zero. No mention is made of the discount rate in the mere computation. However, the second statement is false. To *apply* IRR, you must compare the internal rate of return with the discount rate. Thus the discount rate is needed for making a decision under either the NPV or IRR approach.

6.7 The Profitability Index

Another method used to evaluate projects is called the **profitability index**. It is the ratio of the present value of the future expected cash flows *after* initial investment divided by the amount of the initial investment. The profitability index can be represented like this:

$$\text{Profitability index (PI)} = \frac{\text{PV of cash flows } \textit{subsequent} \text{ to initial investment}}{\text{Initial investment}}$$

EXAMPLE 6.5

Profitability Index   Hiram Finnegan Inc. (HFI) applies a 12 percent discount rate to two investment opportunities.

Project	Cash Flows ($000,000)			PV @ 12% of Cash Flows Subsequent to Initial Investment ($000,000)	Profitability Index	NPV @12% ($000,000)
	C_0	C_1	C_2			
1	−$20	$70	$10	$70.5	3.53	$50.5
2	− 10	15	40	45.3	4.53	35.3

Calculation of Profitability Index

The profitability index is calculated for project 1 as follows. The present value of the cash flows *after* the initial investment is:

$$\$70.5 = \frac{\$70}{1.12} + \frac{\$10}{(1.12)^2}$$

The profitability index is obtained by dividing this result by the initial investment of $20. This yields:

$$3.53 = \frac{\$70.5}{\$20}$$

Application of the Profitability Index   How do we use the profitability index? We consider three situations:

1. *Independent projects*: Assume that HFI's two projects are independent. According to the NPV rule, both projects should be accepted because NPV is positive in each case. The profitability index (PI) is greater than 1 whenever the NPV is positive. Thus, the PI *decision rule* is

   - Accept an independent project if PI > 1.

   - Reject it if PI < 1.

2. *Mutually exclusive projects*: Let us now assume that HFI can only accept one of its two projects. NPV analysis says accept project 1 because this project has the bigger NPV. Because project 2 has the higher PI, the profitability index leads to the wrong selection.

The problem with the profitability index for mutually exclusive projects is the same as the scale problem with the IRR that we mentioned earlier. Project 2 is smaller than project 1. Because the PI is a ratio, this index misses the fact that project 1 has a larger investment than project 2 has. Thus, like IRR, PI ignores differences of scale for mutually exclusive projects.

However, like IRR, the flaw with the PI approach can be corrected using incremental analysis. We write the incremental cash flows after subtracting project 2 from project 1 as follows:

	Cash Flows ($000,000)			PV @ 12% of Cash Flows Subsequent to Initial Investment ($000,000)	Profit-ability Index	NPV @12% ($000,000)
Project	C_0	C_1	C_2			
1–2	−$10	$55	−$30	$25.2	2.52	$15.2

Because the profitability index on the incremental cash flows is greater than 1.0, we should choose the bigger project—that is, project 1. This is the same decision we get with the NPV approach.

3. *Capital rationing*: The first two cases implicitly assumed that HFI could always attract enough capital to make any profitable investments. Now consider the case when the firm does not have enough capital to fund all positive NPV projects. This is the case of **capital rationing**.

   Imagine that the firm has a third project, as well as the first two. Project 3 has the following cash flows:

	Cash Flows ($000,000)			PV @ 12% of Cash Flows Subsequent to Initial Investment ($000,000)	Profit-ability Index	NPV @12% ($000,000)
Project	C_0	C_1	C_2			
3	−$10	−$5	$60	$43.4	4.34	$33.4

Further, imagine that (1) the projects of Hiram Finnegan Inc. are independent, but (2) the firm has only $20 million to invest. Because project 1 has an initial investment of $20 million, the firm cannot select both this project and another one. Conversely, because projects 2 and 3 have initial investments of $10 million each, both these projects can be chosen. In other words, the cash constraint forces the firm to choose either project 1 or projects 2 and 3.

What should the firm do? Individually, projects 2 and 3 have lower NPVs than project 1 has. However, when the NPVs of projects 2 and 3 are added together, the sum is higher than the NPV of project 1. Thus, common sense dictates that projects 2 and 3 should be accepted.

What does our conclusion have to say about the NPV rule or the PI rule? In the case of limited funds, we cannot rank projects according to their NPVs. Instead we should rank them according to the ratio of present value to initial investment. This is the PI rule. Both project 2 and project 3 have higher PI ratios than does project 1. Thus they should be ranked ahead of project 1 when capital is rationed.

The usefulness of the profitability index under capital rationing can be explained in military terms. The Pentagon speaks highly of a weapon with a lot of "bang for the buck." In capital budgeting, the profitability index measures the bang (the dollar return) for the buck invested. Hence it is useful for capital rationing.

It should be noted that the profitability index does not work if funds are also limited beyond the initial time period. For example, if heavy cash outflows elsewhere in the firm were to occur at date 1, project 3, which also has a cash outflow at date 1, might need to be rejected. In other words, the profitability index cannot handle capital rationing over multiple time periods.

In addition, what economists term *indivisibilities* may reduce the effectiveness of the PI rule. Imagine that HFI has $30 million available for capital investment, not just $20 million. The firm now has enough cash for projects 1 and 2. Because the sum of the NPVs of these two projects is greater than the sum of the NPVs of projects 2 and 3, the firm would be better served by accepting projects 1 and 2. But because projects 2 and 3 still have the highest profitability indexes, the PI rule now leads to the wrong decision. Why does the PI rule lead us astray here? The key is that projects 1 and 2 use up all of the $30 million, whereas projects 2 and 3 have a combined initial investment of only $20 million (= $10 + 10). If projects 2 and 3 are accepted, the remaining $10 million must be left in the bank.

This situation points out that care should be exercised when using the profitability index in the real world. Nevertheless, while not perfect, the profitability index goes a long way toward handling capital rationing.

6.8 The Practice of Capital Budgeting

So far this chapter has asked "Which capital budgeting methods should companies be using?" An equally important question is this: Which methods *are* companies using? Table 6.4 helps answer this question. As can be seen from the table, approximately three-quarters of U.S. and Canadian companies use the IRR and NPV methods. This is not surprising, given the theoretical advantages of these approaches. Over half of these companies use the payback method, a rather surprising result given the conceptual problems with this approach. And while discounted payback represents a theoretical improvement over regular payback,

Table 6.4

Percentage of CFOs Who Always or Almost Always Use a Given Technique

	% Always or Almost Always
Internal rate of return (IRR)	75.6%
Net present value (NPV)	74.9
Payback method	56.7
Discounted payback	29.5
Accounting rate of return	30.3
Profitability index	11.9

SOURCE: Figure 2 from John R. Graham and Campbell R. Harvey, "The Theory and Practice of Corporate Finance: Evidence from the Field," *Journal of Financial Economics* 60 (2001). Based on a survey of 392 CFOs.

In Their Own Words

KITCHEN CONFIDENTIAL: ADVENTURES IN THE CULINARY UNDERBELLY BY ANTHONY BOURDAIN (BLOOMSBURY PRESS, 2000)

To want to own a restaurant can be a strange and terrible affliction. What causes such a destructive urge in so many otherwise sensible people? Why would anyone who has worked hard, saved money, and often been successful in other fields want to pump their hard-earned cash down a hole that statistically, at least, will almost surely prove dry? Why venture into an industry with enormous fixed expenses (rent, electricity, gas, water, linen, maintenance, insurance, license fees, trash removal, etc.), a notoriously transient and unstable workforce, and a highly perishable inventory of assets? The chances of ever seeing a return on your investment are about one in five. What insidious spongiform bacteria so riddles the brains of men and women that they stand there on the tracks, watching the lights of the oncoming locomotive, knowing full well it will eventually run them over? After all these years in the business, I still don't know.

Anthony Bourdain is also the author of the novels *Bone in the Throat*, *Gone Bamboo*, and *The Bobby Gold Stories*. He is the executive chef at Brasserie Les Halles in New York.

the usage here is far less. Perhaps companies are attracted to the user-friendly nature of payback. In addition, the flaws of this approach, as mentioned in the current chapter, may be relatively easy to correct. For example, while the payback method ignores all cash flows after the payback period, an alert manager can make ad hoc adjustments for a project with back-loaded cash flows.

Capital expenditures by individual corporations can add up to enormous sums for the economy as a whole. For example, in late 2005, Royal Dutch Shell announced it expected to increase its capital spending in 2006 to $19 billion, an increase of 17 percent over the previous year. About the same time, competitor Chevron Corp. announced it would increase its capital budget for 2006 to $14.8 billion, up from $11 billion in 2005. Other companies with large capital spending budgets in 2006 were ConocoPhillips, which projected capital spending of $11.4 billion, and Canadian-based Suncor Energy, which projected capital spending of $3.5 billion.

Capital spending is often an industrywide occurrence. For example, in 2006, capital spending by dynamic random access memory (DRAM) chip makers was expected to reach $16.84 billion. This amount represented only a 5 percent increase from 2005 and was a major slowdown for capital spending growth. From 2003 to 2004, the DRAM industry's capital spending had grown by an astonishing 65 percent.

According to information released by the Census Bureau in 2006, capital investment for the economy as a whole was actually $1.05 trillion in 2004, $975 billion in 2003, and $953 billion in 2002. The totals for the three years therefore were about $3 trillion! Given the sums at stake, it is not too surprising that careful analysis of capital expenditures is something at which successful corporations seek to become adept.

One might expect the capital budgeting methods of large firms to be more sophisticated than the methods of small firms. After all, large firms have the financial resources to hire more sophisticated employees. Table 6.5 provides some support for this idea. Here firms indicate frequency of use of the various capital budgeting methods on a scale of 0 (never) to 4 (always). Both the IRR and NPV methods are used more frequently, and payback less frequently, in large firms than in small firms. Conversely, large and small firms employ the last three approaches about equally.

Table 6.5

Frequency of Use of Various Capital Budgeting Methods

	Large Firms	Small Firms
Internal rate of return (IRR)	3.41	2.87
Net present value (NPV)	3.42	2.83
Payback method	2.25	2.72
Discounted payback	1.55	1.58
Accounting rate of return	1.25	1.41
Profitability index	0.75	0.78

Firms indicate frequency of use on a scale from 0 (never) to 4 (always). Numbers in table are averages across respondents.

SOURCE: Table 2 from Graham and Harvey (2001), op. cit.

The use of quantitative techniques in capital budgeting varies with the industry. As one would imagine, firms that are better able to estimate cash flows are more likely to use NPV. For example, estimation of cash flow in certain aspects of the oil business is quite feasible. Because of this, energy-related firms were among the first to use NPV analysis. Conversely, the cash flows in the motion picture business are very hard to project. The grosses of the great hits like *Titanic, Harry Potter,* and *Star Wars* were far, far greater than anyone imagined. The big failures like *Alamo* and *Waterworld* were unexpected as well. Because of this, NPV analysis is frowned upon in the movie business.

How does Hollywood perform capital budgeting? The information that a studio uses to accept or reject a movie idea comes from the *pitch*. An independent movie producer schedules an extremely brief meeting with a studio to pitch his or her idea for a movie. Consider the following four paragraphs of quotes concerning the pitch from the thoroughly delightful book *Reel Power*:[12]

"They [studio executives] don't want to know too much," says Ron Simpson. "They want to know concept. . . . They want to know what the three-liner is, because they want it to suggest the ad campaign. They want a title. . . . They don't want to hear any esoterica. And if the meeting lasts more than five minutes, they're probably not going to do the project."

"A guy comes in and says this is my idea: '*Jaws* on a spaceship,'" says writer Clay Frohman (*Under Fire*). "And they say, 'Brilliant, fantastic.' Becomes *Alien*. That is *Jaws* on a spaceship, ultimately. . . . And that's it. That's all they want to hear. Their attitude is 'Don't confuse us with the details of the story.'"

". . . Some high-concept stories are more appealing to the studios than others. The ideas liked best are sufficiently original that the audience will not feel it has already seen the movie, yet similar enough to past hits to reassure executives wary of anything too far-out. Thus, the frequently used shorthand: It's *Flashdance* in the country (*Footloose*) or *High Noon* in outer space (*Outland*)."

". . . One gambit not to use during a pitch," says executive Barbara Boyle, "is to talk about big box-office grosses your story is sure to make. Executives know as well as anyone that it's impossible to predict how much money a movie will make, and declarations to the contrary are considered pure malarkey."

---

[12]Mark Litwak, *Reel Power: The Struggle for Influence and Success in the New Hollywood* (New York: William Morrow and Company, Inc., 1986), pp. 73, 74, and 77.

Summary and Conclusions

1. In this chapter, we covered different investment decision rules. We evaluated the most popular alternatives to the NPV: the payback period, the discounted payback period, the accounting rate of return, the internal rate of return, and the profitability index. In doing so we learned more about the NPV.

2. While we found that the alternatives have some redeeming qualities, when all is said and done, they are not the NPV rule; for those of us in finance, that makes them decidedly second-rate.

3. Of the competitors to NPV, IRR must be ranked above both payback and accounting rate of return. In fact, IRR always reaches the same decision as NPV in the normal case where the initial outflows of an independent investment project are followed only by a series of inflows.

4. We classified the flaws of IRR into two types. First, we considered the general case applying to both independent and mutually exclusive projects. There appeared to be two problems here:
   a. Some projects have cash inflows followed by one or more outflows. The IRR rule is inverted here: One should accept when the IRR is *below* the discount rate.
   b. Some projects have a number of changes of sign in their cash flows. Here, there are likely to be multiple internal rates of return. The practitioner must use either NPV or modified internal rate of return here.

5. Next, we considered the specific problems with the NPV for mutually exclusive projects. We showed that, due to differences in either size or timing, the project with the highest IRR need not have the highest NPV. Hence, the IRR rule should not be applied. (Of course, NPV can still be applied.)

   However, we then calculated incremental cash flows. For ease of calculation, we suggested subtracting the cash flows of the smaller project from the cash flows of the larger project. In that way the incremental initial cash flow is negative. One can always reach a correct decision by accepting the larger project if the incremental IRR is greater than the discount rate.

6. We described capital rationing as the case where funds are limited to a fixed dollar amount. With capital rationing the profitability index is a useful method of adjusting the NPV.

Concept Questions

1. **Payback Period and Net Present Value**   If a project with conventional cash flows has a payback period less than the project's life, can you definitively state the algebraic sign of the NPV? Why or why not? If you know that the discounted payback period is less than the project's life, what can you say about the NPV? Explain.

2. **Net Present Value**   Suppose a project has conventional cash flows and a positive NPV. What do you know about its payback? Its discounted payback? Its profitability index? Its IRR? Explain.

3. **Comparing Investment Criteria**   Define each of the following investment rules and discuss any potential shortcomings of each. In your definition, state the criterion for accepting or rejecting independent projects under each rule.
   a. Payback period.
   b. Average accounting return.
   c. Internal rate of return.
   d. Profitability index.
   e. Net present value.

4. **Payback and Internal Rate of Return**   A project has perpetual cash flows of C per period, a cost of I, and a required return of R. What is the relationship between the project's payback and its IRR? What implications does your answer have for long-lived projects with relatively constant cash flows?

5. **International Investment Projects**   In November 2004, automobile manufacturer Honda announced plans to build an automatic transmission plant in Georgia and expand its transmission plant in Ohio. Honda apparently felt that it would be better able to compete and create value with U.S.-based facilities. Other companies such as Fuji Film and Swiss chemical company Lonza have reached similar conclusions and taken similar actions. What are some of the reasons that foreign manufacturers of products as diverse as automobiles, film, and chemicals might arrive at this same conclusion?

6. **Capital Budgeting Problems**   What are some of the difficulties that might come up in actual applications of the various criteria we discussed in this chapter? Which one would be the easiest to implement in actual applications? The most difficult?

7. **Capital Budgeting in Not-for-Profit Entities**   Are the capital budgeting criteria we discussed applicable to not-for-profit corporations? How should such entities make capital budgeting decisions? What about the U.S. government? Should it evaluate spending proposals using these techniques?

8. **Net Present Value**   The investment in project A is $1 million, and the investment in project B is $2 million. Both projects have a unique internal rate of return of 20 percent. Is the following statement true or false?

   For any discount rate from 0 percent to 20 percent, project B has an NPV twice as great as that of project A.

   Explain your answer.

9. **Net Present Value versus Profitability Index**   Consider the following two mutually exclusive projects available to Global Investments, Inc.:

	C_0	C_1	C_2	Profitability Index	NPV
A	−$1,000	$1,000	$500	1.32	$322
B	−500	500	400	1.57	285

   The appropriate discount rate for the projects is 10 percent. Global Investments chose to undertake project A. At a luncheon for shareholders, the manager of a pension fund that owns a substantial amount of the firm's stock asks you why the firm chose project A instead of project B when project B has a higher profitability index.

   How would you, the CFO, justify your firm's action? Are there any circumstances under which Global Investments should choose project B?

10. **Internal Rate of Return**   Projects A and B have the following cash flows:

Year	Project A	Project B
0	−$1,000	−$2,000
1	C1A	C1B
2	C2A	C2B
3	C3A	C3B

   a. If the cash flows from the projects are identical, which of the two projects would have a higher IRR? Why?
   b. If C1B = 2C1A, C2B = 2C2A, and C3B = 2C3A, then is $IRR_A = IRR_B$?

11. **Net Present Value**   You are evaluating project A and project B. Project A has a short period of future cash flows, while project B has relatively long future cash flows. Which project will be more sensitive to changes in the required return? Why?

12. **Modified Internal Rate of Return**   One of the less flattering interpretations of the acronym MIRR is "meaningless internal rate of return." Why do you think this term is applied to MIRR?

13. **Net Present Value**   It is sometimes stated that "the net present value approach assumes reinvestment of the intermediate cash flows at the required return." Is this claim correct? To answer, suppose you calculate the NPV of a project in the usual way. Next, suppose you do the following:
   a. Calculate the future value (as of the end of the project) of all the cash flows other than the initial outlay assuming they are reinvested at the required return, producing a single future value figure for the project.
   b. Calculate the NPV of the project using the single future value calculated in the previous step and the initial outlay. It is easy to verify that you will get the same NPV as in your original calculation only if you use the required return as the reinvestment rate in the previous step.

14. **Internal Rate of Return**   It is sometimes stated that "the internal rate of return approach assumes reinvestment of the intermediate cash flows at the internal rate of return." Is this claim correct? To answer, suppose you calculate the IRR of a project in the usual way. Next, suppose you do the following:
   a. Calculate the future value (as of the end of the project) of all the cash flows other than the initial outlay assuming they are reinvested at the IRR, producing a single future value figure for the project.
   b. Calculate the IRR of the project using the single future value calculated in the previous step and the initial outlay. It is easy to verify that you will get the same IRR as in your original calculation only if you use the IRR as the reinvestment rate in the previous step.

Questions and Problems

BASIC
(Questions 1–10)

1. **Calculating Payback Period and NPV**   Fuji Software, Inc., has the following mutually exclusive projects.

Year	Project A	Project B
0	−$7,500	−$5,000
1	4,000	2,500
2	3,500	1,200
3	1,500	3,000

   a. Suppose Fuji's payback period cutoff is two years. Which of these two projects should be chosen?
   b. Suppose Fuji uses the NPV rule to rank these two projects. Which project should be chosen if the appropriate discount rate is 15 percent?

2. **Calculating Payback**   An investment project provides cash inflows of $840 per year for eight years. What is the project payback period if the initial cost is $3,000? What if the initial cost is $5,000? What if it is $7,000?

3. **Calculating Discounted Payback**   An investment project has annual cash inflows of $7,000, $7,500, $8,000, and $8,500, and a discount rate of 14 percent. What is the discounted payback period for these cash flows if the initial cost is $8,000? What if the initial cost is $13,000? What if it is $18,000?

4. **Calculating Discounted Payback**   An investment project costs $10,000 and has annual cash flows of $2,100 for six years. What is the discounted payback period if the discount rate is 0 percent? What if the discount rate is 5 percent? If it is 15 percent?

5.   **Average Accounting Return**   Your firm is considering purchasing a machine with the following annual, end-of-year, book investment accounts:

	Purchase Date	Year 1	Year 2	Year 3	Year 4
Gross investment	$16,000	$16,000	$16,000	$16,000	$16,000
Less: Accumulated depreciation	0	4,000	8,000	12,000	16,000
Net investment	$16,000	$12,000	$ 8,000	$ 4,000	$ 0

The machine generates, on average, $4,500 per year in additional net income.
   a. What is the average accounting return for this machine?
   b. What three flaws are inherent in this decision rule?

6.   **Average Accounting Return**   The Bluerock Group has invested $8,000 in a high-tech project lasting three years. Depreciation is $4,000, $2,500, and $1,500 in years 1, 2, and 3, respectively. The project generates pretax income of $2,000 each year. The pretax income already includes the depreciation expense. If the tax rate is 25 percent, what is the project's average accounting return (AAR)?

7.   **Calculating IRR**   Teddy Bear Planet, Inc., has a project with the following cash flows:

Year	Cash Flows ($)
0	−$8,000
1	4,000
2	3,000
3	2,000

The company evaluates all projects by applying the IRR rule. If the appropriate interest rate is 8 percent, should the company accept the project?

8.   **Calculating IRR**   Compute the internal rate of return for the cash flows of the following two projects:

	Cash Flows ($)	
Year	Project A	Project B
0	−$2,000	−$1,500
1	1,000	500
2	1,500	1,000
3	2,000	1,500

9.   **Calculating Profitability Index**   Bill plans to open a self-serve grooming center in a storefront. The grooming equipment will cost $160,000, to be paid immediately. Bill expects after-tax cash inflows of $40,000 annually for seven years, after which he plans to scrap the equipment and retire to the beaches of Nevis. The first cash inflow occurs at the end of the first year. Assume the required return is 15 percent. What is the project's PI? Should it be accepted?

10. **Calculating Profitability Index**   Suppose the following two independent investment opportunities are available to Greenplain, Inc. The appropriate discount rate is 10 percent.

Year	Project Alpha	Project Beta
0	−$500	−$2,000
1	300	300
2	700	1,800
3	600	1,700

a. Compute the profitability index for each of the two projects.
b. Which project(s) should Greenplain accept based on the profitability index rule?

INTERMEDIATE
(Questions 11–23)

11. **Cash Flow Intuition**   A project has an initial cost of I, has a required return of R, and pays C annually for N years.
   a. Find C in terms of I and N such that the project has a payback period just equal to its life.
   b. Find C in terms of I, N, and R such that this is a profitable project according to the NPV decision rule.
   c. Find C in terms of I, N, and R such that the project has a benefit–cost ratio of 2.

12. **Problems with IRR**   Suppose you are offered $5,000 today but must make the following payments:

Year	Cash Flows ($)
0	$5,000
1	−2,500
2	−2,000
3	−1,000
4	−1,000

   a. What is the IRR of this offer?
   b. If the appropriate discount rate is 10 percent, should you accept this offer?
   c. If the appropriate discount rate is 20 percent, should you accept this offer?
   d. What is the NPV of the offer if the appropriate discount rate is 10 percent? 20 percent?
   e. Are the decisions under the NPV rule in part (d) consistent with those of the IRR rule?

13. **NPV versus IRR**   Consider the following cash flows on two mutually exclusive projects for the Bahamas Recreation Corporation (BRC). Both projects require an annual return of 15 percent.

Year	Deepwater Fishing	New Submarine Ride
0	−$600,000	−$1,800,000
1	270,000	1,000,000
2	350,000	700,000
3	300,000	900,000

As a financial analyst for BRC, you are asked the following questions:
   a. If your decision rule is to accept the project with the greater IRR, which project should you choose?
   b. Because you are fully aware of the IRR rule's scale problem, you calculate the incremental IRR for the cash flows. Based on your computation, which project should you choose?
   c. To be prudent, you compute the NPV for both projects. Which project should you choose? Is it consistent with the incremental IRR rule?

14. Problems with Profitability Index   The Robb Computer Corporation is trying to choose between the following two mutually exclusive design projects:

Year	Cash Flow (I)	Cash Flow (II)
0	−$30,000	−$5,000
1	15,000	2,800
2	15,000	2,800
3	15,000	2,800

   a. If the required return is 10 percent and Robb Computer applies the profitability index decision rule, which project should the firm accept?
   b. If the company applies the NPV decision rule, which project should it take?
   c. Explain why your answers in (a) and (b) are different.

15. Problems with IRR   Cutler Petroleum, Inc., is trying to evaluate a generation project with the following cash flows:

Year	Cash Flow
0	−$28,000,000
1	53,000,000
2	−8,000,000

   a. If the company requires a 10 percent return on its investments, should it accept this project? Why?
   b. Compute the IRR for this project. How many IRRs are there? If you apply the IRR decision rule, should you accept the project or not? What's going on here?

16. Comparing Investment Criteria   Mario Brothers, a game manufacturer, has a new idea for an adventure game. It can market the game either as a traditional board game or as an interactive CD-ROM, but not both. Consider the following cash flows of the two mutually exclusive projects for Mario Brothers. Assume the discount rate for Mario Brothers is 10 percent.

Year	Board Game	CD-ROM
0	−$300	−$1,500
1	400	1,100
2	100	800
3	100	400

   a. Based on the payback period rule, which project should be chosen?
   b. Based on the NPV, which project should be chosen?
   c. Based on the IRR, which project should be chosen?
   d. Based on the incremental IRR, which project should be chosen?

17. Profitability Index versus NPV   Hanmi Group, a consumer electronics conglomerate, is reviewing its annual budget in wireless technology. It is considering investments in three different technologies to develop wireless communication devices. Consider the following cash flows of the three independent projects for Hanmi. Assume the discount rate for Hanmi is 10 percent. Further, Hanmi Group has only $30 million to invest in new projects this year.

Cash Flows (in $ millions)			
Year	CDMA	G4	Wi-Fi
0	−$10	−$20	−$ 30
1	25	20	20
2	15	50	40
3	5	40	100

   a. Based on the profitability index decision rule, rank these investments.
   b. Based on the NPV, rank these investments.
   c. Based on your findings in (a) and (b), what would you recommend to the CEO of Hanmi Group and why?

18. **Comparing Investment Criteria**   Consider the following cash flows of two mutually exclusive projects for AZ-Motorcars. Assume the discount rate for AZ-Motorcars is 10 percent.

Year	AZM Mini-SUV	AZF Full-SUV
0	−$200,000	−$500,000
1	200,000	200,000
2	150,000	300,000
3	150,000	300,000

   a. Based on the payback period, which project should be taken?
   b. Based on the NPV, which project should be taken?
   c. Based on the IRR, which project should be taken?
   d. Based on this analysis, is incremental IRR analysis necessary? If yes, please conduct the analysis.

19. **Comparing Investment Criteria**   The treasurer of Amaro Canned Fruits, Inc., has projected the cash flows of projects A, B, and C as follows.

Year	Project A	Project B	Project C
0	−$100,000	−$200,000	−$100,000
1	70,000	130,000	75,000
2	70,000	130,000	60,000

Suppose the relevant discount rate is 12 percent a year.
   a. Compute the profitability index for each of the three projects.
   b. Compute the NPV for each of the three projects.
   c. Suppose these three projects are independent. Which project(s) should Amaro accept based on the profitability index rule?
   d. Suppose these three projects are mutually exclusive. Which project(s) should Amaro accept based on the profitability index rule?
   e. Suppose Amaro's budget for these projects is $300,000. The projects are not divisible. Which project(s) should Amaro accept?

20. Comparing Investment Criteria Consider the following cash flows of two mutually exclusive projects for Tokyo Rubber Company. Assume the discount rate for Tokyo Rubber Company is 10 percent.

Year	Dry Prepreg	Solvent Prepreg
0	−$1,000,000	−$500,000
1	600,000	300,000
2	400,000	500,000
3	1,000,000	100,000

    a. Based on the payback period, which project should be taken?
    b. Based on the NPV, which project should be taken?
    c. Based on the IRR, which project should be taken?
    d. Based on this analysis, is incremental IRR analysis necessary? If yes, please conduct the analysis.

21. Comparing Investment Criteria Consider two mutually exclusive new product launch projects that Nagano Golf is considering. Assume the discount rate for Nagano Golf is 15 percent.

    Project *A*:   Nagano NP-30.
               Professional clubs that will take an initial investment of $100,000 at time 0.
               Next five years (years 1–5) of sales will generate a consistent cash flow of $40,000 per year.
               Introduction of new product at year 6 will terminate further cash flows from this project.

    Project *B*:   Nagano NX-20.
               High-end amateur clubs that will take an initial investment of $30,000 at time 0.
               Cash flow at year 1 is $20,000. In each subsequent year cash flow will grow at 15 percent per year.
               Introduction of new product at year 6 will terminate further cash flows from this project.

Year	NP-30	NX-20
0	−$100,000	−$30,000
1	40,000	20,000
2	40,000	23,000
3	40,000	26,450
4	40,000	30,418
5	40,000	34,980

Please fill in the following table:

	NP-30	NX-20	Implications
NPV			
IRR			
Incremental IRR			
PI			

www.mhhe.com/rwj

22. **Comparing Investment Criteria**   Consider two mutually exclusive R&D projects that ADM is considering. Assume the discount rate for ADM is 15 percent.

    Project *A*:   Server CPU .13 micron processing project.

               By shrinking the die size to .13 micron, ADM will be able to offer server CPU chips with lower power consumption and heat generation, meaning faster CPUs.

    Project *B*:   New telecom chip project.

               Entry into this industry will require introduction of a new chip for cellphones. The know-how will require a lot of upfront capital, but success of the project will lead to large cash flows later on.

Year	A	B
0	−$100,000	−$200,000
1	50,000	60,000
2	50,000	60,000
3	40,000	60,000
4	30,000	100,000
5	20,000	200,000

Please fill in the following table:

	A	B	Implications
NPV			
IRR			
Incremental IRR			
PI			

23. **Comparing Investment Criteria**   You are a senior manager at Poeing Aircraft and have been authorized to spend up to $200,000 for projects. The three projects you are considering have the following characteristics:

    Project *A*:   Initial investment of $150,000. Cash flow of $50,000 at year 1 and $100,000 at year 2. This is a plant expansion project, where the required rate of return is 10 percent.

    Project *B*:   Initial investment of $200,000. Cash flow of $200,000 at year 1 and $111,000 at year 2. This is a new product development project, where the required rate of return is 20 percent.

    Project *C*:   Initial investment of $100,000. Cash flow of $100,000 at year 1 and $100,000 at year 2. This is a market expansion project, where the required rate of return is 20 percent.

Assume the corporate discount rate is 10 percent.

Please offer your recommendations, backed by your analysis:

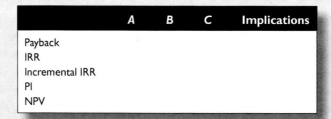

	A	B	C	Implications
Payback				
IRR				
Incremental IRR				
PI				
NPV				

24. **Payback and NPV** An investment under consideration has a payback of seven years and a cost of $483,000. If the required return is 12 percent, what is the worst-case NPV? The best-case NPV? Explain. Assume the cash flows are conventional.

25. **Multiple IRRs** This problem is useful for testing the ability of financial calculators and computer software. Consider the following cash flows. How many different IRRs are there? (*Hint*: Search between 20 percent and 70 percent.) When should we take this project?

Year	Cash Flow
0	−$ 504
1	2,862
2	−6,070
3	5,700
4	−2,000

26. **NPV Valuation** The Yurdone Corporation wants to set up a private cemetery business. According to the CFO, Barry M. Deep, business is "looking up." As a result, the cemetery project will provide a net cash inflow of $50,000 for the firm during the first year, and the cash flows are projected to grow at a rate of 6 percent per year forever. The project requires an initial investment of $780,000.
   a. If Yurdone requires a 13 percent return on such undertakings, should the cemetery business be started?
   b. The company is somewhat unsure about the assumption of a 6 percent growth rate in its cash flows. At what constant growth rate would the company just break even if it still required a 13 percent return on investment?

27. **Calculating IRR** The Utah Mining Corporation is set to open a gold mine near Provo, Utah. According to the treasurer, Monty Goldstein, "This is a golden opportunity." The mine will cost $600,000 to open and will have an economic life of 11 years. It will generate a cash inflow of $100,000 at the end of the first year, and the cash inflows are projected to grow at 8 percent per year for the next 10 years. After 11 years, the mine will be abandoned. Abandonment costs will be $50,000 at the end of year 11.
   a. What is the IRR for the gold mine?
   b. The Utah Mining Corporation requires a 10 percent return on such undertakings. Should the mine be opened?

28. **Calculating IRR** Consider two streams of cash flows, *A* and *B*. Stream *A*'s first cash flow is $5,000 and is received three years from today. Future cash flows in stream *A* grow by 4 percent in perpetuity. Stream *B*'s first cash flow is −$6,000, is received two years from today, and will continue in perpetuity. Assume that the appropriate discount rate is 12 percent.
   a. What is the present value of each stream?
   b. Suppose that the two streams are combined into one project, called *C*. What is the IRR of project *C*?
   c. What is the correct IRR rule for project *C*?

29. **Calculating Incremental Cash Flows** Darin Clay, the CFO of MakeMoney.com, has to decide between the following two projects:

Year	Project Million	Project Billion
0	−$1,500	−$$I_o$
1	I_o + 200	I_o + 500
2	1,200	1,500
3	1,500	2,000

196   **Part II**   Valuation and Capital Budgeting

The expected rate of return for either of the two projects is 12 percent. What is the range of initial investment (I_0) for which Project Billion is more financially attractive than Project Million?

30.   **Problems with IRR**   McKeekin Corp. has a project with the following cash flows:

Year	Cash Flow
0	$20,000
1	−26,000
2	13,000

What is the IRR of the project? What is happening here?

Bullock Gold Mining

Mini Case

Seth Bullock, the owner of Bullock Gold Mining, is evaluating a new gold mine in South Dakota. Dan Dority, the company's geologist, has just finished his analysis of the mine site. He has estimated that the mine would be productive for eight years, after which the gold would be completely mined. Dan has taken an estimate of the gold deposits to Alma Garrett, the company's financial officer. Alma has been asked by Seth to perform an analysis of the new mine and present her recommendation on whether the company should open the new mine.

Alma has used the estimates provided by Dan to determine the revenues that could be expected from the mine. She has also projected the expense of opening the mine and the annual operating expenses. If the company opens the mine, it will cost $500 million today, and it will have a cash outflow of $80 million nine years from today in costs associated with closing the mine and reclaiming the area surrounding it. The expected cash flows each year from the mine are shown in the following table. Bullock Mining has a 12 percent required return on all of its gold mines.

Year	Cash Flow
0	−$500,000,000
1	60,000,000
2	90,000,000
3	170,000,000
4	230,000,000
5	205,000,000
6	140,000,000
7	110,000,000
8	70,000,000
9	−80,000,000

1. Construct a spreadsheet to calculate the payback period, internal rate of return, modified internal rate of return, and net present value of the proposed mine.

2. Based on your analysis, should the company open the mine?

3. Bonus question: Most spreadsheets do not have a built-in formula to calculate the payback period. Write a VBA script that calculates the payback period for a project.

CHAPTER 6
NET PRESENT VALUE AND OTHER INVESTMENT CRITERIA

Answers to Concepts Review and Critical Thinking Questions

1. Assuming conventional cash flows, a payback period less than the project's life means that the NPV is positive for a zero discount rate, but nothing more definitive can be said. For discount rates greater than zero, the payback period will still be less than the project's life, but the NPV may be positive, zero, or negative, depending on whether the discount rate is less than, equal to, or greater than the IRR. The discounted payback includes the effect of the relevant discount rate. If a project's discounted payback period is less than the project's life, it must be the case that NPV is positive.

2. Assuming conventional cash flows, if a project has a positive NPV for a certain discount rate, then it will also have a positive NPV for a zero discount rate; thus, the payback period must be less than the project life. Since discounted payback is calculated at the same discount rate as is NPV, if NPV is positive, the discounted payback period must be less than the project's life. If NPV is positive, then the present value of future cash inflows is greater than the initial investment cost; thus, PI must be greater than 1. If NPV is positive for a certain discount rate R, then it will be zero for some larger discount rate $R*$; thus, the IRR must be greater than the required return.

3. *a.* Payback period is simply the accounting break-even point of a series of cash flows. To actually compute the payback period, it is assumed that any cash flow occurring during a given period is realized continuously throughout the period, and not at a single point in time. The payback is then the point in time for the series of cash flows when the initial cash outlays are fully recovered. Given some predetermined cutoff for the payback period, the decision rule is to accept projects that pay back before this cutoff, and reject projects that take longer to pay back. The worst problem associated with the payback period is that it ignores the time value of money. In addition, the selection of a hurdle point for the payback period is an arbitrary exercise that lacks any steadfast rule or method. The payback period is biased towards short-term projects; it fully ignores any cash flows that occur after the cutoff point.

    b. The average accounting return is interpreted as an average measure of the accounting performance of a project over time, computed as some average profit measure attributable to the project divided by some average balance sheet value for the project. This text computes AAR as average net income with respect to average (total) book value. Given some predetermined cutoff for AAR, the decision rule is to accept projects with an AAR in excess of the target measure, and reject all other projects. AAR is not a measure of cash flows or market value, but is rather a measure of financial statement accounts that often bear little resemblance to the relevant value of a project. In addition, the selection of a cutoff is arbitrary, and the time value of money is ignored. For a financial manager, both the reliance on accounting numbers rather than relevant market data and the exclusion of time value of money considerations are troubling. Despite these problems, AAR continues to be used in practice because (1) the accounting information is usually available, (2) analysts often use accounting ratios to analyze

B-124 SOLUTIONS

firm performance, and (3) managerial compensation is often tied to the attainment of target accounting ratio goals.

c. The IRR is the discount rate that causes the NPV of a series of cash flows to be identically zero. IRR can thus be interpreted as a financial break-even rate of return; at the IRR discount rate, the net value of the project is zero. The acceptance and rejection criteria are:

If $C_0 < 0$ and all future cash flows are positive, accept the project if the internal rate of return is greater than or equal to the discount rate.

If $C_0 < 0$ and all future cash flows are positive, reject the project if the internal rate of return is less than the discount rate.

If $C_0 > 0$ and all future cash flows are negative, accept the project if the internal rate of return is less than or equal to the discount rate.

If $C_0 > 0$ and all future cash flows are negative, reject the project if the internal rate of return is greater than the discount rate.

IRR is the discount rate that causes NPV for a series of cash flows to be zero. NPV is preferred in all situations to IRR; IRR can lead to ambiguous results if there are non-conventional cash flows, and it also may ambiguously rank some mutually exclusive projects. However, for stand-alone projects with conventional cash flows, IRR and NPV are interchangeable techniques.

d. The profitability index is the present value of cash inflows relative to the project cost. As such, it is a benefit/cost ratio, providing a measure of the relative profitability of a project. The profitability index decision rule is to accept projects with a PI greater than one, and to reject projects with a PI less than one. The profitability index can be expressed as: PI = (NPV + cost)/cost = 1 + (NPV/cost). If a firm has a basket of positive NPV projects and is subject to capital rationing, PI may provide a good ranking measure of the projects, indicating the "bang for the buck" of each particular project.

e. NPV is simply the present value of a project's cash flows, including the initial outlay. NPV specifically measures, after considering the time value of money, the net increase or decrease in firm wealth due to the project. The decision rule is to accept projects that have a positive NPV, and reject projects with a negative NPV. NPV is superior to the other methods of analysis presented in the text because it has no serious flaws. The method unambiguously ranks mutually exclusive projects, and it can differentiate between projects of different scale and time horizon. The only drawback to NPV is that it relies on cash flow and discount rate values that are often estimates and thus not certain, but this is a problem shared by the other performance criteria as well. A project with NPV = $2,500 implies that the total shareholder wealth of the firm will increase by $2,500 if the project is accepted.

4. For a project with future cash flows that are an annuity:

Payback = I / C

And the IRR is:

0 = – I + C / IRR

CHAPTER 6 B-125

Solving the IRR equation for IRR, we get:

IRR = C / I

Notice this is just the reciprocal of the payback. So:

IRR = 1 / PB

For long-lived projects with relatively constant cash flows, the sooner the project pays back, the greater is the IRR, and the IRR is approximately equal to the reciprocal of the payback period.

5. There are a number of reasons. Two of the most important have to do with transportation costs and exchange rates. Manufacturing in the U.S. places the finished product much closer to the point of sale, resulting in significant savings in transportation costs. It also reduces inventories because goods spend less time in transit. Higher labor costs tend to offset these savings to some degree, at least compared to other possible manufacturing locations. Of great importance is the fact that manufacturing in the U.S. means that a much higher proportion of the costs are paid in dollars. Since sales are in dollars, the net effect is to immunize profits to a large extent against fluctuations in exchange rates. This issue is discussed in greater detail in the chapter on international finance.

6. The single biggest difficulty, by far, is coming up with reliable cash flow estimates. Determining an appropriate discount rate is also not a simple task. These issues are discussed in greater depth in the next several chapters. The payback approach is probably the simplest, followed by the AAR, but even these require revenue and cost projections. The discounted cash flow measures (discounted payback, NPV, IRR, and profitability index) are really only slightly more difficult in practice.

7. Yes, they are. Such entities generally need to allocate available capital efficiently, just as for-profits do. However, it is frequently the case that the "revenues" from not-for-profit ventures are not tangible. For example, charitable giving has real opportunity costs, but the benefits are generally hard to measure. To the extent that benefits are measurable, the question of an appropriate required return remains. Payback rules are commonly used in such cases. Finally, realistic cost/benefit analysis along the lines indicated should definitely be used by the U.S. government and would go a long way toward balancing the budget!

8. The statement is false. If the cash flows of Project B occur early and the cash flows of Project A occur late, then for a low discount rate the NPV of A can exceed the NPV of B. Observe the following example.

	C_0	C_1	C_2	IRR	NPV @ 0%
Project A	−$1,000,000	$0	$1,440,000	20%	$440,000
Project B	−$2,000,000	$2,400,000	$0	20%	400,000

However, in one particular case, the statement is true for equally risky projects. If the lives of the two projects are equal and the cash flows of Project B are twice the cash flows of Project A in every time period, the NPV of Project B will be twice the NPV of Project A.

9. Although the profitability index (PI) is higher for Project B than for Project A, Project A should be chosen because it has the greater NPV. Confusion arises because Project B requires a smaller investment than Project A. Since the denominator of the PI ratio is lower for Project B than for Project A, B can have a higher PI yet have a lower NPV. Only in the case of capital rationing could the company's decision have been incorrect.

B-126 SOLUTIONS

10. *a.* Project A would have a higher IRR since initial investment for Project A is less than that of Project B, if the cash flows for the two projects are identical.

    b. Yes, since both the cash flows as well as the initial investment are twice that of Project B.

11. Project B's NPV would be more sensitive to changes in the discount rate. The reason is the time value of money. Cash flows that occur further out in the future are always more sensitive to changes in the interest rate. This sensitivity is similar to the interest rate risk of a bond.

12. The MIRR is calculated by finding the present value of all cash outflows, the future value of all cash inflows to the end of the project, and then calculating the IRR of the two cash flows. As a result, the cash flows have been discounted or compounded by one interest rate (the required return), and then the interest rate between the two remaining cash flows is calculated. As such, the MIRR is not a true interest rate. In contrast, consider the IRR. If you take the initial investment, and calculate the future value at the IRR, you can replicate the future cash flows of the project exactly.

13. The statement is incorrect. It is true that if you calculate the future value of all intermediate cash flows to the end of the project at the required return, then calculate the NPV of this future value and the initial investment, you will get the same NPV. However, NPV says nothing about reinvestment of intermediate cash flows. The NPV is the present value of the project cash flows. What is actually done with those cash flows once they are generated is not relevant. Put differently, the value of a project depends on the cash flows generated by the project, not on the future value of those cash flows. The fact that the reinvestment "works" only if you use the required return as the reinvestment rate is also irrelevant simply because reinvestment is not relevant in the first place to the value of the project.

    One caveat: Our discussion here assumes that the cash flows are truly available once they are generated, meaning that it is up to firm management to decide what to do with the cash flows. In certain cases, there may be a requirement that the cash flows be reinvested. For example, in international investing, a company may be required to reinvest the cash flows in the country in which they are generated and not "repatriate" the money. Such funds are said to be "blocked" and reinvestment becomes relevant because the cash flows are not truly available.

14. The statement is incorrect. It is true that if you calculate the future value of all intermediate cash flows to the end of the project at the IRR, then calculate the IRR of this future value and the initial investment, you will get the same IRR. However, as in the previous question, what is done with the cash flows once they are generated does not affect the IRR. Consider the following example:

	C_0	C_1	C_2	IRR
Project A	–$100	$10	$110	10%

Suppose this $100 is a deposit into a bank account. The IRR of the cash flows is 10 percent. Does the IRR change if the Year 1 cash flow is reinvested in the account, or if it is withdrawn and spent on pizza? No. Finally, consider the yield to maturity calculation on a bond. If you think about it, the YTM is the IRR on the bond, but no mention of a reinvestment assumption for the bond coupons is suggested. The reason is that reinvestment is irrelevant to the YTM calculation; in the same way, reinvestment is irrelevant in the IRR calculation. Our caveat about blocked funds applies here as well.

Solutions to Questions and Problems

NOTE: All end-of-chapter problems were solved using a spreadsheet. Many problems require multiple steps. Due to space and readability constraints, when these intermediate steps are included in this solutions manual, rounding may appear to have occurred. However, the final answer for each problem is found without rounding during any step in the problem.

Basic

1.   *a.*   The payback period is the time that it takes for the cumulative undiscounted cash inflows to equal the initial investment.

Project A:

Cumulative cash flows Year 1 = $4,000   = $4,000
Cumulative cash flows Year 2 = $4,000 +3,500   = $7,500

Payback period = 2 years

Project B:

Cumulative cash flows Year 1 = $2,500   = $2,500
Cumulative cash flows Year 2 = $2,500 + 1,200   = $3,700
Cumulative cash flows Year 3 = $2,500 + 1,200 + 3,000   = $6,700

Companies can calculate a more precise value using fractional years. To calculate the fractional payback period, find the fraction of year 3's cash flows that is needed for the company to have cumulative undiscounted cash flows of $5,000. Divide the difference between the initial investment and the cumulative undiscounted cash flows as of year 2 by the undiscounted cash flow of year 3.

Payback period = 2 + ($5,000 – $3,700) / $3,000
Payback period = 2.43

Since project A has a shorter payback period than project B has, the company should choose project A.

   b.   Discount each project's cash flows at 15 percent. Choose the project with the highest NPV.

Project A:
$NPV = -\$7,500 + \$4,000 / 1.15 + \$3,500 / 1.15^2 + \$1,500 / 1.15^3$
$NPV = -\$388.96$

Project B:
$NPV = -\$5,000 + \$2,500 / 1.15 + \$1,200 / 1.15^2 + \$3,000 / 1.15^3$
$NPV = \$53.83$

The firm should choose Project B since it has a higher NPV than Project A has.

192

Ross–Westerfield–Jaffe:
Corporate Finance, Eighth
Edition

II. Valuation and Capital
Budgeting

Answers for Chapter 6

© The McGraw–Hill
Companies, 2008

B-128 SOLUTIONS

2. To calculate the payback period, we need to find the time that the project has recovered its initial investment. The cash flows in this problem are an annuity, so the calculation is simpler. If the initial cost is $3,000, the payback period is:

Payback = 3 + ($480 / $840) = 3.57 years

There is a shortcut to calculate the payback period if the future cash flows are an annuity. Just divide the initial cost by the annual cash flow. For the $3,000 cost, the payback period is:

Payback = $3,000 / $840 = 3.57 years

For an initial cost of $5,000, the payback period is:

Payback = 5 + ($800 / $840) = 5.95 years

The payback period for an initial cost of $7,000 is a little trickier. Notice that the total cash inflows after eight years will be:

Total cash inflows = 8($840) = $6,720

If the initial cost is $7,000, the project never pays back. Notice that if you use the shortcut for annuity cash flows, you get:

Payback = $7,000 / $840 = 8.33 years.

This answer does not make sense since the cash flows stop after eight years, so there is no payback period.

3. When we use discounted payback, we need to find the value of all cash flows today. The value today of the project cash flows for the first four years is:

Value today of Year 1 cash flow = $7,000/1.14 = $6,140.35
Value today of Year 2 cash flow = $7,500/1.14^2 = $5,771.01
Value today of Year 3 cash flow = $8,000/1.14^3 = $5,399.77
Value today of Year 4 cash flow = $8,500/1.14^4 = $5,032.68

To find the discounted payback, we use these values to find the payback period. The discounted first year cash flow is $6,140.35, so the discounted payback for an $8,000 initial cost is:

Discounted payback = 1 + ($8,000 – 6,140.35)/$5,771.01 = 1.32 years

For an initial cost of $13,000, the discounted payback is:

Discounted payback = 2 + ($13,000 – 6,140.35 – 5,771.01)/$5,399.77 = 2.20 years

Notice the calculation of discounted payback. We know the payback period is between two and three years, so we subtract the discounted values of the Year 1 and Year 2 cash flows from the initial cost. This is the numerator, which is the discounted amount we still need to make to recover our initial investment. We divide this amount by the discounted amount we will earn in Year 3 to get the fractional portion of the discounted payback.

If the initial cost is $18,000, the discounted payback is:

Discounted payback = 3 + ($18,000 – 6,140.35 – 5,771.01 – 5,399.77) / $5,032.68 = 3.14 years

4. To calculate the discounted payback, discount all future cash flows back to the present, and use these discounted cash flows to calculate the payback period. Doing so, we find:

R = 0%: 4 + ($1,600 / $2,100) = 4.76 years
Discounted payback = Regular payback = 4.76 years

R = 5%: $2,100/1.05 + $2,100/1.05^2 + $2,100/1.05^3 + $2,100/1.05^4 + $2,100/1.05^5 = $9,091.90
$2,100/1.05^6 = $1,567.05
Discounted payback = 5 + ($10,000 – 9,091.90) / $1,567.05 = 5.58 years

R = 15%: $2,100/1.15 + $2,100/1.15^2 + $2,100/1.15^3 + $2,100/1.15^4 + $2,100/1.15^5 + $2,100/1.15^6
= $7,947.41; The project never pays back.

5. a. The average accounting return is the average project earnings after taxes, divided by the average book value, or average net investment, of the machine during its life. The book value of the machine is the gross investment minus the accumulated depreciation.

Average book value = (Book value$_0$ + Book value$_1$ + Book value$_2$ + Book value$_3$ +
Book value$_4$ + Book value$_5$) / (Economic life)
Average book value = ($16,000 + 12,000 + 8,000 + 4,000 + 0) / (5 years)
Average book value = $8,000

Average project earnings = $4,500

To find the average accounting return, we divide the average project earnings by the average book value of the machine to calculate the average accounting return. Doing so, we find:

Average accounting return = Average project earnings / Average book value
Average accounting return = $4,500 / $8,000
Average accounting return = 0.5625 or 56.25%

6. First, we need to determine the average book value of the project. The book value is the gross investment minus accumulated depreciation.

	Purchase Date	Year 1	Year 2	Year 3
Gross Investment	$8,000	$8,000	$8,000	$8,000
Less: Accumulated depreciation	0	4,000	6,500	8,000
Net Investment	$8,000	$4,000	$1,500	$0

Now, we can calculate the average book value as:

Average book value = ($8,000 + 4,000 + 1,500 + 0) / (4 years)
Average book value = $3,375

B-130 SOLUTIONS

To calculate the average accounting return, we must remember to use the aftertax average net income when calculating the average accounting return. So, the average aftertax net income is:

Average aftertax net income = $(1 - t_c)$ Annual pretax net income
Average aftertax net income = $(1 - 0.25)$ $2,000
Average aftertax net income = $1,500

The average accounting return is the average after-tax net income divided by the average book value, which is:

Average accounting return = $1,500 / $3,375
Average accounting return = 0.4444 or 44.44%

7. The IRR is the interest rate that makes the NPV of the project equal to zero. So, the equation that defines the IRR for this project is:

$$0 = C_0 + C_1 / (1 + IRR) + C_2 / (1 + IRR)^2 + C_3 / (1 + IRR)^3$$
$$0 = -\$8,000 + \$4,000/(1 + IRR) + \$3,000/(1 + IRR)^2 + \$2,000/(1 + IRR)^3$$

Using a spreadsheet, financial calculator, or trial and error to find the root of the equation, we find that:

IRR = 6.93%

Since the IRR is less than the required return we would reject the project.

8. The IRR is the interest rate that makes the NPV of the project equal to zero. So, the equation that defines the IRR for this Project A is:

$$0 = C_0 + C_1 / (1 + IRR) + C_2 / (1 + IRR)^2 + C_3 / (1 + IRR)^3$$
$$0 = -\$2,000 + \$1,000/(1 + IRR) + \$1,500/(1 + IRR)^2 + \$2,000/(1 + IRR)^3$$

Using a spreadsheet, financial calculator, or trial and error to find the root of the equation, we find that:

IRR = 47.15%

And the IRR for Project B is:

$$0 = C_0 + C_1 / (1 + IRR) + C_2 / (1 + IRR)^2 + C_3 / (1 + IRR)^3$$
$$0 = -\$1,500 + \$500/(1 + IRR) + \$1,000/(1 + IRR)^2 + \$1,500/(1 + IRR)^3$$

Using a spreadsheet, financial calculator, or trial and error to find the root of the equation, we find that:

IRR = 36.19%

9. The profitability index is defined as the PV of the cash inflows divided by the PV of the cash outflows. The cash flows from this project are an annuity, so the equation for the profitability index is:

$PI = C(PVIFA_{R,t}) / C_0$
$PI = \$40,000(PVIFA_{15\%,7}) / \$160,000$
$PI = 1.0401$

10. *a.* The profitability index is the present value of the future cash flows divided by the initial cost. So, for Project Alpha, the profitability index is:

$$PI_{Alpha} = [\$300 / 1.10 + \$700 / 1.10^2 + \$600 / 1.10^3] / \$500 = 2.604$$

And for Project Beta the profitability index is:

$$PI_{Beta} = [\$300 / 1.10 + \$1,800 / 1.10^2 + \$1,700 / 1.10^3] / \$2,000 = 1.519$$

b. According to the profitability index, you would accept Project Alpha. However, remember the profitability index rule can lead to an incorrect decision when ranking mutually exclusive projects.

Intermediate

11. *a.* To have a payback equal to the project's life, given C is a constant cash flow for N years:

$$C = I/N$$

b. To have a positive NPV, $I < C \, (PVIFA_{R\%, \, N})$. Thus, $C > I / (PVIFA_{R\%, \, N})$.

c. Benefits = $C \, (PVIFA_{R\%, \, N}) = 2 \times$ costs = 2I
$C = 2I / (PVIFA_{R\%, \, N})$

12. *a.* The IRR is the interest rate that makes the NPV of the project equal to zero. So, the equation that defines the IRR for this project is:

$$0 = C_0 + C_1 / (1 + IRR) + C_2 / (1 + IRR)^2 + C_3 / (1 + IRR)^3 + C_4 / (1 + IRR)^4$$
$$0 = \$5,000 - \$2,500 / (1 + IRR) - \$2,000 / (1 + IRR)^2 - \$1,000 / (1 + IRR)^3$$
$$- \$1,000 / (1 + IRR)^4$$

Using a spreadsheet, financial calculator, or trial and error to find the root of the equation, we find that:

IRR = 13.99%

b. This problem differs from previous ones because the initial cash flow is positive and all future cash flows are negative. In other words, this is a financing-type project, while previous projects were investing-type projects. For financing situations, accept the project when the IRR is less than the discount rate. Reject the project when the IRR is greater than the discount rate.

IRR = 13.99%
Discount Rate = 10%

IRR > Discount Rate

Reject the offer when the discount rate is less than the IRR.

B-132 SOLUTIONS

    c.   Using the same reason as part *b.*, we would accept the project if the discount rate is 20 percent.

IRR = 13.99%
Discount Rate = 20%

IRR < Discount Rate

Accept the offer when the discount rate is greater than the IRR.

    d.   The NPV is the sum of the present value of all cash flows, so the NPV of the project if the discount rate is 10 percent will be:

$$\text{NPV} = \$5,000 - \$2,500 / 1.1 - \$2,000 / 1.1^2 - \$1,000 / 1.1^3 - \$1,000 / 1.1^4$$
$$\text{NPV} = -\$359.95$$

When the discount rate is 10 percent, the NPV of the offer is –$359.95. Reject the offer.

And the NPV of the project is the discount rate is 20 percent will be:

$$\text{NPV} = \$5,000 - \$2,500 / 1.2 - \$2,000 / 1.2^2 - \$1,000 / 1.2^3 - \$1,000 / 1.2^4$$
$$\text{NPV} = \$466.82$$

When the discount rate is 20 percent, the NPV of the offer is $466.82. Accept the offer.

    e.   Yes, the decisions under the NPV rule are consistent with the choices made under the IRR rule since the signs of the cash flows change only once.

13. *a.*   The IRR is the interest rate that makes the NPV of the project equal to zero. So, the IRR for each project is:

Deepwater Fishing IRR:

$$0 = C_0 + C_1 / (1 + \text{IRR}) + C_2 / (1 + \text{IRR})^2 + C_3 / (1 + \text{IRR})^3$$
$$0 = -\$600,000 + \$270,000 / (1 + \text{IRR}) + \$350,000 / (1 + \text{IRR})^2 + \$300,000 / (1 + \text{IRR})^3$$

Using a spreadsheet, financial calculator, or trial and error to find the root of the equation, we find that:

IRR = 24.30%

Submarine Ride IRR:

$$0 = C_0 + C_1 / (1 + \text{IRR}) + C_2 / (1 + \text{IRR})^2 + C_3 / (1 + \text{IRR})^3$$
$$0 = -\$1,800,000 + \$1,000,000 / (1 + \text{IRR}) + \$700,000 / (1 + \text{IRR})^2 + \$900,000 / (1 + \text{IRR})^3$$

Using a spreadsheet, financial calculator, or trial and error to find the root of the equation, we find that:

IRR = 21.46%

Based on the IRR rule, the deepwater fishing project should be chosen because it has the higher IRR.

b. To calculate the incremental IRR, we subtract the smaller project's cash flows from the larger project's cash flows. In this case, we subtract the deepwater fishing cash flows from the submarine ride cash flows. The incremental IRR is the IRR of these incremental cash flows. So, the incremental cash flows of the submarine ride are:

	Year 0	Year 1	Year 2	Year 3
Submarine Ride	−$1,800,000	$1,000,000	$700,000	$900,000
Deepwater Fishing	−600,000	270,000	350,000	300,000
Submarine − Fishing	−$1,200,000	$730,000	$350,000	$600,000

Setting the present value of these incremental cash flows equal to zero, we find the incremental IRR is:

$$0 = C_0 + C_1 / (1 + IRR) + C_2 / (1 + IRR)^2 + C_3 / (1 + IRR)^3$$
$$0 = -\$1,200,000 + \$730,000 / (1 + IRR) + \$350,000 / (1 + IRR)^2 + \$600,000 / (1 + IRR)^3$$

Using a spreadsheet, financial calculator, or trial and error to find the root of the equation, we find that:

Incremental IRR = 19.92%

For investing-type projects, accept the larger project when the incremental IRR is greater than the discount rate. Since the incremental IRR, 19.92%, is greater than the required rate of return of 15 percent, choose the submarine ride project. Note that this is the choice when evaluating only the IRR of each project. The IRR decision rule is flawed because there is a scale problem. That is, the submarine ride has a greater initial investment than does the deepwater fishing project. This problem is corrected by calculating the IRR of the incremental cash flows, or by evaluating the NPV of each project.

c. The NPV is the sum of the present value of the cash flows from the project, so the NPV of each project will be:

Deepwater fishing:

$$NPV = -\$600,000 + \$270,000 / 1.15 + \$350,000 / 1.15^2 + \$300,000 / 1.15^3$$
$$NPV = \$96,687.76$$

B-134 SOLUTIONS

Submarine ride:

$$NPV = -\$1,800,000 + \$1,000,000 / 1.15 + \$700,000 / 1.15^2 + \$900,000 / 1.15^3$$
$$NPV = \$190,630.39$$

Since the NPV of the submarine ride project is greater than the NPV of the deepwater fishing project, choose the submarine ride project. The incremental IRR rule is always consistent with the NPV rule.

14. *a.* The profitability index is the PV of the future cash flows divided by the initial investment. The cash flows for both projects are an annuity, so:

$$PI_I = \$15,000(PVIFA_{10\%,3}) / \$30,000 = 1.243$$

$$PI_{II} = \$2,800(PVIFA_{10\%,3}) / \$5,000 = 1.393$$

The profitability index decision rule implies that we accept project II, since PI_{II} is greater than the PI_I.

b. The NPV of each project is:

$$NPV_I = -\$30,000 + \$15,000(PVIFA_{10\%,3}) = \$7,302.78$$

$$NPV_{II} = -\$5,000 + \$2,800(PVIFA_{10\%,3}) = \$1,963.19$$

The NPV decision rule implies accepting Project I, since the NPV_I is greater than the NPV_{II}.

c. Using the profitability index to compare mutually exclusive projects can be ambiguous when the magnitudes of the cash flows for the two projects are of different scale. In this problem, project I is roughly 3 times as large as project II and produces a larger NPV, yet the profitability index criterion implies that project II is more acceptable.

15. *a.* The equation for the NPV of the project is:

$$NPV = -\$28,000,000 + \$53,000,000/1.1 - \$8,000,000/1.1^2 = \$13,570,247.93$$

The NPV is greater than 0, so we would accept the project.

b. The equation for the IRR of the project is:

$$0 = -\$28,000,000 + \$53,000,000/(1+IRR) - \$8,000,000/(1+IRR)^2$$

From Descartes rule of signs, we know there are two IRRs since the cash flows change signs twice. From trial and error, the two IRRs are:

$$IRR = 72.75\%, -83.46\%$$

When there are multiple IRRs, the IRR decision rule is ambiguous. Both IRRs are correct; that is, both interest rates make the NPV of the project equal to zero. If we are evaluating whether or not to accept this project, we would not want to use the IRR to make our decision.

16. *a.* The payback period is the time that it takes for the cumulative undiscounted cash inflows to equal the initial investment.

Board game:

Cumulative cash flows Year 1 = $400 = $400

Payback period = $300 / $400 = .75 years

CD-ROM:

Cumulative cash flows Year 1 = $1,100 = $1,100
Cumulative cash flows Year 2 = $1,100 + 800 = $1,900

Payback period = 1 + ($1,500 – $1,100) / $800
Payback period = 1.50 years

Since the board game has a shorter payback period than the CD-ROM project, the company should choose the board game.

b. The NPV is the sum of the present value of the cash flows from the project, so the NPV of each project will be:

Board game:

$NPV = -\$300 + \$400 / 1.10 + \$100 / 1.10^2 + \$100 / 1.10^3$
$NPV = \$221.41$

CD-ROM:

$NPV = -\$1,500 + \$1,100 / 1.10 + \$800 / 1.10^2 + \$400 / 1.10^3$
$NPV = \$461.68$

Since the NPV of the CD-ROM is greater than the NPV of the board game, choose the CD-ROM.

c. The IRR is the interest rate that makes the NPV of a project equal to zero. So, the IRR of each project is:

Board game:

$0 = -\$300 + \$400 / (1 + IRR) + \$100 / (1 + IRR)^2 + \$100 / (1 + IRR)^3$

Using a spreadsheet, financial calculator, or trial and error to find the root of the equation, we find that:

$IRR = 65.61\%$

B-136 SOLUTIONS

CD-ROM:

$$0 = -\$1,500 + \$1,100 / (1 + IRR) + \$800 / (1 + IRR)^2 + \$400 / (1 + IRR)^3$$

Using a spreadsheet, financial calculator, or trial and error to find the root of the equation, we find that:

IRR = 30.09%

Since the IRR of the board game is greater than the IRR of the CD-ROM, IRR implies we choose the board game.

d. To calculate the incremental IRR, we subtract the smaller project's cash flows from the larger project's cash flows. In this case, we subtract the board game cash flows from the CD-ROM cash flows. The incremental IRR is the IRR of these incremental cash flows. So, the incremental cash flows of the submarine ride are:

	Year 0	Year 1	Year 2	Year 3
CD-ROM	–$1,500	$1,100	$800	$400
Board game	–300	400	100	100
CD-ROM – Board game	–$1,200	$700	$700	$300

Setting the present value of these incremental cash flows equal to zero, we find the incremental IRR is:

$$0 = C_0 + C_1 / (1 + IRR) + C_2 / (1 + IRR)^2 + C_3 / (1 + IRR)^3$$
$$0 = -\$1,200 + \$700 / (1 + IRR) + \$700 / (1 + IRR)^2 + \$300 / (1 + IRR)^3$$

Using a spreadsheet, financial calculator, or trial and error to find the root of the equation, we find that:

Incremental IRR = 22.57%

For investing-type projects, accept the larger project when the incremental IRR is greater than the discount rate. Since the incremental IRR, 22.57%, is greater than the required rate of return of 10 percent, choose the CD-ROM project. Note that this is the choice when evaluating only the IRR of each project. The IRR decision rule is flawed because there is a scale problem. That is, the CD-ROM has a greater initial investment than does the board game. This problem is corrected by calculating the IRR of the incremental cash flows, or by evaluating the NPV of each project.

17. *a.* The profitability index is the PV of the future cash flows divided by the initial investment. The profitability index for each project is:

$$PI_{CDMA} = [\$25,000,000 / 1.10 + \$15,000,000 / 1.10^2 + \$5,000,000 / 1.10^3] / \$10,000,000 = 3.89$$

$$PI_{G4} = [\$20,000,000 / 1.10 + \$50,000,000 / 1.10^2 + \$40,000,000 / 1.10^3] / \$20,000,000 = 4.48$$

$$PI_{Wi\text{-}Fi} = [\$20,000,000 / 1.10 + \$40,000,000 / 1.10^2 + \$100,000,000 / 1.10^3] / \$30,000,000 = 4.21$$

The profitability index implies we accept the G4 project. Remember this is not necessarily correct because the profitability index does not necessarily rank projects with different initial investments correctly.

b. The NPV of each project is:

$$NPV_{CDMA} = -\$10,000,000 + \$25,000,000 / 1.10 + \$15,000,000 / 1.10^2 + \$5,000,000 / 1.10^3$$
$$NPV_{CDMA} = \$28,880,540.95$$

$$NPV_{G4} = -\$20,000,000 + \$20,000,000 / 1.10 + \$50,000,000 / 1.10^2 + \$40,000,000 / 1.10^3$$
$$NPV_{G4} = \$69,556,724.27$$

$$PI_{Wi\text{-}Fi} = -\$30,000,000 + \$20,000,000 / 1.10 + \$40,000,000 / 1.10^2 + \$100,000,000 / 1.10^3$$
$$PI_{Wi\text{-}Fi} = \$96,371,149.51$$

NPV implies we accept the Wi-Fi project since it has the highest NPV. This is the correct decision if the projects are mutually exclusive.

c. We would like to invest in all three projects since each has a positive NPV. If the budget is limited to $30 million, we can only accept the CDMA project and the G4 project, or the Wi-Fi project. NPV is additive across projects and the company. The total NPV of the CDMA project and the G4 project is:

$$NPV_{CDMA \text{ and } G4} = \$28,880,540.95 + 69,556,724.27$$
$$NPV_{CDMA \text{ and } G4} = \$98,437,265.21$$

This is greater than the Wi-Fi project, so we should accept the CDMA project and the G4 project.

18. *a.* The payback period is the time that it takes for the cumulative undiscounted cash inflows to equal the initial investment.

AZM Mini-SUV:

Cumulative cash flows Year 1 = $200,000   = $200,000

Payback period = $200,000 / $200,000 = 1 year

B-138 SOLUTIONS

AZF Full-SUV:

Cumulative cash flows Year 1 = $200,000   = $200,000
Cumulative cash flows Year 2 = $200,000 + 300,000   = $500,000

Payback period = 2 years

Since the AZM has a shorter payback period than the AZF, the company should choose the AZF. Remember the payback period does not necessarily rank projects correctly.

b.   The NPV of each project is:

$$NPV_{AZM} = -\$200{,}000 + \$200{,}000 / 1.10 + \$150{,}000 / 1.10^2 + \$150{,}000 / 1.10^3$$
$$NPV_{AZM} = \$218{,}482.34$$

$$NPV_{AZF} = -\$500{,}000 + \$200{,}000 / 1.10 + \$300{,}000 / 1.10^2 + \$300{,}000 / 1.10^3$$
$$NPV_{AZF} = \$155{,}146.51$$

The NPV criteria implies we accept the AZM because it has the highest NPV.

c.   The IRR is the interest rate that makes the NPV of the project equal to zero. So, the IRR of each AZM is:

$$0 = -\$200{,}000 + \$200{,}000 / (1 + IRR) + \$150{,}000 / (1 + IRR)^2 + \$150{,}000 / (1 + IRR)^3$$

Using a spreadsheet, financial calculator, or trial and error to find the root of the equation, we find that:

$$IRR_{AZM} = 70.04\%$$

And the IRR of the AZF is:

$$0 = -\$500{,}000 + \$200{,}000 / (1 + IRR) + \$300{,}000 / (1 + IRR)^2 + \$300{,}000 / (1 + IRR)^3$$

Using a spreadsheet, financial calculator, or trial and error to find the root of the equation, we find that:

$$IRR_{AZF} = 25.70\%$$

The IRR criteria implies we accept the AZM because it has the highest NPV. Remember the IRR does not necessarily rank projects correctly.

d.   Incremental IRR analysis is not necessary. The AZM has the smallest initial investment, and the largest NPV, so it should be accepted.

19. *a.* The profitability index is the PV of the future cash flows divided by the initial investment. The profitability index for each project is:

$$PI_A = [\$70,000 / 1.12 + \$70,000 / 1.12^2] / \$100,000 = 1.18$$

$$PI_B = [\$130,000 / 1.12 + \$130,000 / 1.12^2] / \$200,000 = 1.10$$

$$PI_C = [\$75,000 / 1.12 + \$60,000 / 1.12^2] / \$100,000 = 1.15$$

b. The NPV of each project is:

$$NPV_A = -\$100,000 + \$70,000 / 1.12 + \$70,000 / 1.12^2$$
$$NPV_A = \$18,303.57$$

$$NPV_B = -\$200,000 + \$130,000 / 1.12 + \$130,000 / 1.12^2$$
$$NPV_B = \$19,706.63$$

$$NPV_C = -\$100,000 + \$75,000 / 1.12 + \$60,000 / 1.12^2$$
$$NPV_C = \$14,795.92$$

c. Accept projects A, B, and C. Since the projects are independent, accept all three projects because the respective profitability index of each is greater than one.

d. Accept Project B. Since the Projects are mutually exclusive, choose the Project with the highest PI, while taking into account the scale of the Project. Because Projects A and C have the same initial investment, the problem of scale does not arise when comparing the profitability indices. Based on the profitability index rule, Project C can be eliminated because its PI is less than the PI of Project A. Because of the problem of scale, we cannot compare the PIs of Projects A and B. However, we can calculate the PI of the incremental cash flows of the two projects, which are:

Project	C_0	C_1	C_2
B – A	–$100,000	$60,000	$60,000

When calculating incremental cash flows, remember to subtract the cash flows of the project with the smaller initial cash outflow from those of the project with the larger initial cash outflow. This procedure insures that the incremental initial cash outflow will be negative. The incremental PI calculation is:

$$PI(B - A) = [\$60,000 / 1.12 + \$60,000 / 1.12^2] / \$100,000$$
$$PI(B - A) = 1.014$$

The company should accept Project B since the PI of the incremental cash flows is greater than one.

e. Remember that the NPV is additive across projects. Since we can spend $300,000, we could take two of the projects. In this case, we should take the two projects with the highest NPVs, which are Project B and Project A.

204

Ross–Westerfield–Jaffe:
Corporate Finance, Eighth
Edition

II. Valuation and Capital
Budgeting

Answers for Chapter 6

© The McGraw–Hill
Companies, 2008

B-140 SOLUTIONS

20. *a.* The payback period is the time that it takes for the cumulative undiscounted cash inflows to equal the initial investment.

Dry Prepeg:

Cumulative cash flows Year 1 = $600,000   = $600,000
Cumulative cash flows Year 2 = $600,000 + 400,000   = $1,000,000

Payback period = 2 years

Solvent Prepeg:

Cumulative cash flows Year 1 = $300,000   = $300,000
Cumulative cash flows Year 2 = $300,000 + 500,000   = $800,000

Payback period = 1 + ($200,000/$500,000) = 1.4 years

Since the solvent prepeg has a shorter payback period than the dry prepeg, the company should choose the solvent prepeg. Remember the payback period does not necessarily rank projects correctly.

b. The NPV of each project is:

$\text{NPV}_{\text{Dry prepeg}} = -\$1,000,000 + \$600,000 / 1.10 + \$400,000 / 1.10^2 + \$1,000,000 / 1.10^3$
$\text{NPV}_{\text{Dry prepeg}} = \$627,347.86$

$\text{NPV}_{\text{G4}} = -\$500,000 + \$300,000 / 1.10 + \$500,000 / 1.10^2 + \$100,000 / 1.10^3$
$\text{NPV}_{\text{G4}} = \$261,081.89$

The NPV criteria implies accepting the dry prepeg because it has the highest NPV.

c. The IRR is the interest rate that makes the NPV of the project equal to zero. So, the IRR of each dry prepeg is:

$0 = -\$1,000,000 + \$600,000 / (1 + \text{IRR}) + \$400,000 / (1 + \text{IRR})^2 + \$1,000,000 / (1 + \text{IRR})^3$

Using a spreadsheet, financial calculator, or trial and error to find the root of the equation, we find that:

$\text{IRR}_{\text{Dry prepeg}} = 39.79\%$

And the IRR of the solvent prepeg is:

$0 = -\$500,000 + \$300,000 / (1 + \text{IRR}) + \$500,000 / (1 + \text{IRR})^2 + \$100,000 / (1 + \text{IRR})^3$

Using a spreadsheet, financial calculator, or trial and error to find the root of the equation, we find that:

$\text{IRR}_{\text{Solvent prepeg}} = 40.99\%$

The IRR criteria implies accepting the solvent prepeg because it has the highest NPV. Remember the IRR does not necessarily rank projects correctly.

d. Incremental IRR analysis is necessary. The solvent prepeg has a higher IRR, but is relatively smaller in terms of investment and NPV. In calculating the incremental cash flows, we subtract the cash flows from the project with the smaller initial investment from the cash flows of the project with the large initial investment, so the incremental cash flows are:

	Year 0	Year 1	Year 2	Year 3
Dry prepeg	–$1,000,000	$600,000	$400,000	$1,000,000
Solvent prepeg	–500,000	300,000	500,000	100,000
Dry prepeg – Solvent prepeg	–$500,000	$300,000	–$100,000	$900,000

Setting the present value of these incremental cash flows equal to zero, we find the incremental IRR is:

$$0 = -\$500,000 + \$300,000 / (1 + IRR) - \$100,000 / (1 + IRR)^2 + \$900,000 / (1 + IRR)^3$$

Using a spreadsheet, financial calculator, or trial and error to find the root of the equation, we find that:

Incremental IRR = 38.90%

For investing-type projects, we accept the larger project when the incremental IRR is greater than the discount rate. Since the incremental IRR, 38.90%, is greater than the required rate of return of 10 percent, we choose the dry prepeg. Note that this is the choice when evaluating only the IRR of each project. The IRR decision rule is flawed because there is a scale problem. That is, the dry prepeg has a greater initial investment than does the solvent prepeg. This problem is corrected by calculating the IRR of the incremental cash flows, or by evaluating the NPV of each project.

By the way, as an aside: The cash flows for the incremental IRR change signs three times, so we would expect up to three real IRRs. In this particular case, however, two of the IRRs are not real numbers. For the record, the other IRRs are:

$$IRR = [1/(-.30442 + .08240i)] - 1$$
$$IRR = [1/(-.30442 - .08240i)] - 1$$

21. *a.* The NPV of each project is:

$$NPV_{NP-30} = -\$100,000 + \$40,000\{[1 - (1/1.15)^5] / .15 \}$$
$$NPV_{NP-30} = \$34,086.20$$

$$NPV_{NX-20} = -\$30,000 + \$20,000 / 1.15 + \$23,000 / 1.15^2 + \$26,450 / 1.15^3 + \$30,418 / 1.15^4$$
$$\qquad\qquad + \$34,980 / 1.15^5$$
$$NPV_{NX-20} = \$56,956.75$$

The NPV criteria implies accepting the NX-20.

B-142 SOLUTIONS

b. The IRR is the interest rate that makes the NPV of the project equal to zero, so the IRR of each project is:

NP-30:
$$0 = -\$100,000 + \$40,000(\{1 - [1/(1 + IRR)^5]\} / IRR)$$

Using a spreadsheet, financial calculator, or trial and error to find the root of the equation, we find that:

$$IRR_{NP-30} = 28.65\%$$

And the IRR of the NX-20 is:

$$0 = -\$30,000 + \$20,000 / (1 + IRR) + \$23,000 / (1 + IRR)^2 + \$26,450 / (1 + IRR)^3$$
$$+ \$30,418 / (1 + IRR)^4 + \$34,980 / (1 + IRR)^5$$

Using a spreadsheet, financial calculator, or trial and error to find the root of the equation, we find that:

$$IRR_{NX-20} = 73.02\%$$

The IRR criteria implies accepting the NX-20.

c. Incremental IRR analysis is not necessary. The NX-20 has a higher IRR, and but is relatively smaller in terms of investment, with a larger NPV. Nonetheless, we will calculate the incremental IRR. In calculating the incremental cash flows, we subtract the cash flows from the project with the smaller initial investment from the cash flows of the project with the large initial investment, so the incremental cash flows are:

Year	Incremental cash flow
0	–$70,000
1	20,000
2	17,000
3	13,550
4	9,582
5	5,020

Setting the present value of these incremental cash flows equal to zero, we find the incremental IRR is:

$$0 = -\$70,000 + \$20,000 / (1 + IRR) + \$17,000 / (1 + IRR)^2 + \$13,550 / (1 + IRR)^3$$
$$+ \$9,582 / (1 + IRR)^4 + \$5,020 / (1 + IRR)^5$$

Using a spreadsheet, financial calculator, or trial and error to find the root of the equation, we find that:

Incremental IRR = –2.89%

For investing-type projects, accept the larger project when the incremental IRR is greater than the discount rate. Since the incremental IRR, –2.89%, is less than the required rate of return of 15 percent, choose the NX-20.

d. The profitability index is the present value of all subsequent cash flows, divided by the initial investment, so the profitability index of each project is:

$PI_{NP-30} = (\$40,000\{[1 - (1/1.15)^5]/.15\})/\$100,000$
$PI_{NP-30} = 1.341$

$PI_{NX-20} = [\$20,000/1.15 + \$23,000/1.15^2 + \$26,450/1.15^3 + \$30,418/1.15^4$
$\qquad\qquad + \$34,980/1.15^5]/\$30,000$
$PI_{NX-20} = 2.899$

The PI criteria implies accepting the NX-20.

22. *a.* The NPV of each project is:

$NPV_A = -\$100,000 + \$50,000/1.15 + \$50,000/1.15^2 + \$40,000/1.15^3 + \$30,000/1.15^4$
$\qquad\qquad + \$20,000/1.15^5$
$NPV_A = \$34,682.23$

$NPV_B = -\$200,000 + \$60,000/1.15 + \$60,000/1.15^2 + \$60,000/1.15^3 + \$100,000/1.15^4$
$\qquad\qquad + \$200,000/1.15^5$
$NPV_B = \$93,604.18$

The NPV criteria implies accepting Project B.

b. The IRR is the interest rate that makes the NPV of the project equal to zero, so the IRR of each project is:

Project A:

$0 = -\$100,000 + \$50,000/(1 + IRR) + \$50,000/(1 + IRR)^2 + \$40,000/(1 + IRR)^3$
$\qquad\qquad + \$30,000/(1 + IRR)^4 + \$20,000/(1 + IRR)^5$

Using a spreadsheet, financial calculator, or trial and error to find the root of the equation, we find that:

$IRR_A = 31.28\%$

And the IRR of the Project B is:

$0 = -\$200,000 + \$60,000/(1 + IRR) + \$60,000/(1 + IRR)^2 + \$60,000/(1 + IRR)^3$
$\qquad\qquad + \$100,000/(1 + IRR)^4 + \$200,000/(1 + IRR)^5$

B-144 SOLUTIONS

Using a spreadsheet, financial calculator, or trial and error to find the root of the equation, we find that:

$IRR_B = 29.54\%$

The IRR criteria implies accepting Project A.

c. Incremental IRR analysis is not necessary. The NX-20 has a higher IRR, and is relatively smaller in terms of investment, with a larger NPV. Nonetheless, we will calculate the incremental IRR. In calculating the incremental cash flows, we subtract the cash flows from the project with the smaller initial investment from the cash flows of the project with the large initial investment, so the incremental cash flows are:

Year	Incremental cash flow
0	–$100,000
1	10,000
2	10,000
3	20,000
4	70,000
5	180,000

Setting the present value of these incremental cash flows equal to zero, we find the incremental IRR is:

$$0 = -\$100,000 + \$10,000 / (1 + IRR) + \$10,000 / (1 + IRR)^2 + \$20,000 / (1 + IRR)^3$$
$$+ \$70,000 / (1 + IRR)^4 + \$180,000 / (1 + IRR)^5$$

Using a spreadsheet, financial calculator, or trial and error to find the root of the equation, we find that:

Incremental IRR = 28.60%

For investing-type projects, accept the larger project when the incremental IRR is greater than the discount rate. Since the incremental IRR, 28.60%, is greater than the required rate of return of 15 percent, choose the Project B.

d. The profitability index is the present value of all subsequent cash flows, divided by the initial investment, so the profitability index of each project is:

$$PI_A = [50,000 / 1.15 + \$50,000 / 1.15^2 + \$40,000 / 1.15^3 + \$30,000 / 1.15^4$$
$$+ \$20,000 / 1.15^5] / \$100,000$$
$$PI_A = 1.347$$

$$PI_B = [\$60,000 / 1.15 + \$60,000 / 1.15^2 + \$60,000 / 1.15^3 + \$100,000 / 1.15^4$$
$$+ \$200,000 / 1.15^5] / \$200,000$$
$$PI_B = 1.468$$

The PI criteria implies accepting Project B.

23. *a.* The payback period is the time that it takes for the cumulative undiscounted cash inflows to equal the initial investment.

Project A:

Cumulative cash flows Year 1 = $50,000   = $50,000
Cumulative cash flows Year 2 = $50,000 + 100,000   = $150,000

Payback period = 2 years

Project B:

Cumulative cash flows Year 1 = $200,000   = $200,000

Payback period = 1 year

Project C:

Cumulative cash flows Year 1 = $100,000   = $100,000

Payback period = 1 year

Project B and Project C have the same payback period, so the projects cannot be ranked. Regardless, the payback period does not necessarily rank projects correctly.

b. The IRR is the interest rate that makes the NPV of the project equal to zero, so the IRR of each project is:

Project A:

$$0 = -\$150,000 + \$50,000 / (1 + IRR) + \$100,000 / (1 + IRR)^2$$

Using a spreadsheet, financial calculator, or trial and error to find the root of the equation, we find that:

$$IRR_A = 0.00\%$$

And the IRR of the Project B is:

$$0 = -\$200,000 + \$200,000 / (1 + IRR) + \$111,000 / (1 + IRR)^2$$

Using a spreadsheet, financial calculator, or trial and error to find the root of the equation, we find that:

$$IRR_B = 39.72\%$$

B-146 SOLUTIONS

And the IRR of the Project C is:

$$0 = -\$100,000 + \$100,000 / (1 + IRR) + \$100,000 / (1 + IRR)^2$$

Using a spreadsheet, financial calculator, or trial and error to find the root of the equation, we find that:

$IRR_C = 61.80\%$

The IRR criteria implies accepting Project C.

c. Project A can be excluded from the incremental IRR analysis. Since the project has a negative NPV, and an IRR less than its required return, the project is rejected. We need to calculate the incremental IRR between Project B and Project C. In calculating the incremental cash flows, we subtract the cash flows from the project with the smaller initial investment from the cash flows of the project with the large initial investment, so the incremental cash flows are:

Year	Incremental cash flow
0	–$100,000
1	100,000
2	11,000

Setting the present value of these incremental cash flows equal to zero, we find the incremental IRR is:

$$0 = -\$100,000 + \$100,000 / (1 + IRR) + \$11,000 / (1 + IRR)^2$$

Using a spreadsheet, financial calculator, or trial and error to find the root of the equation, we find that:

Incremental IRR = 10.00%

For investing-type projects, accept the larger project when the incremental IRR is greater than the discount rate. Since the incremental IRR, 10.00 percent, is less than the required rate of return of 20 percent, choose the Project C.

d. The profitability index is the present value of all subsequent cash flows, divided by the initial investment. We need to discount the cash flows of each project by the required return of each project. The profitability index of each project is:

$PI_A = [\$50,000 / 1.10 + \$100,000 / 1.10^2] / \$150,000$
$PI_A = 0.85$

$PI_B = [\$200,000 / 1.20 + \$111,000 / 1.20^2] / \$200,000$
$PI_B = 1.22$

$PI_C = [\$100,000 / 1.20 + \$100,000 / 1.20^2] / \$100,000$
$PI_C = 1.53$

The PI criteria implies accepting Project C.

e.   We need to discount the cash flows of each project by the required return of each project. The NPV of each project is:

$NPV_A = -\$150,000 + \$50,000 / 1.10 + \$100,000 / 1.10^2$
$NPV_A = -\$21,900.83$

$NPV_B = -\$200,000 + \$200,000 / 1.20 + \$111,000 / 1.20^2$
$NPV_B = \$43,750.00$

$NPV_C = -\$100,000 + \$100,000 / 1.20 + \$100,000 / 1.20^2$
$NPV_C = \$52,777.78$

The NPV criteria implies accepting Project C.

Challenge

24. Given the seven-year payback, the worst case is that the payback occurs at the end of the seventh year. Thus, the worst case:

$NPV = -\$483,000 + \$483,000/1.12^7 = -\$264,515.33$

The best case has infinite cash flows beyond the payback point. Thus, the best-case NPV is infinite.

25. The equation for the IRR of the project is:

$0 = -\$504 + \$2,862/(1 + IRR) - \$6,070/(1 + IRR)^2 + \$5,700/(1 + IRR)^3 - \$2,000/(1 + IRR)^4$

Using Descartes rule of signs, from looking at the cash flows we know there are four IRRs for this project. Even with most computer spreadsheets, we have to do some trial and error. From trial and error, IRRs of 25%, 33.33%, 42.86%, and 66.67% are found.

We would accept the project when the NPV is greater than zero. See for yourself that the NPV is greater than zero for required returns between 25% and 33.33% or between 42.86% and 66.67%.

26. *a.*   Here the cash inflows of the project go on forever, which is a perpetuity. Unlike ordinary perpetuity cash flows, the cash flows here grow at a constant rate forever, which is a growing perpetuity. If you remember back to the chapter on stock valuation, we presented a formula for valuing a stock with constant growth in dividends. This formula is actually the formula for a growing perpetuity, so we can use it here. The PV of the future cash flows from the project is:

PV of cash inflows $= C_1/(R - g)$
PV of cash inflows $= \$50,000/(.13 - .06) = \$714,285.71$

NPV is the PV of the outflows minus by the PV of the inflows, so the NPV is:

NPV of the project $= -\$780,000 + 714,285.71 = -\$65,714.29$

The NPV is negative, so we would reject the project.

B-148 SOLUTIONS

b.   Here we want to know the minimum growth rate in cash flows necessary to accept the project. The minimum growth rate is the growth rate at which we would have a zero NPV. The equation for a zero NPV, using the equation for the PV of a growing perpetuity is:

$$0 = -\$780,000 + \$50,000/(.13 - g)$$

Solving for g, we get:

$$g = 6.59\%$$

27. *a.*   The project involves three cash flows: the initial investment, the annual cash inflows, and the abandonment costs. The mine will generate cash inflows over its 11-year economic life. To express the PV of the annual cash inflows, apply the growing annuity formula, discounted at the IRR and growing at eight percent.

$$\text{PV(Cash Inflows)} = C\,\{[1/(r-g)] - [1/(r-g)] \times [(1+g)/(1+r)]^t\}$$
$$\text{PV(Cash Inflows)} = \$100,000\{[1/(\text{IRR}-.08)] - [1/(\text{IRR}-.08)] \times [(1+.08)/(1+\text{IRR})]^{11}\}$$

At the end of 11 years, the Utah Mining Corporate will abandon the mine, incurring a $50,000 charge. Discounting the abandonment costs back 11 years at the IRR to express its present value, we get:

$$\text{PV(Abandonment)} = C_{11}/(1+\text{IRR})^{11}$$
$$\text{PV(Abandonment)} = -\$50,000/(1+\text{IRR})^{11}$$

So, the IRR equation for this project is:

$$0 = -\$600,000 + \$100,000\{[1/(\text{IRR}-.08)] - [1/(\text{IRR}-.08)] \times [(1+.08)/(1+\text{IRR})]^{11}\}$$
$$-\$50,000/(1+\text{IRR})^{11}$$

Using a spreadsheet, financial calculator, or trial and error to find the root of the equation, we find that:

$$\text{IRR} = 18.56\%$$

b.   Yes. Since the mine's IRR exceeds the required return of 10 percent, the mine should be opened. The correct decision rule for an investment-type project is to accept the project if the discount rate is above the IRR. Although it appears there is a sign change at the end of the project because of the abandonment costs, the last cash flow is actually positive because the operating cash in the last year.

28. *a.*   We can apply the growing perpetuity formula to find the PV of stream *A*. The perpetuity formula values the stream as of one year before the first payment. Therefore, the growing perpetuity formula values the stream of cash flows as of year 2. Next, discount the PV as of the end of year 2 back two years to find the PV as of today, year 0. Doing so, we find:

$$\text{PV(A)} = [C_3/(R-g)]/(1+R)^2$$
$$\text{PV(A)} = [\$5,000/(0.12-0.04)]/(1.12)^2$$
$$\text{PV(A)} = \$49,824.62$$

We can apply the perpetuity formula to find the PV of stream B. The perpetuity formula discounts the stream back to year 1, one period prior to the first cash flow. Discount the PV as of the end of year 1 back one year to find the PV as of today, year 0. Doing so, we find:

$$PV(B) = [C_2 / R] / (1 + R)$$
$$PV(B) = [-\$6,000 / 0.12] / (1.12)$$
$$PV(B) = -\$44,642.86$$

b. If we combine the cash flow streams to form Project C, we get:

Project A $= [C_3 / (R - G)] / (1 + R)^2$

Project B $= [C_2 / R] / (1 + R)$

Project C = Project A + Project B
Project C $= [C_3 / (R - g)] / (1 + R)^2 + [C_2 / R] / (1 + R)$
$0 = [\$5,000 / (IRR - .04)] / (1 + IRR)^2 + [-\$6,000 / IRR] / (1 + IRR)$

Using a spreadsheet, financial calculator, or trial and error to find the root of the equation, we find that:

IRR = 14.65%

c. The correct decision rule for an investing-type project is to accept the project if the discount rate is below the IRR. Since there is one IRR, a decision can be made. At a point in the future, the cash flows from stream A will be greater than those from stream B. Therefore, although there are many cash flows, there will be only one change in sign. When the sign of the cash flows change more than once over the life of the project, there may be multiple internal rates of return. In such cases, there is no correct decision rule for accepting and rejecting projects using the internal rate of return.

29. To answer this question, we need to examine the incremental cash flows. To make the projects equally attractive, Project Billion must have a larger initial investment. We know this because the subsequent cash flows from Project Billion are larger than the subsequent cash flows from Project Million. So, subtracting the Project Million cash flows from the Project Billion cash flows, we find the incremental cash flows are:

Year	Incremental cash flows
0	$-I_0 + \$1,500$
1	300
2	300
3	500

Now we can find the present value of the subsequent incremental cash flows at the discount rate, 12 percent. The present value of the incremental cash flows is:

$$PV = \$1,500 + \$300 / 1.12 + \$300 / 1.12^2 + \$500 / 1.12^3$$
$$PV = \$2,362.91$$

B-150 SOLUTIONS

So, if I_0 is greater than \$2,362.91, the incremental cash flows will be negative. Since we are subtracting Project Million from Project Billion, this implies that for any value over \$2,362.91 the NPV of Project Billion will be less than that of Project Billion, so I_0 must be less than \$2,362.91.

30. The IRR is the interest rate that makes the NPV of the project equal to zero. So, the IRR of the project is:

$$0 = \$20,000 - \$26,000 / (1 + IRR) + \$13,000 / (1 + IRR)^2$$

Even though it appears there are two IRRs, a spreadsheet, financial calculator, or trial and error will not give an answer. The reason is that there is no real IRR for this set of cash flows. If you examine the IRR equation, what we are really doing is solving for the roots of the equation. Going back to high school algebra, in this problem we are solving a quadratic equation. In case you don't remember, the quadratic equation is:

$$x = \frac{-b \pm \sqrt{b^2 - 4ac}}{2a}$$

In this case, the equation is:

$$x = \frac{-(-26,000) \pm \sqrt{(-26,000)^2 - 4(20,000)(13,000)}}{2(26,000)}$$

The square root term works out to be:

$$676,000,000 - 1,040,000,000 = -364,000,000$$

The square root of a negative number is a complex number, so there is no real number solution, meaning the project has no real IRR.

Calculator Solutions

1. *b.*

Project A

CF₀	–$7,500
C01	$4,000
F01	1
C02	$3,500
F02	1
C03	$1,500
F03	1

I = 15%
NPV CPT
–$388.96

CF₀	–$5,000
C01	$2,500
F01	1
C02	$1,200
F02	1
C03	$3,000
F03	1

I = 15%
NPV CPT
$53.83

7.

CF₀	–$8,000
C01	$4,000
F01	1
C02	$3,000
F02	1
C03	$2,000
F03	1

IRR CPT
6.93%

8.

Project A

CF₀	–$2,000
C01	$1,000
F01	1
C02	$1,500
F02	1
C03	$2,000
F03	1

IRR CPT
47.15%

Project B

CF₀	–$1,500
C01	$500
F01	1
C02	$1,000
F02	1
C03	$1,500
F03	1

IRR CPT
36.19%

B-152 SOLUTIONS

9.

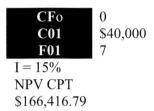

CFo	0
C01	$40,000
F01	7

I = 15%
NPV CPT
$166,416.79

PI = $166,416.79 / $160,000 = 1.0401

12.

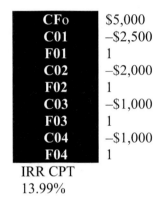

CFo	$5,000
C01	–$2,500
F01	1
C02	–$2,000
F02	1
C03	–$1,000
F03	1
C04	–$1,000
F04	1

IRR CPT
13.99%

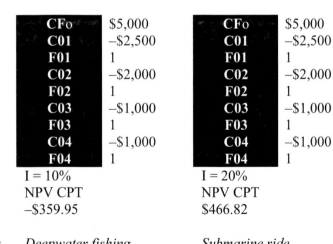

CFo	$5,000		**CFo**	$5,000
C01	–$2,500		**C01**	–$2,500
F01	1		**F01**	1
C02	–$2,000		**C02**	–$2,000
F02	1		**F02**	1
C03	–$1,000		**C03**	–$1,000
F03	1		**F03**	1
C04	–$1,000		**C04**	–$1,000
F04	1		**F04**	1

I = 10%   I = 20%
NPV CPT   NPV CPT
–$359.95 $466.82

13. *a.*   *Deepwater fishing*   *Submarine ride*

CFo	–$600,000		**CFo**	–$1,800,000
C01	$270,000		**C01**	$1,000,000
F01	1		**F01**	1
C02	$350,000		**C02**	$700,000
F02	1		**F02**	1
C03	$300,000		**C03**	$900,000
F03	1		**F03**	1

IRR CPT   IRR CPT
24.30%   21.46%

b.

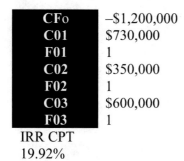

CFo	–$1,200,000
C01	$730,000
F01	1
C02	$350,000
F02	1
C03	$600,000
F03	1

IRR CPT
19.92%

c.

Deepwater fishing			*Submarine ride*	
CFo	–$600,000		CFo	–$1,800,000
C01	$270,000		C01	$1,000,000
F01	1		F01	1
C02	$350,000		C02	$700,000
F02	1		F02	1
C03	$300,000		C03	$900,000
F03	1		F03	1

I = 15%   I = 15%
NPV CPT   NPV CPT
$96,687.76 $190,630.39

14.

Project I

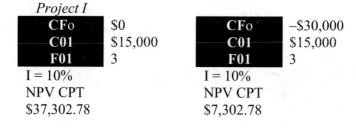

CFo	$0		CFo	–$30,000
C01	$15,000		C01	$15,000
F01	3		F01	3

I = 10%   I = 10%
NPV CPT   NPV CPT
$37,302.78 $7,302.78

PI = $37,302.78 / $30,000 = 1.243

Project II

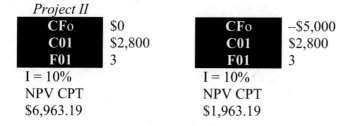

CFo	$0		CFo	–$5,000
C01	$2,800		C01	$2,800
F01	3		F01	3

I = 10%   I = 10%
NPV CPT   NPV CPT
$6,963.19 $1,963.19

PI = $6,963.19 / $5,000 = 1.393

B-154 SOLUTIONS

15.

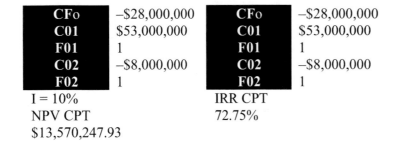

CFo	−$28,000,000		CFo	−$28,000,000
C01	$53,000,000		C01	$53,000,000
F01	1		F01	1
C02	−$8,000,000		C02	−$8,000,000
F02	1		F02	1

I = 10%
NPV CPT
$13,570,247.93

IRR CPT
72.75%

Financial calculators will only give you one IRR, even if there are multiple IRRs. Using trial and error, or a root solving calculator, the other IRR is −83.46%.

16. *b.*

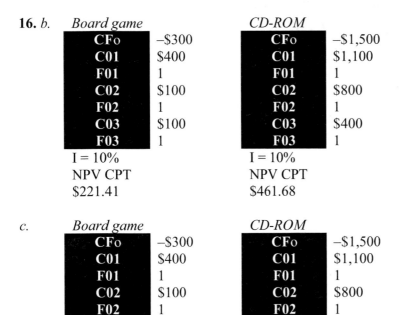

Board game			*CD-ROM*	
CFo	−$300		CFo	−$1,500
C01	$400		C01	$1,100
F01	1		F01	1
C02	$100		C02	$800
F02	1		F02	1
C03	$100		C03	$400
F03	1		F03	1

I = 10% 　　　　　　 I = 10%
NPV CPT 　　　　　 NPV CPT
$221.41 　　　　　　 $461.68

c.

Board game			*CD-ROM*	
CFo	−$300		CFo	−$1,500
C01	$400		C01	$1,100
F01	1		F01	1
C02	$100		C02	$800
F02	1		F02	1
C03	$100		C03	$400
F03	1		F03	1

IRR CPT 　　　　　 IRR CPT
65.61% 　　　　　　 30.09%

c.

CFo	−$1,200
C01	$700
F01	1
C02	$700
F02	1
C03	$300
F03	1

IRR CPT
22.57%

17. *a.*

CDMA			G4			Wi-Fi	
CF0	0		**CF0**	0		**CF0**	0
C01	$25,000,000		**C01**	$20,000,000		**C01**	$20,000,000
F01	1		**F01**	1		**F01**	1
C02	$15,000,000		**C02**	$50,000,000		**C02**	$40,000,000
F02	1		**F02**	1		**F02**	1
C03	$5,000,000		**C03**	$40,000,000		**C03**	$100,000,000
F03	1		**F03**	1		**F03**	1

I = 10%
NPV CPT
$38,880,540.95

I = 10%
NPV CPT
$89,556,724.27

I = 10%
NPV CPT
$126,371,149.51

PI_{CDMA} = $38,880,540.95 / $10,000,000 = 3.89
PI_{G4} = $89,556,724.27 / $20,000,000 = 4.48
$PI_{Wi\text{-}Fi}$ = $126,371,149.51 / $30,000,000 = 4.21

b.

CDMA			G4			Wi-Fi	
CF0	–$10,000,000		**CF0**	–$20,000,000		**CF0**	–$30,000,000
C01	$25,000,000		**C01**	$20,000,000		**C01**	$20,000,000
F01	1		**F01**	1		**F01**	1
C02	$15,000,000		**C02**	$50,000,000		**C02**	$40,000,000
F02	1		**F02**	1		**F02**	1
C03	$5,000,000		**C03**	$40,000,000		**C03**	$100,000,000
F03	1		**F03**	1		**F03**	1

I = 10%
NPV CPT
$28,880,540.95

I = 10%
NPV CPT
$69,556,724.27

I = 10%
NPV CPT
$96,371,149.51

18. *b.*

AZM			AZF	
CF0	–$200,000		**CF0**	–$500,000
C01	$200,000		**C01**	$200,000
F01	1		**F01**	1
C02	$150,000		**C02**	$300,000
F02	1		**F02**	1
C03	$150,000		**C03**	$300,0000
F03	1		**F03**	1

I = 10%
NPV CPT
$218,482.34

I = 10%
NPV CPT
$155,146.51

c.

AZM			AZF	
CF0	–$200,000		**CF0**	–$500,000
C01	$200,000		**C01**	$200,000
F01	1		**F01**	1
C02	$150,000		**C02**	$300,000
F02	1		**F02**	1
C03	$150,000		**C03**	$300,000
F03	1		**F03**	1

IRR CPT
70.04%

IRR CPT
25.70%

B-156 SOLUTIONS

19. *a.*

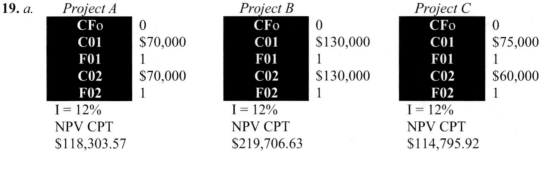

Project A		*Project B*		*Project C*	
CF0	0	**CF0**	0	**CF0**	0
C01	$70,000	**C01**	$130,000	**C01**	$75,000
F01	1	**F01**	1	**F01**	1
C02	$70,000	**C02**	$130,000	**C02**	$60,000
F02	1	**F02**	1	**F02**	1
I = 12%		I = 12%		I = 12%	
NPV CPT		NPV CPT		NPV CPT	
$118,303.57		$219,706.63		$114,795.92	

$PI_A = \$118,303.57 / \$100,000 = 1.18$
$PI_B = \$219,706.63 / \$200,000 = 1.10$
$PI_C = \$114,795.72 / \$100,000 = 1.15$

b.

Project A		*Project B*		*Project C*	
CF0	–$100,000	**CF0**	–$200,000	**CF0**	–$100,000
C01	$70,000	**C01**	$130,000	**C01**	$75,000
F01	1	**F01**	1	**F01**	1
C02	$130,000	**C02**	$130,000	**C02**	$60,000
F02	1	**F02**	1	**F02**	1
I = 12%		I = 12%		I = 12%	
NPV CPT		NPV CPT		NPV CPT	
$18,303.57		$19,706.63		$14,795.92	

d.

Project B – A	
CF0	–$100,000
C01	$60,000
F01	1
C02	$60,000
F02	1
I = 12%	
NPV CPT	
$101,403.06	

$PI(B – A) = \$101,403.06 / \$100,000 = 1.014$

20. *b.*

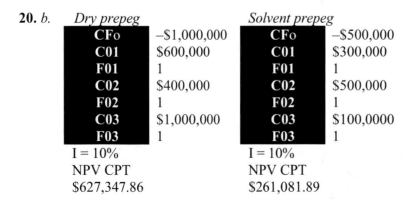

Dry prepeg		*Solvent prepeg*	
CF0	–$1,000,000	**CF0**	–$500,000
C01	$600,000	**C01**	$300,000
F01	1	**F01**	1
C02	$400,000	**C02**	$500,000
F02	1	**F02**	1
C03	$1,000,000	**C03**	$100,0000
F03	1	**F03**	1
I = 10%		I = 10%	
NPV CPT		NPV CPT	
$627,347.86		$261,081.89	

c.

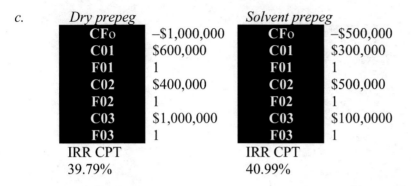

Dry prepeg

CF₀	−$1,000,000
C01	$600,000
F01	1
C02	$400,000
F02	1
C03	$1,000,000
F03	1

IRR CPT
39.79%

Solvent prepeg

CF₀	−$500,000
C01	$300,000
F01	1
C02	$500,000
F02	1
C03	$100,0000
F03	1

IRR CPT
40.99%

d.

CF₀	−$500,000
C01	$300,000
F01	1
C02	−$100,000
F02	1
C03	$900,000
F03	1

IRR CPT
38.90%

21. a.

NP-30

CF₀	−$100,000
C01	$40,000
F01	5
C02	
F02	
C03	
F03	
C04	
F04	
C05	
F05	

I = 15%
NPV CPT
$34,086.20

NX-20

CF₀	−$30,000
C01	$20,000
F01	1
C02	$23,000
F02	1
C03	$26,450
F03	1
C04	$30,418
F04	1
C05	$34,890
F05	1

I = 15%
NPV CPT
$56,956.75

B-158 SOLUTIONS

b.

NP-30			NX-20	
CF₀	−$100,000		CF₀	−$30,000
C01	$40,000		C01	$20,000
F01	5		F01	1
C02			C02	$23,000
F02			F02	1
C03			C03	$26,450
F03			F03	1
C04			C04	$30,418
F04			F04	1
C05			C05	$34,890
F05			F05	1
IRR CPT			IRR CPT	
26.85%			73.02%	

c.

CF₀	−$70,000
C01	$20,000
F01	1
C02	$17,000
F02	1
C03	$13,550
F03	1
C04	$9,582
F04	1
C05	$5,020
F05	1
IRR CPT	
−2.89%	

d.

NP-30			NX-20	
CF₀	0		CF₀	0
C01	$40,000		C01	$20,000
F01	5		F01	1
C02			C02	$23,000
F02			F02	1
C03			C03	$26,450
F03			F03	1
C04			C04	$30,418
F04			F04	1
C05			C05	$34,890
F05			F05	1
I = 15%			I = 15%	
NPV CPT			NPV CPT	
$134,086.20			$86,956.75	

$PI_{NP-30} = \$134,086.20 / \$100,000 = 1.341$

$PI_{NX-20} = \$86,959.75 / \$30,000 = 2.899$

Ross–Westerfield–Jaffe:
Corporate Finance, Eighth
Edition

II. Valuation and Capital
Budgeting

Answers for Chapter 6

© The McGraw–Hill
Companies, 2008

223

22. *a.*

Project A			*Project B*	
CF₀	–$100,000		**CF₀**	–$200,000
C01	$50,000		**C01**	$60,000
F01	2		**F01**	3
C02	$40,000		**C02**	$100,000
F02	1		**F02**	1
C03	$30,000		**C03**	$200,000
F03	1		**F03**	1
C04	$20,000		**C04**	
F04	1		**F04**	

I = 15% NPV CPT $34,682.23

I = 15% NPV CPT $93,604.18

b.

Project A			*Project B*	
CF₀	–$100,000		**CF₀**	–$200,000
C01	$50,000		**C01**	$60,000
F01	2		**F01**	3
C02	$40,000		**C02**	$100,000
F02	1		**F02**	1
C03	$30,000		**C03**	$200,000
F03	1		**F03**	1
C04	$20,000		**C04**	
F04	1		**F04**	

IRR CPT 31.28%

I = 15% 29.54%

c.

CF₀	–$100,000
C01	$10,000
F01	2
C02	$20,000
F02	1
C03	$70,000
F03	1
C04	$180,000
F04	1

IRR CPT 28.60%

B-160 SOLUTIONS

d.

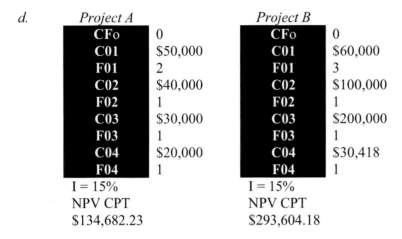

Project A

CFo	0
C01	$50,000
F01	2
C02	$40,000
F02	1
C03	$30,000
F03	1
C04	$20,000
F04	1

I = 15%
NPV CPT
$134,682.23

Project B

CFo	0
C01	$60,000
F01	3
C02	$100,000
F02	1
C03	$200,000
F03	1
C04	$30,418
F04	1

I = 15%
NPV CPT
$293,604.18

PI_A = $134,682.23 / $100,000 = 1.347
PI_B = $293,604.18 / $200,000 = 1.468

23. *b.*

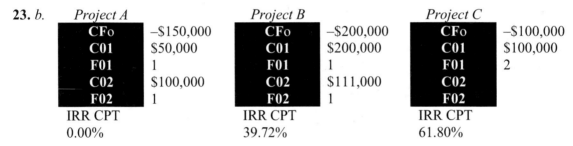

Project A

CFo	–$150,000
C01	$50,000
F01	1
C02	$100,000
F02	1

IRR CPT
0.00%

Project B

CFo	–$200,000
C01	$200,000
F01	1
C02	$111,000
F02	1

IRR CPT
39.72%

Project C

CFo	–$100,000
C01	$100,000
F01	2
C02	
F02	

IRR CPT
61.80%

c.

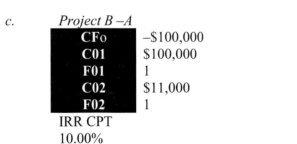

Project B –A

CFo	–$100,000
C01	$100,000
F01	1
C02	$11,000
F02	1

IRR CPT
10.00%

d.

Project A

CFo	0
C01	$50,000
F01	1
C02	$100,000
F02	1

I = 10%
NPV CPT
$128,099.17

Project B

CFo	0
C01	$200,000
F01	1
C02	$111,000
F02	1

I = 00%
NPV CPT
$243,750.00

Project C

CFo	0
C01	$100,000
F01	2
C02	
F02	

I = 00%
NPV CPT
$152,777.78

PI_A = $128,099.17 / $150,000 = 0.85
PI_B = $243,750.00 / $200,000 = 1.22
PI_C = $152,777.75 / $100,000 = 1.53

e.

Project A			Project B			Project C	
CF₀	–$150,000		**CF₀**	–$200,000		**CF₀**	–$100,000
C01	$50,000		**C01**	$200,000		**C01**	$100,000
F01	1		**F01**	1		**F01**	2
C02	$100,000		**C02**	$111,000		**C02**	
F02	1		**F02**	1		**F02**	

Project A: I = 10%, NPV CPT, –$21,900.83

Project B: I = 20%, NPV CPT, $43,750.00

Project C: I = 20%, NPV CPT, $52,777.78

30.

CF₀	$20,000
C01	–$26,000
F01	1
C02	$13,000
F02	1

IRR CPT
ERROR 7

CHAPTER 7

Making Capital Investment Decisions

In January 2006, Sharp Corporation, the world's leading producer of flat panel LCD TVs, announced that it would spend an additional 200 billion yen ($1.75 billion) to build a new plant to produce LCD panels. This addition brought the total investment in the new plant to 350 billion yen ($3.07 billion). The extra investment increased the production capacity of the new plant from 30,000 glass substrates per month to 90,000 glass substrates per month, and the new plant would have the capacity to produce the equivalent of 22 million 32-inch TV sets by 2008. Just several days earlier, Matsushita Electric Industrial Co., the world's leading plasma TV manufacturer, announced that it would invest 180 billion

yen ($1.57 billion) to build a new plant to produce plasma panels. The new plasma plant would more than double the company's production capacity to 11.1 million units per year.

This chapter follows up on our previous one by delving more deeply into capital budgeting and the evaluation of projects such as these flat panel manufacturing facilities. We identify the relevant cash flows of a project, including initial investment outlays, requirements for net working capital, and operating cash flows. Further, we look at the effects of depreciation and taxes. We also examine the impact of inflation, and show how to evaluate consistently the NPV analysis of a project.

7.1 Incremental Cash Flows

Cash Flows—Not Accounting Income

You may not have thought about it, but there is a big difference between corporate finance courses and financial accounting courses. Techniques in corporate finance generally use cash flows, whereas financial accounting generally stresses income or earnings numbers. Certainly our text follows this tradition: Our net present value techniques discount cash flows, not earnings. When considering a single project, we discount the cash flows that the firm receives from the project. When valuing the firm as a whole, we discount dividends—not earnings—because dividends are the cash flows that an investor receives.

EXAMPLE 7.1

Relevant Cash Flows The Weber-Decker Co. just paid $1 million in cash for a building as part of a new capital budgeting project. This entire $1 million is an immediate cash outflow. However, assuming straight-line depreciation over 20 years, only $50,000 (=$1 million/20) is considered an accounting expense in the current year. Current earnings are thereby reduced by only $50,000. The remaining $950,000 is expensed over the following 19 years. For capital budgeting purposes, the relevant cash outflow at date 0 is the full $1 million, not the reduction in earnings of only $50,000.

Always discount cash flows, not earnings, when performing a capital budgeting calculation. Earnings do not represent real money. You can't spend out of earnings, you can't eat out of earnings, and you can't pay dividends out of earnings. You can do these things only out of cash flow.

In addition, it is not enough to use cash flows. In calculating the NPV of a project, only cash flows that are *incremental* to the project should be used. These cash flows are the changes in the firm's cash flows that occur as a direct consequence of accepting the project. That is, we are interested in the difference between the cash flows of the firm with the project and the cash flows of the firm without the project.

The use of incremental cash flows sounds easy enough, but pitfalls abound in the real world. We describe how to avoid some of the pitfalls of determining incremental cash flows.

Sunk Costs

A **sunk cost** is a cost that has already occurred. Because sunk costs are in the past, they cannot be changed by the decision to accept or reject the project. Just as we "let bygones be bygones," we should ignore such costs. Sunk costs are not incremental cash outflows.

EXAMPLE 7.2

Sunk Costs   The General Milk Company is currently evaluating the NPV of establishing a line of chocolate milk. As part of the evaluation, the company had paid a consulting firm $100,000 to perform a test marketing analysis. This expenditure was made last year. Is this cost relevant for the capital budgeting decision now confronting the management of General Milk Company?

The answer is no. The $100,000 is not recoverable, so the $100,000 expenditure is a sunk cost, or spilled milk. Of course, the decision to spend $100,000 for a marketing analysis was a capital budgeting decision itself and was perfectly relevant *before* it was sunk. Our point is that once the company incurred the expense, the cost became irrelevant for any future decision.

Opportunity Costs

Your firm may have an asset that it is considering selling, leasing, or employing elsewhere in the business. If the asset is used in a new project, potential revenues from alternative uses are lost. These lost revenues can meaningfully be viewed as costs. They are called **opportunity costs** because, by taking the project, the firm forgoes other opportunities for using the assets.

EXAMPLE 7.3

Opportunity Costs   Suppose the Weinstein Trading Company has an empty warehouse in Philadelphia that can be used to store a new line of electronic pinball machines. The company hopes to sell these machines to affluent Northeastern consumers. Should the warehouse be considered a cost in the decision to sell the machines?

The answer is yes. The company could sell the warehouse if the firm decides not to market the pinball machines. Thus, the sales price of the warehouse is an opportunity cost in the pinball machine decision.

Side Effects

Another difficulty in determining incremental cash flows comes from the side effects of the proposed project on other parts of the firm. A side effect is classified as either **erosion** or **synergy**. Erosion occurs when a new product reduces the sales and, hence, the cash flows of existing products. Synergy occurs when a new project increases the cash flows of existing projects.

EXAMPLE 7.4

Synergies Suppose the Innovative Motors Corporation (IMC) is determining the NPV of a new convertible sports car. Some of the customers who would purchase the car are owners of IMC's compact sedans. Are all sales and profits from the new convertible sports car incremental?

The answer is no because some of the cash flow represents transfers from other elements of IMC's product line. This is erosion, which must be included in the NPV calculation. Without taking erosion into account, IMC might erroneously calculate the NPV of the sports car to be, say, $100 million. If half the customers are transfers from the sedan and lost sedan sales have an NPV of −$150 million, the true NPV is −$50 million (=$100 million − $150 million).

IMC is also contemplating the formation of a racing team. The team is forecast to lose money for the foreseeable future, with perhaps the best projection showing an NPV of −$35 million for the operation. However, IMC's managers are aware that the team will likely generate great publicity for all of IMC's products. A consultant estimates that the increase in cash flows elsewhere in the firm has a present value of $65 million. Assuming that the consultant's estimates of synergy are trustworthy, the net present value of the team is $30 million (=$65 million − $35 million). The managers should form the team.

Allocated Costs

Frequently a particular expenditure benefits a number of projects. Accountants allocate this cost across the different projects when determining income. However, for capital budgeting purposes, this **allocated cost** should be viewed as a cash outflow of a project only if it is an incremental cost of the project.

EXAMPLE 7.5

Allocated Costs The Voetmann Consulting Corp. devotes one wing of its suite of offices to a library requiring a cash outflow of $100,000 a year in upkeep. A proposed capital budgeting project is expected to generate revenue equal to 5 percent of the overall firm's sales. An executive at the firm, H. Sears, argues that $5,000 (=5 percent × $100,000) should be viewed as the proposed project's share of the library's costs. Is this appropriate for capital budgeting?

The answer is no. One must ask what the difference is between the cash flows of the entire firm with the project and the cash flows of the entire firm without the project. The firm will spend $100,000 on library upkeep whether or not the proposed project is accepted. Because acceptance of the proposed project does not affect this cash flow, the cash flow should be ignored when calculating the NPV of the project.

7.2 The Baldwin Company: An Example

We next consider the example of a proposed investment in machinery and related items. Our example involves the Baldwin Company and colored bowling balls.

The Baldwin Company, originally established in 1965 to make footballs, is now a leading producer of tennis balls, baseballs, footballs, and golf balls. In 1973 the company introduced "High Flite," its first line of high-performance golf balls. Baldwin management has sought opportunities in whatever businesses seem to have some potential for cash flow. Recently W. C. Meadows, vice president of the Baldwin Company, identified another segment of the sports ball market that looked promising and that he felt was not adequately served by larger manufacturers. That market was for brightly colored bowling balls, and he believed many bowlers valued appearance and style above performance. He also believed that it would be difficult for competitors to take advantage of the opportunity because of both Baldwin's cost advantages and its highly developed marketing skills.

As a result, the Baldwin Company investigated the marketing potential of brightly colored bowling balls. Baldwin sent a questionnaire to consumers in three markets: Philadelphia, Los Angeles, and New Haven. The results of the three questionnaires were much better than expected and supported the conclusion that the brightly colored bowling balls could achieve a 10 to 15 percent share of the market. Of course, some people at Baldwin complained about the cost of the test marketing, which was $250,000. (As we shall see later, this is a sunk cost and should not be included in project evaluation.)

In any case, the Baldwin Company is now considering investing in a machine to produce bowling balls. The bowling balls would be manufactured in a building owned by the firm and located near Los Angeles. This building, which is vacant, and the land can be sold for $150,000 after taxes.

Working with his staff, Meadows is preparing an analysis of the proposed new product. He summarizes his assumptions as follows: The cost of the bowling ball machine is $100,000. The machine has an estimated market value at the end of five years of $30,000. Production by year during the five-year life of the machine is expected to be as follows: 5,000 units, 8,000 units, 12,000 units, 10,000 units, and 6,000 units. The price of bowling balls in the first year will be $20. The bowling ball market is highly competitive, so Meadows believes that the price of bowling balls will increase at only 2 percent per year, as compared to the anticipated general inflation rate of 5 percent. Conversely, the plastic used to produce bowling balls is rapidly becoming more expensive. Because of this, production cash outflows are expected to grow at 10 percent per year. First-year production costs will be $10 per unit. Meadows has determined, based on Baldwin's taxable income, that the appropriate incremental corporate tax rate in the bowling ball project is 34 percent.

Net working capital is defined as the difference between current assets and current liabilities. Like any other manufacturing firm, Baldwin finds that it must maintain an investment in working capital. It will purchase raw materials before production and sale, giving rise to an investment in inventory. It will maintain cash as a buffer against unforeseen expenditures. And, its credit sales will generate accounts receivable. Management determines that an immediate (year 0) investment in the different items of working capital of $10,000 is required. Working capital is forecast to rise in the early years of the project but to fall to $0 by the project's end. In other words, the investment in working capital is to be completely recovered by the end of the project's life.

Projections based on these assumptions and Meadows's analysis appear in Tables 7.1 through 7.4. In these tables all cash flows are assumed to occur at the *end* of the year. Because of the large amount of information in these tables, it is important to see how the tables are related. Table 7.1 shows the basic data for both investment and income. Supplementary schedules on operations and depreciation, as presented in Tables 7.2 and 7.3, help explain where the numbers in Table 7.1 come from. Our goal is to obtain projections of cash flow. The data in Table 7.1 are all that are needed to calculate the relevant cash flows, as shown in Table 7.4.

An Analysis of the Project

Investments   The investment outlays for the project are summarized in the top segment of Table 7.1. They consist of three parts:

1. *The bowling ball machine*: The purchase requires an immediate (year 0) cash outflow of $100,000. The firm realizes a cash inflow when the machine is sold in year 5. These cash flows are shown in line 1 of Table 7.1. As indicated in the footnote to the table, taxes are incurred when the asset is sold.

...orksheet for Cash Flows of the Baldwin Company (in $ thousands). (All cash flows occur at ...e *end* of the year.)

	Year 0	Year I	Year 2	Year 3	Year 4	Year 5
Investments:						
(1) Bowling ball machine	−$100.00					$21.76*
(2) Accumulated depreciation		$ 20.00	$ 52.00	$ 71.20	$ 82.72	94.24
(3) Adjusted basis of machine after depreciation (end of year)		80.00	48.00	28.80	17.28	5.76
(4) Opportunity cost (warehouse)	−150.00					150.00
(5) Net working capital (end of year)	10.00	10.00	16.32	24.97	21.22	0
(6) Change in net working capital	−10.00		−6.32	−8.65	3.75	21.22
(7) Total cash flow of investment [(1) + (4) + (6)]	−260.00		−6.32	−8.65	3.75	192.98
Income:						
(8) Sales revenues		$100.00	$163.20	$249.72	$212.20	$129.90
(9) Operating costs		−50.00	−88.00	−145.20	−133.10	−87.84
(10) Depreciation		−20.00	−32.00	−19.20	−11.52	−11.52
(11) Income before taxes [(8) + (9) + (10)]		30.00	43.20	85.32	67.58	30.54
(12) Tax at 34 percent		−10.20	−14.69	−29.01	−22.98	−10.38
(13) Net income		19.80	28.51	56.31	44.60	20.16

*We assume that the ending market value of the capital investment at year 5 is $30 (in thousands). The taxable amount is $24.24 ($=$30 − 5.76). The aftertax salvage value is $30 − [.34 \times ($30 − $5.76)] = 21.76.

Table 7.2

Operating Revenues and Costs of the Baldwin Company

(1) Year	(2) Quantity Produced	(3) Price	(4) Sales Revenues	(5) Cost Per Unit	(6) Operating Costs
1	5,000	$20.00	$100,000	$10.00	$ 50,000
2	8,000	20.40	163,200	11.00	88,000
3	12,000	20.81	249,720	12.10	145,200
4	10,000	21.22	212,200	13.31	133,100
5	6,000	21.65	129,900	14.64	87,840

Prices rise at 2% a year.
Unit costs rise at 10% a year.

2. *The opportunity cost of not selling the warehouse*: If Baldwin accepts the bowling ball project, it will use a warehouse and land that could otherwise be sold. The estimated sales price of the warehouse and land is therefore included as an *opportunity cost* in year 0, as presented in line 4. Opportunity costs are treated as cash outflows for purposes of capital budgeting. However, note that if the project is accepted, management assumes that the warehouse will be sold for $150,000 (after taxes) in year 5.

   The test marketing cost of $250,000 is not included. The tests occurred in the past and should be viewed as a *sunk cost*.

Table 7.3

Depreciation (in percent) under Modified Accelerated Cost Recovery System (MACRS)

	Recovery Period Class					
Year	**3 Years**	**5 Years**	**7 Years**	**10 Years**	**15 Years**	**20 Years**
1	.333	.200	.143	.100	.050	.038
2	.444	.320	.245	.180	.095	.072
3	.148	.192	.175	.144	.086	.067
4	.074	.115	.125	.115	.077	.062
5		.115	.089	.092	.069	.057
6		.058	.089	.074	.062	.053
7			.089	.066	.059	.049
8			.045	.066	.059	.045
9				.066	.059	.045
10				.066	.059	.045
11				.033	.059	.045
12–15					.059	.045
16					.030	.045
17–20						.045
21						.022

Depreciation is expressed as a percentage of the asset's cost. These schedules are based on the IRS publication *Depreciation*. Details of depreciation are presented later in the chapter. Three-year depreciation actually carries over four years because the IRS assumes the purchase is made in midyear.

Table 7.4   Incremental Cash Flows for the Baldwin Company (in $ thousands)

	Year 0	Year 1	Year 2	Year 3	Year 4	Year 5
(1) Sales revenue [line 8, Table 7.1]		$100.00	$163.20	$249.72	$212.20	$129.90
(2) Operating costs [line 9, Table 7.1]		−50.00	−88.00	−145.20	−133.10	−87.84
(3) Taxes [line 12, Table 7.1]		−10.20	−14.69	−29.01	−22.98	−10.38
(4) Cash flow from operations [(1) + (2) + (3)]		39.80	60.51	75.51	56.12	31.68
(5) Total cash flow of investment [line 7, Table 7.1]	−$260.00		−6.32	−8.65	3.75	192.98
(6) Total cash flow of project [(4) + (5)]	−260.00	39.80	54.19	66.86	59.87	224.66

NPV @		
	4%	$123.641
	10%	$51.588
	15%	$5.472
	15.67%	$0
	20%	−$31.351

3. *The investment in working capital*: Required working capital appears in line 5. Working capital rises over the early years of the project as expansion occurs. However, all working capital is assumed to be recovered at the end, a common assumption in capital budgeting. In other words, all inventory is sold by the end, the cash balance maintained as a buffer is liquidated, and all accounts receivable are collected. Increases in working capital in the early years must be funded by cash generated elsewhere in the firm. Hence, these increases are viewed as cash *outflows*. To reiterate, it is the *increase* in working capital over a year that leads to a cash outflow in that year. Even if working

capital is at a high level, there will be no cash outflow over a year if working capital stays constant over that year. Conversely, decreases in working capital in the later years are viewed as cash inflows. All of these cash flows are presented in line 6 of Table 7.1. A more complete discussion of working capital is provided later in this section.

To recap, there are three investments in this example: the bowling ball machine (line 1 in Table 7.1), the opportunity cost of the warehouse (line 4), and the changes in working capital (line 6). The total cash flow from these three investments is shown in line 7.

Income and Taxes   Next the determination of income is presented in the bottom segment of Table 7.1. While we are ultimately interested in cash flow—not income—we need the income calculation to determine taxes. Lines 8 and 9 of Table 7.1 show sales revenues and operating costs, respectively. The projections in these lines are based on the sales revenues and operating costs computed in columns 4 and 6 of Table 7.2. The estimates of revenues and costs follow from assumptions made by the corporate planning staff at Baldwin. In other words, the estimates critically depend on the fact that product prices are projected to increase at 2 percent per year and costs per unit are projected to increase at 10 percent per year.

Depreciation of the $100,000 capital investment is shown in line 10 of Table 7.1. Where do these numbers come from? Depreciation for tax purposes for U.S. companies is based on the Modified Accelerated Cost Recovery System (MACRS). Each asset is assigned a useful life under MACRS, with an accompanying depreciation schedule as shown in Table 7.3. The IRS ruled that Baldwin is to depreciate its capital investment over five years, so the second column of the table applies in this case. Because depreciation in the table is expressed as a percentage of the asset's cost, multiply the percentages in this column by $100,000 to arrive at depreciation in dollars.

Income before taxes is calculated in line 11 of Table 7.1. Taxes are provided in line 12 of this table, and net income is calculated in line 13.

Salvage Value   In calculating depreciation under current tax law, the expected economic life and future value of an asset are not issues. As a result, the book value of an asset can differ substantially from its actual market value. For example, consider the bowling machine the Baldwin Company is considering for its new project. The book value after the first year is $100,000 less the first year's depreciation of $20,000, or $80,000. After six years, the book value of the machine is zero.

Suppose, at the end of the project, Baldwin sold the machine. At the end of the fifth year, the book value of the machine would be $5,760; but based on Baldwin's experience, it would probably be worth about $30,000. If the company actually sold it for this amount, then it would pay taxes at the ordinary income tax rate on the difference between the sale price of $30,000 and the book value of $5,760. With a 34 percent tax rate, the tax liability would be $.34 \times (\$30,000 - 5,760) = \$8,241.60$. So, the aftertax salvage value of the equipment, a cash inflow to the company, would be $30,000 - 8,241.60 = \$21,758.40$.

Taxes must be paid in this case because the difference between the market value and the book value is "excess" depreciation, and it must be "recaptured" when the asset is sold. In this case, Baldwin would have over depreciated the asset by $30,000 - 5,760 = \$24,240$. Because the depreciation was too high, the company paid too little in taxes.

Notice this is not a tax on a long-term capital gain. Further, what is and what is not a capital gain is ultimately up to taxing authorities, and the specific rules can be very complex. We will ignore capital gains taxes for the most part.

Finally, if the book value exceeds the market value, then the difference is treated as a loss for tax purposes. For example, if Baldwin sold the machine for $4,000, then the book value exceeds the market value by $1,760. In this case, a tax savings of $.34 \times \$1,760 = \$598.40$ occurs.

Cash Flow   Cash flow is finally determined in Table 7.4. We begin by reproducing lines 8, 9, and 12 in Table 7.1 as lines 1, 2, and 3 in Table 7.4. Cash flow from operations, which is sales minus both operating costs and taxes, is provided in line 4 of Table 7.4. Total investment cash flow, taken from line 7 of Table 7.1, appears as line 5 of Table 7.4. Cash flow from operations plus total cash flow of the investment equals total cash flow of the project, which is displayed as line 6 of Table 7.4.

Net Present Value   The NPV of the Baldwin bowling ball project can be calculated from the cash flows in line 6. As can be seen at the bottom of Table 7.4, the NPV is $51,588 if 10 percent is the appropriate discount rate and −$31,351 if 20 percent is the appropriate discount rate. If the discount rate is 15.67 percent, the project will have a zero NPV. In other words, the project's internal rate of return is 15.67 percent. If the discount rate of the Baldwin bowling ball project is above 15.67 percent, it should not be accepted because its NPV would be negative.

Which Set of Books?

It should be noted that the firm's management generally keeps two sets of books, one for the IRS (called the *tax books*) and another for its annual report (called the *stockholders' books*). The tax books follow the rules of the IRS. The stockholders' books follow the rules of the *Financial Accounting Standards Board* (FASB), the governing body in accounting. The two sets of rules differ widely in certain areas. For example, income on municipal bonds is ignored for tax purposes while being treated as income by the FASB. The differences almost always benefit the firm: The rules permit income on the stockholders' books to be higher than income on the tax books. That is, management can look profitable to the stockholders without needing to pay taxes on all of the reported profit. In fact, plenty of large companies consistently report positive earnings to the stockholders while reporting losses to the IRS.

A Note about Net Working Capital

The investment in net working capital is an important part of any capital budgeting analysis. While we explicitly considered net working capital in lines 5 and 6 of Table 7.1, students may be wondering where the numbers in these lines came from. An investment in net working capital arises whenever (1) inventory is purchased, (2) cash is kept in the project as a buffer against unexpected expenditures, and (3) credit sales are made, generating accounts receivable rather than cash. (The investment in net working capital is reduced by credit purchases, which generate accounts payable.) This investment in net working capital represents a cash outflow because cash generated elsewhere in the firm is tied up in the project.

To see how the investment in net working capital is built from its component parts, we focus on year 1. We see in Table 7.1 that Baldwin's managers predict sales in year 1 to be $100,000 and operating costs to be $50,000. If both the sales and costs were cash transactions, the firm would receive $50,000 (=$100,000 − $50,000). As stated earlier, this cash flow would occur at the *end* of year 1.

Now let's give you more information. The managers:

1. Forecast that $9,000 of the sales will be on credit, implying that cash receipts at the end of year 1 will be only $91,000 (=$100,000 − $9,000). The accounts receivable of $9,000 will be collected at the end of year 2.

2. Believe that they can defer payment on $3,000 of the $50,000 of costs, implying that cash disbursements at the end of year 1 will be only $47,000 (=$50,000 − $3,000). Baldwin will pay off the $3,000 of accounts payable at the end of year 2.

3. Decide that inventory of $2,500 should be left on hand at the end of year 1 to avoid *stockouts* (that is, running out of inventory).

4. Decide that cash of $1,500 should be earmarked for the project at the end of year 1 to avoid running out of cash.

Thus, net working capital at the end of year 1 is:

$$
\underset{\substack{\text{Accounts} \\ \text{receivable}}}{\$9,000} \quad - \quad \underset{\substack{\text{Accounts} \\ \text{payable}}}{\$3,000} \quad + \quad \underset{\text{Inventory}}{\$2,500} \quad + \quad \underset{\text{Cash}}{\$1,500} \quad = \quad \underset{\substack{\text{Net working} \\ \text{capital}}}{\$10,000}
$$

Because $10,000 of cash generated elsewhere in the firm must be used to offset this requirement for net working capital, Baldwin's managers correctly view the investment in net working capital as a cash outflow of the project. As the project grows over time, needs for net working capital increase. *Changes* in net working capital from year to year represent further cash flows, as indicated by the negative numbers for the first few years on line 6 of Table 7.1. However, in the declining years of the project, net working capital is reduced—ultimately to zero. That is, accounts receivable are finally collected, the project's cash buffer is returned to the rest of the corporation, and all remaining inventory is sold off. This frees up cash in the later years, as indicated by positive numbers in years 4 and 5 on line 6.

Typically corporate worksheets (such as Table 7.1) treat net working capital as a whole. The individual components of working capital (receivables, inventory, and the like) do not generally appear in the worksheets. However, the reader should remember that the working capital numbers in the worksheets are not pulled out of thin air. Rather, they result from a meticulous forecast of the components, just as we illustrated for year 1.

A Note about Depreciation

The Baldwin case made some assumptions about depreciation. Where did these assumptions come from? Assets are currently depreciated for tax purposes according to the provisions of the 1986 Tax Reform Act. There are seven classes of depreciable property:

- The three-year class includes certain specialized short-lived property. Tractor units and racehorses over two years old are among the very few items fitting into this class.

- The five-year class includes (a) cars and trucks; (b) computers and peripheral equipment, as well as calculators, copiers, and typewriters; and (c) specific items used for research.

- The seven-year class includes office furniture, equipment, books, and single-purpose agricultural structures. It is also a catchall category because any asset not designated to be in another class is included here.

- The 10-year class includes vessels, barges, tugs, and similar equipment related to water transportation.

- The 15-year class encompasses a variety of specialized items. Included are equipment of telephone distribution plants and similar equipment used for voice and data communications, and sewage treatment plants.

- The 20-year class includes farm buildings, sewer pipe, and other very long-lived equipment.
- Real property that is depreciable is separated into two classes: residential and non-residential. The cost of residential property is recovered over 27½ years and nonresidential property over 31½ years.

Items in the three-, five-, and seven-year classes are depreciated using the 200 percent declining-balance method, with a switch to straight-line depreciation at a point specified in the Tax Reform Act. Items in the 15- and 20-year classes are depreciated using the 150 percent declining-balance method, with a switch to straight-line depreciation at a specified point. All real estate is depreciated on a straight-line basis.

All calculations of depreciation include a half-year convention, which treats all property as if it were placed in service at midyear. To be consistent, the IRS allows half a year of depreciation for the year in which property is disposed of or retired. The effect of this is to spread the deductions for property over one year more than the name of its class—for example, six tax years for five-year property.

Interest Expense

It may have bothered you that interest expense was ignored in the Baldwin example. After all, many projects are at least partially financed with debt, particularly a bowling ball machine that is likely to increase the debt capacity of the firm. As it turns out, our approach of assuming no debt financing is rather standard in the real world. Firms typically calculate a project's cash flows under the assumption that the project is financed only with equity. Any adjustments for debt financing are reflected in the discount rate, not the cash flows. The treatment of debt in capital budgeting will be covered in depth later in the text. Suffice it to say at this time that the full ramifications of debt financing are well beyond our current discussion.

7.3　Inflation and Capital Budgeting

Inflation is an important fact of economic life, and it must be considered in capital budgeting. We begin our examination of inflation by considering the relationship between interest rates and inflation.

Interest Rates and Inflation

Suppose a bank offers a one-year interest rate of 10 percent. This means that an individual who deposits $1,000 will receive $1,100 (=$1,000 × 1.10) in one year. Although 10 percent may seem like a handsome return, one can put it in perspective only after examining the rate of inflation.

Imagine that the rate of inflation is 6 percent over the year and it affects all goods equally. For example, a restaurant that charges $1.00 for a hamburger today will charge $1.06 for the same hamburger at the end of the year. You can use your $1,000 to buy 1,000 hamburgers today (date 0). Alternatively, if you put your money in the bank, you can buy 1,038 (=$1,100/$1.06) hamburgers at date 1. Thus, lending increases your hamburger consumption by only 3.8 percent.

Because the prices of all goods rise at this 6 percent rate, lending lets you increase your consumption of any single good or any combination of goods by only 3.8 percent. Thus, 3.8 percent is what you are *really* earning through your savings account, after adjusting for

Figure 7.1

Calculation of Real Rate of Interest

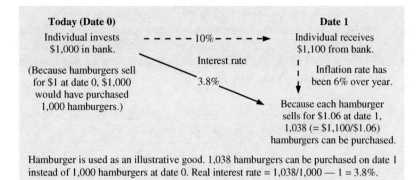

Today (Date 0)

Individual invests $1,000 in bank.

(Because hamburgers sell for $1 at date 0, $1,000 would have purchased 1,000 hamburgers.)

- - - - - 10% - - - - - →

Interest rate

3.8%

Date 1

Individual receives $1,100 from bank.

Inflation rate has been 6% over year.

Because each hamburger sells for $1.06 at date 1, 1,038 (= $1,100/$1.06) hamburgers can be purchased.

Hamburger is used as an illustrative good. 1,038 hamburgers can be purchased on date 1 instead of 1,000 hamburgers at date 0. Real interest rate = 1,038/1,000 — 1 = 3.8%.

inflation. Economists refer to the 3.8 percent number as the *real interest rate*. Economists refer to the 10 percent rate as the *nominal interest rate* or simply the *interest rate*. This discussion is illustrated in Figure 7.1.

We have used an example with a specific nominal interest rate and a specific inflation rate. In general, the formula between real and nominal interest rates can be written as follows:

$$1 + \text{Nominal interest rate} = (1 + \text{Real interest rate}) \times (1 + \text{Inflation rate})$$

Rearranging terms, we have:

$$\text{Real interest rate} = \frac{1 + \text{Nominal interest rate}}{1 + \text{Inflation rate}} - 1 \qquad \textbf{(7.1)}$$

The formula indicates that the real interest rate in our example is 3.8 percent (=1.10/ 1.06 − 1).

Equation 7.1 determines the real interest rate precisely. The following formula is an approximation:

$$\text{Real interest rate} \cong \text{Nominal interest rate} - \text{Inflation rate} \qquad \textbf{(7.2)}$$

The symbol $\cong$ indicates that the equation is approximately true. This latter formula calculates the real rate in our example like this:

$$4\% = 10\% - 6\%$$

The student should be aware that, although Equation 7.2 may seem more intuitive than Equation 7.1, 7.2 is only an approximation. This approximation is reasonably accurate for low rates of interest and inflation. In our example the difference between the approximate calculation and the exact one is only 0.2 percent (=4 percent − 3.8 percent). Unfortunately, the approximation becomes poor when rates are higher.

EXAMPLE 7.6

Real and Nominal Rates   The little-known monarchy of Gerberovia recently had a nominal interest rate of 300 percent and an inflation rate of 280 percent. According to Equation 7.2, the real interest rate is:

$$300\% - 280\% = 20\% \text{ (Approximate formula)}$$

However, according to Equation 7.1 this rate is:

$$\frac{1 + 300\%}{1 + 280\%} - 1 = 5.26\% \quad \text{(Exact formula)}$$

(continued)

How do we know that the second formula is indeed the exact one? Let's think in terms of hamburgers again. Had you deposited $1,000 in a Gerberovian bank a year ago, the account would be worth $4,000 [=$1,000 × (1 + 300%)] today. However, while a hamburger cost $1 a year ago, it costs $3.80 (=1 + 280%) today. Therefore, you would now be able to buy 1,052.6 (=$4,000/3.80) hamburgers, implying a real interest rate of 5.26 percent.

Cash Flow and Inflation

The previous analysis defines two types of interest rates, nominal rates and real rates, and relates them through Equation 7.1. Capital budgeting requires data on cash flows as well as on interest rates. Like interest rates, cash flows can be expressed in either nominal or real terms.

A **nominal cash flow** refers to the actual dollars to be received (or paid out). A **real cash flow** refers to the cash flow's purchasing power. These definitions are best explained by examples.

EXAMPLE 7.7

Nominal versus Real Cash Flow   Burrows Publishing has just purchased the rights to the next book of famed romantic novelist Barbara Musk. Still unwritten, the book should be available to the public in four years. Currently, romantic novels sell for $10.00 in softcover. The publishers believe that inflation will be 6 percent a year over the next four years. Because romantic novels are so popular, the publishers anticipate that their prices will rise about 2 percent per year more than the inflation rate over the next four years. Burrows Publishing plans to sell the novel at $13.60 [=(1.08)^4 × $10.00] four years from now, anticipating sales of 100,000 copies.

The expected cash flow in the fourth year of $1.36 million (=$13.60 × 100,000) is a *nominal cash flow*. That is, the firm expects to receive $1.36 million at that time. In other words, a nominal cash flow refers to the actual dollars to be received in the future.

The purchasing power of $1.36 million in four years is:

$$\$1.08 \text{ million} = \frac{\$1.36 \text{ million}}{(1.06)^4}$$

The figure of $1.08 million is a *real cash flow* because it is expressed in terms of purchasing power. Extending our hamburger example, the $1.36 million to be received in four years will only buy 1.08 million hamburgers because the price of a hamburger will rise from $1 to $1.26 [=$1 × (1.06)^4] over the period.

EXAMPLE 7.8

Depreciation   EOBII Publishers, a competitor of Burrows, recently bought a printing press for $2,000,000 to be depreciated by the straight-line method over five years. This implies yearly depreciation of $400,000 (=$2,000,000/5). Is this $400,000 figure a real or a nominal quantity?

Depreciation is a *nominal* quantity because $400,000 is the actual tax deduction over each of the next four years. Depreciation becomes a real quantity if it is adjusted for purchasing power. Hence, $316,837 [=$400,000/(1.06)^4] is depreciation in the fourth year, expressed as a real quantity.

Discounting: Nominal or Real?

Our previous discussion showed that interest rates can be expressed in either nominal or real terms. Similarly, cash flows can be expressed in either nominal or real terms. Given these choices, how should one express interest rates and cash flows when performing capital budgeting?

Financial practitioners correctly stress the need to maintain *consistency* between cash flows and discount rates. That is:

Nominal cash flows must be discounted at the *nominal* rate.

Real cash flows must be discounted at the *real* rate.

As long as one is consistent, either approach is correct. To minimize computational error, it is generally advisable in practice to choose the approach that is easiest. This idea is illustrated in the following two examples.

EXAMPLE 7.9

Real and Nominal Discounting Shields Electric forecasts the following nominal cash flows on a particular project:

	0	1	2
Cash flow	−$1,000	$600	$650

The nominal discount rate is 14 percent, and the inflation rate is forecast to be 5 percent. What is the value of the project?

Using Nominal Quantities The NPV can be calculated as:

$$\$26.47 = -\$1,000 + \frac{\$600}{1.14} + \frac{\$650}{(1.14)^2}$$

The project should be accepted.

Using Real Quantities The real cash flows are these:

	0	1	2
Cash flow	−$1,000	$571.43 $\left(\frac{\$600}{1.05}\right)$	$589.57 $\left(\frac{\$650}{(1.05)^2}\right)$

As we have discussed, the real discount rate is 8.57143 percent ($=1.14/1.05 - 1$).
The NPV can be calculated as:

$$\$26.47 = -\$1,000 + \frac{\$571.43}{1.0857143} + \frac{\$589.57}{(1.0857143)^2}$$

The NPV is the same whether cash flows are expressed in nominal or in real quantities. It must always be the case that the NPV is the same under the two different approaches.

Because both approaches always yield the same result, which one should be used? Use the approach that is simpler because the simpler approach generally leads to fewer computational errors. The Shields Electric example begins with nominal cash flows, so nominal quantities produce a simpler calculation here.

EXAMPLE 7.10

Real and Nominal NPV   Altshuler, Inc., generated the following forecast for a capital budgeting project:

	Year		
	0	**1**	**2**
Capital expenditure	$1,210		
Revenues (in real terms)		$1,900	$2,000
Cash expenses (in real terms)		950	1,000
Depreciation (straight-line)		605	605

The president, David Altshuler, estimates inflation to be 10 percent per year over the next two years. In addition, he believes that the cash flows of the project should be discounted at the nominal rate of 15.5 percent. His firm's tax rate is 40 percent.

Mr. Altshuler forecasts all cash flows in *nominal* terms, leading to the following spreadsheet:

	Year		
	0	**1**	**2**
Capital expenditure	−$1,210		
Revenues		$2,090 (= 1,900 × 1.10)	$2,420 [= 2,000 × (1.10)^2]
−Expenses		−1,045 (= 950 × 1.10)	−1,210 [= 1,000 × (1.10)^2]
−Depreciation		−605 (= 1,210/2)	−605
Taxable income		$ 440	$ 605
−Taxes (40%)		−176	−242
Income after taxes		$ 264	$ 363
+Depreciation		+605	+605
Cash flow		$ 869	$ 968

$$\text{NPV} = -\$1,210 + \frac{\$869}{1.155} + \frac{\$968}{(1.155)^2} = \$268$$

Mr. Altshuler's sidekick, Stuart Weiss, prefers working in real terms. He first calculates the real rate to be 5 percent (=1.155/1.10 − 1). Next, he generates the following spreadsheet in *real* quantities:

	Year		
	0	**1**	**2**
Capital expenditure	−$1,210		
Revenues		$1,900	$ 2,000
−Expenses		−950	−1,000
−Depreciation		−550 (=605/1.1)	−500 [=605/(1.1)^2]
Taxable income		$ 400	$ 500
−Taxes (40%)		−160	−200
Income after taxes		$ 240	$ 300
+Depreciation		+550	+500
Cash flow		$ 790	$ 800

(continued)

$$NPV = -\$1,210 + \frac{\$790}{1.05} + \frac{\$800}{(1.05)^2} = \$268$$

In explaining his calculations to Mr. Altshuler, Mr. Weiss points out these facts:

1. The capital expenditure occurs at date 0 (today), so its nominal value and its real value are equal.

2. Because yearly depreciation of $605 is a nominal quantity, one converts it to a real quantity by discounting at the inflation rate of 10 percent.

It is no coincidence that both Mr. Altshuler and Mr. Weiss arrive at the same NPV number. Both methods must always generate the same NPV.

7.4 Alternative Definitions of Operating Cash Flow

The analysis we went through in the previous section is quite general and can be adapted to just about any capital investment problem. In the next section, we illustrate a particularly useful variation. Before we do so, we need to discuss the fact that different definitions of project operating cash flow are commonly used, both in practice and in finance texts.

As we will see, the different approaches to operating cash flow all measure the same thing. If they are used correctly, they all produce the same answer, and one is not necessarily any better or more useful than another. Unfortunately, the fact that alternative definitions are used sometimes leads to confusion. For this reason, we examine several of these variations next to see how they are related.

In the discussion that follows, keep in mind that when we speak of cash flow, we literally mean dollars in less dollars out. This is all we are concerned with. Different definitions of operating cash flow simply amount to different ways of manipulating basic information about sales, costs, depreciation, and taxes to get at cash flow.

For a particular project and year under consideration, suppose we have the following estimates:

$$Sales = \$1,500$$
$$Costs = \$700$$
$$Depreciation = \$600$$

With these estimates, notice that EBIT is:

$$EBIT = Sales - Costs - Depreciation$$
$$= \$1,500 - 700 - 600$$
$$= \$200$$

Once again, we assume that no interest is paid, so the tax bill is:

$$Taxes = EBIT \times t_c$$
$$= \$200 \times .34 = \$68$$

where t_c, the corporate tax rate, is 34 percent.

When we put all of this together, we see that project operating cash flow, OCF, is:

$$OCF = EBIT + Depreciation - Taxes$$
$$= \$200 + 600 - 68 = \$732$$

It turns out there are some other ways to determine OCF that could be (and are) used. We consider these next.

The Bottom-Up Approach

Because we are ignoring any financing expenses, such as interest, in our calculations of project OCF, we can write project net income as:

$$\text{Project net income} = \text{EBIT} - \text{Taxes}$$
$$= \$200 - 68$$
$$= \$132$$

If we simply add the depreciation to both sides, we arrive at a slightly different and very common expression for OCF:

$$\text{OCF} = \text{Net income} + \text{Depreciation}$$
$$= \$132 + 600 \tag{7.3}$$
$$= \$732$$

This is the *bottom-up* approach. Here, we start with the accountant's bottom line (net income) and add back any noncash deductions such as depreciation. It is crucial to remember that this definition of operating cash flow as net income plus depreciation is correct only if there is no interest expense subtracted in the calculation of net income.

The Top-Down Approach

Perhaps the most obvious way to calculate OCF is this:

$$\text{OCF} = \text{Sales} - \text{Costs} - \text{Taxes}$$
$$= \$1,500 - 700 - 68 = \$732 \tag{7.4}$$

This is the *top-down* approach, the second variation on the basic OCF definition. Here we start at the top of the income statement with sales and work our way down to net cash flow by subtracting costs, taxes, and other expenses. Along the way, we simply leave out any strictly noncash items such as depreciation.

The Tax Shield Approach

The third variation on our basic definition of OCF is the *tax shield* approach. This approach will be very useful for some problems we consider in the next chapter. The tax shield definition of OCF is:

$$\text{OCF} = (\text{Sales} - \text{Costs}) \times (1 - t_c) + \text{Depreciation} \times t_c \tag{7.5}$$

where t_c is again the corporate tax rate. Assuming that $t_c = 34$ percent, the OCF works out to be:

$$\text{OCF} = (\$1,500 - 700) \times .66 + 600 \times .34$$
$$= \$528 + 204$$
$$= \$732$$

This is just as we had before.

This approach views OCF as having two components. The first part is what the project's cash flow would be if there were no depreciation expense. In this case, this would-have-been cash flow is $528.

The second part of OCF in this approach is the depreciation deduction multiplied by the tax rate. This is called the **depreciation tax shield**. We know that depreciation is a non-cash expense. The only cash flow effect of deducting depreciation is to reduce our taxes, a benefit to us. At the current 34 percent corporate tax rate, every dollar in depreciation expense saves us 34 cents in taxes. So, in our example, the $600 depreciation deduction saves us $600 × .34 = $204 in taxes.

Conclusion

Now that we've seen that all of these approaches are the same, you're probably wondering why everybody doesn't just agree on one of them. One reason is that different approaches are useful in different circumstances. The best one to use is whichever happens to be the most convenient for the problem at hand.

7.5   Investments of Unequal Lives: The Equivalent Annual Cost Method

Suppose a firm must choose between two machines of unequal lives. Both machines can do the same job, but they have different operating costs and will last for different time periods. A simple application of the NPV rule suggests taking the machine whose costs have the lower present value. This choice might be a mistake, however, because the lower-cost machine may need to be replaced before the other one.

Let's consider an example. The Downtown Athletic Club must choose between two mechanical tennis ball throwers. Machine *A* costs less than machine *B* but will not last as long. The cash *outflows* from the two machines are shown here:

Machine	0	1	2	3	4
			Date		
A	$500	$120	$120	$120	
B	$600	$100	$100	$100	$100

Machine *A* costs $500 and lasts three years. There will be maintenance expenses of $120 to be paid at the end of each of the three years. Machine *B* costs $600 and lasts four years. There will be maintenance expenses of $100 to be paid at the end of each of the four years. We place all costs in real terms, an assumption greatly simplifying the analysis. Revenues per year are assumed to be the same, regardless of machine, so they are ignored in the analysis. Note that all numbers in the previous chart are *outflows*.

To get a handle on the decision, let's take the present value of the costs of each of the two machines. Assuming a discount rate of 10 percent, we have:

$$\text{Machine } A: \$798.42 = \$500 + \frac{\$120}{1.1} + \frac{\$120}{(1.1)^2} + \frac{\$120}{(1.1)^3}$$

$$\text{Machine } B: \$916.99 = \$600 + \frac{\$100}{1.1} + \frac{\$100}{(1.1)^2} + \frac{\$100}{(1.1)^3} + \frac{\$100}{(1.1)^4}$$

Machine *B* has a higher present value of outflows. A naive approach would be to select machine *A* because of its lower present value. However, machine *B* has a longer life, so perhaps its cost per year is actually lower.

How might one properly adjust for the difference in useful life when comparing the two machines? Perhaps the easiest approach involves calculating something called the *equivalent annual cost* of each machine. This approach puts costs on a per-year basis.

The previous equation showed that payments of ($500, $120, $120, $120) are equivalent to a single payment of $798.42 at date 0. We now wish to equate the single payment of $798.42 at date 0 with a three-year annuity. Using techniques of previous chapters, we have:

$$\$798.42 = C \times A_{.10}^3$$

$A_{.10}^3$ is an annuity of $1 a year for three years, discounted at 10 percent. C is the unknown—the annuity payment per year such that the present value of all payments equals $798.42. Because $A_{.10}^3$ equals 2.4869, C equals $321.05 (=$798.42/2.4869). Thus, a payment stream of ($500, $120, $120, $120) is equivalent to annuity payments of $321.05 made at the *end* of each year for three years. We refer to $321.05 as the *equivalent annual cost* of machine A.

This idea is summarized in the following chart:

	Date			
	0	**1**	**2**	**3**
Cash outflows of machine A	$500	$120	$120	$120
Equivalent annual cost of machine A		$321.05	$321.05	$321.05

The Downtown Athletic Club should be indifferent between cash outflows of ($500, $120, $120, $120) and cash outflows of ($0, $321.05, $321.05, $321.05). Alternatively, one can say that the purchase of the machine is financially equivalent to a rental agreement calling for annual lease payments of $321.05.

Now let's turn to machine B. We calculate its equivalent annual cost from:

$$\$916.99 = C \times A_{.10}^4$$

Because $A_{.10}^4$ equals 3.1699, C equals $916.99/3.1699, or $289.28.

As we did for machine A, we can create the following chart for machine B:

	Date				
	0	**1**	**2**	**3**	**4**
Cash outflows of machine B	$600	$100	$100	$100	$100
Equivalent annual cost of machine B		$289.28	$289.28	$289.28	$289.28

The decision is easy once the charts of the two machines are compared. Would you rather make annual lease payments of $321.05 or $289.28? Put this way, the problem becomes a no-brainer: A rational person would rather pay the lower amount. Thus, machine B is the preferred choice.

Two final remarks are in order. First, it is no accident that we specified the costs of the tennis ball machines in real terms. Although B would still have been the preferred machine had the costs been stated in nominal terms, the actual solution would have been much more difficult. As a general rule, always convert cash flows to real terms when working through problems of this type.

Second, such analysis applies only if one anticipates that both machines can be replaced. The analysis would differ if no replacement were possible. For example, imagine that the only company that manufactured tennis ball throwers just went out of business and no new producers are expected to enter the field. In this case, machine *B* would generate revenues in the fourth year whereas machine *A* would not. Here, simple net present value analysis for mutually exclusive projects including both revenues and costs would be appropriate.

The General Decision to Replace

The previous analysis concerned the choice between machine *A* and machine *B*, both of which were new acquisitions. More typically firms must decide when to replace an existing machine with a new one. This decision is actually quite straightforward. One should replace if the annual cost of the new machine is less than the annual cost of the old machine. As with much else in finance, an example clarifies this approach better than further explanation.

EXAMPLE 7.11

Replacement Decisions   Consider the situation of BIKE, which must decide whether to replace an existing machine. BIKE currently pays no taxes. The replacement machine costs $9,000 now and requires maintenance of $1,000 at the end of every year for eight years. At the end of eight years, the machine would be sold for $2,000 after taxes.

The existing machine requires increasing amounts of maintenance each year, and its salvage value falls each year, as shown:

Year	Maintenance	Aftertax Salvage
Present	$ 0	$4,000
1	1,000	2,500
2	2,000	1,500
3	3,000	1,000
4	4,000	0

This chart tells us that the existing machine can be sold for $4,000 now after taxes. If it is sold one year from now, the resale price will be $2,500 after taxes, and $1,000 must be spent on maintenance during the year to keep it running. For ease of calculation, we assume that this maintenance fee is paid at the end of the year. The machine will last for four more years before it falls apart. In other words, salvage value will be zero at the end of year 4. If BIKE faces an opportunity cost of capital of 15 percent, when should it replace the machine?

Our approach is to compare the annual cost of the replacement machine with the annual cost of the old machine. The annual cost of the replacement machine is simply its *equivalent annual cost* (EAC). Let's calculate that first.

Equivalent Annual Cost of New Machine   The present value of the cost of the new replacement machine is as follows:

$$PV_{costs} = \$9,000 + \$1,000 \times A^8_{.15} - \frac{\$2,000}{(1.15)^8}$$
$$= \$9,000 + \$1,000 \times (4.4873) - \$2,000 \times (.3269)$$
$$= \$12,833$$

(continued)

Notice that the $2,000 salvage value is an inflow. It is treated as a *negative* number in this equation because it *offsets* the cost of the machine.

The EAC of a new replacement machine equals:

$$\text{PV/8-year annuity factor at 15\%} = \frac{PV}{A_{.15}^{8}} = \frac{\$12,833}{4.4873} = \$2,860$$

This calculation implies that buying a replacement machine is financially equivalent to renting this machine for $2,860 per year.

Cost of Old Machine   This calculation is a little trickier. If BIKE keeps the old machine for one year, the firm must pay maintenance costs of $1,000 a year from now. But this is not BIKE's only cost from keeping the machine for one year. BIKE will receive $2,500 at date 1 if the old machine is kept for one year but would receive $4,000 today if the old machine were sold immediately. This reduction in sales proceeds is clearly a cost as well.

Thus the PV of the costs of keeping the machine one more year before selling it equals:

$$\$4,000 + \frac{\$1,000}{1.15} - \frac{\$2,500}{1.15} = \$2,696$$

That is, if BIKE holds the old machine for one year, BIKE does *not* receive the $4,000 today. This $4,000 can be thought of as an opportunity cost. In addition, the firm must pay $1,000 a year from now. Finally, BIKE does receive $2,500 a year from now. This last item is treated as a negative number because it offsets the other two costs.

Although we normally express cash flows in terms of present value, the analysis to come is easier if we express the cash flow in terms of its future value one year from now. This future value is:

$$\$2,696 \times 1.15 = \$3,100$$

In other words, the cost of keeping the machine for one year is equivalent to paying $3,100 at the end of the year.

Making the Comparison   Now let's review the cash flows. If we replace the machine immediately, we can view our annual expense as $2,860, beginning at the end of the year. This annual expense occurs forever if we replace the new machine every eight years. This cash flow stream can be written as follows:

	Year 1	Year 2	Year 3	Year 4	...
Expenses from replacing machine immediately	$2,860	$2,860	$2,860	$2,860	...

If we replace the old machine in one year, our expense from using the old machine for that final year can be viewed as $3,100, payable at the end of the year. After replacement, our annual expense is $2,860, beginning at the end of two years. This annual expense occurs forever if we replace the new machine every eight years. This cash flow stream can be written like this:

	Year 1	Year 2	Year 3	Year 4	...
Expenses from using old machine for one year and then replacing it	$3,100	$2,860	$2,860	$2,860	...

(continued)

Put this way, the choice is a no-brainer. Anyone would rather pay $2,860 at the end of the year than $3,100 at the end of the year. Thus, BIKE should replace the old machine immediately to minimize the expense at year 1.[1]

Two final points should be made about the decision to replace. First, we have examined a situation where both the old machine and the replacement machine generate the same revenues. Because revenues are unaffected by the choice of machine, revenues do not enter our analysis. This situation is common in business. For example, the decision to replace either the heating system or the air conditioning system in one's home office will likely not affect firm revenues. However, sometimes revenues will be greater with a new machine. The approach here can easily be amended to handle differential revenues.

Second, we want to stress the importance of the current approach. Applications of this approach are pervasive in business because *every* machine must be replaced at some point.

---

[1] One caveat is in order. Perhaps the old machine's maintenance is high in the first year but drops after that. A decision to replace immediately might be premature in that case. Therefore, we need to check the cost of the old machine in future years.

The cost of keeping the existing machine a second year is:

$$\text{PV of costs at time } 1 = \$2,500 + \frac{\$2,000}{1.15} - \frac{\$1,500}{1.15} = \$2,935$$

which has a future value of $3,375 (=$2,935 × 1.15).

The costs of keeping the existing machine for years 3 and 4 are also greater than the EAC of buying a new machine. Thus, BIKE's decision to replace the old machine immediately is still valid.

Summary and Conclusions

This chapter discussed a number of practical applications of capital budgeting.

1. Capital budgeting must be placed on an incremental basis. This means that sunk costs must be ignored, whereas both opportunity costs and side effects must be considered.

2. In the Baldwin case we computed NPV using the following two steps:
   a. Calculate the net cash flow from all sources for each period.
   b. Calculate the NPV using these cash flows.

3. Inflation must be handled consistently. One approach is to express both cash flows and the discount rate in nominal terms. The other approach is to express both cash flows and the discount rate in real terms. Because either approach yields the same NPV calculation, the simpler method should be used. The simpler method will generally depend on the type of capital budgeting problem.

4. A firm should use the equivalent annual cost approach when choosing between two machines of unequal lives.

Concept Questions

1. **Opportunity Cost**   In the context of capital budgeting, what is an opportunity cost?

2. **Incremental Cash Flows**   Which of the following should be treated as an incremental cash flow when computing the NPV of an investment?
   a. A reduction in the sales of a company's other products caused by the investment.
   b. An expenditure on plant and equipment that has not yet been made and will be made only if the project is accepted.
   c. Costs of research and development undertaken in connection with the product during the past three years.
   d. Annual depreciation expense from the investment.

    e. Dividend payments by the firm.

    f. The resale value of plant and equipment at the end of the project's life.

    g. Salary and medical costs for production personnel who will be employed only if the project is accepted.

3.   **Incremental Cash Flows**   Your company currently produces and sells steel shaft golf clubs. The board of directors wants you to consider the introduction of a new line of titanium bubble woods with graphite shafts. Which of the following costs are *not* relevant?

    a. Land you already own that will be used for the project, but otherwise will be sold for $700,000, its market value.

    b. A $300,000 drop in your sales of steel shaft clubs if the titanium woods with graphite shafts are introduced.

    c. $200,000 spent on research and development last year on graphite shafts.

4.   **Depreciation**   Given the choice, would a firm prefer to use MACRS depreciation or straight-line depreciation? Why?

5.   **Net Working Capital**   In our capital budgeting examples, we assumed that a firm would recover all of the working capital it invested in a project. Is this a reasonable assumption? When might it not be valid?

6.   **Stand-Alone Principle**   Suppose a financial manager is quoted as saying, "Our firm uses the stand-alone principle. Because we treat projects like minifirms in our evaluation process, we include financing costs because they are relevant at the firm level." Critically evaluate this statement.

7.   **Equivalent Annual Cost**   When is EAC analysis appropriate for comparing two or more projects? Why is this method used? Are there any implicit assumptions required by this method that you find troubling? Explain.

8.   **Cash Flow and Depreciation**   "When evaluating projects, we're only concerned with the relevant incremental aftertax cash flows. Therefore, because depreciation is a noncash expense, we should ignore its effects when evaluating projects." Critically evaluate this statement.

9.   **Capital Budgeting Considerations**   A major college textbook publisher has an existing finance textbook. The publisher is debating whether to produce an "essentialized" version, meaning a shorter (and lower-priced) book. What are some of the considerations that should come into play?

To answer the next three questions, refer to the following example. In 2003, Porsche unveiled its new sports utility vehicle (SUV), the Cayenne. With a price tag of over $40,000, the Cayenne goes from zero to 62 mph in 8.5 seconds. Porsche's decision to enter the SUV market was in response to the runaway success of other high-priced SUVs such as the Mercedes-Benz M class. Vehicles in this class had generated years of very high profits. The Cayenne certainly spiced up the market, and, in 2006, Porsche introduced the Cayenne Turbo S, which goes from zero to 60 mph in 4.8 seconds and has a top speed of 168 mph. The base price for the Cayenne Turbo S? Almost $112,000!

Some analysts questioned Porsche's entry into the luxury SUV market. The analysts were concerned because not only was Porsche a late entry into the market, but also the introduction of the Cayenne might damage Porsche's reputation as a maker of high-performance automobiles.

10.   **Erosion**   In evaluating the Cayenne, would you consider the possible damage to Porsche's reputation as erosion?

11.   **Capital Budgeting**   Porsche was one of the last manufacturers to enter the sports utility vehicle market. Why would one company decide to proceed with a product when other companies, at least initially, decide not to enter the market?

12.   **Capital Budgeting**   In evaluating the Cayenne, what do you think Porsche needs to assume regarding the substantial profit margins that exist in this market? Is it likely that they will be maintained as the market becomes more competitive, or will Porsche be able to maintain the profit margin because of its image and the performance of the Cayenne?

Questions and Problems

BASIC
(Questions 1–10)

1. **Calculating Project NPV**   Raphael Restaurant is considering the purchase of a $10,000 souffle maker. The souffle maker has an economic life of five years and will be fully depreciated by the straight-line method. The machine will produce 2,000 souffles per year, with each costing $2 to make and priced at $5. Assume that the discount rate is 17 percent and the tax rate is 34 percent. Should Raphael make the purchase?

2. **Calculating Project NPV**   The Best Manufacturing Company is considering a new investment. Financial projections for the investment are tabulated here. The corporate tax rate is 34 percent. Assume all sales revenue is received in cash, all operating costs and income taxes are paid in cash, and all cash flows occur at the end of the year. All net working capital is recovered at the end of the project.

	Year 0	Year 1	Year 2	Year 3	Year 4
Investment	$10,000	–	–	–	–
Sales revenue	–	$7,000	$7,000	$7,000	$7,000
Operating costs	–	2,000	2,000	2,000	2,000
Depreciation	–	2,500	2,500	2,500	2,500
Net working capital spending	200	250	300	200	?

   a. Compute the incremental net income of the investment for each year.
   b. Compute the incremental cash flows of the investment for each year.
   c. Suppose the appropriate discount rate is 12 percent. What is the NPV of the project?

3. **Calculating Project NPV**   Down Under Boomerang, Inc., is considering a new three-year expansion project that requires an initial fixed asset investment of $2.7 million. The fixed asset will be depreciated straight-line to zero over its three-year tax life, after which it will be worthless. The project is estimated to generate $2,400,000 in annual sales, with costs of $960,000. The tax rate is 35 percent and the required return is 15 percent. What is the project's NPV?

4. **Calculating Project Cash Flow from Assets**   In the previous problem, suppose the project requires an initial investment in net working capital of $300,000 and the fixed asset will have a market value of $210,000 at the end of the project. What is the project's year 0 net cash flow? Year 1? Year 2? Year 3? What is the new NPV?

5. **NPV and Modified ACRS**   In the previous problem, suppose the fixed asset actually falls into the three-year MACRS class. All the other facts are the same. What is the project's year 1 net cash flow now? Year 2? Year 3? What is the new NPV?

6. **Project Evaluation**   Your firm is contemplating the purchase of a new $925,000 computer-based order entry system. The system will be depreciated straight-line to zero over its five-year life. It will be worth $90,000 at the end of that time. You will save $360,000 before taxes per year in order processing costs, and you will be able to reduce working capital by $125,000 (this is a one-time reduction). If the tax rate is 35 percent, what is the IRR for this project?

7. **Project Evaluation**   Dog Up! Franks is looking at a new sausage system with an installed cost of $390,000. This cost will be depreciated straight-line to zero over the project's five-year life, at the end of which the sausage system can be scrapped for $60,000. The sausage system will save the firm $120,000 per year in pretax operating costs, and the system requires an initial investment in net working capital of $28,000. If the tax rate is 34 percent and the discount rate is 10 percent, what is the NPV of this project?

8. **Calculating Salvage Value**   An asset used in a four-year project falls in the five-year MACRS class for tax purposes. The asset has an acquisition cost of $9,300,000 and will be sold for

$2,100,000 at the end of the project. If the tax rate is 35 percent, what is the aftertax salvage value of the asset?

9. **Calculating NPV**   Howell Petroleum is considering a new project that complements its existing business. The machine required for the project costs $2 million. The marketing department predicts that sales related to the project will be $1.2 million per year for the next four years, after which the market will cease to exist. The machine will be depreciated down to zero over its four-year economic life using the straight-line method. Cost of goods sold and operating expenses related to the project are predicted to be 25 percent of sales. Howell also needs to add net working capital of $100,000 immediately. The additional net working capital will be recovered in full at the end of the project's life. The corporate tax rate is 35 percent. The required rate of return for Howell is 14 percent. Should Howell proceed with the project?

10. **Calculating EAC**   You are evaluating two different silicon wafer milling machines. The Techron I costs $210,000, has a three-year life, and has pretax operating costs of $34,000 per year. The Techron II costs $320,000, has a five-year life, and has pretax operating costs of $23,000 per year. For both milling machines, use straight-line depreciation to zero over the project's life and assume a salvage value of $20,000. If your tax rate is 35 percent and your discount rate is 14 percent, compute the EAC for both machines. Which do you prefer? Why?

INTERMEDIATE
(Questions 11–29)

11. **Cost-Cutting Proposals**   Massey Machine Shop is considering a four-year project to improve its production efficiency. Buying a new machine press for $480,000 is estimated to result in $160,000 in annual pretax cost savings. The press falls in the MACRS five-year class, and it will have a salvage value at the end of the project of $70,000. The press also requires an initial investment in spare parts inventory of $20,000, along with an additional $3,000 in inventory for each succeeding year of the project. If the shop's tax rate is 35 percent and its discount rate is 14 percent, should Massey buy and install the machine press?

12. **Comparing Mutually Exclusive Projects**   Hagar Industrial Systems Company (HISC) is trying to decide between two different conveyor belt systems. System A costs $430,000, has a four-year life, and requires $120,000 in pretax annual operating costs. System B costs $540,000, has a six-year life, and requires $80,000 in pretax annual operating costs. Both systems are to be depreciated straight-line to zero over their lives and will have zero salvage value. Whichever system is chosen, it will *not* be replaced when it wears out. If the tax rate is 34 percent and the discount rate is 20 percent, which system should the firm choose?

13. **Comparing Mutually Exclusive Projects**   Suppose in the previous problem that HISC always needs a conveyor belt system; when one wears out, it must be replaced. Which system should the firm choose now?

14. **Comparing Mutually Exclusive Projects**   Vandalay Industries is considering the purchase of a new machine for the production of latex. Machine A costs $2,100,000 and will last for six years. Variable costs are 35 percent of sales, and fixed costs are $150,000 per year. Machine B costs $4,500,000 and will last for nine years. Variable costs for this machine are 30 percent and fixed costs are $100,000 per year. The sales for each machine will be $9 million per year. The required return is 10 percent and the tax rate is 35 percent. Both machines will be depreciated on a straight-line basis. If the company plans to replace the machine when it wears out on a perpetual basis, which machine should you choose?

15. **Capital Budgeting with Inflation**   Consider the following cash flows on two mutually exclusive projects:

Year	Project A	Project B
0	−$40,000	−$50,000
1	20,000	10,000
2	15,000	20,000
3	15,000	40,000

The cash flows of project A are expressed in real terms, whereas those of project B are expressed in nominal terms. The appropriate nominal discount rate is 15 percent and the inflation rate is 4 percent. Which project should you choose?

16. **Inflation and Company Value** Sparkling Water, Inc., expects to sell 2 million bottles of drinking water each year in perpetuity. This year each bottle will sell for $1.25 in real terms and will cost $0.70 in real terms. Sales income and costs occur at year-end. Revenues will rise at a real rate of 6 percent annually, while real costs will rise at a real rate of 5 percent annually. The real discount rate is 10 percent. The corporate tax rate is 34 percent. What is Sparkling worth today?

17. **Calculating Nominal Cash Flow** Etonic Inc. is considering an investment of $250,000 in an asset with an economic life of five years. The firm estimates that the nominal annual cash revenues and expenses at the end of the first year will be $200,000 and $50,000, respectively. Both revenues and expenses will grow thereafter at the annual inflation rate of 3 percent. Etonic will use the straight-line method to depreciate its asset to zero over five years. The salvage value of the asset is estimated to be $30,000 in nominal terms at that time. The one-time net working capital investment of $10,000 is required immediately and will be recovered at the end of the project. All corporate cash flows are subject to a 34 percent tax rate. What is the project's total nominal cash flow from assets for each year?

18. **Cash Flow Valuation** Phillips Industries runs a small manufacturing operation. For this fiscal year, it expects real net cash flows of $120,000. Phillips is an ongoing operation, but it expects competitive pressures to erode its real net cash flows at 6 percent per year in perpetuity. The appropriate real discount rate for Phillips is 11 percent. All net cash flows are received at year-end. What is the present value of the net cash flows from Phillips's operations?

19. **Equivalent Annual Cost** Bridgton Golf Academy is evaluating different golf practice equipment. The "Dimple-Max" equipment costs $45,000, has a three-year life, and costs $5,000 per year to operate. The relevant discount rate is 12 percent. Assume that the straight-line depreciation method is used and that the equipment is fully depreciated to zero. Furthermore, assume the equipment has a salvage value of $10,000 at the end of the project's life. The relevant tax rate is 34 percent. All cash flows occur at the end of the year. What is the equivalent annual cost (EAC) of this equipment?

20. **Equivalent Annual Cost** Harwell University must purchase word processors for its typing lab. The university can buy 10 EVF word processors that cost $8,000 each and have annual, year-end maintenance costs of $2,000 per machine. The EVF word processors will be replaced at the end of year 4 and have no value at that time. Alternatively, Harwell can buy 11 AEH word processors to accomplish the same work. The AEH word processors will be replaced after three years. They each cost $5,000 and have annual, year-end maintenance costs of $2,500 per machine. Each AEH word processor will have a resale value of $500 at the end of three years. The university's opportunity cost of funds for this type of investment is 14 percent. Because the university is a nonprofit institution, it does not pay taxes. It is anticipated that whichever manufacturer is chosen now will be the supplier of future machines. Would you recommend purchasing 10 EVF word processors or 11 AEH machines?

21. **Calculating Project NPV** Scott Investors, Inc., is considering the purchase of a $500,000 computer with an economic life of five years. The computer will be fully depreciated over five years using the straight-line method. The market value of the computer will be $100,000 in five years. The computer will replace five office employees whose combined annual salaries are $120,000. The machine will also immediately lower the firm's required net working capital by $100,000. This amount of net working capital will need to be replaced once the machine is sold. The corporate tax rate is 34 percent. Is it worthwhile to buy the computer if the appropriate discount rate is 12 percent?

22. **Calculating NPV and IRR for a Replacement** A firm is considering an investment in a new machine with a price of $32 million to replace its existing machine. The current machine has a book value of $1 million and a market value of $9 million. The new machine is expected

to have a four-year life, and the old machine has four years left in which it can be used. If the firm replaces the old machine with the new machine, it expects to save $8 million in operating costs each year over the next four years. Both machines will have no salvage value in four years. If the firm purchases the new machine, it will also need an investment of $500,000 in net working capital. The required return on the investment is 18 percent, and the tax rate is 39 percent.

a. What are the NPV and IRR of the decision to replace the old machine?

b. The new machine saves $32 million over the next four years and has a cost of $32 million. When you consider the time value of money, how is it possible that the NPV of the decision to replace the old machine has a positive NPV?

23. **Project Analysis and Inflation**   Sanders Enterprises, Inc., has been considering the purchase of a new manufacturing facility for $120,000. The facility is to be fully depreciated on a straight-line basis over seven years. It is expected to have no resale value after the seven years. Operating revenues from the facility are expected to be $50,000, in nominal terms, at the end of the first year. The revenues are expected to increase at the inflation rate of 5 percent. Production costs at the end of the first year will be $20,000, in nominal terms, and they are expected to increase at 7 percent per year. The real discount rate is 14 percent. The corporate tax rate is 34 percent. Sanders has other ongoing profitable operations. Should the company accept the project?

24. **Calculating Project NPV**   With the growing popularity of casual surf print clothing, two recent MBA graduates decided to broaden this casual surf concept to encompass a "surf lifestyle for the home." With limited capital, they decided to focus on surf print table and floor lamps to accent people's homes. They projected unit sales of these lamps to be 5,000 in the first year, with growth of 15 percent each year for the next five years. Production of these lamps will require $28,000 in net working capital to start. Total fixed costs are $75,000 per year, variable production costs are $20 per unit, and the units are priced at $45 each. The equipment needed to begin production will cost $60,000. The equipment will be depreciated using the straight-line method over a five-year life and is not expected to have a salvage value. The effective tax rate is 34 percent, and the required rate of return is 25 percent. What is the NPV of this project?

25. **Calculating Project NPV**   You have been hired as a consultant for Pristine Urban-Tech Zither, Inc. (PUTZ), manufacturers of fine zithers. The market for zithers is growing quickly. The company bought some land three years ago for $1 million in anticipation of using it as a toxic waste dump site but has recently hired another company to handle all toxic materials. Based on a recent appraisal, the company believes it could sell the land for $800,000 on an aftertax basis. The company also hired a marketing firm to analyze the zither market, at a cost of $125,000. An excerpt of the marketing report is as follows:

> The zither industry will have a rapid expansion in the next four years. With the brand name recognition that PUTZ brings to bear, we feel that the company will be able to sell 2,900, 3,800, 2,700, and 1,900 units each year for the next four years, respectively. Again, capitalizing on the name recognition of PUTZ, we feel that a premium price of $700 can be charged for each zither. Because zithers appear to be a fad, we feel at the end of the four-year period, sales should be discontinued.

PUTZ feels that fixed costs for the project will be $350,000 per year, and variable costs are 15 percent of sales. The equipment necessary for production will cost $3.8 million and will be depreciated according to a three-year MACRS schedule. At the end of the project, the equipment can be scrapped for $400,000. Net working capital of $120,000 will be required by the end of the first year. PUTZ has a 38 percent tax rate, and the required return on the project is 13 percent. What is the NPV of the project? Assume the company has other profitable projects.

26. **Calculating Project NPV**   Pilot Plus Pens is deciding when to replace its old machine. The machine's current salvage value is $2 million. Its current book value is $1 million. If not sold, the old machine will require maintenance costs of $400,000 at the end of the year for the next five years. Depreciation on the old machine is $200,000 per year. At the end of five years, it will have a salvage value of $200,000 and a book value of $0. A replacement machine costs $3 million now and requires maintenance costs of $500,000 at the end of each year during its

economic life of five years. At the end of the five years, the new machine will have a salvage value of $500,000. It will be fully depreciated by the straight-line method. In five years a replacement machine will cost $3,500,000. Pilot will need to purchase this machine regardless of what choice it makes today. The corporate tax rate is 34 percent and the appropriate discount rate is 12 percent. The company is assumed to earn sufficient revenues to generate tax shields from depreciation. Should Pilot Plus Pens replace the old machine now or at the end of five years?

27. **Calculating EAC**   Gold Star Industries is contemplating a purchase of computers. The firm has narrowed its choices to the SAL 5000 and the DET 1000. Gold Star would need 10 SALs, and each SAL costs $3,750 and requires $500 of maintenance each year. At the end of the computer's eight-year life, Gold Star expects to sell each one for $500. Alternatively, Gold Star could buy seven DETs. Each DET costs $5,250 and requires $700 of maintenance every year. Each DET lasts for six years and has a resale value of $600 at the end of its economic life. Gold Star will continue to purchase the model that it chooses today into perpetuity. Gold Star has a 34 percent tax rate. Assume that the maintenance costs occur at year-end. Depreciation is straight-line to zero. Which model should Gold Star buy if the appropriate discount rate is 11 percent?

28. **EAC and Inflation**   Office Automation, Inc., must choose between two copiers, the XX40 or the RH45. The XX40 costs $700 and will last for three years. The copier will require an aftertax cost of $100 per year after all relevant expenses. The RH45 costs $900 and will last five years. The real aftertax cost for the RH45 will be $110 per year. All cash flows occur at the end of the year. The inflation rate is expected to be 5 percent per year, and the nominal discount rate is 14 percent. Which copier should the company choose?

29. **Project Analysis and Inflation**   Dickinson Brothers, Inc., is considering investing in a machine to produce computer keyboards. The price of the machine will be $400,000, and its economic life is five years. The machine will be fully depreciated by the straight-line method. The machine will produce 10,000 keyboards each year. The price of each keyboard will be $40 in the first year and will increase by 5 percent per year. The production cost per keyboard will be $20 in the first year and will increase by 10 percent per year. The project will have an annual fixed cost of $50,000 and require an immediate investment of $25,000 in net working capital. The corporate tax rate for the company is 34 percent. If the appropriate discount rate is 15 percent, what is the NPV of the investment?

CHALLENGE
(Questions 30–40)

30. **Project Evaluation**   Aguilera Acoustics (AAI), Inc., projects unit sales for a new seven-octave voice emulation implant as follows:

Year	Unit Sales
1	85,000
2	98,000
3	106,000
4	114,000
5	93,000

Production of the implants will require $1,500,000 in net working capital to start and additional net working capital investments each year equal to 15 percent of the projected sales increase for the following year. Total fixed costs are $900,000 per year, variable production costs are $240 per unit, and the units are priced at $325 each. The equipment needed to begin production has an installed cost of $21,000,000. Because the implants are intended for professional singers, this equipment is considered industrial machinery and thus qualifies as seven-year MACRS property. In five years, this equipment can be sold for about 20 percent of its acquisition cost. AAI is in the 35 percent marginal tax bracket and has a required return on all its projects of 18 percent. Based on these preliminary project estimates, what is the NPV of the project? What is the IRR?

31. **Calculating Required Savings**   A proposed cost-saving device has an installed cost of $480,000. The device will be used in a five-year project but is classified as three-year MACRS

property for tax purposes. The required initial net working capital investment is $40,000, the marginal tax rate is 35 percent, and the project discount rate is 12 percent. The device has an estimated year 5 salvage value of $45,000. What level of pretax cost savings do we require for this project to be profitable?

32.   **Calculating a Bid Price**   Another utilization of cash flow analysis is setting the bid price on a project. To calculate the bid price, we set the project NPV equal to zero and find the required price. Thus the bid price represents a financial break-even level for the project. Guthrie Enterprises needs someone to supply it with 150,000 cartons of machine screws per year to support its manufacturing needs over the next five years, and you've decided to bid on the contract. It will cost you $780,000 to install the equipment necessary to start production; you'll depreciate this cost straight-line to zero over the project's life. You estimate that in five years this equipment can be salvaged for $50,000. Your fixed production costs will be $240,000 per year, and your variable production costs should be $8.50 per carton. You also need an initial investment in net working capital of $75,000. If your tax rate is 35 percent and you require a 16 percent return on your investment, what bid price should you submit?

33.   **Financial Break-Even Analysis**   The technique for calculating a bid price can be extended to many other types of problems. Answer the following questions using the same technique as setting a bid price; that is, set the project NPV to zero and solve for the variable in question.
    a.   In the previous problem, assume that the price per carton is $13 and find the project NPV. What does your answer tell you about your bid price? What do you know about the number of cartons you can sell and still break even? How about your level of costs?
    b.   Solve the previous problem again with the price still at $13—but find the quantity of cartons per year that you can supply and still break even. (*Hint*: It's less than 150,000.)
    c.   Repeat (b) with a price of $13 and a quantity of 150,000 cartons per year, and find the highest level of fixed costs you could afford and still break even. (*Hint*: It's more than $240,000.)

34.   **Calculating a Bid Price**   Your company has been approached to bid on a contract to sell 10,000 voice recognition (VR) computer keyboards a year for four years. Due to technological improvements, beyond that time they will be outdated and no sales will be possible. The equipment necessary for the production will cost $2.4 million and will be depreciated on a straight-line basis to a zero salvage value. Production will require an investment in net working capital of $75,000 to be returned at the end of the project, and the equipment can be sold for $200,000 at the end of production. Fixed costs are $500,000 per year, and variable costs are $165 per unit. In addition to the contract, you feel your company can sell 3,000, 6,000, 8,000, and 5,000 additional units to companies in other countries over the next four years, respectively, at a price of $275. This price is fixed. The tax rate is 40 percent, and the required return is 13 percent. Additionally, the president of the company will undertake the project only if it has an NPV of $100,000. What bid price should you set for the contract?

35.   **Replacement Decisions**   Suppose we are thinking about replacing an old computer with a new one. The old one cost us $650,000; the new one will cost $780,000. The new machine will be depreciated straight-line to zero over its five-year life. It will probably be worth about $140,000 after five years.
    The old computer is being depreciated at a rate of $130,000 per year. It will be completely written off in three years. If we don't replace it now, we will have to replace it in two years. We can sell it now for $230,000; in two years it will probably be worth $90,000. The new machine will save us $125,000 per year in operating costs. The tax rate is 38 percent, and the discount rate is 14 percent.
    a.   Suppose we recognize that if we don't replace the computer now, we will be replacing it in two years. Should we replace now or should we wait? (*Hint*: What we effectively have here is a decision either to "invest" in the old computer—by not selling it—or to invest in the new one. Notice that the two investments have unequal lives.)
    b.   Suppose we consider only whether we should replace the old computer now without worrying about what's going to happen in two years. What are the relevant cash flows? Should

we replace it or not? (*Hint*: Consider the net change in the firm's aftertax cash flows if we do the replacement.)

36.   Project Analysis   Benson Enterprises is evaluating alternative uses for a three-story manufacturing and warehousing building that it has purchased for $225,000. The company can continue to rent the building to the present occupants for $12,000 per year. The present occupants have indicated an interest in staying in the building for at least another 15 years. Alternatively, the company could modify the existing structure to use for its own manufacturing and warehousing needs. Benson's production engineer feels the building could be adapted to handle one of two new product lines. The cost and revenue data for the two product alternatives are as follows:

	Product A	Product B
Initial cash outlay for building modifications	$ 36,000	$ 54,000
Initial cash outlay for equipment	144,000	162,000
Annual pretax cash revenues (generated for 15 years)	105,000	127,500
Annual pretax expenditures (generated for 15 years)	60,000	75,000

The building will be used for only 15 years for either product *A* or product *B*. After 15 years the building will be too small for efficient production of either product line. At that time, Benson plans to rent the building to firms similar to the current occupants. To rent the building again, Benson will need to restore the building to its present layout. The estimated cash cost of restoring the building if product *A* has been undertaken is $3,750. If product *B* has been manufactured, the cash cost will be $28,125. These cash costs can be deducted for tax purposes in the year the expenditures occur.

Benson will depreciate the original building shell (purchased for $225,000) over a 30-year life to zero, regardless of which alternative it chooses. The building modifications and equipment purchases for either product are estimated to have a 15-year life. They will be depreciated by the straight-line method. The firm's tax rate is 34 percent, and its required rate of return on such investments is 12 percent.

For simplicity, assume all cash flows occur at the end of the year. The initial outlays for modifications and equipment will occur today (year 0), and the restoration outlays will occur at the end of year 15. Benson has other profitable ongoing operations that are sufficient to cover any losses. Which use of the building would you recommend to management?

37.   Project Analysis and Inflation   The Biological Insect Control Corporation (BICC) has hired you as a consultant to evaluate the NPV of its proposed toad ranch. BICC plans to breed toads and sell them as ecologically desirable insect control mechanisms. They anticipate that the business will continue into perpetuity. Following the negligible start-up costs, BICC expects the following nominal cash flows at the end of the year:

Revenues	$150,000
Labor costs	80,000
Other costs	40,000

The company will lease machinery for $20,000 per year. The lease payments start at the end of year 1 and are expressed in nominal terms. Revenues will increase by 5 percent per year in real terms. Labor costs will increase by 3 percent per year in real terms. Other costs will decrease by 1 percent per year in real terms. The rate of inflation is expected to be 6 percent per year. BICC's required rate of return is 10 percent in real terms. The company has a 34 percent tax rate. All cash flows occur at year-end. What is the NPV of BICC's proposed toad ranch today?

38.   Project Analysis and Inflation   Sony International has an investment opportunity to produce a new stereo color TV. The required investment on January 1 of this year is $32 million. The firm will depreciate the investment to zero using the straight-line method over four years. The investment has no resale value after completion of the project. The firm is in the 34 percent tax

www.mhhe.com/rwj

bracket. The price of the product will be $400 per unit, in real terms, and will not change over the life of the project. Labor costs for year 1 will be $15.30 per hour, in real terms, and will increase at 2 percent per year in real terms. Energy costs for year 1 will be $5.15 per physical unit, in real terms, and will increase at 3 percent per year in real terms. The inflation rate is 5 percent per year. Revenues are received and costs are paid at year-end. Refer to the following table for the production schedule:

	Year 1	Year 2	Year 3	Year 4
Physical production, in units	100,000	200,000	200,000	150,000
Labor input, in hours	2,000,000	2,000,000	2,000,000	2,000,000
Energy input, physical units	200,000	200,000	200,000	200,000

The real discount rate for Sony is 8 percent. Calculate the NPV of this project.

39. **Project Analysis and Inflation**   After extensive medical and marketing research, Pill, Inc., believes it can penetrate the pain reliever market. It is considering two alternative products. The first is a medication for headache pain. The second is a pill for headache and arthritis pain. Both products would be introduced at a price of $4 per package in real terms. The headache-only medication is projected to sell 5 million packages a year, whereas the headache and arthritis remedy would sell 10 million packages a year. Cash costs of production in the first year are expected to be $1.50 per package in real terms for the headache-only brand. Production costs are expected to be $1.70 in real terms for the headache and arthritis pill. All prices and costs are expected to rise at the general inflation rate of 5 percent.

Either product requires further investment. The headache-only pill could be produced using equipment costing $10.2 million. That equipment would last three years and have no resale value. The machinery required to produce the broader remedy would cost $12 million and last three years. The firm expects that equipment to have a $1 million resale value (in real terms) at the end of year 3.

Pill, Inc., uses straight-line depreciation. The firm faces a corporate tax rate of 34 percent and believes that the appropriate real discount rate is 13 percent. Which pain reliever should the firm produce?

40. **Calculating Project NPV**   J. Smythe, Inc., manufactures fine furniture. The company is deciding whether to introduce a new mahogany dining room table set. The set will sell for $5,600, including a set of eight chairs. The company feels that sales will be 1,300; 1,325; 1,375; 1,450; and 1,320 sets per year for the next five years, respectively. Variable costs will amount to 45 percent of sales, and fixed costs are $1.7 million per year. The new tables will require inventory amounting to 10 percent of sales, produced and stockpiled in the year prior to sales. It is believed that the addition of the new table will cause a loss of 200 tables per year of the oak tables the company produces. These tables sell for $4,500 and have variable costs of 40 percent of sales. The inventory for this oak table is also 10 percent. J. Smythe currently has excess production capacity. If the company buys the necessary equipment today, it will cost $10.5 million. However, the excess production capacity means the company can produce the new table without buying the new equipment. The company controller has said that the current excess capacity will end in two years with current production. This means that if the company uses the current excess capacity for the new table, it will be forced to spend the $10.5 million in two years to accommodate the increased sales of its current products. In five years, the new equipment will have a market value of $2.8 million if purchased today, and $6.1 million if purchased in two years. The equipment is depreciated on a seven-year MACRS schedule. The company has a tax rate of 38 percent, and the required return for the project is 14 percent.

a. Should J. Smythe undertake the new project?

b. Can you perform an IRR analysis on this project? How many IRRs would you expect to find?

c. How would you interpret the profitability index?

Bethesda Mining Company

Bethesda Mining is a midsized coal mining company with 20 mines located in Ohio, Pennsylvania, West Virginia, and Kentucky. The company operates deep mines as well as strip mines. Most of the coal mined is sold under contract, with excess production sold on the spot market.

The coal mining industry, especially high-sulfur coal operations such as Bethesda, has been hard-hit by environmental regulations. Recently, however, a combination of increased demand for coal and new pollution reduction technologies has led to an improved market demand for high-sulfur coal. Bethesda has just been approached by Mid-Ohio Electric Company with a request to supply coal for its electric generators for the next four years. Bethesda Mining does not have enough excess capacity at its existing mines to guarantee the contract. The company is considering opening a strip mine in Ohio on 5,000 acres of land purchased 10 years ago for $6 million. Based on a recent appraisal, the company feels it could receive $5 million on an aftertax basis if it sold the land today.

Strip mining is a process where the layers of topsoil above a coal vein are removed and the exposed coal is removed. Some time ago, the company would simply remove the coal and leave the land in an unusable condition. Changes in mining regulations now force a company to reclaim the land; that is, when the mining is completed, the land must be restored to near its original condition. The land can then be used for other purposes. Because it is currently operating at full capacity, Bethesda will need to purchase additional necessary equipment, which will cost $30 million. The equipment will be depreciated on a seven-year MACRS schedule. The contract runs for only four years. At that time the coal from the site will be entirely mined. The company feels that the equipment can be sold for 60 percent of its initial purchase price. However, Bethesda plans to open another strip mine at that time and will use the equipment at the new mine.

The contract calls for the delivery of 600,000 tons of coal per year at a price of $34 per ton. Bethesda Mining feels that coal production will be 650,000 tons, 725,000 tons, 810,000 tons, and 740,000 tons, respectively, over the next four years. The excess production will be sold in the spot market at an average of $40 per ton. Variable costs amount to $13 per ton, and fixed costs are $2,500,000 per year. The mine will require a net working capital investment of 5 percent of sales. The NWC will be built up in the year prior to the sales.

Bethesda will be responsible for reclaiming the land at termination of the mining. This will occur in year 5. The company uses an outside company for reclamation of all the company's strip mines. It is estimated the cost of reclamation will be $4 million. After the land is reclaimed, the company plans to donate the land to the state for use as a public park and recreation area. This will occur in year 6 and result in a charitable expense deduction of $6 million. Bethesda faces a 38 percent tax rate and has a 12 percent required return on new strip mine projects. Assume that a loss in any year will result in a tax credit.

You have been approached by the president of the company with a request to analyze the project. Calculate the payback period, profitability index, average accounting return, net present value, internal rate of return, and modified internal rate of return for the new strip mine. Should Bethesda Mining take the contract and open the mine?

Goodweek Tires, Inc.

After extensive research and development, Goodweek Tires, Inc., has recently developed a new tire, the SuperTread, and must decide whether to make the investment necessary to produce and market it. The tire would be ideal for drivers doing a large amount of wet weather and off-road driving in addition to normal freeway usage. The research and development costs so far have totaled about $10 million. The SuperTread would be put on the market beginning this year, and Goodweek expects it to stay on the market for a total of four years. Test marketing costing $5 million has shown that there is a significant market for a SuperTread-type tire.

As a financial analyst at Goodweek Tires, you have been asked by your CFO, Adam Smith, to evaluate the SuperTread project and provide a recommendation on whether to go ahead with the investment. Except for the initial investment that will occur immediately, assume all cash flows will occur at year-end.

Goodweek must initially invest $120 million in production equipment to make the Super-Tread. This equipment can be sold for $51 million at the end of four years. Goodweek intends to sell the SuperTread to two distinct markets:

1. *The original equipment manufacturer (OEM) market*: The OEM market consists primarily of the large automobile companies (like General Motors) that buy tires for new cars. In the OEM market, the SuperTread is expected to sell for $36 per tire. The variable cost to produce each tire is $18.

2. *The replacement market*: The replacement market consists of all tires purchased after the automobile has left the factory. This market allows higher margins; Goodweek expects to sell the SuperTread for $59 per tire there. Variable costs are the same as in the OEM market.

Goodweek Tires intends to raise prices at 1 percent above the inflation rate; variable costs will also increase at 1 percent above the inflation rate. In addition, the SuperTread project will incur $25 million in marketing and general administration costs the first year. This cost is expected to increase at the inflation rate in the subsequent years.

Goodweek's corporate tax rate is 40 percent. Annual inflation is expected to remain constant at 3.25 percent. The company uses a 15.9 percent discount rate to evaluate new product decisions. Automotive industry analysts expect automobile manufacturers to produce 2 million new cars this year and production to grow at 2.5 percent per year thereafter. Each new car needs four tires (the spare tires are undersized and are in a different category). Goodweek Tires expects the SuperTread to capture 11 percent of the OEM market.

Industry analysts estimate that the replacement tire market size will be 14 million tires this year and that it will grow at 2 percent annually. Goodweek expects the SuperTread to capture an 8 percent market share.

The appropriate depreciation schedule for the equipment is the seven-year MACRS depreciation schedule. The immediate initial working capital requirement is $11 million. Thereafter, the net working capital requirements will be 15 percent of sales. What are the NPV, payback period, discounted payback period, AAR, IRR, and PI on this project?

CHAPTER 7
MAKING CAPITAL INVESTMENT DECISIONS

Answers to Concepts Review and Critical Thinking Questions

1. In this context, an opportunity cost refers to the value of an asset or other input that will be used in a project. The relevant cost is what the asset or input is actually worth today, not, for example, what it cost to acquire.

2. *a.* Yes, the reduction in the sales of the company's other products, referred to as erosion, should be treated as an incremental cash flow. These lost sales are included because they are a cost (a revenue reduction) that the firm must bear if it chooses to produce the new product.

    b. Yes, expenditures on plant and equipment should be treated as incremental cash flows. These are costs of the new product line. However, if these expenditures have already occurred (and cannot be recaptured through a sale of the plant and equipment), they are sunk costs and are not included as incremental cash flows.

    c. No, the research and development costs should not be treated as incremental cash flows. The costs of research and development undertaken on the product during the past three years are sunk costs and should not be included in the evaluation of the project. Decisions made and costs incurred in the past cannot be changed. They should not affect the decision to accept or reject the project.

    d. Yes, the annual depreciation expense must be taken into account when calculating the cash flows related to a given project. While depreciation is not a cash expense that directly affects cash flow, it decreases a firm's net income and hence, lowers its tax bill for the year. Because of this depreciation tax shield, the firm has more cash on hand at the end of the year than it would have had without expensing depreciation.

    e. No, dividend payments should not be treated as incremental cash flows. A firm's decision to pay or not pay dividends is independent of the decision to accept or reject any given investment project. For this reason, dividends are not an incremental cash flow to a given project. Dividend policy is discussed in more detail in later chapters.

    f. Yes, the resale value of plant and equipment at the end of a project's life should be treated as an incremental cash flow. The price at which the firm sells the equipment is a cash inflow, and any difference between the book value of the equipment and its sale price will create accounting gains or losses that result in either a tax credit or liability.

    g. Yes, salary and medical costs for production employees hired for a project should be treated as incremental cash flows. The salaries of all personnel connected to the project must be included as costs of that project.

3. Item I is a relevant cost because the opportunity to sell the land is lost if the new golf club is produced. Item II is also relevant because the firm must take into account the erosion of sales of existing products when a new product is introduced. If the firm produces the new club, the earnings from the existing clubs will decrease, effectively creating a cost that must be included in the decision. Item III is not relevant because the costs of research and development are sunk costs. Decisions made in the past cannot be changed. They are not relevant to the production of the new club.

4. For tax purposes, a firm would choose MACRS because it provides for larger depreciation deductions earlier. These larger deductions reduce taxes, but have no other cash consequences. Notice that the choice between MACRS and straight-line is purely a time value issue; the total depreciation is the same; only the timing differs.

5. It's probably only a mild over-simplification. Current liabilities will all be paid, presumably. The cash portion of current assets will be retrieved. Some receivables won't be collected, and some inventory will not be sold, of course. Counterbalancing these losses is the fact that inventory sold above cost (and not replaced at the end of the project's life) acts to increase working capital. These effects tend to offset one another.

6. Management's discretion to set the firm's capital structure is applicable at the firm level. Since any one particular project could be financed entirely with equity, another project could be financed with debt, and the firm's overall capital structure would remain unchanged. Financing costs are not relevant in the analysis of a project's incremental cash flows according to the stand-alone principle.

7. The EAC approach is appropriate when comparing mutually exclusive projects with different lives that will be replaced when they wear out. This type of analysis is necessary so that the projects have a common life span over which they can be compared. For example, if one project has a three-year life and the other has a five-year life, then a 15-year horizon is the minimum necessary to place the two projects on an equal footing, implying that one project will be repeated five times and the other will be repeated three times. Note the shortest common life may be quite long when there are more than two alternatives and/or the individual project lives are relatively long. Assuming this type of analysis is valid implies that the project cash flows remain the same over the common life, thus ignoring the possible effects of, among other things: (1) inflation, (2) changing economic conditions, (3) the increasing unreliability of cash flow estimates that occur far into the future, and (4) the possible effects of future technology improvement that could alter the project cash flows.

8. Depreciation is a non-cash expense, but it is tax-deductible on the income statement. Thus depreciation causes taxes paid, an actual cash outflow, to be reduced by an amount equal to the depreciation tax shield, t_cD. A reduction in taxes that would otherwise be paid is the same thing as a cash inflow, so the effects of the depreciation tax shield must be added in to get the total incremental aftertax cash flows.

9. There are two particularly important considerations. The first is erosion. Will the "essentialized" book simply displace copies of the existing book that would have otherwise been sold? This is of special concern given the lower price. The second consideration is competition. Will other publishers step in and produce such a product? If so, then any erosion is much less relevant. A particular concern to book publishers (and producers of a variety of other product types) is that the publisher only makes money from the sale of new books. Thus, it is important to examine whether the new book would displace sales of used books (good from the publisher's perspective) or new books (not good). The concern arises any time there is an active market for used product.

B-164 SOLUTIONS

10. Definitely. The damage to Porsche's reputation is a factor the company needed to consider. If the reputation was damaged, the company would have lost sales of its existing car lines.

11. One company may be able to produce at lower incremental cost or market better. Also, of course, one of the two may have made a mistake!

12. Porsche would recognize that the outsized profits would dwindle as more products come to market and competition becomes more intense.

Solutions to Questions and Problems

NOTE: All end-of-chapter problems were solved using a spreadsheet. Many problems require multiple steps. Due to space and readability constraints, when these intermediate steps are included in this solutions manual, rounding may appear to have occurred. However, the final answer for each problem is found without rounding during any step in the problem.

   Basic

1. Using the tax shield approach to calculating OCF, we get:

   $OCF = (Sales - Costs)(1 - t_C) + t_C Depreciation$
   $OCF = [(\$5 \times 2,000) - (\$2 \times 2,000)](1 - 0.34) + 0.34(\$10,000/5)$
   $OCF = \$4,640$

   So, the NPV of the project is:

   $NPV = -\$10,000 + \$4,640(PVIFA_{17\%,5})$
   $NPV = \$4,844.97$

2. We will use the bottom-up approach to calculate the operating cash flow for each year. We also must be sure to include the net working capital cash flows each year. So, the total cash flow each year will be:

		Year 1	Year 2	Year 3	Year 4
Sales		$7,000	$7,000	$7,000	$7,000
Costs		2,000	2,000	2,000	2,000
Depreciation		2,500	2,500	2,500	2,500
EBT		$2,500	$2,500	$2,500	$2,500
Tax		850	850	850	850
Net income		$1,650	$1,650	$1,650	$1,650
OCF	0	$4,150	$4,150	$4,150	$4,150
Capital spending	−$10,000	0	0	0	0
NWC	−200	−250	−300	−200	950
Incremental cash flow	−$10,200	$3,900	$3,850	$3,950	$5,100

The NPV for the project is:

$$NPV = -\$10,200 + \$3,900 / 1.12 + \$3,850 / 1.12^2 + \$3,950 / 1.12^3 + \$5,100 / 1.12^4$$
$$NPV = \$2,404.01$$

3. Using the tax shield approach to calculating OCF, we get:

$$OCF = (Sales - Costs)(1 - t_C) + t_C Depreciation$$
$$OCF = (\$2,400,000 - 960,000)(1 - 0.35) + 0.35(\$2,700,000/3)$$
$$OCF = \$1,251,000$$

So, the NPV of the project is:

$$NPV = -\$2,700,000 + \$1,251,000(PVIFA_{15\%,3})$$
$$NPV = \$156,314.62$$

4. The cash outflow at the beginning of the project will increase because of the spending on NWC. At the end of the project, the company will recover the NWC, so it will be a cash inflow. The sale of the equipment will result in a cash inflow, but we also must account for the taxes which will be paid on this sale. So, the cash flows for each year of the project will be:

Year	Cash Flow	
0	– $3,000,000	$= -\$2.7M - 300K$
1	1,251,000	
2	1,251,000	
3	1,687,500	$= \$1,251,000 + 300,000 + 210,000 + (0 - 210,000)(.35)$

And the NPV of the project is:

$$NPV = -\$3,000,000 + \$1,251,000(PVIFA_{15\%,2}) + (\$1,687,500 / 1.15^3)$$
$$NPV = \$143,320.46$$

5. First we will calculate the annual depreciation for the equipment necessary for the project. The depreciation amount each year will be:

Year 1 depreciation = $2.7M(0.3330) = $899,100
Year 2 depreciation = $2.7M(0.4440) = $1,198,800
Year 3 depreciation = $2.7M(0.1480) = $399,600

So, the book value of the equipment at the end of three years, which will be the initial investment minus the accumulated depreciation, is:

Book value in 3 years = $2.7M – ($899,100 + 1,198,800 + 399,600)
Book value in 3 years = $202,500

The asset is sold at a gain to book value, so this gain is taxable.

Aftertax salvage value = $202,500 + ($210,000 – 202,500)(0.35)
Aftertax salvage value = $207,375

B-166 SOLUTIONS

To calculate the OCF, we will use the tax shield approach, so the cash flow each year is:

$$OCF = (Sales - Costs)(1 - t_C) + t_C Depreciation$$

Year	Cash Flow	
0	– $3,000,000	= –$2.7M – 300K
1	1,250,685.00	= ($1,440,000)(.65) + 0.35($899,100)
2	1,355,580.00	= ($1,440,000)(.65) + 0.35($1,198,800)
3	1,583,235.00	= ($1,440,000)(.65) + 0.35($399,600) + $207,375 + 300,000

Remember to include the NWC cost in Year 0, and the recovery of the NWC at the end of the project. The NPV of the project with these assumptions is:

$$NPV = - \$3.0M + (\$1,250,685/1.15) + (\$1,355,580/1.15^2) + (\$1,583,235/1.15^3)$$
$$NPV = \$153,568.12$$

6. First, we will calculate the annual depreciation of the new equipment. It will be:

Annual depreciation charge = $925,000/5
Annual depreciation charge = $185,000

The aftertax salvage value of the equipment is:

Aftertax salvage value = $90,000(1 – 0.35)
Aftertax salvage value = $58,500

Using the tax shield approach, the OCF is:

OCF = $360,000(1 – 0.35) + 0.35($185,000)
OCF = $298,750

Now we can find the project IRR. There is an unusual feature that is a part of this project. Accepting this project means that we will reduce NWC. This reduction in NWC is a cash inflow at Year 0. This reduction in NWC implies that when the project ends, we will have to increase NWC. So, at the end of the project, we will have a cash outflow to restore the NWC to its level before the project. We also must include the aftertax salvage value at the end of the project. The IRR of the project is:

$$NPV = 0 = -\$925,000 + 125,000 + \$298,750(PVIFA_{IRR\%,5}) + [(\$58,500 - 125,000) / (1+IRR)^5]$$

IRR = 23.85%

7. First, we will calculate the annual depreciation of the new equipment. It will be:

Annual depreciation = $390,000/5
Annual depreciation = $78,000

Now, we calculate the aftertax salvage value. The aftertax salvage value is the market price minus (or plus) the taxes on the sale of the equipment, so:

Aftertax salvage value = $MV + (BV - MV)t_c$

Very often, the book value of the equipment is zero as it is in this case. If the book value is zero, the equation for the aftertax salvage value becomes:

Aftertax salvage value = $MV + (0 - MV)t_c$
Aftertax salvage value = $MV(1 - t_c)$

We will use this equation to find the aftertax salvage value since we know the book value is zero. So, the aftertax salvage value is:

Aftertax salvage value = $60,000(1 - 0.34)$
Aftertax salvage value = $39,600

Using the tax shield approach, we find the OCF for the project is:

OCF = $120,000(1 - 0.34) + 0.34($78,000)
OCF = $105,720

Now we can find the project NPV. Notice that we include the NWC in the initial cash outlay. The recovery of the NWC occurs in Year 5, along with the aftertax salvage value.

NPV = $-$390,000 - 28,000 + $105,720(PVIFA_{10\%,5}) + [($39,600 + 28,000) / 1.1^5]$
NPV = $24,736.26

8. To find the BV at the end of four years, we need to find the accumulated depreciation for the first four years. We could calculate a table with the depreciation each year, but an easier way is to add the MACRS depreciation amounts for each of the first four years and multiply this percentage times the cost of the asset. We can then subtract this from the asset cost. Doing so, we get:

$BV_4 = $9,300,000 - 9,300,000(0.2000 + 0.3200 + 0.1920 + 0.1150)$
$BV_4 = $1,608,900$

The asset is sold at a gain to book value, so this gain is taxable.

Aftertax salvage value = $2,100,000 + ($1,608,900 - 2,100,000)(.35)$
Aftertax salvage value = $1,928,115

9. We will begin by calculating the initial cash outlay, that is, the cash flow at Time 0. To undertake the project, we will have to purchase the equipment and increase net working capital. So, the cash outlay today for the project will be:

Equipment	–$2,000,000
NWC	–100,000
Total	–$2,100,000

B-168 SOLUTIONS

Using the bottom-up approach to calculating the operating cash flow, we find the operating cash flow each year will be:

Sales	$1,200,000
Costs	300,000
Depreciation	500,000
EBT	$400,000
Tax	140,000
Net income	$260,000

The operating cash flow is:

OCF = Net income + Depreciation
OCF = $260,000 + 500,000
OCF = $760,000

To find the NPV of the project, we add the present value of the project cash flows. We must be sure to add back the net working capital at the end of the project life, since we are assuming the net working capital will be recovered. So, the project NPV is:

$NPV = -\$2,100,000 + \$760,000(PVIFA_{14\%,4}) + \$100,000 / 1.14^4$
$NPV = \$173,629.38$

10. We will need the aftertax salvage value of the equipment to compute the EAC. Even though the equipment for each product has a different initial cost, both have the same salvage value. The aftertax salvage value for both is:

Both cases: aftertax salvage value = $20,000(1 − 0.35) = $13,000

To calculate the EAC, we first need the OCF and NPV of each option. The OCF and NPV for Techron I is:

$OCF = -\$34,000(1 - 0.35) + 0.35(\$210,000/3) = \$2,400$

$NPV = -\$210,000 + \$2,400(PVIFA_{14\%,3}) + (\$13,000/1.14^3) = -\$195,653.45$

$EAC = -\$195,653.45 / (PVIFA_{14\%,3}) = -\$84,274.10$

And the OCF and NPV for Techron II is:

$OCF = -\$23,000(1 - 0.35) + 0.35(\$320,000/5) = \$7,450$

$NPV = -\$320,000 + \$7,450(PVIFA_{14\%,5}) + (\$13,000/1.14^5) = -\$287,671.75$

$EAC = -\$287,671.75 / (PVIFA_{14\%,5}) = -\$83,794.05$

The two milling machines have unequal lives, so they can only be compared by expressing both on an equivalent annual basis, which is what the EAC method does. Thus, you prefer the Techron II because it has the lower (less negative) annual cost.

Intermediate

11. First, we will calculate the depreciation each year, which will be:

$D_1 = \$480,000(0.2000) = \$96,000$
$D_2 = \$480,000(0.3200) = \$153,600$
$D_3 = \$480,000(0.1920) = \$92,160$
$D_4 = \$480,000(0.1150) = \$55,200$

The book value of the equipment at the end of the project is:

$BV_4 = \$480,000 - (\$96,000 + 153,600 + 92,160 + 55,200) = \$83,040$

The asset is sold at a loss to book value, so this creates a tax refund.
After-tax salvage value = $\$70,000 + (\$83,040 - 70,000)(0.35) = \$74,564.00$

So, the OCF for each year will be:

$OCF_1 = \$160,000(1 - 0.35) + 0.35(\$96,000) = \$137,600.00$
$OCF_2 = \$160,000(1 - 0.35) + 0.35(\$153,600) = \$157,760.00$
$OCF_3 = \$160,000(1 - 0.35) + 0.35(\$92,160) = \$136,256.00$
$OCF_4 = \$160,000(1 - 0.35) + 0.35(\$55,200) = \$123,320.00$

Now we have all the necessary information to calculate the project NPV. We need to be careful with the NWC in this project. Notice the project requires $20,000 of NWC at the beginning, and $3,000 more in NWC each successive year. We will subtract the $20,000 from the initial cash flow and subtract $3,000 each year from the OCF to account for this spending. In Year 4, we will add back the total spent on NWC, which is $29,000. The $3,000 spent on NWC capital during Year 4 is irrelevant. Why? Well, during this year the project required an additional $3,000, but we would get the money back immediately. So, the net cash flow for additional NWC would be zero. With all this, the equation for the NPV of the project is:

$$NPV = -\$480,000 - 20,000 + (\$137,600 - 3,000)/1.14 + (\$157,760 - 3,000)/1.14^2$$
$$+ (\$136,256 - 3,000)/1.14^3 + (\$123,320 + 29,000 + 74,564)/1.14^4$$
$$NPV = -\$38,569.48$$

12. If we are trying to decide between two projects that will not be replaced when they wear out, the proper capital budgeting method to use is NPV. Both projects only have costs associated with them, not sales, so we will use these to calculate the NPV of each project. Using the tax shield approach to calculate the OCF, the NPV of System A is:

$OCF_A = -\$120,000(1 - 0.34) + 0.34(\$430,000/4)$
$OCF_A = -\$42,650$

$NPV_A = -\$430,000 - \$42,650(PVIFA_{20\%,4})$
$NPV_A = -\$540,409.53$

B-170 SOLUTIONS

And the NPV of System B is:

$OCF_B = -\$80,000(1 - 0.34) + 0.34(\$540,000/6)$
$OCF_B = -\$22,200$

$NPV_B = -\$540,000 - \$22,200(PVIFA_{20\%,6})$
$NPV_B = -\$613,826.32$

If the system will not be replaced when it wears out, then System A should be chosen, because it has the less negative NPV.

13. If the equipment will be replaced at the end of its useful life, the correct capital budgeting technique is EAC. Using the NPVs we calculated in the previous problem, the EAC for each system is:

$EAC_A = -\$540,409.53 / (PVIFA_{20\%,4})$
$EAC_A = -\$208,754.32$

$EAC_B = -\$613,826.32 / (PVIFA_{20\%,6})$
$EAC_B = -\$184,581.10$

If the conveyor belt system will be continually replaced, we should choose System B since it has the less negative EAC.

14. Since we need to calculate the EAC for each machine, sales are irrelevant. EAC only uses the costs of operating the equipment, not the sales. Using the bottom up approach, or net income plus depreciation, method to calculate OCF, we get:

	Machine A	Machine B
Variable costs	–$3,150,000	–$2,700,000
Fixed costs	–150,000	–100,000
Depreciation	–350,000	–500,000
EBT	–$3,650,000	–$3,300,000
Tax	1,277,500	1,155,000
Net income	–$2,372,500	–$2,145,000
+ Depreciation	350,000	500,000
OCF	–$2,022,500	–$1,645,000

The NPV and EAC for Machine A is:

$NPV_A = -\$2,100,000 - \$2,022,500(PVIFA_{10\%,6})$
$NPV_A = -\$10,908,514.76$

$EAC_A = -\$10,908,514.76 / (PVIFA_{10\%,6})$
$EAC_A = -\$2,504,675.50$

And the NPV and EAC for Machine B is:

$NPV_B = -\$4,500,000 - 1,645,000(PVIFA_{10\%,9})$
$NPV_B = -\$13,973,594.18$

$EAC_B = -\$13,973,594.18 / (PVIFA_{10\%,9})$
$EAC_B = -\$2,426,382.43$

You should choose Machine B since it has a less negative EAC.

15. When we are dealing with nominal cash flows, we must be careful to discount cash flows at the nominal interest rate, and we must discount real cash flows using the real interest rate. Project A's cash flows are in real terms, so we need to find the real interest rate. Using the Fisher equation, the real interest rate is:

$1 + R = (1 + r)(1 + h)$
$1.15 = (1 + r)(1 + .04)$
$r = .1058$ or 10.58%

So, the NPV of Project A's real cash flows, discounting at the real interest rate, is:

$NPV = -\$40,000 + \$20,000 / 1.1058 + \$15,000 / 1.1058^2 + \$15,000 / 1.1058^3$
$NPV = \$1,448.88$

Project B's cash flow are in nominal terms, so the NPV discount at the nominal interest rate is:

$NPV = -\$50,000 + \$10,000 / 1.15 + \$20,000 / 1.15^2 + \$40,000 / 1.15^3$
$NPV = \$119.17$

We should accept Project A if the projects are mutually exclusive since it has the highest NPV.

16. To determine the value of a firm, we can simply find the present value of the firm's future cash flows. No depreciation is given, so we can assume depreciation is zero. Using the tax shield approach, we can find the present value of the aftertax revenues, and the present value of the aftertax costs. The required return, growth rates, price, and costs are all given in real terms. Subtracting the costs from the revenues will give us the value of the firm's cash flows. We must calculate the present value of each separately since each is growing at a different rate. First, we will find the present value of the revenues. The revenues in year 1 will be the number of bottles sold, times the price per bottle, or:

Aftertax revenue in year 1 in real terms = $(2,000,000 \times \$1.25)(1 - 0.34)$
Aftertax revenue in year 1 in real terms = $\$1,650,000$

Revenues will grow at six percent per year in real terms forever. Apply the growing perpetuity formula, we find the present value of the revenues is:

PV of revenues = $C_1 / (R - g)$
PV of revenues = $\$1,650,000 / (0.10 - 0.06)$
PV of revenues = $\$41,250,000$

B-172 SOLUTIONS

The real aftertax costs in year 1 will be:

Aftertax costs in year 1 in real terms = (2,000,000 × $0.70)(1 – 0.34)
Aftertax costs in year 1 in real terms = $924,000

Costs will grow at five percent per year in real terms forever. Applying the growing perpetuity formula, we find the present value of the costs is:

PV of costs = $C_1 / (R – g)$
PV of costs = $924,000 / (0.10 – 0.05)
PV of costs = $18,480,000

Now we can find the value of the firm, which is:

Value of the firm = PV of revenues – PV of costs
Value of the firm = $41,250,000 – 18,480,000
Value of the firm = $22,770,000

17. To calculate the nominal cash flows, we simple increase each item in the income statement by the inflation rate, except for depreciation. Depreciation is a nominal cash flow, so it does not need to be adjusted for inflation in nominal cash flow analysis. Since the resale value is given in nominal terms as of the end of year 5, it does not need to be adjusted for inflation. Also, no inflation adjustment is needed for either the depreciation charge or the recovery of net working capital since these items are already expressed in nominal terms. Note that an increase in required net working capital is a negative cash flow whereas a decrease in required net working capital is a positive cash flow. We first need to calculate the taxes on the salvage value. Remember, to calculate the taxes paid (or tax credit) on the salvage value, we take the book value minus the market value, times the tax rate, which, in this case, would be:

Taxes on salvage value = $(BV – MV)t_C$
Taxes on salvage value = ($0 – 30,000)(.34)
Taxes on salvage value = –$10,200

So, the nominal aftertax salvage value is:

Market price	$30,000
Tax on sale	−10,200
Aftertax salvage value	$19,800

Now we can find the nominal cash flows each year using the income statement. Doing so, we find:

	Year 0	Year 1	Year 2	Year 3	Year 4	Year 5
Sales		$200,000	$206,000	$212,180	$218,545	$225,102
Expenses		50,000	51,500	53,045	54,636	56,275
Depreciation		50,000	50,000	50,000	50,000	50,000
EBT		$100,000	$104,500	$109,135	$113,909	$118,826
Tax		34,000	35,530	37,106	38,729	40,401
Net income		$66,000	$68,970	$72,029	$75,180	$78,425
OCF		$116,000	$118,970	$122,029	$125,180	$128,425
Capital spending	–$250,000					$19,800
NWC	–10,000					10,000
Total cash flow	–$260,000	$116,000	$118,970	$122,029	$125,180	$158,225

18. The present value of the company is the present value of the future cash flows generated by the company. Here we have real cash flows, a real interest rate, and a real growth rate. The cash flows are a growing perpetuity, with a negative growth rate. Using the growing perpetuity equation, the present value of the cash flows are:

$PV = C_1 / (R - g)$
$PV = \$120,000 / [.11 - (-.06)]$
$PV = \$705,882.35$

19. To find the EAC, we first need to calculate the NPV of the incremental cash flows. We will begin with the aftertax salvage value, which is:

$Taxes\ on\ salvage\ value = (BV - MV)t_C$
$Taxes\ on\ salvage\ value = (\$0 - 10,000)(.34)$
$Taxes\ on\ salvage\ value = -\$3,400$

Market price	$10,000
Tax on sale	–3,400
Aftertax salvage value	$6,600

Now we can find the operating cash flows. Using the tax shield approach, the operating cash flow each year will be:

$OCF = -\$5,000(1 - 0.34) + 0.34(\$45,000/3)$
$OCF = \$1,800$

So, the NPV of the cost of the decision to buy is:

$NPV = -\$45,000 + \$1,800(PVIFA_{12\%,3}) + (\$6,600/1.12^3)$
$NPV = -\$35,987.95$

B-174 SOLUTIONS

In order to calculate the equivalent annual cost, set the NPV of the equipment equal to an annuity with the same economic life. Since the project has an economic life of three years and is discounted at 12 percent, set the NPV equal to a three-year annuity, discounted at 12 percent.

EAC = –$35,987.95 / (PVIFA$_{12\%,3}$)
EAC = –$14,979.80

20. We will find the EAC of the EVF first. There are no taxes since the university is tax-exempt, so the maintenance costs are the operating cash flows. The NPV of the decision to buy one EVF is:

NPV = –$8,000 – $2,000(PVIFA$_{14\%,4}$)
NPV = –$13,827.42

In order to calculate the equivalent annual cost, set the NPV of the equipment equal to an annuity with the same economic life. Since the project has an economic life of four years and is discounted at 14 percent, set the NPV equal to a three-year annuity, discounted at 14 percent. So, the EAC per unit is:

EAC = –$13,827.42 / (PVIFA$_{14\%,4}$)
EAC = –$4,745.64

Since the university must buy 10 of the word processors, the total EAC of the decision to buy the EVF word processor is:

Total EAC = 10(–$4,745.64)
Total EAC = –$47,456.38

Note, we could have found the total EAC for this decision by multiplying the initial cost by the number of word processors needed, and multiplying the annual maintenance cost of each by the same number. We would have arrived at the same EAC.

We can find the EAC of the AEH word processors using the same method, but we need to include the salvage value as well. There are no taxes on the salvage value since the university is tax-exempt, so the NPV of buying one AEH will be:

NPV = –$5,000 – $2,500(PVIFA$_{14\%,3}$) + ($500/1.14^3)
NPV = –$10,466.59

So, the EAC per machine is:

EAC = –$10,466.59 / (PVIFA$_{14\%,3}$)
EAC = –$4,508.29

Since the university must buy 11 of the word processors, the total EAC of the decision to buy the AEH word processor is:

Total EAC = 11(–$4,508.29)
Total EAC = –$49,591.21

The university should buy the EVF word processors since the EAC is less negative. Notice that the EAC of the AEH is lower on a per machine basis, but because the university needs more of these word processors, the total EAC is higher.

21. We will calculate the aftertax salvage value first. The aftertax salvage value of the equipment will be:

Taxes on salvage value = $(BV - MV)t_C$
Taxes on salvage value = ($0 – 100,000)(.34)
Taxes on salvage value = –$34,000

Market price	$100,000
Tax on sale	–34,000
Aftertax salvage value	$66,000

Next, we will calculate the initial cash outlay, that is, the cash flow at Time 0. To undertake the project, we will have to purchase the equipment. The new project will decrease the net working capital, so this is a cash inflow at the beginning of the project. So, the cash outlay today for the project will be:

Equipment	–$500,000
NWC	100,000
Total	–$400,000

Now we can calculate the operating cash flow each year for the project. Using the bottom up approach, the operating cash flow will be:

Saved salaries	$120,000
Depreciation	100,000
EBT	$20,000
Taxes	6,800
Net income	$13,200

And the OCF will be:

OCF = $13,200 + 100,000
OCF = $113,200

Now we can find the NPV of the project. In Year 5, we must replace the saved NWC, so:

NPV = –$400,000 + $113,200(PVIFA$_{12\%,5}$) – $34,000 / 1.12^5
NPV = –$11,231.85

B-176 SOLUTIONS

22. Replacement decision analysis is the same as the analysis of two competing projects, in this case, keep the current equipment, or purchase the new equipment. We will consider the purchase of the new machine first.

Purchase new machine:

The initial cash outlay for the new machine is the cost of the new machine, plus the increased net working capital. So, the initial cash outlay will be:

Purchase new machine	−$32,000,000
Net working capital	−500,000
Total	−$32,500,000

Next, we can calculate the operating cash flow created if the company purchases the new machine. The saved operating expense is an incremental cash flow. Additionally, the reduced operating expense is a cash inflow, so it should be treated as such in the income statement. The pro forma income statement, and adding depreciation to net income, the operating cash flow created by purchasing the new machine each year will be:

Operating expense	$5,000,000
Depreciation	8,000,000
EBT	−$3,000,000
Taxes	−1,170,000
Net income	−$1,830,000
OCF	$6,170,000

So, the NPV of purchasing the new machine, including the recovery of the net working capital, is:

$NPV = -\$32,500,000 + \$6,170,000(PVIFA_{10\%,4}) + \$500,000 / 1.10^4$
$NPV = -\$12,600,423.47$

And the IRR is:

$0 = -\$32,500,000 + \$6,170,000(PVIFA_{IRR,4}) + \$500,000 / (1 + IRR)^4$

Using a spreadsheet or financial calculator, we find the IRR is:

$IRR = -9.38\%$

Now we can calculate the decision to keep the old machine:

Keep old machine:

The initial cash outlay for the old machine is the market value of the old machine, including any potential tax consequence. The decision to keep the old machine has an opportunity cost, namely, the company could sell the old machine. Also, if the company sells the old machine at its current value, it will incur taxes. Both of these cash flows need to be included in the analysis. So, the initial cash flow of keeping the old machine will be:

Keep machine	–$9,000,000
Taxes	390,000
Total	–$8,610,000

Next, we can calculate the operating cash flow created if the company keeps the old machine. There are no incremental cash flows from keeping the old machine, but we need to account for the cash flow effects of depreciation. The income statement, adding depreciation to net income to calculate the operating cash flow will be:

Depreciation	$2,000,000
EBT	–$2,000,000
Taxes	–780,000
Net income	–$1,220,000
OCF	$780,000

So, the NPV of the decision to keep the old machine will be:

$$NPV = -\$8,610,000 + \$780,000(PVIFA_{10\%,4})$$
$$NPV = -\$6,137,504.95$$

And the IRR is:

$$0 = -\$8,610,000 + \$780,000(PVIFA_{IRR,4})$$

Since the project never pays pay back, there is no IRR.

The company should not purchase the new machine since it has a lower NPV.

B-178 SOLUTIONS

There is another way to analyze a replacement decision that is often used. It is an incremental cash flow analysis of the change in cash flows from the existing machine to the new machine, assuming the new machine is purchased. In this type of analysis, the initial cash outlay would be the cost of the new machine, the increased inventory, and the cash inflow (including any applicable taxes) of selling the old machine. In this case, the initial cash flow under this method would be:

Purchase new machine	−$32,000,000
Net working capital	−500,000
Sell old machine	9,000,000
Taxes on old machine	−390,000
Total	−$23,890,000

The cash flows from purchasing the new machine would be the saved operating expenses. We would also need to include the change in depreciation. The old machine has a depreciation of $2 million per year, and the new machine has a depreciation of $8 million per year, so the increased depreciation will be $6 million per year. The pro forma income statement and operating cash flow under this approach will be:

Operating expense savings	$5,000,000
Depreciation	−6,000,000
EBT	−$1,000,000
Taxes	−390,000
Net income	−$610,000
OCF	$5,390,000

The NPV under this method is:

$$NPV = -\$23,890,000 + \$5,390,000(PVIFA_{10\%,4}) + \$500,000 / 1.10^4$$
$$NPV = -\$6,462,918.52$$

And the IRR is:

$$0 = -\$23,890,000 + \$5,390,000(PVIFA_{IRR,4}) + \$500,000 / (1 + IRR)^4$$

Using a spreadsheet or financial calculator, we find the IRR is:

$$IRR = -3.07\%$$

So, this analysis still tells us the company should not purchase the new machine. This is really the same type of analysis we originally did. Consider this: Subtract the NPV of the decision to keep the old machine from the NPV of the decision to purchase the new machine. You will get:

$$\text{Differential NPV} = -\$12,600,423.47 - (-6,137,504.95) = -\$6,462,918.52$$

This is the exact same NPV we calculated when using the second analysis method.

b.   The purchase of a new machine can have a positive NPV because of the depreciation tax shield. Without the depreciation tax shield, the new machine would have a negative NPV since the saved expenses from the machine do not exceed the cost of the machine when we consider the time value of money.

23.   We can find the NPV of a project using nominal cash flows or real cash flows. Either method will result in the same NPV. For this problem, we will calculate the NPV using both nominal and real cash flows. The initial investment in either case is $120,000 since it will be spent today. We will begin with the nominal cash flows. The revenues and production costs increase at different rates, so we must be careful to increase each at the appropriate growth rate. The nominal cash flows for each year will be:

	Year 0	Year 1	Year 2	Year 3
Revenues		$50,000.00	$52,500.00	$55,125.00
Costs		20,000.00	21,400.00	22,898.00
Depreciation		17,142.86	17,142.86	17,142.86
EBT		$12,857.14	$13,957.14	$15,084.14
Taxes		4,371.43	4,745.43	5,128.61
Net income		$8,485.71	$9,211.71	$9,955.53
OCF		$25,628.57	$26,354.57	$27,098.39
Capital spending	–$120,000			
Total cash flow	–$120,000	$25,628.57	$26,354.57	$27,098.39

	Year 4	Year 5	Year 6	Year 7
Revenues	$57,881.25	$60,775.31	$63,814.08	$67,004.78
Costs	24,500.86	26,215.92	28,051.03	30,014.61
Depreciation	17,142.86	17,142.86	17,142.86	17,142.86
EBT	$16,237.53	$17,416.54	$18,620.19	$19,847.32
Taxes	5,520.76	5,921.62	6,330.86	6,748.09
Net income	$10,716.77	$11,494.91	$12,289.32	$13,099.23
OCF	$27,859.63	$28,637.77	$29,432.18	$30,242.09
Capital spending				
Total cash flow	$27,859.63	$28,637.77	$29,432.18	$30,242.09

Now that we have the nominal cash flows, we can find the NPV. We must use the nominal required return with nominal cash flows. Using the Fisher equation to find the nominal required return, we get:

$(1 + R) = (1 + r)(1 + h)$
$(1 + R) = (1 + .14)(1 + .05)$
$R = .1970$ or 19.70%

B-180 SOLUTIONS

So, the NPV of the project using nominal cash flows is:

$$NPV = -\$120,000 + \$25,625.57 / 1.1970 + \$26,354.57 / 1.1970^2 + \$27,098.39 / 1.1970^3$$
$$+ \$27,859.63 / 1.1970^4 + \$28,637.77 / 1.1970^5 + \$29,432.18 / 1.1970^6 + \$30,242.09 / 1.1970^7$$
$$NPV = -\$20,576.00$$

We can also find the NPV using real cash flows and the real required return. This will allow us to find the operating cash flow using the tax shield approach. Both the revenues and expenses are growing annuities, but growing at different rates. This means we must find the present value of each separately. We also need to account for the effect of taxes, so we will multiply by one minus the tax rate. So, the present value of the aftertax revenues using the growing annuity equation is:

$$PV \text{ of aftertax revenues} = C \{[1/(r-g)] - [1/(r-g)] \times [(1+g)/(1+r)]^t\}(1-t_C)$$
$$PV \text{ of aftertax revenues} = \$50,000\{[1/(.14-.05)] - [1/(.14-.05)] \times [(1+.05)/(1+.14)]^7\}(1-.34)$$
$$PV \text{ of aftertax revenues} = \$134,775.29$$

And the present value of the aftertax costs will be:

$$PV \text{ of aftertax costs} = C \{[1/(r-g)] - [1/(r-g)] \times [(1+g)/(1+r)]^t\}(1-t_C)$$
$$PV \text{ of aftertax costs} = \$20,000\{[1/(.14-.07)] - [1/(.14-.07)] \times [(1+.07)/(1+.14)]^7\}(1-.34)$$
$$PV \text{ of aftertax costs} = \$56,534.91$$

Now we need to find the present value of the depreciation tax shield. The depreciation amount in the first year is a real value, so we can find the present value of the depreciation tax shield as an ordinary annuity using the real required return. So, the present value of the depreciation tax shield will be:

$$PV \text{ of depreciation tax shield} = (\$120,000/7)(.34)(PVIFA_{19.70\%,7})$$
$$PV \text{ of depreciation tax shield} = \$21,183.61$$

Using the present value of the real cash flows to find the NPV, we get:

$$NPV = \text{Initial cost} + \text{PV of revenues} - \text{PV of costs} + \text{PV of depreciation tax shield}$$
$$NPV = -\$120,000 + \$134,775.29 - 56,534.91 + 21,183.61$$
$$NPV = -\$20,576.00$$

Notice, the NPV using nominal cash flows or real cash flows is identical, which is what we would expect.

24. Here we have a project in which the quantity sold each year increases. First, we need to calculate the quantity sold each year by increasing the current year's quantity by the growth rate. So, the quantity sold each year will be:

Year 1 quantity = 5,000
Year 2 quantity = 5,000(1 + .15) = 5,750
Year 3 quantity = 5,750(1 + .15) = 6,613
Year 4 quantity = 6,613(1 + .15) = 7,604
Year 5 quantity = 7,604(1 + .15) = 8,745

CHAPTER 7 B-181

Now we can calculate the sales revenue and variable costs each year. The pro forma income statements and operating cash flow each year will be:

	Year 0	Year 1	Year 2	Year 3	Year 4	Year 5
Revenues		$225,000.00	$258,750.00	$297,562.50	$342,196.88	$393,526.41
Fixed costs		75,000.00	75,000.00	75,000.00	75,000.00	75,000.00
Variable costs		100,000.00	115,000.00	132,250.00	152,087.50	174,900.63
Depreciation		12,000.00	12,000.00	12,000.00	12,000.00	12,000.00
EBT		$38,000.00	$56,750.00	$78,312.50	$103,109.38	$131,625.78
Taxes		12,920.00	19,295.00	26,626.25	35,057.19	44,752.77
Net income		$25,080.00	$37,455.00	$51,686.25	$68,052.19	$86,873.02
OCF		$37,080.00	$49,455.00	$63,686.25	$80,052.19	$98,873.02
Capital spending	–$60,000					
NWC	–28,000					$28,000
Total cash flow	–$88,000	$37,080.00	$49,455.00	$63,686.25	$80,052.19	$126,873.02

So, the NPV of the project is:

$$NPV = -\$88,000 + \$37,080 / 1.25 + \$49,455 / 1.25^2 + \$63,686.25 / 1.25^3 + \$80,052.19 / 1.25^4$$
$$+ \$126,873.02 / 1.25^5$$
$$NPV = \$80,285.69$$

We could also have calculated the cash flows using the tax shield approach, with growing annuities and ordinary annuities. The sales and variable costs increase at the same rate as sales, so both are growing annuities. The fixed costs and depreciation are both ordinary annuities. Using the growing annuity equation, the present value of the revenues is:

PV of revenues = $C \{[1/(r-g)] - [1/(r-g)] \times [(1+g)/(1+r)]^t\}(1-t_C)$
PV of revenues = $\$225,000\{[1/(.25-.15)] - [1/(.25-.15)] \times [(1+.15)/(1+.25)]^5\}$
PV of revenues = $\$767,066.57$

And the present value of the variable costs will be:

PV of variable costs = $C \{[1/(r-g)] - [1/(r-g)] \times [(1+g)/(1+r)]^t\}(1-t_C)$
PV of variable costs = $\$100,000\{[1/(.25-.15)] - [1/(.25-.15)] \times [(1+.15)/(1+.25)]^5\}$
PV of variable costs = $\$340,918.48$

The fixed costs and depreciation are both ordinary annuities. The present value of each is:

PV of fixed costs = $C(\{1 - [1/(1+r)]^t\} / r)$
PV of fixed costs = $\$75,000(PVIFA_{25\%,5})$
PV of fixed costs = $\$201,696.00$

B-182 SOLUTIONS

PV of depreciation $= C(\{1 - [1/(1 + r)]^t\} / r)$
PV of depreciation $= \$12,000(\text{PVIFA}_{25\%,5})$
PV of depreciation $= \$32,271.36$

Now, we can use the depreciation tax shield approach to find the NPV of the project, which is:

NPV $= -\$88,000 + (\$767,066.57 - 340,918.48 - 201,696.00)(1 - .34) + (\$32,271.36)(.34)$
$\qquad + \$28,000 / 1.25^5$
NPV $= \$80,285.69$

25. We will begin by calculating the aftertax salvage value of the equipment at the end of the project's life. The aftertax salvage value is the market value of the equipment minus any taxes paid (or refunded), so the aftertax salvage value in four years will be:

Taxes on salvage value $= (\text{BV} - \text{MV})t_C$
Taxes on salvage value $= (\$0 - 400,000)(.34)$
Taxes on salvage value $= -\$152,000$

Market price	$400,000
Tax on sale	−152,000
Aftertax salvage value	$248,000

Now we need to calculate the operating cash flow each year. Note, we assume that the net working capital cash flow occurs immediately. Using the bottom up approach to calculating operating cash flow, we find:

	Year 0	Year 1	Year 2	Year 3	Year 4
Revenues		$2,030,000	$2,660,000	$1,890,000	$1,330,000
Fixed costs		350,000	350,000	350,000	350,000
Variable costs		304,500	399,000	283,500	199,500
Depreciation		1,265,400	1,687,200	562,400	281,200
EBT		$110,100	$223,800	$694,100	$499,300
Taxes		41,838	85,044	263,758	189,734
Net income		$68,262	$138,756	$430,342	$309,566
OCF		$1,333,662	$1,825,956	$992,742	$590,766
Capital spending	−$3,800,000				$248,000
Land	−800,000				800,000
NWC	−$120,000				120,000
Total cash flow	−$4,720,000	$1,333,662	$1,825,956	$992,742	$1,758,766

Notice the calculation of the cash flow at time 0. The capital spending on equipment and investment in net working capital are cash outflows. The aftertax selling price of the land is also a cash outflow. Even though no cash is actually spent on the land because the company already owns it, the aftertax cash flow from selling the land is an opportunity cost, so we need to include it in the analysis. With all the project cash flows, we can calculate the NPV, which is:

$$NPV = -\$4,720,000 + \$1,333,662 / 1.13 + \$1,825,956 / 1.13^2 + \$992,742 / 1.13^3$$
$$+ \$1,758,766 / 1.13^4$$
$$NPV = -\$343,072.63$$

The company should reject the new product line.

26. Replacement decision analysis is the same as the analysis of two competing projects, in this case, keep the current equipment, or purchase the new equipment. We will consider the purchase of the new machine first.

Purchase new machine:

The initial cash outlay for the new machine is the cost of the new machine. We can calculate the operating cash flow created if the company purchases the new machine. The maintenance cost is an incremental cash flow, so using the pro forma income statement, and adding depreciation to net income, the operating cash flow created by purchasing the new machine each year will be:

Maintenance cost	−$500,000
Depreciation	−600,000
EBT	−$1,100,000
Taxes	−374,000
Net income	−$726,000
OCF	−$126,000

Notice the taxes are negative, implying a tax credit. The new machine also has a salvage value at the end of five years, so we need to include this in the cash flows analysis. The aftertax salvage value will be:

Sell machine	$500,000
Taxes	−170,000
Total	$330,000

The NPV of purchasing the new machine is:

$$NPV = -\$3,000,000 - \$126,000(PVIFA_{12\%,5}) + \$330,000 / 1.12^5$$
$$NPV = -\$3,266,950.54$$

Notice the NPV is negative. This does not necessarily mean we should not purchase the new machine. In this analysis, we are only dealing with costs, so we would expect a negative NPV. The revenue is not included in the analysis since it is not incremental to the machine. Similar to an EAC analysis, we will use the machine with the least negative NPV. Now we can calculate the decision to keep the old machine:

B-184 SOLUTIONS

Keep old machine:

The initial cash outlay for the new machine is the market value of the old machine, including any potential tax. The decision to keep the old machine has an opportunity cost, namely, the company could sell the old machine. Also, if the company sells the old machine at its current value, it will incur taxes. Both of these cash flows need to be included in the analysis. So, the initial cash flow of keeping the old machine will be:

Keep machine	–$2,000,000
Taxes	–340,000
Total	–$2,340,000

Next, we can calculate the operating cash flow created if the company keeps the old machine. We need to account for the cost of maintenance, as well as the cash flow effects of depreciation. The incomes statement, adding depreciation to net income to calculate the operating cash flow will be:

Maintenance cost	–$400,000
Depreciation	–200,000
EBT	–$600,000
Taxes	–204,000
Net income	–$396,000
OCF	–$196,000

The old machine also has a salvage value at the end of five years, so we need to include this in the cash flows analysis. The aftertax salvage value will be:

Sell machine	$200,000
Taxes	–68,000
Total	$132,000

So, the NPV of the decision to keep the old machine will be:

NPV = –$2,340,000 – $196,000(PVIFA$_{12\%,5}$) + $132,000 / 1.12^5
NPV = –$2,971,635.79

The company should not purchase the new machine since it has a lower NPV.

There is another way to analyze a replacement decision that is often used. It is an incremental cash flow analysis of the change in cash flows from the existing machine to the new machine, assuming the new machine is purchased. In this type of analysis, the initial cash outlay would be the cost of the new machine, and the cash inflow (including any applicable taxes) of selling the old machine. In this case, the initial cash flow under this method would be:

Purchase new machine	–$3,000,000
Sell old machine	2,000,000
Taxes on old machine	–340,000
Total	–$1,340,000

The cash flows from purchasing the new machine would be the difference in the operating expenses. We would also need to include the change in depreciation. The old machine has a depreciation of $200,000 per year, and the new machine has a depreciation of $600,000 per year, so the increased depreciation will be $400,000 per year. The pro forma income statement and operating cash flow under this approach will be:

Maintenance cost	–$100,000
Depreciation	–400,000
EBT	–$500,000
Taxes	–170,000
Net income	–$330,000
OCF	$70,000

The salvage value of the differential cash flow approach is more complicated. The company will sell the new machine, and incur taxes on the sale in five years. However, we must also include the lost sale of the old machine. Since we assumed we sold the old machine in the initial cash outlay, we lose the ability to sell the machine in five years. This is an opportunity loss that must be accounted for. So, the salvage value is:

Sell machine	$500,000
Taxes	–170,000
Lost sale of old	–200,000
Taxes on lost sale of old	68,000
Total	$198,000

The NPV under this method is:

$$\text{NPV} = -\$1,340,000 + \$70,000(\text{PVIFA}_{12\%,5}) + \$198,000 / 1.12^4$$
$$\text{NPV} = -\$975,315.15$$

So, this analysis still tells us the company should not purchase the new machine. This is really the same type of analysis we originally did. Consider this: Subtract the NPV of the decision to keep the old machine from the NPV of the decision to purchase the new machine. You will get:

Differential NPV = –$3,266,950.94 – (–2,971,635.79) = –$975,315.15

This is the exact same NPV we calculated when using the second analysis method.

27. Here we have a situation where a company is going to buy one of two assets, so we need to calculate the EAC of each asset. To calculate the EAC, we can calculate the EAC of the combined costs of each computer, or calculate the EAC of an individual computer, then multiply by the number of computers the company is purchasing. In this instance, we will calculate the EAC of each individual computer. For the SAL 5000, we will begin by calculating the aftertax salvage value, then the operating cash flows. So:

B-186 SOLUTIONS

SAL 5000:

Taxes on salvage value = $(BV - MV)t_C$
Taxes on salvage value = $(\$0 - 500)(.34)$
Taxes on salvage value = $-\$170$

Market price	$500
Tax on sale	−170
Aftertax salvage value	$330

The incremental costs will include the maintenance costs, depreciation, and taxes. Notice the taxes are negative, signifying a lower tax bill. So, the incremental cash flows will be:

Maintenance cost	−$500.00
Depreciation	−468.75
EBT	−$968.75
Tax	−329.38
Net income	−$639.38
OCF	−$170.63

So, the NPV of the decision to buy one unit is:

NPV = −$3,750 − $170.63(PVIFA$_{11\%,8}$) + $330 / 1.11^8
NPV = −$4,484.86

And the EAC on a per unit basis is:

−$4,484.86 = EAC(PVIFA$_{11\%,8}$)
EAC = −$871.50

Since the company must buy 10 units, the total EAC of the decision is:

Total EAC = 10(−$871.50)
Total EAC = −$8,715.03

And the EAC for the DET 1000:

Taxes on salvage value = $(BV - MV)t_C$
Taxes on salvage value = $(\$0 - 500)(.34)$
Taxes on salvage value = $-\$204$

Market price	$600
Tax on sale	−204
Aftertax salvage value	$396

The incremental costs will include the maintenance costs, depreciation, and taxes. Notice the taxes are negative, signifying a lower tax bill. So, the incremental cash flows will be:

Maintenance cost	–$700.00
Depreciation	–875.00
EBT	–$1,575.00
Tax	–535.50
Net income	–$1,039.50
OCF	–$164.50

So, the NPV of the decision to buy one unit is:

$$NPV = -\$5,250 - \$164.50(PVIFA_{11\%,6}) + \$396 / 1.11^6$$
$$NPV = -\$5,734.21$$

And the EAC on a per unit basis is:

$$-\$5,734.21 = EAC(PVIFA_{11\%,6})$$
$$EAC = -\$1,355.43$$

Since the company must buy 7 units, the total EAC of the decision is:

$$Total\ EAC = 7(-\$1,355.43)$$
$$Total\ EAC = -\$9,488.02$$

The company should choose the SAL 5000 since the total EAC is greater.

28. Here we are comparing two mutually exclusive assets, with inflation. Since each will be replaced when it wears out, we need to calculate the EAC for each. We have real cash flows. Similar to other capital budgeting projects, when calculating the EAC, we can use real cash flows with the real interest rate, or nominal cash flows and the nominal interest rate. Using the Fisher equation to find the real required return, we get:

$$(1 + R) = (1 + r)(1 + h)$$
$$(1 + .14) = (1 + r)(1 + .05)$$
$$r = .0857\ or\ 8.57\%$$

This is the interest rate we need to use with real cash flows. We are given the real aftertax cash flows for each asset, so the NPV for the XX40 is:

$$NPV = -\$700 - \$100(PVIFA_{8.57\%,3})$$
$$NPV = -\$955.08$$

So, the EAC for the XX40 is:

$$-\$955.08 = EAC(PVIFA_{8.57\%,3})$$
$$EAC = -\$374.43$$

B-188 SOLUTIONS

And the EAC for the RH45 is:

NPV = –$900 – $110(PVIFA$_{8.57\%,5}$)
NPV = –$1,322.66

–$1,322.66 = EAC(PVIFA$_{8.57\%,5}$)
EAC = –$338.82

The company should choose the RH45 because it has the greater EAC.

29. The project has a sales price that increases at five percent per year, and a variable cost per unit that increases at 10 percent per year. First, we need to find the sales price and variable cost for each year. The table below shows the price per unit and the variable cost per unit each year.

	Year 1	Year 2	Year 3	Year 4	Year 5
Sales price	$40.00	$42.00	$44.10	$46.31	$48.62
Cost per unit	$20.00	$22.00	$24.20	$26.62	$29.28

Using the sales price and variable cost, we can now construct the pro forma income statement for each year. We can use this income statement to calculate the cash flow each year. We must also make sure to include the net working capital outlay at the beginning of the project, and the recovery of the net working capital at the end of the project. The pro forma income statement and cash flows for each year will be:

	Year 0	Year 1	Year 2	Year 3	Year 4	Year 5
Revenues		$400,000.00	$420,000.00	$441,000.00	$463,050.00	$486,202.50
Fixed costs		50,000.00	50,000.00	50,000.00	50,000.00	50,000.00
Variable costs		200,000.00	220,000.00	242,000.00	266,200.00	292,820.00
Depreciation		80,000.00	80,000.00	80,000.00	80,000.00	80,000.00
EBT		$70,000.00	$70,000.00	$69,000.00	$66,850.00	$63,382.50
Taxes		23,800.00	23,800.00	23,460.00	22,729.00	21,550.05
Net income		$46,200.00	$46,200.00	$45,540.00	$44,121.00	$41,832.45
OCF		$126,200.00	$126,200.00	$125,540.00	$124,121.00	$121,832.45
Capital spending	–$400,000					
NWC	–25,000					25,000
Total cash flow	–$425,000	$126,200.00	$126,200.00	$125,540.00	$124,121.00	$146,832.45

With these cash flows, the NPV of the project is:

NPV = –$425,000 + $126,200 / 1.15 + $126,200 / 1.15^2 + $125,540 / 1.15^3 + $124,121 / 1.15^4
        +$146,832.45 / 1.15^5
NPV = $6,677.31

We could also answer this problem using the depreciation tax shield approach. The revenues and variable costs are growing annuities, growing at different rates. The fixed costs and depreciation are ordinary annuities. Using the growing annuity equation, the present value of the revenues is:

PV of revenues = $C \{[1/(r - g)] - [1/(r - g)] \times [(1 + g)/(1 + r)]^t\}(1 - t_C)$
PV of revenues = $\$400,000\{[1/(.15 - .05)] - [1/(.15 - .05)] \times [(1 + .05)/(1 + .15)]^5\}$
PV of revenues = $\$1,461,850.00$

And the present value of the variable costs will be:

PV of variable costs = $C \{[1/(r - g)] - [1/(r - g)] \times [(1 + g)/(1 + r)]^t\}(1 - t_C)$
PV of variable costs = $\$200,000\{[1/(.15 - .10)] - [1/(.15 - .10)] \times [(1 + .10)/(1 + .15)]^5\}$
PV of variable costs = $\$797,167.58$

The fixed costs and depreciation are both ordinary annuities. The present value of each is:

PV of fixed costs = $C(\{1 - [1/(1 + r)]^t\} / r)$
PV of fixed costs = $\$50,000(\{1 - [1/(1 + .15)]^5\} / .15)$
PV of fixed costs = $\$167,607.75$

PV of depreciation = $C(\{1 - [1/(1 + r)]^t\} / r)$
PV of depreciation = $\$80,000(\{1 - [1/(1 + .15)]^5\} / .15)$
PV of depreciation = $\$268,172.41$

Now, we can use the depreciation tax shield approach to find the NPV of the project, which is:

NPV = $-\$425,000 + (\$1,461,850.00 - 797,167.58 - 167,607.75)(1 - .34) + (\$268,172.41)(.34)$
       $+ \$25,000 / 1.15^5$
NPV = $\$6,677.31$

Challenge

30. This is an in-depth capital budgeting problem. Probably the easiest OCF calculation for this problem is the bottom up approach, so we will construct an income statement for each year. Beginning with the initial cash flow at time zero, the project will require an investment in equipment. The project will also require an investment in NWC. The NWC investment will be 15 percent of the next year's sales. In this case, it will be Year 1 sales. Realizing we need Year 1 sales to calculate the required NWC capital at time 0, we find that Year 1 sales will be $27,625,000. So, the cash flow required for the project today will be:

Capital spending	–$21,000,000
Change in NWC	–1,500,000
Total cash flow	–$22,500,000

B-190 SOLUTIONS

Now we can begin the remaining calculations. Sales figures are given for each year, along with the price per unit. The variable costs per unit are used to calculate total variable costs, and fixed costs are given at $900,000 per year. To calculate depreciation each year, we use the initial equipment cost of $21 million, times the appropriate MACRS depreciation each year. The remainder of each income statement is calculated below. Notice at the bottom of the income statement we added back depreciation to get the OCF for each year. The section labeled "Net cash flows" will be discussed below:

Year	1	2	3	4	5
Ending book value	$17,997,000	$12,852,000	$9,177,000	$6,552,000	$4,683,000
Sales	$27,625,000	$31,850,000	$34,450,000	$37,050,000	$30,225,000
Variable costs	20,400,000	23,520,000	25,440,000	27,360,000	22,320,000
Fixed costs	900,000	900,000	900,000	900,000	900,000
Depreciation	3,003,000	5,145,000	3,675,000	2,625,000	1,869,000
EBIT	3,322,000	2,285,000	4,435,000	6,165,000	5,136,000
Taxes	1,162,700	799,750	1,552,250	2,157,750	1,797,600
Net income	2,159,300	1,485,250	2,882,750	4,007,250	3,338,400
Depreciation	3,003,000	5,145,000	3,675,000	2,625,000	1,869,000
Operating cash flow	$5,162,300	$6,630,250	$6,557,750	$6,632,250	$5,207,400
Net cash flows					
Operating cash flow	$5,162,300	$6,630,250	$6,557,750	$6,632,250	$5,207,400
Change in NWC	(633,750)	(390,000)	(390,000)	1,023,750	1,890,000
Capital spending	-	-	-	-	4,369,050
Total cash flow	$4,528,550	$6,240,250	$6,167,750	$7,656,000	$11,466,450

After we calculate the OCF for each year, we need to account for any other cash flows. The other cash flows in this case are NWC cash flows and capital spending, which is the aftertax salvage of the equipment. The required NWC capital is 15 percent of the sales in the next year. We will work through the NWC cash flow for Year 1. The total NWC in Year 1 will be 15 percent of sales increase from Year 1 to Year 2, or:

Increase in NWC for Year 1 = .15($31,850,000 – 27,625,000)
Increase in NWC for Year 1 = $633,750

Notice that the NWC cash flow is negative. Since the sales are increasing, we will have to spend more money to increase NWC. In Year 4, the NWC cash flow is positive since sales are declining. And, in Year 5, the NWC cash flow is the recovery of all NWC the company still has in the project.

To calculate the aftertax salvage value, we first need the book value of the equipment. The book value at the end of the five years will be the purchase price, minus the total depreciation. So, the ending book value is:

Ending book value = $21,000,000 – ($3,003,000 + 5,145,000 + 3,675,000 + 2,625,000 + 1,869,000)
Ending book value = $4,683,000

The market value of the used equipment is 20 percent of the purchase price, or $4.2 million, so the aftertax salvage value will be:

Aftertax salvage value = $4,200,000 + ($4,683,000 – 4,200,000)(.35)
Aftertax salvage value = $4,369,050

The aftertax salvage value is included in the total cash flows are capital spending. Now we have all of the cash flows for the project. The NPV of the project is:

$$NPV = -\$22,500,000 + \$4,528,550/1.18 + \$6,240,250/1.18^2 + \$6,167,750/1.18^3 + \$7,655,000/1.18^4 + \$11,466,450/1.18^5$$
$$NPV = -\$1,465,741.71$$

And the IRR is:

$$NPV = 0 = -\$22,500,000 + \$4,528,550/(1 + IRR) + \$6,240,250/(1 + IRR)^2 + \$6,167,750/(1 + IRR)^3 + \$7,655,000/(1 + IRR)^4 + \$11,466,450/(1 + IRR)^5$$
$$IRR = 15.47\%$$

We should reject the project.

31. To find the initial pretax cost savings necessary to buy the new machine, we should use the tax shield approach to find the OCF. We begin by calculating the depreciation each year using the MACRS depreciation schedule. The depreciation each year is:

$D_1 = \$480,000(0.3330) = \$159,840$
$D_2 = \$480,000(0.4440) = \$213,120$
$D_3 = \$480,000(0.1480) = \$71,040$
$D_4 = \$480,000(0.0740) = \$35,520$

Using the tax shield approach, the OCF each year is:

$OCF_1 = (S - C)(1 - 0.35) + 0.35(\$159,840)$
$OCF_2 = (S - C)(1 - 0.35) + 0.35(\$213,120)$
$OCF_3 = (S - C)(1 - 0.35) + 0.35(\$71,040)$
$OCF_4 = (S - C)(1 - 0.35) + 0.35(\$35,520)$
$OCF_5 = (S - C)(1 - 0.35)$

Now we need the aftertax salvage value of the equipment. The aftertax salvage value is:

After-tax salvage value = $45,000(1 – 0.35) = $29,250

To find the necessary cost reduction, we must realize that we can split the cash flows each year. The OCF in any given year is the cost reduction (S – C) times one minus the tax rate, which is an annuity for the project life, and the depreciation tax shield. To calculate the necessary cost reduction, we would require a zero NPV. The equation for the NPV of the project is:

$$NPV = 0 = -\$480,000 - 40,000 + (S - C)(0.65)(PVIFA_{12\%,5}) + 0.35(\$159,840/1.12 + \$213,120/1.12^2 + \$71,040/1.12^3 + \$35,520/1.12^4) + (\$40,000 + 29,250)/1.12^5$$

B-192 SOLUTIONS

Solving this equation for the sales minus costs, we get:

$(S - C)(0.65)(PVIFA_{12\%,5}) = \$345,692.94$
$(S - C) = \$147,536.29$

32. To find the bid price, we need to calculate all other cash flows for the project, and then solve for the bid price. The aftertax salvage value of the equipment is:

Aftertax salvage value $= \$50,000(1 - 0.35) = \$32,500$

Now we can solve for the necessary OCF that will give the project a zero NPV. The equation for the NPV of the project is:

$NPV = 0 = - \$780,000 - 75,000 + OCF(PVIFA_{16\%,5}) + [(\$75,000 + 32,500) / 1.16^5]$

Solving for the OCF, we find the OCF that makes the project NPV equal to zero is:

$OCF = \$803,817.85 / PVIFA_{16\%,5} = \$245,493.51$

The easiest way to calculate the bid price is the tax shield approach, so:

$OCF = \$245,493.51 = [(P - v)Q - FC](1 - t_c) + t_c D$
$\$245,493.51 = [(P - \$8.50)(150,000) - \$240,000](1 - 0.35) + 0.35(\$780,000/5)$
$P = \$12.06$

33. *a.* This problem is basically the same as the previous problem, except that we are given a sales price. The cash flow at Time 0 for all three parts of this question will be:

Capital spending	–$780,000
Change in NWC	–75,000
Total cash flow	–$855,000

We will use the initial cash flow and the salvage value we already found in that problem. Using the bottom up approach to calculating the OCF, we get:

Assume price per unit = $13 and units/year = 150,000

Year	1	2	3	4	5
Sales	$1,950,000	$1,950,000	$1,950,000	$1,950,000	$1,950,000
Variable costs	1,275,000	1,275,000	1,275,000	1,275,000	1,275,000
Fixed costs	240,000	240,000	240,000	240,000	240,000
Depreciation	156,000	156,000	156,000	156,000	156,000
EBIT	279,000	279,000	279,000	279,000	279,000
Taxes (35%)	97,650	97,650	97,650	97,650	97,650
Net Income	181,350	181,350	181,350	181,350	181,350
Depreciation	156,000	156,000	156,000	156,000	156,000
Operating CF	$337,350	$337,350	$337,350	$337,350	$337,350

Year	1	2	3	4	5
Operating CF	$337,350	$337,350	$337,350	$337,350	$337,350
Change in NWC	0	0	0	0	75,000
Capital spending	0	0	0	0	32,500
Total CF	$337,350	$337,350	$337,350	$337,350	$444,850

With these cash flows, the NPV of the project is:

$$NPV = - \$780,000 - 75,000 + \$337,350(PVIFA_{16\%,5}) + [(\$75,000 + 32,500) / 1.16^5]$$
$$NPV = \$300,765.11$$

If the actual price is above the bid price that results in a zero NPV, the project will have a positive NPV. As for the cartons sold, if the number of cartons sold increases, the NPV will increase, and if the costs increase, the NPV will decrease.

b. To find the minimum number of cartons sold to still breakeven, we need to use the tax shield approach to calculating OCF, and solve the problem similar to finding a bid price. Using the initial cash flow and salvage value we already calculated, the equation for a zero NPV of the project is:

$$NPV = 0 = - \$780,000 - 75,000 + OCF(PVIFA_{16\%,5}) + [(\$75,000 + 32,500) / 1.16^5]$$

So, the necessary OCF for a zero NPV is:

$$OCF = \$803,817.85 / PVIFA_{16\%,5} = \$245,493.51$$

Now we can use the tax shield approach to solve for the minimum quantity as follows:

$$OCF = \$245,493.51 = [(P - v)Q - FC](1 - t_C) + t_C D$$
$$\$245,493.51 = [(\$13.00 - 8.50)Q - 240,000](1 - 0.35) + 0.35(\$780,000/5)$$
$$Q = 118,596$$

As a check, we can calculate the NPV of the project with this quantity. The calculations are:

Year	1	2	3	4	5
Sales	$1,541,749	$1,541,749	$1,541,749	$1,541,749	$1,541,749
Variable costs	1,008,067	1,008,067	1,008,067	1,008,067	1,008,067
Fixed costs	240,000	240,000	240,000	240,000	240,000
Depreciation	156,000	156,000	156,000	156,000	156,000
EBIT	137,682	137,682	137,682	137,682	137,682
Taxes (35%)	48,189	48,189	48,189	48,189	48,189
Net Income	89,493	89,493	89,493	89,493	89,493
Depreciation	156,000	156,000	156,000	156,000	156,000
Operating CF	$245,494	$245,494	$245,494	$245,494	$245,494

B-194 SOLUTIONS

Year	1	2	3	4	5
Operating CF	$245,494	$245,494	$245,494	$245,494	$245,494
Change in NWC	0	0	0	0	75,000
Capital spending	0	0	0	0	32,500
Total CF	$245,494	$245,494	$245,494	$245,494	$352,994

$$\text{NPV} = -\$780,000 - 75,000 + \$245,494(\text{PVIFA}_{16\%,5}) + [(\$75,000 + 32,500) / 1.16^5] \approx \$0$$

Note that the NPV is not exactly equal to zero because we had to round the number of cartons sold; you cannot sell one-half of a carton.

c. To find the highest level of fixed costs and still breakeven, we need to use the tax shield approach to calculating OCF, and solve the problem similar to finding a bid price. Using the initial cash flow and salvage value we already calculated, the equation for a zero NPV of the project is:

$$\text{NPV} = 0 = -\$780,000 - 75,000 + \text{OCF}(\text{PVIFA}_{16\%,5}) + [(\$75,000 + 32,500) / 1.16^5]$$
$$\text{OCF} = \$803,817.85 / \text{PVIFA}_{16\%,5} = \$245,494.51$$

Notice this is the same OCF we calculated in part *b*. Now we can use the tax shield approach to solve for the maximum level of fixed costs as follows:

$$\text{OCF} = \$245,494.51 = [(P-v)Q - FC\ ](1 - t_C) + t_C D$$
$$\$245,494.51 = [(\$13.00 - \$8.50)(150,000) - FC](1 - 0.35) + 0.35(\$780,000/5)$$
$$FC = \$381,317.67$$

As a check, we can calculate the NPV of the project with this quantity. The calculations are:

Year	1	2	3	4	5
Sales	$1,950,000	$1,950,000	$1,950,000	$1,950,000	$1,950,000
Variable costs	1,275,000	1,275,000	1,275,000	1,275,000	1,275,000
Fixed costs	381,318	381,318	381,318	381,318	381,318
Depreciation	156,000	156,000	156,000	156,000	156,000
EBIT	137,682	137,682	137,682	137,682	137,682
Taxes (35%)	48,189	48,189	48,189	48,189	48,189
Net Income	89,494	89,494	89,494	89,494	89,494
Depreciation	156,000	156,000	156,000	156,000	156,000
Operating CF	$245,494	$245,494	$245,494	$245,494	$245,494

Year	1	2	3	4	5
Operating CF	$245,494	$245,494	$245,494	$245,494	$245,494
Change in NWC	0	0	0	0	75,000
Capital spending	0	0	0	0	32,500
Total CF	$245,494	$245,494	$245,494	$245,494	$352,994

$$\text{NPV} = -\$780,000 - 75,000 + \$245,494(\text{PVIFA}_{16\%,5}) + [(\$75,000 + 32,500) / 1.16^5] \approx \$0$$

34. We need to find the bid price for a project, but the project has extra cash flows. Since we don't already produce the keyboard, the sales of the keyboard outside the contract are relevant cash flows. Since we know the extra sales number and price, we can calculate the cash flows generated by these sales. The cash flow generated from the sale of the keyboard outside the contract is:

	Year 1	Year 2	Year 3	Year 4
Sales	$825,000	$1,650,000	$2,200,000	$1,375,000
Variable costs	495,000	990,000	1,320,000	825,000
EBT	$330,000	$660,000	$880,000	$550,000
Tax	132,000	264,000	352,000	220,000
Net income (and OCF)	$198,000	$396,000	$528,000	$330,000

So, the addition to NPV of these market sales is:

NPV of market sales = $198,000/1.13 + $396,000/1.13^2 + $528,000/1.13^3 + $330,000/1.13^4
NPV of market sales = $1,053,672.99

You may have noticed that we did not include the initial cash outlay, depreciation, or fixed costs in the calculation of cash flows from the market sales. The reason is that it is irrelevant whether or not we include these here. Remember that we are not only trying to determine the bid price, but we are also determining whether or not the project is feasible. In other words, we are trying to calculate the NPV of the project, not just the NPV of the bid price. We will include these cash flows in the bid price calculation. The reason we stated earlier that whether we included these costs in this initial calculation was irrelevant is that you will come up with the same bid price if you include these costs in this calculation, or if you include them in the bid price calculation.

Next, we need to calculate the aftertax salvage value, which is:

Aftertax salvage value = $200,000(1 − .40) = $120,000

Instead of solving for a zero NPV as is usual in setting a bid price, the company president requires an NPV of $100,000, so we will solve for a NPV of that amount. The NPV equation for this project is (remember to include the NWC cash flow at the beginning of the project, and the NWC recovery at the end):

NPV = $100,000 = –$2,400,000 – 75,000 + 1,053,672.99 + OCF (PVIFA$_{13\%,4}$) + [($120,000 + 75,000) / 1.13^4]

Solving for the OCF, we get:

OCF = $1,401,729.86 / PVIFA$_{13\%,4}$ = $471,253.44

Now we can solve for the bid price as follows:

OCF = $471,253.44 = [(P − v)Q − FC](1 − t$_C$) + t$_C$D
$471,253.44 = [(P − $165)(10,000) − $500,000](1 − 0.40) + 0.40($2,400,000/4)
P = $253.54

B-196 SOLUTIONS

35. Since the two computers have unequal lives, the correct method to analyze the decision is the EAC. We will begin with the EAC of the new computer. Using the depreciation tax shield approach, the OCF for the new computer system is:

OCF = ($125,000)(1 − .38) + ($780,000 / 5)(.38) = $136,780

Notice that the costs are positive, which represents a cash inflow. The costs are positive in this case since the new computer will generate a cost savings. The only initial cash flow for the new computer is cost of $780,000. We next need to calculate the aftertax salvage value, which is:

Aftertax salvage value = $140,000(1 − .38) = $86,800

Now we can calculate the NPV of the new computer as:

NPV = −$780,000 + $136,780(PVIFA$_{14\%,5}$) + $86,800 / 1.14^5
NPV = −$265,341.99

And the EAC of the new computer is:

EAC = − $265,341.99 / (PVIFA$_{14\%,5}$) = −$77,289.75

Analyzing the old computer, the only OCF is the depreciation tax shield, so:

OCF = $130,000(.38) = $49,400

The initial cost of the old computer is a little trickier. You might assume that since we already own the old computer there is no initial cost, but we can sell the old computer, so there is an opportunity cost. We need to account for this opportunity cost. To do so, we will calculate the aftertax salvage value of the old computer today. We need the book value of the old computer to do so. The book value is not given directly, but we are told that the old computer has depreciation of $130,000 per year for the next three years, so we can assume the book value is the total amount of depreciation over the remaining life of the system, or $390,000. So, the aftertax salvage value of the old computer is:

Aftertax salvage value = $230,000 + ($390,000 − 230,000)(.38) = $290,800

This is the initial cost of the old computer system today because we are forgoing the opportunity to sell it today. We next need to calculate the aftertax salvage value of the computer system in two years since we are "buying" it today. The aftertax salvage value in two years is:

Aftertax salvage value = $90,000 + ($130,000 − 90,000)(.38) = $105,200

Now we can calculate the NPV of the old computer as:

NPV = −$290,800 + $49,400(PVIFA$_{14\%,2}$) + 105,200 / 1.14^2
NPV = −$128,506.99

And the EAC of the old computer is:

$$EAC = -\$128,506.99 / (PVIFA_{14\%,2}) = -\$78,040.97$$

If we are going to replace the system in two years no matter what our decision today, we should instead replace it today since the EAC is lower.

b. If we are only concerned with whether or not to replace the machine now, and are not worrying about what will happen in two years, the correct analysis is NPV. To calculate the NPV of the decision on the computer system now, we need the difference in the total cash flows of the old computer system and the new computer system. From our previous calculations, we can say the cash flows for each computer system are:

t	New computer	Old computer	Difference
0	–$780,000	$290,800	–$489,200
1	136,780	–49,400	87,380
2	136,780	–154,600	–17,820
3	136,780	0	136,780
4	136,780	0	136,780
5	223,580	0	223,580

Since we are only concerned with marginal cash flows, the cash flows of the decision to replace the old computer system with the new computer system are the differential cash flows. The NPV of the decision to replace, ignoring what will happen in two years is:

$$NPV = -\$489,200 + \$87,380/1.14 - \$17,820/1.14^2 + \$136,780/1.14^3 + \$136,780/1.14^4$$
$$+ \$223,580/1.14^5$$
$$NPV = -\$136,835.00$$

If we are not concerned with what will happen in two years, we should not replace the old computer system.

36. To answer this question, we need to compute the NPV of all three alternatives, specifically, continue to rent the building, Project A, or Project B. We would choose the project with the highest NPV. If all three of the projects have a positive NPV, the project that is more favorable is the one with the highest NPV

There are several important cash flows we should not consider in the incremental cash flow analysis. The remaining fraction of the value of the building and depreciation are not incremental and should not be included in the analysis of the two alternatives. The $225,000 purchase price of the building is a sunk cost and should be ignored. In effect, what we are doing is finding the NPV of the future cash flows of each option, so the only cash flow today would be the building modifications needed for Project A and Project B. If we did include these costs, the effect would be to lower the NPV of all three options by the same amount, thereby leading to the same conclusion. The cash flows from renting the building after year 15 are also irrelevant. No matter what the company chooses today, it will rent the building after year 15, so these cash flows are not incremental to any project.

B-198 SOLUTIONS

We will begin by calculating the NPV of the decision of continuing to rent the building first.

Continue to rent:

Rent	$12,000
Taxes	4,080
Net income	$7,920

Since there is no incremental depreciation, the operating cash flow is simply the net income. So, the NPV of the decision to continue to rent is:

$$NPV = \$7,920(PVIFA_{12\%,15})$$
$$NPV = \$53,942.05$$

Product A:

Next, we will calculate the NPV of the decision to modify the building to produce Product A. The income statement for this modification is the same for the first 14 years, and in year 15, the company will have an additional expense to convert the building back to its original form. This will be an expense in year 15, so the income statement for that year will be slightly different. The cash flow at time zero will be the cost of the equipment, and the cost of the initial building modifications, both of which are depreciable on a straight-line basis. So, the pro forma cash flows for Product A are:

Initial cash outlay:

Building modifications	–$36,000
Equipment	–144,000
Total cash flow	–$180,000

	Years 1-14	Year 15
Revenue	$105,000	$105,000
Expenditures	60,000	60,000
Depreciation	12,000	12,000
Restoration cost	0	3,750
EBT	$33,000	$29,250
Tax	11,220	9,945
NI	$21,780	$19,305
OCF	$33,780	$31,305

The OCF each year is net income plus depreciation. So, the NPV for modifying the building to manufacture Product A is:

$$NPV = -\$180,000 + \$33,780(PVIFA_{12\%,14}) + \$31,305 / 1.12^{15}$$
$$NPV = \$49,618.83$$

Product B:

Now we will calculate the NPV of the decision to modify the building to produce Product B. The income statement for this modification is the same for the first 14 years, and in year 15, the company will have an additional expense to convert the building back to its original form. This will be an expense in year 15, so the income statement for that year will be slightly different. The cash flow at time zero will be the cost of the equipment, and the cost of the initial building modifications, both of which are depreciable on a straight-line basis. So, the pro forma cash flows for Product A are:

Initial cash outlay:

Building modifications	–$54,000
Equipment	–162,000
Total cash flow	–$216,000

	Years 1-14	Year 15
Revenue	$127,500	$127,500
Expenditures	75,000	75,000
Depreciation	14,400	14,400
Restoration cost	0	28,125
EBT	$38,100	$9,975
Tax	12,954	3,392
NI	$25,146	$6,584
OCF	$39,546	$20,984

The OCF each year is net income plus depreciation. So, the NPV for modifying the building to manufacture Product B is:

$NPV = -\$216,000 + \$39,546(PVIFA_{12\%,14}) + \$20,984 / 1.12^{15}$
$NPV = \$49,951.15$

We could have also done the analysis as the incremental cash flows between Product A and continuing to rent the building, and the incremental cash flows between Product B and continuing to rent the building. The results of this type of analysis would be:

NPV of differential cash flows between Product A and continuing to rent:

$NPV = NPV_{Product A} - NPV_{Rent}$
$NPV = \$49,618.83 - 53,942.05$
$NPV = -\$4,323.22$

NPV of differential cash flows between Product B and continuing to rent:

$NPV = NPV_{Product B} - NPV_{Rent}$
$NPV = \$49,951.15 - 53,942.05$
$NPV = -\$3,990.90$

Both of these incremental analyses have a negative NPV, so the company should continue to rent, which is the same as our original result.

B-200 SOLUTIONS

37. The discount rate is expressed in real terms, and the cash flows are expressed in nominal terms. We can answer this question by converting all of the cash flows to real dollars. We can then use the real interest rate. The real value of each cash flow is the present value of the year 1 nominal cash flows, discounted back to the present at the inflation rate. So, the real value of the revenue and costs will be:

Revenue in real terms = $150,000 / 1.06 = $141,509.43
Labor costs in real terms = $80,000 / 1.06 = $75,471.70
Other costs in real terms = $40,000 / 1.06 = $37,735.85
Lease payment in real terms = $20,000 / 1.06 = $18,867.92

Revenues, labor costs, and other costs are all growing perpetuities. Each has a different growth rate, so we must calculate the present value of each separately. Other costs are a growing perpetuity with a negative growth rate. Using the real required return, the present value of each of these is:

$PV_{Revenue}$ = $141,509.43 / (0.10 – 0.05) = $2,830,188.68
$PV_{Labor\ costs}$ = $75,471.70 / (0.10 – 0.03) = $1,078,167.12
$PV_{Other\ costs}$ = $37,735.85 / [0.10 – (–0.01)] = $343,053.17

The lease payments are constant in nominal terms, so they are declining in real terms by the inflation rate. Therefore, the lease payments form a growing perpetuity with a negative growth rate. The real present value of the lease payments is:

$PV_{Lease\ payments}$ = $18,867.92 / [0.10 – (–0.06)] = $117,924.53

Now we can use the tax shield approach to calculate the net present value. Since there is no investment in equipment, there is no depreciation; therefore, no depreciation tax shield, so we will ignore this in our calculation. This means the cash flows each year are equal to net income. There is also no initial cash outlay, so the NPV is the present value of the future aftertax cash flows. The NPV of the project is:

NPV = $PV_{Revenue}$ – $PV_{Labor\ costs}$ – $PV_{Other\ costs}$ – $PV_{Lease\ payments}$
NPV = ($2,830,188.68 – 1,078,167.12 – 343,053.17 – 117,924.53)(1 – .34)
NPV = $852,088.95

Alternatively, we could have solved this problem by expressing everything in nominal terms. This approach yields the same answer as given above. However, in this case, the computation would have been much more difficult. The reason is that we are dealing with growing perpetuities. In other problems, when calculating the NPV of nominal cash flows, we could simply calculate the nominal cash flow each year since the cash flows were finite. Because of the perpetual nature of the cash flows in this problem, we cannot calculate the nominal cash flows each year until the end of the project. When faced with two alternative approaches, where both are equally correct, always choose the simplest one.

38. We are given the real revenue and costs, and the real growth rates, so the simplest way to solve this problem is to calculate the NPV with real values. While we could calculate the NPV using nominal values, we would need to find the nominal growth rates, and convert all values to nominal terms. The real labor costs will increase at a real rate of two percent per year, and the real energy costs will increase at a real rate of three percent per year, so the real costs each year will be:

	Year 1	Year 2	Year 3	Year 4
Real labor cost each year	$15.30	$15.61	$15.92	$16.24
Real energy cost each year	$5.15	$5.30	$5.46	$5.63

Remember that the depreciation tax shield also affects a firm's aftertax cash flows. The present value of the depreciation tax shield must be added to the present value of a firm's revenues and expenses to find the present value of the cash flows related to the project. The depreciation the firm will recognize each year is:

Annual depreciation = Investment / Economic Life
Annual depreciation = $32,000,000 / 4
Annual depreciation = $8,000,000

Depreciation is a nominal cash flow, so to find the real value of depreciation each year, we discount the real depreciation amount by the inflation rate. Doing so, we find the real depreciation each year is:

Year 1 real depreciation = $8,000,000 / 1.05 = $7,619,047.62
Year 2 real depreciation = $8,000,000 / 1.05^2 = $7,256,235.83
Year 3 real depreciation = $8,000,000 / 1.05^3 = $6,910,700.79
Year 4 real depreciation = $8,000,000 / 1.05^4 = $6,581,619.80

Now we can calculate the pro forma income statement each year in real terms. We can then add back depreciation to net income to find the operating cash flow each year. Doing so, we find the cash flow of the project each year is:

	Year 0	Year 1	Year 2	Year 3	Year 4
Revenues		$40,000,000.00	$80,000,000.00	$80,000,000.00	$60,000,000.00
Labor cost		30,600,000.00	31,212,000.00	31,836,240.00	32,472,964.80
Energy cost		1,030,000.00	1,060,900.00	1,092,727.00	1,125,508.81
Depreciation		7,619,047.62	7,256,235.83	6,910,700.79	6,581,619.80
EBT		$750,952.38	$40,470,864.17	$40,160,332.21	$19,819,906.59
Taxes		255,323.81	13,760,093.82	13,654,512.95	6,738,768.24
Net income		$495,628.57	$26,710,770.35	$26,505,819.26	$13,081,138.35
OCF		$8,114,676.19	$33,967,006.18	$33,416,520.05	$19,662,758.15
Capital spending	−$32,000,000				
Total cash flow	−$32,000,000	$8,114,676.19	$33,967,006.18	$33,416,520.05	$19,662,758.15

B-202 SOLUTIONS

We can use the total cash flows each year to calculate the NPV, which is:

$$\text{NPV} = -\$32,000,000 + \$8,114,676.19 / 1.08 + \$33,967,006.18 / 1.08^2 + \$33,416,520.05 / 1.08^3$$
$$+ \$19,662,758.15 / 1.08^4$$
$$\text{NPV} = \$45,614,647.30$$

39. Here we have the sales price and production costs in real terms. The simplest method to calculate the project cash flows is to use the real cash flows. In doing so, we must be sure to adjust the depreciation, which is in nominal terms. We could analyze the cash flows using nominal values, which would require calculating the nominal discount rate, nominal price, and nominal production costs. This method would be more complicated, so we will use the real numbers. We will first calculate the NPV of the headache only pill.

Headache only:

We can find the real revenue and production costs by multiplying each by the units sold. We must be sure to discount the depreciation, which is in nominal terms. We can then find the pro forma net income, and add back depreciation to find the operating cash flow. Discounting the depreciation each year by the inflation rate, we find the following cash flows each year:

	Year 1	Year 2	Year 3
Sales	$20,000,000	$20,000,000	$20,000,000
Production costs	7,500,000	7,500,000	7,500,000
Depreciation	3,238,095	3,083,900	2,937,048
EBT	$9,261,905	$9,416,100	$9,562,952
Tax	3,149,048	3,201,474	3,251,404
Net income	$6,112,857	$6,214,626	$6,311,548
OCF	$9,350,952	$9,298,526	$9,248,596

And the NPV of the headache only pill is:

$$\text{NPV} = -\$10,200,000 + \$9,350,952 / 1.13 + \$9,298,526 / 1.13^2 + \$9,248,596 / 1.13^3$$
$$\text{NPV} = \$11,767,030.10$$

Headache and arthritis:

For the headache and arthritis pill project, the equipment has a salvage value. We will find the aftertax salvage value of the equipment first, which will be:

Market value	$1,000,000
Taxes	−340,000
Total	$660,000

Remember, to calculate the taxes on the equipment salvage value, we take the book value minus the market value, times the tax rate. Using the same method as the headache only pill, the cash flows each year for the headache and arthritis pill will be:

	Year 1	Year 2	Year 3
Sales	$40,000,000	$40,000,000	$40,000,000
Production costs	17,000,000	17,000,000	17,000,000
Depreciation	3,809,524	3,628,118	3,455,350
EBT	$19,190,476	$19,371,882	$19,544,650
Tax	6,524,762	6,586,440	6,645,181
Net income	$12,665,714	$12,785,442	$12,899,469
OCF	$16,475,238	$16,413,560	$16,354,819

So, the NPV of the headache and arthritis pill is:

$$NPV = -\$12,000,000 + \$16,475,238 / 1.13 + \$16,413,560 / 1.13^2 + (\$16,354,819 + 660,000) / 1.13^3$$
$$NPV = \$27,226,205.03$$

The company should manufacture the headache and arthritis remedy since the project has a higher NPV.

40. This is an in-depth capital budgeting problem. Since the project requires an initial investment in inventory as a percentage of sales, we will calculate the sales figures for each year first. The incremental sales will include the sales of the new table, but we also need to include the lost sales of the existing model. This is an erosion cost of the new table. The lost sales of the existing table are constant for every year, but the sales of the new table change every year. So, the total incremental sales figure for the five years of the project will be:

	Year 1	Year 2	Year 3	Year 4	Year 5
New	$7,280,000	$7,420,000	$7,700,000	$8,120,000	$7,392,000
Lost sales	–900,000	–900,000	–900,000	–900,000	–900,000
Total	$6,380,000	$6,520,000	$6,800,000	$7,220,000	$6,492,000

Now we will calculate the initial cash outlay that will occur today. The company has the necessary production capacity to manufacture the new table without adding equipment today. So, the equipment will not be purchased today, but rather in two years. The reason is that the existing capacity is not being used. If the existing capacity were being used, the new equipment would be required, so it would be a cash flow today. The old equipment would have an opportunity cost if it could be sold. As there is no discussion that the existing equipment could be sold, we must assume it cannot be sold. The only initial cash flow is the cost of the inventory. The company will have to spend money for inventory in the new table, but will be able to reduce inventory of the existing table. So, the initial cash flow today is:

New table	–$728,000
Old table	90,000
Total	–$638,000

B-204 SOLUTIONS

In year 2, the company will have a cash outflow to pay for the cost of the new equipment. Since the equipment will be purchased in two years rather than now, the equipment will have a higher salvage value. The book value of the equipment in five years will be the initial cost, minus the accumulated depreciation, or:

Book value = $10,500,000 – 1,500,500 – 2,572,500 – 1,838,445
Book value = $4,587,555

The taxes on the salvage value will be:

Taxes on salvage = ($4,591,650 – 6,100,000)(.40)
Taxes on salvage = –$603,340

So, the aftertax salvage value of the equipment in five years will be:

Sell equipment	$6,100,000
Taxes	–603,340
Salvage value	$5,496,660

Next, we need to calculate the variable costs each year. The variable costs of the lost sales are included as a variable cost savings, so the variable costs will be:

	Year 1	Year 2	Year 3	Year 4	Year 5
New	$3,276,000	$3,339,000	$3,465,000	$3,654,000	$3,326,400
Lost sales	–360,000	–360,000	–360,000	–360,000	–360,000
Variable costs	$2,916,000	$2,979,000	$3,105,000	$3,294,000	$2,966,400

Now we can prepare the rest of the pro forma income statements for each year. The project will have no incremental depreciation for the first two years as the equipment is not purchased for two years. Adding back depreciation to net income to calculate the operating cash flow, we get:

	Year 1	Year 2	Year 3	Year 4	Year 5
Sales	$6,380,000	$6,520,000	$6,800,000	$7,220,000	$6,492,000
VC	2,916,000	2,979,000	3,105,000	3,294,000	2,966,400
Fixed costs	1,700,000	1,700,000	1,700,000	1,700,000	1,700,000
Dep.	-	-	1,501,500	2,572,500	1,838,445
EBT	$1,764,000	$1,841,000	$493,500	–$346,500	–$12,845
Tax	705,600	736,400	197,400	–138,600	–5,138
NI	$1,058,400	$1,104,600	$296,100	–$207,900	–$7,707
Dep.	-	-	1,501,500	2,572,500	1,838,445
OCF	$1,058,400	$1,104,600	$1,797,600	$2,364,600	$1,830,738

Next, we need to account for the changes in inventory each year. The inventory is a percentage of sales. The way we will calculate the change in inventory is the beginning of period inventory minus the end of period inventory. The sign of this calculation will tell us whether the inventory change is a cash inflow, or a cash outflow. The inventory each year, and the inventory change, will be:

	Year 1	Year 2	Year 3	Year 4	Year 5
Beginning	$728,000	$742,000	$770,000	$812,000	$739,200
Ending	742,000	770,000	812,000	739,200	0
Change	–$14,000	–$28,000	–$42,000	$72,800	$739,200

Notice that we recover the remaining inventory at the end of the project. The total cash flows for the project will be the sum of the operating cash flow, the capital spending, and the inventory cash flows, so:

	Year 1	Year 2	Year 3	Year 4	Year 5
OCF	$1,058,400	$1,104,600	$1,797,600	$2,364,600	$1,830,738
Equipment	0	–10,500,000	0	0	5,496,660
Inventory	–14,000	–28,000	–42,000	72,800	739,200
Total	$1,044,400	–$9,423,400	$1,755,600	$2,437,400	$8,064,960

The NPV of the project, including the inventory cash flow at the beginning of the project, will be:

$$NPV = -\$638,000 + \$1,044,400 \,/\, 1.14 - \$9,423,400 \,/\, 1.14^2 + \$1,755,600 \,/\, 1.14^3$$
$$+ \$2,437,400 \,/\, 1.14^4 + \$8,064,960 \,/\, 1.14^5$$
$$NPV = -\$156,055.99$$

The company should not go ahead with the new table.

b. You can perform an IRR analysis, and would expect to find three IRRs since the cash flows change signs three times.

c. The profitability index is intended as a "bang for the buck" measure; that is, it shows how much shareholder wealth is created for every dollar of initial investment. In this case, the largest investment is not at the beginning of the project, but later in its life. However, since the future negative cash flow is discounted, the profitability index will still measure the amount of shareholder wealth created for every dollar spent today.

CHAPTER 8

Risk Analysis, Real Options, and Capital Budgeting

In 1836, defenders of the Alamo in San Antonio, Texas, held out for 13 days against great odds, and "Remember the Alamo!" became a part of U.S. history. In contrast, Disney's 2004 movie *The Alamo*, starring Billy Bob Thornton as Davy Crockett, barely lasted a weekend at the box office, and the last thing Disney's management wants to do is remember that particular bomb. Disney spent close to $100 million making the movie, plus millions more for marketing and distribution, but the film pulled in only about $22.5 million. In fact, about 4 of 10 movies lose money at the box office, though DVD sales often help the final tally. Of course there are movies that do quite well. In 2005, the last of the Star Wars movies, *Revenge of the Sith*, pulled in about $849 million at a cost of $115 million.

Obviously, Disney didn't *plan* to lose $80 or so million on *The Alamo*, but it happened. As the short life and quick death of *The Alamo* show, projects don't always go as companies think they will. This chapter explores how this can happen, and what companies can do to analyze and possibly avoid these situations.

8.1 Sensitivity Analysis, Scenario Analysis, and Break-Even Analysis

One main point of this book is that NPV analysis is a superior capital budgeting technique. In fact, because the NPV approach uses cash flows rather than profits, uses all the cash flows, and discounts the cash flows properly, it is hard to find any theoretical fault with it. However, in our conversations with practical businesspeople, we hear the phrase "a false sense of security" frequently. These people point out that the documentation for capital budgeting proposals is often quite impressive. Cash flows are projected down to the last thousand dollars (or even the last dollar) for each year (or even each month). Opportunity costs and side effects are handled quite properly. Sunk costs are ignored—also quite properly. When a high net present value appears at the bottom, one's temptation is to say yes immediately. Nevertheless, the projected cash flow often goes unmet in practice, and the firm ends up with a money loser.

Sensitivity Analysis and Scenario Analysis

How can the firm get the net present value technique to live up to its potential? One approach is **sensitivity analysis**, which examines how sensitive a particular NPV calculation is to changes in underlying assumptions. Sensitivity analysis is also known as *what-if* analysis and *bop* (best, optimistic, and pessimistic) analysis.

Table 8.1

Cash Flow Forecasts for Solar Electronics Corporation's Jet Engine: Base Case (millions)*

	Year 1	Years 2–6
Revenues		$6,000
Variable costs		3,000
Fixed costs		1,791
Depreciation		300
Pretax profit		909
Tax ($t_c = 0.34$)		309
Net profit		$ 600
Cash flow		$ 900
Initial investment costs	$1,500	

*Assumptions: (1) Investment is depreciated in years 2 through 6 using the straight-line method; (2) tax rate is 34 percent; (3) the company receives no tax benefits for initial development costs.

Consider the following example. Solar Electronics Corporation (SEC) has recently developed a solar-powered jet engine and wants to go ahead with full-scale production. The initial (year 1)[1] investment is $1,500 million, followed by production and sales over the next five years. The preliminary cash flow projection appears in Table 8.1. Should SEC go ahead with investment in and production of the jet engine, the NPV at a discount rate of 15 percent is (in millions):

$$\text{NPV} = -\$1,500 + \sum_{t=1}^{5} \frac{\$900}{(1.15)^t}$$
$$= -\$1,500 + \$900 \times A_{0.15}^{5}$$
$$= \$1,517$$

Because the NPV is positive, basic financial theory implies that SEC should accept the project. However, is this all there is to say about the venture? Before actual funding, we ought to check out the project's underlying assumptions about revenues and costs.

Revenues   Let's assume that the marketing department has projected annual sales to be:

$$\frac{\text{Number of jet engines}}{\text{sold per year}} = \text{Market share} \times \frac{\text{Size of jet engine}}{\text{market per year}}$$

$$3,000 \quad = \quad 0.30 \quad \times \quad 10,000$$

$$\frac{\text{Annual sales}}{\text{revenues}} = \frac{\text{Number of jet}}{\text{engines sold}} \times \frac{\text{Price per}}{\text{engine}}$$

$$\$6,000 \text{ million} \quad = \quad 3,000 \quad \times \quad \$2 \text{ million}$$

Thus, it turns out that the revenue estimates depend on three assumptions:

1. Market share.
2. Size of jet engine market.
3. Price per engine.

---

[1] Financial custom generally designates year 0 as "today." However, we use year 1 as today in this example because later in this chapter we will consider another decision made a year earlier. That decision will have occurred at year 0.

Table 8.2

Different Estimates for Solar Electronics' Solar Plane Engine

Variable	Pessimistic	Expected or Best	Optimistic
Market size (per year)	5,000	10,000	20,000
Market share	20%	30%	50%
Price	$1.9 million	$2 million	$2.2 million
Variable cost (per plane)	$1.2 million	$1 million	$0.8 million
Fixed cost (per year)	$1,891 million	$1,791 million	$1,741 million
Investment	$1,900 million	$1,500 million	$1,000 million

Costs   Financial analysts frequently divide costs into two types: variable costs and fixed costs. **Variable costs** change as the output changes, and they are zero when production is zero. Costs of direct labor and raw materials are usually variable. It is common to assume that a variable cost is constant per unit of output, implying that total variable costs are proportional to the level of production. For example, if direct labor is variable and one unit of final output requires $10 of direct labor, then 100 units of final output should require $1,000 of direct labor.

Fixed costs are not dependent on the amount of goods or services produced during the period. Fixed costs are usually measured as costs per unit of time, such as rent per month or salaries per year. Naturally, fixed costs are not fixed forever. They are fixed only over a predetermined time period.

The engineering department has estimated variable costs to be $1 million per engine. Fixed costs are $1,791 million per year. The cost breakdowns are:

$$\frac{\text{Variable}}{\text{cost per year}} = \frac{\text{Variable cost}}{\text{per unit}} \times \frac{\text{Number of jet engines}}{\text{sold per year}}$$

$$\$3,000 \text{ million} = \$1 \text{ million} \times 3,000$$

$$\frac{\text{Total cost before}}{\text{taxes per year}} = \frac{\text{Variable cost}}{\text{per year}} + \text{Fixed cost per year}$$

$$\$4,791 \text{ million} = \$3,000 \text{ million} + \$1,791 \text{ million}$$

These estimates for market size, market share, price, variable cost, and fixed cost, as well as the estimate of initial investment, are presented in the middle column of Table 8.2. These figures represent the firm's expectations or best estimates of the different parameters. For comparison, the firm's analysts also prepared both optimistic and pessimistic forecasts for each of the different variables. These forecasts are provided in the table as well.

Standard sensitivity analysis calls for an NPV calculation for all three possibilities of a single variable, along with the expected forecast for all other variables. This procedure is illustrated in Table 8.3. For example, consider the NPV calculation of $8,154 million provided in the upper right corner of this table. This NPV occurs when the optimistic forecast of 20,000 units per year is used for market size while all other variables are set at their expected forecasts from Table 8.2. Note that each row of the middle column of Table 8.3 shows a value of $1,517 million. This occurs because the expected forecast is used for the variable that was singled out, as well as for all other variables.

Table 8.3 can be used for a number of purposes. First, taken as a whole, the table can indicate whether NPV analysis should be trusted. In other words, it reduces the false sense of security we spoke of earlier. Suppose that NPV is positive when the expected forecast for each variable is used. However, further suppose that every number in the pessimistic

Table 8.3

NPV Calculations (in $ millions) for the Solar Plane Engine Using Sensitivity Analysis

	Pessimistic	Expected or Best	Optimistic
Market size	−$1,802*	$1,517	$8,154
Market share	−696*	1,517	5,942
Price	853	1,517	2,844
Variable cost	189	1,517	2,844
Fixed cost	1,295	1,517	1,628
Investment	1,208	1,517	1,903

Under sensitivity analysis, one input is varied while all other inputs are assumed to meet their expectation. For example, an NPV of −$1,802 occurs when the pessimistic forecast of 5,000 is used for market size, while all other variables are set at their expected forecasts from Table 8.2.

*We assume that the other divisions of the firm are profitable, implying that a loss on this project can offset income elsewhere in the firm, thereby reducing the overall taxes of the firm.

column is highly negative and every number in the optimistic column is highly positive. A change in a single forecast greatly alters the NPV estimate, making one leery of the net present value approach. A conservative manager might well scrap the entire NPV analysis in this situation. Fortunately, the solar plane engine does not exhibit this wide dispersion because all but two of the numbers in Table 8.3 are positive. Managers viewing the table will likely consider NPV analysis to be useful for the solar-powered jet engine.

Second, sensitivity analysis shows where more information is needed. For example, error in the estimate of investment appears to be relatively unimportant because, even under the pessimistic scenario, the NPV of $1,208 million is still highly positive. By contrast, the pessimistic forecast for market share leads to a negative NPV of −$696 million, and a pessimistic forecast for market size leads to a substantially negative NPV of −$1,802 million. Because the effect of incorrect estimates on revenues is so much greater than the effect of incorrect estimates on costs, more information about the factors determining revenues might be needed.

Because of these advantages, sensitivity analysis is widely used in practice. Graham and Harvey[2] report that slightly over 50 percent of the 392 firms in their sample subject their capital budgeting calculations to sensitivity analysis. This number is particularly large when one considers that only about 75 percent of the firms in their sample use NPV analysis.

Unfortunately, sensitivity analysis also suffers from some drawbacks. For example, sensitivity analysis may unwittingly *increase* the false sense of security among managers. Suppose all pessimistic forecasts yield positive NPVs. A manager might feel that there is no way the project can lose money. Of course the forecasters may simply have an optimistic view of a pessimistic forecast. To combat this, some companies do not treat optimistic and pessimistic forecasts subjectively. Rather, their pessimistic forecasts are always, say, 20 percent less than expected. Unfortunately, the cure in this case may be worse than the disease: A deviation of a fixed percentage ignores the fact that some variables are easier to forecast than others.

In addition, sensitivity analysis treats each variable in isolation when, in reality, the different variables are likely to be related. For example, if ineffective management allows costs to get out of control, it is likely that variable costs, fixed costs, and investment will all rise above expectation at the same time. If the market is not receptive to a solar plane engine, both market share and price should decline together.

---

[2] See Figure 2 of John Graham and Campbell Harvey, "The Theory and Practice of Corporate Finance: Evidence from the Field," *Journal of Financial Economics* (May/June 2001).

Table 8.4

Cash Flow Forecast (in $ millions) under the Scenario of a Plane Crash*

	Year I	Years 2–5
Revenues		$2,800
Variable costs		1,400
Fixed costs		1,791
Depreciation		300
Pretax profit		−691
Tax ($t_c = 0.34$)[†]		235
Net profit		−$456
Cash flow		−$156
Initial investment cost	−$1,500	

*Assumptions are
  Market size   7,000 (70 percent of expectation)
  Market share   20% (2/3 of expectation)
Forecasts for all other variables are the expected forecasts as given in Table 8.2.
[†]Tax loss offsets income elsewhere in firm.

Managers frequently perform **scenario analysis**, a variant of sensitivity analysis, to minimize this problem. Simply put, this approach examines a number of different likely scenarios, where each scenario involves a confluence of factors. As a simple example, consider the effect of a few airline crashes. These crashes are likely to reduce flying in total, thereby limiting the demand for any new engines. Furthermore, even if the crashes do not involve solar-powered aircraft, the public could become more averse to any innovative and controversial technologies. Hence, SEC's market share might fall as well. Perhaps the cash flow calculations would look like those in Table 8.4 under the scenario of a plane crash. Given the calculations in the table, the NPV (in millions) would be:

$$-\$2,023 = -\$1,500 - \$156 \times A_{0.15}^5$$

A series of scenarios like this might illuminate issues concerning the project better than the standard application of sensitivity analysis would.

Break-Even Analysis

Our discussion of sensitivity analysis and scenario analysis suggests that there are many ways to examine variability in forecasts. We now present another approach, **break-even analysis**. As its name implies, this approach determines the sales needed to break even. The approach is a useful complement to sensitivity analysis because it also sheds light on the severity of incorrect forecasts. We calculate the break-even point in terms of both accounting profit and present value.

Accounting Profit   Annual net profit under four different sales forecasts is as follows:

Annual Unit Sales	Net Profit (in $ millions)
0	−$1,380
1,000	−720
3,000	600
10,000	5,220

Table 8.5   Revenues and Costs of Project under Different Sales Assumptions (in $ millions, except unit sales)

Year 1			Years 2–6						
Initial Invest-ment	Annual Unit Sales	Revenues	Variable Costs	Fixed Costs	Depreci-ation	Taxes* ($t_c = 0.34$)	Net Profit	Operating Cash Flows	NPV (evaluated date 1)
$1,500	0	$ 0	$ 0	−$1,791	−$300	$ 711	−$1,380	−$1,080	−$ 5,120
1,500	1,000	2,000	−1,000	−1,791	−300	371	−720	−420	−2,908
1,500	3,000	6,000	−3,000	−1,791	−300	−309	600	900	1,517
1,500	10,000	20,000	−10,000	−1,791	−300	−2,689	5,220	5,520	17,004

*Loss is incurred in the first two rows. For tax purposes, this loss offsets income elsewhere in the firm.

Figure 8.1

Break-Even Point Using Accounting Numbers

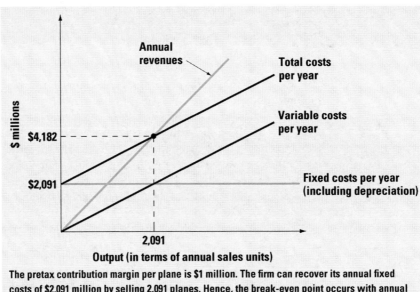

The pretax contribution margin per plane is $1 million. The firm can recover its annual fixed costs of $2,091 million by selling 2,091 planes. Hence, the break-even point occurs with annual sales of 2,091 planes.

A more complete presentation of costs and revenues appears in Table 8.5.

We plot the revenues, costs, and profits under the different assumptions about sales in Figure 8.1. The revenue and cost curves cross at 2,091 jet engines. This is the break-even point—that is, the point where the project generates no profits or losses. As long as annual sales are above 2,091 jet engines, the project will make a profit.

This break-even point can be calculated very easily. Because the sales price is $2 million per engine and the variable cost is $1 million per engine,[3] the difference between sales price and variable cost per engine is:

$$\text{Sales price} - \text{Variable cost} = \$2 \text{ million} - \$1 \text{ million}$$
$$= \$1 \text{ million}$$

This difference is called the pretax **contribution margin** because each additional engine contributes this amount to pretax profit. (Contribution margin can also be expressed on an aftertax basis.)

---

[3]Though the previous section considered both optimistic and pessimistic forecasts for sales price and variable cost, break-even analysis uses just the expected or best estimates of these variables.

Fixed costs are $1,791 million and depreciation is $300 million, implying that the sum of these costs is:

$$\text{Fixed costs} + \text{Depreciation} = \$1{,}791 \text{ million} + \$300 \text{ million}$$
$$= \$2{,}091 \text{ million}$$

That is, the firm incurs costs of $2,091 million per year, regardless of the number of sales. Because each engine contributes $1 million, annual sales must reach the following level to offset the costs:

Accounting Profit Break-Even Point:

$$\frac{\text{Fixed costs} + \text{Depreciation}}{\text{Sales price} - \text{Variable costs}} = \frac{\$2{,}091 \text{ million}}{\$1 \text{ million}} = 2{,}091$$

Thus, 2,091 engines is the break-even point required for an accounting profit.

The astute reader might be wondering why taxes have been ignored in the calculation of break-even accounting profit. The reason is that a firm with a pretax profit of $0 will also have an aftertax profit of $0 because no taxes are paid if no pretax profit is reported. Thus, the number of units needed to break even on a pretax basis must be equal to the number of units needed to break even on an aftertax basis.

Present Value   As we have stated many times, we are more interested in present value than we are in profit. Therefore, we should calculate breakeven in terms of present value. Given a discount rate of 15 percent, the solar plane engine has the following net present values for different levels of annual sales:

Annual Unit Sales	NPV ($ millions)
0	−5,120
1,000	−2,908
3,000	1,517
10,000	17,004

These NPV calculations are reproduced from the last column of Table 8.5.

Figure 8.2 relates the net present value of both the revenues and the costs to output. There are at least two differences between Figure 8.2 and Figure 8.1, one of which is quite important and the other is much less so. First the less important point: The dollar amounts on the vertical dimension of Figure 8.2 are greater than those on the vertical dimension of Figure 8.1 because the net present values are calculated over five years. More important, accounting breakeven occurs when 2,091 units are sold annually, whereas NPV breakeven occurs when 2,315 units are sold annually.

Of course the NPV break-even point can be calculated directly. The firm originally invested $1,500 million. This initial investment can be expressed as a five-year equivalent annual cost (EAC), determined by dividing the initial investment by the appropriate five-year annuity factor:

$$\text{EAC} = \frac{\text{Initial investment}}{\text{5-year annuity factor at 15\%}} = \frac{\text{Initial investment}}{A^5_{.15}}$$
$$= \frac{\$1{,}500 \text{ million}}{3.3522} = \$447.5 \text{ million}$$

Figure 8.2

Break-Even Point
Using Net Present
Value*

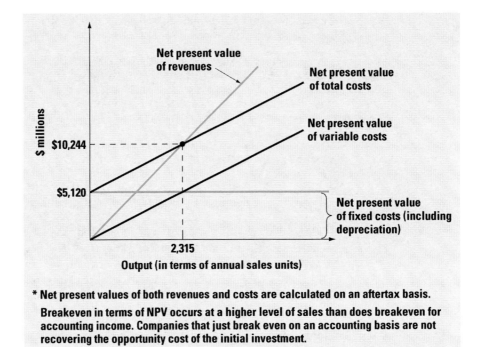

* Net present values of both revenues and costs are calculated on an aftertax basis.

Breakeven in terms of NPV occurs at a higher level of sales than does breakeven for accounting income. Companies that just break even on an accounting basis are not recovering the opportunity cost of the initial investment.

Note that the EAC of $447.5 million is greater than the yearly depreciation of $300 million. This must occur because the calculation of EAC implicitly assumes that the $1,500 million investment could have been invested at 15 percent.

Aftertax costs, regardless of output, can be viewed like this:

$$\begin{aligned}\$1,528 \text{ million} &= \frac{\$447.5}{\text{million}} + \frac{\$1,791}{\text{million}} \times .66 - \frac{\$300}{\text{million}} \times .34 \\ &= \text{EAC} + \text{Fixed costs} \times (1 - t_c) - \text{Depreciation} \times t_c\end{aligned}$$

That is, in addition to the initial investment's equivalent annual cost of $447.5 million, the firm pays fixed costs each year and receives a depreciation tax shield each year. The depreciation tax shield is written as a negative number because it offsets the costs in the equation. Each plane contributes $.66 million to aftertax profit, so it will take the following sales to offset the costs:

Present Value Break-Even Point:

$$\frac{\text{EAC} + \text{Fixed costs} \times (1 - t_c) - \text{Depreciation} \times t_c}{(\text{Sales price} - \text{Variable costs}) \times (1 - t_c)} = \frac{\$1,528 \text{ million}}{\$.66 \text{ million}} = 2,315$$

Thus, 2,315 planes is the break-even point from the perspective of present value.

Why is the accounting break-even point different from the financial break-even point? When we use accounting profit as the basis for the break-even calculation, we subtract depreciation. Depreciation for the solar jet engines project is $300 million per year. If 2,091 solar jet engines are sold per year, SEC will generate sufficient revenues to cover the $300 million depreciation expense plus other costs. Unfortunately, at this level of sales SEC will not cover the economic opportunity costs of the $1,500 million laid out for the investment. If we take into account that the $1,500 million could have been invested at 15 percent, the true annual cost of the investment is $447.5 million, not $300 million. Depreciation understates the true costs of recovering the initial investment. Thus companies that break even on an accounting basis are really losing money. They are losing the opportunity cost of the initial investment.

Is break-even analysis important? Very much so: All corporate executives fear losses. Break-even analysis determines how far down sales can fall before the project is losing money, either in an accounting sense or an NPV sense.

8.2   Monte Carlo Simulation

Both sensitivity analysis and scenario analysis attempt to answer the question "What if?" However, while both analyses are frequently used in the real world, each has its own limitations. Sensitivity analysis allows only one variable to change at a time. By contrast, many variables are likely to move at the same time in the real world. Scenario analysis follows specific scenarios, such as changes in inflation, government regulation, or the number of competitors. Although this methodology is often quite helpful, it cannot cover all sources of variability. In fact, projects are likely to exhibit a lot of variability under just one economic scenario.

Monte Carlo simulation is a further attempt to model real-world uncertainty. This approach takes its name from the famous European casino because it analyzes projects the way one might analyze gambling strategies. Imagine a serious blackjack player who wonders if he should take a third card whenever his first two cards total 16. Most likely, a formal mathematical model would be too complex to be practical here. However, he could play thousands of hands in a casino, sometimes drawing a third card when his first two cards add to 16 and sometimes not drawing that third card. He could compare his winnings (or losings) under the two strategies to determine which were better. Of course he would probably lose a lot of money performing this test in a real casino, so simulating the results from the two strategies on a computer might be cheaper. Monte Carlo simulation of capital budgeting projects is in this spirit.

Imagine that Backyard Barbeques, Inc. (BBI), a manufacturer of both charcoal and gas grills, has a blueprint for a new grill that cooks with compressed hydrogen. The CFO, Edward H. Comiskey, being dissatisfied with simpler capital budgeting techniques, wants a Monte Carlo simulation for this new grill. A consultant specializing in the Monte Carlo approach, Lester Mauney, takes him through the five basic steps of the method.

Step 1: Specify the Basic Model

Les Mauney breaks up cash flow into three components: annual revenue, annual costs, and initial investment. The revenue in any year is viewed as:

$$\text{Number of grills sold} \atop \text{by entire industry} \times {\text{Market share of BBI's} \atop \text{hydrogen grill (in percent)}} \times {\text{Price per} \atop \text{hydrogen grill}} \qquad (8.1)$$

The cost in any year is viewed as:

$$\text{Fixed manufacturing costs} + \text{Variable manufacturing costs} + \text{Marketing costs} + \text{Selling costs}$$

Initial investment is viewed as:

$$\text{Cost of patent} + \text{Test marketing costs} + \text{Cost of production facility}$$

Step 2: Specify a Distribution for Each Variable in the Model

Here comes the hard part. Let's start with revenue, which has three components in Equation 8.1. The consultant first models overall market size—that is, the number of grills sold

Figure 8.3

Probability Distributions for Industrywide Unit Sales, Market Share of BBI's Hydrogen Grill, and Price of Hydrogen Grill

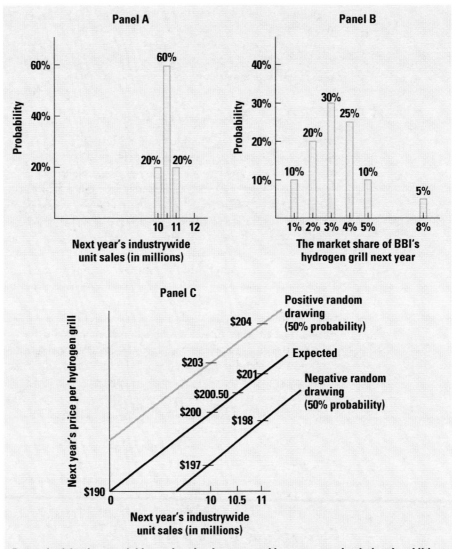

For each of the three variables, a drawing is generated by computer simulation. In addition, price per grill is dependent on industrywide unit sales.

by the entire industry. The trade publication *Outdoor Food (OF)* reported that 10 million grills of all types were sold in the continental United States last year, and it forecasts sales of 10.5 million next year. Mr. Mauney, using *OF*'s forecast and his own intuition, creates the following distribution for next year's sales of grills by the entire industry:

Probability	20%	60%	20%
Next Year's Industrywide Unit Sales	10 million	10.5 million	11 million

The tight distribution here reflects the slow but steady historical growth in the grill market. This probability distribution is graphed in Panel A of Figure 8.3.

Lester Mauney realizes that estimating the market share of BBI's hydrogen grill is more difficult. Nevertheless, after a great deal of analysis, he determines the distribution of next year's market share:

Probability	10%	20%	30%	25%	10%	5%
Market Share of BBI's Hydrogen Grill Next Year	1%	2%	3%	4%	5%	8%

Whereas the consultant assumed a symmetrical distribution for industrywide unit sales, he believes a skewed distribution makes more sense for the project's market share. In his mind there is always the small possibility that sales of the hydrogen grill will really take off. This probability distribution is graphed in Panel B of Figure 8.3.

These forecasts assume that unit sales for the overall industry are unrelated to the project's market share. In other words, the two variables are *independent* of each other. Mr. Mauney reasons that although an economic boom might increase industrywide grill sales and a recession might decrease them, the project's market share is unlikely to be related to economic conditions.

Now Mr. Mauney must determine the distribution of price per grill. Mr. Comiskey, the CFO, informs him that the price will be in the area of $200 per grill, given what other competitors are charging. However, the consultant believes that the price per hydrogen grill will almost certainly depend on the size of the overall market for grills. As in any business, you can usually charge more if demand is high.

After rejecting a number of complex models for price, Mr. Mauney settles on the following specification:

$$\frac{\text{Next year's price}}{\text{per hydrogen grill}} = \$190 + \$1 \times \frac{\text{Industrywide unit sales}}{\text{(in millions)}} +/- \$3 \qquad (8.2)$$

The grill price in Equation 8.2 depends on the unit sales of the industry. In addition, random variation is modeled via the term "$+/-\$3$," where a drawing of $+\$3$ and a drawing of $-\$3$ each occur 50 percent of the time. For example, if industrywide unit sales are 11 million, the price per share would be either of the following:

$$\$190 + \$11 + \$3 = \$204 \quad (50\% \text{ probability})$$
$$\$190 + \$11 - \$3 = \$198 \quad (50\% \text{ probability})$$

The relationship between the price of a hydrogen grill and industrywide unit sales is graphed in Panel C of Figure 8.3.

The consultant now has distributions for each of the three components of next year's revenue. However, he needs distributions for future years as well. Using forecasts from *Outdoor Food* and other publications, Mr. Mauney forecasts the distribution of growth rates for the entire industry over the second year:

Probability	20%	60%	20%
Growth Rate of Industrywide Unit Sales in Second Year	1%	3%	5%

Given both the distribution of next year's industrywide unit sales and the distribution of growth rates for this variable over the second year, we can generate the distribution of industrywide unit sales for the second year. A similar extension should give Mr. Mauney a distribution for later years as well, though we won't go into the details here. And just as the consultant extended the first component of revenue (industrywide unit sales) to later years, he would want to do the same thing for market share and unit price.

The preceding discussion shows how the three components of revenue can be modeled. Step 2 would be complete once the components of cost and investment are modeled in a similar way. Special attention must be paid to the interactions between variables here because ineffective management will likely allow the different cost components to rise together. However, you are probably getting the idea now, so we will skip the rest of this step.

Step 3: The Computer Draws One Outcome

As we said, next year's revenue in our model is the product of three components. Imagine that the computer randomly picks industrywide unit sales of 10 million, a market share for BBI's hydrogen grill of 2 percent, and a $+\$3$ random price variation. Given these drawings, next year's price per hydrogen grill will be:

$$\$190 + \$10 + \$3 = \$203$$

and next year's revenue for BBI's hydrogen grill will be:

$$10 \text{ million} \times 0.02 \times \$203 = \$40.6 \text{ million}$$

Of course, we are not done with the entire *outcome* yet. We would have to perform drawings for revenue in each future year. In addition, we would perform drawings for costs in each future year. Finally, a drawing for initial investment would have to be made as well. In this way, a single outcome, made up of a drawing for each variable in the model, would generate a cash flow from the project in each future year.

How likely is it that the specific outcome discussed would be drawn? We can answer this because we know the probability of each component. Because industry sales of $10 million has a 20 percent probability, a market share of 2 percent also has a 20 percent probability, and a random price variation of $+\$3$ has a 50 percent probability, the probability of these three drawings together in the same outcome is:

$$0.02 = 0.20 \times 0.20 \times 0.50 \tag{8.3}$$

Of course the probability would get even smaller once drawings for future revenues, future costs, and the initial investment are included in the outcome.

This step generates the cash flow for each year from a single outcome. What we are ultimately interested in is the *distribution* of cash flow each year across many outcomes. We ask the computer to randomly draw over and over again to give us this distribution, which is just what is done in the next step.

Step 4: Repeat the Procedure

The first three steps generate one outcome, but the essence of Monte Carlo simulation is repeated outcomes. Depending on the situation, the computer may be called on to generate thousands or even millions of outcomes. The result of all these drawings is a distribution of cash flow for each future year. This distribution is the basic output of Monte Carlo simulation.

Consider Figure 8.4. Here, repeated drawings have produced the simulated distribution of the third year's cash flow. There would be, of course, a distribution like the one in this figure for each future year. This leaves us with just one more step.

Step 5: Calculate NPV

Given the distribution of cash flow for the third year in Figure 8.4, one can determine the expected cash flow for this year. In a similar manner, one can also determine the expected

Figure 8.4

Simulated Distribution of the Third Year's Cash Flow for BBI's New Hydrogen Grill

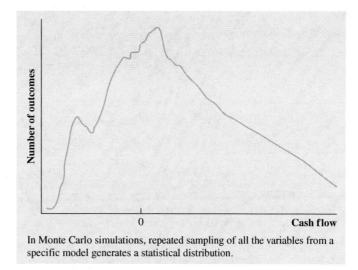

In Monte Carlo simulations, repeated sampling of all the variables from a specific model generates a statistical distribution.

cash flow for each future year and then calculate the net present value of the project by discounting these expected cash flows at an appropriate rate.

Monte Carlo simulation is often viewed as a step beyond either sensitivity analysis or scenario analysis. Interactions between the variables are explicitly specified in Monte Carlo; so (at least in theory) this methodology provides a more complete analysis. And, as a by-product, having to build a precise model deepens the forecaster's understanding of the project.

Because Monte Carlo simulations have been around for at least 35 years, you might think that most firms would be performing them by now. Surprisingly, this does not seem to be the case. In our experience, executives are frequently skeptical of the complexity. It is difficult to model either the distributions of each variable or the interactions between variables. In addition, the computer output is often devoid of economic intuition. Thus while Monte Carlo simulations are used in certain real-world situations,[4] the approach is not likely to be "the wave of the future." In fact, Graham and Harvey[5] report that only about 15 percent of the firms in their sample use capital budgeting simulations.

8.3 Real Options

In Chapter 6, we stressed the superiority of net present value (NPV) analysis over other approaches when valuing capital budgeting projects. However, both scholars and practitioners have pointed out problems with NPV. The basic idea here is that NPV analysis, as well as all the other approaches in Chapter 6, ignores the adjustments that a firm can make after a project is accepted. These adjustments are called **real options**. In this respect NPV underestimates the true value of a project. NPV's conservatism is best explained through a series of examples.

The Option to Expand

Conrad Willig, an entrepreneur, recently learned of a chemical treatment causing water to freeze at 100 degrees Fahrenheit rather than 32 degrees. Of all the many practical

---

[4]More than perhaps any other, the pharmaceutical industry has pioneered applications of this methodology. For example, see Nancy A. Nichols, "Scientific Management at Merck: An Interview with CFO Judy Lewent," *Harvard Business Review* (January/February 1994).

[5]See Figure 2 of Graham and Harvey, op. cit.

Figure 8.5

Decision Tree for Ice Hotel

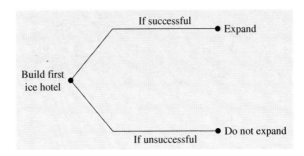

applications for this treatment, Mr. Willig liked the idea of hotels made of ice more than anything else. Conrad estimated the annual cash flows from a single ice hotel to be $2 million, based on an initial investment of $12 million. He felt that 20 percent was an appropriate discount rate, given the risk of this new venture. Believing that the cash flows would be perpetual, Mr. Willig determined the NPV of the project to be:

$$-\$12,000,000 + \$2,000,000/0.20 = -\$2 \text{ million}$$

Most entrepreneurs would have rejected this venture, given its negative NPV. But Conrad was not your typical entrepreneur. He reasoned that NPV analysis missed a hidden source of value. While he was pretty sure that the initial investment would cost $12 million, there was some uncertainty concerning annual cash flows. His cash flow estimate of $2 million per year actually reflected his belief that there was a 50 percent probability that annual cash flows will be $3 million and a 50 percent probability that annual cash flows will be $1 million.

The NPV calculations for the two forecasts are given here:

> **Optimistic forecast:** $-\$12 \text{ million} + \$3 \text{ million}/0.20 = \$3 \text{ million}$
>
> **Pessimistic forecast:** $-\$12 \text{ million} + \$1 \text{ million}/0.20 = -\$7 \text{ million}$

On the surface, this new calculation doesn't seem to help Mr. Willig much. An average of the two forecasts yields an NPV for the project of:

$$50\% \times \$3 \text{ million} + 50\% \times (-\$7 \text{ million}) = -\$2 \text{ million}$$

which is just the value he calculated in the first place.

However, if the optimistic forecast turns out to be correct, Mr. Willig would want to *expand*. If he believes that there are, say, 10 locations in the country that can support an ice hotel, the true NPV of the venture would be:

$$50\% \times 10 \times \$3 \text{ million} + 50\% \times (-\$7 \text{ million}) = \$11.5 \text{ million}$$

Figure 8.5, which represents Mr. Willig's decision, is often called a **decision tree**. The idea expressed in the figure is both basic and universal. The entrepreneur has the option to expand if the pilot location is successful. For example, think of all the people that start restaurants, most of them ultimately failing. These individuals are not necessarily overly optimistic. They may realize the likelihood of failure but go ahead anyway because of the small chance of starting the next McDonald's or Burger King.

The Option to Abandon

Managers also have the option to abandon existing projects. Abandonment may seem cowardly, but it can often save companies a great deal of money. Because of this, the option to abandon increases the value of any potential project.

Ross−Westerfield−Jaffe:
Corporate Finance, Eighth
Edition

II. Valuation and Capital
Budgeting

8. Risk Analysis, Real
Options, and Capital
Budgeting

© The McGraw−Hill
Companies, 2008

317

Figure 8.6

The Abandonment Option in the Movie Industry

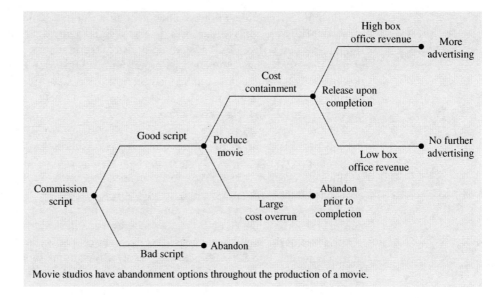

Movie studios have abandonment options throughout the production of a movie.

The example of ice hotels, which illustrated the option to expand, can also illustrate the option to abandon. To see this, imagine that Mr. Willig now believes that there is a 50 percent probability that annual cash flows will be $6 million and a 50 percent probability that annual cash flows will be −$2 million. The NPV calculations under the two forecasts become:

Optimistic forecast: −$12 million + $6 million/0.2 = $18 million

Pessimistic forecast: −$12 million − $2 million/0.2 = −$22 million

yielding an NPV for the project of:

$$50\% \times \$18 \text{ million} + 50\% \times (-\$22 \text{ million}) = -\$2 \text{ million} \qquad \textbf{(8.4)}$$

Furthermore, now imagine that Mr. Willig wants to own, at most, just one ice hotel, implying that there is no option to expand. Because the NPV in Equation 8.4 is negative, it looks as if he will not build the hotel.

But things change when we consider the abandonment option. As of date 1, the entrepreneur will know which forecast has come true. If cash flows equal those under the optimistic forecast, Conrad will keep the project alive. If, however, cash flows equal those under the pessimistic forecast, he will abandon the hotel. If Mr. Willig knows these possibilities ahead of time, the NPV of the project becomes:

$$50\% \times \$18 \text{ million} + 50\% \times (-\$12 \text{ million} - \$2 \text{ million}/1.20) = \$2.17 \text{ million}$$

Because Mr. Willig abandons after experiencing the cash flow of −$2 million at date 1, he does not have to endure this outflow in any of the later years. The NPV is now positive, so Conrad will accept the project.

The example here is clearly a stylized one. Whereas many years may pass before a project is abandoned in the real world, our ice hotel was abandoned after just one year. And, while salvage values generally accompany abandonment, we assumed no salvage value for the ice hotel. Nevertheless, abandonment options are pervasive in the real world.

For example, consider the moviemaking industry. As shown in Figure 8.6, movies begin with either the purchase or development of a script. A completed script might cost a movie studio a few million dollars and potentially lead to actual production. However, the great majority of scripts (perhaps well in excess of 80 percent) are abandoned. Why would studios abandon scripts that they commissioned in the first place? The studios know ahead of time that only a few scripts will be promising, and they don't know which ones. Thus, they cast a wide net, commissioning many scripts to get a few good ones. The studios must be ruthless with the bad scripts because the expenditure here pales in comparison to the huge losses from producing a bad movie.

The few lucky scripts then move into production, where costs might be budgeted in the tens of millions of dollars, if not much more. At this stage, the dreaded phrase is that on-location production gets "bogged down," creating cost overruns. But the studios are equally ruthless here. Should these overruns become excessive, production is likely to be abandoned midstream. Interestingly, abandonment almost always occurs due to high costs, not due to the fear that the movie won't be able to find an audience. Little information on that score will be obtained until the movie is actually released.

Release of the movie is accompanied by significant advertising expenditures, perhaps in the range of $10 to $20 million. Advertising will continue following strong ticket sales, but it will likely be abandoned after a few weeks of poor box office performance.

Moviemaking is one of the riskiest businesses around, with studios receiving hundreds of millions of dollars in a matter of weeks from a blockbuster while receiving practically nothing during this period from a flop. The abandonment options contain costs that might otherwise bankrupt the industry.

To illustrate some of these ideas, consider the case of Euro Disney. The deal to open Euro Disney occurred in 1987, and the park opened its doors outside Paris in 1992. Disney's management thought Europeans would go goofy over the new park, but trouble soon began. The number of visitors never met expectations, in part because the company priced tickets too high. Disney also decided not to serve alcohol in a country that was accustomed to wine with meals. French labor inspectors fought Disney's strict dress codes, and so on.

After several years of operations, the park began serving wine in its restaurants, lowered ticket prices, and made other adjustments. In other words, management exercised its option to reformulate the product. The park began to make a small profit. Then the company exercised the option to expand by adding a "second gate," which was another theme park next to Euro Disney named Walt Disney Studios. The second gate was intended to encourage visitors to extend their stays. But the new park flopped. The reasons ranged from high ticket prices, attractions geared toward Hollywood rather than European filmmaking, labor strikes in Paris, and a summer heat wave.

By the summer of 2003, Euro Disney was close to bankruptcy again. Executives discussed a range of options. These options ranged from letting the company go broke (the option to abandon) to pulling the Disney name from the park. In 2005, the company finally agreed to a restructuring with the help of the French government.

The whole idea of managerial options was summed up aptly by Jay Rasulo, the overseer of Disney's theme parks, when he said, "One thing we know for sure is that you never get it 100 percent right the first time. We open every one of our parks with the notion that we're going to add content."

A recent example of a company actually exercising the option to abandon occurred in 2005 when Sony Corporation announced that it was withdrawing from the handheld computer, or PDA, market in Japan. What was somewhat surprising was that the company was the market leader in sales at the time, with about one-third of the market. However, PDA sales had been shrinking over the past three years, in large part due to increased competition from smart phones that have PDA capabilities. So, Sony concluded that the future market for stand-alone devices was limited and bailed out.

Figure 8.7

Decision Tree for Vacant Land

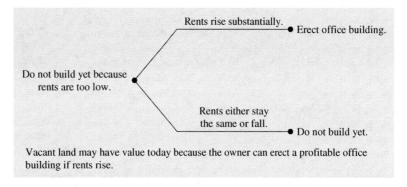

Vacant land may have value today because the owner can erect a profitable office building if rents rise.

Timing Options

One often finds urban land that has been vacant for many years. Yet this land is bought and sold from time to time. Why would anyone pay a positive price for land that has no source of revenue? Certainly, one could not arrive at a positive price through NPV analysis. However, the paradox can easily be explained in terms of real options.

Suppose that the land's highest and best use is as an office building. Total construction costs for the building are estimated to be $1 million. Currently, net rents (after all costs) are estimated to be $90,000 per year in perpetuity, and the discount rate is 10 percent. The NPV of this proposed building would be:

$$-\$1 \text{ million} + \$90,000/.10 = -\$100,000$$

Because this NPV is negative, one would not currently want to build. However, suppose that the federal government is planning various urban revitalization programs for the city. Office rents will likely increase if the programs succeed. In this case the property's owner might want to erect the office building after all. Conversely, office rents will remain the same, or even fall, if the programs fail. The owner will not build in this case.

We say that the property owner has a *timing option*. Although she does not currently want to build, she will want to build in the future should rents in the area rise substantially. This timing option explains why vacant land often has value. There are costs, such as taxes, from holding raw land, but the value of an office building after a substantial rise in rents may more than offset these holding costs. Of course the exact value of the vacant land depends on both the probability of success in the revitalization program and the extent of the rent increase. Figure 8.7 illustrates this timing option.

Mining operations almost always provide timing options as well. Suppose you own a copper mine where the cost of mining each ton of copper exceeds the sales revenue. It's a no-brainer to say that you would not want to mine the copper currently. And because there are costs of ownership such as property taxes, insurance, and security, you might actually want to pay someone to take the mine off your hands. However, we would caution you not to do so hastily. Copper prices in the future might increase enough so that production is profitable. Given that possibility, you could likely find someone to pay a positive price for the property today.

8.4 Decision Trees

As shown in the previous section, managers adjust their decisions on the basis of new information. For example, a project may be expanded if early experience is promising, whereas the same project might be abandoned in the wake of bad results. As we said earlier, the choices available to managers are called *real options* and an individual project can often be

320

Ross–Westerfield–Jaffe:
Corporate Finance, Eighth
Edition

II. Valuation and Capital
Budgeting

8. Risk Analysis, Real
Options, and Capital
Budgeting

© The McGraw–Hill
Companies, 2008

Figure 8.8

Decision Tree
for SEC ($ millions)

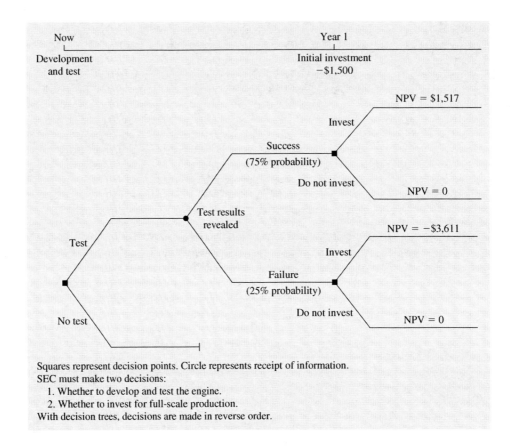

Squares represent decision points. Circle represents receipt of information.
SEC must make two decisions:
   1. Whether to develop and test the engine.
   2. Whether to invest for full-scale production.
With decision trees, decisions are made in reverse order.

viewed as a series of real options, leading to valuation approaches beyond the basic present value methodology of earlier chapters.

Earlier in this chapter, we considered Solar Electronics Corporation's (SEC's) solar-powered jet engine project, with cash flows as shown in Table 8.1. In that example, SEC planned to invest $1,500 million at year 1 and expected to receive $900 million per year in each of the next five years. Our calculations showed an NPV of $1,517 million, so the firm would presumably want to go ahead with the project.

To illustrate decision trees in more detail, let's move back one year to year 0, when SEC's decision was more complicated. At that time, the engineering group had developed the technology for a solar-powered plane engine, but test marketing had not begun. The marketing department proposed that SEC develop some prototypes and conduct test marketing of the engine. A corporate planning group, including representatives from production, marketing, and engineering, estimated that this preliminary phase would take a year and cost $100 million. Furthermore, the group believed there was a 75 percent chance that the marketing test would prove successful. After completion of the marketing tests, SEC would decide whether to engage in full-scale production, necessitating the investment of $1,500 million.

The marketing tests add a layer of complexity to the analysis. Our previous work on the example assumed that the marketing tests had already proved successful. How do we analyze whether we want to go ahead with the marketing tests in the first place? This is where decision trees come in.

To recap, SEC faces two decisions, both of which are represented in Figure 8.8. First the firm must decide whether to go ahead with the marketing tests. And if the tests are performed, the firm must decide whether the results of the tests warrant full-scale production.

The important point here, as we will see, is that decision trees answer the two questions in *reverse* order. So let's work backward, first considering what to do with the results of the tests, which can be either successful or unsuccessful.

Assume tests have been successful (75 percent probability). Table 8.1 tells us that full-scale production will cost $1,500 million and will generate an annual cash flow of $900 million for five years, yielding an NPV of:

$$= -\$1,500 + \sum_{t=1}^{5} \frac{\$900}{(1.15)^t}$$
$$= -\$1,500 + \$900 \times A_{0.15}^5$$
$$= \$1.517$$

Because the NPV is positive, successful marketing tests should lead to full-scale production. (Note that the NPV is calculated as of year 1, the time at which the investment of $1,500 million is made. Later we will discount this number back to year 0, when the decision on test marketing is to be made.)

Assume tests have not been successful (25 percent probability). Here, SEC's $1,500 million investment would produce an NPV of −$3,611 million, calculated as of year 1. (To save space, we will not provide the raw numbers leading to this calculation.) Because the NPV here is negative, SEC will not want full-scale production if the marketing tests are unsuccessful.

Decision on marketing tests. Now we know what to do with the results of the marketing tests. Let's use these results to move back one year. That is, we now want to figure out whether SEC should invest $100 million for the test marketing costs in the first place.

The expected payoff evaluated at date 1 (in millions) is:

$$
\begin{aligned}
\text{Expected payoff} &= \begin{pmatrix} \text{Probability} \\ \text{of} \\ \text{success} \end{pmatrix} \times \begin{pmatrix} \text{Payoff} \\ \text{if} \\ \text{successful} \end{pmatrix} + \begin{pmatrix} \text{Probability} \\ \text{of} \\ \text{failure} \end{pmatrix} \times \begin{pmatrix} \text{Payoff} \\ \text{if} \\ \text{failure} \end{pmatrix} \\
&= (0.75 \times \$1,517) + (0.25 \times \$0) \\
&= \$1,138
\end{aligned}
$$

The NPV of testing computed at date 0 (in millions) is:

$$
\begin{aligned}
\text{NPV} &= -\$100 + \frac{\$1,138}{1.15} \\
&= \$890
\end{aligned}
$$

Because the NPV is positive, the firm should test the market for solar-powered jet engines.

Warning We have used a discount rate of 15 percent for both the testing and the investment decisions. Perhaps a higher discount rate should have been used for the initial test marketing decision, which is likely to be riskier than the investment decision.

Recap As mentioned above, the analysis is graphed in Figure 8.8. As can be seen from the figure, SEC must make the following two decisions:

1. Whether to develop and test the solar-powered jet engine.
2. Whether to invest for full-scale production following the results of the test.

Using a decision tree, we answered the second question before we answered the first one.

Decision trees represent the best approach to solving SEC's problem, given the information presented so far in the text. However, we will examine a more sophisticated approach to valuing options in a later chapter. Though this approach was first used to value financial options traded on organized option exchanges, it can be used to value real options as well.

Summary and Conclusions

This chapter discussed a number of practical applications of capital budgeting.

1. Though NPV is the best capital budgeting approach conceptually, it has been criticized in practice for giving managers a false sense of security. Sensitivity analysis shows NPV under varying assumptions, giving managers a better feel for the project's risks. Unfortunately sensitivity analysis modifies only one variable at a time, but many variables are likely to vary together in the real world. Scenario analysis examines a project's performance under different scenarios (such as war breaking out or oil prices skyrocketing). Finally, managers want to know how bad forecasts must be before a project loses money. Break-even analysis calculates the sales figure at which the project breaks even. Though break-even analysis is frequently performed on an accounting profit basis, we suggest that a net present value basis is more appropriate.

2. Monte Carlo simulation begins with a model of the firm's cash flows, based on both the interactions between different variables and the movement of each individual variable over time. Random sampling generates a distribution of these cash flows for each period, leading to a net present value calculation.

3. We analyzed the hidden options in capital budgeting, such as the option to expand, the option to abandon, and timing options.

4. Decision trees represent an approach for valuing projects with these hidden, or real, options.

Concept Questions

1. **Forecasting Risk**   What is forecasting risk? In general, would the degree of forecasting risk be greater for a new product or a cost-cutting proposal? Why?

2. **Sensitivity Analysis and Scenario Analysis**   What is the essential difference between sensitivity analysis and scenario analysis?

3. **Marginal Cash Flows**   A coworker claims that looking at all this marginal this and incremental that is just a bunch of nonsense, and states, "Listen, if our average revenue doesn't exceed our average cost, then we will have a negative cash flow, and we will go broke!" How do you respond?

4. **Break-Even Point**   As a shareholder of a firm that is contemplating a new project, would you be more concerned with the accounting break-even point, the cash break-even point (the point at which operating cash flow is zero), or the financial break-even point? Why?

5. **Break-Even Point**   Assume a firm is considering a new project that requires an initial investment and has equal sales and costs over its life. Will the project reach the accounting, cash, or financial break-even point first? Which will it reach next? Last? Will this order always apply?

6. **Real Options**   Why does traditional NPV analysis tend to underestimate the true value of a capital budgeting project?

7. **Real Options**   The Mango Republic has just liberalized its markets and is now permitting foreign investors. Tesla Manufacturing has analyzed starting a project in the country and has determined that the project has a negative NPV. Why might the company go ahead with the project? What type of option is most likely to add value to this project?

8. **Sensitivity Analysis and Breakeven**   How does sensitivity analysis interact with break-even analysis?

www.mhhe.com/rwj

9. **Option to Wait** An option can often have more than one source of value. Consider a logging company. The company can log the timber today or wait another year (or more) to log the timber. What advantages would waiting one year potentially have?

10. **Project Analysis** You are discussing a project analysis with a coworker. The project involves real options, such as expanding the project if successful, or abandoning the project if it fails. Your coworker makes the following statement: "This analysis is ridiculous. We looked at expanding or abandoning the project in two years, but there are many other options we should consider. For example, we could expand in one year, and expand further in two years. Or we could expand in one year, and abandon the project in two years. There are too many options for us to examine. Because of this, anything this analysis would give us is worthless." How would you evaluate this statement? Considering that with any capital budgeting project there are an infinite number of real options, when do you stop the option analysis on an individual project?

Questions and Problems

BASIC
(Questions 1–10)

1. **Sensitivity Analysis and Break-Even Point** We are evaluating a project that costs $896,000, has an eight-year life, and has no salvage value. Assume that depreciation is straight-line to zero over the life of the project. Sales are projected at 100,000 units per year. Price per unit is $38, variable cost per unit is $25, and fixed costs are $900,000 per year. The tax rate is 35 percent, and we require a 15 percent return on this project.
   a. Calculate the accounting break-even point.
   b. Calculate the base-case cash flow and NPV. What is the sensitivity of NPV to changes in the sales figure? Explain what your answer tells you about a 500-unit decrease in projected sales.
   c. What is the sensitivity of OCF to changes in the variable cost figure? Explain what your answer tells you about a $1 decrease in estimated variable costs.

2. **Scenario Analysis** In the previous problem, suppose the projections given for price, quantity, variable costs, and fixed costs are all accurate to within ±10 percent. Calculate the best-case and worst-case NPV figures.

3. **Calculating Breakeven** In each of the following cases, find the unknown variable. Ignore taxes.

Accounting Breakeven	Unit Price	Unit Variable Cost	Fixed Costs	Depreciation
130,200	$41	$30	$ 820,000	?
135,000	?	56	3,200,000	$1,150,000
5,478	105	?	160,000	105,000

4. **Financial Breakeven** L.J.'s Toys Inc. just purchased a $200,000 machine to produce toy cars. The machine will be fully depreciated by the straight-line method over its five-year economic life. Each toy sells for $25. The variable cost per toy is $5, and the firm incurs fixed costs of $350,000 each year. The corporate tax rate for the company is 25 percent. The appropriate discount rate is 12 percent. What is the financial break-even point for the project?

5. **Option to Wait** Your company is deciding whether to invest in a new machine. The new machine will increase cash flow by $280,000 per year. You believe the technology used in the machine has a 10-year life; in other words, no matter when you purchase the machine, it will be obsolete 10 years from today. The machine is currently priced at $1,500,000. The cost of the machine will decline by $125,000 per year until it reaches $1,000,000, where it will remain. If your required return is 12 percent, should you purchase the machine? If so, when should you purchase it?

Part II   Valuation and Capital Budgeting

6.   **Decision Trees**   Ang Electronics, Inc., has developed a new DVDR. If the DVDR is successful, the present value of the payoff (when the product is brought to market) is $20 million. If the DVDR fails, the present value of the payoff is $5 million. If the product goes directly to market, there is a 50 percent chance of success. Alternatively, Ang can delay the launch by one year and spend $2 million to test market the DVDR. Test marketing would allow the firm to improve the product and increase the probability of success to 75 percent. The appropriate discount rate is 15 percent. Should the firm conduct test marketing?

7.   **Decision Trees**   The manager for a growing firm is considering the launch of a new product. If the product goes directly to market, there is a 50 percent chance of success. For $120,000 the manager can conduct a focus group that will increase the product's chance of success to 70 percent. Alternatively, the manager has the option to pay a consulting firm $400,000 to research the market and refine the product. The consulting firm successfully launches new products 90 percent of the time. If the firm successfully launches the product, the payoff will be $1.2 million. If the product is a failure, the NPV is zero. Which action will result in the highest expected payoff to the firm?

8.   **Decision Trees**   B&B has a new baby powder ready to market. If the firm goes directly to the market with the product, there is only a 55 percent chance of success. However, the firm can conduct customer segment research, which will take a year and cost $1 million. By going through research, B&B will be able to better target potential customers and will increase the probability of success to 70 percent. If successful, the baby powder will bring a present value profit (at time of initial selling) of $30 million. If unsuccessful, the present value payoff is only $3 million. Should the firm conduct customer segment research or go directly to market? The appropriate discount rate is 15 percent.

9.   **Financial Break-Even Analysis**   You are considering investing in a company that cultivates abalone for sale to local restaurants. Use the following information:

Sales price per abalone	= $2.00
Variable costs per abalone	= $.72
Fixed costs per year	= $340,000
Depreciation per year	= $20,000
Tax rate	= 35%

The discount rate for the company is 15 percent, the initial investment in equipment is $140,000, and the project's economic life is seven years. Assume the equipment is depreciated on a straight-line basis over the project's life.
a. What is the accounting break-even level for the project?
b. What is the financial break-even level for the project?

10.   **Financial Breakeven**   Niko has purchased a brand new machine to produce its High Flight line of shoes. The machine has an economic life of five years. The depreciation schedule for the machine is straight-line with no salvage value. The machine costs $300,000. The sales price per pair of shoes is $60, while the variable cost is $8. $100,000 of fixed costs per year are attributed to the machine. Assume that the corporate tax rate is 34 percent and the appropriate discount rate is 8 percent. What is the financial break-even point?

INTERMEDIATE (Questions 11–25)

11.   **Break-Even Intuition**   Consider a project with a required return of R percent that costs $\$I$ and will last for N years. The project uses straight-line depreciation to zero over the N-year life; there are neither salvage value nor net working capital requirements.
a. At the accounting break-even level of output, what is the IRR of this project? The payback period? The NPV?
b. At the cash break-even level of output, what is the IRR of this project? The payback period? The NPV?
c. At the financial break-even level of output, what is the IRR of this project? The payback period? The NPV?

12. **Sensitivity Analysis**   Consider a four-year project with the following information: initial fixed asset investment = $420,000; straight-line depreciation to zero over the four-year life; zero salvage value; price = $28; variable costs = $19; fixed costs = $190,000; quantity sold = 110,000 units; tax rate = 34 percent. How sensitive is OCF to changes in quantity sold?

13. **Project Analysis**   You are considering a new product launch. The project will cost $720,000, have a four-year life, and have no salvage value; depreciation is straight-line to zero. Sales are projected at 190 units per year; price per unit will be $21,000; variable cost per unit will be $15,000; and fixed costs will be $225,000 per year. The required return on the project is 15 percent, and the relevant tax rate is 35 percent.

    a. Based on your experience, you think the unit sales, variable cost, and fixed cost projections given here are probably accurate to within ±10 percent. What are the upper and lower bounds for these projections? What is the base-case NPV? What are the best-case and worst-case scenarios?

    b. Evaluate the sensitivity of your base-case NPV to changes in fixed costs.

    c. What is the accounting break-even level of output for this project?

14. **Project Analysis**   McGilla Golf has decided to sell a new line of golf clubs. The clubs will sell for $700 per set and have a variable cost of $320 per set. The company has spent $150,000 for a marketing study that determined the company will sell 55,000 sets per year for seven years. The marketing study also determined that the company will lose sales of 13,000 sets of its high-priced clubs. The high-priced clubs sell at $1,100 and have variable costs of $600. The company will also increase sales of its cheap clubs by 10,000 sets. The cheap clubs sell for $400 and have variable costs of $180 per set. The fixed costs each year will be $7,500,000. The company has also spent $1,000,000 on research and development for the new clubs. The plant and equipment required will cost $18,200,000 and will be depreciated on a straight-line basis. The new clubs will also require an increase in net working capital of $950,000 that will be returned at the end of the project. The tax rate is 40 percent, and the cost of capital is 14 percent. Calculate the payback period, the NPV, and the IRR.

15. **Scenario Analysis**   In the previous problem, you feel that the values are accurate to within only ±10 percent. What are the best-case and worst-case NPVs? (*Hint:* The price and variable costs for the two existing sets of clubs are known with certainty; only the sales gained or lost are uncertain.)

16. **Sensitivity Analysis**   McGilla Golf would like to know the sensitivity of NPV to changes in the price of the new clubs and the quantity of new clubs sold. What is the sensitivity of the NPV to each of these variables?

17. **Abandonment Value**   We are examining a new project. We expect to sell 7,000 units per year at $60 net cash flow apiece for the next 10 years. In other words, the annual operating cash flow is projected to be $60 × 7,000 = $420,000. The relevant discount rate is 16 percent, and the initial investment required is $1,800,000.

    a. What is the base-case NPV?

    b. After the first year, the project can be dismantled and sold for $1,400,000. If expected sales are revised based on the first year's performance, when would it make sense to abandon the investment? In other words, at what level of expected sales would it make sense to abandon the project?

    c. Explain how the $1,400,000 abandonment value can be viewed as the opportunity cost of keeping the project in one year.

18. **Abandonment**   In the previous problem, suppose you think it is likely that expected sales will be revised upward to 9,000 units if the first year is a success and revised downward to 4,000 units if the first year is not a success.

    a. If success and failure are equally likely, what is the NPV of the project? Consider the possibility of abandonment in answering.

    b. What is the value of the option to abandon?

19. **Abandonment and Expansion**   In the previous problem, suppose the scale of the project can be doubled in one year in the sense that twice as many units can be produced and sold.

Naturally, expansion would be desirable only if the project were a success. This implies that if the project is a success, projected sales after expansion will be 18,000. Again assuming that success and failure are equally likely, what is the NPV of the project? Note that abandonment is still an option if the project is a failure. What is the value of the option to expand?

20. **Break-Even Analysis**   Your buddy comes to you with a sure-fire way to make some quick money and help pay off your student loans. His idea is to sell T-shirts with the words "I get" on them. "You get it?" He says, "You see all those bumper stickers and T-shirts that say 'got milk' or 'got surf.' So this says, 'I get.' It's funny! All we have to do is buy a used silk screen press for $2,000 and we are in business!" Assume there are no fixed costs, and you depreciate the $2,000 in the first period. Taxes are 30 percent.

    a. What is the accounting break-even point if each shirt costs $8 to make and you can sell them for $10 apiece?

    Now assume one year has passed and you have sold 5,000 shirts! You find out that the Dairy Farmers of America have copyrighted the "got milk" slogan and are requiring you to pay $10,000 to continue operations. You expect this craze will last for another three years and that your discount rate is 12 percent.

    b. What is the financial break-even point for your enterprise now?

21. **Decision Trees**   Young screenwriter Carl Draper has just finished his first script. It has action, drama, and humor, and he thinks it will be a blockbuster. He takes the script to every motion picture studio in town and tries to sell it but to no avail. Finally, ACME studios offers to buy the script for either (a) $5,000 or (b) 1 percent of the movie's profits. There are two decisions the studio will have to make. First is to decide if the script is good or bad, and second if the movie is good or bad. First, there is a 90 percent chance that the script is bad. If it is bad, the studio does nothing more and throws the script out. If the script is good, they will shoot the movie. After the movie is shot, the studio will review it, and there is a 70 percent chance that the movie is bad. If the movie is bad, the movie will not be promoted and will not turn a profit. If the movie is good, the studio will promote heavily; the average profit for this type of movie is $10 million. Carl rejects the $5,000 and says he wants the 1 percent of profits. Was this a good decision by Carl?

22. **Accounting Breakeven**   Samuelson, Inc., has just purchased a $600,000 machine to produce calculators. The machine will be fully depreciated by the straight-line method over its economic life of five years and will produce 20,000 calculators each year. The variable production cost per calculator is $15, and total fixed costs are $900,000 per year. The corporate tax rate for the company is 30 percent. For the firm to break even in terms of accounting profit, how much should the firm charge per calculator?

23. **Abandonment Decisions**   Allied Products, Inc., is considering a new product launch. The firm expects to have an annual operating cash flow of $25 million for the next 10 years. Allied Products uses a discount rate of 20 percent for new product launches. The initial investment is $100 million. Assume that the project has no salvage value at the end of its economic life.

    a. What is the NPV of the new product?

    b. After the first year, the project can be dismantled and sold for $50 million. If the estimates of remaining cash flows are revised based on the first year's experience, at what level of expected cash flows does it make sense to abandon the project?

24. **Expansion Decisions**   Applied Nanotech is thinking about introducing a new surface cleaning machine. The marketing department has come up with the estimate that Applied Nanotech can sell 10 units per year at $.3 million net cash flow per unit for the next five years. The engineering department has come up with the estimate that developing the machine will take a $10 million initial investment. The finance department has estimated that a 25 percent discount rate should be used.

    a. What is the base-case NPV?

    b. If unsuccessful, after the first year the project can be dismantled and will have an aftertax salvage value of $5 million. Also, after the first year, expected cash flows will be revised up to 20 units per year or to 0 units per year, with equal probability. What is the revised NPV?

Chapter 8 Risk Analysis, Real Options, and Capital Budgeting | **253**

25. **Scenario Analysis** You are the financial analyst for a tennis racket manufacturer. The company is considering using a graphitelike material in its tennis rackets. The company has estimated the information in the following table about the market for a racket with the new material. The company expects to sell the racket for five years. The equipment required for the project has no salvage value. The required return for projects of this type is 13 percent, and the company has a 40 percent tax rate. Should you recommend the project?

	Pessimistic	Expected	Optimistic
Market size	110,000	120,000	130,000
Market share	22%	25%	27%
Selling price	$ 115	$ 120	$ 125
Variable costs per unit	$ 72	$ 70	$ 68
Fixed costs per year	$ 850,000	$ 800,000	$ 750,000
Initial investment	$1,500,000	$1,500,000	$1,500,000

CHALLENGE
(Questions 26–30)

26. **Scenario Analysis** Consider a project to supply Detroit with 40,000 tons of machine screws annually for automobile production. You will need an initial $1,700,000 investment in threading equipment to get the project started; the project will last for five years. The accounting department estimates that annual fixed costs will be $450,000 and that variable costs should be $210 per ton; accounting will depreciate the initial fixed asset investment straight-line to zero over the five-year project life. It also estimates a salvage value of $500,000 after dismantling costs. The marketing department estimates that the automakers will let the contract at a selling price of $230 per ton. The engineering department estimates you will need an initial net working capital investment of $450,000. You require a 13 percent return and face a marginal tax rate of 38 percent on this project.
    a. What is the estimated OCF for this project? The NPV? Should you pursue this project?
    b. Suppose you believe that the accounting department's initial cost and salvage value projections are accurate only to within ±15 percent; the marketing department's price estimate is accurate only to within ±10 percent; and the engineering department's net working capital estimate is accurate only to within ±5 percent. What is your worst-case scenario for this project? Your best-case scenario? Do you still want to pursue the project?

27. **Sensitivity Analysis** In Problem 26, suppose you're confident about your own projections, but you're a little unsure about Detroit's actual machine screw requirement. What is the sensitivity of the project OCF to changes in the quantity supplied? What about the sensitivity of NPV to changes in quantity supplied? Given the sensitivity number you calculated, is there some minimum level of output below which you wouldn't want to operate? Why?

28. **Abandonment Decisions** Consider the following project for Hand Clapper, Inc. The company is considering a four-year project to manufacture clap-command garage door openers. This project requires an initial investment of $8 million that will be depreciated straight-line to zero over the project's life. An initial investment in net working capital of $2 million is required to support spare parts inventory; this cost is fully recoverable whenever the project ends. The company believes it can generate $7 million in pretax revenues with $3 million in total pretax operating costs. The tax rate is 38 percent, and the discount rate is 16 percent. The market value of the equipment over the life of the project is as follows:

Year	Market Value ($ millions)
1	$6.50
2	6.00
3	3.00
4	0.00

a. Assuming Hand Clapper operates this project for four years, what is the NPV?

b. Now compute the project NPVs assuming the project is abandoned after only one year, after two years, and after three years. What economic life for this project maximizes its value to the firm? What does this problem tell you about not considering abandonment possibilities when evaluating projects?

29. **Abandonment Decisions** M.V.P. Games, Inc., has hired you to perform a feasibility study of a new video game that requires a $4 million initial investment. M.V.P. expects a total annual operating cash flow of $750,000 for the next 10 years. The relevant discount rate is 10 percent. Cash flows occur at year-end.

a. What is the NPV of the new video game?

b. After one year, the estimate of remaining annual cash flows will be revised either upward to $1.5 million or downward to $120,000. Each revision has an equal probability of occurring. At that time, the video game project can be sold for $800,000. What is the revised NPV given that the firm can abandon the project after one year?

30. **Financial Breakeven** The Cornchopper Company is considering the purchase of a new harvester. Cornchopper has hired you to determine the break-even purchase price in terms of present value of the harvester. This break-even purchase price is the price at which the project's NPV is zero. Base your analysis on the following facts:

- The new harvester is not expected to affect revenues, but pretax operating expenses will be reduced by $10,000 per year for 10 years.
- The old harvester is now 5 years old, with 10 years of its scheduled life remaining. It was originally purchased for $45,000 and has been depreciated by the straight-line method.
- The old harvester can be sold for $20,000 today.
- The new harvester will be depreciated by the straight-line method over its 10-year life.
- The corporate tax rate is 34 percent.
- The firm's required rate of return is 15 percent.
- The initial investment, the proceeds from selling the old harvester, and any resulting tax effects occur immediately.
- All other cash flows occur at year-end.
- The market value of each harvester at the end of its economic life is zero.

Bunyan Lumber, LLC

Bunyan Lumber, LLC, harvests timber and delivers logs to timber mills for sale. The company was founded 70 years ago by Pete Bunyan. The current CEO is Paula Bunyan, the granddaughter of the founder. The company is currently evaluating a 5,000-acre forest it owns in Oregon. Paula has asked Steve Boles, the company's finance officer, to evaluate the project. Paula's concern is when the company should harvest the timber.

Lumber is sold by the company for its "pond value." Pond value is the amount a mill will pay for a log delivered to the mill location. The price paid for logs delivered to a mill is quoted in dollars per thousands of board feet (MBF), and the price depends on the grade of the logs. The forest Bunyan Lumber is evaluating was planted by the company 20 years ago and is made up entirely of Douglas fir trees. The table here shows the current price per MBF for the three grades of timber the company feels will come from the stand:

Timber Grade	Price Per MBF
1P	$1,050
2P	925
3P	770

Ross–Westerfield–Jaffe:
Corporate Finance, Eighth
Edition

II. Valuation and Capital
Budgeting

8. Risk Analysis, Real
Options, and Capital
Budgeting

© The McGraw–Hill
Companies, 2008

329

Steve believes that the pond value of lumber will increase at the inflation rate. The company is planning to thin the forest today, and it expects to realize a positive cash flow of $1,000 per acre from thinning. The thinning is done to increase the growth rate of the remaining trees, and it is always done 20 years following a planting.

The major decision the company faces is when to log the forest. When the company logs the forest, it will immediately replant saplings, which will allow for a future harvest. The longer the forest is allowed to grow, the larger the harvest becomes per acre. Additionally, an older forest has a higher grade of timber. Steve has compiled the following table with the expected harvest per acre in thousands of board feet, along with the breakdown of the timber grades:

Years from Today to Begin Harvest	Harvest (MBF) Per Acre	Timber Grade		
		1P	2P	3P
20	6	10%	40%	50%
25	7.6	12	42	46
30	9	15	42	43
35	10	16	43	41

The company expects to lose 5 percent of the timber it cuts due to defects and breakage.

The forest will be clear-cut when the company harvests the timber. This method of harvesting allows for faster growth of replanted trees. All of the harvesting, processing, replanting, and transportation are to be handled by subcontractors hired by Bunyan Lumber. The cost of the logging is expected to be $140 per MBF. A road system has to be constructed and is expected to cost $50 per MBF on average. Sales preparation and administrative costs, excluding office overhead costs, are expected to be $18 per MBF.

As soon as the harvesting is complete, the company will reforest the land. Reforesting costs include the following:

	Per Acre Cost
Excavator piling	$150
Broadcast burning	300
Site preparation	145
Planting costs	225

All costs are expected to increase at the inflation rate.

Assume all cash flows occur at the year of harvest. For example, if the company begins harvesting the timber 20 years from today, the cash flow from the harvest will be received 20 years from today. When the company logs the land, it will immediately replant the land with new saplings. The harvest period chosen will be repeated for the foreseeable future. The company's nominal required return is 10 percent, and the inflation rate is expected to be 3.7 percent per year. Bunyan Lumber has a 35 percent tax rate.

Clear-cutting is a controversial method of forest management. To obtain the necessary permits, Bunyan Lumber has agreed to contribute to a conservation fund every time it harvests the lumber. If the company harvested the forest today, the required contribution would be $100,000. The company has agreed that the required contribution will grow by 3.2 percent per year. When should the company harvest the forest?

CHAPTER 8
RISK ANALYSIS, REAL OPTIONS, AND CAPITAL BUDGETING

Answers to Concepts Review and Critical Thinking Questions

1. Forecasting risk is the risk that a poor decision is made because of errors in projected cash flows. The danger is greatest with a new product because the cash flows are probably harder to predict.

2. With a sensitivity analysis, one variable is examined over a broad range of values. With a scenario analysis, all variables are examined for a limited range of values.

3. It is true that if average revenue is less than average cost, the firm is losing money. This much of the statement is therefore correct. At the margin, however, accepting a project with marginal revenue in excess of its marginal cost clearly acts to increase operating cash flow.

4. From the shareholder perspective, the financial break-even point is the most important. A project can exceed the accounting and cash break-even points but still be below the financial break-even point. This causes a reduction in shareholder (your) wealth.

5. The project will reach the cash break-even first, the accounting break-even next and finally the financial break-even. For a project with an initial investment and sales aftewardr, this ordering will always apply. The cash break-even is achieved first since it excludes depreciation. The accounting break-even is next since it includes depreciation. Finally, the financial break-even, which includes the time value of money, is achieved.

6. Traditional NPV analysis is often too conservative because it ignores profitable options such as the ability to expand the project if it is profitable, or abandon the project if it is unprofitable. The option to alter a project when it has already been accepted has a value, which increases the NPV of the project.

7. The type of option most likely to affect the decision is the option to expand. If the country just liberalized its markets, there is likely the potential for growth. First entry into a market, whether an entirely new market, or with a new product, can give a company name recognition and market share. This may make it more difficult for competitors entering the market.

8. Sensitivity analysis can determine how the financial break-even point changes when some factors (such as fixed costs, variable costs, or revenue) change.

9. There are two sources of value with this decision to wait. Potentially, the price of the timber can potentially increase, and the amount of timber will almost definitely increase, barring a natural catastrophe or forest fire. The option to wait for a logging company is quite valuable, and companies in the industry have models to estimate the future growth of a forest depending on its age.

10. When the additional analysis has a negative NPV. Since the additional analysis is likely to occur almost immediately, this means when the benefits of the additional analysis outweigh the costs. The benefits of the additional analysis are the reduction in the possibility of making a bad decision. Of course, the additional benefits are often difficult, if not impossible, to measure, so much of this decision is based on experience.

Solutions to Questions and Problems

NOTE: All end-of-chapter problems were solved using a spreadsheet. Many problems require multiple steps. Due to space and readability constraints, when these intermediate steps are included in this solutions manual, rounding may appear to have occurred. However, the final answer for each problem is found without rounding during any step in the problem.

Basic

1. *a.* To calculate the accounting breakeven, we first need to find the depreciation for each year. The depreciation is:

Depreciation = $896,000/8
Depreciation = $112,000 per year

And the accounting breakeven is:

Q_A = ($900,000 + 112,000)/($38 – 25)
Q_A = 77,846 units

b. We will use the tax shield approach to calculate the OCF. The OCF is:

OCF_{base} = [(P – v)Q – FC](1 – t_c) + t_cD
OCF_{base} = [($38 – 25)(100,000) – $900,000](0.65) + 0.35($112,000)
OCF_{base} = $299,200

Now we can calculate the NPV using our base-case projections. There is no salvage value or NWC, so the NPV is:

NPV_{base} = –$896,000 + $299,200(PVIFA$_{15\%,8}$)
NPV_{base} = $446,606.60

To calculate the sensitivity of the NPV to changes in the quantity sold, we will calculate the NPV at a different quantity. We will use sales of 105,000 units. The NPV at this sales level is:

OCF_{new} = [($38 – 25)(105,000) – $900,000](0.65) + 0.35($112,000)
OCF_{new} = $341,450

And the NPV is:

NPV_{new} = –$896,000 + $341,450(PVIFA$_{15\%,8}$)
NPV_{new} = $636,195.93

B-208 SOLUTIONS

So, the change in NPV for every unit change in sales is:

$\Delta NPV/\Delta S = (\$636,195.93 - 446,606.60)/(105,000 - 100,000)$
$\Delta NPV/\Delta S = +\$37.918$

If sales were to drop by 500 units, then NPV would drop by:

NPV drop = $\$37.918(500) = \$18,958.93$

You may wonder why we chose 105,000 units. Because it doesn't matter! Whatever sales number we use, when we calculate the change in NPV per unit sold, the ratio will be the same.

c. To find out how sensitive OCF is to a change in variable costs, we will compute the OCF at a variable cost of $24. Again, the number we choose to use here is irrelevant: We will get the same ratio of OCF to a one dollar change in variable cost no matter what variable cost we use. So, using the tax shield approach, the OCF at a variable cost of $24 is:

$OCF_{new} = [(\$38 - 24)(100,000) - 900,000](0.65) + 0.35(\$112,000)$
$OCF_{new} = \$364,200$

So, the change in OCF for a $1 change in variable costs is:

$\Delta OCF/\Delta v = (\$299,200 - 364,200)/(\$25 - 24)$
$\Delta OCF/\Delta v = -\$65,000$

If variable costs decrease by $1 then, OCF would increase by $65,000

2. We will use the tax shield approach to calculate the OCF for the best- and worst-case scenarios. For the best-case scenario, the price and quantity increase by 10 percent, so we will multiply the base case numbers by 1.1, a 10 percent increase. The variable and fixed costs both decrease by 10 percent, so we will multiply the base case numbers by .9, a 10 percent decrease. Doing so, we get:

$OCF_{best} = \{[(\$38)(1.1) - (\$25)(0.9)](100K)(1.1) - \$900K(0.9)\}(0.65) + 0.35(\$112K)$
$OCF_{best} = \$892,650$

The best-case NPV is:

$NPV_{best} = -\$896,000 + \$892,650(PVIFA_{15\%,8})$
$NPV_{best} = \$3,109,607.54$

For the worst-case scenario, the price and quantity decrease by 10 percent, so we will multiply the base case numbers by .9, a 10 percent decrease. The variable and fixed costs both increase by 10 percent, so we will multiply the base case numbers by 1.1, a 10 percent increase. Doing so, we get:

$OCF_{worst} = \{[(\$38)(0.9) - (\$25)(1.1)](100K)(0.9) - \$900K(1.1)\}(0.65) + 0.35(\$112K)$
$OCF_{worst} = -\$212,350$

The worst-case NPV is:

$NPV_{worst} = -\$896,000 - \$212,350(PVIFA_{15\%,8})$
$NPV_{worst} = -\$1,848,882.72$

3. We can use the accounting breakeven equation:

$Q_A = (FC + D)/(P - v)$

to solve for the unknown variable in each case. Doing so, we find:

(1): $Q_A = 130,200 = (\$820,000 + D)/(\$41 - 30)$
     $D = \$612,200$

(2): $Q_A = 135,000 = (\$3.2M + 1.15M)/(P - \$56)$
     $P = \$88.22$

(3): $Q_A = 5,478 = (\$160,000 + 105,000)/(\$105 - v)$
     $v = \$56.62$

4. When calculating the financial breakeven point, we express the initial investment as an equivalent annual cost (EAC). Dividing the in initial investment by the seven-year annuity factor, discounted at 12 percent, the EAC of the initial investment is:

$EAC =$ Initial Investment $/ PVIFA_{12\%,5}$
$EAC = \$200,000 / 3.60478$
$EAC = \$55,481.95$

Note that this calculation solves for the annuity payment with the initial investment as the present value of the annuity. In other words:

$PVA = C(\{1 - [1/(1 + R)]^t\} / R)$
$\$200,000 = C\{[1 - (1/1.12)^5] / .12\}$
$C = \$55,481.95$

The annual depreciation is the cost of the equipment divided by the economic life, or:

Annual depreciation $= \$200,000 / 5$
Annual depreciation $= \$40,000$

Now we can calculate the financial breakeven point. The financial breakeven point for this project is:

$Q_F = [EAC + FC(1 - t_C) - Depreciation(t_C)] / [(P - VC)(1 - t_C)]$
$Q_F = [\$55,481.95 + \$350,000(1 - 0.25) - \$40,000(0.25)] / [(\$25 - 5)(1 - 0.25)]$
$Q_F = 20,532.13$ or about 20,532 units

5. If we purchase the machine today, the NPV is the cost plus the present value of the increased cash flows, so:

$NPV_0 = -\$1,500,000 + \$280,000(PVIFA_{12\%,10})$
$NPV_0 = \$82,062.45$

B-210 SOLUTIONS

We should not purchase the machine today. We would want to purchase the machine when the NPV is the highest. So, we need to calculate the NPV each year. The NPV each year will be the cost plus the present value of the increased cash savings. We must be careful, however. In order to make the correct decision, the NPV for each year must be taken to a common date. We will discount all of the NPVs to today. Doing so, we get:

Year 1: $NPV_1 = [-\$1,375,000 + \$280,000(PVIFA_{12\%,9})] / 1.12$
    $NPV_1 = \$104,383.88$

Year 2: $NPV_2 = [-\$1,250,000 + \$280,000(PVIFA_{12\%,8})] / 1.12^2$
    $NPV_2 = \$112,355.82$

Year 3: $NPV_3 = [-\$1,125,000 + \$280,000(PVIFA_{12\%,7})] / 1.12^3$
    $NPV_3 = \$108,796.91$

Year 4: $NPV_4 = [-\$1,000,000 + \$280,000(PVIFA_{12\%,6})] / 1.12^4$
    $NPV_4 = \$96,086.55$

Year 5: $NPV_5 = [-\$1,000,000 + \$280,000(PVIFA_{12\%,5})] / 1.12^5$
    $NPV_5 = \$5,298.26$

Year 6: $NPV_6 = [-\$1,000,000 + \$280,000(PVIFA_{12\%,4})] / 1.12^6$
    $NPV_6 = -\$75,762.72$

The company should purchase the machine two years from now when the NPV is the highest.

6. We need to calculate the NPV of the two options, go directly to market now, or utilize test marketing first. The NPV of going directly to market now is:

$NPV = C_{Success} (Prob.\ of\ Success) + C_{Failure} (Prob.\ of\ Failure)$
$NPV = \$20,000,000(0.50) + \$5,000,000(0.50)$
$NPV = \$12,500,000$

Now we can calculate the NPV of test marketing first. Test marketing requires a \$2 million cash outlay. Choosing the test marketing option will also delay the launch of the product by one year. Thus, the expected payoff is delayed by one year and must be discounted back to year 0.

$NPV = C_0 + \{[C_{Success} (Prob.\ of\ Success)] + [C_{Failure} (Prob.\ of\ Failure)]\} / (1 + R)^t$
$NPV = -\$2,000,000 + \{[\$20,000,000 (0.75)] + [\$5,000,000 (0.25)]\} / 1.15$
$NPV = \$12,130,434.78$

The company should go directly to market with the product since that option has the highest expected payoff.

7. We need to calculate the NPV of each option, and choose the option with the highest NPV. So, the NPV of going directly to market is:

$NPV = C_{Success} (Prob.\ of\ Success)$
$NPV = \$1,200,000 (0.50)$
$NPV = \$600,000$

The NPV of the focus group is:

NPV = C_0 + $C_{Success}$ (Prob. of Success)
NPV = –$120,000 + $1,200,000 (0.70)
NPV = $720,000

And the NPV of using the consulting firm is:

NPV = C_0 + $C_{Success}$ (Prob. of Success)
NPV = –$400,000 + $1,200,000 (0.90)
NPV = $680,000

The firm should conduct a focus group since that option has the highest NPV.

8. The company should analyze both options, and choose the option with the greatest NPV. So, if the company goes to market immediately, the NPV is:

NPV = $C_{Success}$ (Prob. of Success) + $C_{Failure}$ (Prob. of Failure)
NPV = $30,000,000(.55) + $3,000,000(.45)
NPV = $17,850,000.00

Customer segment research requires a $1 million cash outlay. Choosing the research option will also delay the launch of the product by one year. Thus, the expected payoff is delayed by one year and must be discounted back to year 0. So, the NPV of the customer segment research is:

NPV= C_0 + {[$C_{Success}$ (Prob. of Success)] + [$C_{Failure}$ (Prob. of Failure)]} / $(1 + R)^t$
NPV = –$1,000,000 + {[$30,000,000 (0.70)] + [$3,000,000 (0.30)]} / 1.15
NPV = $18,043,478.26

Graphically, the decision tree for the project is:

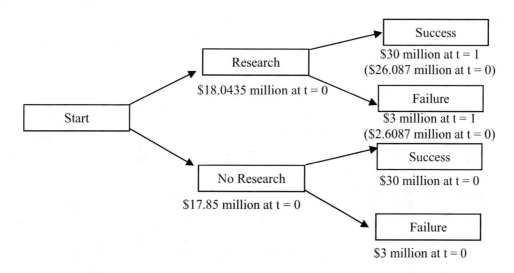

The company should undertake the market segment research since it has the largest NPV.

B-212 SOLUTIONS

9. *a.* The accounting breakeven is the aftertax sum of the fixed costs and depreciation charge divided by the aftertax contribution margin (selling price minus variable cost). So, the accounting breakeven level of sales is:

Q_A = [(FC + Depreciation)$(1 - t_C)$] / [$(P - VC)(1 - t_C)$]
Q_A = [($340,000 + $20,000) $(1 - 0.35)$] / [($2.00 - 0.72) $(1 - 0.35)$]
Q_A = 281,250.00

b. When calculating the financial breakeven point, we express the initial investment as an equivalent annual cost (EAC). Dividing the in initial investment by the seven-year annuity factor, discounted at 15 percent, the EAC of the initial investment is:

EAC = Initial Investment / $PVIFA_{15\%,7}$
EAC = $140,000 / 4.1604
EAC = $33,650.45

Note that this calculation solves for the annuity payment with the initial investment as the present value of the annuity. In other words:

$PVA = C(\{1 - [1/(1 + R)]^t\} / R)$
$\$140,000 = C\{[1 - (1/1.15)^7] / .15\}$
$C = \$33,650.45$

Now we can calculate the financial breakeven point. The financial breakeven point for this project is:

Q_F = [EAC + FC$(1 - t_C)$ – Depreciation(t_C)] / [$(P - VC)(1 - t_C)$]
Q_F = [$33,650.45 + $340,000(.65) – $20,000(.35)] / [($2 – 0.72) (.65)]
Q_F = 297,656.79 or about 297,657 units

10. When calculating the financial breakeven point, we express the initial investment as an equivalent annual cost (EAC). Dividing the in initial investment by the five-year annuity factor, discounted at 8 percent, the EAC of the initial investment is:

EAC = Initial Investment / $PVIFA_{8\%,5}$
EAC = $300,000 / 3.60478
EAC = $75,136.94

Note that this calculation solves for the annuity payment with the initial investment as the present value of the annuity. In other words:

$PVA = C(\{1 - [1/(1 + R)]^t\} / R)$
$\$300,000 = C\{[1 - (1/1.08)^5] / .08\}$
$C = \$75,136.94$

The annual depreciation is the cost of the equipment divided by the economic life, or:

Annual depreciation = $300,000 / 5
Annual depreciation = $60,000

Now we can calculate the financial breakeven point. The financial breakeven point for this project is:

Q_F = [EAC + FC(1 – t_C) – Depreciation(t_C)] / [(P – VC)(1 – t_C)]
Q_F = [$75,136.94 + $100,000(1 – 0.34) – $60,000(0.34)] / [($60 – 8) (1 – 0.34)]
Q_F = 3,517.98 or about 3,518 units

Intermediate

11. *a.* At the accounting breakeven, the IRR is zero percent since the project recovers the initial investment. The payback period is N years, the length of the project since the initial investment is exactly recovered over the project life. The NPV at the accounting breakeven is:

NPV = I [(1/N)(PVIFA$_{R\%,N}$) – 1]

b. At the cash breakeven level, the IRR is –100 percent, the payback period is negative, and the NPV is negative and equal to the initial cash outlay.

c. The definition of the financial breakeven is where the NPV of the project is zero. If this is true, then the IRR of the project is equal to the required return. It is impossible to state the payback period, except to say that the payback period must be less than the length of the project. Since the discounted cash flows are equal to the initial investment, the undiscounted cash flows are greater than the initial investment, so the payback must be less than the project life.

12. Using the tax shield approach, the OCF at 110,000 units will be:

OCF = [(P – v)Q – FC](1 – t_C) + t_C(D)
OCF = [($28 – 19)(110,000) – 190,000](0.66) + 0.34($420,000/4)
OCF = $563,700

We will calculate the OCF at 111,000 units. The choice of the second level of quantity sold is arbitrary and irrelevant. No matter what level of units sold we choose, we will still get the same sensitivity. So, the OCF at this level of sales is:

OCF = [($28 – 19)(111,000) – 190,000](0.66) + 0.34($420,000/4)
OCF = $569,640

The sensitivity of the OCF to changes in the quantity sold is:

Sensitivity = ΔOCF/ΔQ = ($569,640 – 563,700)/(111,000 – 110,000)
ΔOCF/ΔQ = +$5.94

OCF will increase by $5.94 for every additional unit sold.

13. *a.* The base-case, best-case, and worst-case values are shown below. Remember that in the best-case, sales and price increase, while costs decrease. In the worst-case, sales and price decrease, and costs increase.

Scenario	Unit sales	Variable cost	Fixed costs
Base	190	$15,000	$225,000
Best	209	$13,500	$202,500
Worst	171	$16,500	$247,500

B-214 SOLUTIONS

Using the tax shield approach, the OCF and NPV for the base case estimate are:

$OCF_{base} = [(\$21,000 - 15,000)(190) - \$225,000](0.65) + 0.35(\$720,000/4)$
$OCF_{base} = \$657,750$

$NPV_{base} = -\$720,000 + \$657,750(PVIFA_{15\%,4})$
$NPV_{base} = \$1,157,862.02$

The OCF and NPV for the worst case estimate are:

$OCF_{worst} = [(\$21,000 - 16,500)(171) - \$247,500](0.65) + 0.35(\$720,000/4)$
$OCF_{worst} = \$402,300$

$NPV_{worst} = -\$720,000 + \$402,300(PVIFA_{15\%,4})$
$NPV_{worst} = \$428,557.80$

And the OCF and NPV for the best case estimate are:

$OCF_{best} = [(\$21,000 - 13,500)(209) - \$202,500](0.65) + 0.35(\$720,000/4)$
$OCF_{best} = \$950,250$

$NPV_{best} = -\$720,000 + \$950,250(PVIFA_{15\%,4})$
$NPV_{best} = \$1,992,943.19$

b.   To calculate the sensitivity of the NPV to changes in fixed costs, we choose another level of fixed costs. We will use fixed costs of $230,000. The OCF using this level of fixed costs and the other base case values with the tax shield approach, we get:

$OCF = [(\$21,000 - 15,000)(190) - \$230,000](0.65) + 0.35(\$720,000/4)$
$OCF = \$654,500$

And the NPV is:

$NPV = -\$720,000 + \$654,500(PVIFA_{15\%,4})$
$NPV = \$1,148,583.34$

The sensitivity of NPV to changes in fixed costs is:

$\Delta NPV/\Delta FC = (\$1,157,862.02 - 1,148,583.34)/(\$225,000 - 230,000)$
$\Delta NPV/\Delta FC = -\$1.856$

For every dollar FC increase, NPV falls by $1.86.

c. The accounting breakeven is:

$$Q_A = (FC + D)/(P - v)$$
$$Q_A = [\$225{,}000 + (\$720{,}000/4)]/(\$21{,}000 - 15{,}000)$$
$$Q_A = 68$$

At the accounting breakeven, the DOL is:

$$DOL = 1 + FC/OCF$$
$$DOL = 1 + (\$225{,}000/\$180{,}000) = 2.25$$

For each 1% increase in unit sales, OCF will increase by 2.25%.

14. The marketing study and the research and development are both sunk costs and should be ignored. We will calculate the sales and variable costs first. Since we will lose sales of the expensive clubs and gain sales of the cheap clubs, these must be accounted for as erosion. The total sales for the new project will be:

Sales		
New clubs	$700 × 55,000 =	$38,500,000
Exp. clubs	$1,100 × (−13,000) =	−14,300,000
Cheap clubs	$400 × 10,000 =	4,000,000
		$28,200,000

For the variable costs, we must include the units gained or lost from the existing clubs. Note that the variable costs of the expensive clubs are an inflow. If we are not producing the sets any more, we will save these variable costs, which is an inflow. So:

Var. costs		
New clubs	−$320 × 55,000 =	−$17,600,000
Exp. clubs	−$600 × (−13,000) =	7,800,000
Cheap clubs	−$180 × 10,000 =	−1,800,000
		−$11,600,000

The pro forma income statement will be:

Sales	$28,200,000
Variable costs	11,600,000
Fixed costs	7,500,000
Depreciation	2,600,000
EBT	6,500,000
Taxes	2,600,000
Net income	$ 3,900,000

Using the bottom up OCF calculation, we get:

$$OCF = NI + Depreciation = \$3{,}900{,}000 + 2{,}600{,}000$$
$$OCF = \$6{,}500{,}000$$

B-216 SOLUTIONS

So, the payback period is:

Payback period = 2 + \$6.15M/\$6.5M
Payback period = 2.946 years

The NPV is:

$NPV = -\$18.2M - .95M + \$6.5M(PVIFA_{14\%,7}) + \$0.95M/1.14^7$
NPV = \$9,103,636.91

And the IRR is:

$IRR = -\$18.2M - .95M + \$6.5M(PVIFA_{IRR\%,7}) + \$0.95M/(1 + IRR)^7$
IRR = 28.24%

15. The upper and lower bounds for the variables are:

	Base Case	Lower Bound	Upper Bound
Unit sales (new)	55,000	49,500	60,500
Price (new)	\$700	\$630	\$770
VC (new)	\$320	\$288	\$352
Fixed costs	\$7,500,000	\$6,750,000	\$8,250,000
Sales lost (expensive)	13,000	11,700	14,300
Sales gained (cheap)	10,000	9,000	11,000

Best-case

We will calculate the sales and variable costs first. Since we will lose sales of the expensive clubs and gain sales of the cheap clubs, these must be accounted for as erosion. The total sales for the new project will be:

Sales
New clubs	$\$770 \times 60,500 =$	\$46,585,000
Exp. clubs	$\$1,100 \times (-11,700) =$	$-12,870,000$
Cheap clubs	$\$400 \times 11,000 =$	4,400,000
		\$38,115,000

For the variable costs, we must include the units gained or lost from the existing clubs. Note that the variable costs of the expensive clubs are an inflow. If we are not producing the sets any more, we will save these variable costs, which is an inflow. So:

Var. costs
New clubs	$\$288 \times 60,500 =$	\$17,424,000
Exp. clubs	$\$600 \times (-11,700) =$	$-7,020,000$
Cheap clubs	$\$180 \times 11,000 =$	1,980,000
		\$12,384,000

The pro forma income statement will be:

Sales	$38,115,000
Variable costs	12,384,000
Costs	6,750,000
Depreciation	2,600,000
EBT	16,381,000
Taxes	6,552,400
Net income	$9,828,600

Using the bottom up OCF calculation, we get:

OCF = Net income + Depreciation = $9,828,600 + 2,600,000
OCF = $12,428,600

And the best-case NPV is:

$NPV = -\$18.2M - .95M + \$12,428,600(PVIFA_{14\%,7}) + .95M/1.14^7$
NPV = $34,527,280.98

Worst-case

We will calculate the sales and variable costs first. Since we will lose sales of the expensive clubs and gain sales of the cheap clubs, these must be accounted for as erosion. The total sales for the new project will be:

Sales		
New clubs	$630 × 49,500 =	$31,185,000
Exp. clubs	$1,100 × (− 14,300) =	− 15,730,000
Cheap clubs	$400 × 9,000 =	3,600,000
		$19,055,000

For the variable costs, we must include the units gained or lost from the existing clubs. Note that the variable costs of the expensive clubs are an inflow. If we are not producing the sets any more, we will save these variable costs, which is an inflow. So:

Var. costs		
New clubs	$352 × 49,500 =	$17,424,000
Exp. clubs	$600 × (− 14,300) =	− 8,580,000
Cheap clubs	$180 × 9,000 =	1,620,000
		$10,464,000

B-218 SOLUTIONS

The pro forma income statement will be:

Sales	$19,055,000
Variable costs	10,464,000
Costs	8,250,000
Depreciation	2,600,000
EBT	– 2,259,000
Taxes	903,600 *assumes a tax credit
Net income	–$1,355,400

Using the bottom up OCF calculation, we get:

OCF = NI + Depreciation = –$1,355,400 + 2,600,000
OCF = $1,244,600

And the worst-case NPV is:

NPV = –$18.2M – .95M + $1,244,600(PVIFA$_{14\%,7}$) + .95M/1.14^7
NPV = –$13,433,120.34

16. To calculate the sensitivity of the NPV to changes in the price of the new club, we simply need to change the price of the new club. We will choose $750, but the choice is irrelevant as the sensitivity will be the same no matter what price we choose.

We will calculate the sales and variable costs first. Since we will lose sales of the expensive clubs and gain sales of the cheap clubs, these must be accounted for as erosion. The total sales for the new project will be:

Sales		
New clubs	$750 × 55,000 =	$41,250,000
Exp. clubs	$1,100 × (– 13,000) =	–14,300,000
Cheap clubs	$400 × 10,000 =	4,000,000
		$30,950,000

For the variable costs, we must include the units gained or lost from the existing clubs. Note that the variable costs of the expensive clubs are an inflow. If we are not producing the sets any more, we will save these variable costs, which is an inflow. So:

Var. costs		
New clubs	$320 × 55,000 =	$17,600,000
Exp. clubs	$600 × (–13,000) =	–7,800,000
Cheap clubs	$180 × 10,000 =	1,800,000
		$11,600,000

The pro forma income statement will be:

Sales	$30,950,000
Variable costs	11,600,000
Costs	7,500,000
Depreciation	2,600,000
EBT	9,250,000
Taxes	3,700,000
Net income	$ 5,550,000

Using the bottom up OCF calculation, we get:

OCF = NI + Depreciation = $5,550,000 + 2,600,000
OCF = $8,150,000

And the NPV is:

$$NPV = -\$18.2M - 0.95M + \$8.15M(PVIFA_{14\%,7}) + .95M/1.14^7$$
NPV = $16,179,339.89

So, the sensitivity of the NPV to changes in the price of the new club is:

$$\Delta NPV/\Delta P = (\$16,179,339.89 - 9,103,636.91)/(\$750 - 700)$$
$$\Delta NPV/\Delta P = \$141,514.06$$

For every dollar increase (decrease) in the price of the clubs, the NPV increases (decreases) by $141,514.06.

To calculate the sensitivity of the NPV to changes in the quantity sold of the new club, we simply need to change the quantity sold. We will choose 60,000 units, but the choice is irrelevant as the sensitivity will be the same no matter what quantity we choose.

We will calculate the sales and variable costs first. Since we will lose sales of the expensive clubs and gain sales of the cheap clubs, these must be accounted for as erosion. The total sales for the new project will be:

Sales		
New clubs	$700 × 60,000 =	$42,000,000
Exp. clubs	$1,100 × (− 13,000) =	−14,300,000
Cheap clubs	$400 × 10,000 =	4,000,000
		$31,700,000

B-220 SOLUTIONS

For the variable costs, we must include the units gained or lost from the existing clubs. Note that the variable costs of the expensive clubs are an inflow. If we are not producing the sets any more, we will save these variable costs, which is an inflow. So:

Var. costs		
New clubs	$320 × 60,000 =	$19,200,000
Exp. clubs	$600 × (–13,000) =	–7,800,000
Cheap clubs	$180 × 10,000 =	1,800,000
		$13,200,000

The pro forma income statement will be:

Sales	$31,700,000
Variable costs	13,200,000
Costs	7,500,000
Depreciation	2,600,000
EBT	8,400,000
Taxes	3,360,000
Net income	$ 5,040,000

Using the bottom up OCF calculation, we get:

OCF = NI + Depreciation = $5,040,000 + 2,600,000
OCF = $7,640,000

The NPV at this quantity is:

$$NPV = -\$18.2M - \$0.95M + \$7.64M(PVIFA_{14\%,7}) + \$0.95M/1.14^7$$
NPV = $13,992,304.43

So, the sensitivity of the NPV to changes in the quantity sold is:

$$\Delta NPV/\Delta Q = (\$13,992,304.43 - 9,103,636.91)/(60,000 - 55,000)$$
$$\Delta NPV/\Delta Q = \$977.73$$

For an increase (decrease) of one set of clubs sold per year, the NPV increases (decreases) by $977.73.

17. *a.* The base-case NPV is:

$$NPV = -\$1,800,000 + \$420,000(PVIFA_{16\%,10})$$
NPV = $229,955.54

Ross–Westerfield–Jaffe:
Corporate Finance, Eighth
Edition

II. Valuation and Capital
Budgeting

Answers for Chapter 8

© The McGraw–Hill
Companies, 2008

345

b. We would abandon the project if the cash flow from selling the equipment is greater than the present value of the future cash flows. We need to find the sale quantity where the two are equal, so:

$1,400,000 = ($60)Q(PVIFA$_{16\%,9}$)
Q = $1,400,000/[$60(4.6065)]
Q = 5,065

Abandon the project if Q < 5,065 units, because the NPV of abandoning the project is greater than the NPV of the future cash flows.

c. The $1,400,000 is the market value of the project. If you continue with the project in one year, you forego the $1,400,000 that could have been used for something else.

18. a. If the project is a success, present value of the future cash flows will be:

PV future CFs = $60(9,000)(PVIFA$_{16\%,9}$)
PV future CFs = $2,487,533.69

From the previous question, if the quantity sold is 4,000, we would abandon the project, and the cash flow would be $1,400,000. Since the project has an equal likelihood of success or failure in one year, the expected value of the project in one year is the average of the success and failure cash flows, plus the cash flow in one year, so:

Expected value of project at year 1 = [($2,487,533.69 + $1,400,000)/2] + $420,000
Expected value of project at year 1 = $2,363,766.85

The NPV is the present value of the expected value in one year plus the cost of the equipment, so:

NPV = –$1,800,000 + ($2,363,766.85)/1.16
NPV = $237,730.04

b. If we couldn't abandon the project, the present value of the future cash flows when the quantity is 4,000 will be:

PV future CFs = $60(4,000)(PVIFA$_{16\%,9}$)
PV future CFs = $1,105,570.53

The gain from the option to abandon is the abandonment value minus the present value of the cash flows if we cannot abandon the project, so:

Gain from option to abandon = $1,400,000 – 1,105,570.53
Gain from option to abandon = $294,429.47

We need to find the value of the option to abandon times the likelihood of abandonment. So, the value of the option to abandon today is:

Option value = (.50)($294,429.47)/1.16
Option value = $126,909.25

B-222 SOLUTIONS

19. If the project is a success, present value of the future cash flows will be:

PV future CFs = $60(18,000)(PVIFA$_{16\%,9}$)
PV future CFs = $4,975,067.39

If the sales are only 4,000 units, from Problem #14, we know we will abandon the project, with a value of $1,400,000. Since the project has an equal likelihood of success or failure in one year, the expected value of the project in one year is the average of the success and failure cash flows, plus the cash flow in one year, so:

Expected value of project at year 1 = [($4,975,067.39 + $1,400,000)/2] + $420,000
Expected value of project at year 1 = $3,607,533.69

The NPV is the present value of the expected value in one year plus the cost of the equipment, so:

NPV = –$1,800,000 + $3,607,533.69/1.16
NPV = $1,309,942.84

The gain from the option to expand is the present value of the cash flows from the additional units sold, so:

Gain from option to expand = $60(9,000)(PVIFA$_{16\%,9}$)
Gain from option to expand = $2,487,533.69

We need to find the value of the option to expand times the likelihood of expansion. We also need to find the value of the option to expand today, so:

Option value = (.50)($2,487,533.69)/1.16
Option value = $1,072,212.80

20. *a.* The accounting breakeven is the aftertax sum of the fixed costs and depreciation charge divided by the contribution margin (selling price minus variable cost). In this case, there are no fixed costs, and the depreciation is the entire price of the press in the first year. So, the accounting breakeven level of sales is:

Q_A = [(FC + Depreciation)(1 – t_C)] / [(P – VC)(1 – t_C)]
Q_A = [($0 + 2,000) (1 – 0.30)] / [($10 – 8) (1 – 0.30)]
Q_A = 1,000 units

b. When calculating the financial breakeven point, we express the initial investment as an equivalent annual cost (EAC). The initial investment is the $10,000 in licensing fees. Dividing the in initial investment by the three-year annuity factor, discounted at 12 percent, the EAC of the initial investment is:

EAC = Initial Investment / PVIFA$_{12\%,3}$
EAC = $10,000 / 2.4018
EAC = $4,163.49

Note, this calculation solves for the annuity payment with the initial investment as the present value of the annuity, in other words:

$PVA = C(\{1 - [1/(1 + R)]^t \} / R)$
$\$10,000 = C\{[1 - (1/1.12)^3] / .12\}$
$C = \$4,163.49$

Now we can calculate the financial breakeven point. Notice that there are no fixed costs or depreciation. The financial breakeven point for this project is:

$Q_F = [EAC + FC(1 - t_C) - Depreciation(t_C)] / [(P - VC)(1 - t_C)]$
$Q_F = (\$4,163.49 + 0 - 0) / [(\$10 - 8) (.70)]$
$Q_F = 2,973.92$ or about 2,974 units

21. The payoff from taking the lump sum is $5,000, so we need to compare this to the expected payoff from taking one percent of the profit. The decision tree for the movie project is:

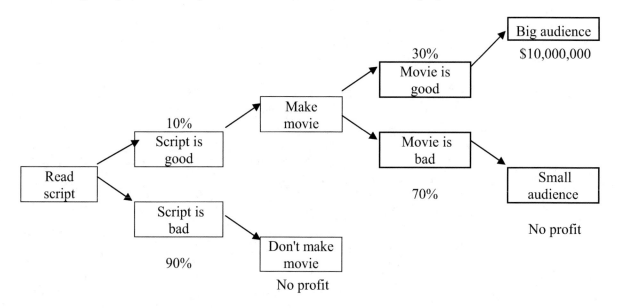

The value of one percent of the profits as follows. There is a 30 percent probability the movie is good, and the audience is big, so the expected value of this outcome is:

Value = $10,000,000 × .30
Value = $3,000,000

The value that the movie is good, and has a big audience, assuming the script is good is:

Value = $3,000,000 × .10
Value = $300,000

B-224 SOLUTIONS

This is the expected value for the studio, but the screenwriter will only receive one percent of this amount, so the payment to the screenwriter will be:

Payment to screenwriter = $300,000 × .01
Payment to screenwriter = $3,000

The screenwriter should take the upfront offer of $5,000.

22. Apply the accounting profit break-even point formula and solve for the sales price, P, that allows the firm to break even when producing 20,000 calculators. In order for the firm to break even, the revenues from the calculator sales must equal the total annual cost of producing the calculators. The depreciation charge each year will be:

Depreciation = Initial investment / Economic life
Depreciation = $600,000 / 5
Depreciation = $120,000 per year

Now we can solve the accounting break-even equation for the sales price at 20,000 units. The accounting break-even is the point at which the net income of the product is zero. So, solving the accounting break-even equation for the sales price, we get:

Q_A = [(FC + Depreciation) $(1 - t_C)$] / [(P − VC)$(1 - t_C)$]
20,000 = [($900,000 + 120,000)(1 − .30)] / [(P − 15)(1 − .30)]
P = $66

23. *a.* The NPV of the project is sum of the present value of the cash flows generated by the project. The cash flows from this project are an annuity, so the NPV is:

NPV = −$100,000,000 + $25,000,000(PVIFA$_{20\%,10}$)
NPV = $4,811,802.14

b. The company should abandon the project if the PV of the revised cash flows for the next nine years is less than the project's aftertax salvage value. Since the option to abandon the project occurs in year 1, discount the revised cash flows to year 1 as well. To determine the level of expected cash flows below which the company should abandon the project, calculate the equivalent annual cash flows the project must earn to equal the aftertax salvage value. We will solve for C_2, the revised cash flow beginning in year 2. So, the revised annual cash flow below which it makes sense to abandon the project is:

Aftertax salvage value = C_2(PVIFA$_{20\%,9}$)
$50,000,000 = C_2(PVIFA$_{20\%,9}$)
C_2 = $50,000,000 / PVIFA$_{20\%,9}$
C_2 = $12,403,973.08

24. *a.* The NPV of the project is sum of the present value of the cash flows generated by the project. The annual cash flow for the project is the number of units sold times the cash flow per unit, which is:

Annual cash flow = 10($300,000)
Annual cash flow = $3,000,000

The cash flows from this project are an annuity, so the NPV is:

NPV = –$10,000,000 + $3,000,000(PVIFA$_{25\%,5}$)
NPV = –$1,932,160.00

b. The company will abandon the project if unit sales are not revised upward. If the unit sales are revised upward, the aftertax cash flows for the project over the last four years will be:

New annual cash flow = 20($300,000)
New annual cash flow = $6,000,000

The NPV of the project will be the initial cost, plus the expected cash flow in year one based on 10 unit sales projection, plus the expected value of abandonment, plus the expected value of expansion. We need to remember that the abandonment value occurs in year 1, and the present value of the expansion cash flows are in year one, so each of these must be discounted back to today. So, the project NPV under the abandonment or expansion scenario is:

NPV = –$10,000,000 + $3,000,000 / 1.25 + .50($5,000,000) / 1.25
        + [.50($6,000,000)(PVIFA$_{25\%,4}$)] / 1.25
NPV = $67,840.00

25. To calculate the unit sales for each scenario, we multiply the market sales times the company's market share. We can then use the quantity sold to find the revenue each year, and the variable costs each year. After doing these calculations, we will construct the pro forma income statement for each scenario. We can then find the operating cash flow using the bottom up approach, which is net income plus depreciation. Doing so, we find:

	Pessimistic	*Expected*	*Optimistic*
Units per year	24,200	30,000	35,100
Revenue	$2,783,000	$3,600,000	$4,387,500
Variable costs	1,742,400	2,100,000	2,386,800
Fixed costs	850,000	800,000	750,000
Depreciation	300,000	300,000	300,000
EBT	–$109,400	$400,000	$950,700
Tax	–43,760	160,000	380,280
Net income	–$65,640	$240,000	$570,420
OCF	$234,360	$540,000	$870,420

B-226 SOLUTIONS

Note that under the pessimistic scenario, the taxable income is negative. We assumed a tax credit in the case. Now we can calculate the NPV under each scenario, which will be:

$NPV_{Pessimistic} = -\$1,500,000 + \$234,360(PVIFA_{13\%,5})$
$NPV = -\$675,701.68$

$NPV_{Expected} = -\$1,500,000 + \$540,000(PVIFA_{13\%,5})$
$NPV = \$399,304.88$

$NPV_{Optimistic} = -\$1,500,000 + \$870,420(PVIFA_{13\%,5})$
$NPV = \$1,561,468.43$

The NPV under the pessimistic scenario is negative, but the company should probably accept the project.

Challenge

26. *a.* Using the tax shield approach, the OCF is:

$OCF = [(\$230 - 210)(40,000) - \$450,000](0.62) + 0.38(\$1,700,000/5)$
$OCF = \$346,200$

And the NPV is:

$NPV = -\$1.7M - 450K + \$346,200(PVIFA_{13\%,5}) + [\$450K + \$500K(1 - .38)]/1.13^5$
$NPV = -\$519,836.99$

b. In the worst-case, the OCF is:

$OCF_{worst} = \{[(\$230)(0.9) - 210](40,000) - \$450,000\}(0.62) + 0.38(\$1,955,000/5)$
$OCF_{worst} = -\$204,820$

And the worst-case NPV is:

$NPV_{worst} = -\$1,955,000 - \$450,000(1.05) + -\$204,820(PVIFA_{13\%,5}) +$
$\qquad [\$450,000(1.05) + \$500,000(0.85)(1 - .38)]/1.13^5$
$NPV_{worst} = -\$2,748,427.99$

The best-case OCF is:

$OCF_{best} = \{[\$230(1.1) - 210](40,000) - \$450,000\}(0.62) + 0.38(\$1,445,000/5)$
$OCF_{best} = \$897,220$

And the best-case NPV is:

$NPV_{best} = -\$1,445,000 - \$450,000(0.95) + \$897,220(PVIFA_{13\%,5}) +$
$\qquad [\$450,000(0.95) + \$500,000(1.15)(1 - .38)]/1.13^5$
$NPV_{best} = \$1,708,754.02$

27. To calculate the sensitivity to changes in quantity sold, we will choose a quantity of 41,000. The OCF at this level of sale is:

OCF = [($230 − 210)(41,000) − $450,000](0.62) + 0.38($1,700,000/5)
OCF = $358,600

The sensitivity of changes in the OCF to quantity sold is:

ΔOCF/ΔQ = ($358,600 − 346,200)/(41,000 − 40,000)
ΔOCF/ΔQ = +$12.40

The NPV at this level of sales is:

NPV = −$1.7M − $450,000 + $358,600(PVIFA$_{13\%,5}$) + [$450K + $500K(1 − .38)]/1.13^5
NPV = −$476,223.32

And the sensitivity of NPV to changes in the quantity sold is:

ΔNPV/ΔQ = (−$476,223.32 − (−$519,836.99))/(41,000 − 40,000)
ΔNPV/ΔQ = +$43.61

You wouldn't want the quantity to fall below the point where the NPV is zero. We know the NPV changes $43.61 for every unit sale, so we can divide the NPV for 40,000 units by the sensitivity to get a change in quantity. Doing so, we get:

−$519,836.99 = $43.61($\Delta$Q)
ΔQ = −11,919

For a zero NPV, we need to increase sales by 11,919 units, so the minimum quantity is:

Q$_{Min}$ = 40,000 + 11,919
Q$_{Min}$ = 51,919

B-228 SOLUTIONS

28. We will use the bottom up approach to calculate the operating cash flow. Assuming we operate the project for all four years, the cash flows are:

Year	0	1	2	3	4
Sales		$7,000,000	$7,000,000	$7,000,000	$7,000,000
Operating costs		3,000,000	3,000,000	3,000,000	3,000,000
Depreciation		2,000,000	2,000,000	2,000,000	2,000,000
EBT		$2,000,000	$2,000,000	$2,000,000	$2,000,000
Tax		760,000	760,000	760,000	760,000
Net income		$1,240,000	$1,240,000	$1,240,000	$1,240,000
+Depreciation		2,000,000	2,000,000	2,000,000	2,000,000
Operating CF		$3,240,000	$3,240,000	$3,240,000	$3,240,000
Change in NWC	–$2,000,000	0	0	0	$2,000,000
Capital spending	–8,000,000	0	0	0	0
Total cash flow	–$10,000,000	$3,240,000	$3,240,000	$3,240,000	$5,240,000

There is no salvage value for the equipment. The NPV is:

$$\text{NPV} = -\$10,000,000 + \$3,240,000(\text{PVIFA}_{16\%,4}) + \$5,240,000/1.16^4$$
$$\text{NPV} = \$170,687.46$$

The cash flows if we abandon the project after one year are:

Year	0	1
Sales		$7,000,000
Operating costs		3,000,000
Depreciation		2,000,000
EBT		$2,000,000
Tax		760,000
Net income		$1,240,000
+Depreciation		2,000,000
Operating CF		$3,240,000
Change in NWC	–$2,000,000	$2,000,000
Capital spending	–8,000,000	6,310,000
Total cash flow	–$10,000,000	$11,550,000

The book value of the equipment is:

Book value = $8,000,000 – (1)($8,000,000/4)
Book value = $6,000,000

So the taxes on the salvage value will be:

Taxes = ($6,000,000 – 6,500,000)(.38)
Taxes = –$190,000

This makes the aftertax salvage value:

Aftertax salvage value = $6,500,000 – 190,000
Aftertax salvage value = $6,310,000

The NPV if we abandon the project after one year is:

NPV = –$10,000,000 + $11,550,000/1.16
NPV = –$43,103.45

If we abandon the project after two years, the cash flows are:

Year	0	1	2
Sales		$7,000,000	$7,000,000
Operating costs		3,000,000	3,000,000
Depreciation		2,000,000	2,000,000
EBT		$2,000,000	$2,000,000
Tax		760,000	760,000
Net income		$1,240,000	$1,240,000
+Depreciation		2,000,000	2,000,000
Operating CF		$3,240,000	$3,240,000
Change in NWC	–$2,000,000	0	$2,000,000
Capital spending	–8,000,000	0	5,240,000
Total cash flow	–$10,000,000	$3,240,000	$10,480,000

The book value of the equipment is:

Book value = $8,000,000 – (2)($8,000,000/4)
Book value = $4,000,000

So the taxes on the salvage value will be:

Taxes = ($4,000,000 – 6,000,000)(.38)
Taxes = –$760,000

This makes the aftertax salvage value:

Aftertax salvage value = $6,000,000 – 760,000
Aftertax salvage value = $5,240,000

B-230 SOLUTIONS

The NPV if we abandon the project after two years is:

$NPV = -\$10,000,000 + \$3,240,000/1.16 + \$10,480,000/1.16^2$
$NPV = \$581,450.65$

If we abandon the project after three years, the cash flows are:

Year	0	1	2	3
Sales		$7,000,000	$7,000,000	$7,000,000
Operating costs		3,000,000	3,000,000	3,000,000
Depreciation		2,000,000	2,000,000	2,000,000
EBT		$2,000,000	$2,000,000	$2,000,000
Tax		760,000	760,000	760,000
Net income		$1,240,000	$1,240,000	$1,240,000
+Depreciation		2,000,000	2,000,000	2,000,000
Operating CF		$3,240,000	$3,240,000	$3,240,000
Change in NWC	–$2,000,000	0	0	$2,000,000
Capital spending	–8,000,000	0	0	2,620,000
Total cash flow	–$10,000,000	$3,240,000	$3,240,000	$7,860,000

The book value of the equipment is:

Book value = $8,000,000 – (3)($8,000,000/4)
Book value = $2,000,000

So the taxes on the salvage value will be:

Taxes = ($2,000,000 – 3,000,000)(.38)
Taxes = –$380,000

This makes the aftertax salvage value:

Aftertax salvage value = $3,000,000 – 380,000
Aftertax salvage value = $2,620,000

The NPV if we abandon the project after two years is:

$NPV = -\$10,000,000 + \$3,240,000(PVIFA_{16\%,2}) + \$7,860,000/1.16^3$
$NPV = \$236,520.56$

We should abandon the equipment after two years since the NPV of abandoning the project after two years has the highest NPV.

29. *a.* The NPV of the project is sum of the present value of the cash flows generated by the project. The cash flows from this project are an annuity, so the NPV is:

NPV = –$4,000,000 + $750,000(PVIFA$_{10\%,10}$)
NPV = $608,425.33

b. The company will abandon the project if value of abandoning the project is greater than the value of the future cash flows. The present value of the future cash flows if the company revises it sales downward will be:

PV of downward revision = $120,000(PVIFA$_{10\%,9}$)
PV of downward revision = $691,082.86

Since this is less than the value of abandoning the project, the company should abandon in one year. So, the revised NPV of the project will be the initial cost, plus the expected cash flow in year one based on upward sales projection, plus the expected value of abandonment. We need to remember that the abandonment value occurs in year 1, and the present value of the expansion cash flows are in year one, so each of these must be discounted back to today. So, the project NPV under the abandonment or expansion scenario is:

NPV = –$4,000,000 + $750,000 / 1.10 + .50($800,000) / 1.10
         + [.50($1,500,000)(PVIFA$_{10\%,9}$)] / 1.10
NPV = $972,061.69

30. First, determine the cash flow from selling the old harvester. When calculating the salvage value, remember that tax liabilities or credits are generated on the difference between the resale value and the book value of the asset. Using the original purchase price of the old harvester to determine annual depreciation, the annual depreciation for the old harvester is:

Depreciation$_{Old}$ = $45,000 / 15
Depreciation$_{Old}$ = $3,000

Since the machine is five years old, the firm has accumulated five annual depreciation charges, reducing the book value of the machine. The current book value of the machine is equal to the initial purchase price minus the accumulated depreciation, so:

Book value = Initial Purchase Price – Accumulated Depreciation
Book value = $45,000 – ($3,000 × 5 years)
Book value = $30,000

Since the firm is able to resell the old harvester for $20,000, which is less than the $30,000 book value of the machine, the firm will generate a tax credit on the sale. The aftertax salvage value of the old harvester will be:

Aftertax salvage value = Market value + t$_C$(Book value – Market value)
Aftertax salvage value = $20,000 + .34($30,000 – 20,000)
Aftertax salvage value = $23,400

B-232 SOLUTIONS

Next, we need to calculate the incremental depreciation. We need to calculate depreciation tax shield generated by the new harvester less the forgone depreciation tax shield from the old harvester. Let P be the break-even purchase price of the new harvester. So, we find:

Depreciation tax shield$_{New}$ = (Initial Investment / Economic Life) $\times$ t_C
Depreciation tax shield$_{New}$ = (P / 10) (.34)

And the depreciation tax shield on the old harvester is:

Depreciation tax shield$_{Old}$ = (\$45,000 / 15) (.34)
Depreciation tax shield$_{Old}$ = (\$3,000)(0.34)

So, the incremental depreciation tax, which is the depreciation tax shield from the new harvester, minus the depreciation tax shield from the old harvester, is:

Incremental depreciation tax shield = (P / 10)(.34) – (\$3,000)(.34)
Incremental depreciation tax shield = (P / 10 – \$3,000)(.34)

The present value of the incremental depreciation tax shield will be:

PV$_{Depreciation\ tax\ shield}$ = (P / 10)(.34)(PVIFA$_{15\%,10}$) – \$3,000(.34)(PVIFA$_{15\%,10}$)

The new harvester will generate year-end pre-tax cash flow savings of \$10,000 per year for 10 years. We can find the aftertax present value of the cash flows savings as:

PV$_{Ssavings}$ = C_1(1 – t_C)(PVIFA$_{15\%,10}$)
PV$_{Ssavings}$ = \$10,000(1 – 0.34)(PVIFA$_{15\%,10}$)
PV$_{Ssavings}$ = \$33,123.87

The break-even purchase price of the new harvester is the price, P, which makes the NPV of the machine equal to zero.

NPV = –P + Salvage value$_{Old}$ + PV$_{Depreciation\ tax\ shield}$ + PV$_{Savings}$
\$0 = –P + \$23,400 + (P / 10)(.34)(PVIFA$_{15\%,10}$) – \$3,000(.34)(PVIFA$_{15\%,10}$) + \$33,123.87
P – (P / 10)(.34)(PVIFA$_{15\%,10}$) = \$56,523.87 – \$3,000(.34)(PVIFA$_{15\%,10}$)
P[1 – (1 / 10)(.34)(PVIFA$_{15\%,10}$) = \$51,404.73
P = \$61,981.06

CHAPTER 9

Risk and Return

Lessons from Market History

PART THREE

With the S&P 500 index up about 3 percent and the NASDAQ stock market index up about 1.4 percent in 2005, stock market performance overall was well below average. However, it was a great year for investors in pharmaceutical manufacturer ViroPharma, Inc., which gained a whopping 469 percent! And investors in Hansen Natural, makers of Monster energy drinks, had to be energized by the 333 percent gain of that stock. Of course, not all stocks increased in value. Stock in video game manufacturer Majesco Entertainment fell 92 percent during the year, and stock in Aphton, a biotechnology company, dropped 89 percent. These examples show that there were tremendous potential profits to be made during 2005, but there was also the risk of losing money—lots of it. So what should you, as a stock market investor, expect when you invest your own money? In this chapter, we study eight decades of market history to find out.

9.1 Returns

Dollar Returns

Suppose the Video Concept Company has several thousand shares of stock outstanding and you are a shareholder. Further suppose that you purchased some of the shares of stock in the company at the beginning of the year; it is now year-end and you want to figure out how well you have done on your investment. The return you get on an investment in stocks, like that in bonds or any other investment, comes in two forms.

First, over the year most companies pay dividends to shareholders. As the owner of stock in the Video Concept Company, you are a part owner of the company. If the company is profitable, it generally will distribute some of its profits to the shareholders. Therefore, as the owner of shares of stock, you will receive some cash, called a *dividend,* during the year. This cash is the *income component* of your return. In addition to the dividends, the other part of your return is the *capital gain*—or, if it is negative, the *capital loss* (negative capital gain)—on the investment.

For example, suppose we are considering the cash flows of the investment in Figure 9.1, showing that you purchased 100 shares of stock at the beginning of the year at a price of $37 per share. Your total investment, then, was:

$$C_0 = \$37 \times 100 = \$3,700$$

How did the market do today? Find out at **finance.yahoo.com.**

Figure 9.1

Dollar Returns

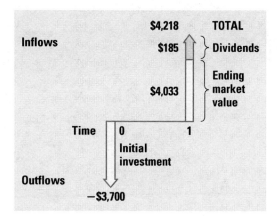

Suppose that over the year the stock paid a dividend of $1.85 per share. During the year, then, you received income of:

$$\text{Div} = \$1.85 \times 100 = \$185$$

Suppose, finally, that at the end of the year the market price of the stock is $40.33 per share. Because the stock increased in price, you had a capital gain of:

$$\text{Gain} = (\$40.33 - \$37) \times 100 = \$333$$

The capital gain, like the dividend, is part of the return that shareholders require to maintain their investment in the Video Concept Company. Of course, if the price of Video Concept stock had dropped in value to, say, $34.78, you would have recorded this capital loss:

$$\text{Loss} = (\$34.78 - \$37) \times 100 = -\$222$$

The *total dollar return* on your investment is the sum of the dividend income and the capital gain or loss on the investment:

$$\text{Total dollar return} = \text{Dividend income} + \text{Capital gain (or loss)}$$

(From now on we will refer to *capital losses* as *negative capital gains* and not distinguish them.) In our first example the total dollar return is given by:

$$\text{Total dollar return} = \$185 + \$333 = \$518$$

Notice that if you sold the stock at the end of the year, your total amount of cash would be the initial investment plus the total dollar return. In the preceding example you would have:

$$\text{Total cash if stock is sold} = \text{Initial investment} + \text{Total dollar return}$$
$$= \$3,700 + \$518$$
$$= \$4,218$$

As a check, notice that this is the same as the proceeds from the sale of stock plus the dividends:

$$\text{Proceeds from stock sale} + \text{Dividends}$$
$$= \$40.33 \times 100 + \$185$$
$$= \$4,033 + \$185$$
$$= \$4,218$$

Figure 9.2

Percentage Returns

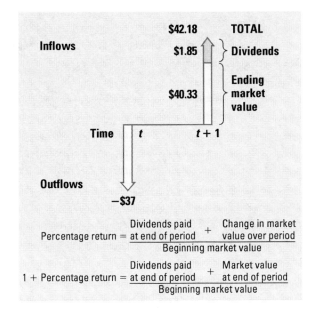

$$\text{Percentage return} = \frac{\text{Dividends paid at end of period} + \text{Change in market value over period}}{\text{Beginning market value}}$$

$$1 + \text{Percentage return} = \frac{\text{Dividends paid at end of period} + \text{Market value at end of period}}{\text{Beginning market value}}$$

Suppose, however, that you hold your Video Concept stock and don't sell it at year-end. Should you still consider the capital gain as part of your return? Does this violate our previous present value rule that only cash matters?

The answer to the first question is a strong yes, and the answer to the second question is an equally strong no. The capital gain is every bit as much a part of your return as is the dividend, and you should certainly count it as part of your total return. That you have decided to hold onto the stock and not sell or *realize* the gain or the loss in no way changes the fact that, if you want to, you could get the cash value of the stock. After all, you could always sell the stock at year-end and immediately buy it back. The total amount of cash you would have at year-end would be the $518 gain plus your initial investment of $3,700. You would not lose this return when you bought back 100 shares of stock. In fact, you would be in exactly the same position as if you had not sold the stock (assuming, of course, that there are no tax consequences and no brokerage commissions from selling the stock).

Percentage Returns

It is more convenient to summarize the information about returns in percentage terms than in dollars because the percentages apply to any amount invested. The question we want to answer is this: How much return do we get for each dollar invested? To find this out, let t stand for the year we are looking at, let P_t be the price of the stock at the beginning of the year, and let Div_{t+1} be the dividend paid on the stock during the year. Consider the cash flows in Figure 9.2.

Go to **www.smartmoney.com/marketmap** for a Java applet that shows today's returns by market sector.

In our example, the price at the beginning of the year was $37 per share and the dividend paid during the year on each share was $1.85. Hence the percentage income return, sometimes called the *dividend yield*, is:

$$\text{Dividend yield} = \text{Div}_{t+1}/P_t$$
$$= \$1.85/\$37$$
$$= .05$$
$$= 5\%$$

The **capital gain** (or loss) is the change in the price of the stock divided by the initial price. Letting P_{t+1} be the price of the stock at year-end, we can compute the capital gain as follows:

$$\text{Capital gain} = (P_{t+1} - P_t)/P_t$$
$$= (\$40.33 - \$37)/\$37$$
$$= \$3.33/\$37$$
$$= .09$$
$$= 9\%$$

Combining these two results, we find that the *total return* on the investment in Video Concept stock over the year, which we will label R_{t+1}, was:

$$R_{t+1} = \frac{\text{Div}_{t+1}}{P_t} + \frac{(P_{t+1} - P_t)}{P_t}$$
$$= 5\% + 9\%$$
$$= 14\%$$

From now on, we will refer to returns in percentage terms.

To give a more concrete example, stock in Goldman Sachs (GS), the well-known financial services company, began 2005 at $102.90 a share. Goldman Sachs paid dividends of $1.00 during 2005, and the stock price at the end of the year was $127.47. What was the return on GS for the year? For practice, see if you agree that the answer is 24.85 percent. Of course, negative returns occur as well. For example, in 2005, General Motor's stock price at the beginning of the year was $37.64 per share, and dividends of $2.00 were paid. The stock ended the year at $19.42 per share. Verify that the loss was 43.09 percent for the year.

EXAMPLE 9.1

Calculating Returns Suppose a stock begins the year with a price of $25 per share and ends with a price of $35 per share. During the year it paid a $2 dividend per share. What are its dividend yield, its capital gain, and its total return for the year? We can imagine the cash flows in Figure 9.3.

$$R_1 = \frac{\text{Div}_1}{P_0} + \frac{P_1 - P_0}{P_0}$$
$$= \frac{\$2}{\$25} + \frac{\$35 - 25}{\$25} = \frac{\$12}{\$25}$$
$$= 8\% + 40\% = 48\%$$

Figure 9.3 Cash Flow—An Investment Example

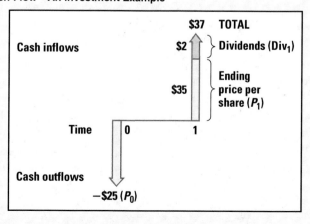

(continued)

362

Ross–Westerfield–Jaffe:
Corporate Finance, Eighth
Edition

III. Risk

9. Risk and Return: Lessons
from Market History

© The McGraw–Hill
Companies, 2008

Thus, the stock's dividend yield, its capital gain yield, and its total return are 8 percent, 40 percent, and 48 percent, respectively.

Suppose you had $5,000 invested. The total dollar return you would have received on an investment in the stock is $5,000 × .48 = $2,400. If you know the total dollar return on the stock, you do not need to know how many shares you would have had to purchase to figure out how much money you would have made on the $5,000 investment. You just use the total dollar return.

9.2 Holding Period Returns

A famous set of studies dealing with rates of return on common stocks, bonds, and Treasury bills was conducted by Roger Ibbotson and Rex Sinquefield.[1] They present year-by-year historical rates of return for the following five important types of financial instruments in the United States:

1. *Large-company common stocks*: The common stock portfolio is based on the Standard & Poor's (S&P) composite index. At present the S&P composite includes 500 of the largest (in terms of market value) stocks in the United States.

For more about market
history, visit **www.
globalfindata.com.**

2. *Small-company common stocks*: This is a portfolio corresponding to the bottom fifth of stocks traded on the New York Stock Exchange in which stocks are ranked by market value (that is, the price of the stock multiplied by the number of shares outstanding).

3. *Long-term corporate bonds*: This is a portfolio of high-quality corporate bonds with a 20-year maturity.

4. *Long-term U.S. government bonds*: This is based on U.S. government bonds with a maturity of 20 years.

5. *U.S. Treasury bills*: This is based on Treasury bills with a three-month maturity.

None of the returns are adjusted for taxes or transaction costs. In addition to the year-by-year returns on financial instruments, the year-to-year change in the consumer price index is computed. This is a basic measure of inflation. We can calculate year-by-year real returns by subtracting annual inflation.

Before looking closely at the different portfolio returns, we graphically present the returns and risks available from U.S. capital markets in the 80-year period from 1926 to 2005. Figure 9.4 shows the growth of $1 invested at the beginning of 1926. Notice that the vertical axis is logarithmic, so that equal distances measure the same percentage change. The figure shows that if $1 were invested in large-company common stocks and all dividends were reinvested, the dollar would have grown to $2,657.56 by the end of 2005. The biggest growth was in the small stock portfolio. If $1 were invested in small stocks in 1926, the investment would have grown to $13,706.15. However, when you look carefully at Figure 9.4, you can see great variability in the returns on small stocks, especially in the earlier part of the period. A dollar in long-term government bonds was very stable as compared with a dollar in common stocks. Figures 9.5 to 9.8 plot each year-to-year percentage return as a vertical bar drawn from the horizontal axis for large-company common stocks, for small-company stocks, for long-term bonds and Treasury bills, and for inflation, respectively.

Figure 9.4 gives the growth of a dollar investment in the stock market from 1926 through 2005. In other words, it shows what the worth of the investment would have been if

---

[1] The most recent update of this work is *Stocks, Bonds, Bills and Inflation: 2006 Yearbook*™ (Chicago: Ibbotson Associates). All rights reserved.

Figure 9.4   Wealth Indexes of Investments in the U.S. Capital Markets (Year-End 1925 = $1.00)

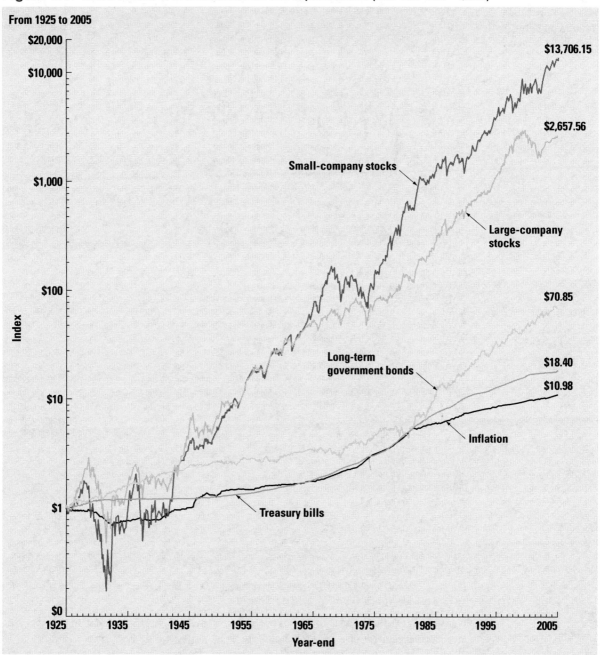

the dollar had been left in the stock market and if each year the dividends from the previous year had been reinvested in more stock. If R_t is the return in year t (expressed in decimals), the value you would have at the end of year T is the product of 1 plus the return in each of the years:

$$(1 + R_1) \times (1 + R_2) \times \cdots \times (1 + R_t) \times \cdots \times (1 + R_T)$$

Figure 9.5

Year-by-Year Total Returns on Large-Company Common Stocks

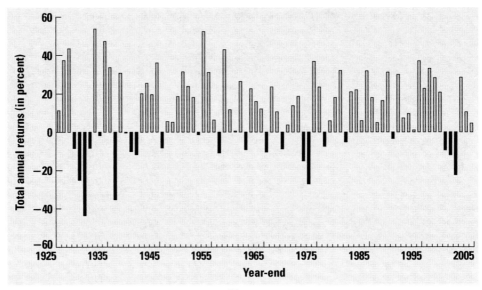

Figure 9.6

Year-by-Year Total Returns on Small-Company Common Stocks

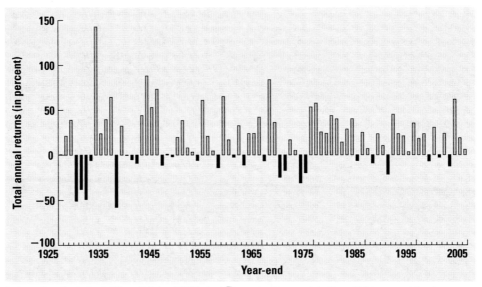

For example, if the returns were 11 percent, -5 percent, and 9 percent in a three-year period, an investment of $1 at the beginning of the period would be worth:

$$(1 + R_1) \times (1 + R_2) \times (1 + R_3) = (\$1 + .11) \times (\$1 - .05) \times (\$1 + .09)$$
$$= \$1.11 \times \$.95 \times \$1.09$$
$$= \$1.15$$

Go to **bigcharts. marketwatch.com** to see both intraday and long-term charts.

at the end of the three years. Notice that .15 or 15 percent is the total return and that it includes the return from reinvesting the first-year dividends in the stock market for two more years and reinvesting the second-year dividends for the final year. The 15 percent is called a three-year **holding period return**. Table 9.1 gives the annual returns each year for selected investments from 1926 to 2005. From this table, you can determine holding period returns for any combination of years.

Figure 9.7

Year-by-Year Total Returns on Bonds and Bills

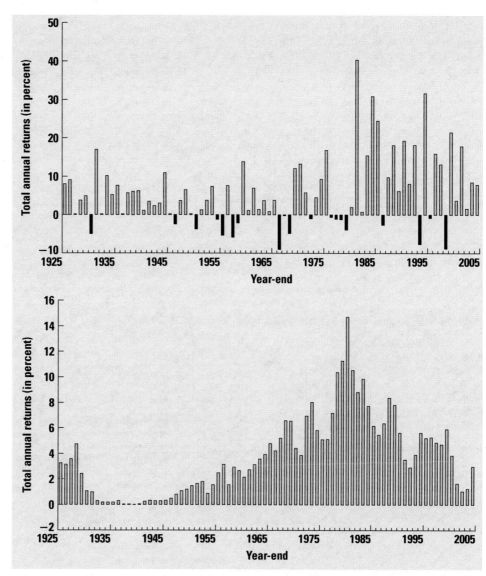

9.3   Return Statistics

The history of capital market returns is too complicated to be handled in its undigested form. To use the history, we must first find some manageable ways of describing it, dramatically condensing the detailed data into a few simple statements.

This is where two important numbers summarizing the history come in. The first and most natural number is some single measure that best describes the past annual returns on the stock market. In other words, what is our best estimate of the return that an investor could have realized in a particular year over the 1926 to 2005 period? This is the *average return*.

Figure 9.9 plots the histogram of the yearly stock market returns given in Table 9.1. This plot is the **frequency distribution** of the numbers. The height of the graph gives the number of sample observations in the range on the horizontal axis.

366

Ross–Westerfield–Jaffe:
Corporate Finance, Eighth
Edition

III. Risk

9. Risk and Return: Lessons
from Market History

© The McGraw–Hill
Companies, 2008

Figure 9.8

Year-by-Year Inflation

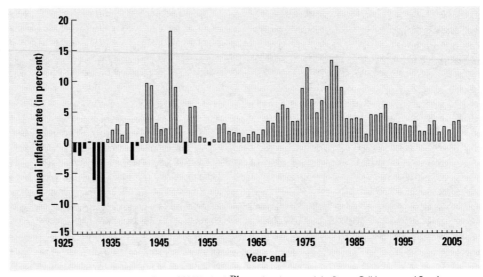

Figure 9.9   **Histogram of Returns on Common Stocks, 1926–2005**

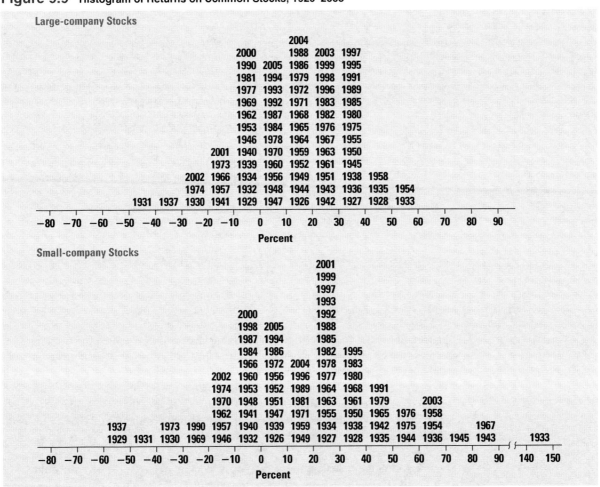

Chapter 9   Risk and Return   265

Table 9.1

Year-by-Year Total Returns, 1926–2005

Year	Large-Company Stocks	Long-Term Government Bonds	U.S. Treasury Bills	Consumer Price Index
1926	13.75%	5.69%	3.30%	−1.12%
1927	35.70	6.58	3.15	−2.26
1928	45.08	1.15	4.05	−1.16
1929	−8.80	4.39	4.47	0.58
1930	−25.13	4.47	2.27	−6.40
1931	−43.60	−2.15	1.15	−9.32
1932	−8.75	8.51	0.88	−10.27
1933	52.95	1.92	0.52	0.76
1934	−2.31	7.59	0.27	1.52
1935	46.79	4.20	0.17	2.99
1936	32.49	5.13	0.17	1.45
1937	−35.45	1.44	0.27	2.86
1938	31.63	4.21	0.06	−2.78
1939	−1.43	3.84	0.04	0.00
1940	−10.36	5.70	0.04	0.71
1941	−12.02	0.47	0.14	9.93
1942	20.75	1.80	0.34	9.03
1943	25.38	2.01	0.38	2.96
1944	19.49	2.27	0.38	2.30
1945	36.21	5.29	0.38	2.25
1946	−8.42	0.54	0.38	18.13
1947	5.05	−1.02	0.62	8.84
1948	4.99	2.66	1.06	2.99
1949	17.81	4.58	1.12	−2.07
1950	30.05	−0.98	1.22	5.93
1951	23.79	−0.20	1.56	6.00
1952	18.39	2.43	1.75	0.75
1953	−1.07	2.28	1.87	0.75
1954	52.23	3.08	0.93	−0.74
1955	31.62	−0.73	1.80	0.37
1956	6.91	−1.72	2.66	2.99
1957	−10.50	6.82	3.28	2.90
1958	43.57	−1.72	1.71	1.76
1959	12.01	−2.02	3.48	1.73
1960	0.47	11.21	2.81	1.36
1961	26.84	2.20	2.40	0.67
1962	−8.75	5.72	2.82	1.33
1963	22.70	1.79	3.23	1.64
1964	16.43	3.71	3.62	0.97
1965	12.38	0.93	4.06	1.92
1966	−10.06	5.12	4.94	3.46
1967	23.98	−2.86	4.39	3.04
1968	11.03	2.25	5.49	4.72
1969	−8.43	−5.63	6.90	6.20
1970	3.94	18.92	6.50	5.57
1971	14.30	11.24	4.36	3.27
1972	18.99	2.39	4.23	3.41
1973	−14.69	3.30	7.29	8.71
1974	−26.47	4.00	7.99	12.34
1975	37.23	5.52	5.87	6.94

(*continued*)

368

Ross–Westerfield–Jaffe:
Corporate Finance, Eighth
Edition

III. Risk

9. Risk and Return: Lessons
from Market History

© The McGraw–Hill
Companies, 2008

Table 9.1

Year-by-Year Total
Returns, 1926–2005

(concluded)

Year	Large-Company Stocks	Long-Term Government Bonds	U.S. Treasury Bills	Consumer Price Index
1976	23.93%	15.56%	5.07%	4.86%
1977	−7.16	0.38	5.45	6.70
1978	6.57	−1.26	7.64	9.02
1979	18.61	1.26	10.56	13.29
1980	32.50	−2.48	12.10	12.52
1981	−4.92	4.04	14.60	8.92
1982	21.55	44.28	10.94	3.83
1983	22.56	1.29	8.99	3.79
1984	6.27	15.29	9.90	3.95
1985	31.73	32.27	7.71	3.80
1986	18.67	22.39	6.09	1.10
1987	5.25	−3.03	5.88	4.43
1988	16.61	6.84	6.94	4.42
1989	31.69	18.54	8.44	4.65
1990	−3.10	7.74	7.69	6.11
1991	30.46	19.36	5.43	3.06
1992	7.62	7.34	3.48	2.90
1993	10.08	13.06	3.03	2.75
1994	1.32	−7.32	4.39	2.67
1995	37.58	25.94	5.61	2.54
1996	22.96	0.13	5.14	3.32
1997	33.36	12.02	5.19	1.70
1998	28.58	14.45	4.86	1.61
1999	21.04	−7.51	4.80	2.68
2000	−9.10	17.22	5.98	3.39
2001	−11.89	5.51	3.33	1.55
2002	−22.10	15.15	1.61	2.4
2003	28.89	2.01	0.94	1.9
2004	10.88	8.12	1.14	3.3
2005	4.91	6.89	2.79	3.4

SOURCE: Author calculations based on data obtained from *Global Financial Data*, Bloomberg, Standard and Poor's, and other sources.

Given a frequency distribution like that in Figure 9.9, we can calculate the **average** or **mean** of the distribution. To compute the average of the distribution, we add up all of the values and divide by the total ($\mathcal{T}$) number (80 in our case because we have 80 years of data). The bar over the R is used to represent the mean, and the formula is the ordinary formula for the average:

$$\text{Mean} = \bar{R} = \frac{(R_1 + \cdots + R_T)}{\mathcal{T}}$$

The mean of the 80 annual large-company stocks returns from 1926 to 2005 is 12.2 percent.

EXAMPLE 9.2

Calculating Average Returns Suppose the returns on common stock from 1926 to 1929 are .1370, .3580, .4514, and −.0888, respectively. The average, or mean, return over these four years is:

$$\bar{R} = \frac{.1370 + .3580 + .4514 - .0888}{4} = .2144 \text{ or } 21.44\%$$

9.4 Average Stock Returns and Risk-Free Returns

Now that we have computed the average return on the stock market, it seems sensible to compare it with the returns on other securities. The most obvious comparison is with the low-variability returns in the government bond market. These are free of most of the volatility we see in the stock market.

The government borrows money by issuing bonds, which the investing public holds. As we discussed in an earlier chapter, these bonds come in many forms, and the ones we will look at here are called *Treasury bills*, or *T-bills*. Once a week the government sells some bills at an auction. A typical bill is a pure discount bond that will mature in a year or less. Because the government can raise taxes to pay for the debt it incurs—a trick that many of us would like to be able to perform—this debt is virtually free of the risk of default. Thus we will call this the *risk-free return* over a short time (one year or less).

An interesting comparison, then, is between the virtually risk-free return on T-bills and the very risky return on common stocks. This difference between risky returns and risk-free returns is often called the *excess return on the risky asset*. It is called *excess* because it is the additional return resulting from the riskiness of common stocks and is interpreted as an equity **risk premium**.

Table 9.2 shows the average stock return, bond return, T-bill return, and inflation rate for the period from 1926 through 2005. From this we can derive excess returns. The average excess return from large-company common stocks for the entire period was 8.5 percent (12.3 percent − 3.8 percent).

One of the most significant observations of stock market data is this long-term excess of the stock return over the risk-free return. An investor for this period was rewarded for investment in the stock market with an extra or excess return over what would have been achieved by simply investing in T-bills.

Why was there such a reward? Does it mean that it never pays to invest in T-bills and that someone who invested in them instead of in the stock market needs a course in finance? A complete answer to these questions lies at the heart of modern finance, and Chapter 10 is devoted entirely to this. However, part of the answer can be found in the variability of the various types of investments. We see in Table 9.1 many years when an investment in T-bills achieved higher returns than an investment in large common stocks. Also, we note that the returns from an investment in common stocks are frequently negative, whereas an investment in T-bills never produces a negative return. So, we now turn our attention to measuring the variability of returns and an introductory discussion of risk.

We first look more closely at Table 9.2. We see that the standard deviation of T-bills is substantially less than that of common stocks. This suggests that the risk of T-bills is less than that of common stocks. Because the answer turns on the riskiness of investments in common stock, we next turn our attention to measuring this risk.

9.5 Risk Statistics

The second number that we use to characterize the distribution of returns is a measure of the risk in returns. There is no universally agreed-upon definition of risk. One way to think about the risk of returns on common stock is in terms of how spread out the frequency distribution in Figure 9.9 is. The spread, or dispersion, of a distribution is a measure of how much a particular return can deviate from the mean return. If the distribution

Table 9.2   Total Annual Returns, 1926–2005

Series	Arithmetic Mean	Risk Premium (relative to U.S. Treasury bills)	Standard Deviation	Distribution
Large-company stocks	12.3%	8.5%	20.2%	
Small-company stocks	17.4	13.6	32.9	*
Long-term corporate bonds	6.2	2.4	8.5	
Long-term government	5.8	2.0	9.2	
Intermediate-term government	5.5	1.7	5.7	
U.S. Treasury bills	3.8		3.1	
Inflation	3.1		4.3	
				−90% 0% 90%

*The 1933 small-company stock total return was 142.9 percent.

SOURCE: Modified from *Stocks, Bonds, Bills and Inflation: 2006 Yearbook*,™ annual updates work by Roger G. Ibbotson and Rex A. Sinquefield (Chicago: Ibbotson Associates). All rights reserved.

is very spread out, the returns that will occur are very uncertain. By contrast, a distribution whose returns are all within a few percentage points of each other is tight, and the returns are less uncertain. The measures of risk we will discuss are variance and standard deviation.

Variance

The **variance** and its square root, the **standard deviation**, are the most common measures of variability or dispersion. We will use Var and σ^2 to denote the variance and SD and σ to represent the standard deviation. σ is, of course, the Greek letter sigma.

EXAMPLE 9.3

Volatility Suppose the returns on common stocks from 1926 to 1929 are (in decimals) .1370, .3580, .4514, and −.0888, respectively. The variance of this sample is computed as follows:

$$\text{Var} = \frac{1}{T-1}[(R_1 - \bar{R})^2 + (R_2 - \bar{R})^2 + (R_3 - \bar{R})^2 + (R_4 - \bar{R})^2]$$

$$.0582 = \frac{1}{3}[(.1370 - .2144)^2 + (.3580 - .2144)^2$$
$$+ (.4514 - .2144)^2 + (-.0888 - .2144)^2]$$
$$\text{SD} = \sqrt{.0582} = .2413 \text{ or } 24.13\%$$

This formula tells us just what to do: Take the T individual returns (R_1, R_2, ...) and subtract the average return $\bar{R}$, square the result, and add them up. Finally, this total must be divided by the number of returns less one ($T - 1$). The standard deviation is always just the square root of the variance.

Using the stock returns for the 80-year period from 1926 through 2005 in this formula, the resulting standard deviation of large stock returns is 20.2 percent. The standard deviation is the standard statistical measure of the spread of a sample, and it will be the measure we use most of the time. Its interpretation is facilitated by a discussion of the normal distribution.

Standard deviations are widely reported for mutual funds. For example, the Fidelity Magellan Fund is one of the largest mutual funds in the United States. How volatile is it? To find out, we went to www.morningstar.com, entered the ticker symbol FMAGX, and hit the "Risk/Measures" link. Here is what we found:

Fidelity Magellan FMAGX   See Fund Family Data ▸▸

Volatility Measurements	Trailing 3-Yr through 12-31-05 | *Trailing 5-Yr through 12-31-05		
Standard Deviation	8.89	Sharpe Ratio	1.17
Mean	12.61	Bear Market Decile Rank*	7

Modern Portfolio Theory Statistics		Trailing 3-Yr through 12-31-05
	Standard Index S&P 500	Best Fit Index S&P 500
R-Squared	96	96
Beta	0.95	0.95
Alpha	-1.01	-1.01

Over the last three years, the standard deviation of the return on the Fidelity Magellan Fund was 8.89 percent. When you consider the average stock has a standard deviation of about 50 percent, this seems like a low number. But the Magellan fund is a relatively well-diversified portfolio, so this is an illustration of the power of diversification, a subject we will discuss in detail later. The mean is the average return; so over the last three years, investors in the Magellan Fund earned a 12.61 percent return per year. Also under the Volatility Measurements section, you will see the Sharpe ratio. The Sharpe ratio is calculated as the risk premium of the asset divided by the standard deviation. As such, it is a measure of return to the level of risk taken (as measured by standard deviation). The "beta" for the Fidelity Magellan Fund is .95. We will have more to say about this number—lots more—in the next chapter.

Figure 9.10

The Normal Distribution

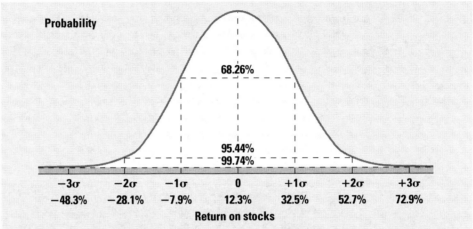

In the case of a normal distribution, there is a 68.26 percent probability that a return will be within one standard deviation of the mean. In this example, there is a 68.26 percent probability that a yearly return will be between –7.9 percent and 32.5 percent.

There is a 95.44 percent probability that a return will be within two standard deviations of the mean. In this example, there is a 95.44 percent probability that a yearly return will be between –28.1 percent and 52.7 percent.

Finally, there is a 99.74 percent probability that a return will be within three standard deviations of the mean. In this example, there is a 99.74 percent probability that a yearly return will be between –48.3 percent and 72.99 percent.

Normal Distribution and Its Implications for Standard Deviation

A large enough sample drawn from a **normal distribution** looks like the bell-shaped curve drawn in Figure 9.10. As you can see, this distribution is *symmetric* about its mean, not *skewed,* and has a much cleaner shape than the actual distribution of yearly returns drawn in Figure 9.9. Of course, if we had been able to observe stock market returns for 1,000 years, we might have filled in a lot of the jumps and jerks in Figure 9.9 and had a smoother curve.

In classical statistics, the normal distribution plays a central role, and the standard deviation is the usual way to represent the spread of a normal distribution. For the normal distribution, the probability of having a return that is above or below the mean by a certain amount depends only on the standard deviation. For example, the probability of having a return that is within one standard deviation of the mean of the distribution is approximately .68 or 2/3, and the probability of having a return that is within two standard deviations of the mean is approximately .95.

The 20.2 percent standard deviation we found for stock returns from 1926 through 2005 can now be interpreted in the following way: If stock returns are roughly normally distributed, the probability that a yearly return will fall within 20.2 percent of the mean of 12.3 percent will be approximately 2/3. That is, about 2/3 of the yearly returns will be between −7.9 percent and 32.5 percent. (Note that −7.9 = 12.3 − 20.2 and 32.5 = 12.3 + 20.2.) The probability that the return in any year will fall within two standard deviations is about .95. That is, about 95 percent of yearly returns will be between −28.1 percent and 52.7 percent.

9.6   More on Average Returns

Thus far in this chapter we have looked closely at simple average returns. But there is another way of computing an average return. The fact that average returns are calculated two different ways leads to some confusion, so our goal in this section is to explain the two approaches and also the circumstances under which each is appropriate.

Arithmetic versus Geometric Averages

Let's start with a simple example. Suppose you buy a particular stock for $100. Unfortunately, the first year you own it, it falls to $50. The second year you own it, it rises back to $100, leaving you where you started (no dividends were paid).

What was your average return on this investment? Common sense seems to say that your average return must be exactly zero because you started with $100 and ended with $100. But if we calculate the returns year-by-year, we see that you lost 50 percent the first year (you lost half of your money). The second year, you made 100 percent (you doubled your money). Your average return over the two years was thus $(-50$ percent $+ 100$ percent$)/2 = 25$ percent!

So which is correct, 0 percent or 25 percent? The answer is that both are correct; they just answer different questions. The 0 percent is called the **geometric average return**. The 25 percent is called the **arithmetic average return**. The geometric average return answers the question, *"What was your average compound return per year over a particular period?"* The arithmetic average return answers the question, *"What was your return in an average year over a particular period?"*

Notice that in previous sections, the average returns we calculated were all arithmetic averages, so we already know how to calculate them. What we need to do now is (1) learn how to calculate geometric averages and (2) learn the circumstances under which one average is more meaningful than the other.

Calculating Geometric Average Returns

First, to illustrate how we calculate a geometric average return, suppose a particular investment had annual returns of 10 percent, 12 percent, 3 percent, and −9 percent over the last four years. The geometric average return over this four-year period is calculated as $(1.10 \times 1.12 \times 1.03 \times .91)^{1/4} - 1 = 3.66$ percent. In contrast, the average arithmetic return we have been calculating is $(.10 + .12 + .03 - .09)/4 = 4.0$ percent.

In general, if we have T years of returns, the geometric average return over these T years is calculated using this formula:

$$\text{Geometric average return} = [(1 + R_1) \times (1 + R_2) \times \cdots \times (1 + R_T)]^{1/T} - 1 \qquad (9.1)$$

This formula tells us that four steps are required:

1. Take each of the T annual returns $R_1, R_2, \ldots, R_T$ and add 1 to each (after converting them to decimals).
2. Multiply all the numbers from step 1 together.
3. Take the result from step 2 and raise it to the power of $1/T$.
4. Finally, subtract 1 from the result of step 3. The result is the geometric average return.

EXAMPLE 9.4

Calculating the Geometric Average Return   Calculate the geometric average return for S&P 500 large-cap stocks for 1926–1930 using the numbers given here.

First convert percentages to decimal returns, add 1, and then calculate their product:

S&P 500 Returns	Product
13.75%	1.1375
35.70	× 1.3570
45.08	× 1.4508
−8.80	× .9120
−25.13	× .7487
	1.5291

(continued)

Notice that the number 1.5291 is what our investment is worth after five years if we started with a $1 investment. The geometric average return is then calculated as:

$$\text{Geometric average return} = 1.5291^{1/5} - 1 = .0887, \text{ or } 8.87\%$$

Thus the geometric average return is about 8.87 percent in this example. Here is a tip: If you are using a financial calculator, you can put $1 in as the present value, $1.5291 as the future value, and 5 as the number of periods. Then solve for the unknown rate. You should get the same answer we did.

You may have noticed in our examples thus far that the geometric average returns seem to be smaller. It turns out that this will always be true (as long as the returns are not all identical, in which case the two "averages" would be the same). To illustrate, Table 9.3 shows the arithmetic averages and standard deviations from Table 9.2, along with the geometric average returns.

As shown in Table 9.3, the geometric averages are all smaller, but the magnitude of the difference varies quite a bit. The reason is that the difference is greater for more volatile investments. In fact, there is a useful approximation. Assuming all the numbers are expressed in decimals (as opposed to percentages), the geometric average return is approximately equal to the arithmetic average return minus half the variance. For example, looking at the large-company stocks, the arithmetic average is 12.3 and the standard deviation is 20.2, implying that the variance is .0408. The approximate geometric average is thus 12.3% − .0408/2 = 10.26%, which is quite close to the actual value.

EXAMPLE 9.5

More Geometric Averages   Take a look back at Figure 9.4. There we showed the value of a $1 investment after 80 years. Use the value for the large-company stock investment to check the geometric average in Table 9.3.

In Figure 9.4, the large-company investment grew to $2,657.56 over 80 years. The geometric average return is thus:

$$\text{Geometric average return} = \$2,657.56^{1/80} - 1 = .1036, \text{ or } 10.4\%$$

This 10.4 percent is the value shown in Table 9.3. For practice, check some of the other numbers in Table 9.3 the same way.

Arithmetic Average Return or Geometric Average Return?

When we look at historical returns, the difference between the geometric and arithmetic average returns isn't too hard to understand. To put it slightly differently, the geometric average tells you what you actually earned per year on average, compounded annually. The arithmetic average tells you what you earned in a typical year. You should use whichever one answers the question you want answered.

A somewhat trickier question concerns forecasting the future, and there's a lot of confusion about this point among analysts and financial planners. The problem is this: If we

Table 9.3

Geometric versus Arithmetic Average Returns: 1926–2005

Series	Geometric Mean	Arithmetic Mean	Standard Deviation
Large-company stocks	10.4%	12.3%	20.2%
Small-company stocks	12.6	17.4	32.9
Long-term corporate bonds	5.9	6.2	8.5
Long-term government bonds	5.5	5.8	9.2
Intermediate-term government bonds	5.3	5.5	5.7
U.S. Treasury bills	3.7	3.8	3.1
Inflation	3.0	3.1	4.3

have *estimates* of both the arithmetic and geometric average returns, then the arithmetic average is probably too high for longer periods and the geometric average is probably too low for shorter periods.

The good news is that there is a simple way of combining the two averages, which we will call *Blume's formula*.[2] Suppose we calculated geometric and arithmetic return averages from N years of data and we wish to use these averages to form a T-year average return forecast, $R(T)$, where T is less than N. Here's how we do it:

$$R(T) = \frac{T-1}{N-1} \times \text{Geometric average} + \frac{N-T}{N-1} \times \text{Arithmetic average} \qquad (9.2)$$

For example, suppose that from 25 years of annual returns data, we calculate an arithmetic average return of 12 percent and a geometric average return of 9 percent. From these averages, we wish to make 1-year, 5-year, and 10-year average return forecasts. These three average return forecasts are calculated as follows:

$$R(1) = \frac{1-1}{24} \times 9\% + \frac{25-1}{24} \times 12\% = 12\%$$

$$R(5) = \frac{5-1}{24} \times 9\% + \frac{25-5}{24} \times 12\% = 11.5\%$$

$$R(10) = \frac{10-1}{24} \times 9\% + \frac{25-10}{24} \times 12\% = 10.875\%$$

Thus, we see that 1-year, 5-year, and 10-year forecasts are 12 percent, 11.5 percent, and 10.875 percent, respectively.

This concludes our discussion of geometric versus arithmetic averages. One last note: In the future, when we say "average return," we mean arithmetic average unless we explicitly say otherwise.

---

[2]This elegant result is due to Marshal Blume ("Unbiased Estimates of Long-Run Expected Rates of Return," *Journal of the American Statistical Association*, September 1974, pp. 634–638).

Summary and Conclusions

1. This chapter presented returns for a number of different asset classes. The general conclusion is that stocks have outperformed bonds over most of the 20th century, though stocks have also exhibited more risk.

2. The statistical measures in this chapter are necessary building blocks for the material of the next three chapters. In particular, standard deviation and variance measure the variability of the return on an individual security and on portfolios of securities. In the next chapter, we will argue that standard deviation and variance are appropriate measures of the risk of an individual security if an investor's portfolio is composed of that security only.

Concept Questions

1. **Investment Selection**   Given that ViroPharma was up by almost 469 percent for 2005, why didn't all investors hold ViroPharma?

2. **Investment Selection**   Given that Majesco Entertainment was down by 92 percent for 2005, why did some investors hold the stock? Why didn't they sell out before the price declined so sharply?

3. **Risk and Return**   We have seen that over long periods stock investments have tended to substantially outperform bond investments. However, it is not at all uncommon to observe investors with long horizons holding their investments entirely in bonds. Are such investors irrational?

4. **Stocks versus Gambling**   Critically evaluate the following statement: Playing the stock market is like gambling. Such speculative investing has no social value, other than the pleasure people get from this form of gambling.

5. **Effects of Inflation**   Look at Table 9.1 and Figure 9.7 in the text. When were T-bill rates at their highest over the period from 1926 through 2005? Why do you think they were so high during this period? What relationship underlies your answer?

6. **Risk Premiums**   Is it possible for the risk premium to be negative before an investment is undertaken? Can the risk premium be negative after the fact? Explain.

7. **Returns**   Two years ago, General Materials' and Standard Fixtures' stock prices were the same. During the first year, General Materials' stock price increased by 10 percent while Standard Fixtures' stock price decreased by 10 percent. During the second year, General Materials' stock price decreased by 10 percent and Standard Fixtures' stock price increased by 10 percent. Do these two stocks have the same price today? Explain.

8. **Returns**   Two years ago, the Lake Minerals and Small Town Furniture stock prices were the same. The annual return for both stocks over the past two years was 10 percent. Lake Minerals' stock price increased 10 percent each year. Small Town Furniture's stock price increased 25 percent in the first year and lost 5 percent last year. Do these two stocks have the same price today?

9. **Arithmetic versus Geometric Returns**   What is the difference between arithmetic and geometric returns? Suppose you have invested in a stock for the last 10 years. Which number is more important to you, the arithmetic or geometric return?

10. **Historical Returns**   The historical asset class returns presented in the chapter are not adjusted for inflation. What would happen to the estimated risk premium if we did account for inflation? The returns are also not adjusted for taxes. What would happen to the returns if we accounted for taxes? What would happen to the volatility?

Questions and Problems

BASIC
(Questions 1–20)

1. **Calculating Returns**   Suppose a stock had an initial price of $83 per share, paid a dividend of $1.40 per share during the year, and had an ending share price of $91. Compute the percentage total return.

2. **Calculating Yields**   In Problem 1, what was the dividend yield? The capital gains yield?

3. **Calculating Returns**   Rework Problems 1 and 2 assuming the ending share price is $76.

4. **Calculating Returns**   Suppose you bought a 9 percent coupon bond one year ago for $1,120. The bond sells for $1,074 today.
   a. Assuming a $1,000 face value, what was your total dollar return on this investment over the past year?
   b. What was your total nominal rate of return on this investment over the past year?
   c. If the inflation rate last year was 3 percent, what was your total real rate of return on this investment?

5. **Nominal versus Real Returns**   What was the arithmetic average annual return on large-company stocks from 1926 through 2005
   a. In nominal terms?
   b. In real terms?

6. **Bond Returns**   What is the historical real return on long-term government bonds? On long-term corporate bonds?

7. **Calculating Returns and Variability**   Using the following returns, calculate the average returns, the variances, and the standard deviations for X and Y:

	Returns	
Year	X	Y
1	11%	36%
2	6	−7
3	−8	21
4	28	−12
5	13	43

8. **Risk Premiums** Refer to Table 9.1 in the text and look at the period from 1973 through 1978.
   a. Calculate the arithmetic average returns for large-company stocks and T-bills over this period.
   b. Calculate the standard deviation of the returns for large-company stocks and T-bills over this period.
   c. Calculate the observed risk premium in each year for the large-company stocks versus the T-bills. What was the arithmetic average risk premium over this period? What was the standard deviation of the risk premium over this period?

9. **Calculating Returns and Variability** You've observed the following returns on Mary Ann Data Corporation's stock over the past five years: 216 percent, 21 percent, 4 percent, 16 percent, and 19 percent.
   a. What was the arithmetic average return on Mary Ann's stock over this five-year period?
   b. What was the variance of Mary Ann's returns over this period? The standard deviation?

10. **Calculating Real Returns and Risk Premiums** In Problem 9, suppose the average inflation rate over this period was 4.2 percent and the average T-bill rate over the period was 5.1 percent.
    a. What was the average real return on Mary Ann's stock?
    b. What was the average nominal risk premium on Mary Ann's stock?

11. **Calculating Real Rates** Given the information in Problem 10, what was the average real risk-free rate over this time period? What was the average real risk premium?

12. **Holding Period Return** A stock has had returns of −4.91 percent, 21.67 percent, 22.57 percent, 6.19 percent, and 31.85 percent over the past five years, respectively. What was the holding period return for the stock?

13. **Calculating Returns** You purchased a zero coupon bond one year ago for $152.37. The market interest rate is now 10 percent. If the bond had 20 years to maturity when you originally purchased it, what was your total return for the past year?

14. **Calculating Returns** You bought a share of 5 percent preferred stock for $84.12 last year. The market price for your stock is now $80.27. What is your total return for last year?

15. **Calculating Returns** You bought a stock three months ago for $38.65 per share. The stock paid no dividends. The current share price is $42.02. What is the APR of your investment? The EAR?

16. **Calculating Real Returns** Refer to Table 9.1. What was the average real return for Treasury bills from 1926 through 1932?

17. **Return Distributions** Refer back to Figure 9.10. What range of returns would you expect to see 68 percent of the time for long-term corporate bonds? What about 95 percent of the time?

18. **Return Distributions** Refer back to Figure 9.10. What range of returns would you expect to see 68 percent of the time for large-company stocks? What about 95 percent of the time?

19. **Blume's Formula** Over a 30-year period an asset had an arithmetic return of 12.8 percent and a geometric return of 10.7 percent. Using Blume's formula, what is your best estimate of the future annual returns over 5 years? 10 years? 20 years?

20. **Blume's Formula** Assume that the historical return on large-company stocks is a predictor of the future returns. What return would you estimate for large-company stocks over the next year? The next 5 years? 20 years? 30 years?

INTERMEDIATE
(Questions 21–28)

21. **Calculating Returns and Variability** You find a certain stock that had returns of 8 percent, −13 percent, −7 percent, and 29 percent for four of the last five years. If the average return of the stock over this period was 11 percent, what was the stock's return for the missing year? What is the standard deviation of the stock's returns?

22. **Arithmetic and Geometric Returns** A stock has had returns of 29 percent, 14 percent, 23 percent, −8 percent, 9 percent, and −14 percent over the last six years. What are the arithmetic and geometric returns for the stock?

23. Arithmetic and Geometric Returns A stock has had the following year-end prices and dividends:

Year	Price	Dividend
1	$43.12	—
2	49.07	$0.55
3	51.19	0.60
4	47.24	0.63
5	56.09	0.72
6	67.21	0.81

What are the arithmetic and geometric returns for the stock?

24. Calculating Returns Refer to Table 9.1 in the text and look at the period from 1973 through 1980.
   a. Calculate the average return for Treasury bills and the average annual inflation rate (consumer price index) for this period.
   b. Calculate the standard deviation of Treasury bill returns and inflation over this period.
   c. Calculate the real return for each year. What is the average real return for Treasury bills?
   d. Many people consider Treasury bills to be risk-free. What do these calculations tell you about the potential risks of Treasury bills?

25. Calculating Investment Returns You bought one of Bergen Manufacturing Co.'s 8 percent coupon bonds one year ago for $1,028.50. These bonds make annual payments and mature six years from now. Suppose you decide to sell your bonds today, when the required return on the bonds is 7 percent. If the inflation rate was 4.8 percent over the past year, what would be your total real return on the investment?

26. Using Return Distributions Suppose the returns on long-term government bonds are normally distributed. Based on the historical record, what is the approximate probability that your return on these bonds will be less than −3.5 percent in a given year? What range of returns would you expect to see 95 percent of the time? What range would you expect to see 99 percent of the time?

27. Using Return Distributions Assuming that the returns from holding small-company stocks are normally distributed, what is the approximate probability that your money will double in value in a single year? Triple in value?

28. Distributions In the previous problem, what is the probability that the return is less than −100 percent? (Think.) What are the implications for the distribution of returns?

CHALLENGE
(Questions 29–30)

29. Using Probability Distributions Suppose the returns on large-company stocks are normally distributed. Based on the historical record, use the cumulative normal probability table (rounded to the nearest table value) in Chapter 22 to determine the probability that in any given year you will lose money by investing in common stock.

30. Using Probability Distributions Suppose the returns on long-term corporate bonds and T-bills are normally distributed. Based on the historical record, use the cumulative normal probability table (rounded to the nearest table value) in Chapter 22 to answer the following questions:
   a. What is the probability that in any given year, the return on long-term corporate bonds will be greater than 10 percent? Less than 0 percent?
   b. What is the probability that in any given year, the return on T-bills will be greater than 10 percent? Less than 0 percent?
   c. In 1979, the return on long-term corporate bonds was −4.18 percent. How likely is it that this low of a return will recur at some point in the future? T-bills had a return of 10.32 percent in this same year. How likely is it that this high of a return on T-bills will recur at some point in the future?

www.mhhe.com/rwj

S&P Problems

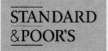

www.mhhe.com/edumarketinsight

1. **Calculating Yields**   Download the historical stock prices for Duke Energy (DUK) under the "Mthly. Adj. Prices" link. Find the closing stock price for the beginning and end of the prior two years. Now use the annual financial statements to find the dividend for each of these years. What was the capital gains yield and dividend yield for Duke Energy stock for each of these years? Now calculate the capital gains yield and dividend yield for Abercrombie & Fitch (ANF). How do the returns for these two companies compare?

2. **Calculating Average Returns**   Download the Monthly Adjusted Prices for Microsoft (MSFT). What is the return on the stock over the past 12 months? Now use the 1 Month Total Return and calculate the average monthly return. Is this one-twelfth of the annual return you calculated? Why or why not? What is the monthly standard deviation of Microsoft's stock over the past year?

Mini Case

A Job at East Coast Yachts

You recently graduated from college, and your job search led you to East Coast Yachts. Because you felt the company's business was seaworthy, you accepted a job offer. The first day on the job, while you are finishing your employment paperwork, Dan Ervin, who works in Finance, stops by to inform you about the company's 401(k) plan.

A 401(k) plan is a retirement plan offered by many companies. Such plans are tax-deferred savings vehicles, meaning that any deposits you make into the plan are deducted from your current pretax income, so no current taxes are paid on the money. For example, assume your salary will be $50,000 per year. If you contribute $3,000 to the 401(k) plan, you will pay taxes on only $47,000 in income. There are also no taxes paid on any capital gains or income while you are invested in the plan, but you do pay taxes when you withdraw money at retirement. As is fairly common, the company also has a 5 percent match. This means that the company will match your contribution up to 5 percent of your salary, but you must contribute to get the match.

The 401(k) plan has several options for investments, most of which are mutual funds. A mutual fund is a portfolio of assets. When you purchase shares in a mutual fund, you are actually purchasing partial ownership of the fund's assets. The return of the fund is the weighted average of the return of the assets owned by the fund, minus any expenses. The largest expense is typically the management fee, paid to the fund manager. The management fee is compensation for the manager, who makes all of the investment decisions for the fund.

East Coast Yachts uses Bledsoe Financial Services as its 401(k) plan administrator. Here are the investment options offered for employees:

Company Stock   One option in the 401(k) plan is stock in East Coast Yachts. The company is currently privately held. However, when you interviewed with the owner, Larissa Warren, she informed you the company stock was expected to go public in the next three to four years. Until then, a company stock price is simply set each year by the board of directors.

Bledsoe S&P 500 Index Fund   This mutual fund tracks the S&P 500. Stocks in the fund are weighted exactly the same as the S&P 500. This means the fund return is approximately the return on the S&P 500, minus expenses. Because an index fund purchases assets based on the compensation of the index it is following, the fund manager is not required to research stocks and make investment decisions. The result is that the fund expenses are usually low. The Bledsoe S&P 500 Index Fund charges expenses of .15 percent of assets per year.

Bledsoe Small-Cap Fund   This fund primarily invests in small-capitalization stocks. As such, the returns of the fund are more volatile. The fund can also invest 10 percent of its assets in companies based outside the United States. This fund charges 1.70 percent in expenses.

Bledsoe Large-Company Stock Fund   This fund invests primarily in large-capitalization stocks of companies based in the United States. The fund is managed by Evan Bledsoe and has outperformed the market in six of the last eight years. The fund charges 1.50 percent in expenses.

Bledsoe Bond Fund   This fund invests in long-term corporate bonds issued by U.S.–domiciled companies. The fund is restricted to investments in bonds with an investment-grade credit rating. This fund charges 1.40 percent in expenses.

Bledsoe Money Market Fund   This fund invests in short-term, high–credit quality debt instruments, which include Treasury bills. As such, the return on the money market fund is only slightly higher than the return on Treasury bills. Because of the credit quality and short-term nature of the investments, there is only a very slight risk of negative return. The fund charges .60 percent in expenses.

1. What advantages do the mutual funds offer compared to the company stock?

2. Assume that you invest 5 percent of your salary and receive the full 5 percent match from East Coast Yachts. What EAR do you earn from the match? What conclusions do you draw about matching plans?

3. Assume you decide you should invest at least part of your money in large-capitalization stocks of companies based in the United States. What are the advantages and disadvantages of choosing the Bledsoe Large-Company Stock Fund compared to the Bledsoe S&P 500 Index Fund?

4. The returns on the Bledsoe Small-Cap Fund are the most volatile of all the mutual funds offered in the 401(k) plan. Why would you ever want to invest in this fund? When you examine the expenses of the mutual funds, you will notice that this fund also has the highest expenses. Does this affect your decision to invest in this fund?

5. A measure of risk-adjusted performance that is often used is the Sharpe ratio. The Sharpe ratio is calculated as the risk premium of an asset divided by its standard deviation. The standard deviation and return of the funds over the past 10 years are listed here. Calculate the Sharpe ratio for each of these funds. Assume that the expected return and standard deviation of the company stock will be 18 percent and 70 percent, respectively. Calculate the Sharpe ratio for the company stock. How appropriate is the Sharpe ratio for these assets? When would you use the Sharpe ratio?

	10-Year Annual Return	Standard Deviation
Bledsoe S&P 500 Index Fund	11.48%	15.82%
Bledsoe Small-Cap Fund	16.68	19.64
Bledsoe Large-Company Stock Fund	11.85	15.41
Bledsoe Bond Fund	9.67	10.83

6. What portfolio allocation would you choose? Why? Explain your thinking carefully.

Appendix 9A   The Historical Market Risk Premium: The Very Long Run

To access Appendix 9A, please go to www.mhhe.com/rwj.

CHAPTER 9
SOME LESSONS FROM CAPITAL MARKET HISTORY

Answers to Concepts Review and Critical Thinking Questions

1. They all wish they had! Since they didn't, it must have been the case that the stellar performance was not foreseeable, at least not by most.

2. As in the previous question, it's easy to see after the fact that the investment was terrible, but it probably wasn't so easy ahead of time.

3. No, stocks are riskier. Some investors are highly risk averse, and the extra possible return doesn't attract them relative to the extra risk.

4. Unlike gambling, the stock market is a positive sum game; everybody can win. Also, speculators provide liquidity to markets and thus help to promote efficiency.

5. T-bill rates were highest in the early eighties. This was during a period of high inflation and is consistent with the Fisher effect.

6. Before the fact, for most assets, the risk premium will be positive; investors demand compensation over and above the risk-free return to invest their money in the risky asset. After the fact, the observed risk premium can be negative if the asset's nominal return is unexpectedly low, the risk-free return is unexpectedly high, or if some combination of these two events occurs.

7. Yes, the stock prices are currently the same. Below is a diagram that depicts the stocks' price movements. Two years ago, each stock had the same price, P_0. Over the first year, General Materials' stock price increased by 10 percent, or $(1.1) \times P_0$. Standard Fixtures' stock price declined by 10 percent, or $(0.9) \times P_0$. Over the second year, General Materials' stock price decreased by 10 percent, or $(0.9)(1.1) \times P_0$, while Standard Fixtures' stock price increased by 10 percent, or $(1.1)(0.9) \times P_0$. Today, each of the stocks is worth 99 percent of its original value.

	2 years ago	1 year ago	Today	
General Materials	P_0	$(1.1)P_0$	$(1.1)(0.9)P_0$	$= (0.99)P_0$
Standard Fixtures	P_0	$(0.9)P_0$	$(0.9)(1.1)P_0$	$= (0.99)P_0$

8. The stock prices are not the same. The return quoted for each stock is the arithmetic return, not the geometric return. The geometric return tells you the wealth increase from the beginning of the period to the end of the period, assuming the asset had the same return each year. As such, it is a better measure of ending wealth. To see this, assuming each stock had a beginning price of $100 per share, the ending price for each stock would be:

    Lake Minerals ending price = $100(1.10)(1.10) = $121.00
    Small Town Furniture ending price = $100(1.25)(.95) = $118.75

B-234 SOLUTIONS

Whenever there is any variance in returns, the asset with the larger variance will always have the greater difference between the arithmetic and geometric return.

9. To calculate an arithmetic return, you simply sum the returns and divide by the number of returns. As such, arithmetic returns do not account for the effects of compounding. Geometric returns do account for the effects of compounding. As an investor, the more important return of an asset is the geometric return.

10. Risk premiums are about the same whether or not we account for inflation. The reason is that risk premiums are the difference between two returns, so inflation essentially nets out. Returns, risk premiums, and volatility would all be lower than we estimated because aftertax returns are smaller than pretax returns.

Solutions to Questions and Problems

NOTE: All end of chapter problems were solved using a spreadsheet. Many problems require multiple steps. Due to space and readability constraints, when these intermediate steps are included in this solutions manual, rounding may appear to have occurred. However, the final answer for each problem is found without rounding during any step in the problem.

Basic

1. The return of any asset is the increase in price, plus any dividends or cash flows, all divided by the initial price. The return of this stock is:

    R = [($91 − 83) + 1.40] / $83
    R = .1133 or 11.33%

2. The dividend yield is the dividend divided by price at the beginning of the period, so:

    Dividend yield = $1.40 / $83
    Dividend yield = .0169 or 1.69%

    And the capital gains yield is the increase in price divided by the initial price, so:

    Capital gains yield = ($91 − 83) / $83
    Capital gains yield = .0964 or 9.64%

3. Using the equation for total return, we find:

    R = [($76 − 83) + 1.40] / $83
    R = −.0675 or −6.75%

    And the dividend yield and capital gains yield are:

    Dividend yield = $1.40 / $83
    Dividend yield = .0169 or 1.69%

Capital gains yield = ($76 – 83) / $83
Capital gains yield = –.0843 or –8.43%

Here's a question for you: Can the dividend yield ever be negative? No, that would mean you were paying the company for the privilege of owning the stock. It has happened on bonds. Remember the Buffett bond's we discussed in the bond chapter.

4. The total dollar return is the change in price plus the coupon payment, so:

Total dollar return = $1,074 – 1,120 + 90
Total dollar return = $44

The total percentage return of the bond is:

R = [($1,074 – 1,120) + 90] / $1,120
R = .0393 or 3.93%

Notice here that we could have simply used the total dollar return of $44 in the numerator of this equation.

Using the Fisher equation, the real return was:

$(1 + R) = (1 + r)(1 + h)$

r = (1.0393 / 1.030) – 1
r = .0090 or 0.90%

5. The nominal return is the stated return, which is 12.40 percent. Using the Fisher equation, the real return was:

$(1 + R) = (1 + r)(1 + h)$

r = (1.1240)/(1.031) – 1
r = .0902 or 9.02%

6. Using the Fisher equation, the real returns for government and corporate bonds were:

$(1 + R) = (1 + r)(1 + h)$

r_G = 1.058/1.031 – 1
r_G = .0262 or 2.62%

r_C = 1.062/1.031 – 1
r_C = .0301 or 3.01%

B-236 SOLUTIONS

7. The average return is the sum of the returns, divided by the number of returns. The average return for each stock was:

$$\overline{X} = \left[\sum_{i=1}^{N} x_i\right]\bigg/N = \frac{[.11 + .06 - .08 + .28 + .13]}{5} = .1000 \text{ or } 10.00\%$$

$$\overline{Y} = \left[\sum_{i=1}^{N} y_i\right]\bigg/N = \frac{[.36 - .07 + .21 - .12 + .43]}{5} = .1620 \text{ or } 16.20\%$$

We calculate the variance of each stock as:

$$s_X^2 = \left[\sum_{i=1}^{N}(x_i - \overline{x})^2\right]\bigg/(N-1)$$

$$s_X^2 = \frac{1}{5-1}\left\{(.11 - .100)^2 + (.06 - .100)^2 + (-.08 - .100)^2 + (.28 - .100)^2 + (.13 - .100)^2\right\} = .016850$$

$$s_Y^2 = \frac{1}{5-1}\left\{(.36 - .162)^2 + (-.07 - .162)^2 + (.21 - .162)^2 + (-.12 - .162)^2 + (.43 - .162)^2\right\} = .061670$$

The standard deviation is the square root of the variance, so the standard deviation of each stock is:

$s_X = (.016850)^{1/2}$
$s_X = .1298 \text{ or } 12.98\%$

$s_Y = (.061670)^{1/2}$
$s_Y = .2483 \text{ or } 24.83\%$

8. We will calculate the sum of the returns for each asset and the observed risk premium first. Doing so, we get:

Year	Large co. stock return	T-bill return	Risk premium
1973	−14.69%	7.29%	−21.98%
1974	−26.47	7.99	−34.46
1975	37.23	5.87	31.36
1976	23.93	5.07	18.86
1977	−7.16	5.45	−12.61
1978	6.57	7.64	−1.07
	19.41	39.31	−19.90

a. The average return for large company stocks over this period was:

Large company stock average return = 19.41% /6
Large company stock average return = 3.24%

CHAPTER 9 B-237

And the average return for T-bills over this period was:

T-bills average return = 39.31% / 6
T-bills average return = 6.55%

b. Using the equation for variance, we find the variance for large company stocks over this period was:

$$\text{Variance} = 1/5[(-.1469 - .0324)^2 + (-.2647 - .0324)^2 + (.3723 - .0324)^2 + (.2393 - .0324)^2 + (-.0716 - .0324)^2 + (.0657 - .0324)^2]$$
Variance = 0.058136

And the standard deviation for large company stocks over this period was:

Standard deviation = $(0.058136)^{1/2}$
Standard deviation = 0.2411 or 24.11%

Using the equation for variance, we find the variance for T-bills over this period was:

$$\text{Variance} = 1/5[(.0729 - .0655)^2 + (.0799 - .0655)^2 + (.0587 - .0655)^2 + (.0507 - .0655)^2 + (.0545 - .0655)^2 + (.0764 - .0655)^2]$$
Variance = 0.000153

And the standard deviation for T-bills over this period was:

Standard deviation = $(0.000153)^{1/2}$
Standard deviation = 0.0124 or 1.24%

c. The average observed risk premium over this period was:

Average observed risk premium = –19.90% / 6
Average observed risk premium = –3.32%

The variance of the observed risk premium was:

$$\text{Variance} = 1/5[(-.2198 - .0332)^2 + (-.3446 - .0332)^2 + (.3136 - .0332)^2 + (.1886 - .0332)^2 + (-.1261 - .0332)^2 + (-.0107 - .0332)^2]$$
Variance = 0.062078

And the standard deviation of the observed risk premium was:

Standard deviation = $(0.06278)^{1/2}$
Standard deviation = 0.2492 or 24.92%

9. a. To find the average return, we sum all the returns and divide by the number of returns, so:

Arithmetic average return = (2.16 +.21 + .04 + .16 + .19)/5
Arithmetic average return = .5520 or 55.20%

B-238 SOLUTIONS

    b.   Using the equation to calculate variance, we find:

$$\text{Variance} = 1/4[(2.16 - .552)^2 + (.21 - .552)^2 + (.04 - .552)^2 + (.16 - .552)^2 + (.19 - .552)^2]$$

Variance = 0.081237

So, the standard deviation is:

Standard deviation = $(0.81237)^{1/2}$
Standard deviation = 0.9013 or 90.13%

10. *a.*   To calculate the average real return, we can use the average return of the asset and the average inflation rate in the Fisher equation. Doing so, we find:

$$(1 + R) = (1 + r)(1 + h)$$

$\bar{r}$ = (1.5520/1.042) − 1
$\bar{r}$ = .4894 or 48.94%

    b.   The average risk premium is simply the average return of the asset, minus the average risk-free rate, so, the average risk premium for this asset would be:

$$\overline{RP} = \overline{R} - \overline{R}_f$$
$\overline{RP}$ = .5520 − .0510
$\overline{RP}$ = .5010 or 50.10%

11.   We can find the average real risk-free rate using the Fisher equation. The average real risk-free rate was:

$$(1 + R) = (1 + r)(1 + h)$$

$\bar{r}_f$ = (1.051/1.042) − 1
$\bar{r}_f$ = .0086 or 0.86%

And to calculate the average real risk premium, we can subtract the average risk-free rate from the average real return. So, the average real risk premium was:

$$\overline{rp} = \bar{r} - \bar{r}_f = 4.41\% - 0.86\%$$
$\overline{rp}$ = 3.55%

12.   Apply the five-year holding-period return formula to calculate the total return of the stock over the five-year period, we find:

5-year holding-period return = $[(1 + R_1)(1 + R_2)(1 + R_3)(1 + R_4)(1 + R_5)] - 1$
5-year holding-period return = $[(1 - .0491)(1 + .2167)(1 + .2257)(1 + .0619)(1 + .3185)] - 1$
5-year holding-period return = 0.9855 or 98.55%

13. To find the return on the zero coupon bond, we first need to find the price of the bond today. Since one year has elapsed, the bond now has 19 years to maturity, so the price today is:

$P_1 = \$1,000/1.10^{19}$
$P_1 = \$163.51$

There are no intermediate cash flows on a zero coupon bond, so the return is the capital gains, or:

$R = (\$163.51 - 152.37) / \$152.37$
$R = .0731$ or 7.31%

14. The return of any asset is the increase in price, plus any dividends or cash flows, all divided by the initial price. This preferred stock paid a dividend of $5, so the return for the year was:

$R = (\$80.27 - 84.12 + 5.00) / \$84.12$
$R = .0137$ or 1.37%

15. The return of any asset is the increase in price, plus any dividends or cash flows, all divided by the initial price. This stock paid no dividend, so the return was:

$R = (\$42.02 - 38.65) / \$38.65$
$R = .0872$ or 8.72%

This is the return for three months, so the APR is:

$APR = 4(8.72\%)$
$APR = 34.88\%$

And the EAR is:

$EAR = (1 + .0872)^4 - 1$
$EAR = .3971$ or 39.71%

16. To find the real return each year, we will use the Fisher equation, which is:

$1 + R = (1 + r)(1 + h)$

Using this relationship for each year, we find:

	T-bills	Inflation	Real Return
1926	0.0330	(0.0112)	0.0447
1927	0.0315	(0.0226)	0.0554
1928	0.0405	(0.0116)	0.0527
1929	0.0447	0.0058	0.0387
1930	0.0227	(0.0640)	0.0926
1931	0.0115	(0.0932)	0.1155
1932	0.0088	(0.1027)	0.1243

B-240 SOLUTIONS

So, the average real return was:

Average = (.0447 + .0554 + .0527 + .0387 + .0926 + .1155 + .1243) / 7
Average = .0748 or 7.48%

Notice the real return was higher than the nominal return during this period because of deflation, or negative inflation.

17. Looking at the long-term corporate bond return history in Figure 9.2, we see that the mean return was 6.2 percent, with a standard deviation of 8.6 percent. The range of returns you would expect to see 68 percent of the time is the mean plus or minus 1 standard deviation, or:

$$R \in \mu \pm 1\sigma = 6.2\% \pm 8.6\% = -2.40\% \text{ to } 14.80\%$$

The range of returns you would expect to see 95 percent of the time is the mean plus or minus 2 standard deviations, or:

$$R \in \mu \pm 2\sigma = 6.2\% \pm 2(8.6\%) = -11.00\% \text{ to } 23.40\%$$

18. Looking at the large-company stock return history in Figure 9.2, we see that the mean return was 12.4 percent, with a standard deviation of 20.3 percent. The range of returns you would expect to see 68 percent of the time is the mean plus or minus 1 standard deviation, or:

$$R \in \mu \pm 1\sigma = 12.4\% \pm 20.3\% = -7.90\% \text{ to } 32.70\%$$

The range of returns you would expect to see 95 percent of the time is the mean plus or minus 2 standard deviations, or:

$$R \in \mu \pm 2\sigma = 12.4\% \pm 2(20.3\%) = -28.20\% \text{ to } 53.00\%$$

19. To find the best forecast, we apply Blume's formula as follows:

$$R(5) = \frac{5-1}{29} \times 10.7\% + \frac{30-5}{29} \times 12.8\% = 12.51\%$$

$$R(10) = \frac{10-1}{29} \times 10.7\% + \frac{30-10}{29} \times 12.8\% = 12.15\%$$

$$R(20) = \frac{20-1}{29} \times 10.7\% + \frac{30-20}{29} \times 12.8\% = 11.42\%$$

20. The best forecast for a one year return is the arithmetic average, which is 12.4 percent. The geometric average, found in Table 9.3 is 10.4 percent. To find the best forecast for other periods, we apply Blume's formula as follows:

$$R(5) = \frac{5-1}{80-1} \times 10.4\% + \frac{80-5}{80-1} \times 12.4\% = 12.30\%$$

$$R(20) = \frac{20-1}{80-1} \times 10.4\% + \frac{80-20}{80-1} \times 12.4\% = 11.92\%$$

$$R(30) = \frac{30-1}{80-1} \times 10.4\% + \frac{80-30}{80-1} \times 12.4\% = 11.67\%$$

Intermediate

21. Here we know the average stock return, and four of the five returns used to compute the average return. We can work the average return equation backward to find the missing return. The average return is calculated as:

.55 = .08 – .13 – .07 + .29 + R
R = .38 or 38%

The missing return has to be 38 percent. Now we can use the equation for the variance to find:

Variance = $1/4[(.08 - .11)^2 + (-.13 - .11)^2 + (-.07 - .11)^2 + (.29 - .11)^2 + (.38 - .11)^2]$
Variance = 0.049050

And the standard deviation is:

Standard deviation = $(0.049050)^{1/2}$
Standard deviation = 0.2215 or 22.15%

22. The arithmetic average return is the sum of the known returns divided by the number of returns, so:

Arithmetic average return = (.29 + .14 + .23 –.08 + .09 –.14) / 6
Arithmetic average return = .0883 or 8.83%

Using the equation for the geometric return, we find:

Geometric average return = $[(1 + R_1) \times (1 + R_2) \times \ldots \times (1 + R_T)]^{1/T} - 1$
Geometric average return = $[(1 + .29)(1 + .14)(1 + .23)(1 - .08)(1 + .09)(1 - .14)]^{(1/6)} - 1$
Geometric average return = .0769 or 7.69%

Remember, the geometric average return will always be less than the arithmetic average return if the returns have any variation.

B-242 SOLUTIONS

23. To calculate the arithmetic and geometric average returns, we must first calculate the return for each year. The return for each year is:

R_1 = ($49.07 − 43.12 + 0.55) / $43.12 = .1507 or 15.07%
R_2 = ($51.19 − 49.07 + 0.60) / $49.07 = .0554 or 5.54%
R_3 = ($47.24 − 51.19 + 0.63) / $51.19 = −.0649 or −6.49%
R_4 = ($56.09 − 47.24 + 0.72)/ $47.24 = .2026 or 20.26%
R_5 = ($67.21 − 56.09 + 0.81) / $56.09 = .2127 or 21.27%

The arithmetic average return was:

R_A = (0.1507 + 0.0554 − 0.0649 + 0.2026 + 0.2127)/5
R_A = 0.1113 or 11.13%

And the geometric average return was:

$R_G = [(1 + .1507)(1 + .0554)(1 − .0649)(1 + .2026)(1 + .2127)]^{1/5} − 1$
R_G = 0.1062 or 10.62%

24. To find the real return we need to use the Fisher equation. Re-writing the Fisher equation to solve for the real return, we get:

$r = [(1 + R)/(1 + h)] − 1$

So, the real return each year was:

Year	T-bill return	Inflation	Real return
1973	0.0729	0.0871	−0.0131
1974	0.0799	0.1234	−0.0387
1975	0.0587	0.0694	−0.0100
1976	0.0507	0.0486	0.0020
1977	0.0545	0.0670	−0.0117
1978	0.0764	0.0902	−0.0127
1979	0.1056	0.1329	−0.0241
1980	0.1210	0.1252	−0.0037
	0.6197	0.7438	−0.1120

a. The average return for T-bills over this period was:

Average return = 0.619 / 8
Average return = .0775 or 7.75%

And the average inflation rate was:

Average inflation = 0.7438 / 8
Average inflation = .0930 or 9.30%

b. Using the equation for variance, we find the variance for T-bills over this period was:

$$\text{Variance} = 1/7[(.0729 - .0775)^2 + (.0799 - .0775)^2 + (.0587 - .0775)^2 + (.0507 - .0775)^2 +$$
$$(.0545 - .0775)^2 + (.0764 - .0775)^2 + (.1056 - .0775)^2 + (.1210 - .0775)^2]$$
$$\text{Variance} = 0.000616$$

And the standard deviation for T-bills was:

$$\text{Standard deviation} = (0.000616)^{1/2}$$
$$\text{Standard deviation} = 0.0248 \text{ or } 2.48\%$$

The variance of inflation over this period was:

$$\text{Variance} = 1/7[(.0871 - .0930)^2 + (.1234 - .0930)^2 + (.0694 - .0930)^2 + (.0486 - .0930)^2 +$$
$$(.0670 - .0930)^2 + (.0902 - .0930)^2 + (.1329 - .0930)^2 + (.1252 - .0930)^2]$$
$$\text{Variance} = 0.000971$$

And the standard deviation of inflation was:

$$\text{Standard deviation} = (0.000971)^{1/2}$$
$$\text{Standard deviation} = 0.0312 \text{ or } 3.12\%$$

c. The average observed real return over this period was:

$$\text{Average observed real return} = -.1122 / 8$$
$$\text{Average observed real return} = -.0140 \text{ or } -1.40\%$$

d. The statement that T-bills have no risk refers to the fact that there is only an extremely small chance of the government defaulting, so there is little default risk. Since T-bills are short term, there is also very limited interest rate risk. However, as this example shows, there is inflation risk, i.e. the purchasing power of the investment can actually decline over time even if the investor is earning a positive return.

25. To find the return on the coupon bond, we first need to find the price of the bond today. Since one year has elapsed, the bond now has six years to maturity, so the price today is:

$$P_1 = \$80(\text{PVIFA}_{7\%,6}) + \$1,000/1.07^6$$
$$P_1 = \$1,047.67$$

You received the coupon payments on the bond, so the nominal return was:

$$R = (\$1,047.67 - 1,028.50 + 80) / \$1,028.50$$
$$R = .0964 \text{ or } 9.64\%$$

And using the Fisher equation to find the real return, we get:

$$r = (1.0964 / 1.048) - 1$$
$$r = .0462 \text{ or } 4.62\%$$

B-244 SOLUTIONS

26. Looking at the long-term government bond return history in Table 9.2, we see that the mean return was 5.8 percent, with a standard deviation of 9.3 percent. In the normal probability distribution, approximately 2/3 of the observations are within one standard deviation of the mean. This means that 1/3 of the observations are outside one standard deviation away from the mean. Or:

$$Pr(R < -3.5 \text{ or } R > 15.1) \approx \frac{1}{3}$$

But we are only interested in one tail here, that is, returns less than –3.5 percent, so:

$$Pr(R < -3.5) \approx \frac{1}{6}$$

You can use the z-statistic and the cumulative normal distribution table to find the answer as well. Doing so, we find:

$$z = (X - \mu)/\sigma$$

$$z = (-3.5\% - 5.8)/9.3\% = -1.00$$

Looking at the z-table, this gives a probability of 15.87%, or:

$$Pr(R < -3.5) \approx .1587 \text{ or } 15.87\%$$

The range of returns you would expect to see 95 percent of the time is the mean plus or minus 2 standard deviations, or:

95% level: $R \in \mu \pm 2\sigma = 5.8\% \pm 2(9.3\%) = -12.80\%$ to 24.40%

The range of returns you would expect to see 99 percent of the time is the mean plus or minus 3 standard deviations, or:

99% level: $R \in \mu \pm 3\sigma = 5.8\% \pm 3(9.3\%) = -22.10\%$ to 33.70%

27. The mean return for small company stocks was 17.5 percent, with a standard deviation of 33.1 percent. Doubling your money is a 100% return, so if the return distribution is normal, we can use the z-statistic. So:

$$z = (X - \mu)/\sigma$$

$$z = (100\% - 17.5\%)/33.1\% = 2.492 \text{ standard deviations above the mean}$$

This corresponds to a probability of $\approx 0.634\%$, or less than once every 100 years. Tripling your money would be:

$$z = (200\% - 17.5\%)/33.1\% = 5.514 \text{ standard deviations above the mean.}$$

This corresponds to a probability of (much) less than 0.5%, or once every 200 years. The actual answer is $\approx .00000176\%$, or about once every 1 million years.

CHAPTER 9 B-245

28. It is impossible to lose more than 100 percent of your investment. Therefore, return distributions are truncated on the lower tail at −100 percent.

Challenge

29. Using the z-statistic, we find:

$$z = (X - \mu)/\sigma$$

$$z = (0\% - 12.4\%)/20.3\% = -0.6108$$

$$Pr(R \leq 0) \approx 27.07\%$$

30. For each of the questions asked here, we need to use the z-statistic, which is:

$$z = (X - \mu)/\sigma$$

a. $z_1 = (10\% - 6.2\%)/8.6\% = 0.4419$

This z-statistic gives us the probability that the return is less than 10 percent, but we are looking for the probability the return is greater than 10 percent. Given that the total probability is 100 percent (or 1), the probability of a return greater than 10 percent is 1 minus the probability of a return less than 10 percent. Using the cumulative normal distribution table, we get:

$$Pr(R \geq 10\%) = 1 - Pr(R \leq 10\%) = 1 - .6707 \approx 32.93\%$$

For a return less than 0 percent:

$$z_2 = (0\% - 6.2\%)/8.6 = -0.7209$$

$$Pr(R < 10\%) = 1 - Pr(R > 0\%) = 1 - .7645 \approx 23.55\%$$

b. The probability that T-bill returns will be greater than 10 percent is:

$$z_3 = (10\% - 3.8\%)/3.1\% = 2$$

$$Pr(R \geq 10\%) = 1 - Pr(R \leq 10\%) = 1 - .9772 \approx 2.28\%$$

And the probability that T-bill returns will be less than 0 percent is:

$$z_4 = (0\% - 3.8\%)/3.1\% = -1.2258$$

$$Pr(R \leq 0) \approx 11.01\%$$

B-246 SOLUTIONS

   c.   The probability that the return on long-term corporate bonds will be less than –4.18 percent is:

$z_5 = (-4.18\% - 6.2\%)/8.6\% = -1.20698$

$\Pr(R \leq -4.18\%) \approx 11.37\%$

And the probability that T-bill returns will be greater than 10.32 percent is:

$z_6 = (10.32\% - 3.8\%)/3.1\% = 2.1032$

$\Pr(R \geq 10.38\%) = 1 - \Pr(R \leq 10.38\%) = 1 - .9823 \approx 1.77\%$

CHAPTER 10

Return and Risk

The Capital Asset Pricing Model (CAPM)

Expected returns on common stocks can vary quite a bit. One important determinant is the industry in which a company operates. For example, according to recent estimates from Ibbotson Associates, the median expected return for department stores, which includes companies such as Sears and Kohls, is 11.63 percent, whereas computer service companies such as Microsoft and Oracle have a median expected return of 15.46 percent. Air transportation companies such as Delta and Southwest have a median expected return that is even higher: 17.93 percent.

These estimates raise some obvious questions. First, why do these industry expected returns differ so much, and how are these specific numbers calculated? Also, does the higher return offered by airline stocks mean that investors should prefer these to, say, department store stocks? As we will see in this chapter, the Nobel Prize–winning answers to these questions form the basis of our modern understanding of risk and return.

10.1 Individual Securities

In the first part of Chapter 10, we will examine the characteristics of individual securities. In particular, we will discuss:

1. *Expected return*: This is the return that an individual expects a stock to earn over the next period. Of course, because this is only an expectation, the actual return may be either higher or lower. An individual's expectation may simply be the average return per period a security has earned in the past. Alternatively, it may be based on a detailed analysis of a firm's prospects, on some computer-based model, or on special (or inside) information.

2. *Variance and standard deviation*: There are many ways to assess the volatility of a security's return. One of the most common is variance, which is a measure of the squared deviations of a security's return from its expected return. Standard deviation is the square root of the variance.

3. *Covariance and correlation*: Returns on individual securities are related to one another. Covariance is a statistic measuring the interrelationship between two securities. Alternatively, this relationship can be restated in terms of the correlation between the two securities. Covariance and correlation are building blocks to an understanding of the beta coefficient.

10.2 Expected Return, Variance, and Covariance

Expected Return and Variance

Suppose financial analysts believe that there are four equally likely states of the economy: depression, recession, normal, and boom. The returns on the Supertech Company are expected to follow the economy closely, while the returns on the Slowpoke Company are not. The return predictions are as follows:

	Supertech Returns R_{At}	Slowpoke Returns R_{Bt}
Depression	−20%	5%
Recession	10	20
Normal	30	−12
Boom	50	9

Variance can be calculated in four steps. An additional step is needed to calculate standard deviation. (The calculations are presented in Table 10.1.) The steps are these:

1. Calculate the expected return:

    Supertech

    $$\frac{-0.20 + 0.10 + 0.30 + 0.50}{4} = 0.175 = 17.5\% = \overline{R}_A$$

    Slowpoke

    $$\frac{0.05 + 0.20 - 0.12 + 0.09}{4} = 0.055 = 5.5\% = \overline{R}_B$$

2. For each company, calculate the deviation of each possible return from the company's expected return given previously. This is presented in the third column of Table 10.1.

3. The deviations we have calculated are indications of the dispersion of returns. However, because some are positive and some are negative, it is difficult to work with them in this form. For example, if we were to simply add up all the deviations for a single company, we would get zero as the sum.

    To make the deviations more meaningful, we multiply each one by itself. Now all the numbers are positive, implying that their sum must be positive as well. The squared deviations are presented in the last column of Table 10.1.

4. For each company, calculate the average squared deviation, which is the variance:[1]

    Supertech

    $$\frac{0.140625 + 0.005625 + 0.015625 + 0.105625}{4} = 0.066875$$

---

[1] In this example, the four states give rise to four *possible* outcomes for each stock. Had we used past data, the outcomes would have actually occurred. In that case, statisticians argue that the correct divisor is $N - 1$, where N is the number of observations. Thus the denominator would be 3 [$= (4 - 1)$] in the case of past data, not 4. Note that the example in Section 9.5 involved past data and we used a divisor of $N - 1$. While this difference causes grief to both students and textbook writers, it is a minor point in practice. In the real world, samples are generally so large that using N or $N - 1$ in the denominator has virtually no effect on the calculation of variance.

Table 10.1

Calculating Variance and Standard Deviation

(1) State of Economy	(2) Rate of Return	(3) Deviation from Expected Return	(4) Squared Value of Deviation
	Supertech*	**(Expected return = 0.175)**	
	R_{At}	$(R_{At} - \bar{R}_A)$	$(R_{At} - \bar{R}_A)^2$
Depression	−0.20	−0.375	0.140625
		(= −0.20 − 0.175)	[= (−0.375)²]
Recession	0.10	−0.075	0.005625
Normal	0.30	0.125	0.015625
Boom	0.50	0.325	0.105625
			0.267500
	Slowpoke†	**(Expected return = 0.055)**	
	R_{Bt}	$(R_{Bt} - \bar{R}_B)$	$(R_{Bt} - \bar{R}_B)^2$
Depression	0.05	−0.005	0.000025
		(= 0.05 − 0.055)	[= (−0.005)²]
Recession	0.20	0.145	0.021025
Normal	−0.12	−0.175	0.030625
Boom	0.09	0.035	0.001225
			0.052900

$$*\bar{R}_A = \frac{-0.20 + 0.10 + 0.30 + 0.50}{4} = 0.175 = 17.5\%$$

$$\text{Var}(R_A) = \sigma_A^2 = \frac{0.2675}{4} = 0.066875$$

$$\text{SD}(R_A) = \sigma_A = \sqrt{0.066875} = 0.2586 = 25.86\%$$

$$\dagger\bar{R}_B = \frac{0.05 + 0.20 - 0.12 - 0.09}{4} = 0.055 = 5.5\%$$

$$\text{Var}(R_B) = \sigma_B^2 = \frac{0.0529}{4} = 0.013225$$

$$\text{SD}(R_B) = \sigma_B = \sqrt{0.013225} = 0.1150 = 11.50\%$$

Slowpoke

$$\frac{0.000025 + 0.021025 + 0.030625 + 0.001225}{4} = 0.013225$$

Thus, the variance of Supertech is 0.066875, and the variance of Slowpoke is: 0.013225.

5. Calculate standard deviation by taking the square root of the variance:

Supertech

$$\sqrt{0.066875} = 0.2586 = 25.86\%$$

Slowpoke

$$\sqrt{0.013225} = 0.1150 = 11.50\%$$

Algebraically, the formula for variance can be expressed as:

$$\text{Var}(R) = \text{Expected value of } (R - \bar{R})^2$$

where $\bar{R}$ is the security's expected return and R is the actual return.

A look at the four-step calculation for variance makes it clear why it is a measure of the spread of the sample of returns. For each observation we square the difference between the actual return and the expected return. We then take an average of these squared differences. Squaring the differences makes them all positive. If we used the differences between each return and the expected return and then averaged these differences, we would get zero because the returns that were above the mean would cancel the ones below.

However, because the variance is still expressed in squared terms, it is difficult to interpret. Standard deviation has a much simpler interpretation, which was provided in Section 9.5. Standard deviation is simply the square root of the variance. The general formula for the standard deviation is:

$$SD(R) = \sqrt{Var(R)}$$

Covariance and Correlation

Variance and standard deviation measure the variability of individual stocks. We now wish to measure the relationship between the return on one stock and the return on another. Enter **covariance** and **correlation**.

Covariance and correlation measure how two random variables are related. We explain these terms by extending the Supertech and Slowpoke example.

Calculating Covariance and Correlation We have already determined the expected returns and standard deviations for both Supertech and Slowpoke. (The expected returns are 0.175 and 0.055 for Supertech and Slowpoke, respectively. The standard deviations are 0.2586 and 0.1150, respectively.) In addition, we calculated the deviation of each possible return from the expected return for each firm. Using these data, we can calculate covariance in two steps. An extra step is needed to calculate correlation.

1. For each state of the economy, multiply Supertech's deviation from its expected return and Slowpoke's deviation from its expected return together. For example, Supertech's rate of return in a depression is −0.20, which is −0.375 (=−0.20 − 0.175) from its expected return. Slowpoke's rate of return in a depression is 0.05, which is −0.005 (=0.05 − 0.055) from its expected return. Multiplying the two deviations together yields 0.001875 [=(−0.375) × (−0.005)]. The actual calculations are given in the last column of Table 10.2. This procedure can be written algebraically as:

$$(R_{At} - \bar{R}_A) \times (R_{Bt} - \bar{R}_B) \tag{10.1}$$

where R_{At} and R_{Bt} are the returns on Supertech and Slowpoke in state t. $\bar{R}_A$ and $\bar{R}_B$ are the expected returns on the two securities.

2. Calculate the average value of the four states in the last column. This average is the covariance. That is:[2]

$$\sigma_{AB} = Cov(R_A, R_B) = \frac{-0.0195}{4} = -0.004875$$

Note that we represent the covariance between Supertech and Slowpoke as either $Cov(R_A, R_B)$ or σ_{AB}. Equation 10.1 illustrates the intuition of covariance. Suppose Supertech's return is generally above its average when Slowpoke's return is above its average, and Supertech's return is generally

(continued)

---

[2] As with variance, we divided by N (4 in this example) because the four states give rise to four *possible* outcomes. However, had we used past data, the correct divisor would be $N − 1$ (3 in this example).

Ross–Westerfield–Jaffe:
Corporate Finance, Eighth
Edition

III. Risk

10. Return and Risk: The
Capital Asset Pricing
Model (CAPM)

© The McGraw–Hill
Companies, 2008

399

Table 10.2   Calculating Covariance and Correlation

State of Economy	Rate of Return of Supertech R_{At}	Deviation from Expected Return $(R_{At} - \bar{R}_A)$	Rate of Return of Slowpoke R_{Bt}	Deviation from Expected Return $(R_{Bt} - \bar{R}_B)$	Product of Deviations $(R_{At} - \bar{R}_A) \times (R_{Bt} - \bar{R}_B)$
		(Expected return = 0.175)		(Expected return = 0.055)	
Depression	−0.20	−0.375	0.05	−0.005	0.001875
		(= −0.20 − 0.175)		(= 0.05 − 0.055)	(= −0.375 × −0.005)
Recession	0.10	−0.075	0.20	0.145	−0.010875
					(= −0.075 × 0.145)
Normal	0.30	0.125	−0.12	−0.175	−0.021875
					(= 0.125 × −0.175)
Boom	0.50	0.325	0.09	0.035	0.011375
					(= 0.325 × 0.035)
	0.70		0.22		−0.0195

$$\sigma_{AB} = \text{Cov}(R_A, R_B) = \frac{-0.0195}{4} = -0.004875$$

$$\rho_{AB} = \text{Corr}(R_A, R_B) = \frac{\text{Cov}(R_A, R_B)}{\text{SD}(R_A) \times \text{SD}(R_B)} = \frac{-0.004875}{0.2586 \times 0.1150} = -0.1639$$

below its average when Slowpoke's return is below its average. This shows a positive dependency or a positive relationship between the two returns. Note that the term in Equation 10.1 will be *positive* in any state where both returns are *above* their averages. In addition, 10.1 will still be *positive* in any state where both terms are *below* their averages. Thus a positive relationship between the two returns will give rise to a positive value for covariance.

Conversely, suppose Supertech's return is generally above its average when Slowpoke's return is below its average, and Supertech's return is generally below its average when Slowpoke's return is above its average. This demonstrates a negative dependency or a negative relationship between the two returns. Note that the term in Equation 10.1 will be *negative* in any state where one return is above its average and the other return is below its average. Thus a negative relationship between the two returns will give rise to a negative value for covariance.

Finally, suppose there is no relationship between the two returns. In this case, knowing whether the return on Supertech is above or below its expected return tells us nothing about the return on Slowpoke. In the covariance formula, then, there will be no tendency for the deviations to be positive or negative together. On average, they will tend to offset each other and cancel out, making the covariance zero.

Of course, even if the two returns are unrelated to each other, the covariance formula will not equal zero exactly in any actual history. This is due to sampling error; randomness alone will make the calculation positive or negative. But for a historical sample that is long enough, if the two returns are not related to each other, we should expect the covariance to come close to zero.

The covariance formula seems to capture what we are looking for. If the two returns are positively related to each other, they will have a positive covariance, and if they are negatively related to each other, the covariance will be negative. Last, and very important, if they are unrelated, the covariance should be zero.

The formula for covariance can be written algebraically as:

$$\sigma_{AB} = \text{Cov}(R_A, R_B) = \text{Expected value of } [(R_A - \bar{R}_A) \times (R_B - \bar{R}_B)]$$

(*continued*)

where $\bar{R}_A$ and $\bar{R}_B$ are the expected returns for the two securities, and R_A and R_B are the actual returns. The ordering of the two variables is unimportant. That is, the covariance of A with B is equal to the covariance of B with A. This can be stated more formally as $Cov(R_A, R_B) = Cov(R_B, R_A)$ or $\sigma_{AB} = \sigma_{BA}$.

The covariance we calculated is -0.004875. A negative number like this implies that the return on one stock is likely to be above its average when the return on the other stock is below its average, and vice versa. However, the size of the number is difficult to interpret. Like the variance figure, the covariance is in squared deviation units. Until we can put it in perspective, we don't know what to make of it.

We solve the problem by computing the correlation.

3. To calculate the correlation, divide the covariance by the standard deviations of both of the two securities. For our example, we have:

$$\rho_{AB} = Corr(R_A, R_B) = \frac{Cov(R_A, R_B)}{\sigma_A \times \sigma_B} = \frac{-0.004875}{0.2586 \times 0.1150} = -0.1639 \qquad (10.2)$$

where σ_A and σ_B are the standard deviations of Supertech and Slowpoke, respectively. Note that we represent the correlation between Supertech and Slowpoke either as $Corr(R_A, R_B)$ or ρ_{AB}. As with covariance, the ordering of the two variables is unimportant. That is, the correlation of A with B is equal to the correlation of B with A. More formally, $Corr(R_A, R_B) = Corr(R_B, R_A)$ or $\rho_{AB} = \rho_{BA}$.

Figure 10.1

Examples of Different Correlation Coefficients—Graphs Plotting the Separate Returns on Two Securities through Time

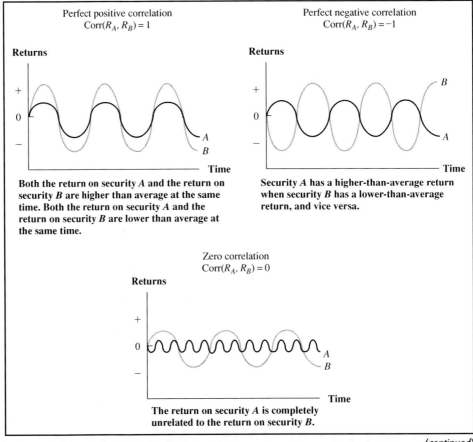

Because the standard deviation is always positive, the sign of the correlation between two variables must be the same as that of the covariance between the two variables. If the correlation is positive, we say that the variables are *positively correlated*; if it is negative, we say that they are *negatively correlated*; and if it is zero, we say that they are *uncorrelated*. Furthermore, it can be proved that the correlation is always between +1 and −1. This is due to the standardizing procedure of dividing by the two standard deviations.

We can compare the correlation between different *pairs* of securities. For example, it turns out that the correlation between General Motors and Ford is much higher than the correlation between General Motors and IBM. Hence, we can state that the first pair of securities is more interrelated than the second pair.

Figure 10.1 shows the three benchmark cases for two assets, A and B. The figure shows two assets with return correlations of +1, −1, and 0. This implies perfect positive correlation, perfect negative correlation, and no correlation, respectively. The graphs in the figure plot the separate returns on the two securities through time.

10.3   The Return and Risk for Portfolios

Suppose an investor has estimates of the expected returns and standard deviations on individual securities and the correlations between securities. How does the investor choose the best combination or **portfolio** of securities to hold? Obviously, the investor would like a portfolio with a high expected return and a low standard deviation of return. It is therefore worthwhile to consider:

1. The relationship between the expected return on individual securities and the expected return on a portfolio made up of these securities.
2. The relationship between the standard deviations of individual securities, the correlations between these securities, and the standard deviation of a portfolio made up of these securities.

To analyze these two relationships, we will use the same example of Supertech and Slowpoke. The relevant calculations follow.

The Expected Return on a Portfolio

The formula for expected return on a portfolio is very simple:

The expected return on a portfolio is simply a weighted average of the expected returns on the individual securities.

Relevant Data from Example of Supertech and Slowpoke		
Item	**Symbol**	**Value**
Expected return on Supertech	$\overline{R}_{Super}$	0.175 = 17.5%
Expected return on Slowpoke	$\overline{R}_{Slow}$	0.055 = 5.5%
Variance of Supertech	σ^2_{Super}	0.066875
Variance of Slowpoke	σ^2_{Slow}	0.013225
Standard deviation of Supertech	σ_{Super}	0.2586 = 25.86%
Standard deviation of Slowpoke	σ_{Slow}	0.1150 = 11.50%
Covariance between Supertech and Slowpoke	$\sigma_{Super, Slow}$	−0.004875
Correlation between Supertech and Slowpoke	$\rho_{Super, Slow}$	−0.1639

Portfolio Expected Returns   Consider Supertech and Slowpoke. From our earlier calculations, we find that the expected returns on these two securities are 17.5 percent and 5.5 percent, respectively.

The expected return on a portfolio of these two securities alone can be written as:

$$\text{Expected return on portfolio} = X_{\text{Super}}\,(17.5\%) + X_{\text{Slow}}\,(5.5\%) = \bar{R}_P$$

where X_{Super} is the percentage of the portfolio in Supertech and X_{Slow} is the percentage of the portfolio in Slowpoke. If the investor with $100 invests $60 in Supertech and $40 in Slowpoke, the expected return on the portfolio can be written as:

$$\text{Expected return on portfolio} = 0.6 \times 17.5\% + 0.4 \times 5.5\% = 12.7\%$$

Algebraically, we can write:

$$\text{Expected return on portfolio} = X_A\bar{R}_A + X_B\bar{R}_B = \bar{R}_P \qquad (10.3)$$

where X_A and X_B are the proportions of the total portfolio in the assets A and B, respectively. (Because our investor can invest in only two securities, $X_A + X_B$ must equal 1 or 100 percent.) $\bar{R}_A$ and $\bar{R}_B$ are the expected returns on the two securities.

Now consider two stocks, each with an expected return of 10 percent. The expected return on a portfolio composed of these two stocks must be 10 percent, regardless of the proportions of the two stocks held. This result may seem obvious at this point, but it will become important later. The result implies that you do not reduce or *dissipate* your expected return by investing in a number of securities. Rather, the expected return on your portfolio is simply a weighted average of the expected returns on the individual assets in the portfolio.

Variance and Standard Deviation of a Portfolio

The Variance   The formula for the variance of a portfolio composed of two securities, A and B, is:

The Variance of the Portfolio

$$\text{Var(portfolio)} = X_A^2\sigma_A^2 + 2X_A X_B\sigma_{A,B} + X_B^2\sigma_B^2$$

Note that there are three terms on the right side of the equation. The first term involves the variance of $A\,(\sigma_A^2)$, the second term involves the covariance between the two securities $(\sigma_{A,B})$, and the third term involves the variance of $B\,(\sigma_B^2)$. (As stated earlier in this chapter, $\sigma_{A,B} = \sigma_{B,A}$. That is, the ordering of the variables is not relevant when we are expressing the covariance between two securities.)

The formula indicates an important point. The variance of a portfolio depends on both the variances of the individual securities and the covariance between the two securities. The variance of a security measures the variability of an individual security's return. Covariance measures the relationship between the two securities. For given variances of the individual securities, a positive relationship or covariance between the two securities increases the variance of the entire portfolio. A negative relationship or covariance between the two securities decreases the variance of the entire portfolio. This important result seems to square with common sense. If one of your securities tends to go up when the other goes down, or vice versa, your two securities are offsetting each other. You are achieving what we call a *hedge* in finance, and the risk of your entire portfolio will be low. However, if both your securities rise and fall together, you are not hedging at all. Hence, the risk of your entire portfolio will be higher.

The variance formula for our two securities, Super and Slow, is:

$$\text{Var(portfolio)} = X^2_{\text{Super}}\sigma^2_{\text{Super}} + 2X_{\text{Super}}X_{\text{Slow}}\sigma_{\text{Super, Slow}} + X^2_{\text{Slow}}\sigma^2_{\text{Slow}} \qquad \textbf{(10.4)}$$

Given our earlier assumption that an individual with $100 invests $60 in Supertech and $40 in Slowpoke, $X_{\text{Super}} = 0.6$ and $X_{\text{Slow}} = 0.4$. Using this assumption and the relevant data from our previous calculations, the variance of the portfolio is:

$$0.023851 = 0.36 \times 0.066875 + 2 \times [0.6 \times 0.4 \times (-0.004875)] + 0.16 \times 0.013225$$
$$\textbf{(10.4}'\textbf{)}$$

The Matrix Approach   Alternatively, Equation 10.4 can be expressed in the following matrix format:

	Supertech	**Slowpoke**
Supertech	$X^2_{\text{Super}}\sigma^2_{\text{Super}}$ $0.024075 = 0.36 \times 0.066875$	$X_{\text{Super}}X_{\text{Slow}}\sigma_{\text{Super, Slow}}$ $-0.00117 = 0.6 \times 0.4 \times (-0.004875)$
Slowpoke	$X_{\text{Super}}X_{\text{Slow}}\sigma_{\text{Super, Slow}}$ $-0.00117 = 0.6 \times 0.4 \times (-0.004875)$	$X^2_{\text{Slow}}\sigma^2_{\text{Slow}}$ $0.002116 = 0.16 \times 0.013225$

There are four boxes in the matrix. We can add the terms in the boxes to obtain Equation 10.4, the variance of a portfolio composed of the two securities. The term in the upper left corner involves the variance of Supertech. The term in the lower right corner involves the variance of Slowpoke. The other two boxes contain the term involving the covariance. These two boxes are identical, indicating why the covariance term is multiplied by 2 in Equation 10.4.

At this point, students often find the box approach to be more confusing than Equation 10.4. However, the box approach is easily generalized to more than two securities, a task we perform later in this chapter.

Standard Deviation of a Portfolio   Given Equation 10.4′, we can now determine the standard deviation of the portfolio's return. This is:

$$\sigma_P = \text{SD(portfolio)} = \sqrt{\text{Var(portfolio)}} = \sqrt{0.023851} \qquad \textbf{(10.5)}$$
$$= 0.1544 = 15.44\%$$

The interpretation of the standard deviation of the portfolio is the same as the interpretation of the standard deviation of an individual security. The expected return on our portfolio is 12.7 percent. A return of -2.74 percent ($=12.7\% - 15.44\%$) is one standard deviation below the mean, and a return of 28.14 percent ($=12.7\% + 15.44\%$) is one standard deviation above the mean. If the return on the portfolio is normally distributed, a return between -2.74 percent and $+28.14$ percent occurs about 68 percent of the time.[3]

The Diversification Effect   It is instructive to compare the standard deviation of the portfolio with the standard deviation of the individual securities. The weighted average of the standard deviations of the individual securities is:

$$\text{Weighted average of standard deviations} = X_{\text{Super}}\sigma_{\text{Super}} + X_{\text{Slow}}\sigma_{\text{Slow}} \qquad \textbf{(10.6)}$$
$$0.2012 = 0.6 \times 0.2586 + 0.4 \times 0.115$$

---

[3]There are only four equally probable returns for Supertech and Slowpoke, so neither security possesses a normal distribution. Thus, probabilities would be slightly different in our example.

One of the most important results in this chapter concerns the difference between Equations 10.5 and 10.6. In our example, the standard deviation of the portfolio is *less* than a weighted average of the standard deviations of the individual securities.

We pointed out earlier that the expected return on the portfolio is a weighted average of the expected returns on the individual securities. Thus, we get a different type of result for the standard deviation of a portfolio than we do for the expected return on a portfolio.

It is generally argued that our result for the standard deviation of a portfolio is due to diversification. For example, Supertech and Slowpoke are slightly negatively correlated ($\rho = -0.1639$). Supertech's return is likely to be a little below average if Slowpoke's return is above average. Similarly, Supertech's return is likely to be a little above average if Slowpoke's return is below average. Thus, the standard deviation of a portfolio composed of the two securities is less than a weighted average of the standard deviations of the two securities.

Our example has negative correlation. Clearly, there will be less benefit from diversification if the two securities exhibit positive correlation. How high must the positive correlation be before all diversification benefits vanish?

To answer this question, let us rewrite Equation 10.4 in terms of correlation rather than covariance. The covariance can be rewritten as:[4]

$$\sigma_{\text{Super, Slow}} = \rho_{\text{Super, Slow}}\sigma_{\text{Super}}\sigma_{\text{Slow}} \tag{10.7}$$

This formula states that the covariance between any two securities is simply the correlation between the two securities multiplied by the standard deviations of each. In other words, covariance incorporates both (1) the correlation between the two assets and (2) the variability of each of the two securities as measured by standard deviation.

From our calculations earlier in this chapter we know that the correlation between the two securities is -0.1639. Given the variances used in Equation 10.4′, the standard deviations are 0.2586 and 0.115 for Supertech and Slowpoke, respectively. Thus, the variance of a portfolio can be expressed as follows:

Variance of the Portfolio's Return

$$= X^2_{\text{Super}}\sigma^2_{\text{Super}} + 2X_{\text{Super}}X_{\text{Slow}}\rho_{\text{Super, Slow}}\sigma_{\text{Super}}\sigma_{\text{Slow}} + X^2_{\text{Slow}}\sigma^2_{\text{Slow}} \tag{10.8}$$
$$0.023851 = 0.36 \times 0.066875 + 2 \times 0.6 \times 0.4 \times (-0.1639)$$
$$\times 0.2586 \times 0.115 + 0.16 \times 0.013225$$

The middle term on the right side is now written in terms of correlation, ρ, not covariance.

Suppose $\rho_{\text{Super, Slow}} = 1$, the highest possible value for correlation. Assume all the other parameters in the example are the same. The variance of the portfolio is:

Variance of the portfolio's return $= 0.040466 = 0.36 \times 0.066875 + 2 \times (0.6 \times 0.4 \times 1 \times 0.2586 \times 0.115) + 0.16 \times 0.013225$

The standard deviation is:

$$\text{Standard deviation of portfolio's return} = \sqrt{0.040466} = 0.2012 = 20.12\% \tag{10.9}$$

Note that Equations 10.9 and 10.6 are equal. That is, the standard deviation of a portfolio's return is equal to the weighted average of the standard deviations of the individual returns when $\rho = 1$. Inspection of Equation 10.8 indicates that the variance and hence the

---

[4]As with covariance, the ordering of the two securities is not relevant when we express the correlation between the two securities. That is, $\rho_{\text{Super,Slow}} = \rho_{\text{Slow,Super}}$.

Table 10.3

Standard Deviations for Standard & Poor's 500 Index and for Selected Stocks in the Index

Asset	Standard Deviation
S&P 500 Index	16.35%
Verizon	33.96
Ford Motor Co.	43.61
Walt Disney Co.	32.55
General Electric	25.18
IBM	35.96
McDonald's	28.61
Sears	44.06
Toys "R" Us Inc.	50.77
Amazon.com	69.19

As long as the correlations between pairs of securities are less than 1, the standard deviation of an index is less than the weighted average of the standard deviations of the individual securities within the index.

standard deviation of the portfolio must fall as the correlation drops below 1. This leads to the following result:

As long as $\rho < 1$, the standard deviation of a portfolio of two securities is *less* than the weighted average of the standard deviations of the individual securities.

In other words, the diversification effect applies as long as there is less than perfect correlation (as long as $\rho < 1$). Thus, our Supertech–Slowpoke example is a case of overkill. We illustrated diversification by an example with negative correlation. We could have illustrated diversification by an example with positive correlation—as long as it was not *perfect* positive correlation.

An Extension to Many Assets The preceding insight can be extended to the case of many assets. That is, as long as correlations between pairs of securities are less than 1, the standard deviation of a portfolio of many assets is less than the weighted average of the standard deviations of the individual securities.

Now consider Table 10.3, which shows the standard deviation of the Standard & Poor's 500 Index and the standard deviations of some of the individual securities listed in the index over a recent 10-year period. Note that all of the individual securities in the table have higher standard deviations than that of the index. In general, the standard deviations of most of the individual securities in an index will be above the standard deviation of the index itself, though a few of the securities could have lower standard deviations than that of the index.

10.4 The Efficient Set for Two Assets

Our results for expected returns and standard deviations are graphed in Figure 10.2. The figure shows a dot labeled Slowpoke and a dot labeled Supertech. Each dot represents both the expected return and the standard deviation for an individual security. As can be seen, Supertech has both a higher expected return and a higher standard deviation.

The box or "□" in the graph represents a portfolio with 60 percent invested in Supertech and 40 percent invested in Slowpoke. You will recall that we previously calculated both the expected return and the standard deviation for this portfolio.

The choice of 60 percent in Supertech and 40 percent in Slowpoke is just one of an infinite number of portfolios that can be created. The set of portfolios is sketched by the curved line in Figure 10.3.

Figure 10.2

Expected Returns and Standard Deviations for Supertech, Slowpoke, and a Portfolio Composed of 60 Percent in Supertech and 40 Percent in Slowpoke

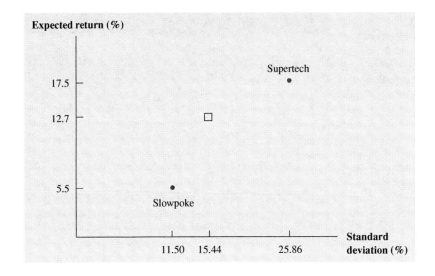

Figure 10.3

Set of Portfolios Composed of Holdings in Supertech and Slowpoke (correlation between the two securities is −0.1639)

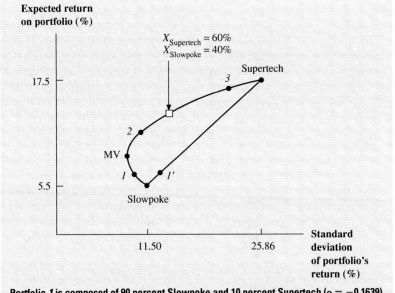

Portfolio *1* is composed of 90 percent Slowpoke and 10 percent Supertech ($\rho = -0.1639$).
Portfolio *2* is composed of 50 percent Slowpoke and 50 percent Supertech ($\rho = -0.1639$).
Portfolio *3* is composed of 10 percent Slowpoke and 90 percent Supertech ($\rho = -0.1639$).
Portfolio *1′* is composed of 90 percent Slowpoke and 10 percent Supertech ($\rho = 1$).
Point **MV** denotes the minimum variance portfolio. This is the portfolio with the lowest possible variance. By definition, the same portfolio must also have the lowest possible standard deviation.

Consider portfolio *1*. This is a portfolio composed of 90 percent Slowpoke and 10 percent Supertech. Because it is weighted so heavily toward Slowpoke, it appears close to the Slowpoke point on the graph. Portfolio *2* is higher on the curve because it is composed of 50 percent Slowpoke and 50 percent Supertech. Portfolio *3* is close to the Supertech point on the graph because it is composed of 90 percent Supertech and 10 percent Slowpoke.

Ross−Westerfield−Jaffe:
Corporate Finance, Eighth
Edition

III. Risk

10. Return and Risk: The
Capital Asset Pricing
Model (CAPM)

© The McGraw−Hill
Companies, 2008

407

There are a few important points concerning this graph:

1. We argued that the diversification effect occurs whenever the correlation between the two securities is below 1. The correlation between Supertech and Slowpoke is −0.1639. The diversification effect can be illustrated by comparison with the straight line between the Supertech point and the Slowpoke point. The straight line represents points that would have been generated had the correlation coefficient between the two securities been 1. The diversification effect is illustrated in the figure because the curved line is always to the left of the straight line. Consider point *1'*. This represents a portfolio composed of 90 percent in Slowpoke and 10 percent in Supertech *if* the correlation between the two were exactly 1. We argue that there is no diversification effect if $\rho = 1$. However, the diversification effect applies to the curved line because point *1* has the same expected return as point *1'* but has a lower standard deviation. (Points *2'* and *3'* are omitted to reduce the clutter of Figure 10.3.)

   Though the straight line and the curved line are both represented in Figure 10.3, they do not simultaneously exist in the same world. *Either* $\rho = -0.1639$ and the curve exists *or* $\rho = 1$ and the straight line exists. In other words, though an investor can choose between different points on the curve if $\rho = -0.1639$, she cannot choose between points on the curve and points on the straight line.

2. The point MV represents the minimum variance portfolio. This is the portfolio with the lowest possible variance. By definition, this portfolio must also have the lowest possible standard deviation. (The term *minimum variance portfolio* is standard in the literature, and we will use that term. Perhaps minimum standard deviation would actually be better because standard deviation, not variance, is measured on the horizontal axis of Figure 10.3.)

3. An individual contemplating an investment in a portfolio of Slowpoke and Supertech faces an **opportunity set** or **feasible set** represented by the curved line in Figure 10.3. That is, he can achieve any point on the curve by selecting the appropriate mix between the two securities. He cannot achieve any point above the curve because he cannot increase the return on the individual securities, decrease the standard deviations of the securities, or decrease the correlation between the two securities. Neither can he achieve points below the curve because he cannot lower the returns on the individual securities, increase the standard deviations of the securities, or increase the correlation. (Of course, he would not want to achieve points below the curve, even if he were able to do so.)

   Were he relatively tolerant of risk, he might choose portfolio *3*. (In fact, he could even choose the end point by investing all his money in Supertech.) An investor with less tolerance for risk might choose portfolio *2*. An investor wanting as little risk as possible would choose MV, the portfolio with minimum variance or minimum standard deviation.

4. Note that the curve is backward bending between the Slowpoke point and MV. This indicates that, for a portion of the feasible set, standard deviation actually decreases as we increase expected return. Students frequently ask, "How can an increase in the proportion of the risky security, Supertech, lead to a reduction in the risk of the portfolio?"

   This surprising finding is due to the diversification effect. The returns on the two securities are negatively correlated with each other. One security tends to go up when the other goes down and vice versa. Thus, an addition of a small amount of Supertech acts as a hedge to a portfolio composed only of Slowpoke. The risk of the portfolio is reduced, implying backward bending. Actually, backward bending always occurs if $\rho \leq 0$. It may or may not occur when $\rho > 0$. Of course, the curve bends backward

408

Ross–Westerfield–Jaffe:
Corporate Finance, Eighth
Edition

III. Risk

10. Return and Risk: The
Capital Asset Pricing
Model (CAPM)

© The McGraw–Hill
Companies, 2008

Figure 10.4

Opportunity
Sets Composed
of Holdings in
Supertech and
Slowpoke

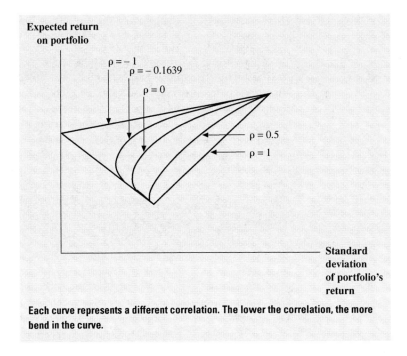

Each curve represents a different correlation. The lower the correlation, the more
bend in the curve.

only for a portion of its length. As we continue to increase the percentage of Supertech in the portfolio, the high standard deviation of this security eventually causes the
standard deviation of the entire portfolio to rise.

5. No investor would want to hold a portfolio with an expected return below that of the
   minimum variance portfolio. For example, no investor would choose portfolio *1*. This
   portfolio has less expected return but more standard deviation than the minimum
   variance portfolio has. We say that portfolios such as portfolio *1* are *dominated* by the
   minimum variance portfolio. Though the entire curve from Slowpoke to Supertech is
   called the *feasible set*, investors consider only the curve from MV to Supertech. Hence
   the curve from MV to Supertech is called the **efficient set** or the **efficient frontier**.

Figure 10.3 represents the opportunity set where $\rho = -0.1639$. It is worthwhile to
examine Figure 10.4, which shows different curves for different correlations. As can be
seen, the lower the correlation, the more bend there is in the curve. This indicates that
the diversification effect rises as ρ declines. The greatest bend occurs in the limiting case
where $\rho = -1$. This is perfect negative correlation. While this extreme case where $\rho = -1$
seems to fascinate students, it has little practical importance. Most pairs of securities exhibit positive correlation. Strong negative correlations, let alone perfect negative correlation, are unlikely occurrences indeed.[5]

Note that there is only one correlation between a pair of securities. We stated earlier that the correlation between Slowpoke and Supertech is -0.1639. Thus, the curve in
Figure 10.4 representing this correlation is the correct one, and the other curves should be
viewed as merely hypothetical.

The graphs we examined are not mere intellectual curiosities. Rather, efficient sets can
easily be calculated in the real world. As mentioned earlier, data on returns, standard deviations, and correlations are generally taken from past observations, though subjective no-
tions can be used to determine the values of these parameters as well. Once the parameters

---

[5]A major exception occurs with derivative securities. For example, the correlation between a stock and a put on
the stock is generally strongly negative. Puts will be treated later in the text.

Figure 10.5

Return/Risk Trade-off for World Stocks: Portfolio of U.S. and Foreign Stocks

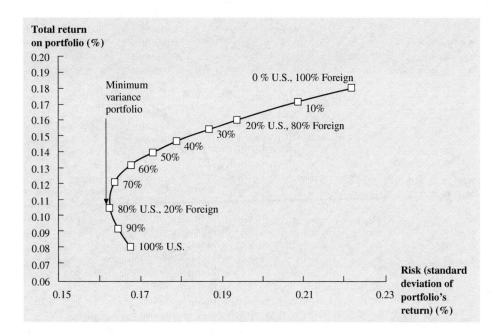

have been determined, any one of a whole host of software packages can be purchased to generate an efficient set. However, the choice of the preferred portfolio within the efficient set is up to you. As with other important decisions like what job to choose, what house or car to buy, and how much time to allocate to this course, there is no computer program to choose the preferred portfolio.

An efficient set can be generated where the two individual assets are portfolios themselves. For example, the two assets in Figure 10.5 are a diversified portfolio of American stocks and a diversified portfolio of foreign stocks. Expected returns, standard deviations, and the correlation coefficient were calculated over the recent past. No subjectivity entered the analysis. The U.S. stock portfolio with a standard deviation of about 0.173 is less risky than the foreign stock portfolio, which has a standard deviation of about 0.222. However, combining a small percentage of the foreign stock portfolio with the U.S. portfolio actually reduces risk, as can be seen by the backward-bending nature of the curve. In other words, the diversification benefits from combining two different portfolios more than offset the introduction of a riskier set of stocks into our holdings. The minimum variance portfolio occurs with about 80 percent of our funds in American stocks and about 20 percent in foreign stocks. Addition of foreign securities beyond this point increases the risk of the entire portfolio.

The backward-bending curve in Figure 10.5 is important information that has not bypassed American money managers. In recent years, pension fund and mutual fund managers in the United States have sought investment opportunities overseas. Another point worth pondering concerns the potential pitfalls of using only past data to estimate future returns. The stock markets of many foreign countries have had phenomenal growth in the past 25 years. Thus, a graph like Figure 10.5 makes a large investment in these foreign markets seem attractive. However, because abnormally high returns cannot be sustained forever, some subjectivity must be used in forecasting future expected returns.

10.5 The Efficient Set for Many Securities

The previous discussion concerned two securities. We found that a simple curve sketched out all the possible portfolios. Because investors generally hold more than two securities, we should look at the same graph when more than two securities are held. The shaded area in

Figure 10.6

The Feasible
Set of Portfolios
Constructed from
Many Securities

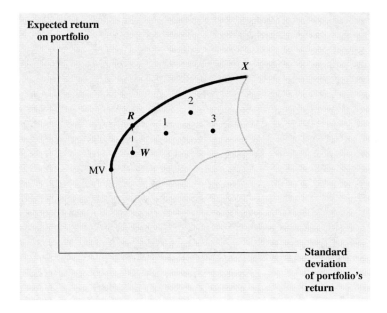

Figure 10.6 represents the opportunity set or feasible set when many securities are considered. The shaded area represents all the possible combinations of expected return and standard deviation for a portfolio. For example, in a universe of 100 securities, point 1 might represent a portfolio of, say, 40 securities. Point 2 might represent a portfolio of 80 securities. Point 3 might represent a different set of 80 securities, or the same 80 securities held in different proportions, or something else. Obviously, the combinations are virtually endless. However, note that all possible combinations fit into a confined region. No security or combination of securities can fall outside the shaded region. That is, no one can choose a portfolio with an expected return above that given by the shaded region. Furthermore, no one can choose a portfolio with a standard deviation below that given in the shaded area. Perhaps more surprisingly, no one can choose an expected return below that given in the curve. In other words, the capital markets actually prevent a self-destructive person from taking on a guaranteed loss.[6]

So far, Figure 10.6 is different from the earlier graphs. When only two securities are involved, all the combinations lie on a single curve. Conversely, with many securities the combinations cover an entire area. However, notice that an individual will want to be somewhere on the upper edge between MV and X. The upper edge, which we indicate in Figure 10.6 by a thick curve, is called the *efficient set*. Any point below the efficient set would receive less expected return and the same standard deviation as a point on the efficient set. For example, consider R on the efficient set and W directly below it. If W contains the risk level you desire, you should choose R instead to receive a higher expected return.

In the final analysis, Figure 10.6 is quite similar to Figure 10.3. The efficient set in Figure 10.3 runs from MV to Supertech. It contains various combinations of the securities Supertech and Slowpoke. The efficient set in Figure 10.6 runs from MV to X. It contains various combinations of many securities. The fact that a whole shaded area appears in Figure 10.6 but not in Figure 10.3 is just not an important difference; no investor would choose any point below the efficient set in Figure 10.6 anyway.

We mentioned before that an efficient set for two securities can be traced out easily in the real world. The task becomes more difficult when additional securities are included

---

[6]Of course, someone dead set on parting with his money can do so. For example, he can trade frequently without purpose, so that commissions more than offset the positive expected returns on the portfolio.

Table 10.4

Matrix Used to Calculate the Variance of a Portfolio

Stock	1	2	3	...	N
1	$X_1^2\sigma_1^2$	$X_1X_2\text{Cov}(R_1,R_2)$	$X_1X_3\text{Cov}(R_1,R_3)$		$X_1X_N\text{Cov}(R_1,R_N)$
2	$X_2X_1\text{Cov}(R_2,R_1)$	$X_2^2\sigma_2^2$	$X_2X_3\text{Cov}(R_2,R_3)$		$X_2X_N\text{Cov}(R_2,R_N)$
3	$X_3X_1\text{Cov}(R_3,R_1)$	$X_3X_2\text{Cov}(R_3,R_2)$	$X_3^2\sigma_3^2$		$X_3X_N\text{Cov}(R_3,R_N)$
.					
.					
.					
N	$X_NX_1\text{Cov}(R_N,R_1)$	$X_NX_2\text{Cov}(R_N,R_2)$	$X_NX_3\text{Cov}(R_N,R_3)$		$X_N^2\sigma_N^2$

The variance of the portfolio is the sum of the terms in all the boxes.

σ_i is the standard deviation of stock i.

$\text{Cov}(R_i, R_j)$ is the covariance between stock i and stock j.

Terms involving the standard deviation of a single security appear on the diagonal. Terms involving covariance between two securities appear off the diagonal.

because the number of observations grows. For example, using subjective analysis to estimate expected returns and standard deviations for, say, 100 or 500 securities may very well become overwhelming, and the difficulties with correlations may be greater still. There are almost 5,000 correlations between pairs of securities from a universe of 100 securities.

Though much of the mathematics of efficient set computation had been derived in the 1950s,[7] the high cost of computer time restricted application of the principles. In recent years this cost has been drastically reduced. A number of software packages allow the calculation of an efficient set for portfolios of moderate size. By all accounts these packages sell quite briskly, so our discussion would appear to be important in practice.

Variance and Standard Deviation in a Portfolio of Many Assets

We earlier calculated the formulas for variance and standard deviation in the two-asset case. Because we considered a portfolio of many assets in Figure 10.6, it is worthwhile to calculate the formulas for variance and standard deviation in the many-asset case. The formula for the variance of a portfolio of many assets can be viewed as an extension of the formula for the variance of two assets.

To develop the formula, we employ the same type of matrix that we used in the two-asset case. This matrix is displayed in Table 10.4. Assuming that there are N assets, we write the numbers 1 through N on the horizontal axis and 1 through N on the vertical axis. This creates a matrix of $N \times N = N^2$ boxes. The variance of the portfolio is the sum of the terms in all the boxes.

Consider, for example, the box in the second row and the third column. The term in the box is $X_2X_3 \text{Cov}(R_2,R_3)$. X_2 and X_3 are the percentages of the entire portfolio that are invested in the second asset and the third asset, respectively. For example, if an individual with a portfolio of $1,000 invests $100 in the second asset, $X_2 = 10\%$ ($=\$100/\$1,000$). $\text{Cov}(R_3,R_2)$ is the covariance between the returns on the third asset and the returns on the second asset. Next, note the box in the third row and the second column. The term in this box is $X_3X_2 \text{Cov}(R_3,R_2)$. Because $\text{Cov}(R_3,R_2) = \text{Cov}(R_2,R_3)$, both boxes have the same value. The second security and the third security make up one pair of stocks. In fact, every pair of stocks appears twice in the table: once in the lower left side and once in the upper right side.

Now consider boxes on the diagonal. For example, the term in the first box on the diagonal is $X_1^2\sigma_1^2$. Here, σ_1^2 is the variance of the return on the first security.

---

[7]The classic treatise is Harry Markowitz, *Portfolio Selection* (New York: John Wiley & Sons, 1959). Markowitz won the Nobel Prize in economics in 1990 for his work on modern portfolio theory.

Table 10.5

Number of Variance and Covariance Terms as a Function of the Number of Stocks in the Portfolio

Number of Stocks in Portfolio	Total Number of Terms	Number of Variance Terms (number of terms on diagonal)	Number of Covariance Terms (number of terms off diagonal)
1	1	1	0
2	4	2	2
3	9	3	6
10	100	10	90
100	10,000	100	9,900
.	.	.	.
.	.	.	.
.	.	.	.
N	N^2	N	$N^2 - N$

In a large portfolio, the number of terms involving covariance between two securities is much greater than the number of terms involving variance of a single security.

Thus, the diagonal terms in the matrix contain the variances of the different stocks. The off-diagonal terms contain the covariances. Table 10.5 relates the numbers of diagonal and off-diagonal elements to the size of the matrix. The number of diagonal terms (number of variance terms) is always the same as the number of stocks in the portfolio. The number of off-diagonal terms (number of covariance terms) rises much faster than the number of diagonal terms. For example, a portfolio of 100 stocks has 9,900 covariance terms. Because the variance of a portfolio's return is the sum of all the boxes, we have the following:

The variance of the return on a portfolio with many securities is more dependent on the covariances between the individual securities than on the variances of the individual securities.

To give a recent example of the impact of diversification, the Dow Jones Industrial Average (DJIA), which contains 30 large, well-known U.S. stocks, was about flat in 2005, meaning no gain or loss. As we saw in our previous chapter, this performance represents a fairly bad year for a portfolio of large-cap stocks. The biggest individual gainers for the year were Hewlett Packard (up 37 percent). Boeing (up 36 percent), and Altria Group (up 22 percent). However, offsetting these nice gains were General Motors (down 52 percent), Verizon Communications (down 26 percent), and IBM (down 17 percent). So, there were big winners and big losers, and they more or less offset in this particular year.

10.6 Diversification: An Example

The preceding point can be illustrated by altering the matrix in Table 10.4 slightly. Suppose we make the following three assumptions:

1. All securities possess the same variance, which we write as $\overline{var}$. In other words, $\sigma_i^2 = \overline{var}$ for every security.

2. All covariances in Table 10.4 are the same. We represent this uniform covariance as $\overline{cov}$. In other words. $Cov(R_i, R_j) = \overline{cov}$ for every pair of securities. It can easily be shown that $\overline{var} > \overline{cov}$.

3. All securities are equally weighted in the portfolio. Because there are N assets, the weight of each asset in the portfolio is $1/N$. In other words, $X_i = 1/N$ for each security i.

Table 10.6 Matrix Used to Calculate the Variance of a Portfolio When (a) All Securities Possess the Same Variance, Which We Represent as $\overline{\text{var}}$; (b) All Pairs of Securities Possess the Same Covariance, Which We Represent as $\overline{\text{cov}}$; (c) All Securities Are Held in the Same Proportion, Which Is 1/N

Stock	1	2	3	⋯	N
1	$(1/N^2)\,\overline{\text{var}}$	$(1/N^2)\,\overline{\text{cov}}$	$(1/N^2)\,\overline{\text{cov}}$		$(1/N^2)\,\overline{\text{cov}}$
2	$(1/N^2)\,\overline{\text{cov}}$	$(1/N^2)\,\overline{\text{var}}$	$(1/N^2)\,\overline{\text{cov}}$		$(1/N^2)\,\overline{\text{cov}}$
3	$(1/N^2)\,\overline{\text{cov}}$	$(1/N^2)\,\overline{\text{cov}}$	$(1/N^2)\,\overline{\text{var}}$		$(1/N^2)\,\overline{\text{cov}}$
.					
.					
.					
N	$(1/N^2)\,\overline{\text{cov}}$	$(1/N^2)\,\overline{\text{cov}}$	$(1/N^2)\,\overline{\text{cov}}$		$(1/N^2)\,\overline{\text{var}}$

Table 10.6 is the matrix of variances and covariances under these three simplifying assumptions. Note that all of the diagonal terms are identical. Similarly, all of the off-diagonal terms are identical. As with Table 10.4, the variance of the portfolio is the sum of the terms in the boxes in Table 10.6. We know that there are N diagonal terms involving variance. Similarly, there are $N \times (N - 1)$ off-diagonal terms involving covariance. Summing across all the boxes in Table 10.6, we can express the variance of the portfolio as:

$$\text{Variance of portfolio} = N \times \left(\frac{1}{N^2}\right)\overline{\text{var}} + N(N-1) \times \left(\frac{1}{N^2}\right)\overline{\text{cov}} \quad \textbf{(10.10)}$$

Number of diagonal terms — Each diagonal term — Number of off-diagonal terms — Each off-diagonal term

$$= \left(\frac{1}{N}\right)\overline{\text{var}} + \left(\frac{N^2 - N}{N^2}\right)\overline{\text{cov}}$$

$$= \left(\frac{1}{N}\right)\overline{\text{var}} + \left(1 - \frac{1}{N}\right)\overline{\text{cov}}$$

Equation 10.10 expresses the variance of our special portfolio as a weighted sum of the average security variance and the average covariance.[8]

Now, let's increase the number of securities in the portfolio without limit. The variance of the portfolio becomes:

$$\text{Variance of portfolio (when } N \to \infty) = \overline{\text{cov}} \quad \textbf{(10.11)}$$

This occurs because (1) the weight on the variance term, $1/N$, goes to 0 as N goes to infinity, and (2) the weight on the covariance term, $1 - 1/N$, goes to 1 as N goes to infinity.

Equation 10.11 provides an interesting and important result. In our special portfolio, the variances of the individual securities completely vanish as the number of securities becomes large. However, the covariance terms remain. In fact, the variance of the portfolio becomes the average covariance, $\overline{\text{cov}}$. We often hear that we should diversify. In other words, we should not put all our eggs in one basket. The effect of diversification on the risk of a portfolio can be illustrated in this example. The variances of the individual securities are diversified away, but the covariance terms cannot be diversified away.

---

[8]Equation 10.10 is actually a weighted *average* of the variance and covariance terms because the weights, $1/N$ and $1 - 1/N$, sum to 1.

Figure 10.7

Relationship between the Variance of a Portfolio's Return and the Number of Securities in the Portfolio*

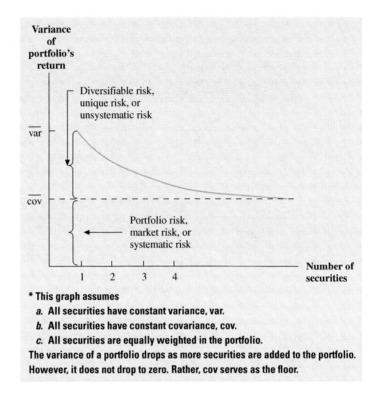

* This graph assumes
   a. All securities have constant variance, var.
   b. All securities have constant covariance, cov.
   c. All securities are equally weighted in the portfolio.
The variance of a portfolio drops as more securities are added to the portfolio.
However, it does not drop to zero. Rather, cov serves as the floor.

The fact that part, but not all, of our risk can be diversified away should be explored. Consider Mr. Smith, who brings $1,000 to the roulette table at a casino. It would be very risky if he put all his money on one spin of the wheel. For example, imagine that he put the full $1,000 on red at the table. If the wheel showed red, he would get $2,000; but if the wheel showed black, he would lose everything. Suppose instead he divided his money over 1,000 different spins by betting $1 at a time on red. Probability theory tells us that he could count on winning about 50 percent of the time. This means he could count on pretty nearly getting all his original $1,000 back.[9] In other words, risk is essentially eliminated with 1,000 different spins.

Now, let's contrast this with our stock market example, which we illustrate in Figure 10.7. The variance of the portfolio with only one security is, of course, $\overline{\text{var}}$ because the variance of a portfolio with one security is the variance of the security. The variance of the portfolio drops as more securities are added, which is evidence of the diversification effect. However, unlike Mr. Smith's roulette example, the portfolio's variance can never drop to zero. Rather it reaches a floor of $\overline{\text{cov}}$, which is the covariance of each pair of securities.[10]

Because the variance of the portfolio asymptotically approaches $\overline{\text{cov}}$, each additional security continues to reduce risk. Thus, if there were neither commissions nor other transactions costs, it could be argued that we can never achieve too much diversification. However, there is a cost to diversification in the real world. Commissions per dollar invested fall as we make larger purchases in a single stock. Unfortunately, we must buy fewer shares of each security when buying more and more different securities. Comparing the costs

---

[9]This example ignores the casino's cut.

[10]Though it is harder to show, this risk reduction effect also applies to the general case where variances and covariances are *not* equal.

and benefits of diversification, Meir Statman argues that a portfolio of about 30 stocks is needed to achieve optimal diversification.[11]

We mentioned earlier that $\overline{\text{var}}$ must be greater than $\overline{\text{cov}}$. Thus, the variance of a security's return can be broken down in the following way:

$$
\begin{array}{ccc}
\text{Total risk of} & & \text{Unsystematic or} \\
\text{individual security} = & \text{Portfolio risk} & + & \text{diversifiable risk} \\
(\overline{\text{var}}) & (\overline{\text{cov}}) & & (\overline{\text{var}} - \overline{\text{cov}})
\end{array}
$$

Total risk, which is $\overline{\text{var}}$ in our example, is the risk we bear by holding onto one security only. *Portfolio risk* is the risk we still bear after achieving full diversification, which is $\overline{\text{cov}}$ in our example. Portfolio risk is often called **systematic** or **market risk** as well. **Diversifiable**, **unique**, or **unsystematic risk** is the risk that can be diversified away in a large portfolio, which must be $(\overline{\text{var}} - \overline{\text{cov}})$ by definition.

To an individual who selects a diversified portfolio, the total risk of an individual security is not important. When considering adding a security to a diversified portfolio, the individual cares about only that portion of the risk of a security that cannot be diversified away. This risk can alternatively be viewed as the *contribution* of a security to the risk of an entire portfolio. We will talk later about the case where securities make different contributions to the risk of the entire portfolio.

Risk and the Sensible Investor

Having gone to all this trouble to show that unsystematic risk disappears in a well-diversified portfolio, how do we know that investors even want such portfolios? What if they like risk and don't want it to disappear?

We must admit that, theoretically at least, this is possible, but we will argue that it does not describe what we think of as the typical investor. Our typical investor is **risk-averse**. Risk-averse behavior can be defined in many ways, but we prefer the following example: A fair gamble is one with zero expected return; a risk-averse investor would prefer to avoid fair gambles.

Why do investors choose well-diversified portfolios? Our answer is that they are risk-averse, and risk-averse people avoid unnecessary risk, such as the unsystematic risk on a stock. If you do not think this is much of an answer, consider whether you would take on such a risk. For example, suppose you had worked all summer and had saved $5,000, which you intended to use for your college expenses. Now, suppose someone came up to you and offered to flip a coin for the money: heads, you would double your money, and tails, you would lose it all.

Would you take such a bet? Perhaps you would, but most people would not. Leaving aside any moral question that might surround gambling and recognizing that some people would take such a bet, it's our view that the average investor would not.

To induce the typical risk-averse investor to take a fair gamble, you must sweeten the pot. For example, you might need to raise the odds of winning from 50–50 to 70–30 or higher. The risk-averse investor can be induced to take fair gambles only if they are sweetened so that they become unfair to the investor's advantage.

10.7 Riskless Borrowing and Lending

Figure 10.6 assumes that all the securities in the efficient set are risky. Alternatively, an investor could combine a risky investment with an investment in a riskless or *risk-free* security, such as an investment in U.S. Treasury bills. This is illustrated in the following example.

---

[11] Meir Statman, "How Many Stocks Make a Diversified Portfolio?" *Journal of Financial and Quantitative Analysis* (September 1987).

EXAMPLE 10.3

Riskless Lending and Portfolio Risk   Ms. Bagwell is considering investing in the common stock of Merville Enterprises. In addition, Ms. Bagwell will either borrow or lend at the risk-free rate. The relevant parameters are these:

	Common Stock of Merville	Risk-Free Asset
Expected return	14%	10%
Standard deviation	0.20	0

Suppose Ms. Bagwell chooses to invest a total of $1,000, $350 of which is to be invested in Merville Enterprises and $650 placed in the risk-free asset. The expected return on her total investment is simply a weighted average of the two returns:

$$\text{Expected return on portfolio composed of one riskless and one risky asset} = 0.114 = (0.35 \times 0.14) + (0.65 \times 0.10) \qquad \textbf{(10.12)}$$

Because the expected return on the portfolio is a weighted average of the expected return on the risky asset (Merville Enterprises) and the risk-free return, the calculation is analogous to the way we treated two risky assets. In other words, Equation 10.3 applies here.

Using Equation 10.4, the formula for the variance of the portfolio can be written as:

$$X^2_{\text{Merville}}\sigma^2_{\text{Merville}} + 2X_{\text{Merville}}X_{\text{Risk-free}}\sigma_{\text{Merville, Risk-free}} + X^2_{\text{Risk-free}}\sigma^2_{\text{Risk-free}}$$

However, by definition, the risk-free asset has no variability. Thus both $\sigma_{\text{Merville, Risk-free}}$ and $\sigma^2_{\text{Risk-free}}$ are equal to zero, reducing the above expression to:

$$\text{Variance of portfolio composed of one riskless and one risky asset} = X^2_{\text{Merville}}\sigma^2_{\text{Merville}} \qquad \textbf{(10.13)}$$

$$= (0.35)^2 \times (0.20)^2$$
$$= 0.0049$$

The standard deviation of the portfolio is:

$$\text{Standard deviation of portfolio composed of one riskless and one risky asset} = X_{\text{Merville}}\sigma_{\text{Merville}} \qquad \textbf{(10.14)}$$

$$= 0.35 \times 0.20$$
$$= 0.07$$

The relationship between risk and expected return for one risky and one riskless asset can be seen in Figure 10.8. Ms. Bagwell's split of 35–65 percent between the two assets is represented on a *straight* line between the risk-free rate and a pure investment in Merville Enterprises. Note that, unlike the case of two risky assets, the opportunity set is straight, not curved.

Suppose that, alternatively, Ms. Bagwell borrows $200 at the risk-free rate. Combining this with her original sum of $1,000, she invests a total of $1,200 in Merville. Her expected return would be:

$$\text{Expected return on portfolio formed by borrowing to invest in risky asset} = 14.8\% = 1.20 \times 0.14 + (-0.2 \times 0.10)$$

Here, she invests 120 percent of her original investment of $1,000 by borrowing 20 percent of her original investment. Note that the return of 14.8 percent is greater than the 14 percent expected return on Merville Enterprises. This occurs because she is borrowing at 10 percent to invest in a security with an expected return greater than 10 percent.

(continued)

Ross–Westerfield–Jaffe:
Corporate Finance, Eighth
Edition

III. Risk

10. Return and Risk: The
Capital Asset Pricing
Model (CAPM)

© The McGraw–Hill
Companies, 2008

417

Figure 10.8   Relationship between Expected Return and Risk for a Portfolio of One Risky Asset and One Riskless Asset

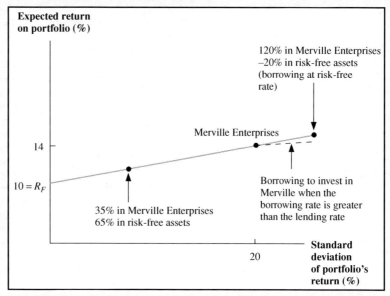

The standard deviation is:

$$\text{Standard deviation of portfolio formed by borrowing to invest in risky asset} = 0.24 = 1.20 \times 0.2$$

The standard deviation of 0.24 is greater than 0.20, the standard deviation of the Merville investment, because borrowing increases the variability of the investment. This investment also appears in Figure 10.8.

So far, we have assumed that Ms. Bagwell is able to borrow at the same rate at which she can lend.[12] Now let us consider the case where the borrowing rate is above the lending rate. The dotted line in Figure 10.8 illustrates the opportunity set for borrowing opportunities in this case. The dotted line is below the solid line because a higher borrowing rate lowers the expected return on the investment.

The Optimal Portfolio

The previous section concerned a portfolio formed between one riskless asset and one risky asset. In reality, an investor is likely to combine an investment in the riskless asset with a *portfolio* of risky assets. This is illustrated in Figure 10.9.

Consider point Q, representing a portfolio of securities. Point Q is in the interior of the feasible set of risky securities. Let us assume the point represents a portfolio of 30 percent in AT&T, 45 percent in General Motors (GM), and 25 percent in IBM. Individuals combining investments in Q with investments in the riskless asset would achieve points along the straight line from R_F to Q. We refer to this as line I. For example, point 1 on the line represents a portfolio of 70 percent in the riskless asset and 30 percent in stocks represented by Q. An investor with $100 choosing point 1 as his portfolio would put $70 in

---

[12]Surprisingly, this appears to be a decent approximation because many investors can borrow from a stockbroker (called *going on margin*) when purchasing stocks. The borrowing rate here is very near the riskless rate of interest, particularly for large investors. More will be said about this in a later chapter.

Figure 10.9

Relationship between Expected Return and Standard Deviation for an Investment in a Combination of Risky Securities and the Riskless Asset

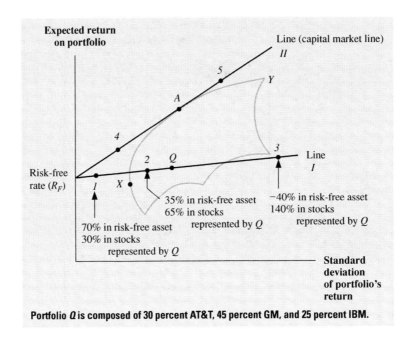

Portfolio *Q* is composed of 30 percent AT&T, 45 percent GM, and 25 percent IBM.

the risk-free asset and $30 in *Q*. This can be restated as $70 in the riskless asset, $9 ($= 0.3 \times$ $30) in AT&T, $13.50 ($= 0.45 \times$ $30) in GM, and $7.50 ($= 0.25 \times$ $30) in IBM. Point *2* also represents a portfolio of the risk-free asset and *Q*, with more (65%) being invested in *Q*.

Point *3* is obtained by borrowing to invest in *Q*. For example, an investor with $100 of her own would borrow $40 from the bank or broker to invest $140 in *Q*. This can be stated as borrowing $40 and contributing $100 of her money to invest $42 ($= 0.3 \times$ $140) in AT&T, $63 ($= 0.45 \times$ $140) in GM, and $35 ($= 0.25 \times$ $140) in IBM.

These investments can be summarized as follows:

	Point Q	Point *I* (Lending $70)	Point *3* (Borrowing $40)
AT&T	$ 30	$ 9	$ 42
GM	45	13.50	63
IBM	25	7.50	35
Risk-free	0	70.00	−40
Total investment	$100	$100	$100

Though any investor can obtain any point on line *I*, no point on the line is optimal. To see this, consider line *II*, a line running from R_F through *A*. Point *A* represents a portfolio of risky securities. Line *II* represents portfolios formed by combinations of the risk-free asset and the securities in *A*. Points between R_F and *A* are portfolios in which some money is invested in the riskless asset and the rest is placed in *A*. Points past *A* are achieved by borrowing at the riskless rate to buy more of *A* than we could with our original funds alone.

As drawn, line *II* is tangent to the efficient set of risky securities. Whatever point an individual can obtain on line *I*, he can obtain a point with the same standard deviation and a higher expected return on line *II*. In fact, because line *II* is tangent to the efficient set of risky assets, it provides the investor with the best possible opportunities. In other words, line *II* can be viewed as the efficient set of *all* assets, both risky and riskless. An investor with a fair degree of risk aversion might choose a point between R_F and A, perhaps point *4*. An individual with less risk aversion might choose a point closer to A or even beyond A. For example, point *5* corresponds to an individual borrowing money to increase investment in A.

The graph illustrates an important point. With riskless borrowing and lending, the portfolio of *risky* assets held by any investor would always be point A. Regardless of the investor's tolerance for risk, she would never choose any other point on the efficient set of risky assets (represented by curve XAY) nor any point in the interior of the feasible region. Rather, she would combine the securities of A with the riskless assets if she had high aversion to risk. She would borrow the riskless asset to invest more funds in A had she low aversion to risk.

This result establishes what financial economists call the **separation principle**. That is, the investor's investment decision consists of two separate steps:

1. After estimating (*a*) the expected returns and variances of individual securities, and (*b*) the covariances between pairs of securities, the investor calculates the efficient set of risky assets, represented by curve XAY in Figure 10.9. He then determines point A, the tangency between the risk-free rate and the efficient set of risky assets (curve XAY). Point A represents the portfolio of risky assets that the investor will hold. This point is determined solely from his estimates of returns, variances, and covariances. No personal characteristics, such as degree of risk aversion, are needed in this step.

2. The investor must now determine how he will combine point A, his portfolio of risky assets, with the riskless asset. He might invest some of his funds in the riskless asset and some in portfolio A. He would end up at a point on the line between R_F and A in this case. Alternatively, he might borrow at the risk-free rate and contribute some of his own funds as well, investing the sum in portfolio A. He would end up at a point on line II beyond A. His position in the riskless asset—that is, his choice of where on the line he wants to be—is determined by his internal characteristics, such as his ability to tolerate risk.

10.8   Market Equilibrium

Definition of the Market Equilibrium Portfolio

The preceding analysis concerns one investor. His estimates of the expected returns and variances for individual securities and the covariances between pairs of securities are his and his alone. Other investors would obviously have different estimates of these variables. However, the estimates might not vary much because all investors would be forming expectations from the same data about past price movements and other publicly available information.

Financial economists often imagine a world where all investors possess the *same* estimates of expected returns, variances, and covariances. Though this can never be literally true, it can be thought of as a useful simplifying assumption in a world where investors have access to similar sources of information. This assumption is called **homogeneous expectations**.[13]

If all investors had homogeneous expectations, Figure 10.9 would be the same for all individuals. That is, all investors would sketch out the same efficient set of risky assets because they would be working with the same inputs. This efficient set of risky assets is

---

[13]The assumption of homogeneous expectations states that all investors have the same beliefs concerning returns, variances, and covariances. It does not say that all investors have the same aversion to risk.

represented by the curve *XAY*. Because the same risk-free rate would apply to everyone, all investors would view point *A* as the portfolio of risky assets to be held.

This point *A* takes on great importance because all investors would purchase the risky securities that it represents. Investors with a high degree of risk aversion might combine *A* with an investment in the riskless asset, achieving point *4*, for example. Others with low aversion to risk might borrow to achieve, say, point *5*. Because this is a very important conclusion, we restate it:

In a world with homogeneous expectations, all investors would hold the portfolio of risky assets represented by point *A*.

If all investors choose the same portfolio of risky assets, it is possible to determine what that portfolio is. Common sense tells us that it is a market value weighted portfolio of all existing securities. It is the **market portfolio**.

In practice, economists use a broad-based index such as the Standard & Poor's (S&P) 500 as a proxy for the market portfolio. Of course all investors do not hold the same portfolio in practice. However, we know that many investors hold diversified portfolios, particularly when mutual funds or pension funds are included. A broad-based index is a good proxy for the highly diversified portfolios of many investors.

Definition of Risk When Investors Hold the Market Portfolio

The previous section states that many investors hold diversified portfolios similar to broad-based indexes. This result allows us to be more precise about the risk of a security in the context of a diversified portfolio.

Researchers have shown that the best measure of the risk of a security in a large portfolio is the *beta* of the security. We illustrate beta by an example.

EXAMPLE 10.4

Beta   Consider the following possible returns both on the stock of Jelco, Inc., and on the market:

State	Type of Economy	Return on Market (percent)	Return on Jelco, Inc. (percent)
I	Bull	15	25
II	Bull	15	15
III	Bear	−5	−5
IV	Bear	−5	−15

Though the return on the market has only two possible outcomes (15% and −5%), the return on Jelco has four possible outcomes. It is helpful to consider the expected return on a security for a given return on the market. Assuming each state is equally likely, we have:

Type of Economy	Return on Market (percent)	Expected Return on Jelco, Inc. (percent)
Bull	15%	$20\% = 25\% \times \frac{1}{2} + 15\% \times \frac{1}{2}$
Bear	−5%	$-10\% = -5\% \times \frac{1}{2} + (-15\%) \times \frac{1}{2}$

(continued)

Figure 10.10   Performance of Jelco, Inc., and the Market Portfolio

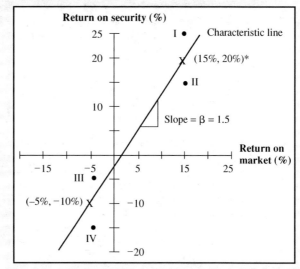

The two points marked X represent the expected return on Jelco for each possible outcome of the market portfolio. The expected return on Jelco is positively related to the return on the market. Because the slop is 1.5, we say that Jelco's beta is 1.5. Beta measures the responsiveness of the security's return to movement in the market.

* (15%, 20%) refers to the point where the return on the market is 15 percent and the return on the security is 20 percent.

Jelco, Inc., responds to market movements because its expected return is greater in bullish states than in bearish states. We now calculate exactly how responsive the security is to market movements. The market's return in a bullish economy is 20 percent [= 15% − (−5%)] greater than the market's return in a bearish economy. However, the expected return on Jelco in a bullish economy is 30 percent [= 20% − (−10%)] greater than its expected return in a bearish state. Thus Jelco, Inc., has a responsiveness coefficient of 1.5 (= 30%/20%).

This relationship appears in Figure 10.10. The returns for both Jelco and the market in each state are plotted as four points. In addition, we plot the expected return on the security for each of the two possible returns on the market. These two points, each of which we designate by an X, are joined by a line called the **characteristic line** of the security. The slope of the line is 1.5, the number calculated in the previous paragraph. This responsiveness coefficient of 1.5 is the **beta** of Jelco.

The interpretation of beta from Figure 10.10 is intuitive. The graph tells us that the returns of Jelco are magnified 1.5 times over those of the market. When the market does well, Jelco's stock is expected to do even better. When the market does poorly, Jelco's stock is expected to do even worse. Now imagine an individual with a portfolio near that of the market who is considering the addition of Jelco to her portfolio. Because of Jelco's *magnification factor* of 1.5, she will view this stock as contributing much to the risk of the portfolio. (We will show shortly that the beta of the average security in the market is 1.) Jelco contributes more to the risk of a large, diversified portfolio than does an average security because Jelco is more responsive to movements in the market.

Further insight can be gleaned by examining securities with negative betas. One should view these securities as either hedges or insurance policies. The security is expected to do well when the market does poorly and vice versa. Because of this, adding a negative-beta security to a large, diversified portfolio actually reduces the risk of the portfolio.[14]

---

[14]Unfortunately, empirical evidence shows that virtually no stocks have negative betas.

Table 10.7

Estimates of Beta for Selected Individual Stocks

Stock	Beta
McGraw-Hill Co.	.52
3M	.66
General Electric	.83
Bed, Bath & Beyond	.98
Dell	1.22
Home Depot	1.44
eBay	2.06
Computer Associates	2.58

The beta is defined as $\text{Cov}(R_i, R_M)/\text{Var}(R_M)$, where $\text{Cov}(R_i, R_M)$ is the covariance of the return on an individual stock, R_i, and the return on the market, R_M. $\text{Var}(R_M)$ is the variance of the return on the market, R_M.

Table 10.7 presents empirical estimates of betas for individual securities. As can be seen, some securities are more responsive to the market than others. For example, eBay has a beta of 2.06. This means that for every 1 percent movement in the market,[15] eBay is expected to move 2.06 percent in the same direction. Conversely, General Electric has a beta of only 0.83. This means that for every 1 percent movement in the market, General Electric is expected to move 0.83 percent in the same direction.

We can summarize our discussion of beta by saying this:

Beta measures the responsiveness of a security to movements in the market portfolio.

The Formula for Beta

Our discussion so far has stressed the intuition behind beta. The actual definition of beta is:

$$\beta_i = \frac{\text{Cov}(R_i, R_M)}{\sigma^2(R_M)} \tag{10.15}$$

where $\text{Cov}(R_i, R_M)$ is the covariance between the return on asset i and the return on the market portfolio and $\sigma^2(R_M)$ is the variance of the market.

One useful property is that the average beta across all securities, when weighted by the proportion of each security's market value to that of the market portfolio, is 1. That is:

$$\sum_{i=1}^{N} X_i \beta_i = 1 \tag{10.16}$$

where X_i is the proportion of security i's market value to that of the entire market and N is the number of securities in the market.

Equation 10.16 is intuitive, once you think about it. If you weight all securities by their market values, the resulting portfolio is the market. By definition, the beta of the market portfolio is 1. That is, for every 1 percent movement in the market, the market must move 1 percent—*by definition*.

A Test

We have put these questions on past corporate finance examinations:

1. What sort of investor rationally views the variance (or standard deviation) of an individual security's return as the security's proper measure of risk?

2. What sort of investor rationally views the beta of a security as the security's proper measure of risk?

---

[15]In Table 10.7, we use the Standard & Poor's 500 Index as a proxy for the market portfolio.

Ross−Westerfield−Jaffe:
Corporate Finance, Eighth
Edition

III. Risk

10. Return and Risk: The
Capital Asset Pricing
Model (CAPM)

© The McGraw−Hill
Companies, 2008

423

A good answer might be something like the following:

> A rational, risk-averse investor views the variance (or standard deviation) of her portfolio's return as the proper measure of the risk of her portfolio. If for some reason the investor can hold only one security, the variance of that security's return becomes the variance of the portfolio's return. Hence, the variance of the security's return is the security's proper measure of risk.
>
> If an individual holds a diversified portfolio, she still views the variance (or standard deviation) of her portfolio's return as the proper measure of the risk of her portfolio. However, she is no longer interested in the variance of each individual security's return. Rather, she is interested in the contribution of an individual security to the variance of the portfolio.

Under the assumption of homogeneous expectations, all individuals hold the market portfolio. Thus, we measure risk as the contribution of an individual security to the variance of the market portfolio. This contribution, when standardized properly, is the beta of the security. Although few investors hold the market portfolio exactly, many hold reasonably diversified portfolios. These portfolios are close enough to the market portfolio so that the beta of a security is likely to be a reasonable measure of its risk.

10.9 Relationship between Risk and Expected Return (CAPM)

It is commonplace to argue that the expected return on an asset should be positively related to its risk. That is, individuals will hold a risky asset only if its expected return compensates for its risk. In this section, we first estimate the expected return on the stock market as a whole. Next, we estimate expected returns on individual securities.

Expected Return on Market

Economists frequently argue that the expected return on the market can be represented as:

$$\overline{R}_M = R_F + \text{Risk premium}$$

In words, the expected return on the market is the sum of the risk-free rate plus some compensation for the risk inherent in the market portfolio. Note that the equation refers to the *expected* return on the market, not the actual return in a particular month or year. Because stocks have risk, the actual return on the market over a particular period can, of course, be below R_F or can even be negative.

Because investors want compensation for risk, the risk premium is presumably positive. But exactly how positive is it? It is generally argued that the place to start looking for the risk premium in the future is the average risk premium in the past. As reported in Chapter 9, Ibbotson and Sinquefield found that the average return on large-company common stocks was 12.3 percent over 1926–2005. The average risk-free rate over the same interval was 3.8 percent. Thus, the average difference between the two was 8.5 percent ($=12.3\% - 3.8\%$). Financial economists find this to be a useful estimate of the difference to occur in the future.

For example, if the risk-free rate, estimated by the current yield on a one-year Treasury bill, is 1 percent, the expected return on the market is:

$$9.5\% = 1\% + 8.5\%$$

424

Ross–Westerfield–Jaffe:
Corporate Finance, Eighth
Edition

III. Risk

10. Return and Risk: The
Capital Asset Pricing
Model (CAPM)

© The McGraw–Hill
Companies, 2008

308

Part III   Risk

Figure 10.11

Relationship between
Expected Return on
an individual Security
and Beta of the
Security

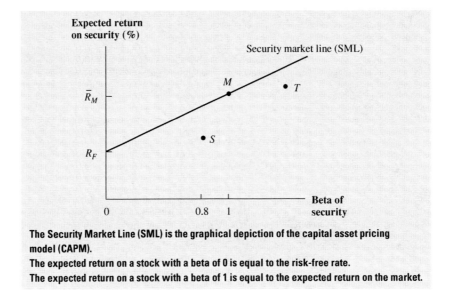

The Security Market Line (SML) is the graphical depiction of the capital asset pricing
model (CAPM).
The expected return on a stock with a beta of 0 is equal to the risk-free rate.
The expected return on a stock with a beta of 1 is equal to the expected return on the market.

Of course, the future equity risk premium could be higher or lower than the historical
equity risk premium. This could be true if future risk is higher or lower than past risk or if
individual risk aversions are higher or lower than those of the past.

Expected Return on Individual Security

Now that we have estimated the expected return on the market as a whole, what is the expected return on an individual security? We have argued that the beta of a security is the
appropriate measure of risk in a large, diversified portfolio. Because most investors are
diversified, the expected return on a security should be positively related to its beta. This
is illustrated in Figure 10.11.

Actually, economists can be more precise about the relationship between expected return and beta. They posit that under plausible conditions the relationship between expected
return and beta can be represented by the following equation:[16]

Capital Asset Pricing Model

$$\overline{R} \quad = \quad R_F \quad + \quad \beta \quad \times \quad (\overline{R}_M - R_F) \qquad \textbf{(10.17)}$$

Expected return on a security	=	Risk-free rate	+	Beta of the security	×	Difference between expected return on market and risk-free rate

This formula, which is called the **capital asset pricing model** (or CAPM for short), implies
that the expected return on a security is linearly related to its beta. Because the average
return on the market has been higher than the average risk-free rate over long periods of
time, $\overline{R}_M - R_F$ is presumably positive. Thus, the formula implies that the expected return
on a security is *positively* related to its beta. The formula can be illustrated by assuming
a few special cases:

• *Assume that* $\beta = 0$. Here $\overline{R} = R_F$—that is, the expected return on the security is
  equal to the risk-free rate. Because a security with zero beta has no relevant risk, its
  expected return should equal the risk-free rate.

[16]This relationship was first proposed independently by John Lintner and William F. Sharpe.

- *Assume that* $\beta = 1$. Equation 10.17 reduces to $\overline{R} = \overline{R}_M$. That is, the expected return on the security is equal to the expected return on the market. This makes sense because the beta of the market portfolio is also 1.

Equation 10.17 can be represented graphically by the upward-sloping line in Figure 10.11. Note that the line begins at R_F and rises to $\overline{R}_M$ when beta is 1. This line is frequently called the **security market line** (SML).

As with any line, the SML has both a slope and an intercept. R_F, the risk-free rate, is the intercept. Because the beta of a security is the horizontal axis, $R_M - R_F$ is the slope. The line will be upward-sloping as long as the expected return on the market is greater than the risk-free rate. Because the market portfolio is a risky asset, theory suggests that its expected return is above the risk-free rate. As mentioned, the empirical evidence of the previous chapter showed that the average return per year on the market portfolio (for large-company stocks as an example) over the past 80 years was 8.5 percent above the risk-free rate.

EXAMPLE 10.5

The stock of Aardvark Enterprises has a beta of 1.5 and that of Zebra Enterprises has a beta of 0.7. The risk-free rate is assumed to be 3 percent, and the difference between the expected return on the market and the risk-free rate is assumed to be 8.0 percent. The expected returns on the two securities are

Expected Return for Aardvark

$$15.0\% = 3\% + 1.5 \times 8.0\% \tag{10.18}$$

Expected Return for Zebra

$$8.6\% = 3\% + 0.7 \times 8.0\%$$

Three additional points concerning the CAPM should be mentioned:

1. *Linearity*: The intuition behind an upwardly sloping curve is clear. Because beta is the appropriate measure of risk, high-beta securities should have an expected return above that of low-beta securities. However, both Figure 10.11 and Equation 10.17 show something more than an upwardly sloping curve: The relationship between expected return and beta corresponds to a *straight* line.

   It is easy to show that the line of Figure 10.11 is straight. To see this, consider security S with, say, a beta of 0.8. This security is represented by a point below the security market line in the figure. Any investor could duplicate the beta of security S by buying a portfolio with 20 percent in the risk-free asset and 80 percent in a security with a beta of 1. However, the homemade portfolio would itself lie on the SML. In other words, the portfolio dominates security S because the portfolio has a higher expected return and the same beta.

   Now consider security T with, say, a beta greater than 1. This security is also below the SML in Figure 10.11. Any investor could duplicate the beta of security T by borrowing to invest in a security with a beta of 1. This portfolio must also lie on the SML, thereby dominating security T.

   Because no one would hold either S or T, their stock prices would drop. This price adjustment would raise the expected returns on the two securities. The price adjustment would continue until the two securities lay on the security market line. The preceding example considered two overpriced stocks and a straight SML. Securities lying above the SML are *underpriced*. Their prices must rise until their expected returns lie on the line. If the SML is itself curved, many stocks would be mispriced. In equilibrium, all securities would be held only when prices changed so that the SML became straight. In other words, linearity would be achieved.

2. *Portfolios as well as securities*: Our discussion of the CAPM considered individual securities. Does the relationship in Figure 10.11 and Equation 10.17 hold for portfolios as well?

Yes. To see this, consider a portfolio formed by investing equally in our two securities from Example 10.5, Aardvark and Zebra. The expected return on the portfolio is:

Expected Return on Portfolio

$$11.8\% = 0.5 \times 15.0\% + 0.5 \times 8.6\% \qquad (10.19)$$

The beta of the portfolio is simply a weighted average of the betas of the two securities. Thus, we have:

Beta of Portfolio

$$1.1 = 0.5 \times 1.5 + 0.5 \times 0.7$$

Under the CAPM, the expected return on the portfolio is

$$11.8\% = 3\% + 1.1 \times 8.0\% \qquad (10.20)$$

Because the expected return in Equation 10.19 is the same as the expected return in Equation 10.20, the example shows that the CAPM holds for portfolios as well as for individual securities.

3. *A potential confusion*: Students often confuse the SML in Figure 10.11 with line *II* in Figure 10.9. Actually, the lines are quite different. Line *II* traces the efficient set of portfolios formed from both risky assets and the riskless asset. Each point on the line represents an entire portfolio. Point *A* is a portfolio composed entirely of risky assets. Every other point on the line represents a portfolio of the securities in *A* combined with the riskless asset. The axes on Figure 10.9 are the expected return on a *portfolio* and the standard deviation of a *portfolio*. Individual securities do not lie along line *II*.

The SML in Figure 10.11 relates expected return to beta. Figure 10.11 differs from Figure 10.9 in at least two ways. First, beta appears in the horizontal axis of Figure 10.11, but standard deviation appears in the horizontal axis of Figure 10.9. Second, the SML in Figure 10.11 holds both for all individual securities and for all possible portfolios, whereas line *II* in Figure 10.9 holds only for efficient portfolios.

We stated earlier that, under homogeneous expectations, point *A* in Figure 10.9 becomes the market portfolio. In this situation, line *II* is referred to as the **capital market line** (CML).

Summary and Conclusions

This chapter set forth the fundamentals of modern portfolio theory. Our basic points are these:

1. This chapter showed us how to calculate the expected return and variance for individual securities, and the covariance and correlation for pairs of securities. Given these statistics, the expected return and variance for a portfolio of two securities A and B can be written as:

$$\text{Expected return on portfolio} = X_A \bar{R}_A + X_B \bar{R}_B$$
$$\text{Var(portfolio)} = X_A^2 \sigma_A^2 + 2 X_A X_B \sigma_{AB} + X_B^2 \sigma_B^2$$

2. In our notation, X stands for the proportion of a security in a portfolio. By varying X we can trace out the efficient set of portfolios. We graphed the efficient set for the two-asset case as a curve, pointing out that the degree of curvature or bend in the graph reflects the diversification effect: The lower the correlation between the two securities, the greater the bend. The same general shape of the efficient set holds in a world of many assets.

3. Just as the formula for variance in the two-asset case is computed from a 2×2 matrix, the variance formula is computed from an $N \times N$ matrix in the N-asset case. We showed that with a large number of assets, there are many more covariance terms than variance terms in the matrix. In fact the variance terms are effectively diversified away in a large portfolio, but the covariance terms are not. Thus, a diversified portfolio can eliminate some, but not all, of the risk of the individual securities.

4. The efficient set of risky assets can be combined with riskless borrowing and lending. In this case a rational investor will always choose to hold the portfolio of risky securities represented by point A in Figure 10.9. Then he can either borrow or lend at the riskless rate to achieve any desired point on line II in the figure.

5. The contribution of a security to the risk of a large, well-diversified portfolio is proportional to the covariance of the security's return with the market's return. This contribution, when standardized, is called the beta. The beta of a security can also be interpreted as the responsiveness of a security's return to that of the market.

6. The CAPM states that:

$$\bar{R} = R_F + \beta(\bar{R}_M - R_F)$$

In other words, the expected return on a security is positively (and linearly) related to the security's beta.

Concept Questions

1. **Diversifiable and Nondiversifiable Risks**   In broad terms, why is some risk diversifiable? Why are some risks nondiversifiable? Does it follow that an investor can control the level of unsystematic risk in a portfolio, but not the level of systematic risk?

2. **Systematic versus Unsystematic Risk**   Classify the following events as mostly systematic or mostly unsystematic. Is the distinction clear in every case?
   a. Short-term interest rates increase unexpectedly.
   b. The interest rate a company pays on its short-term debt borrowing is increased by its bank.
   c. Oil prices unexpectedly decline.
   d. An oil tanker ruptures, creating a large oil spill.
   e. A manufacturer loses a multimillion-dollar product liability suit.
   f. A Supreme Court decision substantially broadens producer liability for injuries suffered by product users.

3. **Expected Portfolio Returns**   If a portfolio has a positive investment in every asset, can the expected return on the portfolio be greater than that on every asset in the portfolio? Can it be less than that on every asset in the portfolio? If you answer yes to one or both of these questions, give an example to support your answer.

4. **Diversification**   True or false: The most important characteristic in determining the expected return of a well-diversified portfolio is the variances of the individual assets in the portfolio. Explain.

5. **Portfolio Risk**   If a portfolio has a positive investment in every asset, can the standard deviation on the portfolio be less than that on every asset in the portfolio? What about the portfolio beta?

6. **Beta and CAPM**   Is it possible that a risky asset could have a beta of zero? Explain. Based on the CAPM, what is the expected return on such an asset? Is it possible that a risky asset could have a negative beta? What does the CAPM predict about the expected return on such an asset? Can you give an explanation for your answer?

7. **Covariance**   Briefly explain why the covariance of a security with the rest of a well-diversified portfolio is a more appropriate measure of the risk of the security than the security's variance.

8. **Beta**   Consider the following quotation from a leading investment manager: "The shares of Southern Co. have traded close to $12 for most of the past three years. Since Southern's stock has demonstrated very little price movement, the stock has a low beta. Texas Instruments, on the other hand, has traded as high as $150 and as low as its current $75. Since TI's stock has demonstrated a large amount of price movement, the stock has a very high beta." Do you agree with this analysis? Explain.

9. **Risk**   A broker has advised you not to invest in oil industry stocks because they have high standard deviations. Is the broker's advice sound for a risk-averse investor like yourself? Why or why not?

10. **Security Selection**   Is the following statement true or false? A risky security cannot have an expected return that is less than the risk-free rate because no risk-averse investor would be willing to hold this asset in equilibrium. Explain.

Questions and Problems

BASIC
(Questions 1–20)

1. **Determining Portfolio Weights**   What are the portfolio weights for a portfolio that has 70 shares of Stock A that sell for $40 per share and 110 shares of Stock B that sell for $22 per share?

2. **Portfolio Expected Return**   You own a portfolio that has $1,200 invested in Stock A and $1,900 invested in Stock B. If the expected returns on these stocks are 11 percent and 16 percent, respectively, what is the expected return on the portfolio?

3. **Portfolio Expected Return**   You own a portfolio that is 50 percent invested in Stock X, 30 percent in Stock Y, and 20 percent in Stock Z. The expected returns on these three stocks are 11 percent, 17 percent, and 14 percent, respectively. What is the expected return on the portfolio?

4. **Portfolio Expected Return**   You have $10,000 to invest in a stock portfolio. Your choices are Stock X with an expected return of 14 percent and Stock Y with an expected return of 9 percent. If your goal is to create a portfolio with an expected return of 12.2 percent, how much money will you invest in Stock X? In Stock Y?

5. **Calculating Expected Return**   Based on the following information, calculate the expected return:

State of Economy	Probability of State of Economy	Rate of Return If State Occurs
Recession	.20	−.05
Normal	.50	.12
Boom	.30	.25

6. **Calculating Returns and Standard Deviations**   Based on the following information, calculate the expected return and standard deviation for the two stocks:

State of Economy	Probability of State of Economy	Rate of Return If State Occurs	
		Stock A	Stock B
Recession	.10	.06	−.20
Normal	.60	.07	.13
Boom	.30	.11	.33

7. **Calculating Returns and Standard Deviations**   Based on the following information, calculate the expected return and standard deviation:

State of Economy	Probability of State of Economy	Rate of Return If State Occurs
Depression	.10	−.045
Recession	.20	.044
Normal	.50	.120
Boom	.20	.207

8. **Calculating Expected Returns**   A portfolio is invested 20 percent in Stock G, 70 percent in Stock J, and 10 percent in Stock K. The expected returns on these stocks are 8 percent, 15 percent, and 24 percent, respectively. What is the portfolio's expected return? How do you interpret your answer?

9. **Returns and Standard Deviations**   Consider the following information:

State of Economy	Probability of State of Economy	Rate of Return If State Occurs		
		Stock A	Stock B	Stock C
Boom	.70	.07	.15	.33
Bust	.30	.13	.03	−.06

    a. What is the expected return on an equally weighted portfolio of these three stocks?
    b. What is the variance of a portfolio invested 20 percent each in A and B, and 60 percent in C?

10. **Returns and Standard Deviations**   Consider the following information:

State of Economy	Probability of State of Economy	Rate of Return If State Occurs		
		Stock A	Stock B	Stock C
Boom	.30	.30	.45	.33
Good	.40	.12	.10	.15
Poor	.25	.01	−.15	−.05
Bust	.05	−.06	−.30	−.09

    a. Your portfolio is invested 30 percent each in A and C, and 40 percent in B. What is the expected return of the portfolio?
    b. What is the variance of this portfolio? The standard deviation?

11. **Calculating Portfolio Betas**   You own a stock portfolio invested 25 percent in Stock Q, 20 percent in Stock R, 15 percent in Stock S, and 40 percent in Stock T. The betas for these four stocks are .6, 1.70, 1.15, and 1.34, respectively. What is the portfolio beta?

12. **Calculating Portfolio Betas**   You own a portfolio equally invested in a risk-free asset and two stocks. If one of the stocks has a beta of 1.9 and the total portfolio is equally as risky as the market, what must the beta be for the other stock in your portfolio?

13. **Using CAPM**   A stock has a beta of 1.3, the expected return on the market is 14 percent, and the risk-free rate is 5 percent. What must the expected return on this stock be?

www.mhhe.com/rwj

14. **Using CAPM** A stock has an expected return of 14 percent, the risk-free rate is 4 percent, and the market risk premium is 6 percent. What must the beta of this stock be?

15. **Using CAPM** A stock has an expected return of 11 percent, its beta is .85, and the risk-free rate is 5.5 percent. What must the expected return on the market be?

16. **Using CAPM** A stock has an expected return of 17 percent, a beta of 1.9, and the expected return on the market is 11 percent. What must the risk-free rate be?

17. **Using CAPM** A stock has a beta of 1.2 and an expected return of 16 percent. A risk-free asset currently earns 5 percent.
    a. What is the expected return on a portfolio that is equally invested in the two assets?
    b. If a portfolio of the two assets has a beta of .75, what are the portfolio weights?
    c. If a portfolio of the two assets has an expected return of 8 percent, what is its beta?
    d. If a portfolio of the two assets has a beta of 2.40, what are the portfolio weights? How do you interpret the weights for the two assets in this case? Explain.

18. **Using the SML** Asset *W* has an expected return of 16 percent and a beta of 1.3. If the risk-free rate is 5 percent, complete the following table for portfolios of Asset *W* and a risk-free asset. Illustrate the relationship between portfolio expected return and portfolio beta by plotting the expected returns against the betas. What is the slope of the line that results?

Percentage of Portfolio in Asset *W*	Portfolio Expected Return	Portfolio Beta
0%		
25		
50		
75		
100		
125		
150		

19. **Reward-to-Risk Ratios** Stock *Y* has a beta of 1.50 and an expected return of 17 percent. Stock *Z* has a beta of .80 and an expected return of 10.5 percent. If the risk-free rate is 5.5 percent and the market risk premium is 7.5 percent, are these stocks correctly priced?

20. **Reward-to-Risk Ratios** In the previous problem, what would the risk-free rate have to be for the two stocks to be correctly priced?

INTERMEDIATE
(Questions 21–33)

21. **Portfolio Returns** Using information from the previous chapter about capital market history, determine the return on a portfolio that is equally invested in large-company stocks and long-term government bonds. What is the return on a portfolio that is equally invested in small-company stocks and Treasury bills?

22. **CAPM** Using the CAPM, show that the ratio of the risk premiums on two assets is equal to the ratio of their betas.

23. **Portfolio Returns and Deviations** Consider the following information about three stocks:

State of Economy	Probability of State of Economy	Rate of Return If State Occurs		
		Stock A	Stock B	Stock C
Boom	.4	.20	.35	.60
Normal	.4	.15	.12	.05
Bust	.2	.01	−.25	−.50

a. If your portfolio is invested 40 percent each in A and B and 20 percent in C, what is the portfolio expected return? The variance? The standard deviation?

b. If the expected T-bill rate is 3.80 percent, what is the expected risk premium on the portfolio?

c. If the expected inflation rate is 3.50 percent, what are the approximate and exact expected real returns on the portfolio? What are the approximate and exact expected real risk premiums on the portfolio?

24. **Analyzing a Portfolio**   You want to create a portfolio equally as risky as the market, and you have $1,000,000 to invest. Given this information, fill in the rest of the following table:

Asset	Investment	Beta
Stock A	$200,000	.80
Stock B	$250,000	1.30
Stock C		1.50
Risk-free asset		

25. **Analyzing a Portfolio**   You have $100,000 to invest in a portfolio containing Stock X, Stock Y, and a risk-free asset. You must invest all of your money. Your goal is to create a portfolio that has an expected return of 13.5 percent and that has only 70 percent of the risk of the overall market. If X has an expected return of 31 percent and a beta of 1.8, Y has an expected return of 20 percent and a beta of 1.3, and the risk-free rate is 7 percent, how much money will you invest in Stock X? How do you interpret your answer?

26. **Covariance and Correlation**   Based on the following information, calculate the expected return and standard deviation of each of the following stocks. Assume each state of the economy is equally likely to happen. What are the covariance and correlation between the returns of the two stocks?

State of Economy	Return on Stock A	Return on Stock B
Bear	.063	−.037
Normal	.105	.064
Bull	.156	.253

27. **Covariance and Correlation**   Based on the following information, calculate the expected return and standard deviation for each of the following stocks. What are the covariance and correlation between the returns of the two stocks?

State of Economy	Probability of State of Economy	Return on Stock J	Return on Stock K
Bear	.25	−.020	.050
Normal	.60	.092	.062
Bull	.15	.154	.074

28. **Portfolio Standard Deviation**   Security F has an expected return of 12 percent and a standard deviation of 34 percent per year. Security G has an expected return of 18 percent and a standard deviation of 50 percent per year.

a. What is the expected return on a portfolio composed of 30 percent of security F and 70 percent of security G?

b. If the correlation between the returns of security F and security G is .2, what is the standard deviation of the portfolio described in part (a)?

29. **Portfolio Standard Deviation** Suppose the expected returns and standard deviations of stocks A and B are $E(R_A) = .15$, $E(R_B) = .25$, $\sigma_A = .40$, and $\sigma_B = .65$, respectively.
    a. Calculate the expected return and standard deviation of a portfolio that is composed of 40 percent A and 60 percent B when the correlation between the returns on A and B is .5.
    b. Calculate the standard deviation of a portfolio that is composed of 40 percent A and 60 percent B when the correlation coefficient between the returns on A and B is $-.5$.
    c. How does the correlation between the returns on A and B affect the standard deviation of the portfolio?

30. **Correlation and Beta** You have been provided the following data about the securities of three firms, the market portfolio, and the risk-free asset:

Security	Expected Return	Standard Deviation	Correlation*	Beta
Firm A	.13	.38	(i)	.9
Firm B	.16	(ii)	.4	1.1
Firm C	.25	.65	.35	(iii)
The market portfolio	.15	.20	(iv)	(v)
The risk-free asset	.05	(vi)	(vii)	(viii)

*With the market portfolio.

    a. Fill in the missing values in the table.
    b. Is the stock of Firm A correctly priced according to the capital asset pricing model (CAPM)? What about the stock of Firm B? Firm C? If these securities are not correctly priced, what is your investment recommendation for someone with a well-diversified portfolio?

31. **CML** The market portfolio has an expected return of 12 percent and a standard deviation of 10 percent. The risk-free rate is 5 percent.
    a. What is the expected return on a well-diversified portfolio with a standard deviation of 7 percent?
    b. What is the standard deviation of a well-diversified portfolio with an expected return of 20 percent?

32. **Beta and CAPM** A portfolio that combines the risk-free asset and the market portfolio has an expected return of 12 percent and a standard deviation of 18 percent. The risk-free rate is 5 percent, and the expected return on the market portfolio is 14 percent. Assume the capital asset pricing model holds. What expected rate of return would a security earn if it had a .45 correlation with the market portfolio and a standard deviation of 40 percent?

33. **Beta and CAPM** Suppose the risk-free rate is 6.3 percent and the market portfolio has an expected return of 14.8 percent. The market portfolio has a variance of .0498. Portfolio Z has a correlation coefficient with the market of .45 and a variance of .1783. According to the capital asset pricing model, what is the expected return on portfolio Z?

CHALLENGE
(Questions 34–39)

34. **Systematic versus Unsystematic Risk** Consider the following information about Stocks I and II:

State of Economy	Probability of State of Economy	Rate of Return If State Occurs	
		Stock I	Stock II
Recession	.15	.09	−.30
Normal	.70	.42	.12
Irrational exuberance	.15	.26	.44

The market risk premium is 10 percent, and the risk-free rate is 4 percent. Which stock has the most systematic risk? Which one has the most unsystematic risk? Which stock is "riskier"? Explain.

35. **SML** Suppose you observe the following situation:

Security	Beta	Expected Return
Pete Corp.	1.3	.23
Repete Co.	.6	.13

Assume these securities are correctly priced. Based on the CAPM, what is the expected return on the market? What is the risk-free rate?

36. **Covariance and Portfolio Standard Deviation** There are three securities in the market. The following chart shows their possible payoffs:

State	Probability of Outcome	Return on Security 1	Return on Security 2	Return on Security 3
1	.10	.25	.25	.10
2	.40	.20	.15	.15
3	.40	.15	.20	.20
4	.10	.10	.10	.25

    a. What are the expected return and standard deviation of each security?
    b. What are the covariances and correlations between the pairs of securities?
    c. What are the expected return and standard deviation of a portfolio with half of its funds invested in security 1 and half in security 2?
    d. What are the expected return and standard deviation of a portfolio with half of its funds invested in security 1 and half in security 3?
    e. What are the expected return and standard deviation of a portfolio with half of its funds invested in security 2 and half in security 3?
    f. What do your answers in parts (a), (c), (d), and (e) imply about diversification?

37. **SML** Suppose you observe the following situation:

State of Economy	Probability of State	Return If State Occurs	
		Stock A	**Stock B**
Bust	.25	−.10	−.30
Normal	.50	.10	.05
Boom	.25	.20	.40

    a. Calculate the expected return on each stock.
    b. Assuming the capital asset pricing model holds and stock *A*'s beta is greater than stock *B*'s beta by .25, what is the expected market risk premium?

38.   Standard Deviation and Beta   There are two stocks in the market, stock A and stock B. The price of stock A today is $50. The price of stock A next year will be $40 if the economy is in a recession, $55 if the economy is normal, and $60 if the economy is expanding. The probabilities of recession, normal times, and expansion are .1, .8, and .1, respectively. Stock A pays no dividends and has a correlation of .8 with the market portfolio. Stock B has an expected return of 9 percent, a standard deviation of 12 percent, a correlation with the market portfolio of .2, and a correlation with stock A of .6. The market portfolio has a standard deviation of 10 percent. Assume the CAPM holds.

a. If you are a typical, risk-averse investor with a well-diversified portfolio, which stock would you prefer? Why?

b. What are the expected return and standard deviation of a portfolio consisting of 70 percent of stock A and 30 percent of stock B?

c. What is the beta of the portfolio in part (b)?

39.   Minimum Variance Portfolio   Assume stocks A and B have the following characteristics:

Stock	Expected Return (%)	Standard Deviation (%)
A	5	10
B	10	20

The covariance between the returns on the two stocks is .001.

a. Suppose an investor holds a portfolio consisting of only stock A and stock B. Find the portfolio weights, X_A and X_B, such that the variance of her portfolio is minimized. (*Hint*: Remember that the sum of the two weights must equal 1.)

b. What is the expected return on the minimum variance portfolio?

c. If the covariance between the returns on the two stocks is $-.02$, what are the minimum variance weights?

d. What is the variance of the portfolio in part (c)?

S&P Problem

www.mhhe.com/edumarketinsight

1.   Using CAPM   You can find estimates of beta for companies under the "Mthly. Val. Data" link. Locate the beta for Amazon.com (AMZN) and Dow Chemical (DOW). How has the beta for each of these companies changed over the period reported? Using the historical risk-free rate and market risk premium found in the chapter, calculate the expected return for each company based on the most recent beta. Is the expected return for each company what you would expect? Why or why not?

Appendix 10A   Is Beta Dead?

To access Appendix 10A, please go to www.mhhe.com/rwj.

Mini Case

A Job at East Coast Yachts, Part 2

You are discussing your 401(k) with Dan Ervin when he mentions that Sarah Brown, a representative from Bledsoe Financial Services, is visiting East Coast Yachts today. You decide that you should meet with Sarah, so Dan sets up an appointment for you later in the day.

When you sit down with Sarah, she discusses the various investment options available in the company's 401(k) account. You mention to Sarah that you researched East Coast Yachts before you accepted your new job. You are confident in management's ability to lead the company. Analysis of the company has led to your belief that the company is growing and will achieve a greater market share in the future. You also feel you should support your employer. Given these considerations, along with the fact that you are a conservative investor, you are leaning toward investing 100 percent of your 401(k) account in East Coast Yachts.

Assume the risk-free rate is the historical average risk-free rate (in Chapter 9). The correlation between the Bledsoe bond fund and large-cap stock fund is .27. Note that the spreadsheet graphing and "solver" functions may assist you in answering the following questions.

1. Considering the effects of diversification, how should Sarah respond to the suggestion that you invest 100 percent of your 401(k) account in East Coast Yachts stock?

2. Sarah's response to investing your 401(k) account entirely in East Coast Yachts stock has convinced you that this may not be the best alternative. Because you are a conservative investor, you tell Sarah that a 100 percent investment in the bond fund may be the best alternative. Is it?

3. Using the returns for the Bledsoe Large-Cap Stock Fund and the Bledsoe Bond Fund, graph the opportunity set of feasible portfolios.

4. After examining the opportunity set, you notice that you can invest in a portfolio consisting of the bond fund and the large-cap stock fund that will have exactly the same standard deviation as the bond fund. This portfolio will also have a greater expected return. What are the portfolio weights and expected return of this portfolio?

5. Examining the opportunity set, notice there is a portfolio that has the lowest standard deviation. This is the minimum variance portfolio. What are the portfolio weights, expected return, and standard deviation of this portfolio? Why is the minimum variance portfolio important?

6. A measure of risk-adjusted performance that is often used is the Sharpe ratio. The Sharpe ratio is calculated as the risk premium of an asset divided by its standard deviation. The portfolio with the highest possible Sharpe ratio on the opportunity set is called the Sharpe optimal portfolio. What are the portfolio weights, expected return, and standard deviation of the Sharpe optimal portfolio? How does the Sharpe ratio of this portfolio compare to the Sharpe ratios of the bond fund and the large-cap stock fund? Do you see a connection between the Sharpe optimal portfolio and the CAPM? What is the connection?

CHAPTER 10
RISK AND RETURN: *THE CAPITAL ASSET PRICING MODEL (CAPM)*

Answers to Concepts Review and Critical Thinking Questions

1. Some of the risk in holding any asset is unique to the asset in question. By investing in a variety of assets, this unique portion of the total risk can be eliminated at little cost. On the other hand, there are some risks that affect all investments. This portion of the total risk of an asset cannot be costlessly eliminated. In other words, systematic risk can be controlled, but only by a costly reduction in expected returns.

2. *a.* systematic
    b. unsystematic
    c. both; probably mostly systematic
    d. unsystematic
    e. unsystematic
    f. systematic

3. No to both questions. The portfolio expected return is a weighted average of the asset's returns, so it must be less than the largest asset return and greater than the smallest asset return.

4. False. The variance of the individual assets is a measure of the total risk. The variance on a well-diversified portfolio is a function of systematic risk only.

5. Yes, the standard deviation can be less than that of every asset in the portfolio. However, β_p cannot be less than the smallest beta because β_p is a weighted average of the individual asset betas.

6. Yes. It is possible, in theory, to construct a zero beta portfolio of risky assets whose return would be equal to the risk-free rate. It is also possible to have a negative beta; the return would be less than the risk-free rate. A negative beta asset would carry a negative risk premium because of its value as a diversification instrument.

7. The covariance is a more appropriate measure of a security's risk in a well-diversified portfolio because the covariance reflects the effect of the security on the variance of the portfolio. Investors are concerned with the variance of their portfolios and not the variance of the individual securities. Since covariance measures the impact of an individual security on the variance of the portfolio, covariance is the appropriate measure of risk.

B-248 SOLUTIONS

8. If we assume that the market has not stayed constant during the past three years, then the lack in movement of Southern Co.'s stock price only indicates that the stock either has a standard deviation or a beta that is very near to zero. The large amount of movement in Texas Instrument' stock price does not imply that the firm's beta is high. Total volatility (the price fluctuation) is a function of both systematic and unsystematic risk. The beta only reflects the systematic risk. Observing the standard deviation of price movements does not indicate whether the price changes were due to systematic factors or firm specific factors. Thus, if you observe large stock price movements like that of TI, you cannot claim that the beta of the stock is high. All you know is that the total risk of TI is high.

9. The wide fluctuations in the price of oil stocks do not indicate that these stocks are a poor investment. If an oil stock is purchased as part of a well-diversified portfolio, only its contribution to the risk of the entire portfolio matters. This contribution is measured by systematic risk or beta. Since price fluctuations in oil stocks reflect diversifiable plus non-diversifiable risk, observing the standard deviation of price movements is not an adequate measure of the appropriateness of adding oil stocks to a portfolio.

10. The statement is false. If a security has a negative beta, investors would want to hold the asset to reduce the variability of their portfolios. Those assets will have expected returns that are lower than the risk-free rate. To see this, examine the Capital Asset Pricing Model:

$$E(R_S) = R_f + \beta_S[E(R_M) - R_f]$$

If $\beta_S < 0$, then the $E(R_S) < R_f$

Solutions to Questions and Problems

NOTE: All end-of-chapter problems were solved using a spreadsheet. Many problems require multiple steps. Due to space and readability constraints, when these intermediate steps are included in this solutions manual, rounding may appear to have occurred. However, the final answer for each problem is found without rounding during any step in the problem.

Basic

1. The portfolio weight of an asset is total investment in that asset divided by the total portfolio value. First, we will find the portfolio value, which is:

    Total value = 70($40) + 110($22) = $5,220

    The portfolio weight for each stock is:

    Weight$_A$ = 70($40)/$5,220 = .5364

    Weight$_B$ = 110($22)/$5,220 = .4636

2. The expected return of a portfolio is the sum of the weight of each asset times the expected return of each asset. The total value of the portfolio is:

Total value = $1,200 + 1,900 = $3,100

So, the expected return of this portfolio is:

$E(R_p) = (\$1,200/\$3,100)(0.11) + (\$1,900/\$3,100)(0.16) = .1406$ or 14.06%

3. The expected return of a portfolio is the sum of the weight of each asset times the expected return of each asset. So, the expected return of the portfolio is:

$E(R_p) = .50(.11) + .30(.17) + .20(.14) = .1340$ or 13.40%

4. Here we are given the expected return of the portfolio and the expected return of each asset in the portfolio and are asked to find the weight of each asset. We can use the equation for the expected return of a portfolio to solve this problem. Since the total weight of a portfolio must equal 1 (100%), the weight of Stock Y must be one minus the weight of Stock X. Mathematically speaking, this means:

$E(R_p) = .122 = .14w_X + .09(1 - w_X)$

We can now solve this equation for the weight of Stock X as:

$.122 = .14w_X + .09 - .09w_X$
$.032 = .05w_X$
$w_X = 0.64$

So, the dollar amount invested in Stock X is the weight of Stock X times the total portfolio value, or:

Investment in X = 0.64($10,000) = $6,400

And the dollar amount invested in Stock Y is:

Investment in Y = (1 – 0.64)($10,000) = $3,600

5. The expected return of an asset is the sum of the probability of each return occurring times the probability of that return occurring. So, the expected return of the asset is:

$E(R) = .2(-.05) + .5(.12) + .3(.25) = .1250$ or 12.50%

B-250 SOLUTIONS

6.   The expected return of an asset is the sum of the probability of each return occurring times the probability of that return occurring. So, the expected return of each stock asset is:

$E(R_A) = .10(.06) + .60(.07) + .30(.11) = .0810$ or 8.10%

$E(R_B) = .10(-.2) + .60(.13) + .30(.33) = .1570$ or 15.70%

To calculate the standard deviation, we first need to calculate the variance. To find the variance, we find the squared deviations from the expected return. We then multiply each possible squared deviation by its probability, and then add all of these up. The result is the variance. So, the variance and standard deviation of each stock are:

$\sigma_A{}^2 = .10(.06 - .0810)^2 + .60(.07 - .0810)^2 + .30(.11 - .0810)^2 = .00037$

$\sigma_A = (.00037)^{1/2} = .0192$ or 1.92%

$\sigma_B{}^2 = .10(-.2 - .1570)^2 + .60(.13 - .1570)^2 + .30(.33 - .1570)^2 = .02216$

$\sigma_B = (.022216)^{1/2} = .1489$ or 14.89%

7.   The expected return of an asset is the sum of the probability of each return occurring times the probability of that return occurring. So, the expected return of the stock is:

$E(R_A) = .10(-.045) + .20(.044) + .50(.12) + .20(.207) = .1057$ or 10.57%

To calculate the standard deviation, we first need to calculate the variance. To find the variance, we find the squared deviations from the expected return. We then multiply each possible squared deviation by its probability, and then add all of these up. The result is the variance. So, the variance and standard deviation are:

$\sigma^2 = .10(-.045 - .1057)^2 + .20(.044 - .1057)^2 + .50(.12 - .1057)^2 + .20(.207 - .1057)^2 = .005187$

$\sigma = (.005187)^{1/2} = .0720$ or 17.20%

8.   The expected return of a portfolio is the sum of the weight of each asset times the expected return of each asset. So, the expected return of the portfolio is:

$E(R_p) = .20(.08) + .70(.15) + .1(.24) = .1450$ or 14.50%

If we own this portfolio, we would expect to get a return of 14.50 percent.

CHAPTER 10 B-251

9. *a.* To find the expected return of the portfolio, we need to find the return of the portfolio in each state of the economy. This portfolio is a special case since all three assets have the same weight. To find the expected return in an equally weighted portfolio, we can sum the returns of each asset and divide by the number of assets, so the expected return of the portfolio in each state of the economy is:

Boom: $E(R_p) = (.07 + .15 + .33)/3 = .1833$ or 18.33%
Bust: $E(R_p) = (.13 + .03 - .06)/3 = .0333$ or 3.33%

To find the expected return of the portfolio, we multiply the return in each state of the economy by the probability of that state occurring, and then sum. Doing this, we find:

$E(R_p) = .70(.1833) + .30(.0333) = .1383$ or 13.83%

b. This portfolio does not have an equal weight in each asset. We still need to find the return of the portfolio in each state of the economy. To do this, we will multiply the return of each asset by its portfolio weight and then sum the products to get the portfolio return in each state of the economy. Doing so, we get:

Boom: $E(R_p)=.20(.07) +.20(.15) + .60(.33) =.2420$ or 24.20%
Bust: $E(R_p) =.20(.13) +.20(.03) + .60(-.06) = -.0040$ or –0.40%

And the expected return of the portfolio is:

$E(R_p) = .70(.2420) + .30(-.004) = .1682$ or 16.82%

To calculate the standard deviation, we first need to calculate the variance. To find the variance, we find the squared deviations from the expected return. We then multiply each possible squared deviation by its probability, and then add all of these up. The result is the variance. So, the variance and standard deviation the portfolio is:

$\sigma_p^2 = .70(.2420 - .1682)^2 + .30(-.0040 - .1682)^2 = .012708$

$\sigma_p = (.012708)^{1/2} = .1127$ or 11.27%

10. *a.* This portfolio does not have an equal weight in each asset. We first need to find the return of the portfolio in each state of the economy. To do this, we will multiply the return of each asset by its portfolio weight and then sum the products to get the portfolio return in each state of the economy. Doing so, we get:

Boom: $E(R_p) = .30(.3) + .40(.45) + .30(.33) = .3690$ or 36.90%
Good: $E(R_p) = .30(.12) + .40(.10) + .30(.15) = .1210$ or 12.10%
Poor: $E(R_p) = .30(.01) + .40(-.15) + .30(-.05) = -.0720$ or –7.20%
Bust: $E(R_p) = .30(-.06) + .40(-.30) + .30(-.09) = -.1650$ or –16.50%

And the expected return of the portfolio is:

$E(R_p) = .30(.3690) + .40(.1210) + .25(-.0720) + .05(-.1650) = .1329$ or 13.29%

B-252 SOLUTIONS

b. To calculate the standard deviation, we first need to calculate the variance. To find the variance, we find the squared deviations from the expected return. We then multiply each possible squared deviation by its probability, and then add all of these up. The result is the variance. So, the variance and standard deviation the portfolio is:

$$\sigma_p^2 = .30(.3690 - .1329)^2 + .40(.1210 - .1329)^2 + .25\,(-.0720 - .1329)^2 + .05(-.1650 - .1329)^2$$
$$\sigma_p^2 = .03171$$

$$\sigma_p = (.03171)^{1/2} = .1781 \text{ or } 17.81\%$$

11. The beta of a portfolio is the sum of the weight of each asset times the beta of each asset. So, the beta of the portfolio is:

$$\beta_p = .25(.6) + .20(1.7) + .15(1.15) + .40(1.34) = 1.20$$

12. The beta of a portfolio is the sum of the weight of each asset times the beta of each asset. If the portfolio is as risky as the market it must have the same beta as the market. Since the beta of the market is one, we know the beta of our portfolio is one. We also need to remember that the beta of the risk-free asset is zero. It has to be zero since the asset has no risk. Setting up the equation for the beta of our portfolio, we get:

$$\beta_p = 1.0 = \tfrac{1}{3}(0) + \tfrac{1}{3}(1.9) + \tfrac{1}{3}(\beta_X)$$

Solving for the beta of Stock X, we get:

$$\beta_X = 1.10$$

13. CAPM states the relationship between the risk of an asset and its expected return. CAPM is:

$$E(R_i) = R_f + [E(R_M) - R_f] \times \beta_i$$

Substituting the values we are given, we find:

$$E(R_i) = .05 + (.14 - .05)(1.3) = .1670 \text{ or } 16.70\%$$

14. We are given the values for the CAPM except for the β of the stock. We need to substitute these values into the CAPM, and solve for the β of the stock. One important thing we need to realize is that we are given the market risk premium. The market risk premium is the expected return of the market minus the risk-free rate. We must be careful not to use this value as the expected return of the market. Using the CAPM, we find:

$$E(R_i) = .14 = .04 + .06\beta_i$$

$$\beta_i = 1.67$$

15. Here we need to find the expected return of the market using the CAPM. Substituting the values given, and solving for the expected return of the market, we find:

$$E(R_i) = .11 = .055 + [E(R_M) - .055](.85)$$

$$E(R_M) = .1197 \text{ or } 11.97\%$$

16. Here we need to find the risk-free rate using the CAPM. Substituting the values given, and solving for the risk-free rate, we find:

$$E(R_i) = .17 = R_f + (.11 - R_f)(1.9)$$

$$.17 = R_f + .209 - 1.9R_f$$

$$R_f = .0433 \text{ or } 4.33\%$$

17. *a.* Again, we have a special case where the portfolio is equally weighted, so we can sum the returns of each asset and divide by the number of assets. The expected return of the portfolio is:

$$E(R_p) = (.16 + .05)/2 = .1050 \text{ or } 10.50\%$$

b. We need to find the portfolio weights that result in a portfolio with a β of 0.75. We know the β of the risk-free asset is zero. We also know the weight of the risk-free asset is one minus the weight of the stock since the portfolio weights must sum to one, or 100 percent. So:

$$\beta_p = 0.75 = w_S(1.2) + (1 - w_S)(0)$$
$$0.75 = 1.2w_S + 0 - 0w_S$$
$$w_S = 0.75/1.2$$
$$w_S = .6250$$

And, the weight of the risk-free asset is:

$$w_{Rf} = 1 - .6250 = .3750$$

c. We need to find the portfolio weights that result in a portfolio with an expected return of 8 percent. We also know the weight of the risk-free asset is one minus the weight of the stock since the portfolio weights must sum to one, or 100 percent. So:

$$E(R_p) = .08 = .16w_S + .05(1 - w_S)$$
$$.08 = .16w_S + .05 - .05w_S$$
$$w_S = .2727$$

So, the β of the portfolio will be:

$$\beta_p = .2727(1.2) + (1 - .2727)(0) = 0.327$$

Ross–Westerfield–Jaffe:
Corporate Finance, Eighth
Edition

III. Risk

Answers for Chapter 10

© The McGraw–Hill
Companies, 2008

443

B-254 SOLUTIONS

d. Solving for the β of the portfolio as we did in part *a*, we find:

$$\beta_p = 2.4 = w_S(1.2) + (1 - w_S)(0)$$

$$w_S = 2.4/1.2 = 2$$

$$w_{Rf} = 1 - 2 = -1$$

The portfolio is invested 200% in the stock and –100% in the risk-free asset. This represents borrowing at the risk-free rate to buy more of the stock.

18. First, we need to find the β of the portfolio. The β of the risk-free asset is zero, and the weight of the risk-free asset is one minus the weight of the stock, the β of the portfolio is:

$$\beta_p = w_W(1.3) + (1 - w_W)(0) = 1.3w_W$$

So, to find the β of the portfolio for any weight of the stock, we simply multiply the weight of the stock times its β.

Even though we are solving for the β and expected return of a portfolio of one stock and the risk-free asset for different portfolio weights, we are really solving for the SML. Any combination of this stock, and the risk-free asset will fall on the SML. For that matter, a portfolio of any stock and the risk-free asset, or any portfolio of stocks, will fall on the SML. We know the slope of the SML line is the market risk premium, so using the CAPM and the information concerning this stock, the market risk premium is:

$$E(R_W) = .16 = .05 + MRP(1.30)$$
$$MRP = .11/1.3 = .0846 \text{ or } 8.46\%$$

So, now we know the CAPM equation for any stock is:

$$E(R_p) = .05 + .0846\beta_p$$

The slope of the SML is equal to the market risk premium, which is 0.0846. Using these equations to fill in the table, we get the following results:

w_W	$E(R_p)$	β_p
0%	.0500	0
25	.0775	0.325
50	.1050	0.650
75	.1325	0.975
100	.1600	1.300
125	.1875	1.625
150	.2150	1.950

19. There are two ways to correctly answer this question. We will work through both. First, we can use the CAPM. Substituting in the value we are given for each stock, we find:

$$E(R_Y) = .055 + .075(1.50) = .1675 \text{ or } 16.75\%$$

It is given in the problem that the expected return of Stock Y is 17 percent, but according to the CAPM, the return of the stock based on its level of risk, the expected return should be 16.75 percent. This means the stock return is too high, given its level of risk. Stock Y plots above the SML and is undervalued. In other words, its price must increase to reduce the expected return to 16.75 percent. For Stock Z, we find:

$$E(R_Z) = .055 + .075(0.80) = .1150 \text{ or } 11.50\%$$

The return given for Stock Z is 10.5 percent, but according to the CAPM the expected return of the stock should be 11.50 percent based on its level of risk. Stock Z plots below the SML and is overvalued. In other words, its price must decrease to increase the expected return to 11.50 percent.

We can also answer this question using the reward-to-risk ratio. All assets must have the same reward-to-risk ratio, that is, every asset must have the same ratio of the asset risk premium to its beta. This follows from the linearity of the SML in Figure 11.11. The reward-to-risk ratio is the risk premium of the asset divided by its β. This is also know as the Treynor ratio or Treynor index. We are given the market risk premium, and we know the β of the market is one, so the reward-to-risk ratio for the market is 0.075, or 7.5 percent. Calculating the reward-to-risk ratio for Stock Y, we find:

$$\text{Reward-to-risk ratio Y} = (.17 - .055) / 1.50 = .0767$$

The reward-to-risk ratio for Stock Y is too high, which means the stock plots above the SML, and the stock is undervalued. Its price must increase until its reward-to-risk ratio is equal to the market reward-to-risk ratio. For Stock Z, we find:

$$\text{Reward-to-risk ratio Z} = (.105 - .055) / .80 = .0625$$

The reward-to-risk ratio for Stock Z is too low, which means the stock plots below the SML, and the stock is overvalued. Its price must decrease until its reward-to-risk ratio is equal to the market reward-to-risk ratio.

20. We need to set the reward-to-risk ratios of the two assets equal to each other (see the previous problem), which is:

$$(.17 - R_f)/1.50 = (.105 - R_f)/0.80$$

We can cross multiply to get:

$$0.80(.17 - R_f) = 1.50(.105 - R_f)$$

Solving for the risk-free rate, we find:

$$0.136 - 0.80R_f = 0.1575 - 1.50R_f$$

$$R_f = .0307 \text{ or } 3.07\%$$

B-256 SOLUTIONS

Intermediate

21. For a portfolio that is equally invested in large-company stocks and long-term bonds:

Return = (12.4% + 5.8%)/2 = 9.1%

For a portfolio that is equally invested in small stocks and Treasury bills:

Return = (17.5% + 3.8%)/2 = 10.65%

22. We know that the reward-to-risk ratios for all assets must be equal (See Question 19). This can be expressed as:

$[E(R_A) - R_f]/\beta_A = [E(R_B) - R_f]/\beta_B$

The numerator of each equation is the risk premium of the asset, so:

$RP_A/\beta_A = RP_B/\beta_B$

We can rearrange this equation to get:

$\beta_B/\beta_A = RP_B/RP_A$

If the reward-to-risk ratios are the same, the ratio of the betas of the assets is equal to the ratio of the risk premiums of the assets.

23. *a.* We need to find the return of the portfolio in each state of the economy. To do this, we will multiply the return of each asset by its portfolio weight and then sum the products to get the portfolio return in each state of the economy. Doing so, we get:

Boom: $E(R_p) = .4(.20) + .4(.35) + .2(.60) = .3400$ or 34.00%
Normal: $E(R_p) = .4(.15) + .4(.12) + .2(.05) = .1180$ or 11.80%
Bust: $E(R_p) = .4(.01) + .4(-.25) + .2(-.50) = -.1960$ or −19.60%

And the expected return of the portfolio is:

$E(R_p) = .4(.34) + .4(.118) + .2(-.196) = .1440$ or 14.40%

To calculate the standard deviation, we first need to calculate the variance. To find the variance, we find the squared deviations from the expected return. We then multiply each possible squared deviation by its probability, than add all of these up. The result is the variance. So, the variance and standard deviation of the portfolio is:

$\sigma^2_p = .4(.34 - .1440)^2 + .4(.118 - .1440)^2 + .2(-.196 - .1440)^2$
$\sigma^2_p = .03876$

$\sigma_p = (.03876)^{1/2} = .1969$ or 19.69%

b. The risk premium is the return of a risky asset, minus the risk-free rate. T-bills are often used as the risk-free rate, so:

$RP_i = E(R_p) - R_f = .1440 - .038 = .1060$ or 10.60%

c. The approximate expected real return is the expected nominal return minus the inflation rate, so:

Approximate expected real return = $.1440 - .035 = .1090$ or 10.90%

To find the exact real return, we will use the Fisher equation. Doing so, we get:

$1 + E(R_i) = (1 + h)[1 + e(r_i)]$
$1.1440 = (1.0350)[1 + e(r_i)]$
$e(r_i) = (1.1440/1.035) - 1 = .1053$ or 10.53%

The approximate real risk premium is the expected return minus the inflation rate, so:

Approximate expected real risk premium = $.1060 - .035 = .0710$ or 7.10%

To find the exact expected real risk premium we use the Fisher effect. Doing do, we find:

Exact expected real risk premium = $(1.1060/1.035) - 1 = .0686$ or 6.86%

24. We know the total portfolio value and the investment of two stocks in the portfolio, so we can find the weight of these two stocks. The weights of Stock A and Stock B are:

$w_A = \$200{,}000 / \$1{,}000{,}000 = .20$

$w_B = \$250{,}000/\$1{,}000{,}000 = .25$

Since the portfolio is as risky as the market, the β of the portfolio must be equal to one. We also know the β of the risk-free asset is zero. We can use the equation for the β of a portfolio to find the weight of the third stock. Doing so, we find:

$\beta_p = 1.0 = w_A(.8) + w_B(1.3) + w_C(1.5) + w_{Rf}(0)$

Solving for the weight of Stock C, we find:

$w_C = .343333$

So, the dollar investment in Stock C must be:

Invest in Stock C = $.343333(\$1{,}000{,}000) = \$343{,}333$

B-258 SOLUTIONS

We also know the total portfolio weight must be one, so the weight of the risk-free asset must be one minus the asset weight we know, or:

$1 = w_A + w_B + w_C + w_{Rf}$
$1 = .20 + .25 + .34333 + w_{Rf}$
$w_{Rf} = .206667$

So, the dollar investment in the risk-free asset must be:

Invest in risk-free asset = $.206667(\$1,000,000) = \$206,667$

25. We are given the expected return and β of a portfolio and the expected return and β of assets in the portfolio. We know the β of the risk-free asset is zero. We also know the sum of the weights of each asset must be equal to one. So, the weight of the risk-free asset is one minus the weight of Stock X and the weight of Stock Y. Using this relationship, we can express the expected return of the portfolio as:

$E(R_p) = .135 = w_X(.31) + w_Y(.20) + (1 - w_X - w_Y)(.07)$

And the β of the portfolio is:

$\beta_p = .7 = w_X(1.8) + w_Y(1.3) + (1 - w_X - w_Y)(0)$

We have two equations and two unknowns. Solving these equations, we find that:

$w_X = -0.0833333$
$w_Y = 0.6538462$
$w_{Rf} = 0.4298472$

The amount to invest in Stock X is:

Investment in stock X = $-0.0833333(\$100,000) = -\$8,333.33$

A negative portfolio weight means that you short sell the stock. If you are not familiar with short selling, it means you borrow a stock today and sell it. You must then purchase the stock at a later date to repay the borrowed stock. If you short sell a stock, you make a profit if the stock decreases in value.

26. The expected return of an asset is the sum of the probability of each return occurring times the probability of that return occurring. So, the expected return of each stock is:

$E(R_A) = .33(.063) + .33(.105) + .33(.156) = .1080$ or 10.80%

$E(R_B) = .33(-.037) + .33(.064) + .33(.253) = .0933$ or 9.33%

To calculate the standard deviation, we first need to calculate the variance. To find the variance, we find the squared deviations from the expected return. We then multiply each possible squared deviation by its probability, and then add all of these up. The result is the variance. So, the variance and standard deviation of Stock A are:

$$\sigma^2 = .33(.063 - .1080)^2 + .33(.105 - .1080)^2 + .33(.156 - .1080)^2 = .00145$$

$$\sigma = (.00145)^{1/2} = .0380 \text{ or } 3.80\%$$

And the standard deviation of Stock B is:

$$\sigma^2 = .33(-.037 - .0933)^2 + .33(.064 - .0933)^2 + .33(.253 - .0933)^2 = .01445$$

$$\sigma = (.01445)^{1/2} = .1202 \text{ or } 12.02\%$$

To find the covariance, we multiply each possible state times the product of each assets' deviation from the mean in that state. The sum of these products is the covariance. So, the covariance is:

$$\text{Cov}(A,B) = .33(.063 - .1080)(-.037 - .0933) + .33(.105 - .1080)(.064 - .0933)$$
$$+ .33(.156 - .1080)(.253 - .0933)$$
$$\text{Cov}(A,B) = .004539$$

And the correlation is:

$$\rho_{A,B} = \text{Cov}(A,B) / \sigma_A \sigma_B$$
$$\rho_{A,B} = .004539 / (.0380)(.1202)$$
$$\rho_{A,B} = .9931$$

27. The expected return of an asset is the sum of the probability of each return occurring times the probability of that return occurring. So, the expected return of each stock is:

$$E(R_A) = .25(-.020) + .60(.092) + .15(.154) = .0733 \text{ or } 7.33\%$$

$$E(R_B) = .25(.050) + .60(.062) + .15(.074) = .0608 \text{ or } 6.08\%$$

To calculate the standard deviation, we first need to calculate the variance. To find the variance, we find the squared deviations from the expected return. We then multiply each possible squared deviation by its probability, and then add all of these up. The result is the variance. So, the variance and standard deviation of Stock A are:

$$\sigma_A^2 = .25(-.020 - .0733)^2 + .60(.092 - .0733)^2 + .15(.154 - .0733)^2 = .00336$$

$$\sigma_A = (.00336)^{1/2} = .0580 \text{ or } 5.80\%$$

And the standard deviation of Stock B is:

$$\sigma_B^2 = .25(.050 - .0608)^2 + .60(.062 - .0608)^2 + .15(.074 - .0608)^2 = .00006$$

$$\sigma_B = (.00006)^{1/2} = .0075 \text{ or } 0.75\%$$

B-260 SOLUTIONS

To find the covariance, we multiply each possible state times the product of each assets' deviation from the mean in that state. The sum of these products is the covariance. So, the covariance is:

$$Cov(A,B) = .25(-.020 - .0733)(.050 - .0608) + .60(.092 - .0733)(.062 - .0608)$$
$$+ .15(.154 - .0733)(.074 - .0608)$$
$$Cov(A,B) = .000425$$

And the correlation is:

$$\rho_{A,B} = Cov(A,B) / \sigma_A \sigma_B$$
$$\rho_{A,B} = .000425 / (.0580)(.0075)$$
$$\rho_{A,B} = .9783$$

28. *a.* The expected return of the portfolio is the sum of the weight of each asset times the expected return of each asset, so:

$$E(R_P) = w_F E(R_F) + w_G E(R_G)$$
$$E(R_P) = .30(.12) + .70(.18)$$
$$E(R_P) = .1620 \text{ or } 16.20\%$$

b. The variance of a portfolio of two assets can be expressed as:

$$\sigma_P^2 = w_F^2 \sigma_F^2 + w_G^2 \sigma_G^2 + 2w_F w_G \sigma_F \sigma_G \rho_{F,G}$$
$$\sigma_P^2 = .30^2(.34^2) + .70^2(.50^2) + 2(.30)(.70)(.34)(.50)(.20)$$
$$\sigma_P^2 = .14718$$

So, the standard deviation is:

$$\sigma = (.14718)^{1/2} = .3836 \text{ or } 38.36\%$$

29. *a.* The expected return of the portfolio is the sum of the weight of each asset times the expected return of each asset, so:

$$E(R_P) = w_A E(R_A) + w_B E(R_B)$$
$$E(R_P) = .40(.15) + .60(.25)$$
$$E(R_P) = .2100 \text{ or } 21.00\%$$

The variance of a portfolio of two assets can be expressed as:

$$\sigma_P^2 = w_A^2 \sigma_A^2 + w_B^2 \sigma_B^2 + 2w_A w_B \sigma_A \sigma_B \rho_{A,B}$$
$$\sigma_P^2 = .40^2(.40^2) + .60^2(.65^2) + 2(.40)(.60)(.40)(.65)(.50)$$
$$\sigma_P^2 = .24010$$

So, the standard deviation is:

$$\sigma = (.24010)^{1/2} = .4900 \text{ or } 49.00\%$$

b. The expected return of the portfolio is the sum of the weight of each asset times the expected return of each asset, so:

$$E(R_P) = w_A E(R_A) + w_B E(R_B)$$
$$E(R_P) = .40(.15) + .60(.25)$$
$$E(R_P) = .2100 \text{ or } 21.00\%$$

The variance of a portfolio of two assets can be expressed as:

$$\sigma_P^2 = w_A^2 \sigma_A^2 + w_B^2 \sigma_B^2 + 2w_A w_B \sigma_A \sigma_B \rho_{A,B}$$
$$\sigma_P^2 = .40^2(.40^2) + .60^2(.65^2) + 2(.40)(.60)(.40)(.65)(-.50)$$
$$\sigma_P^2 = .11530$$

So, the standard deviation is:

$$\sigma = (.11530)^{1/2} = .3396 \text{ or } 33.96\%$$

c. As Stock A and Stock B become less correlated, or more negatively correlated, the standard deviation of the portfolio decreases.

30. a. (i) We can use the equation to calculate beta, we find:

$$\beta_I = (\rho_{I,M})(\sigma_I) / \sigma_M$$
$$0.9 = (\rho_{I,M})(0.38) / 0.20$$
$$\rho_{I,M} = 0.47$$

(ii) Using the equation to calculate beta, we find:

$$\beta_I = (\rho_{I,M})(\sigma_I) / \sigma_M$$
$$1.1 = (.40)(\sigma_I) / 0.20$$
$$\sigma_I = 0.55$$

(iii) Using the equation to calculate beta, we find:

$$\beta_I = (\rho_{I,M})(\sigma_I) / \sigma_M$$
$$\beta_I = (.35)(.65) / 0.20$$
$$\beta_I = 1.14$$

(iv) The market has a correlation of 1 with itself.

(v) The beta of the market is 1.

B-262 SOLUTIONS

(vi) The risk-free asset has zero standard deviation.

(vii) The risk-free asset has zero correlation with the market portfolio.

(viii) The beta of the risk-free asset is 0.

b. Using the CAPM to find the expected return of the stock, we find:

Firm A:
$E(R_A) = R_f + \beta_A[E(R_M) - R_f]$
$E(R_A) = 0.05 + 0.9(0.15 - 0.05)$
$E(R_A) = .1400$ or 14.00%

According to the CAPM, the expected return on Firm A's stock should be 14 percent. However, the expected return on Firm A's stock given in the table is only 13 percent. Therefore, Firm A's stock is overpriced, and you should sell it.

Firm B:
$E(R_B) = R_f + \beta_B[E(R_M) - R_f]$
$E(R_B) = 0.05 + 1.1(0.15 - 0.05)$
$E(R_B) = .1600$ or 16.00%

According to the CAPM, the expected return on Firm B's stock should be 16 percent. The expected return on Firm B's stock given in the table is also 16 percent. Therefore, Firm B's stock is correctly priced.

Firm C:
$E(R_C) = R_f + \beta_C[E(R_M) - R_f]$
$E(R_C) = 0.05 + 1.14(0.15 - 0.05)$
$E(R_C) = .1638$ or 16.38%

According to the CAPM, the expected return on Firm C's stock should be 16.38 percent. However, the expected return on Firm C's stock given in the table is 20 percent. Therefore, Firm C's stock is underpriced, and you should buy it.

31. Because a well-diversified portfolio has no unsystematic risk, this portfolio should lie on the Capital Market Line (CML). The slope of the CML equals:

$Slope_{CML} = [E(R_M) - R_f] / \sigma_M$
$Slope_{CML} = (0.12 - 0.05) / 0.10$
$Slope_{CML} = 0.70$

a. The expected return on the portfolio equals:

$E(R_P) = R_f + Slope_{CML}(\sigma_P)$
$E(R_P) = .05 + .70(.07)$
$E(R_P) = .0990$ or 9.90%

b.   The expected return on the portfolio equals:

$E(R_P) = R_f + Slope_{CML}(\sigma_P)$
$.20 = .05 + .70(\sigma_P)$
$\sigma_P = .2143$ or 21.43%

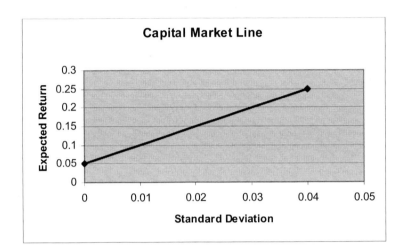

Capital Market Line

32.   First, we can calculate the standard deviation of the market portfolio using the Capital Market Line (CML). We know that the risk-free rate asset has a return of 5 percent and a standard deviation of zero and the portfolio has an expected return of 14 percent and a standard deviation of 18 percent. These two points must lie on the Capital Market Line. The slope of the Capital Market Line equals:

$Slope_{CML} = Rise / Run$
$Slope_{CML} = $ Increase in expected return / Increase in standard deviation
$Slope_{CML} = (.12 - .05) / (.18 - 0)$
$Slope_{CML} = .39$

According to the Capital Market Line:

$E(R_I) = R_f + Slope_{CML}(\sigma_I)$

Since we know the expected return on the market portfolio, the risk-free rate, and the slope of the Capital Market Line, we can solve for the standard deviation of the market portfolio which is:

$E(R_M) = R_f + Slope_{CML}(\sigma_M)$
$.12 = .05 + (.39)(\sigma_M)$
$\sigma_M = (.12 - .05) / .39$
$\sigma_M = .1800$ or 18.00%

B-264 SOLUTIONS

Next, we can use the standard deviation of the market portfolio to solve for the beta of a security using the beta equation. Doing so, we find the beta of the security is:

$\beta_I = (\rho_{I,M})(\sigma_I) / \sigma_M$
$\beta_I = (.45)(.40) / .1800$
$\beta_I = 1.00$

Now we can use the beta of the security in the CAPM to find its expected return, which is:

$E(R_I) = R_f + \beta_I[E(R_M) - R_f]$
$E(R_I) = 0.05 + 1.00(.14 - 0.05)$
$E(R_I) = .1400$ or 14.00%

33. First, we need to find the standard deviation of the market and the portfolio, which are:

$\sigma_M = (.0498)^{1/2}$
$\sigma_M = .2232$ or 22.32%

$\sigma_Z = (.1783)^{1/2}$
$\sigma_Z = .4223$ or 42.23%

Now we can use the equation for beta to find the beta of the portfolio, which is:

$\beta_Z = (\rho_{Z,M})(\sigma_Z) / \sigma_M$
$\beta_Z = (.45)(.4223) / .2232$
$\beta_Z = .85$

Now, we can use the CAPM to find the expected return of the portfolio, which is:

$E(R_Z) = R_f + \beta_Z[E(R_M) - R_f]$
$E(R_Z) = .063 + .85(.148 - .063)$
$E(R_Z) = .1354$ or 13.54%

34. The amount of systematic risk is measured by the β of an asset. Since we know the market risk premium and the risk-free rate, if we know the expected return of the asset we can use the CAPM to solve for the β of the asset. The expected return of Stock I is:

$E(R_I) = .15(.09) + .70(.42) + .15(.26) = .3465$ or 34.65%

Using the CAPM to find the β of Stock I, we find:

$.3465 = .04 + .10\beta_I$
$\beta_I = 3.07$

454

Ross–Westerfield–Jaffe:
Corporate Finance, Eighth
Edition

III. Risk

Answers for Chapter 10

© The McGraw–Hill
Companies, 2008

The total risk of the asset is measured by its standard deviation, so we need to calculate the standard deviation of Stock I. Beginning with the calculation of the stock's variance, we find:

$$\sigma_I^2 = .15(.09 - .3465)^2 + .70(.42 - .3465)^2 + .15(.26 - .3465)^2$$
$$\sigma_I^2 = .01477$$

$$\sigma_I = (.01477)^{1/2} = .1215 \text{ or } 12.15\%$$

Using the same procedure for Stock II, we find the expected return to be:

$$E(R_{II}) = .15(-.30) + .70(.12) + .15(.44) = .1050$$

Using the CAPM to find the β of Stock II, we find:

$$.1050 = .04 + .10\beta_{II}$$
$$\beta_{II} = 0.65$$

And the standard deviation of Stock II is:

$$\sigma_{II}^2 = .15(-.30 - .105)^2 + .70(.12 - .105)^2 + .15(.44 - .105)^2$$
$$\sigma_{II}^2 = .04160$$

$$\sigma_{II} = (.04160)^{1/2} = .2039 \text{ or } 20.39\%$$

Although Stock II has more total risk than I, it has much less systematic risk, since its beta is much smaller than I's. Thus, I has more systematic risk, and II has more unsystematic and more total risk. Since unsystematic risk can be diversified away, I is actually the "riskier" stock despite the lack of volatility in its returns. Stock I will have a higher risk premium and a greater expected return.

35. Here we have the expected return and beta for two assets. We can express the returns of the two assets using CAPM. Now we have two equations and two unknowns. Going back to Algebra, we can solve the two equations. We will solve the equation for Pete Corp. to find the risk-free rate, and solve the equation for Repete Co. to find the expected return of the market. We next substitute the expected return of the market into the equation for Pete Corp., and then solve for the risk-free rate. Now that we have the risk-free rate, we can substitute this into either original CAPM expression and solve for expected return of the market. Doing so, we get:

$$E(R_{\text{Pete Corp.}}) = .23 = R_f + 1.3(R_M - R_f);$$
$$.23 = R_f + 1.3R_M - 1.3R_f = 1.3R_M - .3R_f;$$
$$R_f = (1.3R_M - .23)/.3$$

$$E(R_{\text{Repete Co.}}) = .13 = R_f + .6(R_M - R_f)$$
$$.13 = R_f + .6(R_M - R_f) = R_f + .6R_M - .6R_f$$
$$R_M = (.13 - .4R_f)/.6$$
$$R_M = .217 - .667R_f$$

$$R_f = [1.3(.217 - .667R_f) - .23]/.3$$
$$1.167R_f = .0521$$
$$R_f = .0443 \text{ or } 4.43\%$$

$$.23 = .0443 + 1.3(R_M - .0443)$$
$$R_M = .1871 \text{ or } 18.71\%$$

$$.13 = .0443 + .6(R_M - .0443)$$
$$R_M = .1871 \text{ or } 18.71\%$$

B-266 SOLUTIONS

36. *a.* The expected return of an asset is the sum of the probability of each return occurring times the probability of that return occurring. To calculate the standard deviation, we first need to calculate the variance. To find the variance, we find the squared deviations from the expected return. We then multiply each possible squared deviation by its probability, and then add all of these up. The result is the variance. So, the expected return and standard deviation of each stock are:

Asset 1:
$$E(R_1) = .10(.25) + .40(.20) + .40(.15) + .10(.10) = .1750 \text{ or } 17.50\%$$

$$\sigma_1^2 = .10(.25 - .1750)^2 + .40(.20 - .1750)^2 + .40(.15 - .1750)^2 + .10(.10 - .1750)^2 = .00163$$

$$\sigma_1 = (.00163)^{1/2} = .0403 \text{ or } 4.03\%$$

Asset 2:
$$E(R_2) = .10(.25) + .40(.15) + .40(.20) + .10(.10) = .1750 \text{ or } 17.50\%$$

$$\sigma_2^2 = .10(.25 - .1750)^2 + .40(.15 - .1750)^2 + .40(.20 - .1750)^2 + .10(.10 - .1750)^2 = .00163$$

$$\sigma_2 = (.00163)^{1/2} = .0403 \text{ or } 4.03\%$$

Asset 3:
$$E(R_3) = .10(.10) + .40(.15) + .40(.20) + .10(.25) = .1750 \text{ or } 17.50\%$$

$$\sigma_3^2 = .10(.10 - .1750)^2 + .40(.15 - .1750)^2 + .40(.20 - .1750)^2 + .10(.25 - .1750)^2 = .00163$$

$$\sigma_3 = (.00163)^{1/2} = .0403 \text{ or } 4.03\%$$

b. To find the covariance, we multiply each possible state times the product of each assets' deviation from the mean in that state. The sum of these products is the covariance. The correlation is the covariance divided by the product of the two standard deviations. So, the covariance and correlation between each possible set of assets are:

Asset 1 and Asset 2:
$$\text{Cov}(1,2) = .10(.25 - .1750)(.25 - .1750) + .40(.20 - .1750)(.15 - .1750)$$
$$+ .40(.15 - .1750)(.20 - .1750) + .10(.10 - .1750)(.10 - .1750)$$
$$\text{Cov}(1,2) = .000625$$

$$\rho_{1,2} = \text{Cov}(1,2) / \sigma_1 \sigma_2$$
$$\rho_{1,2} = .000625 / (.0403)(.0403)$$
$$\rho_{1,2} = .3846$$

456

Ross–Westerfield–Jaffe:
Corporate Finance, Eighth
Edition

III. Risk

Answers for Chapter 10

© The McGraw–Hill
Companies, 2008

Asset 1 and Asset 3:
$\text{Cov}(1,3) = .10(.25 - .1750)(.10 - .1750) + .40(.20 - .1750)(.15 - .1750)$
$\qquad\qquad + .40(.15 - .1750)(.20 - .1750) + .10(.10 - .1750)(.25 - .1750)$
$\text{Cov}(1,3) = -.001625$

$\rho_{1,3} = \text{Cov}(1,3) / \sigma_1 \sigma_3$
$\rho_{1,3} = -.001625 / (.0403)(.0403)$
$\rho_{1,3} = -1$

Asset 2 and Asset 3:
$\text{Cov}(2,3) = .10(.25 - .1750)(.10 - .1750) + .40(.15 - .1750)(.15 - .1750)$
$\qquad\qquad + .40(.20 - .1750)(.20 - .1750) + .10(.10 - .1750)(.25 - .1750)$
$\text{Cov}(2,3) = -.000625$

$\rho_{2,3} = \text{Cov}(2,3) / \sigma_2 \sigma_3$
$\rho_{2,3} = -.000625 / (.0403)(.0403)$
$\rho_{2,3} = -.3846$

c. The expected return of the portfolio is the sum of the weight of each asset times the expected return of each asset, so, for a portfolio of Asset 1 and Asset 2:

$E(R_P) = w_1 E(R_1) + w_2 E(R_2)$
$E(R_P) = .50(.1750) + .50(.1750)$
$E(R_P) = .1750$ or 17.50%

The variance of a portfolio of two assets can be expressed as:

$\sigma_P^2 = w_1^2 \sigma_1^2 + w_2^2 \sigma_2^2 + 2w_1 w_2 \sigma_1 \sigma_2 \rho_{1,2}$
$\sigma_P^2 = .50^2(.0403^2) + .50^2(.0403^2) + 2(.50)(.50)(.0403)(.0403)(.3846)$
$\sigma_P^2 = .001125$

And the standard deviation of the portfolio is:

$\sigma_P = (.001125)^{1/2}$
$\sigma_P = .0335$ or 3.35%

d. The expected return of the portfolio is the sum of the weight of each asset times the expected return of each asset, so, for a portfolio of Asset 1 and Asset 3:

$E(R_P) = w_1 E(R_1) + w_3 E(R_3)$
$E(R_P) = .50(.1750) + .50(.1750)$
$E(R_P) = .1750$ or 17.50%

B-268 SOLUTIONS

The variance of a portfolio of two assets can be expressed as:

$$\sigma_P^2 = w_1^2 \sigma_1^2 + w_3^2 \sigma_3^2 + 2w_1 w_3 \sigma_1 \sigma_3 \rho_{1,3}$$
$$\sigma_P^2 = .50^2(.0403^2) + .50^2(.0403^2) + 2(.50)(.50)(.0403)(.0403)(-1)$$
$$\sigma_P^2 = .000000$$

Since the variance is zero, the standard deviation is also zero.

e. The expected return of the portfolio is the sum of the weight of each asset times the expected return of each asset, so, for a portfolio of Asset 1 and Asset 3:

$$E(R_P) = w_2 E(R_2) + w_3 E(R_3)$$
$$E(R_P) = .50(.1750) + .50(.1750)$$
$$E(R_P) = .1750 \text{ or } 17.50\%$$

The variance of a portfolio of two assets can be expressed as:

$$\sigma_P^2 = w_2^2 \sigma_2^2 + w_3^2 \sigma_3^2 + 2w_2 w_3 \sigma_2 \sigma_3 \rho_{1,3}$$
$$\sigma_P^2 = .50^2(.0403^2) + .50^2(.0403^2) + 2(.50)(.50)(.0403)(.0403)(-.3846)$$
$$\sigma_P^2 = .000500$$

And the standard deviation of the portfolio is:

$$\sigma_P = (.000500)^{1/2}$$
$$\sigma_P = .0224 \text{ or } 2.24\%$$

f. As long as the correlation between the returns on two securities is below 1, there is a benefit to diversification. A portfolio with negatively correlated stocks can achieve greater risk reduction than a portfolio with positively correlated stocks, holding the expected return on each stock constant. Applying proper weights on perfectly negatively correlated stocks can reduce portfolio variance to 0.

37. a. The expected return of an asset is the sum of the probability of each return occurring times the probability of that return occurring. So, the expected return of each stock is:

$$E(R_A) = .25(-.10) + .50(.10) + .25(.20) = .0750 \text{ or } 7.50\%$$

$$E(R_B) = .25(-.30) + .50(.05) + .25(.40) = .0500 \text{ or } 5.00\%$$

b. We can use the expected returns we calculated to find the slope of the Security Market Line. We know that the beta of Stock A is .25 greater than the beta of Stock B. Therefore, as beta increases by .25, the expected return on a security increases by .025 (= .075 – .5). The slope of

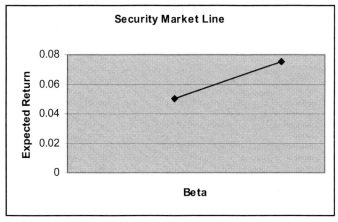

the security market line (SML) equals:

$Slope_{SML}$ = Rise / Run
$Slope_{SML}$ = Increase in expected return / Increase in beta
$Slope_{SML}$ = (.075 – .05) / .25
$Slope_{SML}$ = .1000 or 10%

Since the market's beta is 1 and the risk-free rate has a beta of zero, the slope of the Security Market Line equals the expected market risk premium. So, the expected market risk premium must be 10 percent.

38. *a.* A typical, risk-averse investor seeks high returns and low risks. For a risk-averse investor holding a well-diversified portfolio, beta is the appropriate measure of the risk of an individual security. To assess the two stocks, we need to find the expected return and beta of each of the two securities.

Stock A:
Since Stock A pays no dividends, the return on Stock A is simply: $(P_1 – P_0) / P_0$. So, the return for each state of the economy is:

$R_{Recession}$ = ($40 – 50) / $50 = –.20 or 20%
R_{Normal} = ($55 – 50) / $50 = .10 or 10%
$R_{Expanding}$ = ($60 – 50) / $50 = .20 or 20%

The expected return of an asset is the sum of the probability of each return occurring times the probability of that return occurring. So, the expected return the stock is:

$E(R_A)$ = .10(–.20) + .80(.10) + .10(.20) = .0800 or 8.00%

And the variance of the stock is:

$\sigma_A^2 = .10(-0.20 – 0.08)^2 + .80(.10 – .08)^2 + .10(.20 – .08)^2$
$\sigma_A^2 = 0.0096$

Ross–Westerfield–Jaffe:
Corporate Finance, Eighth
Edition

III. Risk

Answers for Chapter 10

© The McGraw–Hill
Companies, 2008

459

B-270 SOLUTIONS

Which means the standard deviation is:

$\sigma_A = (0.0096)^{1/2}$
$\sigma_A = .098$ or 9.8%

Now we can calculate the stock's beta, which is:

$\beta_A = (\rho_{A,M})(\sigma_A) / \sigma_M$
$\beta_A = (.80)(.098) / .10$
$\beta_A = .784$

For Stock B, we can directly calculate the beta from the information provided. So, the beta for Stock B is:

Stock B:

$\beta_B = (\rho_{B,M})(\sigma_B) / \sigma_M$
$\beta_B = (.20)(.12) / .10$
$\beta_B = .240$

The expected return on Stock B is higher than the expected return on Stock A. The risk of Stock B, as measured by its beta, is lower than the risk of Stock A. Thus, a typical risk-averse investor holding a well-diversified portfolio will prefer Stock B. Note, this situation implies that at least one of the stocks is mispriced since the higher risk (beta) stock has a lower return than the lower risk (beta) stock.

b.   The expected return of the portfolio is the sum of the weight of each asset times the expected return of each asset, so:

$E(R_P) = w_A E(R_A) + w_B E(R_B)$
$E(R_P) = .70(.08) + .30(.09)$
$E(R_P) = .083$ or 8.30%

To find the standard deviation of the portfolio, we first need to calculate the variance. The variance of the portfolio is:

$\sigma_P^2 = w_A^2 \sigma_A^2 + w_B^2 \sigma_B^2 + 2w_A w_B \sigma_A \sigma_B \rho_{A,B}$
$\sigma_P^2 = (.70)^2(.098)^2 + (.30)^2(.12)^2 + 2(.70)(.30)(.098)(.12)(.60)$
$\sigma_P^2 = .00896$

And the standard deviation of the portfolio is:

$\sigma_P = (0.00896)^{1/2}$
$\sigma_P = .0947$ or 9.47%

c. The beta of a portfolio is the weighted average of the betas of its individual securities. So the beta of the portfolio is:

$\beta_P = .70(.784) + .30(0.24)$
$\beta_P = .621$

39. *a.* The variance of a portfolio of two assets equals:

$$\sigma_P^2 = w_A^2 \sigma_A^2 + w_B^2 \sigma_B^2 + 2w_A w_B \sigma_A \sigma_B \text{Cov}(A,B)$$

Since the weights of the assets must sum to one, we can write the variance of the portfolio as:

$$\sigma_P^2 = w_A^2 \sigma_A^2 + (1 - w_A)\sigma_B^2 + 2w_A(1 - w_A)\sigma_A \sigma_B \text{Cov}(A,B)$$

To find the minimum for any function, we find the derivative and set the derivative equal to zero. Finding the derivative of the variance function, setting the derivative equal to zero, and solving for the weight of Asset A, we find:

$$w_A = [\sigma_B^2 - \text{Cov}(A,B)] / [\sigma_A^2 + \sigma_B^2 - 2\text{Cov}(A,B)]$$

Using this expression, we find the weight of Asset A must be:

$w_A = (.20^2 - .001) / [.10^2 + .20^2 - 2(.001)]$
$w_A = .8125$

This implies the weight of Stock B is:

$w_B = 1 - w_A$
$w_B = 1 - .8125$
$w_B = .1875$

b. Using the weights calculated in part *a*, determine the expected return of the portfolio, we find:

$E(R_P) = w_A E(R_A) + w_B E(R_B)$
$E(R_P) = .8125(.05) + .1875(0.10)$
$E(R_P) = 0.0594$

c. Using the derivative from part *a*, with the new covariance, the weight of each stock in the minimum variance portfolio is:

$w_A = [\sigma_B^2 + \text{Cov}(A,B)] / [\sigma_A^2 + \sigma_B^2 - 2\text{Cov}(A,B)]$
$w_A = (.10^2 + -.02) / [.10^2 + .20^2 - 2(-.02)]$
$w_A = .6667$

This implies the weight of Stock B is:

$w_B = 1 - w_A$
$w_B = 1 - .6667$
$w_B = .3333$

Ross–Westerfield–Jaffe:
Corporate Finance, Eighth
Edition

III. Risk

Answers for Chapter 10

© The McGraw–Hill
Companies, 2008

461

B-272 SOLUTIONS

d.   The variance of the portfolio with the weights on part *c* is:

$$\sigma_P^2 = w_A^2 \sigma_A^2 + w_B^2 \sigma_B^2 + 2w_A w_B \sigma_A \sigma_B \text{Cov}(A,B)$$
$$\sigma_P^2 = (.6667)^2(.10)^2 + (.3333)^2(.20)^2 + 2(.6667)(.3333)(.10)(.20)(-.02)$$
$$\sigma_P^2 = .0000$$

Because the stocks have a perfect negative correlation (–1), we can find a portfolio of the two stocks with a zero variance.

CHAPTER 12

Risk, Cost of Capital, and Capital Budgeting

In late 2005, Swiss Re, one of the world's leading reinsurers, published a report discussing how insurance companies create value for shareholders. One of the key components addressed in the report was the cost of capital. According to Swiss Re, the cost of capital for the U.S. non-life insurance industry during the 1980s was about 15 percent. By 2005, the cost of capital for the industry had dropped to 7 to 8 percent. But the cost of capital is important in more than just the insurance industry. One of the major reasons given for the possible sale of General Motors Acceptance Corporation (GMAC) by General Motors was that the lowering of GM's debt rating had increased the cost of capital for GMAC.

In this chapter, we learn how to compute a firm's cost of capital and find out what it means to the firm and its investors. We will also learn when to use the firm's cost of capital—and perhaps more important, when not to use it.

12.1 The Cost of Equity Capital

Whenever a firm has extra cash, it can take one of two actions. It can pay out the cash immediately as a dividend. Alternatively, the firm can invest extra cash in a project, paying out the future cash flows of the project as dividends. Which procedure would the stockholders prefer? If a stockholder can reinvest the dividend in a financial asset (a stock or bond) with the same risk as that of the project, the stockholders would desire the alternative with the highest expected return. In other words, the project should be undertaken only if its expected return is greater than that of a financial asset of comparable risk. This is illustrated in Figure 12.1. This discussion implies a very simple capital budgeting rule:

The discount rate of a project should be the expected return on a financial asset of comparable risk.

From the firm's perspective, the expected return is the cost of equity capital. Under the CAPM, the expected return on the stock can be written as:

$$R_S = R_F + \beta \times (R_M - R_F) \tag{12.1}$$

where R_F is the risk-free rate and $R_M - R_F$ is the difference between the expected return on the market portfolio and the riskless rate. This difference is often called the expected *excess* market return or market risk premium. Note we have dropped the bar denoting expectations from our expression to simplify the notation, but remember that we are always thinking about expected returns with the CAPM.

Figure 12.1

Choices of a Firm with Extra Cash

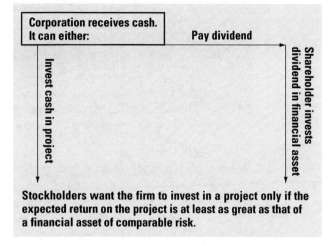

We now have the tools to estimate a firm's cost of equity capital. To do this, we need to know three things:

- The risk-free rate, R_F.
- The market risk premium, $R_M - R_F$.
- The company beta, β.

EXAMPLE 12.1

Cost of Equity Suppose the stock of the Quatram Company, a publisher of college textbooks, has a beta (β) of 1.3. The firm is 100 percent equity financed; that is, it has no debt. Quatram is considering a number of capital budgeting projects that will double its size. Because these new projects are similar to the firm's existing ones, the average beta on the new projects is assumed to be equal to Quatram's existing beta. The risk-free rate is 5 percent. What is the appropriate discount rate for these new projects, assuming a market risk premium of 8.4 percent?

We estimate the cost of equity, R_S, for Quatram as:

$$R_S = 5\% + (8.4\% \times 1.3)$$
$$= 5\% + 10.92\%$$
$$= 15.92\%$$

Two key assumptions were made in this example: (1) The beta risk of the new projects is the same as the risk of the firm, and (2) the firm is all equity financed. Given these assumptions, it follows that the cash flows of the new projects should be discounted at the 15.92 percent rate.

EXAMPLE 12.2

Project Evaluation and Beta Suppose Alpha Air Freight is an all-equity firm with a beta of 1.21. Further suppose the market risk premium is 9.5 percent, and the risk-free rate is 5 percent. We can determine the expected return on the common stock of Alpha Air Freight by using the SML of Equation 12.1. We find that the expected return is:

$$5\% + (1.21 \times 9.5\%) = 16.495\%$$

Because this is the return that shareholders can expect in the financial markets on a stock with a β of 1.21, it is the return they expect on Alpha Air Freight's stock.

(continued)

Further suppose Alpha is evaluating the following non–mutually exclusive projects:

Project	Project's Beta (β)	Project's Expected Cash Flows Next Year	Project's Internal Rate of Return	Project's NPV When Cash Flows Are Discounted At 16.495%	Accept or Reject
A	1.21	$140	40%	$20.2	Accept
B	1.21	120	20	3.0	Accept
C	1.21	110	10	−5.6	Reject

Each project initially costs $100. All projects are assumed to have the same risk as the firm as a whole. Because the cost of equity capital is 16.495 percent, projects in an all-equity firm are discounted at this rate. Projects A and B have positive NPVs, and C has a negative NPV. Thus, only A and B will be accepted. This is illustrated in Figure 12.2.

Figure 12.2   Using the Security Market Line to Estimate the Risk-Adjusted Discount Rate for Risky Projects

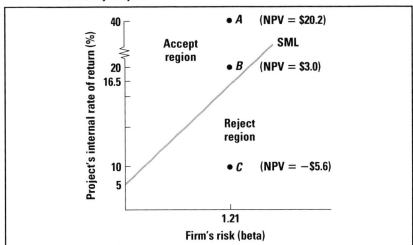

The diagonal line represents the relationship between the cost of equity capital and the firm's beta. An all-equity firm should accept a project whose internal rate of return is greater than the cost of equity capital, and should reject a project whose internal rate of return is less than the cost of equity capital. (This graph assumes that all projects are as risky as the firm.)

12.2 Estimation of Beta

In the previous section, we assumed that the beta of the company was known. Of course, beta must be estimated in the real world. We pointed out earlier that the beta of a security is the standardized covariance of a security's return with the return on the market portfolio. As we have seen, the formula for security i is

$$\text{Beta of security } i = \frac{\text{Cov}(R_i, R_M)}{\text{Var}(R_M)} = \frac{\sigma_{i,M}}{\sigma_M^2}$$

In words, the beta is the covariance of a security with the market, divided by the variance of the market. Because we calculated both covariance and variance in earlier chapters, calculating beta involves no new material.

Measuring Company Betas

The basic method of measuring company betas is to estimate:

$$\frac{\text{Cov}(R_i, R_M)}{\text{Var}(R_M)}$$

using $t = 1, 2, \ldots, T$ observations

Problems

1. Betas may vary over time.
2. The sample size may be inadequate.
3. Betas are influenced by changing financial leverage and business risk.

Solutions

1. Problems 1 and 2 can be moderated by more sophisticated statistical techniques.
2. Problem 3 can be lessened by adjusting for changes in business and financial risk.
3. Look at average beta estimates of several comparable firms in the industry.

Real-World Betas

It is instructive to see how betas are determined for actual real-world companies. Figure 12.3 plots monthly returns for four large firms against monthly returns on the Standard & Poor's (S&P) 500 index. Using a standard regression technique, we fit a straight line through data points. The result is called the "characteristic" line for the security. The slope of the characteristic line is beta. Though we have not shown it in the table, we can also determine the intercept (commonly called alpha) of the characteristic line by regression.

We use five years of monthly data for each plot. Although this choice is arbitrary, it is in line with calculations performed in the real world. Practitioners know that the accuracy of the beta coefficient is suspect when too few observations are used. Conversely, because firms may change their industry over time, observations from the distant past are out of date.

We stated in a previous chapter that the average beta across all stocks in an index is 1. Of course, this need not be true for a subset of the index. For example, of the four securities in our figure, two have betas above 1 and two have betas below 1. Because beta is a measure of the risk of a single security for someone holding a large, diversified portfolio, our results indicate that Philip Morris has relatively low risk and Amazon.com has relatively high risk. A more detailed discussion of the determinants of beta is presented in Section 12.3.

Stability of Beta

We have stated that the beta of a firm is likely to change if the firm changes its industry. It is also interesting to ask the reverse question: Does the beta of a firm stay the same if its industry stays the same?

Take the case of General Electric, a large, diversified firm that for the most part has stayed in the same industries for many decades. Figure 12.4 plots the returns on General Electric and the returns on the S&P 500 for four successive five-year periods. As can be seen from the figure, GE's beta drops slightly from the first to the third subperiod, decreasing

Figure 12.3   Plots of Five Years of Monthly Returns (2000–2004) on Four Individual Securities against Five Years of Monthly Returns on the Standard & Poor's (S&P) 500 Index

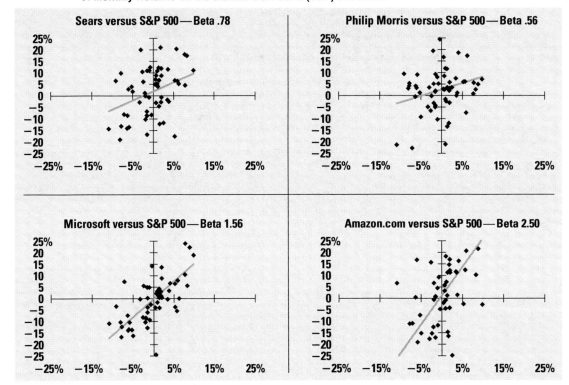

a bit more in the last subperiod. However, this movement in beta is probably nothing more than random variation.[1] Thus, for practical purposes, GE's beta has been approximately constant over the two decades covered in the figure. Although GE is just one company, most analysts argue that betas are generally stable for firms remaining in the same industry.

However, this is not to say that, as long as a firm stays in the same industry, its beta will *never* change. Changes in product line, changes in technology, or changes in the market may affect a firm's beta. For example, the deregulation of the airline industry has increased the betas of airline firms. Furthermore, as we will show in a later section, an increase in the leverage of a firm (i.e., the amount of debt in its capital structure) will increase the firm's beta.

Using an Industry Beta

Our approach to estimating the beta of a company from its own past data may seem commonsensical to you. However, it is frequently argued that people can better estimate a firm's beta by involving the whole industry. Consider Table 12.1, which shows the betas of some prominent firms in the software industry. The average beta across all of the firms in the table is 1.45. Imagine a financial executive at Symantec trying to estimate the firm's beta. Because beta estimation is subject to large random variation in this volatile industry, the executive may be uncomfortable with the estimate of 1.57. However, the error in beta

---

[1]More precisely, we can say that the beta coefficients over the four periods are not statistically different from each other.

Figure 12.4   **Plots of Monthly Returns on General Electric against the Standard & Poor's 500 Index for Four Consecutive Five-Year Periods**

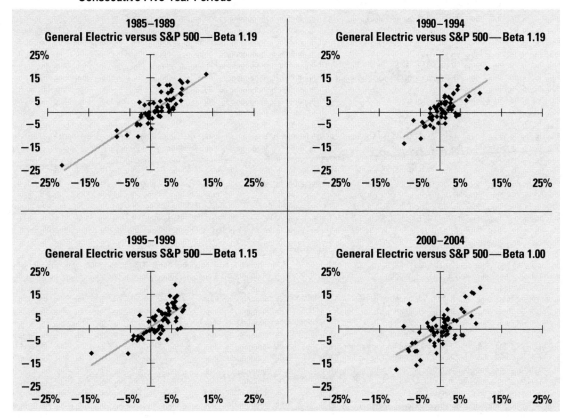

Table 12.1

Betas for Firms in the Computer Software Industry

Company	Beta
Microsoft	1.23
First Data Corp.	.97
Automatic Data Processing	1.07
Electronic Data Systems	1.60
Oracle Corp.	1.40
Computer Sciences	1.76
Computer Associates	2.60
Fiserv Inc.	1.14
Accenture Ltd.	1.71
Symantec Corp.	1.57
Paychex, Inc.	.94
Equally weighted portfolio	1.45

estimation on a single stock is much higher than the error for a portfolio of securities. Thus the executive of Symantec may use the industry beta of 1.45 as the estimate of its own firm's beta. (As it turns out, the choice is unimportant here because the industry beta is so close to that of the firm.)

In contrast, consider Computer Associates. Assuming a risk-free rate of 3.7 percent and a risk premium of 8.7 percent, Computer Associates might estimate its cost of equity capital as:

$$3.7\% + 2.60 \times 8.7\% = 26.32\%$$

However, if Computer Associates believed the industry beta contained less estimation error, it could estimate its cost of equity capital as:

$$3.7\% + 1.45 \times 8.7\% = 16.32\%$$

The difference is substantial here, presenting a difficult choice for a financial executive at Computer Associates.

While there is no formula for selecting the right beta, there is a very simple guideline. If you believe that the operations of a firm are similar to the operations of the rest of the industry, you should use the industry beta simply to reduce estimation error.[2] However, if an executive believes that the operations of the firm are fundamentally different from those in the rest of the industry, the firm's beta should be used.

When we discussed financial statement analysis in Chapter 3, we noted that a problem frequently comes up in practice—namely, what is the industry? For example, Value Line's *Investment Survey* categorizes Accenture, Ltd., as a computer software company, whereas online financial providers such as investor.reuters.com categorize the same company in the business services industry.

12.3 Determinants of Beta

The regression analysis approach in the previous section doesn't tell us where beta comes from. Of course, the beta of a stock does not come out of thin air. Rather, it is determined by the characteristics of the firm. We consider three factors: the cyclical nature of revenues, operating leverage, and financial leverage.

Cyclicality of Revenues

The revenues of some firms are quite cyclical. That is, these firms do well in the expansion phase of the business cycle and do poorly in the contraction phase. Empirical evidence suggests high-tech firms, retailers, and automotive firms fluctuate with the business cycle. Firms in industries such as utilities, railroads, food, and airlines are less dependent on the cycle. Because beta is the standardized covariability of a stock's return with the market's return, it is not surprising that highly cyclical stocks have high betas.

It is worthwhile to point out that cyclicality is not the same as variability. For example, a moviemaking firm has highly variable revenues because hits and flops are not easily predicted. However, because the revenues of a studio are more dependent on the quality of its releases than the phase of the business cycle, motion picture companies are not particularly cyclical. In other words, stocks with high standard deviations need not have high betas, a point we have stressed before.

Operating Leverage

We distinguished fixed costs from variable costs earlier in the text. At that time, we mentioned that fixed costs do not change as quantity changes. Conversely, variable costs increase

---

[2] As we will see later, an adjustment must be made when the debt level in the industry is different from that of the firm. However, we ignore this adjustment here because firms in the software industry generally have little debt.

as the quantity of output rises. This difference between variable and fixed costs allows us to define operating leverage.

EXAMPLE 12.3

Operating Leverage Illustrated   Consider a firm that can choose either technology A or technology B when making a particular product. The relevant differences between the two technologies are displayed here:

Technology A	Technology B
Fixed cost: $1,000/year	Fixed cost: $2,000/year
Variable cost: $8/unit	Variable cost: $6/unit
Price: $10/unit	Price: $10/unit
Contribution margin: $2 (= $10 − $8)	Contribution margin: $4 (= $10 − $6)

Technology A has lower fixed costs and higher variable costs than does technology B. Perhaps technology A involves less mechanization than does B. Or the equipment in A may be leased, whereas the equipment in B must be purchased. Alternatively, perhaps technology A involves few employees but many subcontractors, whereas B involves only highly skilled employees who must be retained in bad times. Because technology B has both lower variable costs and higher fixed costs, we say that it has higher **operating leverage**.[3]

Figure 12.5 graphs the costs under both technologies. The slope of each total cost line represents variable costs under a single technology. The slope of A's line is steeper, indicating greater variable costs.

Figure 12.5   Illustration of Two Different Technologies

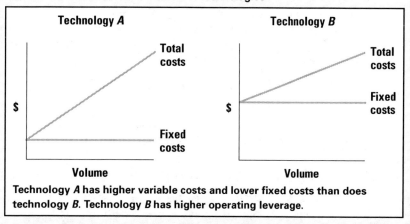

Technology A has higher variable costs and lower fixed costs than does technology B. Technology B has higher operating leverage.

Because the two technologies are used to produce the same products, a unit price of $10 applies for both cases. We mentioned in an earlier chapter that contribution margin is the difference

(continued)

---

[3]The standard definition of operating leverage is

$$\frac{\text{Change in EBIT}}{\text{EBIT}} \times \frac{\text{Sales}}{\text{Change in sales}}$$

where EBIT is the earnings before interest and taxes. That is, operating leverage measures the percentage change in EBIT for a given percentage change in sales or revenues. It can be shown that operating leverage increases as fixed costs rise and as variable costs fall.

350   **Part III**   Risk

Figure 12.6   Illustration of the Effect of a Change in Volume on the Change in Earnings before Interest and Taxes (EBIT)

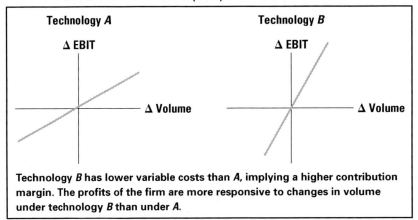

Technology *B* has lower variable costs than *A*, implying a higher contribution margin. The profits of the firm are more responsive to changes in volume under technology *B* than under *A*.

between price and variable cost. It measures the incremental profit from one additional unit. Because the contribution margin in *B* is greater, its technology is riskier. An unexpected sale increases profit by $2 under *A* but increases profit by $4 under *B*. Similarly, an unexpected sale cancellation reduces profit by $2 under *A* but reduces profit by $4 under *B*. This is illustrated in Figure 12.6. This figure shows the change in earnings before interest and taxes for a given change in volume. The slope of the right graph is greater, indicating that technology *B* is riskier.

The cyclicality of a firm's revenues is a determinant of the firm's beta. Operating leverage magnifies the effect of cyclicality on beta. As mentioned earlier, business risk is generally defined as the risk of the firm without financial leverage. Business risk depends both on the responsiveness of the firm's revenues to the business cycle and on the firm's operating leverage.

Although the preceding discussion concerns firms, it applies to projects as well. If we cannot estimate a project's beta in another way, we can examine the project's revenues and operating leverage. Projects whose revenues appear strongly cyclical and whose operating leverage appears high are likely to have high betas. Conversely, weak cyclicality and low operating leverage imply low betas. As mentioned earlier, this approach is unfortunately qualitative in nature. Because start-up projects have little data, quantitative estimates of beta generally are not feasible.

Financial Leverage and Beta

As suggested by their names, operating leverage and financial leverage are analogous concepts. Operating leverage refers to the firm's fixed costs of *production*. Financial leverage is the extent to which a firm relies on debt, and a levered firm is a firm with some debt in its capital structure. Because a *levered* firm must make interest payments regardless of the firm's sales, financial leverage refers to the firm's fixed costs of *finance*.

Consider our discussion in Chapter 10 concerning the beta of Jelco, Inc. In that example, we estimated beta from the returns on Jelco *stock*. Furthermore, the betas in Figures 12.3 and 12.4 from real-world firms were estimated from returns on stock. Thus, in each case, we estimated the firm's stock or **equity beta**. The beta of the assets of a levered firm is different from the beta of its equity. As the name suggests, the **asset beta** is the beta of the assets of the firm. The asset beta could also be thought of as the beta of the common stock had the firm been financed only with equity.

Imagine an individual who owns all the firm's debt and all its equity. In other words, this individual owns the entire firm. What is the beta of her portfolio of the firm's debt and equity?

As with any portfolio, the beta of this portfolio is a weighted average of the betas of the individual items in the portfolio. Let B stand for the market value of the firm's debt and S stand for the market value of the firm's equity. We have:

$$\beta_{Asset} = \frac{S}{B+S} \times \beta_{Equity} + \frac{B}{B+S} \times \beta_{Debt} \qquad (12.2)$$

where β_{Equity} is the beta of the stock of the *levered* firm. Notice that the beta of debt, β_{Debt}, is multiplied by $B/(B + S)$, the percentage of debt in the capital structure. Similarly, the beta of equity is multiplied by the percentage of equity in the capital structure. Because the portfolio contains both the debt of the firm and the equity of the firm, the beta of the portfolio is the *asset beta*. As we just said, the asset beta can also be viewed as the beta of the common stock had the firm been all equity.

The beta of debt is very low in practice. If we make the common assumption that the beta of debt is zero, we have:

$$\beta_{Asset} = \frac{S}{B+S} \times \beta_{Equity} \qquad (12.3)$$

Because $S/(B + S)$ must be below 1 for a levered firm, it follows that $\beta_{Asset} < \beta_{Equity}$. Rearranging this equation, we have:

$$\beta_{Equity} = \beta_{Asset}\left(1 + \frac{B}{S}\right)$$

The equity beta will always be greater than the asset beta with financial leverage (assuming the asset beta is positive).[4]

EXAMPLE 12.4

Asset versus Equity Betas   Consider a tree growing company, Rapid Cedars, Inc., which is currently all equity and has a beta of .8. The firm has decided to move to a capital structure of one part debt to two parts equity. Because the firm is staying in the same industry, its asset beta should remain at .8. However, assuming a zero beta for its debt, its equity beta would become:

$$\beta_{Equity} = \beta_{Asset}\left(1 + \frac{B}{S}\right)$$
$$1.2 = .8\left(1 + \frac{1}{2}\right)$$

If the firm had one part debt to one part equity in its capital structure, its equity beta would be:

$$1.6 = .8(1 + 1)$$

However, as long as it stayed in the same industry, its asset beta would remain at .8. The effect of leverage, then, is to increase the equity beta.

---

[4]It can be shown that the relationship between a firm's asset beta and its equity beta with corporate taxes is

$$\beta_{Equity} = \beta_{Asset}\left[1 + (1 - t_C)\frac{B}{S}\right]$$

In this expression, t_C is the corporate tax rate. Tax effects are considered in more detail in a later chapter.

12.4 Extensions of the Basic Model

The Firm versus the Project: Vive la Différence

We now assume that the risk of a project differs from that of the firm, while going back to the all-equity assumption. We began the chapter by pointing out that each project should be paired with a financial asset of comparable risk. If a project's beta differs from that of the firm, the project should be discounted at the rate commensurate with its own beta. This is a very important point because firms frequently speak of a *corporate discount rate*. (*Hurdle rate, cutoff rate, benchmark,* and *cost of capital* are frequently used synonymously.) Unless all projects in the corporation are of the same risk, choosing the same discount rate for all projects is incorrect.

Project Risk   D. D. Ronnelley Co., a publishing firm, may accept a project in computer software. Noting that computer software companies have high betas, the publishing firm views the software venture as more risky than the rest of its business. It should discount the project at a rate commensurate with the risk of software companies. For example, it might use the average beta of a portfolio of publicly traded software firms. Instead, if all projects in D. D. Ronnelley Co. were discounted at the same rate, a bias would result. The firm would accept too many high-risk projects (software ventures) and reject too many low-risk projects (books and magazines). This point is illustrated in Figure 12.7.

EXAMPLE 12.5

Figure 12.7   Relationship between the Firm's Cost of Capital and the Security Market Line

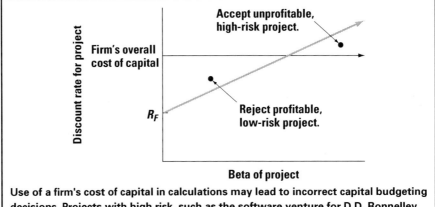

Use of a firm's cost of capital in calculations may lead to incorrect capital budgeting decisions. Projects with high risk, such as the software venture for D.D. Ronnelley Co., should be discounted at a high rate. By using the firm's cost of capital, the firm is likely to accept too many high-risk projects.
   Projects with low risk should be discounted at a low rate. By using the firm's cost of capital, the firm is likely to reject too many low-risk projects.

The D. D. Ronnelley example assumes that the proposed project has identical risk to that of the software industry, allowing the industry beta to be used. However, the beta of a new project may be greater than the beta of existing firms in the same industry because the very newness of the project likely increases its responsiveness to economywide movements. For example, a start-up computer venture may fail in a recession, whereas IBM or Hewlett-Packard will still be around. Conversely, in an economywide expansion, the venture may grow much faster than the old-line computer firms.

Fortunately, a slight adjustment is all that is needed here. The new venture should be assigned a somewhat higher beta than that of the industry to reflect added risk. The adjustment is necessarily ad hoc, so no formula can be given. Our experience indicates that this approach is widespread in practice today.

However, a problem does arise for the rare project constituting its own industry. For example, consider the firms providing consumer shopping by television. Today, we can obtain a reasonable estimate for the beta of this industry because a few of the firms have publicly traded stock. However, when the ventures began in the 1980s, any beta estimate was suspect. At that time, no one knew whether shopping by TV belonged in the television industry, the retail industry, or in an entirely new industry.

What beta should be used in the rare case when an industrywide beta is not appropriate? One approach, which considers the determinants of the project's beta, was treated earlier in this chapter. Unfortunately, that approach is only qualitative in nature.

The Cost of Capital with Debt

Section 12.1 showed how to choose the discount rate when a project is all equity financed. In this section we discuss an adjustment when the project is financed with both debt and equity.

Suppose a firm uses both debt and equity to finance its investments. If the firm pays R_B for its debt financing and R_S for its equity, what is the overall or average cost of its capital? The cost of equity is R_S, as discussed in earlier sections. The cost of debt is the firm's borrowing rate, R_B, which we can often observe by looking at the yield to maturity on the firm's debt. If a firm uses both debt and equity, the cost of capital is a weighted average of each. This works out to be:

$$\frac{S}{S + B} \times R_S + \frac{B}{S + B} \times R_B$$

The weights in the formula are, respectively, the proportion of total value represented by the equity:

$$\left(\frac{S}{S + B} \right)$$

and the proportion of total value represented by debt:

$$\left(\frac{B}{S + B} \right)$$

This is only natural. If the firm had issued no debt and was therefore an all-equity firm, its average cost of capital would equal its cost of equity, R_S. At the other extreme, if the firm had issued so much debt that its equity was valueless, it would be an all-debt firm, and its average cost of capital would be its cost of debt, R_B.

Of course, interest is tax deductible at the corporate level, a point to be treated in more detail in a later chapter. The aftertax cost of debt is:

$$\text{Cost of debt (after corporate tax)} = R_B \times (1 - t_C)$$

where t_C is the corporation's tax rate.

Assembling these results, we get the average cost of capital (after tax) for the firm:

$$\text{Average cost of capital} = \left(\frac{S}{S + B} \right) \times R_S + \left(\frac{B}{S + B} \right) \times R_B \times (1 - t_C) \quad \textbf{(12.4)}$$

Because the average cost of capital is a weighting of its cost of equity and its cost of debt, it is usually referred to as the **weighted average cost of capital**, R_{WACC}, and from now on we will use this term.

EXAMPLE 12.6

WACC   Consider a firm whose debt has a market value of $40 million and whose stock has a market value of $60 million (3 million outstanding shares of stock, each selling for $20 per share). The firm pays a 15 percent rate of interest on its new debt and has a beta of 1.41. The corporate tax rate is 34 percent. (Assume that the SML holds, that the risk premium on the market is 9.5 percent [slightly higher than the historical equity risk premium], and that the current Treasury bill rate is 11 percent [much higher than the current Treasury bill rate].) What is this firm's R_{WACC}?

To compute the R_{WACC} using Equation 12.4, we must know (1) the aftertax cost of debt, $R_B \times (1 - t_C)$, (2) the cost of equity, R_S, and (3) the proportions of debt and equity used by the firm. These three values are computed next:

1. The pretax cost of debt is 15 percent, implying an aftertax cost of 9.9 percent [$15\% \times (1 - .34)$].

2. We compute the cost of equity capital by using the SML:

$$R_S = R_F + \beta \times [R_M - R_F]$$
$$= 11\% + 1.41 \times 9.5\%$$
$$= 24.40\%$$

3. We compute the proportions of debt and equity from the market values of debt and equity. Because the market value of the firm is $100 million (=$40 million + $60 million), the proportions of debt and equity are 40 and 60 percent, respectively.

The cost of equity, R_S, is 24.40 percent, and the aftertax cost of debt, $R_B \times (1 - t_C)$, is 9.9 percent. B is $40 million and S is $60 million. Therefore:

$$R_{WACC} = \frac{S}{B + S} \times R_S + \frac{B}{B + S} \times R_B \times (1 - t_C)$$
$$= \left(\frac{40}{100} \times 9.9\%\right) + \left(\frac{60}{100} \times 24.40\%\right) = 18.60\%$$

This procedure is presented in table form next:

(1) Financing Components	(2) Market Values	(3) Weight	(4) Cost of Capital (after Corporate Tax)	(5) Weighted Cost of Capital
Debt	$ 40,000,000	.40	$15\% \times (1 - .34) =$ 9.9%	3.96%
Equity	60,000,000	.60	$11\% + 1.41 \times 9.5\% =$ 24.40	14.64
	$100,000,000	1.00		18.60%

The weights we used in the previous example were market value weights. Market value weights are more appropriate than book value weights because the market values of the securities are closer to the actual dollars that would be received from their sale. Actually, it is usually useful to think in terms of "target" market weights. These are the market weights expected to prevail over the life of the firm or project.

EXAMPLE 12.7

Project Evaluation and the WACC   Suppose a firm has both a current and a target debt–equity ratio of .6, a cost of debt of 15.15 percent, and a cost of equity of 20 percent. The corporate tax rate is 34 percent.

Our first step calls for transforming the debt–equity (B/S) ratio to a debt–value ratio. A B/S ratio of .6 implies 6 parts debt for 10 parts equity. Because value is equal to the sum of the debt plus the equity, the debt–value ratio is $6/(6 + 10) = .375$. Similarly, the equity–value ratio is $10/(6 + 10) = .625$. The R_{WACC} will then be:

(continued)

$$R_{WACC} = \left(\frac{S}{S+B}\right) \times R_S + \left(\frac{B}{S+B}\right) \times R_B \times (1 - t_C)$$

$$= .625 \times 20\% + .375 \times 15.15\% \times .66 = 16.25\%$$

Suppose the firm is considering taking on a warehouse renovation costing $50 million that is expected to yield cost savings of $12 million a year for six years. Using the NPV equation and discounting the six years of expected cash flows from the renovation at the R_{WACC}, we have:

$$NPV = -\$50 + \frac{\$12}{(1 + R_{WACC})} + \cdots + \frac{\$12}{(1 + R_{WACC})^6}$$

$$= -\$50 + \$12 \times A^6_{.1625}$$

$$= -\$50 + (12 \times 3.66)$$

$$= -\$6.07$$

Should the firm take on the warehouse renovation? The project has a negative NPV using the firm's R_{WACC}. This means that the financial markets offer superior projects in the same risk class (namely, the firm's risk class). The answer is clear: The firm should reject the project.

12.5   Estimating Eastman Chemical's Cost of Capital

In our previous sections, we calculated the cost of capital in examples. We will now calculate the cost of capital for a real company, Eastman Chemical Co., a leading international chemical company and maker of plastics such as that used in soft drink containers. It was created in 1993 when its former parent company, Eastman Kodak, split off the division as a separate company.

Eastman's Cost of Equity

Our first stop for Eastman is investor.reuters.com (ticker: "EMN"). As of February 2006, the relevant pieces of what we found are shown in the next box:

Key Ratios & Statistics

Price & Volume		Valuation Ratios	
Recent Price $	48.45	Price/Earnings (TTM)	7.11
52 Week High $	61.80	Price/Sales (TTM)	0.56
52 Week Low $	44.10	Price/Book (MRQ)	2.45
Avg Daily Vol (Mil)	0.77	Price/Cash Flow (TTM)	4.60
Beta	0.80	**Per Share Data**	
Share Related Items		Earnings (TTM) $	6.82
Mkt. Cap. (Mil) $	3,947.71	Sales (TTM) $	86.32
Shares Out (Mil)	81.48	Book Value (MRQ) $	19.82
Float (Mil)	80.80	Cash Flow (TTM) $	10.53
Dividend Information		Cash (MRQ) $	NM
Yield %	3.63	**Mgmt Effectiveness**	
Annual Dividend	1.76	Return on Equity (TTM)	38.42
Payout Ratio (TTM) %	19.09	Return on Assets (TTM)	9.67
Financial Strength		Return on Investment (TTM)	11.87
Quick Ratio (MRQ)	0.00	**Profitability**	
Current Ratio (MRQ)	1.80	Gross Margin (TTM) %	19.89
LT Debt/Equity (MRQ)	1.00	Operating Margin (TTM) %	10.07
Total Debt/Equity (MRQ)	1.01	Profit Margin (TTM) %	7.89

Mil = Millions   MRQ = Most Recent Quarter   TTM = Trailing Twelve Months
Asterisks (*) Indicates numbers are derived from Earnings Announcements

Table 12.2

Betas for Companies in the Diversified Chemical Industry

Company	Beta
3M Company	.65
Air Products & Chemical	.70
Monsanto Co.	1.05
PPG Industries	.86
Eastman Chemical	.80
Albemarle Corp.	1.00
Cabot Corp.	.84
Pall Corp.	1.23
Cytec Industries	.77
Millipore Corp.	1.10
Cambrex Corp.	.61
Equally weighted portfolio	.87

According to this screen, Eastman has 81.48 million shares of stock outstanding. The book value per share is $19.82, but the stock sells for $48.45. Total equity is therefore about $1.615 billion on a book value basis, but it is closer to $3.948 billion on a market value basis.

To estimate Eastman's cost of equity, we will assume a market risk premium of 8.7 percent, similar to what we calculated in Chapter 9. Eastman's beta on Reuters is .80. Table 12.2 shows the betas for other U.S.-based diversified chemical companies. As you can see, the industry average beta is .87, which is slightly higher than Eastman's beta. According to the bond section of finance.yahoo.com, T-bills were paying about 4.26 percent. Using Eastman's own beta in the CAPM to estimate the cost of equity, we find:

$$R_S = .0426 + .80(.087) = .1122 \text{ or } 11.22\%$$

If we use the industry beta, we would find that the estimate for the cost of equity capital is:

$$R_S = .0426 + .87(.087) = .1183 \text{ or } 11.83\%$$

Notice that the estimates for the cost of equity are close because Eastman's beta is relatively close to the industry beta. The decision of which cost of equity estimate to use is up to the financial executive, based on knowledge and experience of both the company and the industry. In this case, we will choose to use the cost of equity using Eastman's estimated beta.

Eastman's Cost of Debt

Eastman has six long-term bond issues that account for essentially all of its long-term debt. To calculate the cost of debt, we will have to combine these six issues and compute a weighted average. We will go to www.nasdbondinfo.com to find quotes on the bonds. We should note here that finding the yield to maturity for all of a company's outstanding bond issues on a single day is unusual. In our previous discussion of bonds, we found that the bond market is not as liquid as the stock market, and on many days individual bond issues may not trade. To find the book value of the bonds we go to www.sec.gov and find the 10Q report (i.e., the most recent financial report) dated September 30, 2005, and filed with the SEC on November 1, 2005. The basic information is as follows:

Coupon Rate	Maturity	Book Value (Face Value, in Millions)	Price (% of Par)	Yield to Maturity
3.25%	2008	$ 72	96.092%	5.02%
7.00	2012	187	108.515	5.36
6.30	2018	143	100.835	6.20
7.25	2024	497	108.448	6.45
7.625	2024	200	113.006	6.41
7.60	2027	297	113.610	6.41

To calculate the weighted average cost of debt, we take the percentage of the total debt represented by each issue and multiply by the yield on the issue. We then add to get the overall weighted average debt cost. We use both book values and market values here for comparison. The results of the calculations are as follows:

Coupon Rate	Book Value (Face Value, in Millions)	Percentage of Total	Market Value (in Millions)	Percentage of Total	Yield to Maturity	Book Value Weights	Market Value Weights
3.25%	$ 72	0.05	$ 69.19	0.05	5.02%	0.26%	0.23%
7.00	187	0.13	202.92	0.13	5.36	0.72	0.72
6.30	143	0.10	144.19	0.09	6.20	0.64	0.59
7.60	497	0.36	538.99	0.35	6.45	2.30	2.29
7.625	200	0.14	226.01	0.15	6.41	0.92	0.95
7.60	297	0.21	337.42	0.22	6.41	1.36	1.42
Total	$1,396	1.00	$1,518.72	1.00		6.19%	6.20%

As these calculations show, Eastman's cost of debt is 6.19 percent on a book value basis and 6.20 percent on a market value basis. Thus, for Eastman, whether market values or book values are used makes no difference. The reason is simply that the market values and book values are similar. This will often be the case and explains why companies frequently use book values for debt in WACC calculations.

Eastman's WACC

We now have the various pieces necessary to calculate Eastman's WACC. First, we need to calculate the capital structure weights. On a book value basis, Eastman's equity and debt are worth $1.615 billion and $1.396 billion, respectively. The total value is $3.011 billion, so the equity and debt percentages are $1.615 billion/$3.011 billion = .54 and $1.396 billion/$3.011 billion = .46, respectively. Assuming a tax rate of 35 percent, Eastman's WACC is:

$$R_{WACC} = .54 \times 11.22\% + .46 \times 6.20\% \times (1 - .35)$$
$$= 7.91\%$$

Thus, using book value capital structure weights, we get about 7.91 percent for Eastman's R_{WACC}.

If we use market value weights, however, the R_{WACC} will be higher. To see why, notice that on a market value basis, Eastman's equity and debt are worth $3.948 billion and $1.519 billion, respectively. The capital structure weights are therefore $3.948 billion/$5.467 billion = .72

and $1.519 billion/$5.467 billion = .28, so the equity percentage is much higher. With these weights, Eastman's R_{WACC} is:

$$R_{WACC} = .72 \times 11.22\% + .28 \times 6.20\% \times (1 - .35)$$
$$= 9.21\%$$

Thus, using market value weights, we get 9.21 percent for Eastman's R_{WACC}, which is more than a full percent higher than the 7.91 percent R_{WACC} we got using book value weights.

So how does our estimate of the R_{WACC} for Eastman compare to others? One place to find estimates for a company's R_{WACC} is www.valuepro.net. We went there and found the following information for Eastman:

Online Valuation for EMN - 2 / 3 / 2006

Intrinsic Stock Value   `245.16`   [Recalculate]   [Value Another Stock]

Excess Return Period (yrs)	10	Depreciation Rate (% of Rev)	4.89
Revenues ($mil)	6988.0	Investment Rate (% of Rev)	3.77
Growth Rate (%)	29	Working Capital (% of Rev)	11.9
Net Oper. Profit Margin (%)	3.88	Short-Term Assets ($mil)	1844.0
Tax Rate (%)	23.529	Short-Term Liab. ($mil)	889
Stock Price ($)	50.1400	Equity Risk Premium (%)	3
Shares Outstanding (mil)	81.4	Company Beta	1.1025
10-Yr Treasury Yield (%)	5	Value Debt Out. ($mil)	1436
Bond Spread Treasury (%)	1.5	Value Pref. Stock Out. ($mil)	0
Preferred Stock Yield (%)	7.5	Company WACC (%)	7.44

As you can see, ValuePro estimates the R_{WACC} for Eastman as 7.44 percent, which is lower than our estimate of 9.21 percent. The methods used by this site are not identical to ours, but they are similar in many important regards. You can visit the site to learn more if you are so inclined.

12.6   Reducing the Cost of Capital

Chapters 9–12 develop the idea that both the expected return on a stock and the cost of capital of the firm are positively related to risk. Recently, a number of academics have argued that expected return and cost of capital are negatively related to liquidity as well.[5] In addition, these scholars make the interesting point that although it is quite difficult to lower the risk of a firm, it is much easier to increase the liquidity of the firm's stock. Therefore they suggest that a firm can actually lower its cost of capital through liquidity enhancement. We develop this idea next.

What Is Liquidity?

Anyone who owns a home probably thinks of liquidity in terms of the time it takes to buy or sell the home. For example, condominiums in large metropolitan areas are generally quite liquid. Particularly in good times, a condominium may sell within days of being placed on the market. By contrast, single-family homes in suburban areas may take weeks or months to sell. Special properties such as multimillion-dollar mansions may take longer still.

The concept of liquidity is similar, but not identical, in stocks. Here, we speak of the *cost* of buying and selling instead. That is, stocks that are expensive to trade are considered less liquid than those that trade cheaply. What do we mean by the cost to trade? We generally think of three costs here: brokerage fees, the bid–ask spread, and market impact costs.

Brokerage fees are the easiest to understand because you must pay a broker to execute a trade. More difficult is the bid–ask spread. Consider the New York Stock Exchange (NYSE), where all trades on a particular stock must go through the stock's specialist, who is physically on the floor of the exchange. If you want to trade 100 shares of XYZ Co., your broker must get the *quote* from XYZ's specialist. Suppose the specialist provides a quote of 100.00–100.07. This means that you can buy from the specialist at $100.07 per share and sell to the specialist at $100 per share. Note that the specialist makes money here, because she buys from you at $100 and sells to you (or to someone else) at $100.07. The gain to the specialist is a cost to you because you are losing $0.07 per share over a round-trip transaction (over a purchase and a subsequent sale).

Finally, we have *market impact costs*. Suppose a trader wants to sell 10,000 shares instead of just 100 shares. Here, the specialist has to take on extra risk when buying. First, she has to pay out $1,000,000 (=10,000 × $100), cash that may not be easily available to her. Second, the trader may be selling this large amount because she has special information that the stock will fall imminently. The specialist bears the risk of losing a lot of money on that trade. Consequently, to compensate for these risks, the specialist may buy not at $100/share but at a lower price. Similarly, the specialist may be willing to sell a large block of stock only at a price above $100.07. The price drop associated with a large sale and the price rise associated with a large purchase are the market impact costs.

Liquidity, Expected Returns, and the Cost of Capital

The cost of trading a nonliquid stock reduces the total return that an investor receives. That is, if you buy a stock for $100 and sell it later for $105, the gain before trading costs is $5. If you must pay a dollar of commission when buying and another dollar when selling, the gain after trading costs is only $3. Both the bid–ask spread and market impact costs would reduce this gain still further.

As we will see later, trading costs vary across securities. In the last four chapters we have stressed that investors demand a high expected return as compensation when investing in high-risk (e.g., high-beta) stocks. Because the expected return to the investor is the

---

[5]For example, see Y. Amihud and H. Mendelson, "The Liquidity Route to a Lower Cost of Capital," *Journal of Applied Corporate Finance* (Winter 2000), and M. J. Brennan and C. Tamarowski, "Investor Relations, Liquidity, and Stock Prices," *Journal of Applied Corporate Finance* (Winter 2000).

Figure 12.8

Liquidity and the Cost of Capital

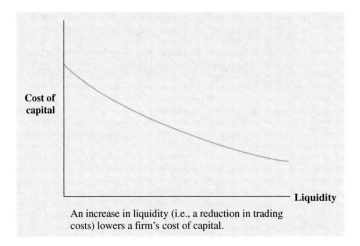

An increase in liquidity (i.e., a reduction in trading costs) lowers a firm's cost of capital.

cost of capital to the firm, the cost of capital is positively related to beta. Now we are saying the same thing for trading costs. Investors demand a high expected return when investing in stocks with high trading costs—that is, with low liquidity. This high expected return implies a high cost of capital to the firm. This idea is illustrated in Figure 12.8.

Liquidity and Adverse Selection

Liquidity varies across stocks because the factors determining liquidity vary across stocks. Although there are a number of factors, we focus on just one: *adverse selection*. As mentioned before, the specialist will lose money on a trade if the trader has information that the specialist does not have. If you have special information that the stock is worth $110 in the preceding example, you will want to buy shares at $100.07. The specialist is obligated to sell to you at this price, which is considerably below the true price of $110. Conversely, if you know that the stock is worth only $90 and you currently own 100 shares, you will be happy to sell these shares to the specialist at $100. Again, the specialist loses because he pays $100/share for a stock worth only $90. In either of these cases, we say that the specialist has been *picked off*, or has been subject to adverse selection.

The specialist must protect himself in some way here. Of course, he cannot forbid informed individuals from trading because he does not know ahead of time who these investors are. His next best alternative is to widen the bid–ask spread, thereby increasing the costs of trading to *all* traders—both informed and uninformed. That is, if the spread is widened to, say, $99.98–$100.11, each trader pays a round-trip cost of $0.13 per share.

The key here is that the spread should be positively related to the ratio of informed to uninformed traders. That is, informed traders will pick off the specialist and uninformed traders will not. Thus, informed traders in a stock raise the required return on equity, thereby increasing the cost of capital.

What the Corporation Can Do

The corporation has an incentive to lower trading costs because (given the preceding discussion) a lower cost of capital should result. Amihud and Mendelson identify two general strategies for corporations. First, they argue that firms should try to bring in more uninformed investors. Stock splits may be a useful tool here. Imagine that a company has 1 million shares outstanding with a price per share of $100. Because investors generally buy in round lots of 100 shares, these investors would need $10,000 (=$100 × 100 shares) for a purchase. A number of small investors might be "priced out" of the stock, although large investors would not be. Thus, the ratio of large investors to small investors would be high. Because large investors are generally more likely than small investors to be informed, the ratio of informed investors to uninformed investors will likely be high.

A 2:1 stock split would give two shares of stock for every one that the investor previously held. Because every investor would still hold the same proportional interest in the firm, each investor would be no better off than before. Thus, it is likely that the price per share will fall to $50 from $100. Here, an individual with 100 shares worth $10,000 (=$100 × 100 shares) finds herself still worth $10,000 (= $50 × 200 shares) after the split.

However, a round lot becomes more affordable, thereby bringing more small and uninformed investors into the firm. Consequently, the adverse selection costs are reduced, allowing the specialist to lower the bid–ask spread. In turn, it is hoped that the expected return on the stock, and the cost of equity capital, will fall as well. If this happens, the stock might actually trade at a price slightly above $50.

This idea is a new one, and empirical evidence is not yet in. Amihud and Mendelson themselves point out the possibility that this strategy might backfire because brokerage commissions are often higher on lower-priced securities. We must await confirmation of this intriguing suggestion.

Companies can also attract small investors by facilitating stock purchases through the Internet. Direct stock purchase plans and dividend reinvestment programs handled online allow small investors to buy securities cheaply. In addition, Amihud and Mendelson state, "And when these plans are administered over the Internet using Web sites like Stockpower .com, moneypaper.com, and Netstockdirect.com, the process is fast and efficient for both the company and the investor."[6]

Second, companies can disclose more information. This narrows the gap between uninformed and informed investors, thereby lowering the cost of capital. Suggestions include providing more financial data about corporate segments and more management forecasts. An interesting study by Coller and Yohn[7] concludes that the bid–ask spread is reduced after the release of these forecasts.

This section would not be complete without a discussion of security analysts. These analysts are employed by brokerage houses to follow the companies in individual industries. For example, an analyst for a particular brokerage house might follow all the firms in, say, the auto industry. This analyst distributes reports and other information to the clients of the brokerage house. Virtually all brokerage houses have analysts following the major industries. Again, through dissemination of the information, these analysts narrow the gap between the informed and the uninformed investors, thereby tending to reduce the bid–ask spread.

Although all major industries are covered, the smaller firms in these industries are often ignored, implying a higher bid–ask spread and a higher cost of capital for these firms. Analysts frequently state that they avoid following companies that release little information, pointing out that these companies are more trouble than they are worth. Thus, it behooves companies that are not followed to release as much information as possible to security analysts to attract their interest. Friendliness toward security analysts would be helpful as well. The argument here is not to get the analysts to make buy recommendations. Rather, it is simply to interest the analysts in following the company, thereby reducing the information asymmetry between informed and uninformed investors.

---

[6]Ibid., p. 19.

[7]M. Coller and T. Yohn, "Management Forecasts and Information Asymmetry: An Examination of Bid–Ask Spreads," *Journal of Accounting Research* (Fall 1997).

Summary and Conclusions

Earlier chapters about capital budgeting assumed that projects generate riskless cash flows. The appropriate discount rate in that case is the riskless interest rate. Of course, most cash flows from real-world capital budgeting projects are risky. This chapter discussed the discount rate when cash flows are risky.

1. A firm with excess cash can either pay a dividend or make a capital expenditure. Because stockholders can reinvest the dividend in risky financial assets, the expected return on a capital budgeting project should be at least as great as the expected return on a financial asset of comparable risk.

2. The expected return on any asset is dependent on its beta. Thus, we showed how to estimate the beta of a stock. The appropriate procedure employs regression analysis on historical returns.

3. We considered the case of a project whose beta risk was equal to that of the firm. If the firm is unlevered, the discount rate on the project is equal to:

$$R_F + \beta \times (R_M - R_F)$$

where R_M is the expected return on the market portfolio and R_F is the risk-free rate. In words, the discount rate on the project is equal to the CAPM's estimate of the expected return on the security.

4. If the project's beta differs from that of the firm, the discount rate should be based on the project's beta. We can generally estimate the project's beta by determining the average beta of the project's industry.

5. The beta of a company is a function of a number of factors. Perhaps the three most important are:
   - Cyclicality of revenues.
   - Operating leverage.
   - Financial leverage.

6. Sometimes we cannot use the average beta of the project's industry as an estimate of the beta of the project. For example, a new project may not fall neatly into any existing industry. In this case, we can estimate the project's beta by considering the project's cyclicality of revenues and its operating leverage. This approach is qualitative.

7. If a firm uses debt, the discount rate to use is the R_{WACC}. To calculate R_{WACC}, we must estimate the cost of equity and the cost of debt applicable to a project. If the project is similar to the firm, the cost of equity can be estimated using the SML for the firm's equity. Conceptually, a dividend growth model could be used as well, though it is likely to be far less accurate in practice.

8. Liquidity probably plays a role in determining a firm's cost of capital. A firm may be able to reduce its cost of capital by taking steps to improve liquidity.

Concept Questions

1. **Project Risk**   If you can borrow all the money you need for a project at 6 percent, doesn't it follow that 6 percent is your cost of capital for the project?

2. **WACC and Taxes**   Why do we use an aftertax figure for cost of debt but not for cost of equity?

3. **SML Cost of Equity Estimation**   If you use the stock beta and the security market line to compute the discount rate for a project, what assumptions are you implicitly making?

4. **SML Cost of Equity Estimation**   What are the advantages of using the SML approach to finding the cost of equity capital? What are the disadvantages? What are the specific pieces of information needed to use this method? Are all of these variables observable, or do they need to be estimated? What are some of the ways in which you could get these estimates?

5. **Cost of Debt Estimation**   How do you determine the appropriate cost of debt for a company? Does it make a difference if the company's debt is privately placed as opposed to being publicly traded? How would you estimate the cost of debt for a firm whose only debt issues are privately held by institutional investors?

6. **Cost of Capital**   Suppose Tom O'Bedlam, president of Bedlam Products, Inc., has hired you to determine the firm's cost of debt and cost of equity capital.

   a. The stock currently sells for $50 per share, and the dividend per share will probably be about $5. Tom argues, "It will cost us $5 per share to use the stockholders' money this year, so the cost of equity is equal to 10 percent ($5/50)." What's wrong with this conclusion?

   b. Based on the most recent financial statements, Bedlam Products' total liabilities are $8 million. Total interest expense for the coming year will be about $1 million. Tom therefore reasons, "We owe $8 million, and we will pay $1 million interest. Therefore, our cost of debt is obviously $1 million/8 million = 12.5 percent." What's wrong with this conclusion?

   c. Based on his own analysis, Tom is recommending that the company increase its use of equity financing because "debt costs 12.5 percent, but equity only costs 10 percent; thus equity is cheaper." Ignoring all the other issues, what do you think about the conclusion that the cost of equity is less than the cost of debt?

7. **Company Risk versus Project Risk**   Both Dow Chemical Company, a large natural gas user, and Superior Oil, a major natural gas producer, are thinking of investing in natural gas wells near Houston. Both are all equity financed companies. Dow and Superior are looking at identical projects. They've analyzed their respective investments, which would involve a negative cash flow now and positive expected cash flows in the future. These cash flows would be the same for both firms. No debt would be used to finance the projects. Both companies estimate that their projects would have a net present value of $1 million at an 18 percent discount rate and a −$1.1 million NPV at a 22 percent discount rate. Dow has a beta of 1.25, whereas Superior has a beta of .75. The expected risk premium on the market is 8 percent, and risk-free bonds are yielding 12 percent. Should either company proceed? Should both? Explain.

8. **Divisional Cost of Capital**   Under what circumstances would it be appropriate for a firm to use different costs of capital for its different operating divisions? If the overall firm WACC were used as the hurdle rate for all divisions, would the riskier divisions or the more conservative divisions tend to get most of the investment projects? Why? If you were to try to estimate the appropriate cost of capital for different divisions, what problems might you encounter? What are two techniques you could use to develop a rough estimate for each division's cost of capital?

9. **Leverage**   Consider a levered firm's projects that have similar risks to the firm as a whole. Is the discount rate for the projects higher or lower than the rate computed using the security market line? Why?

10. **Beta**   What factors determine the beta of a stock? Define and describe each.

Questions and Problems

BASIC
(Questions 1–13)

1. **Calculating Cost of Equity**   The Dybvig Corporation's common stock has a beta of 1.3. If the risk-free rate is 4.5 percent and the expected return on the market is 12 percent, what is Dybvig's cost of equity capital?

2. **Calculating Cost of Debt**   Advance, Inc., is trying to determine its cost of debt. The firm has a debt issue outstanding with 12 years to maturity that is quoted at 105 percent of face value. The issue makes semiannual payments and has a coupon rate of 8 percent annually. What is Advance's pretax cost of debt? If the tax rate is 35 percent, what is the aftertax cost of debt?

3. **Calculating Cost of Debt**   Shanken Corp. issued a 30-year, 10 percent semiannual bond 7 years ago. The bond currently sells for 108 percent of its face value. The company's tax rate is 35 percent.

   a. What is the pretax cost of debt?

   b. What is the aftertax cost of debt?

   c. Which is more relevant, the pretax or the aftertax cost of debt? Why?

4. **Calculating Cost of Debt**   For the firm in the previous problem, suppose the book value of the debt issue is $20 million. In addition, the company has a second debt issue on the market, a zero coupon bond with seven years left to maturity; the book value of this issue is $80 million and the bonds sell for 58 percent of par. What is the company's total book value of debt? The total market value? What is your best estimate of the aftertax cost of debt now?

www.mhhe.com/rwj

5. **Calculating WACC** Mullineaux Corporation has a target capital structure of 55 percent common stock and 45 percent debt. Its cost of equity is 16 percent, and the cost of debt is 9 percent. The relevant tax rate is 35 percent. What is Mullineaux's WACC?

6. **Taxes and WACC** Miller Manufacturing has a target debt–equity ratio of .60. Its cost of equity is 18 percent, and its cost of debt is 10 percent. If the tax rate is 35 percent, what is Miller's WACC?

7. **Finding the Capital Structure** Fama's Llamas has a weighted average cost of capital of 11.5 percent. The company's cost of equity is 16 percent, and its cost of debt is 8.5 percent. The tax rate is 35 percent. What is Fama's debt–equity ratio?

8. **Book Value versus Market Value** Filer Manufacturing has 9.5 million shares of common stock outstanding. The current share price is $53, and the book value per share is $5. Filer Manufacturing also has two bond issues outstanding. The first bond issue has a face value of $75 million and an 8 percent coupon and sells for 93 percent of par. The second issue has a face value of $60 million and a 7.5 percent coupon and sells for 96.5 percent of par. The first issue matures in 10 years, the second in 6 years.
   a. What are Filer's capital structure weights on a book value basis?
   b. What are Filer's capital structure weights on a market value basis?
   c. Which are more relevant, the book or market value weights? Why?

9. **Calculating the WACC** In the previous problem, suppose the company's stock has a beta of 1.2. The risk-free rate is 5.2 percent, and the market risk premium is 9 percent. Assume that the overall cost of debt is the weighted average implied by the two outstanding debt issues. Both bonds make semiannual payments. The tax rate is 35 percent. What is the company's WACC?

10. **WACC** Kose, Inc., has a target debt–equity ratio of .80. Its WACC is 10.5 percent, and the tax rate is 35 percent.
   a. If Kose's cost of equity is 15 percent, what is its pretax cost of debt?
   b. If instead you know that the aftertax cost of debt is 6.4 percent, what is the cost of equity?

11. **Finding the WACC** Given the following information for Huntington Power Co., find the WACC. Assume the company's tax rate is 35 percent.

   Debt: 4,000 7 percent coupon bonds outstanding, $1,000 par value, 20 years to maturity, selling for 103 percent of par; the bonds make semiannual payments.

   Common stock: 90,000 shares outstanding, selling for $57 per share; the beta is 1.10.
   Market: 8 percent market risk premium and 6 percent risk-free rate.

12. **Finding the WACC** Titan Mining Corporation has 9 million shares of common stock outstanding and 120,000 8.5 percent semiannual bonds outstanding, par value $1,000 each. The common stock currently sells for $34 per share and has a beta of 1.20, and the bonds have 15 years to maturity and sell for 93 percent of par. The market risk premium is 10 percent, T-bills are yielding 5 percent, and Titan Mining's tax rate is 35 percent.
   a. What is the firm's market value capital structure?
   b. If Titan Mining is evaluating a new investment project that has the same risk as the firm's typical project, what rate should the firm use to discount the project's cash flows?

13. **SML and WACC** An all-equity firm is considering the following projects:

Project	Beta	Expected Return
W	.60	11%
X	.90	13
Y	1.20	14
Z	1.70	16

Ross–Westerfield–Jaffe:
Corporate Finance, Eighth
Edition

III. Risk

12. Risk, Cost of Capital,
and Capital Budgeting

© The McGraw–Hill
Companies, 2008

485

The T-bill rate is 5 percent, and the expected return on the market is 12 percent.

a. Which projects have a higher expected return than the firm's 12 percent cost of capital?

b. Which projects should be accepted?

c. Which projects would be incorrectly accepted or rejected if the firm's overall cost of capital were used as a hurdle rate?

INTERMEDIATE
(Questions 14–15)

14. WACC and NPV   Och, Inc., is considering a project that will result in initial aftertax cash savings of $3.5 million at the end of the first year, and these savings will grow at a rate of 5 percent per year indefinitely. The firm has a target debt–equity ratio of .65, a cost of equity of 15 percent, and an aftertax cost of debt of 5.5 percent. The cost-saving proposal is somewhat riskier than the usual project the firm undertakes; management uses the subjective approach and applies an adjustment factor of +2 percent to the cost of capital for such risky projects. Under what circumstances should Och take on the project?

15. Preferred Stock and WACC   The Saunders Investment Bank has the following financing outstanding. What is the WACC for the company?

Debt:	50,000 bonds with an 8 percent coupon rate and a quoted price of 119.80; the bonds have 25 years to maturity. 150,000 zero coupon bonds with a quoted price of 13.85 and 30 years until maturity.
Preferred stock:	120,000 shares of 6.5 percent preferred with a current price of $112, and a par value = $100.
Common stock:	2,000,000 shares of common stock; the current price is $65, and the beta of the stock is 1.1.
Market:	The corporate tax rate is 40 percent, the market risk premium is 9 percent, and the risk-free rate is 4 percent.

CHALLENGE
(Questions 16–17)

16. WACC and NPV   Photochronograph Corporation (PC) manufactures time series photographic equipment. It is currently at its target debt–equity ratio of 1.3. It's considering building a new $45 million manufacturing facility. This new plant is expected to generate aftertax cash flows of $5.7 million in perpetuity. There are three financing options:

- A new issue of common stock. The required return on the company's equity is 17 percent.
- A new issue of 20-year bonds. If the company issues these new bonds at an annual coupon rate of 9 percent, they will sell at par.
- Increased use of accounts payable financing. Because this financing is part of the company's ongoing daily business, the company assigns it a cost that is the same as the overall firm WACC. Management has a target ratio of accounts payable to long-term debt of .20. (Assume there is no difference between the pretax and aftertax accounts payable cost.)

What is the NPV of the new plant? Assume that PC has a 35 percent tax rate.

17. Project Evaluation   This is a comprehensive project evaluation problem bringing together much of what you have learned in this and previous chapters. Suppose you have been hired as a financial consultant to Defense Electronics, Inc. (DEI), a large, publicly traded firm that is the market share leader in radar detection systems (RDSs). The company is looking at setting up a manufacturing plant overseas to produce a new line of RDSs. This will be a five-year project. The company bought some land three years ago for $7 million in anticipation of using it as a toxic dump site for waste chemicals, but it built a piping system to safely discard the chemicals instead. If the company sold the land today, it would receive $6.5 million after taxes. In five years the land can be sold for $4.5 million after taxes and reclamation costs. The company wants to build its new manufacturing plant on this land; the plant will cost $15 million to build. The following market data on DEI's securities are current:

Debt:	15,000 7 percent coupon bonds outstanding, 15 years to maturity, selling for 92 percent of par; the bonds have a $1,000 par value each and make semiannual payments.
Common stock:	300,000 shares outstanding, selling for $75 per share; the beta is 1.3.

> *Preferred stock*:   20,000 shares of 5 percent preferred stock outstanding, selling for $72 per share.
>
> *Market*:   8 percent expected market risk premium; 5 percent risk-free rate.

DEI's tax rate is 35 percent. The project requires $900,000 in initial net working capital investment to become operational.

a. Calculate the project's initial time 0 cash flow, taking into account all side effects.

b. The new RDS project is somewhat riskier than a typical project for DEI, primarily because the plant is being located overseas. Management has told you to use an adjustment factor of +2 percent to account for this increased riskiness. Calculate the appropriate discount rate to use when evaluating DEI's project.

c. The manufacturing plant has an eight-year tax life, and DEI uses straight-line depreciation. At the end of the project (i.e., the end of year 5), the plant can be scrapped for $5 million. What is the aftertax salvage value of this manufacturing plant?

d. The company will incur $400,000 in annual fixed costs. The plan is to manufacture 12,000 RDSs per year and sell them at $10,000 per machine; the variable production costs are $9,000 per RDS. What is the annual operating cash flow (OCF) from this project?

e. DEI's comptroller is primarily interested in the impact of DEI's investments on the bottom line of reported accounting statements. What will you tell her is the accounting break-even quantity of RDSs sold for this project?

f. Finally, DEI's president wants you to throw all your calculations, assumptions, and everything else into the report for the chief financial officer; all he wants to know is the RDS project's internal rate of return, IRR, and net present value, NPV. What will you report?

The Cost of Capital for Goff Computer, Inc.

Mini Case

You have recently been hired by Goff Computer, Inc. (GCI), in the finance area. GCI was founded eight years ago by Chris Goff and currently operates 74 stores in the Southeast. GCI is privately owned by Chris and his family and had sales of $97 million last year.

GCI sells primarily to in-store customers. Customers come to the store and talk with a sales representative. The sales representative assists the customer in determining the type of computer and peripherals that are necessary for the individual customer's computing needs. After the order is taken, the customer pays for the order immediately, and the computer is assembled to fill the order. Delivery of the computer averages 15 days but is guaranteed in 30 days.

GCI's growth to date has been financed from its profits. Whenever the company had sufficient capital, it would open a new store. Relatively little formal analysis has been used in the capital budgeting process. Chris has just read about capital budgeting techniques and has come to you for help. The company has never attempted to determine its cost of capital, and Chris would like you to perform the analysis. Because the company is privately owned, it is difficult to determine the cost of equity for the company. You have determined that to estimate the cost of capital for GCI, you will use Dell as a representative company. The following steps will allow you to calculate this estimate:

1. Most publicly traded corporations are required to submit 10Q (quarterly) and 10K (annual) reports to the SEC detailing their financial operations over the previous quarter or year, respectively. These corporate filings are available on the SEC Web site at www.sec.gov. Go to the SEC Web site, follow the "Search for Company Filings" link and the "Companies & Other Filers" link, enter "Dell Computer," and search for SEC filings made by Dell. Find the most recent 10Q and 10K and download the forms. Look on the balance sheet to find the book value of debt and the book value of equity. If you look further down the report, you should find a section titled either "Long-Term Debt" or "Long-Term Debt and Interest Rate Risk Management" that will list a breakdown of Dell's long-term debt.

2. To estimate the cost of equity for Dell, go to finance.yahoo.com and enter the ticker symbol "DELL." Follow the various links to find answers to the following questions: What is the most recent stock price listed for Dell? What is the market value of equity, or market capitalization? How many shares of stock does Dell have outstanding? What is the beta for Dell? Now go back to finance.yahoo.com and follow the "Bonds" link. What is the yield on 3-month Treasury bills? Using the historical market risk premium, what is the cost of equity for Dell using the CAPM?

3. Go to investor.reuters.com and find the list of competitors in the industry. Find the beta for each of these competitors, and then calculate the industry average beta. Using the industry average beta, what is the cost of equity? Does it matter if you use the beta for Dell or the beta for the industry in this case?

4. You now need to calculate the cost of debt for Dell. Go to www.nasdbondinfo.com, enter Dell as the company, and find the yield to maturity for each of Dell's bonds. What is the weighted average cost of debt for Dell using the book value weights and the market value weights? Does it make a difference in this case if you use book value weights or market value weights?

5. You now have all the necessary information to calculate the weighted average cost of capital for Dell. Calculate the weighted average cost of capital for Dell using book value weights and market value weights assuming Dell has a 35 percent marginal tax rate. Which cost of capital number is more relevant?

6. You used Dell as a representative company to estimate the cost of capital for GCI. What are some of the potential problems with this approach in this situation? What improvements might you suggest?

Appendix 12A Economic Value Added and the Measurement of Financial Performance

To access the appendix for this chapter, please visit www.mhhe.com/rwj.

CHAPTER 12
RISK, COST OF CAPITAL, AND CAPITAL BUDGETING

Answers to Concepts Review and Critical Thinking Questions

1. No. The cost of capital depends on the risk of the project, not the source of the money.

2. Interest expense is tax-deductible. There is no difference between pretax and aftertax equity costs.

3. You are assuming that the new project's risk is the same as the risk of the firm as a whole, and that the firm is financed entirely with equity.

4. Two primary advantages of the SML approach are that the model explicitly incorporates the relevant risk of the stock and the method is more widely applicable than is the DCF model, since the SML doesn't make any assumptions about the firm's dividends. The primary disadvantages of the SML method are (1) three parameters (the risk-free rate, the expected return on the market, and beta) must be estimated, and (2) the method essentially uses historical information to estimate these parameters. The risk-free rate is usually estimated to be the yield on very short maturity T-bills and is, hence, observable; the market risk premium is usually estimated from historical risk premiums and, hence, is not observable. The stock beta, which is unobservable, is usually estimated either by determining some average historical beta from the firm and the market's return data, or by using beta estimates provided by analysts and investment firms.

5. The appropriate aftertax cost of debt to the company is the interest rate it would have to pay if it were to issue new debt today. Hence, if the YTM on outstanding bonds of the company is observed, the company has an accurate estimate of its cost of debt. If the debt is privately-placed, the firm could still estimate its cost of debt by (1) looking at the cost of debt for similar firms in similar risk classes, (2) looking at the average debt cost for firms with the same credit rating (assuming the firm's private debt is rated), or (3) consulting analysts and investment bankers. Even if the debt is publicly traded, an additional complication arises when the firm has more than one issue outstanding; these issues rarely have the same yield because no two issues are ever completely homogeneous.

6. *a.*   This only considers the dividend yield component of the required return on equity.
    b.   This is the current yield only, not the promised yield to maturity. In addition, it is based on the book value of the liability, and it ignores taxes.
    c.   Equity is inherently riskier than debt (except, perhaps, in the unusual case where a firm's assets have a negative beta). For this reason, the cost of equity exceeds the cost of debt. If taxes are considered in this case, it can be seen that at reasonable tax rates, the cost of equity does exceed the cost of debt.

7. $R_{Sup} = .12 + .75(.08) = .1800$ or 18.00%
    Both should proceed. The appropriate discount rate does not depend on which company is investing; it depends on the risk of the project. Since Superior is in the business, it is closer to a pure play.

Therefore, its cost of capital should be used. With an 18% cost of capital, the project has an NPV of $1 million regardless of who takes it.

8. If the different operating divisions were in much different risk classes, then separate cost of capital figures should be used for the different divisions; the use of a single, overall cost of capital would be inappropriate. If the single hurdle rate were used, riskier divisions would tend to receive more funds for investment projects, since their return would exceed the hurdle rate despite the fact that they may actually plot below the SML and, hence, be unprofitable projects on a risk-adjusted basis. The typical problem encountered in estimating the cost of capital for a division is that it rarely has its own securities traded on the market, so it is difficult to observe the market's valuation of the risk of the division. Two typical ways around this are to use a pure play proxy for the division, or to use subjective adjustments of the overall firm hurdle rate based on the perceived risk of the division.

9. The discount rate for the projects should be lower that the rate implied by the security market line. The security market line is used to calculate the cost of equity. The appropriate discount rate for projects is the firm's weighted average cost of capital. Since the firm's cost of debt is generally less that the firm's cost of equity, the rate implied by the security market line will be too high.

10. Beta measures the responsiveness of a security's returns to movements in the market. Beta is determined by the cyclicality of a firm's revenues. This cyclicality is magnified by the firm's operating and financial leverage. The following three factors will impact the firm's beta. (1) Revenues. The cyclicality of a firm's sales is an important factor in determining beta. In general, stock prices will rise when the economy expands and will fall when the economy contracts. As we said above, beta measures the responsiveness of a security's returns to movements in the market. Therefore, firms whose revenues are more responsive to movements in the economy will generally have higher betas than firms with less-cyclical revenues. (2) Operating leverage. Operating leverage is the percentage change in earnings before interest and taxes (EBIT) for a percentage change in sales. A firm with high operating leverage will have greater fluctuations in EBIT for a change in sales than a firm with low operating leverage. In this way, operating leverage magnifies the cyclicality of a firm's revenues, leading to a higher beta. (3) Financial leverage. Financial leverage arises from the use of debt in the firm's capital structure. A levered firm must make fixed interest payments regardless of its revenues. The effect of financial leverage on beta is analogous to the effect of operating leverage on beta. Fixed interest payments cause the percentage change in net income to be greater than the percentage change in EBIT, magnifying the cyclicality of a firm's revenues. Thus, returns on highly-levered stocks should be more responsive to movements in the market than the returns on stocks with little or no debt in their capital structure.

Solutions to Questions and Problems

NOTE: All end-of-chapter problems were solved using a spreadsheet. Many problems require multiple steps. Due to space and readability constraints, when these intermediate steps are included in this solutions manual, rounding may appear to have occurred. However, the final answer for each problem is found without rounding during any step in the problem.

Basic

1. With the information given, we can find the cost of equity using the CAPM. The cost of equity is:

$R_E = .045 + 1.30 (.12 - .045) = .1425$ or 14.25%

B-288 SOLUTIONS

2. The pretax cost of debt is the YTM of the company's bonds, so:

$P_0 = \$1,050 = \$40(PVIFA_{R\%,24}) + \$1,000(PVIF_{R\%,24})$
$R = 3.683\%$
$YTM = 2 \times 3.683\% = 7.37\%$

And the aftertax cost of debt is:

$R_D = .0737(1 - .35) = .0479$ or 4.79%

3. *a.* The pretax cost of debt is the YTM of the company's bonds, so:

$P_0 = \$1,080 = \$50(PVIFA_{R\%,46}) + \$1,000(PVIF_{R\%,46})$
$R = 4.58\%$
$YTM = 2 \times 4.58\% = 9.16\%$

b. The aftertax cost of debt is:

$R_D = .0916(1 - .35) = .0595$ or 5.95%

c. The aftertax rate is more relevant because that is the actual cost to the company.

4. The book value of debt is the total par value of all outstanding debt, so:

$BV_D = \$20M + 80M = \$100M$

To find the market value of debt, we find the price of the bonds and multiply by the number of bonds. Alternatively, we can multiply the price quote of the bond times the par value of the bonds. Doing so, we find:

$MV_D = 1.08(\$20M) + .58(\$80M) = \$68M$

The YTM of the zero coupon bonds is:

$P_Z = \$580 = \$1,000(PVIF_{R\%,7})$
$R = 8.09\%$

So, the aftertax cost of the zero coupon bonds is:

$R_Z = .0809(1 - .35) = .0526$ or 5.26%

The aftertax cost of debt for the company is the weighted average of the aftertax cost of debt for all outstanding bond issues. We need to use the market value weights of the bonds. The total aftertax cost of debt for the company is:

$R_D = .0595(\$21.6/\$68) + .0526(\$46.4/\$68) = .0548$ or 5.48%

5. Using the equation to calculate the WACC, we find:

$WACC = .55(.16) + .45(.09)(1 - .35) = .1143$ or 11.43%

6. Here we need to use the debt-equity ratio to calculate the WACC. Doing so, we find:

WACC = .18(1/1.60) + .10(.60/1.60)(1 – .35) = .1369 or 13.69%

7. Here we have the WACC and need to find the debt-equity ratio of the company. Setting up the WACC equation, we find:

WACC = .1150 = .16(E/V) + .085(D/V)(1 – .35)

Rearranging the equation, we find:

.115(V/E) = .16 + .085(.65)(D/E)

Now we must realize that the V/E is just the equity multiplier, which is equal to:

V/E = 1 + D/E

.115(D/E + 1) = .16 + .05525(D/E)

Now we can solve for D/E as:

.05975(D/E) = .0450
D/E = .7531

8. *a.* The book value of equity is the book value per share times the number of shares, and the book value of debt is the face value of the company's debt, so:

BV$_E$ = 9.5M($5) = $47.5M

BV$_D$ = $75M + 60M = $135M

So, the total value of the company is:

V = $47.5M + 135M = $182.5M

And the book value weights of equity and debt are:

E/V = $47.5/$182.5 = .2603

D/V = 1 – E/V = .7397

B-290 SOLUTIONS

b. The market value of equity is the share price times the number of shares, so:

$MV_E = 9.5M(\$53) = \$503.5M$

Using the relationship that the total market value of debt is the price quote times the par value of the bond, we find the market value of debt is:

$MV_D = .93(\$75M) + .965(\$60M) = \$127.65M$

This makes the total market value of the company:

$V = \$503.5M + 127.65M = \$631.15M$

And the market value weights of equity and debt are:

$E/V = \$503.5/\$631.15 = .7978$

$D/V = 1 - E/V = .2022$

c. The market value weights are more relevant.

9. First, we will find the cost of equity for the company. The information provided allows us to solve for the cost of equity using the CAPM, so:

$R_E = .052 + 1.2(.09) = .1600$ or 16.00%

Next, we need to find the YTM on both bond issues. Doing so, we find:

$P_1 = \$930 = \$40(PVIFA_{R\%,20}) + \$1,000(PVIF_{R\%,20})$
$R = 4.54\%$
$YTM = 4.54\% \times 2 = 9.08\%$

$P_2 = \$965 = \$37.5(PVIFA_{R\%,12}) + \$1,000(PVIF_{R\%,12})$
$R = 4.13\%$
$YTM = 4.13\% \times 2 = 8.25\%$

To find the weighted average aftertax cost of debt, we need the weight of each bond as a percentage of the total debt. We find:

$w_{D1} = .93(\$75M)/\$127.65M = .546$

$w_{D2} = .965(\$60M)/\$127.65M = .454$

Now we can multiply the weighted average cost of debt times one minus the tax rate to find the weighted average aftertax cost of debt. This gives us:

$R_D = (1 - .35)[(.546)(.0908) + (.454)(.0825)] = .0566$ or 5.66%

Using these costs and the weight of debt we calculated earlier, the WACC is:

$WACC = .7978(.1600) + .2022(.0566) = .1391$ or 13.91%

10. *a.* Using the equation to calculate WACC, we find:

$$WACC = .105 = (1/1.8)(.15) + (.8/1.8)(1 - .35)R_D$$
$$R_D = .0750 \text{ or } 7.50\%$$

b. Using the equation to calculate WACC, we find:

$$WACC = .105 = (1/1.8)R_E + (.8/1.8)(.064)$$
$$R_E = .1378 \text{ or } 13.78\%$$

11. We will begin by finding the market value of each type of financing. We find:

$$MV_D = 4,000(\$1,000)(1.03) = \$4,120,000$$
$$MV_E = 90,000(\$57) = \$5,130,000$$

And the total market value of the firm is:

$$V = \$4,120,000 + 5,130,000 = \$9,250,000$$

Now, we can find the cost of equity using the CAPM. The cost of equity is:

$$R_E = .06 + 1.10(.08) = .1480 \text{ or } 14.80\%$$

The cost of debt is the YTM of the bonds, so:

$$P_0 = \$1,030 = \$35(PVIFA_{R\%,40}) + \$1,000(PVIF_{R\%,40})$$
$$R = 3.36\%$$
$$YTM = 3.36\% \times 2 = 6.72\%$$

And the aftertax cost of debt is:

$$R_D = (1 - .35)(.0672) = .0437 \text{ or } 4.37\%$$

Now we have all of the components to calculate the WACC. The WACC is:

$$WACC = .0437(4.12/9.25) + .1480(5.13/9.25) = .1015 \text{ or } 10.15\%$$

Notice that we didn't include the $(1 - t_C)$ term in the WACC equation. We simply used the aftertax cost of debt in the equation, so the term is not needed here.

12. *a.* We will begin by finding the market value of each type of financing. We find:

$$MV_D = 120,000(\$1,000)(0.93) = \$111,600,000$$
$$MV_E = 9,000,000(\$34) = \$306,000,000$$

And the total market value of the firm is:

$$V = \$111,600,000 + 306,000,000 = \$417,600,000$$

B-292 SOLUTIONS

So, the market value weights of the company's financing is:

D/V = $111,600,000/$417,600,000 = .2672
E/V = $306,000,000/$417,600,000 = .7328

b. For projects equally as risky as the firm itself, the WACC should be used as the discount rate.

First we can find the cost of equity using the CAPM. The cost of equity is:

R_E = .05 + 1.20(.10) = .1700 or 17.00%

The cost of debt is the YTM of the bonds, so:

P_0 = $930 = $42.5(PVIFA$_{R\%,30}$) + $1,000(PVIF$_{R\%,30}$)
R = 4.69%
YTM = 4.69% × 2 = 9.38%

And the aftertax cost of debt is:

R_D = (1 − .35)(.0938) = .0610 or 6.10%

Now we can calculate the WACC as:

WACC = .1700(.7328) + .0610 (.2672) = .1409 or 14.09%

13. *a.* Projects X, Y and Z.

b. Using the CAPM to consider the projects, we need to calculate the expected return of each project given its level of risk. This expected return should then be compared to the expected return of the project. If the return calculated using the CAPM is higher than the project expected return, we should accept the project; if not, we reject the project. After considering risk via the CAPM:

E[W] = .05 + .60(.12 − .05)   = .0920 < .11, so accept W
E[X] = .05 + .90(.12 − .05)   = .1130 < .13, so accept X
E[Y] = .05 + 1.20(.12 − .05) = .1340 < .14, so accept Y
E[Z] = .05 + 1.70(.12 − .05) = .1690 > .16, so reject Z

c. Project W would be incorrectly rejected; Project Z would be incorrectly accepted.

Intermediate

14. Using the debt-equity ratio to calculate the WACC, we find:

WACC = (.65/1.65)(.055) + (1/1.65)(.15) = .1126 or 11.26%

Since the project is riskier than the company, we need to adjust the project discount rate for the additional risk. Using the subjective risk factor given, we find:

Project discount rate = 11.26% + 2.00% = 13.26%

We would accept the project if the NPV is positive. The NPV is the PV of the cash outflows plus the PV of the cash inflows. Since we have the costs, we just need to find the PV of inflows. The cash inflows are a growing perpetuity. If you remember, the equation for the PV of a growing perpetuity is the same as the dividend growth equation, so:

PV of future CF = $3,500,000/(.1326 − .05) = $42,385,321

The project should only be undertaken if its cost is less than $42,385,321 since costs less than this amount will result in a positive NPV.

15. We will begin by finding the market value of each type of financing. We will use D1 to represent the coupon bond, and D2 to represent the zero coupon bond. So, the market value of the firm's financing is:

MV_{D1} = 50,000($1,000)(1.1980) = $59,900,000
MV_{D2} = 150,000($1,000)(.1385) = $20,775,000
MV_P = 120,000($112) = $13,440,000
MV_E = 2,000,000($65) = $130,000,000

And the total market value of the firm is:

V = $59,900,000 + 20,775,000 + 13,440,000 + 130,000,000 = $224,115,000

Now, we can find the cost of equity using the CAPM. The cost of equity is:

R_E = .04 + 1.10(.09) = .1390 or 13.90%

The cost of debt is the YTM of the bonds, so:

P_0 = $1,198 = $40(PVIFA_{R%,50}) + $1,000(PVIF_{R%,50})
R = 3.20%
YTM = 3.20% × 2 = 6.40%

And the aftertax cost of debt is:

R_{D1} = (1 − .40)(.0640) = .0384 or 3.84%

B-294 SOLUTIONS

And the aftertax cost of the zero coupon bonds is:

$P_0 = \$138.50 = \$1,000(PVIF_{R\%,60})$
$R = 3.35\%$
$YTM = 3.35\% \times 2 = 6.70\%$

$R_{D2} = (1 - .40)(.0670) = .0402$ or 4.02%

Even though the zero coupon bonds make no payments, the calculation for the YTM (or price) still assumes semiannual compounding, consistent with a coupon bond. Also remember that, even though the company does not make interest payments, the accrued interest is still tax deductible for the company.

To find the required return on preferred stock, we can use the preferred stock pricing equation, which is the level perpetuity equation, so the required return on the company's preferred stock is:

$R_P = D_1 / P_0$
$R_P = \$6.50 / \$112$
$R_P = .0580$ or 5.80%

Notice that the required return in the preferred stock is lower than the required on the bonds. This result is not consistent with the risk levels of the two instruments, but is a common occurrence. There is a practical reason for this: Assume Company A owns stock in Company B. The tax code allows Company A to exclude at least 70 percent of the dividends received from Company B, meaning Company A does not pay taxes on this amount. In practice, much of the outstanding preferred stock is owned by other companies, who are willing to take the lower return since it is effectively tax exempt.

Now we have all of the components to calculate the WACC. The WACC is:

$WACC = .0384(59.9/224.115) + .0402(20.775/224.115) + .1390(130/224.115)$
$\qquad + .0580(13.44/224.115)$
$WACC = .0981$ or 9.81%

Challenge

16. We can use the debt-equity ratio to calculate the weights of equity and debt. The debt of the company has a weight for long-term debt and a weight for accounts payable. We can use the weight given for accounts payable to calculate the weight of accounts payable and the weight of long-term debt. The weight of each will be:

Accounts payable weight = .20/1.20 = .17
Long-term debt weight = 1/1.20 = .83

Since the accounts payable has the same cost as the overall WACC, we can write the equation for the WACC as:

$WACC = (1/2.3)(.17) + (1.3/2.3)[(.20/1.2)WACC + (1/1.2)(.09)(1 - .35)]$

Solving for WACC, we find:

WACC = .0739 + .5652[(.20/1.2)WACC + .0488]
WACC = .0739 + (.0942)WACC + .0276
(.9058)WACC = .1015
WACC = .1132 or 11.32%

Since the cash flows go to perpetuity, we can calculate the future cash inflows using the equation for the PV of a perpetuity. The NPV is:

NPV = −$45,000,000 + ($5,700,000/.1132)
NPV = −$45,000,000 + 50,372,552 = $5,372,552

17. The $4 million cost of the land 3 years ago is a sunk cost and irrelevant; the $6.5 million appraised value of the land is an opportunity cost and is relevant. The relevant market value capitalization weights are:

$MV_D = 15,000(\$1,000)(0.92) = \$13,800,000$
$MV_E = 300,000(\$75) = \$22,500,000$
$MV_P = 20,000(\$72) = \$1,440,000$

The total market value of the company is:

V = $13,800,000 + 22,500,000 + 1,440,000 = $37,740,000

Next we need to find the cost of funds. We have the information available to calculate the cost of equity using the CAPM, so:

$R_E = .05 + 1.3(.08) = .1540$ or 15.40%

The cost of debt is the YTM of the company's outstanding bonds, so:

$P_0 = \$920 = \$35(PVIFA_{R\%,30}) + \$1,000(PVIF_{R\%,30})$
R = 3.96%

YTM = 3.96% × 2 = 7.92%

And the aftertax cost of debt is:

$R_D = (1 - .35)(.0792) = .0515$ or 5.15%

The cost of preferred stock is:

$R_P = \$5/\$72 = .0694$ or 6.94%

B-296 SOLUTIONS

a. The initial cost to the company will be the opportunity cost of the land, the cost of the plant, and the net working capital cash flow, so:

$$CF_0 = -\$6,500,000 - 15,000,000 - 900,000 = -\$22,400,000$$

b. To find the required return on this project, we first need to calculate the WACC for the company. The company's WACC is:

$$WACC = [(\$22.5/\$37.74)(.1540) + (\$1.44/\$37.74)(.0694) + (\$13.8/\$37.74)(.0515)] = .1133$$

The company wants to use the subjective approach to this project because it is located overseas. The adjustment factor is 2 percent, so the required return on this project is:

Project required return = .1133 + .02 = .1333

c. The annual depreciation for the equipment will be:

$$\$15,000,000/8 = \$1,875,000$$

So, the book value of the equipment at the end of five years will be:

$$BV_5 = \$15,000,000 - 5(\$1,875,000) = \$5,625,000$$

So, the aftertax salvage value will be:

Aftertax salvage value = $\$5,000,000 + .35(\$5,625,000 - 5,000,000) = \$5,218,750$

d. Using the tax shield approach, the OCF for this project is:

$$OCF = [(P - v)Q - FC](1 - t) + t_C D$$
$$OCF = [(\$10,000 - 9,000)(12,000) - 400,000](1 - .35) + .35(\$15M/8) = \$8,196,250$$

e. The accounting breakeven sales figure for this project is:

$$Q_A = (FC + D)/(P - v) = (\$400,000 + 1,875,000)/(\$10,000 - 9,000) = 2,275 \text{ units}$$

f.   We have calculated all cash flows of the project. We just need to make sure that in Year 5 we add back the aftertax salvage value, the recovery of the initial NWC, and the aftertax value of the land. The cash flows for the project are:

Year	*Flow Cash*
0	–$22,400,000
1	8,196,250
2	8,196,250
3	8,196,250
4	8,196,250
5	18,815,000

Using the required return of 13.33 percent, the NPV of the project is:

$$NPV = -\$22{,}400{,}000 + \$8{,}196{,}250(PVIFA_{13.33\%,4}) + \$18{,}815{,}000/1.1333^5$$
$$NPV = \$11{,}878{,}610.78$$

And the IRR is:

$$NPV = 0 = -\$22{,}400{,}000 + \$8{,}196{,}250(PVIFA_{IRR\%,4}) + \$18{,}815{,}000/(1 + IRR)^5$$
$$IRR = 30.87\%$$

ISBN-13: 978-0-390-80084-8
ISBN-10: 0-390-80084-8

9 780390 800848

90000 >